The New History of Orkney

ORKNEY

North Ronaldsay

Papa Westray
St Boniface
Noltland Cas.
St Tredwell's
Pierowall
Westray
Scar
Burness
Start Point
Sanday
Lady Parish
Lopness
Tuquoy
Rapness
Calf of Eday
Carrick
Tresness
Elsness
Stove
Eday

Quandale
Rousay
Eynhallow
Egilsay
Westness
Papa Stronsay
Brough of Birsay
Birsay
Evie
Wyre
Green Holms
Whitehall
Marwick
Broch of Gurness
Stronsay
Skaill
Gairsay
Skara Brae
Harray
Rendall
Sandwick
Firth
Balfour Village
Shapinsay
Maeshowe
Auskerry
Stromness
Stenness
Kirkwall
Summerdale
Graemsay
Orphir
St Ola
Tankerness
Scapa
St Andrews
Deerness
Bu of Orphir
Skaill
Houton
Holm
St Mary's
Hoy
Cava
Paplay
Copinsay

SCAPA
FLOW

Fara
Hunda
Bu of Burray
Flotta
Burray
Herston
St Margaret's Hope
St Peter's
Walls
Swona
Swona
Burwick
South Ronaldsay

PENTLAND   FIRTH

Pentland Skerries

0   Miles   10
0   Kilometres   15

The New History of Orkney

WILLIAM P. L. THOMSON

ORIGIN

The History of Orkney originally published in 1987 by Mercat Press
Second edition, *The New History of Orkney*, published in 2001 by
Mercat Press

This edition published in 2019 by
Birlinn Origin, an imprint of
Birlinn Limited
West Newington House
10 Newington Road
Edinburgh
EH9 1QS

www.birlinn.co.uk

Reprinted 2021

First published in 2008 by Birlinn Limited

ISBN: 978 1 912476 45 9

The Author

William P. L. Thomson, OBE, MA, M.Univ., Dip.Ed.,
was Rector of Kirkwall Grammar School from 1971-1991, previous
to which he was Principal Teacher of History and Geography
in the Anderson High School, Shetland. He is the author of
The Little General and the Rousay Crofters (1981), *Kelp-making in
Orkney* (1983), *History of Orkney* (1987), *Lord Henry Sinclair's 1492
Rental of Orkney* (1996), *Orkney, Land and People* (2008) and
numerous papers on the economic and social history of
Orkney and Shetland.

Set in Galliard with headings in Tiepolo Book at Birlinn
Printed and bound by Gutenberg Press Ltd, Malta

Contents

List of Maps and Illustrations   vii
Preface   xi
Acknowledgements   xiii

1. Pictish Orkney   1
2. *Orkneyinga Saga* and the Early Jarls   24
3. Place-names and the Pictish-Norse Transition   40
4. Earl Sigurd and the Raven Banner   56
5. Earl Thorfinn and the Christian Earldom   69
6. The Martyrdom of St Magnus   88
7. St Rognvald and Orkney's Twelfth Century Renaissance   101
8. Harald Maddadsson   113
9. Earl John and his Successors   128
10. King Hakon's Expedition and the Loss of the Hebrides   138
11. Angus and Strathearn   148
12. The Sinclair Earldom   160
13. Orkney at the End of the Middle Ages   172
14. The Marriage Treaty and the Pawning of the Islands   189
15. Taxing and Renting Land in Norse Orkney   206
16. Under Scottish Rule, 1468-1513   220
17. The Summerdale Years   233
18. The Reformation   247
19. Earl Robert Stewart   262
20. Earl Patrick Stewart   277
21. The End of the Earldom   287
22. Tacksmen, Lairds and Udallers, 1615-1707   301
23. Old-style Farming   315
24. The False Dawn of Agricultural Improvement   333
25. Merchant-Lairds and the Great Kelp Boom   349

26. Linen, Fishing and the 'Nor Wast'   363
27. The Nineteenth Century Agricultural Revolution   378
28. Orkney Society in the Eighteenth and Nineteenth Centuries   395
29. Farming in the Twentieth Century   416
30. The Twentieth Century: War and Peace   434
Measurement of Land   451
Weights and Measures   451
Glossary   452
Notes to the Text   455
Bibliography and Abbreviations   488
Index   509

Maps and Illustrations

Map of Orkney		Frontispiece
1.	Broch of Gurness	2
2.	Woollen Hood	5
3.	Buckquoy Spindle Whorl	7
4.	Birsay Warriors	12
5.	The Ladykirk Stone	13
6.	Papa-names	15
7.	Eagle from the Knowe of Burrian	18
8.	Eagle from the Corpus Christi Gospel Fragment	18
9.	Peterkirks	19
10.	Papil 'Pony-rider' Stone	21
11.	Early Norse Earls of Orkney, c.900 AD to c.1065	29
12.	Papdale House, Kirkwall	33
13.	Stanley Cursiter and Hugh Marwick	44
14.	Marwick	45
15.	The Bu of Burray	51
16.	Marwick's Place-name 'Chronology'	52
17.	Size and Location of Place-names	54
18.	The Burray Hoard	62
19.	The Scar Plaque	65
20.	Halves, Thirds and Husebys	71
21.	Joseph Storer Clouston	72
22.	The Rulers of Moray	77
23.	The Brough of Birsay	86
24.	Earls of Orkney, c.1065–1230	89
25.	St Magnus Church, Egilsay	94
26.	The Skull of St Magnus	96
27.	Altarpiece from Andenes, Norway	98
28.	St Magnus Cathedral from Broad Street	100
29.	St Rognvald	103
30.	Langskaill, Gairsay	107
31.	Orphir (Mackenzie, *Orcades*)	110
32.	The Bu of Orphir	111
33.	Cubbie Roo's Castle, Wyre	133
34.	The Bishop's Palace, Kirkwall	143
35.	Strathearn and Sinclair Earls, c.1336-1470	151

36. Hawk's Bell   154
37. Kirkwall and the Peedie Sea   161
38. Bridge Street   164
39. Kirkwall   167
40. Sigillum Communitatis Orcadie   183
41. Rosslyn Chapel, Roslin   193
42. Urislands in Rendall   207
43. Sanday (Mackenzie, *Orcades*)   212
44. The Hall of Tankerness   215
45. Earldom Bordlands   223
46. Land Blown to Bergen   229
47. Rapness and its Bordlands   231
48. The Sinclairs, c.1434-1560   235
49. Kirkwall, Centres of Power   250
50. Tankerness House   251
51. Bothwell, Balfour and Bellenden   254
52. Noltland Castle, Westray   255
53. Birsay Village   271
54. Palace of Birsay   272
55. The Earl's Palace, Kirkwall   280
56. Kirbister Farm, Birsay   313
57. The Township of Herston, 1768-9   316
58. Landownership in Herston, 1000 AD to 1850   319
59. Herston Village   320
60. Single-stilt plough   326
61. Grinding Grain with a Quern   330
62. Birsay, 1760   334
63. Ox Cart   338
64. Singling Turnips   338
65. Thomas Balfour's Improvements at Sound   340
66. Fishing Boats at Kirkwall   342
67. The Grain and Meal Trade, 1780-1801   344
68. Scythe   346
69. Kelp Production   353
70. Burning Kelp   354
71. Burning Kelp using a Flaikie   354
72. Kelp Kiln   356
73. The Kelp Trade   357
74. West End Hotel, Kirkwall   359
75. Tangles in North Ronaldsay   361
76. Stromness Piers   367
77. Whitehall Village, Stronsay   370

78. Herring Boats, Stronsay — 371
79. Herring Station, Burray — 372
80. John Rae and his Wife — 373
81. Population, 1755-1991 — 379
82. The Squared Landscape, Shapinsay — 385
83. 'Fossil Dykes', Shapinsay — 387
84. Former North Hill Common, Shapinsay — 387
85. Exports — 389
86. General Burroughs and his Medals — 391
87. Digro, Rousay — 392
88. A Pundlar — 396
89. Sir Laurence Dundas — 397
90. Sir Laurence Dundas's Edinburgh Townhouse — 398
91. David Balfour (1811-1887) — 401
92. Balfour Castle — 402
93. Margaret Brown — 402
94. Rev. George Ritchie — 409
95. The *Lizzie Burroughs* — 413
96. Owner-occupancy — 417
97. Thomas Traill of Holland — 418
98. Crops and Animals, 1900, 1950 and 1998 — 423
99. Travelling Shop — 426
100. Hens — 426
101. Early Tractor — 428
102. Harvesting in Stenness — 432
103. The *Bayern* — 435
104. The *Derfflinger* — 436
105. The Building of the Barriers, 1943 — 437
106. No.2 Barrier — 438
107. Shore Street, Kirkwall — 441
108. The *St Ola* — 443

Preface

When I was invited by James Thin to write the original *History of Orkney* (published by Mercat Press in 1987) it was a chance not to be missed. Equally welcome was the opportunity to undertake a thorough revision, which appeared as *The New History of Orkney* in 2001. The title was intended to indicate that it was based on the previous history and generally followed the same framework but was substantially rewritten, containing several new chapters and additional material based on later research. The opportunity has been taken in this reprint to make some further minor changes.

When the 2001 edition appeared I noted that the bibliography contained 171 entries for books and papers which had been published since the publication of the original history (more than a quarter of all entries) and this flow of new work continues unabated. The bibliography now includes some of the more important books and papers which have appeared since 2001. New translations of some primary sources supplement *Orkneyinga saga*—Ekrem and Mortensen's *Historia Norvegie*, Anderson and Gade's *Morkinskinna* and Finlay's *Fagrskinna*—and recent work in Scandinavian history has been made accessible in English with the appearance of volume 1 of *The Cambridge History of Scandinavia*. A different window on the past is provided by the rapid development of genetic studies including work by James F. Wilson, although it has to be admitted that historians have not altogether come to grips with the findings of the geneticists. Place-names provide another approach to the same problem of the Pictish-Norse transition, and a good deal has recently been published, including papers by Peder Gammeltoft and books edited by him. Barbara Crawford's interdisciplinary Papar Project investigates sites associated with the clergy of the pre-Norse church; the first instalment has been published in *The Papar in the North Atlantic* and more recent developments in the project can be found on a large and informative web-site. A series of books has emerged from a European Union project, 'Destination Viking-Sagalands', including Olwyn Owen's *The World of Orkneyinga Saga*. An apparently endless stream of Viking-age studies continues.

Barbara Crawford has a long and detailed chapter on the bishopric of Orkney in Steinar Imsen's handsome volume on the Archbishopric of Trondheim (Nidaros), and a festchrift presented to her (*West over Sea*, edited by Beverley Ballin Smith et al.) contains a number of papers relevant to

Orkney. Other work on the medieval church includes papers on St Magnus by Phelpstead and Thomson, and a full-scale academic study by Antonsson which places Magnus firmly in the context of the medieval cult of saints.

There are also books of a more general nature and with a wider chronological spread. *The Orkney Book*, edited by Donald Omand, provides a comprehensive survey of Orkney's prehistory, history, economy and culture, and *Stones, Skalds and Saints*, edited by Doreen Waugh, contains a series of conference papers on the natural environment, history and literature of the islands.

It is surprising that rather less has been published on the more recent history of the islands, but the hitherto neglected seventeenth century has been illumined by two publications by James Irvine. His *Blaeu's Orkney and Shetland* not only prints and comments on Blaeu's maps, but includes the hitherto unpublished 'New Chorographic Description of Orkney', which probably dates from 1644 and is one of the earliest descriptions of the islands. Another useful source is his book *The Orkney Poll Taxes of the 1690s*, which transcribes the parish-by-parish returns. Sheena Wenham's book, *A More Enterprising Spirit*, provides a valuable study of the economy and social life on the eighteenth century Graemeshall estate in the parish of Holm.

Two splendid books on the twentieth century have appeared: Howard Hazell's *The Orcadian Book of the Twentieth Century* consists of a large collection of extracts from local newspapers, and it demonstrates what a rich and fascinating source they provide. Virginia Schroder's *Bloody Orkney* takes its title from the wartime poem of that name, and it records the memories of servicemen and women. Although they were far from home and living in bleak surroundings, their impressions of Orkney were not invariably as negative as the poem suggests.

Finally, the author has not been altogether idle in his retirement. My book, *Orkney: Land and People*, to some extent supplements *The New History of Orkney*, having the same chronological spread but dealing less with earls and sagas and more with the day-to-day life of ordinary folk. It describes farming and settlement through the centuries and examines institutions such as the parish bailie courts and kirk sessions which attempted to control the economic, social and moral affairs of the community.

Acknowledgements

In 1987 I acknowledged the help and advice I had received from Dr R.P. Fereday, James Burton and Sue Graves of Kirkwall Grammar School, Dr Barbara Crawford of St Andrews University, Dr Raymond Lamb, then Orkney Archaeologist, Brian Smith, Shetland Archivist, Howie Firth, then of Radio Orkney, Professor Per Sveaas Andersen of Oslo, Dr Gilbert Schrank of New York, and the late Professor Ronald Miller. In 2001 I acknowledged help from Professor Steinar Imsen of Trondheim, Dr Philip Rance, Ann Brundle of Tankerness House Museum, Tom Copland of the Scottish Agricultural College, and Harvey Johnston, Jim Chalmers, Billy Scott and Arthur Cromarty of Orkney College. A special word of thanks goes to Alison Fraser and the staff of Orkney Archives, and David Mackie in the Photographic Archive. Everyone with an interest in Orkney history appreciates the excellent service which these people provide. Thanks are also due to Orkney Islands Council and Orkney Heritage Society for financial support towards the publication of the original volume. It was a pleasure to work with Seán Costello and Tom Johnstone of Mercat Press when the *New History of Orkney* appeared in 2001, and their helpfulness is again gratefully acknowledged.

The Orkney Photographic Archive is the source for figs. 3, 8, 10, 12, 21, 24, 49, 54, 56, 60, 61, 64, 65, 66, 68, 71, 72, 73, 75, 76, 77, 78, 79, 80, 86, 87, 91, 93, 94, 95, 98, 99, 100, 101, 103, 104, 105, 107 and 108. Gunnie Moberg provided figs. 1, 5, 23, 28, 31, 32, 33, 34, 44, 46, 50, 52, 53, 55, 59, 74, 83, 92, 102 and 106. Figs. 2, 13 and 36 are reproduced by permission of the National Museum of Scotland. Figs. 4 and 14 are reproduced by permission of Historic Scotland. I am indebted to the Shetland Museum for fig. 7, the Master and Fellows of Corpus Christi College, Cambridge for fig. 9, Tromsø Museum for fig. 27, Dr Barbara Crawford for fig. 30, Rosslyn Chapel Trust for fig. 41, to Orkney Archive for fig. 57, the Marquis of Zetland for fig. 89 and the Royal Bank of Scotland for fig. 90. Figs. 69 and 70 were drawn by Mrs Anne Brundle.

Pictish Orkney

Orkney people even in recent centuries preserved a knowledge of the Picts, but it was little more than the name which survived. The Picts of Orkney folklore belonged not so much to the real past as to a magical world inhabited by mermaids, finns and seal-folk. In the course of time it was forgotten that they had been human, and they became thoroughly confused with the trows (trolls) who inhabited the mounds and tumuli which were such a prominent feature of the landscape. Farmers who could make little sense of Bronze-Age sub-peat dykes and field boundaries which were unrelated to the present pattern of arable land, spoke of 'picky' (Pictish) dykes, whatever the real age of these structures. These dykes were regularly linked with the supernatural, and along their course were to be found names such as 'the trow's buil' (the troll's lair).[1] Similarly the wild oat grass with which so much of the land was infested until modern times was known as 'Pight oats'; it grew and ripened fast and was believed to make excellent bread if only it could be cut before 'the Picts' threshed it out.[2] The same identification of Picts with mythical creatures is found in Shetland where names incorporating 'Pict' such as Petester, Pettidale and Pettawater were applied to out-of-the-way places well known to be the abode of trows.[3] Another such name is Pickaquoy ('the Picts' field') on the outskirts of Kirkwall, once haunted by 'Picts', but now inhabited by keep-fit enthusiasts at the Pickaquoy sports-centre, and the customers of two of Orkney's largest supermarkets. Nowadays the only 'little people' found at Pickaquoy attend Glaitness Primary School.

The belief that the Orkney Picts were different from other races is not recent. Much the same view is found in the *Historia Norvegiae*, written c.1200 at about the same date as *Orkneyinga saga*:

> These islands were first inhabited by the Picts and Papae. Of these, the one race, the Picts, little exceeded pygmies in stature; they did marvels in the morning and in the evening in building walled towns, but at mid-day they entirely lost all their strength and lurked through fear in little underground houses.[4]

It can be seen that the author of the *Historia* had no real knowledge of the

1. *The Broch of Gurness*

Orkney Picts, but was making deductions from what might be described as 'archaeological evidence'. The remains of a broch such as Gurness with its surrounding settlement must have looked like a 'walled town' to Norse settlers who had no similar buildings, and medieval Orcadians must have wondered what had been the purpose of souterrains (underground chambers); it would have seemed logical to deduce from the low entrances to brochs and chambered cairns that 'the Picts' had been dwarf-like creatures. The deductions which nowadays we are likely to make from the *Historia* are rather different: we are likely to conclude that, since by 1200 ideas about the Picts were so wide of the mark, the pre-Norse population had ceased to exist as a distinct group at an early stage of Norse colonisation.

The same belief that the Picts were an exotic race, altogether more primitive than their neighbours, continues to obscure our understanding of Dark Age Scotland.[5] In a sense the Picts were indeed a vanished race, since by 1200 the kingdom of the Picts had long since been incorporated in Alba, and the kingdom of Alba had subsequently evolved into Scotland. The language of the Picts had also vanished, replaced by Norse in Orkney and Shetland, and by Irish Gaelic even in eastern Scotland. The idea that the Picts had been different also stems in part from their name, *Picti* ('painted people') and from the recurring symbols which appear on Pictish sculpture and which defy interpretation. We are now less certain about some of the other supposed features of Pictish society for which they were once regarded as distinctive: it would now be thought doubtful that Picts practised matrilineal succession whereby kingship descended from the mother, although as in other contemporary kingdoms, kingship did not pass from fathers to sons in a regular fashion. Ideas about the language of the Picts have also been revised: their speech may not have been so outlandish as was once supposed, and perhaps it was not greatly different from the language spoken in some other parts of Britain. Modern opinion regards the Picts c.800 AD as 'a typical north-west European barbarian society with wide connections and parallels'.[6]

Pictish Orkney is unlikely to have been a poverty-stricken place supporting only a primitive population, as those who sought to explain the replacement of the Picts by the Norse at one time supposed.[7] Its fertile boulder clay soils were amenable to cultivation and, by the late Pictish period, scrub-woodland had been removed by upwards of 4,000 years of agriculture. The Picts c.800 AD had a much longer history of agriculture behind them than the period which separates them from the present day. Cultivation was extensive, and the lighter soils and better drained land had long been utilised. In addition to arable land which grew bere on the manured infield and some oats on outfield, there was also good grazing at no great altitude which encouraged a mixed farming economy. Cattle tended to be more important than sheep in most places; other domestic animals included pigs, horses, goats, geese, ducks, dogs and cats, and red deer were hunted both for their meat and for their antlers.[8] The absence of timber was a drawback; perhaps it was supplied by coastwise trade, but to some extent the lack of wood was compensated by the availability of excellent building stone and abundant supplies of peat for fuel. The island environment had the advantage that it combined the resources of land, sea and shore, rather than relying on the land alone—diversity is a distinct advantage in a subsistence economy. Fish were larger in size and probably more abundant than today when commercial fishing has depleted the fishing grounds. We know from the Birsay sites that cod, hake, haddock, saithe, pollack, ballan wrasse and conger eels were caught, showing that, in addition to inshore fishing, there was a capability to engage in offshore line fishing. However, at Howe the relative scarcity of the bones of large cod and ling suggests that the shoreline and nearby waters provided plenty of fish without having to take to the open sea.[9] The cliffs provided seabirds and their eggs, and the beaches were a source of stranded or driven whales, seals, 'spoots' (razor-fish) and limpets both for food and bait.[10] Seaweed was available to manure the land, and driftwood was also plentiful as long as North American forests extended to the banks of rivers and the edge of the tidewater. The drowned landscape of low green islands with long lengths of coast, extensive inshore fishing grounds and access to the open sea provided a uniquely attractive environment. Late Pictish Orkney was a comfortable place by Dark Age standards.

The first information about Orkney from classical writers are statements attributed to the Greek voyager Pytheas of Massilia (Marseilles) who claimed to have sailed round the British Isles c.325 BC.[11] His book, *Concerning the Ocean*, is lost, but several ancient authors quote from it, although not always approvingly. Pytheas recorded the place-name 'Orkas' which he applied to the north-east extremity of Britain (presumably either Dunnett or Duncansby Head). Pomponius Mela, a Roman geographer writing in the early first century AD, supplies the first record of the place-name 'Orcades', and on Ptolemy's map, compiled from information gathered no later than Agricola's campaign of 80-84 AD, these names appear again, although two names are recorded for the headland—Tarvedunum and Cape Orkas.[12] So the name 'Orkney' has an ancestry which stretches back at least as far the broch-building period, although it was apparently not confined to the islands north of the Pentland Firth. The 'Orc' element has been interpreted as a Celtic place-name meaning 'a young pig' or 'a boar'. It seems to fit into a series of animal names in the north of Scotland including the Caerini (rams) in west Sutherland, Cornavii (horned animals, stags) from Caithness, and the Lugi (possibly ravens) from east Sutherland, while Ptolemy's Tarvedunum, ('bull fort') is a name of the same kind, possibly related to 'Thurso' for which a derivation from *Thjorsá* ('bull river') has been suggested.[13] Similarly the 'cats' of Caithness, although not shown on Ptolemy's map, belong to the same naming tradition.[14] The implication is that the Orc were one of a group of peoples, each identified by a totemistic animal name, which later coalesced into the kingdom or kingdoms which we find in the late Pictish period. Perhaps surprisingly, these totems do not appear on later Pictish stones although the sculptors frequently made use of animal themes.

The various references to Orkney by classical writers are bedevilled by the fact that, as seen by most writers, Orkney lay at the farthest extremity of the British Isles, and so there was always a symbolic value in claiming that Roman rule had been established there or enemies pursued to its shores. This is quite the most significant point to bear in mind when dealing not just with classical references but also with Arthurian legends and even some supposed missionary journeys. Thus the story that an Orkney chief was among those who made submission to the emperor Claudius in 43 AD might be true, but there is a strong suspicion that the account is boasting about the completeness of the emperor's conquests, which were not in fact complete and are unlikely to have extended to Orkney. Similarly when Agricola's fleet circum-

2. **Woollen Hood.** *The hood was found in a bog in St Andrews parish in 1867 and has been carbon-dated to between 250 AD and 615 AD.*[15]

navigated the north of Scotland in 84 AD, Tacitus (his son-in-law) tells us that Orkney was 'discovered and subdued', again claiming, with considerable exaggeration, that Roman rule had been extended to the extremities of Britain. The circumnavigation also gave rise to a local tradition that the fleet landed in Shapinsay, where in the eighteenth century the name of the little croft of Grukalty was 'corrected' to 'Agricola'. A reputed find of Roman coins at this site was used as confirmation of this improbable story.[15]

Although Orkney was well beyond the parts of Britain which the Romans occupied, some measure of political interaction is a possibility. The occurrence of Roman objects is only to be expected, since artefacts are frequently found far beyond the frontiers of the empire in a variety of locations ranging from Iceland to southern India. Finds from some of the brochs include much-prized Samian ware, coins, metal artefacts, jewellery and glassware. Some of these finds are surprisingly early, including fragments of amphorae of a first century date from the Broch of Gurness, and first and second century coins from the Broch of Lingro.[16] Perhaps the trade often involved second and third-hand contacts, but there were probably times during the long Roman occupation of southern Britain when links were more direct. The nature of finds indicates an interest in sophisticated Roman fashions and a desire to gain access to Rome's material culture. The occurrence of luxury items, however, is consistent with periodic looting and gift exchange as well as regular trade, while the relatively small number of

Roman artefacts from broch sites and a lack of stylistic influence suggest that Orkney was not greatly Romanised.

While ordinary folk in later centuries lost touch with the real Picts and confused them with supernatural beings, there has also been uncertainty in academic circles about what constitutes a Pict. Gordon Childe's book on Skara Brae, published as late as 1931, was given the unfortunate sub-title 'A Pictish Village in Orkney'.[17] It would now be considered entirely improper to apply the term 'Pict' to the Neolithic period, and the name is now used in a more restricted sense. The name 'Pict' first appears in 297 AD as a name used by the Romans as a collective name for the peoples north of the Antonine Wall,[18] but it avoids the question of Orkney's political and linguistic links with mainland Scotland at this time. Orkney is described as 'islands of the Picts' in the *Bern Chronicle*, when it repeats Bede's account of the 'annexation' of Orkney by Claudius. The statement is valueless as evidence that Orkney was Pictish in 43 AD, but it shows that shows that its English author writing c.800 AD found it natural to assume that Orkney was Pictish, and thus provides evidence which can be taken to show that Orkney was part of a mainland Pictish kingdom in the author's own day.[19] Although the Norse at about the same date approached Orkney from the opposite direction, the place-name 'Pettlandsfjörðr' ('Pictland Firth', Pentland Firth) shows that they too called the inhabitants Picts.[20] To the Romans the meaning of the name was obvious—the 'Picti' were the 'painted people', and one view is that it originated from their custom of tattooing their bodies.

It is not entirely clear which language or languages were spoken in pre-Norse Orkney. The language of the Picts, found from Angus, Fife and Perthshire northwards, was not modern Gaelic but Brittonic or P-Celtic. It was similar to the language once spoken in the Roman province of Britain and was allied to Gaulish. Branches of Brittonic continued to be spoken, not only in Pictland, but also in Strathclyde, Wales, Cumbria, Cornwall and Brittany. Irish Gaelic (Goedelic or Q-Celtic) on the other hand, was the forerunner of modern Gaelic; it had been introduced via the kingdom of Dál Riata (Argyll), and by the late Pictish period it was rapidly replacing Brittonic throughout Pictland. Thus Orkney, presuming that its language was Celtic, is likely to have spoken the Brittonic variety, although in the immediate pre-Norse period some Goedelic influence might be expected (see Chapter 3).

The distribution in modern Scotland of the former Brittonic language is traced through a number of characteristic place-name elements such as *pit* (Pitlochry), *aber* (Aberdeen), *carden* (Cardenden), *lanerc* (Lanark) and *pert* (Perth).[21] These names are very common in the Pictish heartland and their occurrence corresponds in general terms with the distribution of Pictish sculpture, except in the north and in Orkney where Pictish sculpture is still

3. ***Buckquoy Spindle Whorl.*** *Linguistic evidence from modern research suggests that the ogham inscription on this spindle whorl may be written in Old Irish rather than an unknown non-Indo-European language as was at one time believed.*

found but these Brittonic names are missing. The northernmost *pit*-names are in south-east Sutherland (Pitfour, Pitgrundy, Pittentrail). Because these typically Brittonic names are entirely absent from Orkney, and also because of the great difficulty in making sense of Orkney ogham inscriptions, it was once believed that only upper-class incomers spoke Pictish, and the rest of the population spoke an unknown and more primitive language, perhaps as different from other European languages as Basque.[22] However, *aber* is a river-mouth or confluence, *carden* is a thicket, *lanerc* a clearing, and *pert* is a wood. River-mouths, woods, thickets and clearings are not very common in Orkney, so these Brittonic elements might be absent simply because they are topographically inappropriate—they are not found because they describe features absent from the Orkney landscape. Katherine Forsyth's re-interpretation of the ogham-inscribed spindle-whorl from Buckquoy reveals that it may be written in Old Irish rather than in an unintelligible non-Celtic Pictish.[23] The long-held belief that Orkney Picts spoke a primitive non-Indo-European language is now regarded as unlikely.

A twelfth century geographical tract, *De Situ Albanie*, describes the seven divisions of Pictland, which included all of eastern Scotland north of the

Forth.[24] Each division is described as consisting of two parts, a *regio* and a *subregio*, evidently a kingdom and sub-kingdom. What is described is a some-what theoretical model of client kingship, incorporating the idea that a kingdom ought to comprise the king and his *toisech*, and that these regional kings in turn stood in a client relationship to a high king. As central kingship strengthened, the former regional kings later appear as 'mormaers' ('great officials'), and it is a matter of debate how much independence some of them retained in the late Pictish period and even into the Viking Age. The *De Situ Albanie* makes no mention of Orkney; it was written shortly after 1165 and, although some of the information came from the Bishop of Caith-ness who knew that Caithness had been a Pictish province, there was apparently no longer any memory that Orkney had been a part of Pictland. *De Situ Albanie* is as ignorant of the Orkney Picts as is *Orkneyinga saga* and the *Historia Norvegiae*.

We do know, however, that kings of the kind which *De Situ Albanie* describes had existed in Orkney, and that they stood in a client relationship to kings on the Pictish mainland. Soon after Columba arrived in Iona he crossed the 'spine of Britain' and at or near Inverness he visited the court of King Bridei mac Máelchú (King of the Picts c.555–c.585). We are told that Columba was concerned for the safety of Cormac ua Liatháin, an Irish holy man associated with Iona, who was voyaging in northern waters in search of a hermit retreat. Adomnán's *Life of Columba* is a collection of miracles rather than a conventional biography, and for Adomnán the point of the story is to demonstrate that Columba had miraculous foreknowledge of the danger Cormac would face when he arrived in Orkney. We are more likely to be interested in the presence of an unnamed Orkney king at Bridei's court and the light the story sheds on their relationship. Columba addressed the Pictish king:

> Some of our people have recently gone out desiring to find a desert place in the sea which cannot be crossed. Earnestly charge this king ('regulus') whose hostages are in your hand that, if after long wander-ings our people chance to land in the islands of the Orcades, nothing untoward shall happen to them within his territories.[25]

The Orkney king is described using the Latin diminutive 'regulus' (little king or subject-king) whereas Bridei is called 'rex potentissimus' (most pow-erful king). Bridei was evidently King of Pictland, or at least that part of it which lay north of the Mounth, whereas the Orkney *regulus* was in a de-pendent relationship. Bridei held Orkney hostages, and this is sometimes taken as evidence of a hostile relationship, but the holding of hostages was a standard Dark Age precaution which at the less harsh end of the scale was little different from the fostering of the client king's son at the high king's court as a means of creating a lifelong bond between foster-father and foster-son. We therefore cannot assume that Bridei had recently conquered Orkney. As the story reaches us, it seems that Bridei could expect to be obeyed, although the Orkney king's attitude to Christianity appears to have been hostile. We need to remember, however, that Adomnán was writing c.690 AD, and so we might wonder how much he really knew about the relationship of Orkney and Pictland a century and more before he wrote his account. The relationship he describes might well have been more applicable in Adomnán's own day when, only a few years before, a Pictish king (another Bridei) had indeed conquered Orkney (see below). Over the long period from the fifth to ninth centuries there was a gradual decay of petty kingdoms and the emergence of a stronger central authority able to extend its control over ever wider areas, but how far that process had progressed by Columba's time is uncertain.

Another contact with Dál Riata or Argyll (the area from which Columba operated) is an expedition against Orkney by Áedán mac Gabráin (King of Dál Riata 574–608) who had been 'ordained' king by Columba at the command of an angel.[26] Columba was present at a meeting at which Áedán gave up his right to 'expedition and hosting' from the Irish part of his kingdom, but retained his 'tribute and ship-service'.[27] It became apparent to what purpose Áedán could put his ship-service when in 580 AD he launched an attack on Orkney. The reason for the campaign is unknown; the Annals of Ulster merely record 'a campaign in the Orkneys by Áedán mac Gabráin.'[28] A repeat of the entry in the following year might be a continuation of the campaign, but is more likely to be a double entry resulting from careless copying. Áedán might have been using his superior sea-power to attack a vulnerable part of Pictish territory, but for all we know he could have been helping the Picts to subdue a rebellious province. His expedition, however, shows that significant contacts were possible along the Hebridean seaways which the Vikings were later to dominate, although Pictish sculpture points to links with eastern Scotland being even stronger.

A century later there is an equally brief record of an expedition against Orkney in 682 AD. The *Annals of Tigernach* note that 'the Orkneys were destroyed by Bridei'.[29] This was the formidable Bridei mac Bile (king of the Picts 672–693). It has been suggested that the attack on Orkney might be connected with the siege of Dunnottar which was recorded the previous year,[30] and that these events consolidated Bridei's power in the north before his crushing victory at Nechtansmere in 685 AD—the Dark Age Bannockburn —which ended Northumbrian domination of southern Pictland. We are still in the period when we cannot assume that the very limited information which has survived necessarily coincides with events which had the greatest significance at the time. It does, however, seem possible that Bridei mac Bile won more than a temporary victory in Orkney, and that the beginning of a closer political relationship dates from this period. Then in 709 AD the Annals of Ulster record that 'a war was fought in the Orkneys and in it fell the son of Artabláir'.[31] The identity of Artabláir is unknown, but it seems that this entry implies an outside attack either from Pictland or from Dál Riata. Perhaps this war continued, or even completed, the process by which Orkney was integrated with the Pictish kingdom. Closer links with Pictland brought new influences, particularly a strengthened Christian presence, but whether it involved a new ruling class of incomers is unknown. There is some evidence of a more thoroughly Pictish culture, and an incoming aristocracy seemed a likely theory as long as it was believed that two languages were spoken in Orkney, non-Indo-European by the majority and Brittonic by an aristocratic elite, but if that idea is abandoned, there is less reason to suppose there was an influx of mainland Picts. Closer ties could develop within the existing client relationship, and a modification of material culture might also occur. The Pictish high king could probably find compliant members of the royal kinship group in Orkney whose allegiance could be secured by buttressing their position and rewarding their loyalty or, if all else failed, he might threaten to support the claims of competing relatives.

By this date Pictish kings were well capable of exercising authority in Orkney. The wreck of 150 ships in 729 AD at 'Ros-Cuissine' (tentatively identified as Troup Head on the Buchan coast) testifies to the surprisingly large number of ships which it was possible to muster on the direct route northwards from eastern Scotland.[32] Sculpture often deals with land warfare but it rarely depicts ships, suggesting that seafaring was not of much interest to those who commissioned the carved stones. A representation of a ship does appear on the St Orland's stone from Cossans in Angus: it has a high-prow and was probably planked and, although it is shown without sails, it may illustrate the type of ship which the Picts used.[33] Perhaps they were not so entirely land-based as is sometimes supposed, but in the long run Pictish Orkney was vulnerable to Norwegian penetration because its ships were inferior to those of the invaders.

The incorporation of Orkney into a mainland Pictish kingdom was probably at a relatively late date, but we ought not to think that Pictish culture was imposed from outside as a result of the new political link, or indeed that Orkney had hitherto been peripheral or in any way inferior to Pictland in a cultural sense. A ¾ inch crescent and v-rod inscribed on the bone of an ox from the Broch of Burrian, North Ronaldsay, with an even smaller disc and notch on the reverse side, is an example of the informal, almost casual use of Pictish symbols on everyday objects,[34] and similar bone artefacts with the crescent and v-rod and the double disc have been found at Pool, Sanday. A stone bearing the double disc motif was placed face-down in the floor of a building at Pool in a context carbon-dated to the mid-sixth century. It shows the use of typical Pictish symbols well in advance of any likely incorporation of Orkney in a mainland Pictish kingdom.

It has been possible to describe Orkney's changing relationship to mainland Pictland at least in outline, but the limits of our knowledge are demonstrated by the fact that we do not know for certain the name of a single Orkney Pict. There are several mythical kings such as Belus, Gaius and Gunnas,[35] besides the improbable Gunphar who, according to Geoffrey of Monmouth's romance, accompanied King Arthur on an expedition against Rome. Godbold is only marginally less dubious: he was reputedly killed at the Battle of Hatfield in 633 AD in the company of Edwin of Northumbria whose power, according to William of Malmesbury, extended to the Orkney islands.[36] No greater reliance can be put on 'Niva Mac Oirck, prince of the Orcades' who, according to the *Annals of Clonmacnoise,* was among the 7,000 men killed in Ireland in 717 AD.[37]

Although we do not know the names of any Pictish kings with any certainty, we are fortunate to possess a 'portrait' on a slab from the Brough of Birsay, possibly of early eighth century date (Fig.4).[38] The slab was at one time over 6 feet high, but is broken into fragments; it bears the common Pictish symbols of the mirror, crescent and v-rod, the elephant-like 'Pictish beast' and an eagle, below which a procession of three warriors is shown in low relief. All three warriors wear ankle-length robes, drawn in at the waist. They have square shields (which is unusual), they have a sword in a scabbard on their left side, and they carry spears. The warriors appear in order of seniority: the leader is a commanding figure of regal appearance while the last member of the group is a beardless youth. The leader is distinguished by his elaborate curls possibly with a circlet, his robe is trimmed with a fringe, he carries a larger spear and has a decorative shield. Metal objects from Pictish sites suggest additional details which supplement what we see on the sculpture: silver *chapes* to protect the tips of leather scabbards, silver and bronze pommels for sword hilts, and bronze spearheads.[39] It may be that the Birsay sculpture depicts a 'regulus' since Pictish stones have sometimes been thought to record actual events, or the trio might represent heroes from Pictish mythology or figures from an unidentified biblical story. It is reasonable to suppose, however, that the procession shows authentic aristocratic Picts as they wished to be perceived.

In St Mary's church at Burwick, South Ronaldsay, a rough beach stone has been preserved on which a pair of footprints are carefully engraved (Fig.5).[40] The use of stones of this kind in the inauguration of kings is well attested from Ireland and the Hebrides. Stones of this kind were set on a mound and, in a ceremony which was originally pagan and latterly involved Christian clerics, the ancestry of the new king was recited, and he symbolically stepped

*4. **Birsay Warriors.** The figures are on a slab from the Brough of Birsay which also contains Pictish symbols. Although the subject of the carving is not known, the slab probably shows aristocratic Picts as they wished to be perceived. (© Crown Copyright. Reproduced courtesy of Historic Scotland).*

into the footprints of his ancestors. The best known footprint is cut into the rock near the summit of Dunadd where kings of Dál Riata were inaugurated. The existence of similar stones in an Iron Age context at the Broch of Clickhimin, Shetland and in Caithness, and late medieval descriptions of the inauguration of the Lord of the Isles, suggest a long history of ceremonies of this kind.[41]

Since Orkney sculpture, including the Birsay warriors and the symbols which accompany them, is of a kind standard throughout Pictland, it is legitimate to use sculpture from other parts of Pictland to describe the way of life and the values of Pictish aristocrats. It was a society with a passion for warfare and for hunting; the stones regularly represent battle scenes, and they show mettlesome horses, dogs, stags, and all the trappings of the hunt. Warfare and hunting were, of course, universal medieval enthusiasms, but as far as Pictland was concerned the hunt was rooted in the woods and farmland of the Angus and Perthshire countryside, and it is not obvious how hunting translated into insular conditions. Bone remains reveal that red deer were at one stage a surprisingly important source of food at Howe and at Skaill,[42] and the survival of deer in Orkney must have involved a degree of management, perhaps by establishing protected hunting reserves in suitable areas such as Hoy. Perhaps, like their Norse successors, Picts took part in annual deer drives in the Caithness Dales whenever hunting was not interrupted by intermittent low-scale warfare. In the nineteenth century an incoming laird, Archer Fortesque of Swanbister, hunted with hounds in the Orphir hills, and no doubt the Pictish aristocracy were also capable of staging somewhat artificial hunts in the Orkney countryside.

When the Norse arrived in Orkney they were entering a Christian country which apparently had a rich and powerful church. Orkney, however, probably did not have a long history of Christianity, and the formal conversion of the islands may even have been as late as the early years of the eighth century —less than a century before the onset of Viking raids. At one time it would have been assumed that Christianity was much older, having first been established by St Ninian's mission to Orkney and Shetland in the early fifth century.[43] The reason for believing that there had been such a mission is the numerous Ninian dedications and place-names—the St Ninian's chapels in Toab and at Stews in South Ronaldsay, 'Rinansey' (supposedly St Ringan's

5. *The Ladykirk Stone. This stone, preserved in St Mary's Church, Burwick, has a pair of carefully engraved footprints. Stones of this kind were widely used for the inauguration of kings.*

13

island or North Ronaldsay),[44] and further Ninian dedications in Shetland including St Ninian's Isle. It is, however, clear that Ninian's activities (if he existed) were confined to southern Scotland.[45] A revival of Ninian's cult in the twelfth century led to new dedications which laid a false trail and gave rise to mistaken theories about the extent of travels. There must, however, have been occasional Christians in Orkney from Roman times onwards, co-existing with a majority who followed pagan cults, but Christianity made no discernible progress until it received royal support.

In Adomnán's account of Columba's meeting with Bridei mac Máelchú at which the Orkney 'regulus' was present, we learn that the Pictish king was willing to provide protection for Christian travellers throughout the area he controlled including Orkney, although it is by no means certain that Bridei or the *regulus* were converts. We are told that Cormac ua Liatháin did reach Orkney,[46] but we ought not to assume that Christianity was introduced as a result of his visit. Cormac was described by Adomnán as having previously founded a monastery,[47] but on this visit to Orkney he was not the leader of a mission, but a hermit seeking a place of retreat. We are led to believe that Cormac escaped 'imminent death' as a result of Bridei's intervention, although pagans were not usually so hostile to Christianity.

A glimpse of pre-Norse priests is to be found in the *Historia Norvegiae* where, having described the pygmy Picts, the author turned his attention to the Papae:

> And the Papae have been named from their white robes which they wore like priests; whence priests are all called Papae in the Teutonic tongue. An island is still called after them *Papey*. But as is observed from their habit and the writings of their books abandoned there, they were Africans adhering to Judaism.[48]

The author had no better knowledge of the Papae than he had of the Picts, and he believed them to have been a separate 'race'. Whereas he makes deductions from archaeological evidence when he describes the Picts, his information about the Papae seems to come from the place-name, 'Papey', ('priest-island', Papa Westray), and from his knowledge that 'papar' was a general term for priests. It is interesting to find Ninian-dedications associated with *papa*-names as at Papil in Yell and at Papey Geo near Wick.[49] Presumably both the place-name and the dedication result from an 'antiquarian' interest in what the Norse recognised as a pre-Norse Christian site to which they attached a suitable pre-Norse dedication. Viking pirates on their first arrival cannot have had much knowledge of early Christian saints, so perhaps both the *papa*-name and the dedication date from a time when, or after Christianity was re-established. When the author of the *Historia Norvegiae* tells us that the Papae were 'Africans adhering to Judaism' he

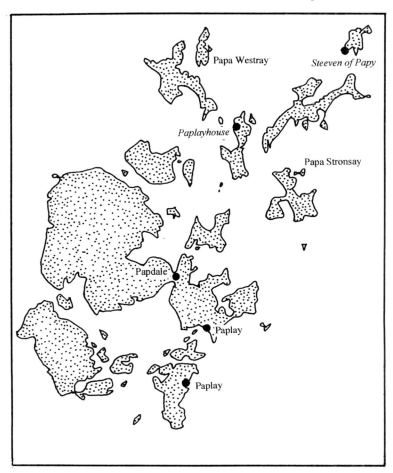

6. **Papa-names.** *Papleyhouse, Eday, and the Steevens of Papy may not be genuine papa-names (H.Marwick* Orkney Farm-names, *50, and 'Place-names of North Ronaldsay', 57). A further papa-name at one time existed, the unidentified island described by Fordun as the 'third Papay'.*

simply shows the extent of his ignorance. The story of the books which were found abandoned is unlikely to be true—a book which might have a silver mount was a rare and valuable object not likely to be abandoned except in the most dire emergency. Of course the arrival of Vikings might have been a dire emergency, but the tradition of the abandoned books is more likely to be an echo of Ari's account in *Islendingabók* of how the first settlers in Iceland were reputed to have found 'Irish books, bells and crosiers' which had been left behind by Irish Papae when their place of retreat was disturbed.[50] A fragment of what may have been a highly ornate book mount

15

of an eighth-century date was found at Munkerhouse, Stromness, although there was nothing to suggest that it had been abandoned in dramatic circumstances.[51] Hermit settlement of the same kind as was found in Iceland was described by the Irish monk Dicuil in his book *Liber de Mensura Orbis Terrarum*, written c.825 AD.[52] He mentions uninhabited islands which from their description must be Faroe and which had been regularly visited by Irish hermits for about a century until Viking attacks led to the abandonment of their settlements.

Adomnán's account of Cormac's travels and the presence of hermits in Iceland and Faroe have unduly influenced ideas about the Orkney Papae, especially since Orkney *papa*-names are identical to Icelandic forms such as Papley and Papyli. It is understandable that scholars lacking a detailed knowledge of Orkney topography have assumed that Orkney *papa*-names also denoted colonies of hermits. However, Orkney and Shetland with their settled population were rather different from the empty lands to the north. A knowledge of the sites reveals that some of the principal *papa*-names are applied to important places on good farming land. Papdale, for example, is the site of Kirkwall and is always likely to have been a central place in relation to the rest of Orkney. Several *papa*-names do show a degree of seclusion insofar as they are relatively small islands—Papa Westray, Papa Stronsay and the unidentified 'third Papa' which Fordun includes in his list of Orkney islands.[53] Papa Westray and Papa Stronsay, however, are fertile and their inhabitants are not likely to have been restricted to a colony of hermits, nor are hermits likely to have commissioned the sculpture found at several of these sites. Later we find that a surprisingly large number of these *papa*-names are associated with the earldom family: Earl Rognvald Brusisson had his residence at Kirkwall (Papdale), we find him collecting his Yule malt from Papa Stronsay, it was there that he was killed, and his place of burial was Papa Westray.[54] Paplay, now in Holm but once a distinct parish, was another big estate with a *papa*-name. Paplay is 'Papa-byli', the settlement of the Papae, and it lies on well-drained south-facing farmland known for its early crop. We find this estate detached from the earldom c.1099 by King Magnus Barelegs to provide a dowry for St Magnus's sister (see Chapter 6) and, since she lived in Norway, Paplay became the residence of her mother.[55] As late as the fifteenth century Earl William Sinclair was at some trouble to acquire Paplay and re-unite it with the earldom estate after a gap of 350 years.[56] We gain the impression that the *papa*-names were estates of a well endowed Pictish church, and it is difficult to avoid the conclusion that much of this church property was at some point confiscated and found its way into the hands of the Norse earls.

The development of a mutually supportive relationship between kings and the church was a general feature throughout north-west Europe at this time. Royal support brought obvious advantages to the church: it led to mass conversion and to the enforcement of Christian practices; kings endowed the church with the land which made it rich and influential, and they provided the protection a property-owning church required. There were equal advantages for the king: his power was sanctified by divine authority and by belief systems which were supportive of his government; he might use the church to bring his kingdom into contact with the wider British and European communities, and a richly endowed church also provided careers and a comfortable life-style for junior members of the royal dynasty whose literacy made them useful supporters of royal power. An alliance of church and state may also have been a particularly effective way of extending the secular rule of mainland Pictland into areas ripe for conversion such as Orkney.[57] The Papae and their landed estates were the products of this kind of church—they were the very antithesis of hermits.

King Nechtán mac Derile (King of the Picts c.706-724 and 728-9) encouraged the institutionally stronger Roman church in Pictland, most famously when c.715 AD he sent messengers to Abbot Ceolfrith in Northumbria seeking advice on conforming the Pictish church to Roman observance. Nechtán's reforms are elaborated in the legend of St Boniface who is reputed to have arrived from Northumbria with seven bishops (symbolically one for each of the Pictish provinces) and to have built 150 churches.[58] This 'Boniface' is not the same person as the better known St Boniface of Crediton who carried Christianity to Germany. It is presumably the Pictish Boniface who is commemorated by the Boniface dedication in Papa Westray. To further complicate matters, this Pictish Boniface seems to be the same person as Curitan who is associated with Rosemarkie.[59] Whereas the Boniface legend emphasises the Northumbrian link, it has been suggested that his *alter ego*, Curitan, actually belonged to a pro-Roman faction within the Columban church, and that direct Northumbrian influence on the organisation of the church in the north of Scotland was limited.[60]

Northumbrian contacts with Orkney are illustrated by the two eagles, the symbol of the evangelist John, one from the Knowe of Burrian, Harray, and the other from a gospel fragment known as Corpus Christi 197b (Figs.7 and 8). The similarities are so great that it is obvious that the Birsay sculpture and the manuscript were executed from a common pattern. Yet on close examination the Orkney sculpture is in several respects the better version. Influences need not necessarily be all in the one direction, so perhaps the gospel was produced at a Northumbrian centre which was receptive to Pictish art.[61] The important point, however, is that the eagles show that Orkney had a direct contact with the area which was then the very heartland of progressive Christianity. On the other hand, Christian influences are unlikely to have been exclusively Northumbrian: if the inscription on the

7 and 8. ***Eagles.*** *The similarities of the eagles from the Knowe of Burrian and from the manuscript gospel fragment (Corpus Christi 197b) suggest that they were executed from a common pattern. This provides evidence of Northumbrian contacts, yet in some respects the Orkney eagle is the better version, for example in the way the legs are depicted.*

spindle-whorl from Buckquoy is Old Irish, it points to an Irish ecclesiastical connection since only a cleric was likely to be able to write. The inscription, however, is on a very portable object and so, although the Irish connection remains valid, the Irish-speaking cleric was not necessarily in Orkney.

The theory that the many Orkney dedications to St Peter are a proto-parochial system associated with these changes has been proposed by Raymond Lamb (Fig.9).[62] The Peter-dedication, of course, emphasises the connection with the Roman church, and we know that this dedication was used at Egglespethir ('Peter-church'), the stone church built near Restenneth in Angus at Nechtán's request by architects sent from Northumbria. A cluster of Peter-dedications is also found near Rosemarkie with which Boniface-Curitan was reputedly associated. In support of the idea that Peterkirks form a contemporaneous network, Lamb sees the distribution as relating to districts a good deal larger than the present parishes; he believes that many are

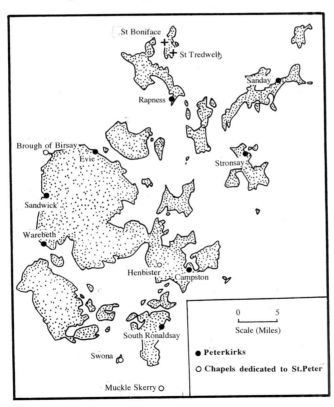

9. **Peterkirks.** *Dedications to St Peter. This distribution has been interpreted as an eighth-century proto-parochial system.*

locally known as 'kirks' rather than chapels, although only a few eventually became parish churches.[63] Another relevant feature is that several of them occupy broch sites, suggesting that secular centres of power were converted to religious purposes and used to endow the church. One Peterkirk for which Pictish origins are particularly convincing is St Peter's, the parish church for the north parish of South Ronaldsay. It occupies a site on sandy land close to the shore, as do many early Orkney churches, and it lies within the extensive and fertile district of Paplay. Furthermore a slab at one time built into the sill of a window is incised with the crescent and v-rod and the mirror symbols.[64] Thus the Peter-dedication is found within a district with a *papa*-name and in association with finds of characteristic Pictish sculpture. Lamb's persuasive Peterkirk theory, however, needs to be treated with a degree of caution, and the way he further elaborates his scheme to pinpoint the actual circumstances of Orkney's official conversion at the hands of the Northumbrian emissary, Ecgbert, is imaginative reconstruction—not necessarily wrong, but venturing beyond the provable facts.[65]

A good reason for believing that the dedication on Papa Westray is to Boniface/Curitan (rather than the better-known St Boniface of Crediton) is the dedication to St Tredwell which is found in the same small island. Tredwell (Triduana or Trolla) was a holy virgin who was a member of Boniface's legendary mission. The dedications cannot be taken as evidence that Boniface/Curitan and Tredwell were active in Orkney but they do show that, either in Pictish times or later, someone wished to add substance to the legend. Tredwell, we are told, attracted the unwelcome attention of a Pictish king who sent messengers to tell her how her beautiful eyes inflamed him; no sooner had Tredwell received the message than she plucked out her eyes, skewered them on a twig and told the king that he could have what he so much admired.[66] Tredwell is a native variant of St Lucy of Syracuse of whom the same story is told, and there is nothing in the legend to connect Tredwell to Orkney. However, in addition to her chapel in Papa Westray, there are other dedications in Caithness (Croit-Trolla) and Sutherland (Kintradwell) and there is a Cairntrodlie near Peterhead which mark the spread of her cult northwards. Whereas all knowledge of Boniface faded, the cult of Tredwell continued to be popular long after the passing of the Picts. When Bishop John of Caithness was attacked and blinded by Earl Harald Maddadsson's men c.1201, his sight was miraculous restored by Tredwell's intervention (Chapter 8).[67] Latter-day Presbyterian ministers in Papa Westray had difficulty in preventing their parishioners from paying their devotions to Tredwell before coming to listen to their sermons.[68]

St Boniface church in Papa Westray is closely associated with the names Munkerhouse (Monks' house) and Binnas Kirk (*boen-hus*, prayer house). Finds from the site include stones inscribed with crosses of a pre-Norse type,

10. *Papil 'Pony-rider' Stone. This slab from Papil, West Burra, Shetland, depicts the 'Papae', the clergy of the late Pictish church.*

and also a fragment of a decorated corner-post shrine.[69] Recent rescue investigations of the eroded coastal location revealed a large and complex site, one phase of which involved a change of use of an Iron Age settlement to ecclesiastical purposes. Lamb has suggested that St Boniface church was the seat of a pre-Norse bishop who was installed as a result of the Northumbrian mission to Pictland; he maintained that a bishop's seat in Papa Westray was not necessarily peripheral, but was conveniently situated on sea routes connecting it to places in Shetland such as Papil in West Burra and St Ninian's Isle.[70] The story of St Findan, if we can believe it, provides possible confirmation that a bishop was found in Papa Westray, or somewhere else in the North Isles of Orkney, in the mid-ninth century (see Chapter 3).

Dedications to Laurence can be seen as a variant of the Peter-dedication. Laurence (Archbishop of Canterbury 606-616 AD) was Augustine's immediate successor and so Laurence-dedications could also be used to demonstrate allegiance to Canterbury and Rome. Laurence came to be known as 'the Apostle to the Picts', apparently on no better a basis than that he sent unfriendly letters to native British churches.[71] The now ruinous St Laurence church in Burray occupies what is possibly an early site, but the best evidence comes from Papil in West Burra, Shetland, where the Laurence-dedication is combined with the *papa*-name and with Pictish sculpture of an ecclesiastical nature.[72] In the same way that the Birsay warriors provide us with a portrait of Pictish aristocrats, one of the stones from Papil provides a picture of the Papae. It shows a procession making its way to a free-standing cross (of which none have survived). The figures wear ankle-length hooded cloaks of a monkish appearance, they each hold a staff or crook, and they carry a satchel which might have contained a precious book. The leader, perhaps an abbot or bishop, is easily identified since he is mounted on a horse—not one of the prancing Pictish horses which appear on scenes of hunting and warfare, but nonetheless a fine-boned thoroughbred. The monks and their leader are not hermits, but well fed and prosperous clerics, conscious of their dignity. Perhaps the distinction between monastic and missionary settlement is somewhat blurred, and priests and monks live in a single community. The members of this group seem to have a pastoral function in relation to the surrounding populace, and to be travelling out to a recognised preaching station. The spiral decorations might even represent waves, suggesting that the community had crossed the sea on a mission to bring organised Christianity to Shetland.

Closely nucleated villages associated with brochs seem to have flourished in the first and second centuries AD, and excavations at Howe indicate a sizeable community.[73] The use of the broch tower at Howe ended in the fourth century and the fortifications were abandoned. Scattered rural settlement always existed in parallel with broch villages and, although settlement on certain broch sites including Howe continued throughout the Pictish period, villages were in decay and there was a reversion to more a dispersed pattern of settlement.

Excavations at Buckquoy (Birsay),[74] Pool (Sanday), and at Skaill (Deerness)[75] reveal in differing degrees that late Pictish society could sustain a comfortable life-style. At Buckquoy a sequence of Pictish houses span the seventh and early eighth century. The first two successive houses have a cellular plan with small rectilinear cells opening off a central living area. House 4 has a 'man-shaped' outline with four chambers in a linear arrangement. The main living chamber had a substantial slab-lined hearth on which peat was burned, and on either side there were wooden benches or sleeping platforms. Buckquoy did not stand alone but was part of a community along the shore of the bay, and it also needs to be interpreted in relation to the Pictish site on what is now the tidal island of the Brough. Buckquoy might be seen as a working part of a manorial estate associated with a royal or aristocratic residence of a kind which was then common in northern Europe. Finds include an inscribed spindle whorl, bone pins, a double-sided comb, a bone spoon and a painted pebble of a type which is widely distributed and is believed to have been used for magical purposes. Good quality Pictish buildings are found at Pool and at Skaill where the building of a prestigious rectilinear house in the late Pictish period was associated with the appearance of a new and relatively fine type of pottery. Peter Gelling, who investigated the site, was impressed by the contrast between the Pictish period and the squalid living conditions of the first Norse settlers on the site —the coming of the Norse in some respects brought a regression in material culture which lasted for the best part of 200 years.

A striking example of the affluence of the upper stratum of Pictish society is to be found in the 28 pieces of ornamented silver found in 1958 at St Ninian's Isle in Shetland.[76] Despite being found on an ecclesiastical site, the treasure appears to be of secular origin and it has been dated to about 800 AD—the very end of the Pictish period. Obvious possibilities are that it was concealed to prevent it falling into the hands of Viking raiders or, alternatively that it was Viking loot, but treasure was concealed as a matter of routine, so we might be mistaken in making a direct connection between the buried treasure and the Viking threat. What may well have been a similar hoard was discovered at the Broch of Burgar in 1840: the items which have now been lost are said to have included a silver vessel, silver combs, pins and brooches, a fragment of a silver chain and a large number of amber beads.[77] Moulds discovered in the Pictish horizon on the Brough of Birsay were designed for the production of brooches similar to those found on St Ninian's Isle,[78] so clearly there were metal-working specialists in Orkney capable of producing work of the same design and quality.

It has been possible to build up a reasonably coherent picture of Pictish Orkney, at least in the last century or so of its existence. Orkney was a successful farming-fishing community which already possessed most of the crops, animals and technological skills which characterised pre-modern farming in recent centuries. It was a society dominated by a warlike aristocracy, but it may not have been greatly disturbed by warfare apart from infrequent external attacks. The islands were ruled by a 'regulus' who was subservient to the a king in mainland Pictland, although for most of the time he was probably free to act as if he was independent. The affluent elite had a lifestyle with interests which were typical of Dark Age society, such as warfare and hunting, and they possessed surplus wealth which enabled them to command the skills of craftsmen who worked in precious metal, in stone, and presumably in more perishable materials. They lived on landed estates, and their wealth probably also derived from food renders and services exacted from the surrounding community. The church in many ways mirrored this secular society and shared its values, and yet, although it reinforced rather than challenged existing power structures, Christianity no doubt was also an effective means of introducing a more outward-looking and enlightened society. This was the society which now had to meet the onslaught of the Viking invasions.

2

Orkneyinga Saga and the Early Jarls

With King Harald Fairhair and the story of his great voyage which established the Orkney earldom, there is a strong sense of a new beginning. We do not know for certain the name of a single Orkney Pict, but events are now illumined by the full light of saga—we have all the detailed stories, the memorable characters, and apparently the very words spoken by the leading protagonists. Yet saga is not always what it seems. *Orkneyinga Saga* was written in Iceland c.1200 AD, some three hundred years after the date of Harald Fairhair, and it was not well informed about early times. The saga as it has come down to us is a composite document, based on a variety of written and oral sources, and the material was revised on more than one occasion.[1] Often the way the story is told reflects both the literary concerns of the writers and the political biases of their sources.

Orkneyinga saga begins with three daunting chapters dealing with the mythical ancestry of the earls. These chapters must have deterred many readers who made the very natural mistake of attempting to read the saga from the beginning. The real action begins in Chapter 4 when King Harald *hárfagre* ('Fairhair') sets out to punish Vikings who are using the islands as a base from which to attack Norway. Thus the first Vikings are not Norwegians appearing over the horizon to raid Orkney, but Vikings who were already in the islands and were attacking the homeland. The saga-audience would know who these people were: they would assume that they were petty kings and defeated chiefs who were continuing their resistance after Harald Fairhair had united Norway by his victory at Hafrsfjord. Icelanders believed that many people emigrated on account of Harald's tyranny, and since they knew that many of their ancestors came from Shetland, Orkney and the Hebrides, they could readily accept that King Harald's power had extended to these parts. Harald's voyage was a triumphal progress: we are told that he subdued Shetland, Orkney and the Hebrides, attacked the Isle of Man and annexed land farther 'west' than any king of Norway had done since. During the course of this expedition Ivarr, a son of Earl Rognvald of Møre, was killed and in compensation the king gave Rognvald Orkney and Shetland. Rognvald did not intend to remain in the islands, so he passed them to his brother, Sigurd *hinn riki* ('the Mighty') who becomes the first of a line of earls who were to rule the islands for the next six hundred years.[2] The great voyage is so thoroughly ingrained in popular and scholarly history, both ancient and modern, that it comes as a bit of a shock to realise that it might not be true.

The kind of information we have from British sources could hardly be more different. In contrast to all the detailed stories of saga, Irish Annals consist of little bullets of information so briefly recorded that it is often difficult to understand the course of events. Annals, however, have the great advantage that they come attached to a date which, if not always entirely accurate, seldom has much margin of error. A typical entry from the *Annals of Ulster* in 794 AD records 'the devastation of all the islands of Britain by the gentiles'[3] (heathen Scandinavians). Other entries point to a sudden on-set of raiding about that time. There are records from the same decade of attacks on Rathlin, Skye, Iona and Ulster,[4] but there is no mention of Ork-ney about which the Irish were less well informed and not much concerned. Harald Fairhair's expedition is much later. Saga seldom contains dates, and it struggles even with such key events as the Battle of Hafrsfjord, but we know that the great battle took place at some date between 880 AD and 900 AD.[5] Harald Fairhair's voyage to Orkney, if it was a real event, was after Hafrsfjord, and so there is a century of Viking activity in the British Isles about which *Orkneyinga saga* is silent.

To some extent the gap can be filled by other sagas. *Eyrbyggia saga* con-tains the same story of a great expedition to punish Vikings who were raiding Norway, but instead of King Harald, it is Ketil *flat-nefr* ('Flatnose') who led the expedition. Ketil was put in command by King Harald and he succeeded in conquering the Hebrides, but apparently as a personal domain, since it was reported that 'he was not doing much to bring the islands under King Harald's rule'.[6] In *Laxdæla saga* we again find Ketil Flatnose, but this time he is on the other side—he is now one of the chiefs fleeing from King Harald's tyranny.[7] Yet another account found in *Landnámabók* attempts to make sense of these conflicting traditions: it describes King Harald's voyage of conquest in terms which echo *Orkneyinga saga*'s account, but we are told that as soon as King Harald returned to Norway, Vikings, Scots and Irishmen swarmed into the Hebrides, and so a second expedition led by Ketil Flatnose was sent to reconquer the islands.[8] However, there are problems with the chronol-ogy of all of these accounts: Sigurd the Mighty, the first Orkney earl, fought a war allied to Thorstein Óláfsson *rauda* ('the Red'), an adult grandson of Ketil,[9] and so it seems that Ketil's activities in the Hebrides actually belong to a period a good deal earlier than the founding of the Orkney earldom as described by *Orkneyinga saga*.

The main problem about accepting King Harald's great voyage as a real historical event is that we read about it only in Icelandic sources of a much later date. If we go to contemporary records in Ireland, England and Scotland we find no mention of this great voyage, although we do find accounts of other royal fleets. The sporadic raids of the 790s had by the mid-ninth century turned into major expeditions of conquest. We are told of 'a great and vast royal fleet' led by 'Tuirgéis' which came to the north of Ireland (c.838 x 845 AD),[10] and in 849 AD a naval expedition of 140 ships led by 'the King of the Foreigners' came to take control over the Scandinavians who were already in Ireland.[11] These expeditions have more than a passing similarity to the events described in *Orkneyinga saga*, although they were a generation earlier than the first possible date for King Harald's great voyage. It is possible, however, that fleets of this size were raised in the Hebrides and Ireland rather than brought across the North Sea. Warfare on a scale which could sustain a prolonged siege of Dumbarton, and which could bring about the temporary submission of southern Pictland, points to the power of Norse kings based in Ireland and western Scotland.[12] The relationship of these ninth century rulers to Orkney and Shetland is largely conjecture, although *Orkneyinga saga* believed that it was with Orkney assistance that they had conquered much of Scotland.[13]

There were, however, implications for Orkney even in the earliest phase of raiding in the Hebrides. Orkney was the landfall after the crossing of the North Sea and it was the launching point for the equally exposed voyage round Cape Wrath into the Minch. There must have been many occasions when ships experienced delay while waiting for weather, provisions were needed, allies and reinforcements might be found, and those caught late on the voyage home might be forced to over-winter. It is possible that the onset of raiding in the 790s was made possible by the acquisition of an Orkney base. By the time large royal fleets are recorded in Ireland in the mid-ninth century, Orkney must have been thoroughly under Norse control.

When we look to Irish Annals in the period 880-900 AD for confirmation of Harald's voyage of conquest, we draw a complete blank. It seems impossible that a major expedition could date from this period. The one piece of contemporary evidence which seems to support the voyage is Norse: a verse in Thorbjorn Hornklove's *Glymsdrapa* refers obliquely to Harald's victory over Scots. It is, however, by no means certain that this victory was during the course of Harald's expedition as described in *Orkneyinga saga*. Snorri Sturlasson offers contradictory opinions: in *King Harald's saga* he quotes the verse to support the great voyage,[14] but in *St Olaf's saga* he takes the verse to refer to Harald's plundering of Scots at a later date after he had made peace with Torf Einar.[15] Haakon Shetelig noted that another poem, also by Thorbjorn Hornklove, which describes the Battle of Hafrsfjord, tells us that Scottish-Irish 'spears' were among Harald's enemies, and so the victory over the Scots commemorated in *Glymsdrapa* might have been at

Hafrsfjord rather than in Scotland.[16] Another possible occasion when Harald might have encountered Scots is a Viking attack on Dunnottar which is around the right date (889 x 900 AD) but about which no details are known.[17] Thus we cannot be sure that *Glymsdrapa*, despite its mention of Scots, refers to the great voyage. On the contrary, it seems more likely that the story of the voyage is a historical deduction or a fictional account which has been reconstructed from this and other verses.

One strand of opinion is that Harald's expedition is entirely apocryphal, the story being shaped by Icelandic prejudices and modelled on the later voyages of King Magnus Barelegs (1098 and 1102).[18] There are certainly numerous points of contact with Magnus Barelegs' expeditions (see Chapter 6). Both King Harald and King Magnus made two voyages to the west; they campaigned in much the same regions, and the claim is made in their respective sagas that they subjected to their rule a wider area than any other Norwegian king;[19] both conquered Orkney, and both established a new regime with someone named Sigurd in charge; both expeditions resulted in the death of an important person (Ivarr and Kali), and on both occasions a relative received generous compensation which had far-reaching consequences for the government of the islands. It seems possible that the saga-writer knew little or nothing about Harald Fairhair's expedition but lifted an 'off-the-peg' account which he used as a historical template for the great voyage. This is further suggested by other Magnus Barelegs parallels in the early part of the saga: the mythical genealogy in *Orkneyinga saga* describes how the sons of the eponymous Nor divided Norway into two parts, the islands and the mainland, in the same way as the west coast of Scotland was divided by Magnus Barelegs' 1098 treaty with Scotland. The myth even includes the annexation of a peninsula when a ship is dragged across an isthmus with the legendary sea-king at the tiller, in the same way that Magnus was reputed to have claimed Kintyre.[20] It seems that the saga-author had King Magnus much in mind when he wrote these early chapters.

The story of the great voyage was politically useful to Norway because King Harald's expedition could be used as a quasi-historical basis for asserting Norway's sovereignty. In 1021 we find King Olaf using the myth for that purpose: Olaf maintained that the first earls had been placed in the islands by King Harald Fairhair, and so their successors held the islands *i lén* (as an administrative fief from the king) rather than by hereditary right (see Chapter 5).[21] Whether or not these arguments were actually used as early as this occasion is uncertain, but the myth was even more relevant at the time the saga was written (c.1200) when the relationship between king and earl was being redefined. In 1195 Earl Harald Maddadsson was forced to make abject submission after Orkney's ill-judged intervention in Norway's civil wars ended in defeat at the Battle of Florevåg (see Chapter 8). King Sverre, who had threatened to make another 'great voyage' to punish Orkney, dictated terms which detached Shetland from the earldom and imposed strict controls on Harald Maddadsson's Orkney.[22] It is common practice to justify arrangements which are in fact innovations by searching for historical precedents: the expedition of Magnus Barelegs had imposed direct royal control, and the fostering of a belief that there had been similar voyages by King Harald Fairhair in the remote past served the purpose of establishing a claim that the earldom of Orkney and the Kingdom of Man and the Hebrides had been integral parts of the king's possessions ever since the very creation of the kingdom of Norway. The way in which this argument is put into the mouth of St Olaf adds the extra authority of Norway's warrior king and patron saint. Thus the story of King Harald's voyage may or may not be based on an ancient legend, but it seems likely that these supposed events had received a good deal of publicity in 1195—only a year or two before the saga-writer wrote his account.

With no details of the conquest of Orkney, nor any mention of its previous inhabitants, the saga plunges straight into a campaign fought in the north of Scotland by Sigurd the Mighty in alliance with Thorstein the Red, grandson of Ketil Flatnose. Their opponent was a fearsome Pict named Maelbrigte Tusk, so called because of a large protruding tooth. It had been agreed that both sides were to meet on an appointed day with 40 men, but Sigurd suspected treachery so he brought 80 men, mounted two to a horse. When Maelbrigte saw two feet on each side of every horse he knew that he had been betrayed, but he was to have posthumous revenge. Sigurd cut off Maelbrigte's head and was riding home in high spirits with the head dangling from his saddle-bow when he grazed his leg on the 'tusk' and as a result contracted blood-poisoning and died.[23]

Set-piece battles are commoner in legend than in reality, and it would be a mistake to take Sigurd's encounter with Maelbrigte too literally. The story, however, relates to the beginnings of a prolonged struggle between native and Norse in the north of Scotland. The name Máel Brigte was later current in the family of the Mormaers of Moray (see Fig.22) whose power-centre was somewhere in the vicinity of Inverness. The author of *Orkneyinga saga* believed that the conflict was in this area: we are told that Sigurd had a fort somewhere well south into the Moray Firth, and that his place of burial was at Ekkjalsbakki, the Dornoch Firth. The farm of Cyderhall near Dornoch appears in the thirteenth century as Syvardhoch ('Sigurd's mound') and so the place-name appears to provide unexpected confirmation of this part of the saga's account.[24]

Sigurd the Mighty was succeeded by his son, Guthorm, who ruled for one winter and died childless. Then Hallad, son of Rognvald of Møre, was sent to rule the islands, but he proved powerless to control Danish Vikings

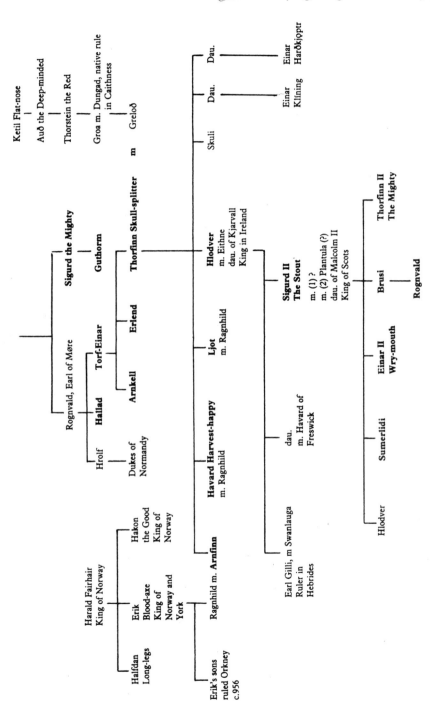

11. *Early Norse Earls of Orkney, c.900 AD to c.1065. Earls of Orkney are shown in bold.*

29

who plundered Orkney and the coast of Caithness, so he gave up the title of 'jarl' and returned to Norway, 'which everyone thought was a huge joke'.[25] The saga tells how, back in Norway, Rognvald gathered his sons in a family conference to discuss what was to be done. The sons one by one step forward to ask Rognvald if it is his will that they should go to Orkney;[26] one by one Rognvald foretells their greater destiny: Thorir will succeed his father as earl in Møre, Hrollaug will emigrate to Iceland where he will be the ancestor of distinguished families, and Hrolf, who is unaccountably absent in *Orkneyinga saga*'s account but present according to *Landnámabók*,[27] is destined to conquer Normandy and become the ancestor of the Kings of England. The outcome is a decision to send Torf Einar, Rognvald's youngest slave-born son. There was no love lost between father and son: Rognvald tells Einar, 'I don't expect you to succeed because all your mother's people were thralls, so the further you go and the longer you stay, the better I'll be pleased'. Einar is given a single ship (in contrast to the great fleet with which King Harald had invaded) yet, despite his limited resources, he immediately defeats the Danish vikings, Kalf *Skurfa* ('Scurvy') and Thórir *Tréskegg* ('Tree-beard') and takes possession of the islands.

Of course, telling the future is not very difficult if you are writing 300 years after the event when everybody knows that important families in Iceland, England and Orkney trace their descent from these people. It is, however, interesting to see the way in which the story is told. It is a common theme in folk tales that brothers are set a difficult task, and that it is the despised youngest son who succeeds where the proud elder brothers fail. When the youngest son is rejected by his father, you know that he is the hero—he is the one who will kill the dragon and marry the princess or whatever the story requires. It shows how saga sometimes makes use of folk-tale motifs which impose their own conventional form on actual events.

There are, however, considerations more important than folk-tale motifs which shape the way the story is told. *Orkneyinga saga* is the *Jarlasaga,* the saga of the earls, and, since the earls are the subject matter, the saga-writer is at pains to establish their status from the outset. This is his main purpose in these early chapters. He is particularly concerned to establish the status of Einar; previous earls, Sigurd the Mighty, Guthorm and Hallad, were a dynastic dead-end, whereas all the earls who follow are in Arnór's phrase 'Torf-Einar's kin'.[28] The saga-writer establishes the status of Einar in two rather different ways:

- He takes every opportunity to emphasise that the Møre family are proper 'earls', legally established in Orkney by King Harald Fairhair, the greatest of early Norwegian kings.

- He depicts Torf Einar as a self-made man, succeeding by his own efforts, owing nothing to anyone, and in some respects capable of dealing with King Harald Fairhair as an equal.

There is bound to be difficulty in combining these contradictory themes of dependence and independence, although they are neatly combined in Einar himself. Royal houses often trace their descent, not just from gods, but also from giantesses—the mythic model requires the prototype king to be the descendant of social opposites.[29] It can be seen how these opposites operate in the case of Torf Einar: his father's ancestry provides a right to rule and confers legitimacy notwithstanding his illegitimate birth, whereas his mother's forebears, because they were unfree, provide him with freedom to carve out a self-made career and break free from the constraints of a dependent relationship to Harald Fairhair. We have already seen some aspects of Einar's self-made image: his mother's people are thralls, he is rejected by his father who apparently has little regard for Orkney, and he succeeds in the conquest of the islands without much help from anyone.

Yet the saga is as much concerned with legality as it is with this self-made theme. We have seen how, according to the saga, the earldom was established in grand style by King Harald Fairhair who personally arrives in Orkney with his fleet. The same concern for legality is found whenever a new earl is appointed: when Harald was about to return to Norway at the close of his great voyage 'he gave Sigurd the title of earl';[30] when Hallad was sent from Norway 'King Harald gave him the title of earl'[31] and, in the case of Torf Einar, 'Harald gave him the title of earl'.[32] Step by step the saga is careful to tell us that each earl's title derives from King Harald Fairhair.

Although the primary purpose of the source which the saga-author was using was to assert the dominion of the Norwegian kings over the Orkney earls, he was also able to use the myth of the great voyage in a way which reflected favourably on the earls. An account which provided such impeccably respectable origins for the Orkney earls was useful because not everyone necessarily agreed. The *Historia Norvegiae*, written about the same date as the saga, described how the Picts and Papae were exterminated by Viking attacks:

> …certain pirates, of the family of the most vigorous prince Ronald, set out with a great fleet, and crossed the Solundic Sea (the North Sea) and stripped these races of their ancient settlements, destroying them wholly, and subduing the islands to themselves.[33]

In this account we again find memories of the 'great fleet' and we find the Møre family, but King Harald Fairhair is missing. The *Historia* is not particularly interested in the status of the rulers of Orkney, so they are not dignified by the title of 'earl' but dismissed as 'certain pirates'. The *Historia* is less partisan than the saga and for that reason its account might be preferred, although, with its fabulous description of the Picts and Papae (Chapter 1), it is not necessarily better informed about the early Viking period.

Because the saga wishes to give a central place to the establishment of the Møre earldom, and particularly to Torf Einar, other traditions which were current about early Orkney history are ignored. We might even describe these traditions as deliberately written out of the saga in order that the establishment of the earldom becomes the beginning of the story. Thus the ninth century Viking raids and the wars which are well documented in Irish Annals are omitted, and there is only the briefest of mentions of the conquests of Ketil Flatnose and Thorstein the Red. Nor does the saga find a place for Ragnar Loðbrók ('Hairy-breeks') although there is compelling evidence that he was well known in Orkney at the time the saga-writer was collecting his information. We find Ragnar, not only in Saxo Grammaticus,[34] but also in *Háttalykill*, the twelfth century poem of which Earl Rognvald Kolsson (St Rognvald) is believed to be joint author, and in *Krákumal* which may also be the work of an Orkney poet.[35] The twelfth century inscription which says of Maeshowe that 'this mound was built before Loðbrók'[36] seems to equate Ragnar, rather than Harald Fairhair, with the beginnings of Norse times. In the Irish *Duald Mac-Firbis Fragment*, which because it mentions an eclipse can date the events it describes to 865 AD (i.e. before Harald Fairhair), a certain 'Rognvald', reputedly the son of Halfdan the Black, King of Norway, remained in Orkney while his older sons made a slave-raid to Spain and North Africa.[37] It has been suggested that this 'Rognvald' might be equated with Ragnar Loðbrók or even with Rognvald of Møre. One theory is that the 'certain pirates of the family of Rognvald of Møre' to whom the *Historia Norvegia* refers, were already established in the islands before the time of King Harald Fairhair, making it easy for King Harald to grant them what they already possessed.[38] Thus there was a corpus of legend, admittedly of a dubious nature, some of which was current in Orkney when the saga-author was gathering his material, but which he chose not to use because he wanted to make the foundation of the earldom the beginning of his story.

The status of the earls is also the main concern of the first three chapters of *Orkneyinga saga* which describe their ancestry. Genealogy in saga-times has been described as 'an imaginative art'[39] whereby some choice of ancestors was usually possible. We certainly ought not to put much reliance on the factual accuracy of this genealogy beyond the most recent generations. There is a natural temptation to dismiss these chapters as being of no real value, and yet it is interesting to see the kind of ancestors which were provided for the Orkney earls. We do not know if this genealogy was devised by

12. **Papdale House, Kirkwall.** *Papdale was the home of Malcolm Laing, the historian, and Samuel Laing, who introduced Norse sagas to the English-speaking world with his translation of* Heimskrigla. *For a time Robert Scarth, the Agricultural Improver, lived there. More recently Papdale was saved from demolition by Orkney Heritage Society and was the home of the author.*

the saga-author, but the ancestors are so well suited to his purpose that we may suspect that he shaped the genealogy, even if it is not entirely his own invention. It would have been easy to have provided a prestigious ancestry by linking the earls to the royal families of Scandinavia, or perhaps tracing their descent from Odin. Instead the forebears of the earls are to be found in the elemental forces of the far north, the Sea, the North Wind, Flame, Frost and Snow. It is a genealogy which serves the purpose of establishing the earls as belonging to an ancient, magical family with a natural right to rule in the northern world. It is, however, a family which exists independently of the royal dynasty of Norway, rather than merely as a junior branch.[40] The genealogy is definitely part of the independence theme.

With such an ancestry Torf Einar was well equipped to deal with King Harald Fairhair almost on terms of equality. Back in Norway Einar's father, Rognvald of Møre, was killed when he was burned in his house by Halfdan *Háleggr* ('Longlegs'), the king's son. Faced with his father's anger, Halfdan fled to Orkney where he made himself king. Torf Einar was expelled and

33

took temporary refuge in Scotland, but then returned and defeated Halfdan in a sea-battle. As darkness fell, Halfdan leapt overboard and swam ashore. The saga describes how the following morning he was discovered and given by Einar as a sacrifice to Odin by the carving of the 'blóðörn' ('blood-eagle'): Halfdan's ribs were hacked from his spine, and his lungs drawn out through his back, thus creating a horrifying and bloody caricature of a winged bird. As events unfolded Einar celebrated his victory by reciting a series of sarcastic verses.[41]

We will return to the blood-eagle in due course, but for the moment we can follow the saga's account of the dealings between Torf Einar and King Harald Fairhair. Harald strongly disapproved of the burning of Rognvald of Møre who was his friend and ally, but he could not ignore the killing of his own son in such humiliating circumstances. Harald descended on the islands for a second time. The outcome was that Harald came to an accommodation with Einar whereby a fine of 60 gold marks was exacted from the islands. We are told that Einar offered to pay the entire fine personally on condition that the odal (or udal) rights of the bonder (leading farmers) were made over to him. The bonder agreed to this arrangement because 'the rich ones expected to be able to buy back their rights and the poor ones had no money to pay the fine'.[42]

This account makes a number of points about Einar's status: Einar is not defeated in battle even when confronted by the great king; Einar pays the entire fine, and he is wealthy enough to do so apparently without difficulty; indeed by acquiring the odal rights of the bonder, he is able to turn the whole affair to his advantage. When faced with the wrath of the king, Einar acquits himself well. The killing of Halfdan and the subsequent peace-making with King Harald are further parts of the 'independence' theme.

The question of the real meaning of these odal rights is difficult, but at one level it is easy to see that the saga-author is comparing Einar's acquisition of odal rights to what the king was reputed to have done in Norway. According to *Harald Fairhair's saga:*

> King Harald made this law over all the lands he conquered that all the udal property should belong to him, and that the bonder should pay him land dues for their possessions.[43]

The *Orkneyinga saga* is making the point that whatever Harald Fairhair could do in Norway, Torf Einar was powerful enough to do in Orkney. It is a story designed to enhance Torf Einar's status by likening him to the Norwegian king. The account in *Orkneyinga saga* (and indeed in *King Harald's saga*) has the effect of indirectly suggesting that the king's authority was less in Orkney than it was in Norway, since it was Torf Einar rather than King Harald who acquired the odal rights. A different version in *St Olaf saga* is designed to emphasise the Norwegian king's feudal superiority over Orkney. In *St Olaf's saga* we are told that it was King Harald who made Orcadians give up their odal rights and hold their land under oath from him.[44]

It would be wise not to accept the acquisition of odal rights by Torf Einar (or King Harald) entirely at face value, especially if we take the story to mean that all property-owners were reduced to the status of tenants.[45] It seems that the real issues in this early period were not so much the latter-day concepts of tenancy and rent which acquiring odal rights might seem to imply, but the question of how new and extended forms of lordship were to operate in a udal society. An extension of lordship depended on expanding the lord's ability to command military service, to exact food renders, and to billet fighting men by means of enforced hospitality. In addition to dependants who lived on the earl's personal lands, there was the larger group of udallers who owned their own farms, but were nevertheless required to accept the earl's lordship and the obligations which that entailed. It appears that enforced military service outside Orkney was particularly contentious. When Torf Einar's great-grandson, Earl Sigurd the Stout (not to be confused with Sigurd the Mighty), was hard pressed in Caithness, Orkneymen initially resisted his attempts to compel them to serve outside the islands. The odal rights come into the story once again: we are told that Sigurd 'gave the Orkneymen their odal rights in return for war-service'.[46] Thus the saga would have us believe that odal rights, whatever they might be, were acquired by Torf Einar but returned to the bonder about a century later.

Odal rights, however, may have less to do with these issues than with events nearer to the saga-author's own time. One source which seems to have been at the writer's disposal is the argument used c.1137 when Earl Rognvald Kolsson was attempting to levy taxation for the building of St Magnus Cathedral (see Chapter 7).[47] The story that earls had acquired rights over the udallers in the remote past seems to be a twelfth century quasi-historical fiction which was used to justify this tax. This useful fiction, however, might have had been constructed from genuine memories of popular resistance to early earls when they attempted to command military service.

It was not enough that Torf Einar was depicted as a great man in his own right, succeeding by his own efforts, and able to deal with Harald Fairhair on something approaching terms of equality—there is more. By means of a series of subtle touches the saga-writer endows Einar with the characteristics of Odin. In doing so, he provides the Orkney earls with a mysterious, archaic and god-like ancestor. Implicit is a comparison between Odin, 'father of the gods' and the founder of royal dynasties, and Torf Einar, the ancestor of all the earls who follow.

Some of these 'Odin-touches' are fairly obvious, but others are so delicately inserted that they have the quality of a literary puzzle. To the saga-audience the first allusion was not difficult: the saga-writer alerts his readers with a one-sentence description of Torf Einar as 'a tall man, and ugly, one-eyed, yet of all men the most keen-sighted'.[48] This is Odin who was one-eyed, having sacrificed the other in order to gain wisdom. Then in the next chapter we are given a demonstration of Torf Einar's keen-sightedness despite the loss of an eye. The morning after Halfdan's defeat, while Einar's ships are searching for him, it is Einar who personally sees something on the shore of North Ronaldsay, now standing up, now lying down. 'It's either a bird or a man', he says, 'Let us go and find out'. This vivid description has sometimes been thought to preserve a real knowledge of how, in the flat landscape of the North Isles of Orkney, movement is magnified on the distant horizon. The man is hideously transformed into the bird by the cutting of the blood-eagle, and this again introduces Odin. The saga tells us that Torf Einar 'gave him to Odin as an offering for victory'. Since the saga has just cast Einar in the *persona* of Odin, the sacrifice of Halfdan to Odin becomes somewhat complicated: Einar is both the giver and receiver of the sacrifice, rather like Odin in the verse in Hávamál which describes how he hanged himself on the world-tree, 'dedicated to Odin, given myself to myself'.[49] Odin's sacrifice of himself gave him a knowledge of poetry, and an ability to speak spontaneously in skaldic verse.[50] Einar has somewhat similar abilities. The saga would have us believe that, as Halfdan was captured and sacrificed, Einar, in a state of continuous elation, poured forth a series of mocking verses in celebration of his revenge. Skaldic verse is in reality a complicated form of poetry, and is not composed spontaneously by mere mortals.

Einar's proud half-brother, Thorir the Silent, had not followed a dishonourable course with regard to the killing of their father by Halfdan Longlegs. Thorir had, in fact, acted in a way which was strictly correct. King Harald, was 'very angry' when he heard his sons had burned Rognvald and he marched against them. Thorir was given the king's daughter in marriage as compensation for his father's death, he was confirmed as earl, and was given his father's lands. It would have been not just impolitic but ungenerous to reject such freely given compensation. Yet it is the unloved youngest son who emerges with the enhanced reputation. The verses tell us that, while Thorir sits at home 'silently drinking', Einar 'makes din of battle' and exacts terrible vengeance. Einar, like Odin, has drunk the mead of poetry, and is far from silent.[51]

The way the saga-writer handles the story of Torf Einar shows something of his methods. He quotes the poetry at length, dividing it into stanzas separated by short prose links which are designed to explain the verses and provide continuity. It is a technique which we see in other parts of the saga when the writer uses poetry as his source. The verses contain factual information which reappear in the prose, but brief phrases in the verses are expanded and some-times completely altered by the saga-author. These explanatory links are not always successful. For example, the verse which gives us Einar's nick-name 'Torf' tells us nothing more, but in the prose link the name is expanded into the story that Einar was the first to cut peat ('torf'), which he imported into Orkney from 'Torfness' in Scotland. The only point to be taken from this absurd legend relates, not to Torf Einar's own time, but to the twelfth cen-tury, when the saga-writer apparently thought that coastwise trade in a low-cost, bulky cargo such as peat was a real possibility. The author, how-ever, usually had access to sufficient oral tradition to make better sense of the verses, perhaps in the form of a generally accepted interpretation of their meaning—or perhaps no additional information is actually needed. The Torf Einar poetry is not particularly obscure by the standards of skaldic verse: it is obvious that it is the killing of Halfdan, King Harald's son, which is being described, and those involved are identified by name rather than disguised by difficult kennings.

We can therefore be sceptical about information which does not receive corroboration in the verses. Whereas King Harald's 'first' voyage seems to be political propaganda designed to proclaim the Norwegian king's domin-ion over Orkney, the Torf Einar verses may provide a better basis for the 'second' voyage to revenge Halfdan. The verses describe the reaction which Einar expects:

> Many men coming from different directions, and not low-born, are eager to take my life... Men say that the brave king is a danger to me. I shall not be afraid of that...[52]

Those 'not low-born' must be high-born, so Einar is referring to the ex-pected hostility of Harald Fairhair and his sons. Strictly the verses speak only of Einar's expectation of an expedition against him, but the expectation is not likely to have been recorded if it had proved groundless. The verses therefore provide an acceptable source for one, but not two expeditions against Orkney, although the extent of King Harald's personal involvement remains unclear.

A central question is whether the blood-eagle derives from mentions of eagles in the verses or whether the saga-writer had independent informa-tion. It is an important question: we want to know whether the blood-eagle was a real event, or whether it is a literary creation. One of the mentions of eagles in the verses reads:

> Many men are eager to take my life, but they certainly do not know before they have killed me, who will come under the eagle's claws.[53]

We might readily assume that the eagle is mentioned in the verse because the poet, ostensibly Torf Einar himself, is alluding to the blood-eagle. But 'coming under the eagle's claws' is a much-used metaphor for violent death, and it is possible that the poet intended nothing more.[54] When the saga-writer was working up his account, it may be that he really did have a tradition that Halfdan was killed by the cutting of the blood-eagle, but another possibility is that the description of the sacrifice in the prose link is simply an imaginative expansion based on the verses.

The blood-eagle, although doubtful as history, serves an important literary purpose. It is, of course, a memorable incident, but its function is more than merely to provide a thrill of horror. To a Christian audience c.1200 with no knowledge of heathen sacrifice, and given the saga's absence of dates, the barbarity of the blood-eagle fixes Einar in the remote heathen past. Although the saga passes no moral judgement, the incident enhances rather than diminishes Einar's reputation. Indeed the sacrifice to Odin 'for victory' in the opening chapters of the saga presages the success of his descendants. In addition, the saga-writer gives his work a unity by the contrast between the heathen Einar at the beginning of the saga and the saintly Magnus whose martyrdom marks the moral high-point of his story.

What then can we make of the myth of King Harald's great voyage and the story of Torf Einar? Until comparatively recently these stories were accepted at face-value. After all, when saga is the only source, it is not immediately obvious that we should distrust what it tells us. However, even when we have only a single source, we can still try to handle it critically. The saga's account was written long after the event, and deals with a period when the relative proportions of myth and history are difficult to determine. The stories rely on skaldic verse from which it is notoriously difficult to create continuous narrative. Folk-tale motifs, historical templates and twelfth century concerns about the relationship between the king of Norway and the earl of Orkney further shape the story. The saga-author is selective in his use of sources, failing to incorporate traditions which did not suit his literary purpose. There are further problems with Torf Einar: no account of his activity outside Orkney has been preserved, and the imprecision of his dates makes it impossible even to speculate about his involvement in wider Viking affairs. Einar emerges from the pages of saga as a memorable figure, ancient, powerful and mysterious—but as a literary figure rather than a real person. The poetry, however, does contain a core content which is probably factual:

Einar belongs to the Møre family; he kills hostile Vikings; he is nick-named 'Torf'; he defeats *Hafoeta* who is King Harald's son; this battle takes place somewhere in 'the islands'; Einar kills him, and thus avenges his father which Thorir, Hrolf and Hrollaug had failed to do; the death of Halfdan provokes the wrath of King Harald and his sons who are expected to mount a formidable expedition against Einar and may actually do so.

This meagre outline is all we know about Torf Einar. The saga story is a sophisticated literary work designed to provide an appropriate prelude to the more historical sections of the saga by creating suitable origins for the earldom and a fitting ancestor for the earls. The most interesting parts of the story are unsubstantiated by the verses: King Harald's great voyage of conquest is political propaganda which may or may not have a real basis; the comparisons of Einar to Odin are, of course, entirely literary; the blood-eagle is probably an imaginative construction which gives a completely new meaning to an innocuous mention of eagles in the verses; the story of the odal rights is very likely a twelfth-century legal argument transplanted to what was thought to be an appropriate chronological point. We may conclude that there was a historical Einar, but he needs to be carefully separated out from the literary creation.

3

Place-names and the Pictish-Norse Transition

Since Orkneyinga saga tells us nothing about the Picts or how the Norse came to establish themselves in Orkney, place-names play an important part in attempting to understand the settlement process. Place-names studies have often tried to establish the relationship between the Norse and their Pictish predecessors; an investigation of common farm-names has been used to describe how Norse settlement expanded and intensified, and attempts have also been made to identify the regions of West Norway which supplied the original colonists.[1]

The Norse, whatever their relationship to the previous population, indelibly stamped the islands with many thousands of their own place-names—the whole vocabulary of today's landscape is unmistakably Norse. The names of the islands generally include the *−øy* ('island') termination as in Westray, Rousay, Sanday, Shapinsay, Flotta, Burray, Gairsay, Egilsay, Fara, Eday, Hoy, Graemsay, Copinsay and Ronaldsay. Hills often incorporate the Norse *fjall*, now in the form 'fea' or 'fiold', giving rise to names such as Kierfea and Blochnie Fiold, while valleys usually have a *dalr*-name ('dale'). Headlands are 'nesses', as in Stromness (the 'stream' or 'tide headland') and round the coast there are innumerable instances of *geo,* often a chasm-like inlet where the roof of a cave has collapsed. Larger inlets and bays have the *−vik* element as in Rackwick, Marwick and Barswick, or else *−vágr* as in Kirkwall, Walls and Osmundwall. These *vágr*-names now have a 'wall' termination, having suffered a misguided attempt to correct what was perceived to be a dialect pronunciation. Kirkwall was still 'Kirkwaa' (Kirk Bay) in 1482-3,[2] but by 1490 it had been 'corrected' to the more proper-sounding 'Kirkwall'.[3] It is interesting that this change took place well in advance of direct English influence. Other names which have undergone a transformation to Scottish forms are the freshwater features. Thus Heldale Water in Hoy appeared as 'Heldale Witten' as late as Johan Blaeu's *Atlas Novus* (1654), and subsequently the 'witten' (vatn) became 'water'. Even more commonly the Scots 'Loch' was adopted, while the standard stream names are the *Burn of …* type (Burn of Swartabreck, Burn of Hillside).[4]

The pioneer of place-name studies was the historian, Per Andreas Munch (1810-1863) whose main interest was the identification of places mentioned in saga as a means to understanding the course of events.[5] As a Norwegian visitor to Orkney he found himself in a landscape littered with names which were often identical to those in Norway, the meaning of which was readily apparent to him, although lost to nineteenth-century Orcadians. The Faroese philologist, Jakob Jakobsen, whose work includes the posthumous translation of his two-volume dictionary of the Norn language in Shetland,[6] made a number of visits to Orkney between 1905 and 1919. The landscape is so thoroughly Norse that Jakobsen initially believed that hardly any place-names could be traced to any other language.[7] However, four years later he changed his mind and produced a list of over 40 Shetland names which he believed contained Celtic elements,[8] and Hugh Marwick followed with a list of nearly 30 names from Orkney.[9] By the time of Jakobsen's final visit he had developed an enthusiasm for Celtic names and, in an off-the-cuff remark, he suggested that between 5% and 10% of Orkney place-names were Celtic – a much greater proportion than anyone would now think possible.[10] The existence or otherwise of a sub-stratum of Celtic place-names is important to our understanding of the Pictish-Norse transition: if a good number of such names survive then the co-existence of the Pictish and Norse populations is implied, whereas if pre-Norse names are missing, or are few in number, it is more likely that there was a sudden break with the past, probably in violent circumstances. A complication is that Celtic names are not necessarily pre-Norse since they are also capable of having been introduced in the Norse period by Gaelic-speakers from the Hebrides and from Ireland, many of whom might have been thralls. In order to identify whether any names could be positively identified as pre-Norse F.T.Wainwright subjected Orkney's Celtic place-names to a stringent test: since any name which is, or might be Gaelic is capable of having been introduced in the Norse period, he searched for names which could only be Brittonic and hence could not be late introductions. His ruthless pruning of Jakobsen and Marwick's lists left one or two names which might be Brittonic, but he concluded that there was not a single name which could beyond doubt be attributed to the Picts.[11]

Words of Celtic origin also occur in Faroe where there was no previous population from whom any words could have been inherited,[12] so the Celtic words which have entered Faroese must have come from Gaelic-speaking thralls, or have been introduced as a result of Norse contacts with the Hebrides and Ireland. Since Orkney had even more frequent contacts, and might have had a bigger thrall-population, it is likely that Orkney's Celtic place-names are Viking-age borrowings rather than pre-Norse survivals. The most convincing loan-word is *airigh* (sheiling) which is found as the place-name 'Airy' in Sanday, Stronsay and Westray.[13] It is likely to reflect the social circumstances in which borrowing occurred: while the Gaelic-speaking thralls were shivering on the sheilings and grazing-places to which they gave *airigh*-names, their masters were warm and snug in a farm with a good Norse name. These Gaelic borrowings, however, are seldom if ever unique to Orkney, but are part of Scandinavian speech throughout the wider North Atlantic area.

Names of large features such as islands are not usually amenable to re-placement, and indeed several of the islands do combine the Norse *øy*, island, with a pre-Norse element. One name of this kind is 'Orkney' itself: we have seen that the element 'Orc' (possibly 'pig') can be traced back to the Roman period; the Norse interpreted the name as *orkn*, seal, and they added 'is-lands' with the plural definite article producing the form 'Orknøyene' ('the Orc or seal islands'). Shetland has some island names, Yell, Unst and Fetlar, which seems very ancient, possibly even non-Indo-European. Although names of this kind are less obvious in Orkney, there are some island-names for which a Norse derivation is not immediately obvious (Shapinsay, Stronsay and Rinansey or North Ronaldsay). However, the great majority of the is-lands do have Norse names often of a simple descriptive type: Hoy (high island), Flotta (flat island), Westray (west island) and Sanday (sandy island). As a general rule place-names survive invasion and colonisation—the fact that even major islands were re-named as a result of Norse settlement is an indication of an unusually drastic process.

It is, however, possible that the decay of Brittonic and its replacement by Goedelic in mainland Pictland somehow created a situation whereby place-names in Orkney were unusually susceptible to replacement or translation. There is a note attached to the *Ravenna Cosmography* which refers to a state of confusion about island names:

> Also in the same ocean are thirty-three islands called the Orchades, not all of which are inhabited. Nevertheless we would wish, Christ willing, to name them, but because of the confusion resulting from this land being controlled by differing peoples who, according to the barbarian fashion, call the same islands by differing names, we leave their names unlisted.[14]

The *Ravenna Cosmography* was able to record the names of 27 islands in the Hebrides, so it seems that the problem was not simply remoteness and a lack of information but something more specific to Orkney. Unfortunately we do not know which languages were causing confusion: the *Ravenna Cosmography* was compiled in the late seventh or early eighth century, so the competing languages ought to be Brittonic and Goedelic (or even Brittonic and the supposed non-Indo-European language). However, it seems quite possible that the note is a later addition, and refers to the Norse period when a wholesale replacement of earlier names was taking place.[15]

The completeness of Norse naming led F.T.Wainwright in his *Northern Isles* (1962) to describe the Picts as 'overwhelmed politically, linguistically, culturally and socially'.[16] As a description of the end result, Wainwright's phrase could not be better. Yet 'overwhelmed' is a very comprehensive term which can be used to disguise our ignorance of what actually happened. On the one hand 'overwhelmed' might mean widespread slaughter, enslavement, and the flight of survivors to mainland Scotland; on the other hand, it might describe an altogether more peaceful process brought about by intermarriage and the disappearance of the Pictish identity under the sheer weight of Norse immigration. Various permutations of the 'War Theory' and the 'Peace Theory' dominate the debate about the relationship between the Picts and the Norse.[17]

The view that Norse settlement was relatively peaceful received a boost from the publication of A.W.Brøgger's *Ancient Emigrants* (1929). Brøgger believed that Norse settlers were ordinary peasant farmers in search of new land rather than Vikings intent on piracy. He pictured the colonists stepping ashore into 'a veritable museum', full of the monuments of a vanished race. He imagined that the Picts were a much-reduced remnant of the broch-builders and, by using adjectives such as 'aboriginal' and 'primitive', he created the impression that they were no great impediment to Norse settlement. He even made the astonishing claim that 'the relation between Celtic and Norse populations in the northern Scottish islands was much the same as in the Faroes and Iceland'.[18] Of course it was absurd to compare Orkney which had a settled population to lands which were devoid of permanent inhabitants when the Norse arrived, and where the only people were hermits. A better knowledge of Pictish Orkney makes it out of the question that Norse settlers occupied the islands simply by default. Brøgger's book is now outdated, but at the time it was much admired and among others it influenced Hugh Marwick. Marwick did not agree with Brøgger's proposed chronology of farm-names, and he was not so dismissive of the Orkney Picts, but he nevertheless was able to envisage settlement proceeding as in Iceland by a series of 'landtakes' which took place without reference to the previous inhabitants much in the way that Brøgger had imagined.[19]

A different kind of 'Peace Theory'—and one not quite so peaceful—resulted from the appearance of Peter Sawyer's book, *The Age of the Vikings* (first published in 1962). Sawyer proposed that, despite the high frequency of Danish place-names in the north of England, the conquest of Danelaw was actually accomplished by relatively small war-bands rather than by the massive influx of new colonists which had previously been envisaged.[20] Orkney was virtually ignored in Sawyer's book, but his views were enormously influential, and created the expectation that Scandinavian settlement in Orkney would similarly have been undertaken by incomers who imposed

13. **Stanley Cursiter and Hugh Marwick.** *Stanley Cursiter (1887–1976), Queen's Limner for Scotland, at work on a portrait of Hugh Marwick (1881–1965), an authority on Orkney's language and place-names.*

themselves on subservient natives who might continue to form the majority of the population. Brian Smith has pointed out that Sawyer's approach was particularly congenial to archaeologists because it came at a time when they were turning away from the old-fashioned view that cultural changes necessarily imply invasions and the arrival of entirely new populations.[21] Yet major movements of population did take place in the Viking Age when Iceland and Faroe were settled, and so mass immigration as in Iceland, rather than domination by an elite as postulated for Danelaw, is a possible model for the settlement of Orkney.

A key archaeological site for understanding the relationship between the Picts and the Norse is Buckquoy, Birsay, where the Pictish houses were described in Chapter 1. Finds from a later phase include a number of bone pins, two combs and fragments of pottery of native manufacture within houses which, from their shape, appeared to be Norse. Anna Ritchie, who excavated the site, interpreted this evidence as indicating that 'some form of social integration between Pict and Norseman existed at least in the ninth century and possibly into the tenth century'.[22] Similar native artefacts have been found nearby on the Brough, and there are also Norse houses built in succession to Pictish settlements at Skaill (Deerness),[23] Pool (Sanday),[24] and

Scatness (Shetland).[25] The current orthodoxy is that is that 'a period of overlap —first indicated at Buckquoy—is the norm'.[26] Notes of caution, however, have been sounded about the Buckquoy evidence as a result of re-evaluating the age of the buildings, and the most recent survey (James Graham-Campbell and Colleen Batey's *Vikings in Scotland*) advises us to be 'somewhat circumspect' about the light which it sheds on the Pictish-Norse transition.[27] Even if there was contact the evidence falls short of explaining the exact nature of the relationship. There seems to be no real justification for the recent statement that 'the cultural traits present in the buildings at Buckquoy can be interpreted as an integration of cultures, probably spurred by intermarriage and trading rather than violent takeover',[28] although for the last 25 years that is how the site has been interpreted.

A cross-slab from Bressay in Shetland is another important piece of evidence for the 'Peace Theory'.[29] It has been taken to show that Christianity and Pictish art continued to exist into the Norse period, at least in attenuated form. A similar stone from Papil, which like the Bressay stone shows the hooded figures of *papae,* was originally dated on stylistic grounds to c.800 AD—the very end of the Pictish period in the Northern Isles. The Bressay stone has been described as an inferior copy of the Papil stone, characterised by 'haphazard scatter of decoration and marked clumsiness of drawing'. It

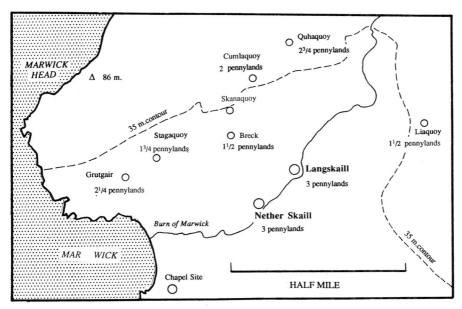

14. **Marwick.** *The pattern of the centrally located* skáli-*name (now divided into Langskaill and Netherskaill) and the peripheral* quoys *was Hugh Marwick's first use of place-names to chart the chronological expansion of settlement.*

has therefore been regarded as being of an even later date, possibly as late as 900 AD which, if correct, places it about a century into the Norse period. Raymond Lamb suggested that an impoverished church lacking secular support still continued to exist, but could no longer afford to commission sculpture of good quality.[30]

It is doubtful if a date well into the Norse era would have been assigned to the Bressay stone quite so confidently were it not for the ogham inscription which appears on the edges of the stone. The inscription is clear, but its interpretation is a matter for debate: it appears to include the Celtic words *meqq* (son of) and *crrossc* (cross) in combination with a personal name which might be Pictish, but it also includes the word *dattrr* which has usually been taken to be the Norse 'daughter'. A further pointer to Norse influence is the use of a colon (:) as a word separator since this is a common characteristic of runic inscriptions.[31] The fact that the short inscription might have words in three languages, Gaelic, Pictish and Norse, caused Wainwright to describe the stone as 'an artistic and linguistic hotch-potch',[32] and it led to the belief that there was a very confused linguistic situation in Shetland at this time. However, the cautionary note by Michael Barnes that the word *dattrr*, for all we know to the contrary, might be Pictish rather than Norse would, if accepted, weaken the whole argument in favour of the very late date, and this in turn might lead to a reconsideration of the theory that Pictish sculpture survived into the Norse period.[33]

It might seem that research into the biological characteristics of present-day Orcadians could settle the proportion of Pict and Viking in their ancestry.[34] These studies have involved measurement of stature, pigmentation of eyes and hair, blood-groups, finger and palm-prints, colour vision deficiencies, and disease patterns. Unlike the popular image of people of Viking descent, Orcadians are not particularly tall; they do tend to have high frequencies of blue and grey eyes, but are less blonde than the Scandinavians, red hair being quite frequent; finger and palm prints relate to Norwegian patterns, but blood groups show marked differences. Recent DNA research into the Y-chromosomes inherited from male ancestors is a promising line of enquiry; it suggests that a significant proportion of the Orcadian populations are likely to be Norse in the male line, although the extent to which the remainder descend from indigenous pre-Norse Picts or from more recent Scots immigrants is not so easy to determine.[35] Genetically, as well as geographically, Orkney lies mid-way between Scotland and Ireland on the one hand, and Scandinavia on the other. It is, however, by no means obvious that this sheds much light on the Pictish-Norse transition. Later immigration from Scandinavia as well as from Scotland (the extent of which a historian would not even attempt to quantify) has no doubt greatly modified the Pictish and Norse populations which existed a thousand years ago. At present geneticists have a rather naive view of history and historians an almost total ignorance of genetics.

Despite the modern tendency to favour various versions of the 'Peace Theory', the opposite view has always had its supporters, and lately they have been re-grouping. Storer Clouston vigorously attacked Brøgger's 'fresh view' of the settlement of Orkney on the grounds that the more historical parts of *Orkneyinga saga* describe a military society of a kind unlikely to have evolved from settlement by leaderless peasant farmers.[36] More recently the 'War Theory' has been re-stated in appropriately belligerent fashion by Iain Crawford, who was dismissive of the archaeological evidence from Buckquoy, and reasserted Wainwright's view that the disappearance of Pictish place-names was a clear indication of a violent take-over.[37] Recently Brian Smith has argued the case for believing that the Norse settlers exterminated or expelled their Pictish predecessors.[38]

The 'War Theory' is also the view which appears in early documentary sources. In 794 AD the Annals of Ulster record 'the devastation of all the islands of Britain by the gentiles'[39] (heathen Scandinavians), and there are numerous other records of extremely violent attacks on the Hebrides and Ireland in that decade and the next. These attacks are unlikely to have bypassed Orkney, and indeed the establishment of bases in the Northern Isles may have been a pre-condition of the sudden outburst of Viking activity farther to the west. At any rate it seems improbable that the early phase of Norse activity could simultaneously take different forms – peaceful colonisation in Orkney and Shetland and violent raids in the Hebrides. In the absence of any evidence to the contrary we ought to conclude that Orkney was subjected to the same brutal attacks.

The settlement of Orkney has sometimes been envisaged as consisting of two phases, first, informal settlement during the period of raiding and, second, overwhelming immigration following the political consolidation of Norse rule and the establishment of the earldom.[40] The place-name evidence, however, is difficult to reconcile with gradual settlement over such a lengthy period.[41] Individual Norse settlers or small groups entering a pre-dominantly Pictish society could not escape using existing place-names, and if further settlers later arrived in overwhelming numbers, they would use the names which were already familiar to their fellow-countrymen. Name replacement is more likely to take place when large numbers settle simultaneously, communicating with each other but having a hostile relationship and minimal contact with the indigenous inhabitants. A persistent feature of written sources is the memory of 'the great fleet' which came to Orkney— and a great fleet might have brought a sudden influx of the kind which causes names replacement. It has been seen that there is reason to doubt the precise details of King Harald Fairhair's voyage when he was reputed to have established the Orkney earldom, but similar 'great fleets' appear in other guises. In the *Historia Norvegiae* we are told that certain pirates of the family of Rognvald of Møre 'set out with a great fleet... and stripped these races (the Picts and Papae) of their ancient settlements, destroying them wholly, and subduing the islands to themselves'.[42] It sounds the kind of circumstances which might result in old place-names being lost and new ones being created. Great fleets also appear at several points in Irish sources, for example c.838 AD when Tuirgéis brought a 'great and vast royal fleet' to the north of Ireland, and in 849 AD when we hear of a fleet of 120 or 140 ships.[43] Even in the tenth century Erik Bloodaxe's large and highly mobile following settled down in Orkney from time to time, the movements of Erik and his family depending on the success or failure of military campaigns in other parts of Britain (see Chapter 4).

A ninth century host of this kind might behave as the Danes did in England when they 'shared out the land of the Northumbrians and proceeded to plough and support themselves'.[44] This would open the way for further immigration into Orkney similar to, but possibly earlier than population movements into Faroe and Iceland. For the indigenous inhabitants enslavement was one possibility. Whereas Brøgger and his contemporaries imagined a society of free peasants and played down the place of slavery in the Viking Age, there has recently been a tendency to emphasise the role of thralldom. Farmers, even on middle-sized holdings, might own several men and women who were typically employed in heavy outdoor work.[45] Medieval Orkney had a good many very large farms which might have needed slave labour, some of which later appear as the earl's bordlands. In some cases the layout of these farms seems to consist of a central core of desmene, peripheral to which there were satellite communities which were differentiated in a way which has been thought to preserve the distinction between free and unfree.[46]

And yet, if the Pictish population was simply enslaved *in situ*, a greater proportion of Pictish names might have been expected to survive. Slavery is certainly a possibility—but it must have been accompanied by a good deal of dislocation which removed Pictish thralls from their familiar surroundings. The other possibility is extermination or wholesale flight. The clearing out of the existing population would be easier in a group of relatively small islands than in a country with a greater land mass. Iain Crawford drew on the analogy of the Australian aborigines, a good number of whose names survive except in Tasmania where there are no names because aborigines were exterminated.[47] The Norse, however, were not simply hunting down a primitive people—they were not noticeably superior to the Picts except, significantly, in their sea-going capacity and their ability to launch devastating attacks on small islands. Another analogy might be found in the Balkans, where at the end of the twentieth century there were many instances of 'ethnic cleansing', when whole populations were deliberately set on the move by massacres and threats of violence in order that their persecutors could take possession of their homelands. The attacks on Iona provide an illustration of how quickly these methods could succeed. In Iona the motivation was plunder rather than the acquisition of land, but the result was the same. The island was attacked in 795 AD, it was 'burned' in 802 AD, and in 806 AD the killing of 68 of its monks led to the withdrawal of the community to the comparative safety of Ireland (807 AD). The martyrdom of Blathmac who deliberately accepted torture and martyrdom on Iona rather than reveal where the church treasure was hidden shows the violence which the raiders were prepared to use when they met resistance.[48]

While place-names lead to the verdict that the Norse takeover was thorough and violent, rather different conclusions have been drawn from the way early church sites were re-used by the Norse. In Papa Westray the Norse gave the island a *Papa*-name, and the Pictish ecclesiastical site was later occupied by St Boniface church which preserved (or was given) a dedication to a Pictish saint (see p.17). Papa Stronsay also has a church, probably of a twelfth century date, which overlies a pre-Norse ecclesiastical site, although the degree of continuity is uncertain. St Peter's in South Ronaldsay also lies within a district with a *Papa*-name (Paplay); it has Pictish sculpture and possibly an early dedication, and it was later rehabilitated as a parish church. St Ninian's Isle in Shetland is another site which bridges the Pictish-Norse period: an early church in which Pictish treasure was concealed was succeeded by an eleventh or twelfth century church which was given a Ninian-dedication, presumably because the existence of a previous church was known and Ninian was regarded as an appropriately early saint. Continuity of this kind can be found at a good many other locations.

The contrast between 'the continuity of resort' on these ecclesiastical sites and the lack of continuity as suggested by place-names is a problem which it is not easy to resolve. Some interpretations simply assume Pictish-Norse continuity without fully taking into account the implications of the place-name evidence, while the opposite view is that 'continuity of resort' on ecclesiastical sites was not really continuity at all, but re-occupation after a period of interruption. The violence of attacks on churches cannot be doubted, at least as long as churches were wealthy, and Vikings were unlikely to have left places like Papa Westray in peace, although that has been suggested.[49] Yet the evidence from graves indicates that the Norse were fairly quick to adopt Christian burial practices, so there was probably a general toleration of Christian beliefs once the church was stripped of its possessions. The evidence of St Ninian's Isle seems to point to a lengthy period of abandonment, but the hiatus on some other sites might have been quite brief, or perhaps Christianity was never really extinguished.[50]

If the legendary adventures of St Findan are to be believed, they provide confirmation of the existence of a Christian community in the mid-ninth century—well into the Norse period. The *Vita Findani* is one of the more factual saint's lives and it describes how, as a young man, Findan was captured in Ireland by Viking slave-traders, but on the voyage back to Norway he was able to escape on an uninhabited island which was apparently located somewhere in the North Isles of Orkney. Eventually he plucked up courage to attempt to escape and, trusting in God and buoyed up by his clothing, he was able to swim and wade to a nearby island where he was found by clerics who took him to an ecclesiastical settlement where he was able to converse with a bishop who had been educated in Ireland. Besides suggesting the possibility of ecclesiastical links with Ireland rather than with mainland Pictland, the story provides a hint about language: since only the bishop could speak Irish we are led to expect that other members of the community were Brittonic-speaking Picts. The important point, however, is the existence of a religious house, apparently somewhere in Orkney, still surviving, or perhaps re-established, at a date when the Norse settlement of the islands was well advanced. One suggestion is that, if Findan's uninhabited island was the Holm of Papay, it would fit very neatly with Papa Westray which Lamb identified as the possible seat of a Pictish bishop.[51]

Orkney place-names studies are dominated by the magisterial figure of Hugh Marwick (1881-1965), Rector of Kirkwall Grammar School and then Director of Education.[52] Marwick met Jakob Jakobsen in 1909, acting as his Orkney informant,[53] and his *Orkney Norn* (1929) was modelled on Jakobsen's Shetland dictionary. Marwick's place-name ideas evolved through a series of 'Antiquarian Notes' which he wrote for the Orkney Antiquarian Society of which he was the first secretary. In his 'Antiquarian Notes on Stronsay'[54] he identified four large settlement units in the island associated with *boer*-names, Everbay, Housebay, Erraby and the Bay, which he described as 'great original settlements', and he discussed similar places in other islands where these '*boers*' had been 'replaced and overlaid'. He also discussed places with *bólstaðr*-names and showed how in relation to the *boers* they were 'secondary and derivative'.

When Hugh Marwick described the Stronsay *bólstaðr*-names as 'secondary' to the *boers,* he assumed that they were secondary, not just in their geographical location, but also in chronological sequence. Over the next few years he used his personal knowledge of the topography and history of Orkney's farms to build up a more elaborate 'chronology' incorporating other place-name elements. His scheme first appeared in his 'Orkney Farm-name

15. ***The Bu of Burray.*** *Hugh Marwick placed Bu of… names in a zone of important Primary settlement (see Fig.16). This imposing farm stood on one of the bordlands of the earls of Orkney.*

Studies'[55] and was not greatly modified when 20 years later it was set out in its final form in *Orkney Farm-names* (1952). He envisaged a zone of 'primary settlement' characterised by the *bœr*-names which he had described in his Stronsay paper; these places were 'greatest in the scale of ancestral dignity'.[56] In this same primary zone he placed *skáli*-names (Skaill, Langskaill, Backaskaill) and farms with *Bu of*…-names (Bu of Burray, Bu of Orphir, Bu of Rendall). In a surrounding zone of secondary settlement Marwick placed *land, garðr and bólstaðr* names (Redland, Trumland, Colligarth, Bressigarth, Isbister, Wasbister). The further class of *staðir*-names, older forms of which preserve a '-staith' ending (Tormiston, Tormistaith, and Costa, Costaith) possibly represented new names on already settled land. A final peripheral zone was characterised by *setr/sætr*-names (Warsetter, Morsetter) and by the very numerous *kví-names* (Pickaquoy, Quoybanks, Queena). This 'chronology' and the outward spread of settlement which Marwick envisaged is shown in Fig.16.

Marwick's model proved to be a fruitful scheme, not only capable of shedding light on the settlement pattern in Orkney, but providing a method which could be used to investigate Norse names in other parts of Scotland,[57]

51

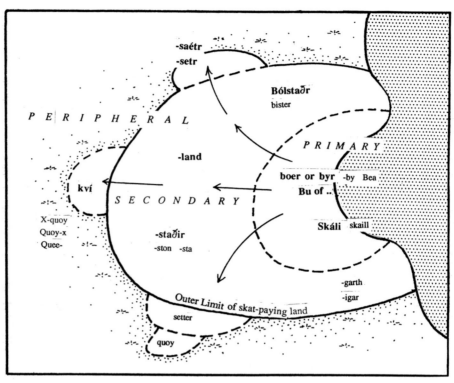

16. Marwick's Place-name 'Chronology' (after Bailey, Orkney, 1971).

yet his scheme is open to serious criticism. Marwick thought of the Norse settlement of Orkney as being a process similar to the settlement of Iceland as described in *Landnámabók*, where the first generation of settlers marked out large settlements on the best land, and their descendants and later arrivals moved outwards from this nucleus to establish a zone of secondary settlement. It is, however, unlikely that the settlement of the empty land of Iceland provides a good model for the settlement of Orkney which had a Pictish population and several thousand years of farming activity. It is unlikely that the Norse settled on prime sites then moved out to establish secondary settlement on new land without reference to the fields and farms created by the native population. The concept of primary and secondary settlement is often used, but it is a model which may not be entirely appropriate to the Norse settlement of Orkney.

Marwick attempted to create, not just a relative chronology, but to connect his scheme to real dates by reference to the skat-paying status of farms. He believed that *skat*, the Norse land tax, had been established during the course of King Harald Fairhair's great voyage of conquest in the late ninth century and consequently, if a farm paid skat, it must already have existed when King Harald put a tax on it c.900 AD. He admitted that the system might have been modified later, but he considered that 'there were difficulties in accepting such a view'.[58] He did not say what these difficulties might be, but possibly he had in mind that *urislands* (ouncelands) could not have remained consistently 18 pennylands if extra pennylands had been created in a piecemeal fashion. The existence of a number of places with the name 'Kirbister' (church farm) caused Marwick some heart-searching. The Kirbisters mostly paid skat, so Marwick's reasoning dated them to a period a good deal earlier than Earl Sigurd's conversion in 995 AD, but perhaps they might have been founded by Viking-age Christians comparable to the Christians recorded in *Landnámabók* who settled in Iceland at a time when most people were still heathen. Skat-paying was an argument which Marwick considered crucial to his chronology; if any of the skat-paying places with *bister*-names could be as late as the official conversion to Christianity then, 'the whole argument must go by the board'.[59]

Seventy years later most of this argument has indeed 'gone by the board'. We have already seen that there is reason to doubt King Harald Fairhair's voyage as a real historical event, nor would it now be thought possible that a system of land assessment and taxation could have been imposed during the course of this voyage, or at anything like so early a date.[60] But if skat was not imposed by Harald Fairhair, there is no longer a need to suppose that all the farms which paid skat had come into existence before 900 AD. This allows us to construct a more credible model of settlement growth. We can now see that the growth of settlement was over a much longer time-scale. Instead of a settlement pattern which was imposed within two or three generations in the Viking Age and thereafter was little changed, we can envisage the pattern of settlement evolving more gradually with a particular need for new names in the eleventh, twelfth and thirteenth centuries as population increased and settlement intensified. Outward expansion on to hill land did occur in times of population growth in the way Marwick envisaged but, in islands of no great land mass, the process of internal division was often more important. This intensification generated a whole host of division-names such as Everbist, Midgarth, Nears, Nistigar, Uttesgarth, North Setter, Symbister and Isbister (respectively upper, middle, lower, lowest, outermost, north, south and east). New settlement strained the language of internal subdivision to its absolute limit, resulting in such linguistic monstrosities as Upper Nisthouse ('the upper lowest house'). At the same time many fields with generics such as *akr* (cultivated field), *kví* (field), *garðr* (enclosure) and *sætr* (grazing place) became permanent settlements.

A compelling reason for rejecting Marwick's scheme as a 'chronology' is that there can be no doubt that farm-generics were active simultaneously

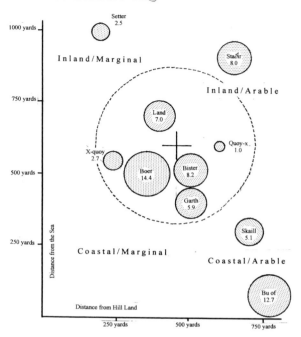

17. **Size and Location of Place-names.** *The graph shows the average size in pennylands, distance from the sea, and the median distance from hill land. It is only setter, staðir, skaill and Bu of ... names which have well defined locational characteristics since places with other generics tend to cluster in an 'average' position. Compare these characteristics to Marwick's scheme in Fig.16.*

rather than consecutively.[61] Marwick's scheme leads us to expect that that many generics had ceased to form new names even before 900 AD, but there is a great deal of evidence that this was not the case. New names continued to be created as late as the nineteenth century when *quoy* (field), *garth* (enclosure) and *bu* (big farm) remained in use as common nouns. Only *staðir* and *skáli* failed to create new farm names in the post-medieval period. In the case of *skáli*, it ceased to be an active name-forming generic because the long open hall designed for the feasting of a military retinue became obsolete in the post-Viking period. It can be seen that, rather than forming a chronological sequence, these place-name generics describe farms of different size, type and location.[62]

Orkney place-name research cannot be said to have produced much in the way of certainty or unanimity. We now have less confidence in our ability to arrange farm-names in a chronological sequence and to assign dates to them. Models of the outward spread of Norse settlement which Hugh Marwick constructed from farm-names have proved inadequate. No one would doubt the importance of place-names in understanding the Pictish-

Norse transition, but there is little agreement how place-names relate to other evidence. Overwhelming Norse naming suggests a more complete break with the Pictish past than most archaeologists have hitherto been prepared to envisage.

4

Earl Sigurd and the Raven Banner

After the death of Torf Einar who, according to *Orkneyinga saga*, 'ruled over Orkney for many years and died in his bed',[1] he was succeeded by his three sons, Arnkell, Erlend and the ominously named Thorfinn *hausakljúfr* ('Skull-splitter'). Two of them, or perhaps all three, ruled as joint earls, but the reign of Arnkell and Erlend was brief. They were killed in England, fighting for King Erik Bloodaxe, and thereafter Thorfinn Skull-splitter ruled as sole earl.

The great voyage of conquest by King Harald Fairhair (Chapter 2) may or may not be a real historical event, but there is no doubt that his son, Erik *blóðäx* ('Blood-axe') regularly used Orkney as a base in the mid-tenth century from which to pursue his ambitions. The history of Erik Blood-axe derives not just from *Orkneyinga saga* and *Heimskringla*, but also from the *Anglo-Saxon Chronicle*. The sagas' accounts are not entirely consistent with English sources, but the existence of independent evidence means that the general course of events is much more secure than the story of Harald Fairhair's voyage. Erik succeeded his father and ruled briefly in Norway, but when his half-brother Hakon the Good arrived from England, Erik's support melted away and he fled overseas. He made himself master of Orkney, and for the next seven years or thereby he used the islands as a secure base from which to pursue his ambitions in the rich Viking kingdom of York. He drew on support from the Hebrides, and his host also included many landless adventurers from Norway.[2] With this new influx, a part of the Orkney population was highly mobile, reacting quickly to the turn of events in Norway and in Britain. Erik seems to have been invited to assume the kingship of York as a counter to threats from Olaf Cuaran, the Norse king of Dublin. However, Erik's rule did not last long, and about 948 AD he was expelled from York when Olaf seized the city. Erik again used Orkney as a base to launch a campaign which saga tells us led to attacks on Scotland, the Hebrides, Ireland, Wales and England. This campaign in the western parts of the British Isles appears to have been directed against Olaf Cuaran with a view to severing the links between Dublin and York. Erik's attack on Ireland cannot have been a success, but he managed to regain York in 952 AD. Two years later he was dead, killed at Stainmore, high in the Pennines on the frontier of his

York kingdom.[3] His York ambitions had ended in disaster: the poem *Eiríksmal* describes Odin waiting to welcome Erik and five kings who died with him.[4] Also among the dead were the Orkney earls, Arnkell and Erlend.[5]

Erik left a wife, Gunnhild, 'the most beautiful of women, clever, with much knowledge and lively, but a very false person, and cruel in disposition'.[6] Since she could no longer live safely in England, Gunnhild and her sons took the ships Erik had possessed, gathered those who were prepared to follow them, and sailed north to Orkney with all the treasure they had accumulated in England from raiding and tribute. This remnant of Erik's army subdued Orkney and Shetland, and used the islands as a base from which to conduct summer raids.[7] A record of Vikings who came with a fleet and were slain in Buchan at about this date may refer to one these raids.[8] An up-turn in their fortunes saw Gunnhild and her sons return to Norway where, with Danish assistance, they defeated and killed Hakon the Good (961 AD). However, two of Erik's sons were again in exile in Orkney c.970 and used the islands to launch an unsuccessful invasion of Norway.[9]

When Erik Blood-axe and his family were in Orkney, the earls were in a distinctly subservient position, in the same way that Torf Einar as an 'earl' had been of lesser status than Halfdan Longlegs who was a 'king'. The host which Erik commanded left the earls no opportunity for independent action. When Erik first arrived from Norway there seems to have been no doubt that he had a right to command the assistance of Orkney,[10] and the death of Arnkell and Erlend who were killed with Erik in his York kingdom suggests that Erik's presence necessarily involved them in his campaigns. There are hints that Orkney support was not always freely given: when Gunnhild and her sons returned to Orkney they 'subdued the isles', and it was only when they returned to Norway that Thorfinn Skull-splitter was 'made earl'.[11] As with earlier earls, the saga for its own reasons is careful to state that his title derives from royal authority (see Chapter 2).

When Gunnhild and her sons left Orkney, Ragnhild, daughter of Erik and Gunnhild, was given in marriage to Arnfinn, son of Earl Thorfinn Skull-splitter. Although this marriage linked Orkney to Gunnhild and her family, other marriages from this early period show that the earls were also entering into British alliances which led to the development of family ties with the native aristocracy. Thorfinn Skull-splitter was married to Greloð (see Fig.11).[12] On her mother's side she had an impressive Norse ancestry, since she was a daughter of Thorstein the Red and a descendant of Ketil Flat-nose. But her paternal descent may have been of greater consequence; her father was Dungad, 'earl' in Caithness, and apparently a member of the pre-Norse ruling family. It has been suggested that this marriage brought subsequent Earls of Orkney within the *derbfíne*, the Celtic kinship group within which members were recognised as legitimate contenders for power.[13] Throughout the next century Orkney earls certainly pursued their claims in Caithness with vigour, and in doing so it is possible that they were no longer regarded as outsiders. Place-names suggests that the north-east corner of Caithness was thoroughly Norse; a scatter of Norse settlement extended at least as far south as the Dornoch Firth, co-existing with a Gaelic population.[14]

After the history of Erik, which deals with events which to some extent can be authenticated, the saga reverts to folk-tale when it tells the story of the evil Ragnhild who plots the death of successive husbands by promising to marry their murderers. No sooner was Thorfinn Skull-splitter dead and buried in his mound at Hoxa than the family tore itself apart. First, Ragnhild had Arnfinn put to death on his estate at Murkle in Caithness, then she married his brother. Havard *hinn arsæli* ('Harvest-happy') was an earl who was remembered as 'lucky with his harvest', but he was less lucky with his new wife. She conspired with his nephew, Einar *klining*, and incited Einar to aim for the earldom, with the result that Havard was defeated and killed at an unidentified place in Stenness known as 'Havarðsteigar' (Havard's rigs).[15] Ragnhild then quarrelled with Einar *klining* and refused to marry him, and persuaded another nephew, Einar *harðkjotr*, to attack and kill him. Finally this female spider and consumer of husbands 'sent for' Ljot, brother of both her late husbands, and married him once he had duly disposed of Einar *harðkjotr*. However, the saga records that Ljot became 'a mighty chief' and nothing more is heard of Ragnhild, so perhaps Ljot was a match for her.[16]

There is no real reason to trust any of the details of this bloodthirsty story, although bloodthirsty stories as well as prosaic events may sometimes be true, and murderous family feuds are a recurring theme of the more historical sections of the saga. Like udal property which was divisible among heirs, the earldom itself was considered to be divisible among co-earls. Up to 1214 there were periods when Orkney was ruled by two, and sometimes three simultaneous earls, either acting jointly or each with his own territory. But inheritance was far from automatic; it was not so much a share of the earldom which heirs inherited as recognition that they had a right to claim a share if they were strong enough to make good their inheritance. Not all descendants exercised this right, and the rule of joint earls was inherently unstable and usually ended in violence, with the result that no collateral branch ever succeeded in establishing itself on a permanent basis. However, the legend of Ragnhild and her husbands was also important to the saga-author in terms of his storytelling technique: these family feuds culminating in the martyrdom of Magnus are the main theme of *Orkneyinga saga*, and so the saga-writer uses these early legends to set in train the doom of 'kindred-slaying' which is to dominate his story.[17] The story also illustrates the general point that Ragnhild represented the continuing authority of the family of Erik Blood-axe. Political power apparently depended on the Norwegian connection—perhaps Ragnhild was not so much the instigator of these troubles as the prize for the winner.

Ljot's reign is only briefly recorded in *Orkneyinga saga* which confines itself to the events of one campaign in the north of Scotland.[18] The Icelandic author of the saga is often at a loss when he deals with Scottish matters—people, places and chronology are hopelessly confused. It is best to postpone unravelling these Scottish entanglements until the next chapter, for the moment noting that Ljot's campaign, during the course of which he disposed of another brother, Skuli, who sided with the Scots, was probably part of an intermittent struggle with the rulers of Moray. Ljot was succeeded by Hlodver, the last remaining brother, about whom the saga tells us even less, merely describing him as 'a mighty chief', and recording his marriage to Eithne, daughter of King Cerbhall of Ossory in Ireland.[19] Hlodver was in turn succeeded by his son Sigurd *digri* ('the Stout'), who came to power without the bitter feuds which had characterised his father's generation and which were to break out among his own sons. When Sigurd inherited the earldom he was in the enviable position of having few surviving relatives.

In the last quarter of the tenth century the main thrust of expeditions from Scandinavia was directed against England, bypassing Orkney and allowing the earls greater scope for independent action. They were no longer forced to play a secondary role, as had been the case when Erik Blood-axe was based in Orkney. In the days of Sigurd (c.980–1014) and his son, Thorfinn (1014-c.1065) the Orkney earldom reached its zenith of power, dominating the north of Scotland, and extending its influence to the Hebrides, the Isle of Man and Ireland. Sigurd's earldom also exerted a magnetic attraction for high-born Icelanders, and several of the Icelandic family sagas contain episodes in which their heroes seek to distinguish themselves in grander military exploits than were available in their native land.

Despite Sigurd's posthumous reputation throughout the Norse world, the treatment of his reign in *Orkneyinga saga* is sketchy, and much of the information comes from other sagas. According to *Njal's saga* (which is later in date than *Orkneyinga saga* and is of little value as a historical source) Sigurd's domain included 'Ross and Moray; Sutherland and the Dales'.[20] Moray at that date was an extensive region, possibly stretching across the Highlands into west coast districts such as Lochaber and if, as has been suggested, 'the Dales' was a term sometimes used for Dál Riata (Argyll), Sigurd's realm was very big indeed. However, the way in which the quotation links Moray with Ross, and Sutherland with the Dales, suggests that in this instance *Njal's saga* is referring to a more northerly region. Probably the Dales were the valleys of the eastward and northward-flowing rivers in northern Scotland, the area which *Orkneyinga saga* elsewhere describes as 'the Caithness dales'.[21] The claim that all these provinces were subject to

Sigurd's rule seems somewhat optimistic. His involvement in Moray might be connected to Fordun's account of a great army of Norwegians, along with a great fleet, which made a long stay and stripped the country before being defeated by Malcolm II, c.1005, somewhere in the vicinity of Mortlach.[22] We should not, however, assume that an army described as Norwegian was necessarily led by Sigurd. At best the conquest of Moray, where Norse place-names are usually absent, can have amounted to little more than a temporary victory and the exacting of tribute. The saga's account of battles fought near Wick and at 'Dungalsnípa'[23] show that there were other occasions when Sigurd was hard pressed by his Moray opponents, and was barely able to retain a foothold even in the Norse parts of Caithness (see Chapter 5).

The area into which we can be more certain that Sigurd's power extended was the Hebrides and the Irish Sea. The Norse could use their maritime superiority to dominate the seaways, and thus impose a greater degree of control on islands, peninsulas and sea lochs than can ever have been possible in the mountainous interior of Moray. By Sigurd's day there had been the best part of two centuries of Norse activity in the region. This had involved not only military expeditions and trade, but also settlement. In Lewis the great majority of settlement names are Norse, suggesting that a Norse population had largely supplanted native Gaelic speakers. Farther south, for example in Islay, the proportion of Norse names is less, but nevertheless some 30% of settlement names are Norse. In Islay and the southern Hebrides a Norse aristocracy ruled over the Gaelic-speaking inhabitants, and a mixed community quickly developed known to the Irish as the *gall-gaedhil* ('foreign Gaels') whom they regarded as a greater scourge than the Vikings proper. Sigurd probably inherited whatever was left of Erik Blood-axe's conquests, but he also inherited Erik's Irish enemies, since the kings of Dublin still tried to extend their influence into the Irish Sea and southern Hebrides. Sigurd had other rivals in the region: it was the Isle of Man which eventually emerged as centre from which the Kingdom of Man and the Isles was ruled, and there were also petty kings after the Irish fashion. Sigurd was a major player in this troubled area, acting not so much an outsider as in conjunction with local factions. He had a consistent ally in his brother-in-law, Earl Gilli, who was based in the island of Colonsay, or perhaps Coll. The large numbers of Orcadians, Islesmen and Scandinavians which Sigurd took to the Battle of Clontarf in 1014 testify that he was sometimes able to provide leadership to a large part of the diverse inhabitants of the area.

Although we are seldom able to follow the details of Sigurd's activities, it appears that he and Earl Gilli conquered the Isle of Man in the years c.986-c.989 AD. The first sign of trouble was a Christmas night attack on Iona and the killing of the bishop.[24] The attackers were described by the Irish as *danair*

('Danes'), a general term for Viking pirates, and they may or may not have been Orcadians—perhaps it would be surprising to find Orcadians campaigning so far from home in the middle of winter. In the following year (987) an invasion of the Isle of Man was reported rather differently by the two sides. The *Annals of Ulster* record the Manx version, claiming that 1,000 of the Norse invaders were killed, along with a great slaughter of the 'Danes' who had attacked Iona.[25] On the other hand, *Njal's saga* describes how Sigurd defeated King Godfrey of Man and returned to Orkney with much treasure.[26] Two years later (989) a second attack was more decisive; *Njal's saga* describes a campaign which involved raids on Anglesey, the Southern Isles, Kintyre, Wales and a final victory on the Isle of Man (all areas within which Erik Blood-axe had been active).[27] Irish Annals report the killing of King Godfrey of Man 'by the men of Dál Riata',[28] presumably Earl Gilli's Gaelic-Norse Hebrideans and their Orcadian allies.

Several of these accounts describe the wealth which Earl Sigurd was able to accumulate from these west-coast campaigns. We read about Sigurd's conquest of the Isle of Man in *Eyrbyggia saga*, which describes how he forced the islanders to pay tribute: we are told that Sigurd sailed back to Orkney 'leaving his agents to collect the tax which was to be paid in refined silver'.[29] *Eyrbyggia Saga* is not a very satisfactory source; its mid-thirteenth century date is long after Sigurd's time, and its latest editors describe it as 'imaginative and interpretative' rather than historical.[30] However, there are other indications of tribute-gathering in the area within which Sigurd was active. According to the Welsh *Brut y Tywysogion*, apparently referring to events around the same date (c.989 AD), a penny was levied from every person as tribute to 'the black host of the Vikings'. Other references to tax-gathering are equally unreliable: we ought not to take too seriously *Njal saga's* account of how Kari Solmundsson, a member of Sigurd's bodyguard, collected *skat* from Earl Gilli, brought the payments to Orkney, and then delivered the skat to Earl Hakon in Norway.[31] *Floamanna saga* contains another dubious reference to attempts to collect skat in Hebrides on behalf of Earl Hakon.[32]

These references to taxation, and particularly to tribute levied in ounces of silver in the Isle of Man and exacted in pennies from households in Wales have led to suggestions that this is the period when we might find the origins of little assessment districts known as *urislands* or ouncelands, each of which in Orkney, Shetland and Caithness was divisible into 18 pennylands. The same units are also found in the Hebrides and the western fringes of the Scottish mainland, where the *unciata terra* or *tir unga* (ounceland), unlike the northern system, has 20 pennylands. Those who search for a time when a single system might have been imposed throughout these scattered districts are attracted to the idea that assessment originates from the reign of

18. **The Burray Hoard.** *The hoard is dated to 997–1010 AD (Earl Sigurd's reign). Much of the treasure is in the form of silver rings of standard weight ('ring-money').*

Sigurd or Thorfinn. It is difficult to identify another period, either earlier or later, when any one person exercised authority throughout the region. However, the question of assessment and taxation is discussed in Chapter 15, where it will be seen that there are difficulties in attributing formal taxation based on land units to quite such an early date. There are also important regional differences, for example between the ouncelands of 18 pennylands in the north and of 20 pennylands in the west. The diversity of the units creates doubts about the advisability of describing it as a 'single system', or looking for one single ruler who imposed the assessment over the whole of the area.

Another interesting possibility is that the warfare and tribute-collection during this period might relate to the famous silver hoards which have been discovered at Skaill in Sandwick and in Burray. The Skaill hoard is the largest in Scotland, weighing over 8 kg., and consisting of over a hundred items, mainly neck-rings, arm-rings and brooches, whereas the 2 kg. of the Burray hoard is largely in the form of ring-money (silver rings of standard weight which could be used as units of exchange). The Skaill treasure can be dated from its coin contents to c.950-970 AD (possibly the Erik Blood-axe period) and the Burray hoard to 997-1010 AD (Earl Sigurd's reign). However, warfare and tribute-collection are not the only explanations for possessing quantities of silver; the large proportion of ring-money is also compatible with wealth which had been accumulated through trade.[33]

The conversion of Orkney to Christianity was, according to saga, accomplished in sudden and dramatic fashion by Olaf Trygvesson.[34] Olaf was a rich and successful Viking leader who had been campaigning in Britain for several years, during the course of which he had exacted an enormous *Danegeld* (tribute) from London. He had been baptised only in the previous year,[35] and in 995 he was returning to Norway where he made himself king. On the voyage round the north of Scotland he put into Osmundwall (Kirk Hope in Walls), as ships frequently did when waiting for a favourable tide to take them through the Pentland Firth. There he found Earl Sigurd who apparently by chance was also in Osmundwall, making ready to go to sea. Olaf invited the earl aboard his ship, then presented him with an ultimatum:

> I want you and all your subjects to be baptised. If you refuse, I'll have you killed on the spot, and I swear that I will ravage every island with fire and steel.[36]

Faced with this stark choice Sigurd chose baptism, and all Orkney immediately became Christian, or so *Orkneyinga saga* tells us.

Olaf's motives are likely to have been primarily political rather than religious. His campaigns in the years 991-994 had included attacks on the Isle of Man and the Hebrides, so he had probably already come into conflict with Sigurd, and their relationship appears to have been hostile.[37] In these circumstances it was an obvious precaution to secure the obedience of the Orkney earl before bidding for kingship in Norway. The taking of Sigurd's son, Hlodver, nicknamed Hundi or 'whelp', as a hostage, was standard practice in these circumstances. However, Hlodver died soon afterwards, whereupon Sigurd threw off his allegiance to Olaf Trygvesson. The saga links the repudiation of Sigurd's allegiance to his remarriage; his new wife was a daughter of Malcolm II, King of Scots. The marriage, however, was not primarily hostile to Norway, but united Scotland and Orkney in the face of a common threat from Moray (see Chapter 5). Scottish support for the Orkney earls and Orkney support for the Scottish crown were important ingredients in the success of Sigurd and Thorfinn.

The sagas do not say that Sigurd relapsed from his enforced baptism but his death, fighting under the raven banner of Odin, gives a deliberate, although possibly misleading, impression that he remained an obdurate heathen at heart. Sigurd's magic banner was made for him by his Irish mother. It depicted a raven and, when the wind blew, the raven appeared to be in full flight. The raven was the symbol of Odin, and its magic ensured the victory of the army before which it was displayed, but it brought death to the standard-bearer who was brave enough to carry it.[38] The banner was first used in Caithness, when it won victory at 'Skiðamyrr' (Skitten Mire, now the Moss of Killimster near Wick). One rather worrying aspect of the story is the possibility that the saga has somehow confused Sigurd of Orkney with Siward of Northumbria. Earl Siward ruled England north of the Humber from 1041 to his death in 1055, so he was rather later in date. However, Sigurd and Siward are forms of the same name, and not only were both named *digri* ('the Stout'), but they both possessed raven banners. A strange Danish legend connects Siward of Northumbria to Orkney, when it inexplicably refers to him as 'dragon-slaying in the Orkneys'.[39] These remarkable points of contact cast doubt on how much the saga-author really knew about Earl Sigurd, and suggest the possibility that a number of stock motifs are embedded in his story.

It is likely that the conversion of Orkney was not such a sudden event as the saga would have us believe. Evidence of heathenism comes mainly from Norse graves, identifiable by jewellery for personal adornment, by swords, daggers, shield-bosses and spear-points in male graves, and by the implements of spinning and weaving in female graves. Besides providing evidence of heathen burial, the contents of graves give information about material culture and the circumstances of everyday life. An extensive series of graves was found on the links at Pierowall in the nineteenth century, but they were so badly recorded that interpretation is difficult.[40] The relatively utilitarian nature of the grave goods has led to the suggestion that Pierowall, the *hofn* of *Orkneyinga saga,* was a trading community based on one of the best harbours in Orkney. The large cemetery at Westness, Rousay, contains heathen graves which are believed to date from the ninth century.[41] The Scar boat-burial also dates from the period between 875 and 950 AD. Those who investigated the Scar site suggested that the burial was 'a late gesture to the old gods and old customs of the homeland', perhaps reflecting the great age of the woman who was one of the three people interred in the grave.[42] She had perhaps lived on into an age when burials of this kind had ceased to be common. The impression is that by Sigurd's time the Norse had generally adopted Christian practices, at least as far as burial was concerned.

If the legendary adventures of St Findan are to be believed, and he really did meet an Orkney bishop (see p.50), Christianity survived the arrival of the Norse or at least was re-established soon afterwards. Place-names associated with heathenism have often been identified but, while some such names may exist, they are not so numerous as is often supposed. The names Odness (supposedly Odin Ness), Torness (Thor) and Freya Geo, all from Stronsay,[43] are probably capable of other derivations—Odness, for example, is more likely to be from *oddr,* a point of land, rather than named from Odin. Similarly the

19. ***The Scar Plaque.*** *This decorative whale-bone plaque was found in the Scar boat burial. Plaques of this kind are associated with female graves, and may have been used as prestigious linen-smoothers.*

names which have been derived from *vé* (sacred) and *hof* (heathen temple) are dubious, the latter being sometimes confused with *haugr* (mound). The name Helliehow in Sanday (*helig haugr*, holy mound) is typical of names which preserve undateable beliefs of a kind which may or may not preserve traces of heathenism: the mound was believed to be haunted by a *hogboon* who was so troublesome that the people in the farm resolved to leave and live elsewhere.[44] Names such as 'the Stone of Odin', applied to a former standing stone in Stenness and another in Shapinsay, have sometimes been connected with an Odin cult,[45] but are more often regarded as fanciful antiquarian explanations with no real connection with Norse heathenism.

One reason why the Norse were easily converted was that their trading voyages regularly brought them into contact with Christians. They were no doubt aware of the commercial advantages of the 'prima signatio', the marking with the cross as a first step towards Christian initiation, which was in theory necessary before heathens were permitted to trade with Christians. Nevertheless the earls themselves, being associated with military activity rather than with trade, might have been slower to convert. It would not have been surprising if the earls had remained heathen until the Kings of Norway turned to Christianity, as indeed *Orkneyinga saga* tells us. It might even be possible, as Raymond Lamb has suggested, that there was in Sigurd's time a 'limited revival of heathenism at the top level of society',[46] associated with the warrior cult of Odin. The evidence for this heathen revival is mainly the story of Sigurd's raven banner, and the fact that some estates with papa-names were later found in the possession of the earls. On this basis Lamb raised the possibility that the earls might have initially ruled through Pictish institutions, but then used heathenism as a convenient pretext to confiscate the estates of the Pictish church.

The Christian church may have attracted a significant part of the population, but, if it lacked the support of the earls, its organisation cannot have been strong. Once the earls converted there is no real evidence that heathenism continued, although *Orkneyinga saga* appears to record isolated instances of heathen practice as late as c.1135. However, the saga's description of how Sweyn *brjóstreip* ('Breastrope') practised the black arts and engaged in *útiseta*[47]—sitting outside at night to conjure up spirits—is a literary device. The saga at that point needed to explain why Sweyn Asleifsson, having killed Sweyn Breastrope, received protection from Bishop William, and so it sets out to blacken Sweyn's character by associating him with heathenism; this allows the bishop to describe the murder as 'a good riddance' and to shelter the killer (see Chapter 7). The incident therefore cannot be taken as an indication that heathen practices were really continuing at the earl's court as late as the first half of the twelfth century. On the other hand a substantial sub-stratum of heathenism was embodied in petty charms recorded in post-Reformation witchcraft trials, and in folklore recorded in the eighteenth, nineteenth and even the twentieth century. Such folklore is seldom associated with the cult of Odin, but is linked to fertility magic. Examples include the carrying of fire round the boundaries of farms and fields, and into byres to frighten off the trolls.

The only information we have about internal events in Orkney comes from a tale in *Flateyjarbók* which illustrates this violent, half-Christian world. Ulf *illi* ('Wolf the Bad') was a great Viking chief who lived in Sanday, apparently before Sigurd's conversion to Christianity.[48] We are told that 'Wolf the Bad... lived up to his name'. When his offer to buy an estate in North Ronaldsay was rejected, he killed the owner and seized the property. Although Earl Sigurd disapproved of the killing, such was Ulf's power that the earl's mediation failed and a blood feud ensued. The story reflects the transition to Christianity: Ulf was heathen, but his grandson converted to Christianity and, after regular visionary encounters with St Peter, he became a bishop in Ireland. Despite the fabulous elements, the story may correctly reflect certain aspects of tenth century society. In later records we find the North Isles of Orkney consisted of a series of large properties, with only a little land in the hands of independent peasant farmers. It is quite likely that Sanday and other islands were dominated by powerful chiefs like Ulf whom the earl had difficulty in controlling.

A dispassionate view of the progress of Christianity in Orkney is obscured by the high drama of Sigurd's death at Clontarf. We need to appreciate, however, that the trappings of heathenism which surround Clontarf are part of the saga-maker's art, and come mainly from *Njal's saga* rather than from *Orkneyinga saga* which has surprisingly little to say about the famous battle.[49] By reading *Njal's saga* in conjunction with *Orkneyinga saga,* a striking contrast emerges between Sigurd, who died clutching the raven banner of Odin, and his son Thorfinn who ended his days by visiting Rome, building the cathedral of Christchurch and superintending the affairs of Orkney's first Norse bishop. The contrast highlights a real transition, not just in terms of religion, but in the transformation of Orkney from a nest of pirates into a Christian earldom which aspired to be fully integrated into European Christendom.

By the time *Njal's saga* was written in the middle of the thirteenth century (about 250 years after the events it purports to describe), the Battle of Clontarf had come to be seen by both the Irish and Norse as an event of enormous significance—it had been transformed into 'one of the most fatal and doom-laden battles in Viking history, the ultimate confrontation between the Irish and the Norse for the soul and sovereignty of Ireland'.[50] Yet Clontarf was not a straightforward contest between Celtic Christianity and Norse heathenism. It was in origin an internal Irish affair, a war between King Brian Boru and the King of Leinster. Both sides sought allies and, while King Sygtrygg of Dublin and a grand alliance of Norsemen sided with Leinster, a contingent of Isle of Man Vikings fought on the side of King Brian. There were Christians and heathens on both sides. Nor did 'Brian's Battle' have any permanent effect on the Norse colony of Dublin; King Sygtrygg continued to rule there, and its market continued to dominate trade as it had done for well over a century. But if the battle failed to bring about major changes, it has to be said that neither long-term political significance nor historical accuracy was of much concern to the saga-maker. For him, the importance of Clontarf lay in an illustrious procession of doomed warriors; he was interested in the story of their famous deeds and the manner of their death. In *Njal's saga* the Battle of Clontarf takes on the qualities of *Ragnarok*—it is the time when the gods are destroyed.

The Viking alliance was formed at Yule 1013 at a gathering in Orkney at which both King Sygtrygg and Earl Gilli were present, and to which came the Icelanders who had been involved in the burning of Njal. According to *Njal's saga*, Sigurd was won over against his better judgement by the promise of a kingdom in Ireland and marriage to Gormflaith, Sygtrygg's mother.[51]

It may be that the preliminaries to Clontarf were rather more complicated than this account suggests; there are stories of a campaign fought by Sigurd in the previous summer when he carried devastation and slaughter to a large area of the west coast of Scotland,[52] possibly indicating that there had been some kind of challenge to his authority which, we may suppose, was never very secure. However, in accordance with his promise, he arrived in Dublin on Palm Sunday 1014, bringing with him a host, not only drawn from Orkney, Shetland and the Hebrides, but containing some of the most famous men from Iceland. The Irish saw the host in a less heroic light: 'the foreigners of Orkney and the Shetland Islands' were 'a levy of fierce, barbarous men —senseless, uncontrollable and unbiddable'.[53]

The nights leading up to the battle were marked by signs and wonders: on the first night men were scalded by sudden showers of boiling blood; the next night swords leapt spontaneously from their sheaths and axes and spears flew about in the air; on the third night the ships were attacked by ferocious ravens with beaks and claws of iron.[54] On the morning of Good Friday 1014 a Caithness man named Dorrud spied on the Valkyries, the grisly 'choosers of the slain'. They worked on their terrible loom with human heads for loom-weights and arrows for shuttles as they wove their web of human entrails. Their chant, the poem *Darraðarljoð*,[55] was, according to Sir Walter Scott, still recited in its original Norn language in the late eighteenth century in North Ronaldsay.[56] As the Valkyries worked on their loom, armies fought in far-off Dublin, controlled by the rhythm of their verses. Sigurd's magic banner was carried before him with the raven of Odin in full flight, but Odin was a fickle god who offered no sure rewards, and in the end his magic failed Sigurd. As one standard-bearer after another fell, Sigurd at last ordered Rafn the Red to take the standard. 'Carry your own fiend', Hrafn replied, so Sigurd took the flag from its staff, rolled it up and put it under his cloak. Shortly afterwards he was dead, pierced through by a spear.

There was a man by the name of Hareck who had been ordered by Sigurd to stay behind in Orkney, much against his will, but Sigurd promised that he would be first to hear the news on his return. That evening Hareck saw Sigurd come riding home at the head of his men. Hareck went out to greet them, they were seen to meet, then the ground opened up and they rode into the hill, and nothing more was ever seen of Hareck.[57] When the hillside closed on Sigurd's ghostly army, it also closed on the whole world of heathen magic.

5

Earl Thorfinn and the Christian Earldom

When Earl Sigurd was killed at Clontarf (1014) he left three adult sons from his first marriage, Sumarlidi, Einar *rangmunnr* ('Wry-mouth') and Brusi, and a younger son, Thorfinn, who was the child of his second marriage. The sagas tell us that Thorfinn was then five years old, but this information can- not altogether be trusted since it is combined with the obviously erroneous statement that he had reigned for 60 or even 70 years, when he died 'in the latter days of King Harald Sigurdsson' (killed 1066).[1] The identity of Thorfinn's mother is not entirely certain: the saga-author, probably correctly, believed her to be a daughter of Malcolm II (King of Scots 1005-1034),[2] but some historians have taken her to be a daughter of one of the Mormaers of Moray.[3] This seems less likely: the course of events in Sigurd's and Thorfinn's reign involved hostility between Orkney and the Moray family and, since the Kings of Scots also faced a threat from Moray, an Orkney- Scottish marriage made strategic sense, besides offering to Malcolm II a means of acquiring some influence in the far north. When Sigurd went off to Clontarf, Thorfinn was left in the care of his Scottish grandfather, who appointed regents to rule in Caithness and Sutherland where Thorfinn was given the title of 'earl'.[4] Although both provinces were regarded as histori- cally part of Scotland,[5] Malcolm II's direct power is likely to have been limited. Probably he was able to make use of a faction in Caithness willing to accept Thorfinn as a means of continuing the Scottish alliance.

It was under the rule of Thorfinn *hinn riki* ('the Mighty') that Orkney attained its maximum influence, dominating large parts of the north and west of Scotland. It was also his achievement that he guided Orkney through the transition from a viking earldom on the fringes of Europe to a Christian principality with the forms of civil and church organisation which made it acceptable in the civilised world. Yet these were the rewards which came to Thorfinn in his old age. First he had to engage in a protracted power strug- gle against his half-brothers and nephew, and when he emerged victorious as sole earl, he had to struggle to retain and eventually to expand Sigurd's conquests. It was only when his internal and external enemies were defeated that Thorfinn in his final peaceful years was able to turn his attention to the reform of church and state.

The saga draws vivid character sketches of those who fought over Sigurd's inheritance. Thorfinn himself grew up to be 'the tallest and strongest of men, with black hair, sharp features and a grisly aspect'; he was energetic, capable, and warlike. We are told less about the eldest brother, the seemingly peace-loving Sumarlidi, who died within a year. The next, Einar Wry-mouth, was harsh, oppressive and belligerent—very different from the remaining brother, Brusi, 'a mild man, equable of temper, unaffected and of good conversation',[6] who often appears in the role of peace-maker. The saga's favourite was Brusi's son, Rognvald, who was fostered by St Olaf and was thus a foster-brother of the Norwegian king Magnus on whose support he could always count. Rognvald was 'the most handsome of men and of such accomplishments that his match was not to be found'.[7] Such was his reputation that, a century later when Kali Kolsson was embarking on his attempt to make himself earl, he found it useful to change his name to 'Rognvald' as a means of identifying himself with his illustrious predecessor (see Chapter 7-).[8]

There were two ways in which the earldom might be shared. Earls could rule jointly as was the case for a brief period with Einar Wry-mouth and Brusi,[9] and later with Paul I and Erlend II (c.1065-c.1098),[10] Rognvald and Harald Maddadsson (c.1138-1152)[11] and probably John and David (1206-1214).[12] In these circumstances one of the earls was usually recognised as the senior partner and was responsible for the conduct of government, the main function of which was military. Joint rule, however, was often unstable, so it was more usual for the islands to be divided territorially. For the first 34 years of Thorfinn's reign the earldom was divided into 'thirds', and it was only after 1046 that he ruled as sole earl.

Despite the interest which the saga takes in the struggle to control the 'halves and thirds' of the earldom, it is never made clear where these shares were located, although there are a number of clues. An attempt by Storer Clouston to identify these shares took as its starting point the saga's statement that Brusi owned 'the northernmost part of the isles';[13] the family connection with this part of Orkney finds confirmation when Brusi's son, Rognvald, fetches malt for his Yule ale from Papa Stronsay and meets his death there, and is buried in Papa Westray.[14] Clouston placed Einar Wry-mouth in the East Mainland and South Isles on the basis of two pieces of information: first, Amundi and his son, Thorkell Fosterer, who lived at 'Hlaupandanes' (apparently Skaill in Deerness),[15] were subject to his rule and, second, Eyvind *úrarhorn*, a Norwegian nobleman, was captured and killed by Einar at Kirk Hope in Walls, so presumably this also was part of his territory. This left the West Mainland as Sumarlidi's third, which seemed

20. *Halves, Thirds and Husebys.* *Clouston's theory that Orkney was shared among co-earls by means of halves and thirds (History, 36) was further developed by Steinnes who related the six districts to four 'huseby' names (Steinnes, 'The Huseby System in Orkney'). His districts are not quite identical to Clouston's scheme, but are equally speculative—no 'husebys' appear in early documentary sources, nor is the evidence for the very existence of six districts very convincing.*

appropriate since, as eldest son, his share might be expected to include Birsay. It was Sumarlidi's share which Thorfinn eventually inherited, and the saga describes how Birsay eventually became his settled residence.[16]

Had Clouston stopped at the point where he had identified the respective territories as being in the north, east and west, no one would take exception to his scheme (although he might have considered that 'north' meant Shetland). However, he proceeded to elaborate his ideas in a way which was theoretical rather than based on hard evidence. Since the earldom was readily divisible into halves as well as thirds, he argued that this implied that there were six recognised divisions which made it possible to share the islands between two earls (three districts each) or between three earls (two

21. *Joseph Storer Clouston (1870–1944). Clouston was a prolific author of popular novels, but he was also an enthusiast for all things Norse and had an unrivalled knowledge of Orkney's history.*

districts each). He then attempted to reconstruct the boundaries of these districts, not on the basis of contemporary evidence, but by lumping together parishes and islands to create districts which were of approximately equal value in terms of their pennylands. However, we need to remember that the saga does not mention parishes or pennylands, neither of which are likely to have existed in Thorfinn's day. Clouston's 'evidence' comes from skat rentals which are separated by nearly 500 years from the events to which they were applied. His over-ingenious scheme was carried a stage further by Asgaut Steinnes who proposed that the six supposed districts were each controlled from a *huseby*, a large military farm with administrative functions in relation to the surrounding area (Fig.20).[17]

A further criticism is that Clouston was preoccupied with Orkney and failed to take account of other areas which also had to be shared, notably Shetland and Caithness. Brian Smith has argued that when the saga tells us that Brusi owned 'the northernmost part of the isles' it is referring to Shetland rather than the North Isles of Orkney.[18] This view is supported by a verse by Thorfinn's poet, Arnór, in which he refers to Rognvald as 'Lord of the Shetlanders'.[19] Since the verse in question describes the battle of

Rauðabjorg when Thorfinn and Rognvald were fighting over their respective shares, it is clear that Shetland was in Rognvald's territory, and no doubt it had previously belonged to his father, Brusi. Later we find this share in the possession of the earls of the Erlend line who consistently commanded the loyalty of the Shetlanders (see Chapter 7).

Although it might have been convenient to treat Shetland, Orkney and Caithness each as a self-contained 'third', it was not easy to use Caithness as part of a comprehensive package. The saga makes a distinction between Orkney and Shetland, which Sigurd's sons had inherited from their father and required to divide, and Caithness, which Thorfinn held as a gift from the King of Scots. It is made clear that Thorfinn held Caithness in addition to his third of Orkney and Shetland, not as part of his share.[20] This indeed was both the source of his power and the cause of ill-feeling between Thorfinn and his brothers. Yet we can see that Caithness, although held from Scotland, was also liable to be shared on occasions. The *De Situ Albanie* describes how Caithness was divided into two provinces, Caithness proper and what is now Sutherland. Although the primary purpose of *De Situ Albanie* was to describe the former provinces of Pictland, it was written c.1165 when the Orkney-Caithness earldoms had recently been divided.[21] Then in 1196 we meet the two provinces again when King William invaded the north of Scotland and 'bowed to his will both provinces of the Caithness men'.[22] The outcome of his invasion was the defeat of Earl Harald Maddadsson who was allowed to hold half of Caithness while the other half was given to his rival, Harald the Younger (see Chapter 8).[23] This episode makes it clear beyond doubt that sharing the earldom sometimes involved a division of Caithness.

In addition to Shetland and Caithness, the division of the earldom must also have taken into account Sigurd's conquests in the Hebrides and perhaps in Ireland. Einar Wry-mouth's preoccupation with Irish affairs suggests that he had inherited these interests. In the aftermath of Clontarf he had serious problems and he suffered a crushing defeat at 'Ulfreksfjorðr' (perhaps Larne).[24] After Einar's death it was Thorfinn who pursued claims in the Hebrides and Ireland, whereas Brusi and Rognvald seem less directly involved. It can thus be seen that there was more to be shared than just Orkney. Although we ought not to be too dogmatic about boundaries, it does seem that Clouston may have been right when he envisaged that the division created a boundary or boundaries which ran through the Orkney Mainland.

In the 32 years which were to pass before the earldom was united under Thorfinn's sole rule, a whole series of arrangements altered the way in which Orkney was shared. It is surprising how often this was achieved by peaceful means, and how important public opinion appears to have been. Certainly disputes occasionally erupted into violence, notably when Einar Wry-mouth was assassinated (c.1020) but only once, at the very end when Rognvald

Brusisson made his final bid for power, did open warfare break out. Disputes between earls were always unpopular, and there were strong pressures to effect a reconciliation. In the absence of agreement, earls might appeal to Norway. Quarrels among competing co-earls and the resulting appeals to royal authority greatly strengthened the King of Norway's ability to intervene in Orkney affairs.

Because of Thorfinn's youth the dispute with his elder brothers was initially conducted on his behalf by Thorkel Fosterer, who had earned Einar's enmity by voicing opposition to the earl's war levies for his Irish campaigns. Thorkel found it prudent to flee to Caithness, where he fostered the youthful Thorfinn and became his inseparable adviser. Disagreement centred on Caithness: the older brothers argued, not unreasonably, that since they were excluded from Caithness, Thorfinn ought to have no share of the Orkney inheritance. Thorfinn, on the other hand, contended that he held Caithness by gift from the King of Scots rather than by inheritance from Sigurd, and so he ought not to be excluded from his father's heritable lands in Orkney. After the death of Sumarlidi, Thorfinn had sufficient strength to force his brothers into a complicated agreement which gave him possession of Sumarlidi's third.[25] Earl Einar resented Thorfinn's return to Orkney, and ill-feeling between Thorkell and Einar reached such a point that, first Thorkell Fosterer, and then Thorfinn, visited Norway to enlist the support of King Olaf.[26]

On Thorkel's return it was agreed that he and Einar should each entertain the other at a feast as a means of sealing peace between them. Thorkell was host at 'Hlaupandanes' (Skaill, Deerness) but when it was time for both to leave for Einar's hall, he claimed to have discovered that there were ambushes laid along the route. Going back into the hall, down the middle of which fires were burning in the long central hearth, Thorkel found the sour-tempered Einar sitting alone on one of the side-benches. 'Are you ready yet?', asked Einar. Thorkel answered, 'I am ready now'. He struck Einar a blow with his sword and the earls' body pitched forward into the fire. Hallvard, an imperturbable Icelander, had come into the hall behind Thorkell. 'It is not very clever to leave the earl in the fire and not pull him out', he remarked, so he drove his pole-axe into the nape of Einar's neck and tossed his smouldering body on to the bench.[27]

Brusi now inherited Einar's third according to an agreement previously made between them, but Thorfinn claimed that Brusi and himself ought each to possess half the earldom.[28] Failing to agree, both parties appealed to King Olaf, and both earls visited Norway to press their claim in person. The circumstantial account in *Orkneyinga saga* probably exaggerates the extent of the king's authority over Orkney; Norway later found it useful to have a definitive statement of its sovereignty over Orkney directly from the mouth of Norway's patron saint (see Chapter 2), and at the same time the subservience of the Orkney earls could be used by the saga-writer to enhance St Olaf's reputation. But the earls' appeal to Norway is not fictitious: *Icelandic Annals* record that 'Earl Thorfinn and Earl Brusi gave Orkney into the power of King Olaf' (1021),[29] and the terms of the settlement are not improbable. This is the first occasion when we are told Orkney earls visited Norway. Appeals to the king marked a new stage in their relationship with their overlord. Olaf claimed that the earls held Orkney *i len* (as a non-heritable administrative fief) not as *eign*, (heritable property), and so he claimed the right to impose a solution. Thorfinn and Brusi were each to possess one third but, because Earl Einar had been responsible for the killing of Eyvind *úrarhorn*, Einar's third was declared forfeit to the crown.[30] Eyvind had assisted Einar's Irish enemies, and on the voyage home he was forced to seek shelter in Osmundwall (Kirk Hope in Walls) where he was captured and put to death by Einar.[31] And yet, although Olaf might judge between the Orkney earls, he was in no position to exercise direct rule. Evidently the king was suspicious of Thorfinn's ambition and his Scottish connections and so, after Thorfinn's departure, he entrusted the royal third to Brusi. Brusi's son Rognvald remained behind as a guarantee of Brusi's good behaviour. However by 1029 Thorfinn succeeded in gaining the dominant position and took over the royal third in return for relieving his less warlike brother of the obligation of defence. However, it is significant that this ultimate reversal was only possible after Olaf's exile from Norway removed the support which Brusi enjoyed.[32]

A large part of *Orkneyinga saga's* account of Thorfinn's long reign is taken up with a campaign against Karl Hundisson, King of Scots.[33] The saga would have us believe that Earl Thorfinn's grandfather, Malcolm II, was succeeded as King of Scots by 'Karl Hundisson'. King Karl, we are told, attempted to install his nephew, Moddan, as 'earl' in Caithness to the exclusion of Thorfinn. The outcome was that Thorfinn was expelled and hurriedly retreated to Orkney with Karl Hundisson in hot pursuit. Although Thorfinn's ships were outnumbered, he was able to defeat Karl in a desperate sea-battle fought off Deerness. Thorfinn then took the offensive, and a surprise attack resulted in the killing of Moddan in Thurso. In his final confrontation with 'King Karl' the saga has a memorable description of Thorfinn with a gilded helmet on his head and a great spear in his hand winning a crushing victory over Karl and his Irish allies in a battle fought at 'Torfness' (usually identified as Tarbatness in Easter Ross where archaeology is at present revealing a rich high-status Pictish site). The saga has no clear knowledge of what happened to Karl after the battle: it tells us that 'some say that he was killed there'. The story ends with Thorfinn everywhere victorious, and he laid waste much of Scotland in a campaign which took him as far south as Fife.

Since there was never a Scottish king by the name of Karl Hundisson, one view is that the whole episode is 'a fabulous story'.[34] That verdict is not entirely justified: the saga-writer's main source is Arnór's poem *Thorfinnsdrápa*[35] which he quotes verbatim, interspersing the relevant verses with narrative which explains and embellishes the action. Arnór is a good witness: he was Thorfinn's court poet and was related to Thorfinn by marriage, and if he was not an actual eye-witness, he was certainly in Orkney a year or two later when he would have heard an account of the Karl Hundisson war from Thorfinn himself and from other participants. The saga-author, however, was faced with the usual difficulties when he attempted to construct narrative from skaldic verse, and he also makes use of another source which is probably later in date and less reliable. Whereas it is Arnór's near-contemporary verse which names the invader 'Karl' and describes him as 'lord' of the Scots, it is the saga-writer's prose written 170 years after the event which tells us that Karl's patronymic was 'Hundisson' and that he was successor to Malcolm, King of Scots.

Either 'Karl Hundisson' was an impenetrable nickname applied to a real king or, more probably, it was bestowed on someone whom the Icelandic saga-author mistakenly believed to have been a King of Scots. The name is not necessarily opprobrious as is often claimed ('peasant son-of-a-dog') since the names 'Karl' and 'Hundi' are elsewhere applied with no disparaging intent.[36] Many attempts have been made to discover Karl's identity. An obvious candidate is Duncan I (King of Scots 1034-1040) since he was the person who actually succeeded on the death of Malcolm II.[37] A case can also be made for Duncan's successor, MacBeth (King of Scots 1040-1057).[38] Before he gained the throne, MacBeth was ruler of Moray, and so he might well have been involved in conflict with Thorfinn's Orkney.

Since in chapter 4 we have already met Hlodver Sigurdsson, nicknamed 'Hundi', who was taken hostage by Olaf Tryggveson in 995 AD, another possibility is that 'Karl Hundisson' was, or claimed to be, a son of Hlodver and therefore a grandson of Earl Sigurd. This son of Hlodver Hundi (if he existed) would have had as good a claim to the earldom as Thorfinn and his brothers, but it was a claim which they might have been reluctant to acknowledge, in which case, it could be argued, Hlodver Hundi's son might have made common cause with Orkney's enemies. It is unlikely that this identification is correct despite the coincidence of the name. When Hlodver Hundi was taken hostage by Olaf Tryggveson, *Orkneyinga saga* does not give his age, but *St Olaf's saga* describes him as 'a lad',[39] and both sagas tell us that he lived only 'a short while'.[40] It is difficult to imagine that Hlodver Hundi lived long enough to have a son, or that a son could have been old enough c.1030 to have had an adult nephew (Moddan). Furthermore, had someone purporting to be Hlodver Hundi's son arrived from Norway, he

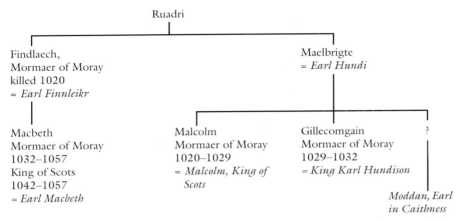

22. **The Rulers of Moray.** *Possible identifications with the Scottish leaders named in* Orkneyinga saga *and* Njal's saga *are shown in italics.*

would claim to be an 'earl' rather than a 'king'. The saga is always careful about the title of 'earl' and would not knowingly describe a claimant as 'king'. Besides, as we will discover, there was another Hundi—'Earl Hundi'— whom it would be difficult to equate with Hlodver 'Hundi' Sigurdsson, and who is more likely to be the parent of the mysterious Karl.

An attempt by A.B.Taylor (translator of *Orkneyinga saga*) to identify King Karl quoted examples of the title *Rí Alban* being applied in Irish sources to people who might be regarded as regional kings, but were not Kings of Scots. His conclusion that Karl Hundisson was based in Argyll is not convincing, but the general premise that he was 'a chief or Mormaer in one or other of the northern provinces of Scotland' is a good starting point.[41] Malcolm, Mormaer of Moray, and his uncle and predecessor Findláech (killed 1020) are both among those described as 'King of Scots' in Irish sources.[42] In the *Annals of Tigernach* we find the entry:

> 1029: Malcolm, king of Scotland, the son of Maelbrigte, son of Ruadri, died.[43]

Despite this description of Malcolm as 'King of Scotland', we can see from the ancestry which is provided that the entry refers to Malcolm of Moray, rather than Malcolm II. Thus *Orkneyinga saga* when it refers to 'Melkolmr Skotakonungr' may be crediting Malcolm of Moray with the same dubious kingship. It may be that the title of 'king' was used rather loosely by those familiar with the petty kingdoms of Ireland and the Hebrides, and that the ruler of Moray, who from central Scotland was regarded as a 'mormaer' ('great official'), appeared to be a king in his own right when viewed from a northern perspective. It is, however, possible that the Moray family claimed and perhaps exercised a wider regional kingship over the parts of northern Scotland which were not directly under Norse rule.[44] A further possibility is that they claimed the kingship of all Scotland as rivals to Malcolm II. MacBeth (King of Scots 1040-1057) and Lulach (1057-8) are members of this Moray family who later really were Kings of Scots.

The campaigns in the north of Scotland which we find at the very beginning of *Orkneyinga saga* can best be understood as recurring warfare between Orkney and this Moray dynasty. The participants in this prolonged struggle are hopelessly confused, but their names, even when wrongly applied, are sufficient to identify Orkney's opponents beyond doubt. One of the very first events recorded in the saga is the set-piece battle between Sigurd the Mighty and Maelbrigte Tusk.[45] Although the story as it appears in the saga is myth rather than history, it contains information we can use: the name 'Máel Brigte' occurs in the Moray family at a later date (see Fig.22), thus Sigurd's opponent might be an earlier member of the family with the same name or, more probably, the name 'Maelbrigte' is simply used out of context. The saga also tells us that Sigurd the Mighty had a fort in Moray, apparently in the inner Moray Firth, so this indicates the area in which this early conflict was believed to have taken place, as does Sigurd's reputed place of burial at Ekjalbakki (the Oykell or Dornoch Firth).

The saga tells us that three generations later Skuli, the renegade Norseman and brother of Earl Ljot, was given the title of 'earl' by the 'King of Scots' (i.e. he was established as a local chief by the ruler of Moray). Together with people described as the 'King of Scots' and 'Earl MacBeth', Skuli was defeated at a battle in the Caithness Dales. Then 'Earl MacBeth' appeared with a huge army and a battle was fought at Skiðamyrr near Wick at which the Norse claimed victory, although Ljot received wounds from which he died (see Chapter 4).[46] The saga uses this story at a point too early for 'Earl Macbeth' to be the historical MacBeth. Once again the name is misapplied, or perhaps the author has inserted the story at the wrong point in his saga. When the struggle was renewed by Earl Sigurd, his opponent at a second battle at Skiðamyrr was Finnleikr who is easily identified as Finnláech, Mormaer of Moray (killed 1020). In *Njal's saga* there is a further account of warfare apparently shortly before 1014, which may or may not be the same battle: it tells us that Sigurd's brother-in-law, Havard of Freswick, was killed by 'Earl Hundi' and 'Earl Melsnati', and at the subsequent battle of 'Dungalsnípa', Melsnati was killed. However, Sigurd withdrew when he heard that Malcolm was gathering a host at Duncansby.[47] 'Melsnati' is probably Máel Snechta, *rí Muréb* ('King of Moray'), who was Lulach's son and whose real date is much later (d.1085).

Little reliance can be placed on the *Orkneyinga saga*'s account of these events, and *Njal's saga* is an even more dubious historical source. Nevertheless the occurrence of the names Maelbrigte, MacBeth, Finnleikr, Malcolm and Melsnati, even when misapplied, indicate a prolonged struggle between Orkney and Moray. It may even be possible to identify Moddan whom Karl tried to install as earl in Caithness to the exclusion of Thorfinn: the name Matáin mac Caerill appears in the *Book of Deer* as a benefactor of the monastery, and he is listed in close proximity to the names of Ruadri, Malcolm, Maelbrigte, Lulach and Maelsnechtai,[48] so he may be a member of the same family. However, the most interesting name in the Moray family is Earl Hundi ('the dog earl'), mentioned only in *Njal's saga*, who it is reasonable to suppose was the father of Karl 'Hundi's son'.

Although *Orkneyinga saga* is remarkably vague about the identity of Karl Hundisson, it is for once quite precise about dates. We are told that 'Malcolm, King of Scots' died just after the brothers Brusi and Thorfinn made their settlement to share the earldom,[49] and that this division took place 'when Cnut got the realm in Norway and Olaf was in exile' (c.1028-9).[50] This confirms that the saga's 'King of Scots' was Malcolm of Moray who died in 1029, rather than Malcolm II whose death was in 1034.[51] Then *Orkneyinga saga* concludes the chapter which deals with Karl Hundisson by stating that 'at that time Earl Brusi died'[52]—we are given to understand that Brusi's death was during or shortly after the Karl Hundisson campaign. According to *St Olaf's saga*, Brusi died in the reign of Cnut (i.e. before 1035), and a short time after the death of Olaf (1030).[53] All this careful dating places the Karl Hundisson war within the years 1029-1035, and probably in the earlier part of that period.

Malcolm was succeeded by his brother Gillacomgain (pronounced 'Gilchoan'), who at the time of his death in 1032 was described as Mormaer of Moray. His three-year rule coincides with the likely date of the Karl Hundisson war, and as Malcolm's successor, he is the person who ought to be 'King Karl'. Gillacomgain's reign was short, and the *Annals of Ulster* record the circumstances of his death:

> 1032: Gillacomgain, Maelbrigte's son, the Mormaer of Moray, was burned with fifty of his men.[54]

This entry is perhaps the ultimate fate of Karl Hundisson. The saga-writer did not know what had happened to Karl, but Arnór's near-contemporary verse describing the aftermath of the Battle of Torfness may be a better source of information:

> Dwellings perish as they put to flame the Scots realm. Red fire leapt in the smoking thatch. That day peril never ceased.[55]

The saga-writer understood this verse to refer to a widespread campaign of devastation in Scotland following the Battle of Torfness. However, when

Arnór refers to 'that day', he may have had a more specific event in mind. The 'red fire leaping from the smoking thatch' may record the burning of Gillacomgain and his 50 men. It sounds a typically Norse killing.

Gillacomgain may have had only a brief three-year rule in Moray, but there are hints of his greater ambitions. His marriage is an indicator of his aspirations: he married Gruoch, daughter of Boite, and thereby he united his own royal credentials (perhaps based on the Cenel Loarn lineage)[56] with an important line of descent from Kenneth II or perhaps from Kenneth III. It was a marriage which seems to have been designed to strengthen his acceptability as a potential King of Scots, and the fact that Gruoch was subsequently married to MacBeth is an indication of her dynastic importance. There were, however, divisions in the Moray family which had resulted in the killing of MacBeth's father, Findláech, in 1020 by Malcolm and Gillacomgain.[57] There are hints that the feud continued, and that MacBeth was claiming the title of king at the same time as we find Gillacomgain described as Mormaer.[58] It is not known who exercised real power in Moray in the period 1029-32, and so MacBeth is also a possible Karl Hundisson. However, if Karl Hundisson was MacBeth who subsequently ruled for 17 years as the real King of Scots, the saga, despite its ignorance of Scottish affairs, might have known more about him. On the other hand, the identification of Gillacomgain with the 'King Karl' is consistent with the saga's rumours of Karl's death soon after the Battle of Torfness.

The ambitions of the Moray family brought them into conflict with Malcolm II,[59] and there are some indications that the Karl Hundisson war was fought to two fronts. Trouble in the south began with the burning of Dunkeld in 1027.[60] The circumstances of Dunkeld's destruction are entirely unknown but the violence may have been directed by Moray against Crinan, Abbot of Dunkeld, who was Malcolm II's son-in-law. The ultimate target might have been Crinan's son, the future Duncan I whose imminent succession to the aged Malcolm II was not regarded as automatic in a country where there had been no recent instance of kingship descending in the direct line. Duncan's position as heir was an obvious impediment to Moray ambitions. Then again, at the end of the war in 1033, the year after the burning of Gillacomgain, we have a record of the killing of an unnamed grandson of Boite (who might have been a son of Gillacomgain) by Malcolm II which perhaps marks the end to the threat which the Karl Hundisson war had posed for Malcolm II's dynasty.[61]

It follows that Orkney is more likely to have been involved in the Karl Hundisson war as an ally of the King of Scots, rather than as an opponent. There are indications that Scottish kings had a consistent strategy of securing allies in Orkney as a means of engaging Moray on its northern front. If, as seems likely, Earl Sigurd's marriage to a daughter of Malcolm II was designed to achieve such an alliance, Thorfinn's victory over Moray marked the spectacular success of this policy. We see the same strategy of a Scottish-Orkney alliance later repeated in the first marriage of Malcolm Canmore (later Malcolm III) to Ingibjorg, said in the saga to be Thorfinn's widow but on the grounds of her age often regarded as more probably his daughter (see Chapter 8).[62] If Ingibjorg was Thorfinn's daughter, this marriage implies that Malcolm Canmore and Thorfinn made common cause during the reign of MacBeth.

One of the problems about Thorfinn is the great extent of his conquests as claimed by *Orkneyinga saga*.[63] Arnór's verses describe his realm as stretching from 'Thursasker' (perhaps Muckle Flugga in the north of Shetland) all the way to Dublin,[64] which is certainly extensive, but it suggests a realm lying on the northern and western fringes of Scotland rather than in its heartland. The saga's prose makes the altogether grander claim that Thorfinn held 'nine earldoms in Scotland'. This has led to the assumption that he overran the greater part of the kingdom, and attempts to identify these earldoms have credited him with districts where Norse rule is not very likely. The statement, if it has any factual basis, must refer, not to the traditional earldoms of Scotland, but to chieftainships of a more local nature. The supposed extent of his realm is difficult to reconcile with the vague account of his conquests in *Orkneyinga saga* and with the scant notice which Thorfinn receives in non-Norse sources. Following the victory over Karl Hundisson at Torfness, the saga simply says that Thorfinn 'marched far and wide throughout the land subduing it'.[65] The description of widespread burnings is a reconstruction based on the imagery in Arnór's verse. The one piece of evidence which suggests that the conquests were extensive is the statement that Thorfinn 'went south as far as Fife'.[66] Thorfinn, however, was not necessarily in Fife at the head of an invading army: he was more likely to have been there as his grandfather's ally.

One possibility is that Thorfinn was in Fife in connection with the visit to Scotland (c.1031) of King Cnut, whose empire included England, Denmark and Norway. During this visit Cnut received the submission of Malcolm II and two other kings whom the *Anglo-Saxon Chronicle* names as Maelbaeth (MacBeth) and Iehmarc (whose identity is less certain).[67] The location of the meeting is known only from an skaldic verse by Sighvatr Thorðarson, which mentions that the kings travelled to Fife to meet Cnut.[68] Since *Orkneyinga saga* tells us that Thorfinn was also in Fife about this time, he may have been one of the regional potentates whose submission Cnut was keen to secure. The purpose of Cnut's expedition to Scotland is not clear, although it seems to have been a matter of some urgency. It has been suggested that one of Cnut's concerns was that those who wished to overthrow his rule in Norway were likely to seek allies in the Norse parts of Britain.[69] It is interesting to note that Brusi, although co-earl, did not play an active part in the Karl Hundisson story. He might, of course, have been terminally ill since he died soon after, but the way events are dated with reference to Brusi suggests that he might somehow have played a more important role than the saga reveals. When Thorfinn and Brusi appealed to King Olaf's judgement in 1021, Brusi's son, Rognvald, had been left in Norway to ensure his father's loyalty. Rognvald was fostered by Olaf, and the future King Magnus was his foster-brother; he fought at Stiklestad (1030) when Olaf was killed, and he shared exile in Novgorod with Magnus. The saga describes how Rognvald was involved in the eventual overthrow of Cnut's government, and how he returned to Norway along with King Magnus.[70] Thus one of Cnut's concerns might well have been the entirely justified fear that the Orkney earldom would assist those who threatened his government in Norway. Thorfinn's presence in Fife may have been required in order to try to counter this threat.

Rognvald's close friendship with Magnus (King of Norway, 1035-47) brought further difficulties for Thorfinn. After Brusi's death, the king gave Rognvald the title of earl in succession to his father. Rognvald received Brusi's 'third', and he was also entrusted with the royal third which King Olaf had previously bestowed on Brusi.[71] Thorfinn greeted Rognvald's return to Orkney with little enthusiasm, but at that time 'he had his hands full with the men of the Hebrides and the Irish'. Thorfinn's victory at Torfness had allowed him to turn to his attention to Ireland, the Hebrides and the west coast of Scotland, all areas which Sigurd had once controlled. Thorfinn grumbled about the way King Olaf had been able to take advantage of the earls, and he was reluctant to acknowledge King Magnus's right to the royal third. However, he needed to avoid outright opposition to King Magnus, and he also needed Rognvald's assistance, so Thorfinn agreed to Rognvald holding two-thirds of the earldom as 'his loyal kinsman' in return for military assistance. Thus he allowed Rognvald to take all the territory he had received from King Magnus, but he implied that it was to be held from himself rather than from the king. For about eight years 'the kinsmen pulled well together', and their joint achievements included a great victory at 'Vatzfjorðr' (c.1039), the location of which is unknown but which might be Loch Vatten in Skye or perhaps Waterford in Ireland.[72]

In the period 1040-2 the earls were campaigning from Galloway 'where Scotland and England meet'. A party was sent south along the English coast, but met a serious defeat when the raiders were captured and all the fighting men were put to death.[73] The following year Thorfinn gathered an army which is reminiscent of the host which Sigurd took to Clontarf: besides his levies from Orkney and Caithness, men came flocking to him from Scotland, the Hebrides and Ireland.[74] The course of events is unclear and is unsupported by independent sources, but it seems that Thorfinn was now in a position to command the military resources of the Hebrides, perhaps as a consequence of his recent victory at 'Vatzfjorðr'. By 1040-2 his campaigning was taking him farther south into regions bordering the Irish Sea where the saga claims major victories. Although there are no details of campaigns in Ireland, Thorfinn's Irish interests seem to have been important. From as early as the Battle of Torfness the Irish are regularly listed among his enemies, and, at the time of his death, the saga credits him with 'a large realm in Ireland'.

The sharing of the earldom between Thorfinn and Rognvald was probably never very stable, but it came under pressure as a result of the arrival in Orkney of the exiled Kalf Arnesson. Thorfinn was related to Kalf by marriage, since his wife, Ingebjorg, was Kalf's niece. Kalf was one of the most powerful men in Norway; he had made a rich marriage and had been created a *lendirman* by King Olaf. He was described as 'a great chief and a man of great understanding',[75] but he had a reputation for inconsistency and disloyalty. He broke with King Olaf and joined Cnut, won over by the prospect that he would be appointed ruler of Norway on Cnut's behalf. Kalf fought against Olaf at Stiklestad, and was reputed to have dealt the saint-king his death-blow. When Kalf's hopes of ruling Norway on behalf of Cnut were not fulfilled, he made peace with King Magnus and assisted his return to Norway, but soon afterwards they quarrelled and Kalf was forced into exile in Orkney. Kalf Arneson was less of a direct threat than Rognvald since he had no territorial claim to Thorfinn's earldom, and he brought with him a large following which provided a welcome addition to Thorfinn's military forces. However, Kalf was so powerful that he was a third force rather than a mere ally. In addition, his relationship with Earl Rognvald was bound to cause difficulties: Kalf was the killer of St Olaf, whereas Rognvald was Olaf's foster-son and was closely associated with King Magnus who had recently driven Kalf into exile.

Kalf was a useful ally in warfare, but his large following was a liability when peace was restored. The end of hostilities also provided Thorfinn with an opportunity to deal with Rognvald, and the cost of Kalf's upkeep provided a pretext for a re-opening the question of how the earldom was divided. Although Rognvald held two of the thirds, he was in no position to resist Thorfinn who could command forces from Caithness and elsewhere. Rognvald therefore visited King Magnus in Norway, and the outcome was a scheme to allow Kalf to return to his Norwegian estates provided he assisted Rognvald against Thorfinn.[76] Kalf was attracted by the proposal, but he had still not made up his mind when Thorfinn and Rognvald met at the Battle of 'Rauðabjorg' ('Red Cliffs', often translated as 'Roeberry') somewhere in the Pentland Firth. Thorfinn sailed from the Caithness shore and Rognvald from

Orkney, and perhaps their ships met on the Orkney side of the firth.[77] While the battle was in the balance, Kalf remained aloof. The ships were close enough to the land for Arnór to be sent ashore to persuade Kalf that he had better prospects from his kinship with Thorfinn than from King Magnus's specious promises. He was won over, and together Thorfinn and Kalf destroyed Rognvald's fleet, forcing him to seek refuge in Norway for a second time.

Affairs reached their climax in the violent events of the winter of 1046. Hugh Marwick said of the saga's story of Rognvald's last days that it was 'as lurid and dramatic an episode as is to be found anywhere in literature'—it was 'sheer art'.[78] Marwick was right to emphasise the literary aspects of the story, for 'sheer art' is not necessarily good history. *Orkneyinga saga* tells how Rognvald rejected King Magnus's offer to equip another expedition, and chose instead to return with a single ship manned by picked men from the king's guard. Thorfinn did not expect a winter attack, so he was easily surprised and his house set ablaze. Unnoticed in the darkness and confusion, Thorfinn and his wife broke out through a loft door, leapt down and escaped to Caithness in a small rowing boat. Everyone believed that they had perished, so Rognvald was unprepared for Thorfinn's equally sudden and violent return. Rognvald was in Papa Stronsay, collecting malt for his Yule ale, when Thorfinn and his men landed on the island, surrounded his house and set fire to it. Rognvald appeared in the barricaded doorway disguised as a priest, then vaulting clear of his enemies, he disappeared into the darkness. The barking of his pet dog betrayed his hiding place among the rocks, where he was caught and killed by the ever-useful Thorkel Fosterer.[79]

The story of Rognvald's killing is saga-fiction, and it contains some stock-episodes which are repeated elsewhere in the saga.[80] Norse earls were, however, vulnerable to an attack pressed home with timing and courage. Their residences were largely unfortified, lacking even the small cell-like stone keeps which appeared in the next century. But whatever the truth of the story, Thorfinn was at last clear of his remaining rival to the earldom. Kalf Arneson's eventual pardon and return to Norway removed another problem; Kalf was killed shortly after on an expedition to Denmark.

By 1046 Thorfinn had put an end to Orkney's internal divisions. The remainder of his reign consisted of nearly 20 peaceful years, the only recorded interruption being the presence of Orkneymen in a Norwegian invasion of England in 1058.[81] While King Magnus was alive, Thorfinn was never forgiven for the killing of Rognvald, but it was easier to come to terms with Harald *hardrada*. Thorfinn visited Harald in Hordaland with two 20-bench ships and more than 100 men in order to put his relationship on a regular footing. From there Thorfinn sailed south to Denmark where he met King

Sweyn at Aalborg, then he continued his journey into Germany to visit the Emperor Henry III. Mounting his men on horses, he crossed the Alps, visited Rome and received absolution for his sins from the Pope (probably Leo IX).[82]

When we are told that Archbishop Adalbert of Hamburg-Bremen was visited by 'legates from Orkney' requesting the provision of a bishop, we readily connect the request with Thorfinn's visit to Germany, and Thorfinn must also have discussed the lack of a bishop with the pope. Information about early episcopal appointments comes mainly from Adam of Bremen, who mentions an even earlier bishop of whom he had no great opinion. This was Bishop Henry, formerly Cnut's treasurer in England, and later a missionary bishop in Iceland and bishop of Lund in Sweden. Henry was presumably consecrated from York, but we do not know whether he ever visited Orkney. According to Adam of Bremen, Henry embezzled Cnut's treasure and spent it on high living until 'delighting in the pestiferous practice of drunkenness and gluttony, he died at last through surfeit'.[83] This jaundiced view reflects the bitterness with which York and Hamburg-Bremen vied with each other for the right to consecrate Orkney bishops. The Archbishop of Hamburg-Bremen now supplied bishops to the people of Orkney, Iceland and Greenland, and it is significant that the appointment of Bishop Turolf to Orkney was explicitly 'by order of the pope'. Turolf's name is Norse which at that date is unusual for a bishop, so Thorfinn had probably gained the pope's approval for the promotion of a relative or a close associate. Turolf was succeeded by Bishops John and Adalbert, both of whom were also Hamburg-Bremen consecrations.[84]

Bishop Turolf's appointment was 'to the city of Blascona'. By 'city' nothing more is implied than the seat of a bishop, and the strange name 'Blascona' is presumably a Latinised corruption of an early form of the name 'Birsay'. On the Brough of Birsay there are archaeological remains which indicate the importance of Thorfinn's capital. It was in Birsay that Thorfinn had his own residence, and it was here that he built his cathedral of Christchurch and installed his new bishop. The pattern in Norway was similar; Christchurch dedications are found in Bergen and Trondheim within the confines of royal residences where bishops were closely associated with the king's household. It is noteworthy that Norwegian Christchurch dedications follow the Orkney model, since they are rather later than Thorfinn's cathedral which can be no later than c.1060 and might indeed be a dozen years earlier.

Controversy surrounds the whereabouts of Thorfinn's Christchurch. For once the problem is not lack of evidence—quite the reverse, since there are two sites either of which can be interpreted as fulfilling the requirements. The claims of the buildings on the tidal island of the Brough were advocated by Cruden,[85] and this view was adopted by Radford in the official guide to

*23. **The Brough of Birsay.** The little church on the tidal island of the Brough is of superior design and construction and is possibly Earl Thorfinn's Christchurch. The buildings immediately to the right may be an episcopal or monastic cloister.*

the site. The Romanesque church on the Brough is small, but it is of superior design and construction, so it has been identified as Christchurch, and substantial buildings nearby have been attributed to Thorfinn and his immediate predecessors (see Fig.23). It is an awkward fact that the church is known to have been dedicated to St Peter, but one possibility is that it might have been re-dedicated after Thorfinn visited Rome.[86]

More recently Raymond Lamb has reasserted the view rooted in local tradition that Christchurch lay on the Mainland shore.[87] Substantial foundations of an earlier church lie below the present-day unassuming parish church, now dedicated to St Magnus.[88] It is well authenticated that later bishops had an residence close by at Mons Bellus, the site remembered by Birsay people as 'the lower palace'.[89] Those who advocate the Mainland site then have to explain what is on the Brough. It has been suggested that it was a contemporary Benedictine monastery, and parallels have been drawn between Thorfinn's Birsay and Thorkell Fosterer's Hlaupandaness (Skaill, Deerness) where there is the same association between a chief's hall on the Mainland and an ecclesiastical settlement on the Brough. The implication is

86

that, in more modest fashion, Thorkell was replicating the pattern of settlement at Thorfinn's Birsay.[90] However, the question of the site remains uncertain: the focus of settlement shifted from the Brough at an early enough stage to generate the name 'Langskaill' ('the long hall') on the Mainland site, but it is perhaps unlikely that it had already done so in Thorfinn's time.

It was here in his 'City of Blascona' that Thorfinn settled down in the final peaceful years of his reign. *Orkneyinga saga* tells how he gave up viking voyages and turned his attention to the government of his realm and the making of new laws.[91] The saga is never much interested in peaceful times, and it gives no details of his system of government or his new laws. A likely concern was the levying of a regular income from his conquered territories, and so the ouncelands which are found throughout what once was his realm might have been created or modified at this time as a basis from which to levy tribute, food renders and obligations of military service (see Chapter 15). New laws must also have been needed to enforce Christian practices. In *St Olaf's saga* we are told that when Olaf enquired about the state of Christianity in Orkney, Shetland and the Faroe Islands, he discovered that 'it was far from being as he could have wished'.[92] The passage is linked to reports from Iceland of the eating of horseflesh and the exposure of unwanted infants, so perhaps Thorfinn's new laws dealt with matters of that kind, as well as enforcing Christian marriage and burial, and outlawing sacrifices to the old gods.

It was Thorfinn's permanent achievement that Orkney was set on a course which led to its integration with western Christendom. His widespread conquests were less permanent: 'in those lands which he brought under him by the sword, it seemed to many a hard lot to live under his rule'.[93] After his death most of his conquered lands reverted to their native rulers.

6
The Martyrdom of St Magnus

The peace of Thorfinn's latter years was brought to an end by the momentous events of 1066 which caught up his sons, the joint earls Paul I and Erlend II (c.1065–1098). It is proof of the regular relationship which Thorfinn had eventually built up with Norway, and the military assistance that his powerful earldom could provide, that King Harald Hardrada's invasion of England sailed via Orkney and that his queen and daughters remained in the isles for the duration of the campaign.[1] Paul and Erlend accompanied the expedition but escaped the general slaughter, being left in charge of the fleet at Riccall when King Harald met his death at Stamford Bridge.[2]

The rule of Paul and Erlend lasted more than 30 years, but it is for the most part a blank in *Orkneyinga saga's* account. Despite the martial beginning to their joint rule, their reign is represented as predominantly peaceful, but it cannot have been entirely so, since the loss of Thorfinn's conquests to native rulers probably involved warfare. At home joint rule seems to have been for once harmonious, and for many years Paul and Erlend together ruled over an undivided realm. It was, however, easier for brothers to agree than for cousins. We are told that their sons, respectively Hakon and Magnus, 'could not be in each other's company without the risk of a quarrel',[3] so Paul and Erlend eventually divided the earldom into two distinct territories in the same way that the islands had been divided between Thorfinn and Brusi.[4] It was a rivalry which was to lead to the spilling of blood one Easter day on the island of Egilsay, which earned Magnus immortality as Orkney's saint and martyr. It also set in train feuds between rival claimants from the 'Paul Line' and the 'Erlend Line' which were still continuing three and four generations later when *Orkneyinga saga* was written (c.1200).

The saga describes how, in an attempt to defuse the cousins' rivalry, Hakon was persuaded to leave the islands and journey to Scandinavia. Throughout the events which followed, Hakon's contacts were entirely Scandinavian, whereas Magnus seems to have had close links with Scotland, and indeed with England and Wales. Hakon's travels took him to Sweden where the saga has a long and circumstantial account of his dealings with a heathen wizard. Hakon prevailed on him to reveal the future and, with some reluctance, the soothsayer foretold that Hakon would commit a crime for which

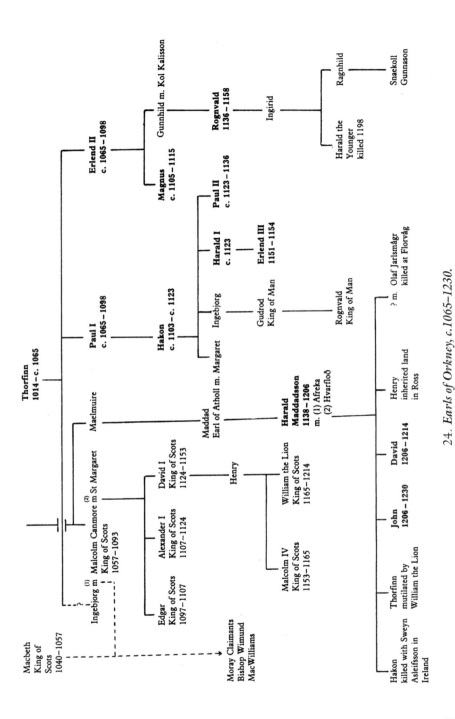

24. *Earls of Orkney, c.1065–1230.*

89

it would be difficult to atone, he would become sole earl of Orkney, he would journey to the extremities of the world but return to die in northern parts.[5]

The way this story is told reminds us that we see the historical Magnus, partly through the filter of a naive 'Saint's Life', but also filtered by the saga-author's sophisticated literary talents. The fortune-telling episode deals with a real person (Hakon) and purports to be a real event, but it is shaped, or more probably entirely invented, for literary reasons. It is obvious that it is intended as a 'table of contents' to alert the reader to the events which follow—the killing of Magnus, and Hakon's search for absolution in Rome and Jerusalem. However, it serves another literary purpose since we are introduced to Hakon in the dubious company of a heathen wizard, and so the idea is implanted that there is a dark side to the man who is destined to kill the saint. This story is an example of the frequent need to disentangle the historical Magnus from the saga's story-telling techniques.

Hakon was in Norway when Magnus *berfætr* ('Barelegs') was preparing the expedition which burst on the west in 1098.[6] Hakon hoped to enlist King Magnus's support, but he was to find the king's plans for Orkney were very different. Arriving in Orkney, King Magnus captured the joint earls and sent them back to Norway where they both died that winter, Paul in Bergen and Erlend in Trondheim. The semi-autonomous earldom was abolished, and the king set up his own system of government with his young son Sigurd as the nominal king, aided by a council to rule in his name.[7] Hakon was given a role as a member of this council.

Magnus Erlendsson was then eighteen years of age,[8] and both he and Hakon accompanied the king on the onward voyage into the Hebrides, and south into the Irish Sea where the fleet arrived on the shores of Anglesey. Anglesey was part of the Welsh kingdom of Gwynedd, ruled over by the Welsh-Irish-Norse king, Gruffydd ap Cynan.[9] Gruffydd had recently been driven out of his kingdom and found refuge with the Norse in Ireland, while two Norman earls, Hugh of Chester and Hugh of Shrewsbury, now dominated Anglesey from the castle of Aberlleiniog at the entrance to the Menai Straits. Although the arrival of Magnus Barelegs was treated as a fortuitous encounter—mere piracy—it seems likely that his intervention was on Gruffudd's behalf. It was in Anglesey at the entrance to the Menai Straits that the battle took place which first marked Magnus for sanctity. It was a somewhat unusual battle since the landing from the Norwegian ships was opposed by Norman horsemen. Archers on both sides played an important role, and the mounted knights splashing out into the shallow water 'fell from their horses like the fruit of figs from the trees'.[10] The king ordered Magnus to prepare for battle, but Magnus declared that he had no quarrel with anyone there. He refused to take shelter, and remained ostentatiously singing from his psalter, unprotected from the spears and arrows which rained down on the ships with deadly effect.[11]

This event is often taken as the very key to Magnus's sainthood, although the saga tells us that the king did not believe that Magnus's motives were religious. Twentieth century writers have generally had no such doubts; both John Mooney's study of the saint and George Mackay Brown's novel, *Magnus*, represent the incident as a moral stand against unprovoked aggression.[12] They might be wrong. We cannot even be entirely sure that Magnus was at Menai. *Orkneyinga saga* and the related *Magnus Sagas* describe Magnus's part in this expedition, but he does not appear in non-Norse sources, although that is hardly conclusive since there was no real reason why his presence should have been recorded. However, the *Saga of Magnus Barelegs*, which we might expected to be better informed, makes no mention of Magnus at Menai, but states that he escaped from the king's presence during a later expedition (1102/3).[13] Peter Foote concluded that the Menai incident might not have been in the original 'Saint's Life' (now lost) and therefore was probably unhistorical.[14]

We might, however, decide that both Hakon and Magnus probably did accompany Magnus Barelegs, not only because they were obliged to serve the king in time of war, but also because it would not have been very prudent to leave them behind given the way Orkney had been treated. If Magnus was at Menai, he had some very obvious and entirely worldly reasons for refusing to fight for Magnus Barelegs: his father and uncle had been taken prisoner in circumstances which led to their death, the earldom had been abolished, and Magnus's expectation of becoming earl had been blighted. But the earls, although they held Orkney from Norway, also held Caithness from Scotland. Since Hakon thought that something might yet be salvaged through the influence of his high-born Norwegian relatives and his friendship with Magnus Barelegs, Magnus's obvious course was to cultivate the Scottish connection. He therefore took an early chance to escape, and made his way to the court of King Edgar where he must have witnessed the religious reforms associated with St Margaret and her sons.[15] If he was influenced by what he saw, the saga fails to tell us.

Magnus's refusal to fight might also be related in some way to his surprisingly frequent involvement in Welsh affairs. Soon after Menai he was back in Wales, residing with 'a certain bishop'.[16] The Welsh bishop with whom Magnus resided might have been Hervé of Bangor. Hervé was a controversial figure whose election was described by Pope Paschal II as 'barbarous'; he was a Norman, closely associated with the Norman earls with whom, the saga tells us, Magnus 'had no quarrel'.[17] For his part King Gruffydd of Gwenydd had strong Norse links and was rumoured to have visited Orkney where he raised a fleet of twenty-four ships to attack Glamorgan.[18] Thus

Magnus's refusal to fight at Menai probably had a political context, although we do not properly understand his involvement. His Welsh connections may explain why his protest was made in Anglesey, whereas reasons of conscience might have led him to object to the brutal plundering and burning of the Western Isles, the violence of which was celebrated with evident relish by Magnus Barelegs' skalds.[19]

Magnus's usefulness to the King of Scots was political rather than religious. He was one of a long line of claimants to the divided earldom whom Scots kings manipulated with the object of making trouble and increasing their own influence. As a preliminary step Magnus became earl in Caithness,[20] then the death of Magnus Barelegs, killed in Ulster in 1102, opened the possibility of a return to Orkney. The young Sigurd Magnusson, nominal king in Orkney for the last five years, was recalled to become joint king of Norway along with his brothers. Orkney appears to have been governed directly from Norway for perhaps a further two years, then Hakon was given the title of earl and was restored to 'such of the realm as was his birthright'.[21] The story that Hakon murdered the royal officials who were entrusted with the management of Magnus's share[22] is probably a late attempt to blacken his reputation. As far as we can see, the respective claims of Hakon and Magnus seem to have resolved with due regard for the law.

Thus Magnus was able to return to Orkney and contest Hakon's possession. The legal process and mediation averted bloodshed, and it was decided that Magnus should visit Norway to obtain a decision from the Norwegian kings. He was successful in pressing his claim, as claimants to the earldom usually were, and Hakon seems to have accepted the decision with a good grace, although it is by no means obvious that Magnus allowed him a share of Caithness at this stage.[23] For several years, possibly as long as from 1105 to about 1114, Hakon and Magnus ruled their respective territories in 'good fellowship'. Joint rule seems to have been reasonably effective. During this period the cousins waged war against an unidentified second cousin Dufnjal (Donald), son of an unidentified Duncan, whom they killed. They also put to death a Shetland viking, Thorbjorn of Burrafirth, by the traditional Norse expedient of setting fire to his house and burning him.[24]

Magnus was married about this time (c.1105) and his marriage may have further bound him to Scotland. *Orkneyinga saga* does not name his wife but describes her as 'of the most noble family in Scotland',[25] which suggests a close link with Scottish royalty. The discovery that she possessed a Norse name, Ingarth,[26] casts doubts, but does not disprove such a connection. The saga makes much of Magnus's chastity within marriage and describes how 'when he felt temptations coming on him to bodily lusts, then he bathed in cold water'.[27] Chastity, of course, is a desirable quality in sainthood, and the story need have no more foundation than that the marriage was childless.

Other royal saints preserved their chastity by bathing in cold water; for example similar stories are told about Edward the Confessor and about the seventh century St Oswald.[28]

The period of co-operation between Hakon and Magnus eventually came to an end. The *Longer Magnus Saga*, alone among the accounts of his life, describes how Magnus left Orkney with two ships and a band of picked men who were maintained for a year at the expense of Henry I of England.[29] The *Longer Magnus Saga*, written in Iceland c.1300, is a late source, not altogether to be trusted when it describes events which do not appear in earlier accounts. However, its story, although undated, may refer to the events of 1114. In that year Alexander I of Scotland accompanied Henry I of England on an expedition into Wales, and strangely King Gruffydd comes into the story once again. Alexander I commanded a separate Scottish army which, according to the Welsh, was drawn from 'the farthest corner of Pictland'.[30] An army drawn from the farthest corner of Pictland is consistent with Alexander I being accompanied by Earl Magnus and a contingent from Caithness or even Orkney. It was this Scottish army which advanced farthest into Gwynedd and compelled King Gruffydd to come to terms, so once again Magnus is found involved in the affairs of this Welsh kingdom.

Orkneyinga saga gives no details of the renewed dispute which eventually led to Magnus's death. We can imagine that joint rule resulted in personal irritations as well as all sorts of practical difficulties. If Magnus was with Henry I for a year, his absence from Orkney may have precipitated the crisis. The fact that the immediate cause of the dispute is withheld from us suggests that there might have been a number of fairly mundane points to be resolved rather than a single clear-cut issue.

Matters came to a head when the earls met with armed followers at a *ting* or assembly. The date was a little before Palm Sunday, but the year is unknown since the saga does not provide us with good enough information to date Magnus's martyrdom.[31] If the breach between the cousins followed Magnus's participation in the Welsh campaign of 1114, the year might have been 1115. When joint-earls threatened to fight there was usually a neutral party in favour of seeking a solution through arbitration, and this group was strong enough to persuade Hakon and Magnus to bind themselves to a settlement. Then there was a call for a further meeting on Egilsay so that the details of the agreement could be finalised. The choice of Egilsay is interesting since Bishop William the Old is on several occasions recorded as living on the island.[32] The location of the meeting suggests Bishop William's involvement.

The choice of an ecclesiastical meeting place might also indicate that there were urgent church matters to discuss—not only did Orkney have two earls, but by this date it seems that each earl had acquired his own bishop.[33]

25. St Magnus Church, Egilsay.

Following Thorfinn's three bishops consecrated from Hamburg-Bremen, the next bishops were appointed from York, possibly because between 1072 and 1100-8 there was no Archbishop of Hamburg-Bremen with metropolitan authority, or simply because disputes between earls caused one of them to look elsewhere. Then in 1102 the York connection was broken by the appointment of Bishop William 'the Old' (Bishop of Orkney 1102-1168).[34] The vacancy occurred at the time when Magnus Barelegs had conquered Orkney, and no doubt the king would want his own nominee at this critical point; it would be advisable to have a bishop whom he could trust to serve on the council which advised his son. Bishop William was described as 'a clerk of Paris', which at that date makes it unlikely that he was a Norwegian, but he seems to have had an Orkney connection through kinship with Sweyn Asleifsson.[35] His episcopate lasted 66 years, so he must have been unusually young when he was appointed, which in turn suggests that he came from an important family. In these circumstances it probably was not difficult to persuade York to support another candidate on the grounds that previous Orkney bishops had been York appointments. At a date between 1109 and 1114 Ralph Novell was elected by 'the men of Orkney' and consecrated from York. Since Hakon's links were with Magnus Barelegs and therefore with Bishop William, it seems that Earl Magnus was the leader of these 'men of Orkney' who sought a rival bishop. We do not know whether Bishop Ralph ever visited his diocese, although it has been suggested that the reason that Bishop William was so often found in Egilsay was that Ralph Novell was installed in Christchurch. Another possibility is that the newly consecrated York bishop accompanied Magnus when he returned from visiting Henry I, in which case his arrival might have been the cause of the crisis. After Magnus's death there was little chance that Ralph would be accepted, although he continued to receive the support of the papacy. Calixtus II c.1119 tried to prevail on the Norwegian kings, Sigurd and Eystein, to defend Ralph and ensure that he was given peaceful possession of his bishopric,[36] and a further papal letter in 1125 continued to mention 'an intruder' (Bishop William).[37] Despite the efforts of the papacy on his behalf, Bishop Ralph Novell ended his days as bishop 'in remotis', a useful assistant in the Archbishopric of York. He was described as 'unacceptable to the people of his diocese, having been chosen by neither clergy, people or ruler'.[38]

If Egilsay as the meeting-place between Hakon and Magnus suggests Bishop William's involvement, the dispute about the rival bishops makes it unlikely that he was a disinterested mediator. The saga makes no mention of him when describing the martyrdom, so we do not know what part, if any, he played in Magnus's death. Bishop William was, however, well placed to influence how the story of the martyrdom was later recorded, and we may imagine that he was anxious to gloss over the fact that he was in any way associated with these events.

Magnus was the first to arrive on Egilsay, having two ships with him in accordance with the agreement. When towards evening Hakon came with 'seven or eight war-ships, all large, filled with men',[39] Magnus knew he had been betrayed. Hakon's ships lay off-shore during the night, and when his men came ashore the following morning, Magnus was captured. Contradictory accounts describe how he was either dragged from the church where he was receiving the sacraments,[40] or else was discovered hiding among the rocks.[41] He was not immediately killed but, if we can believe *Orkneyinga saga's* account which is hagiographical and probably over-formalises the occasion, he was brought before an impromptu assembly which proffered advice to Hakon. It is not clear whether charges were considered, but the saga would have us believe that the assembly had the final say in determining the sentence. When faced with execution, Magnus bargained for his life: first, he offered to leave Orkney and go on pilgrimage to Rome or the Holy Land, but that was rejected; he then offered to agree to imprisonment in Scotland, but that too was unacceptable; his third offer was to suffer maiming, blinding and imprisonment. Although the three offers are a hagiographical device, they remind us of the real fate of Earl Paul who 20

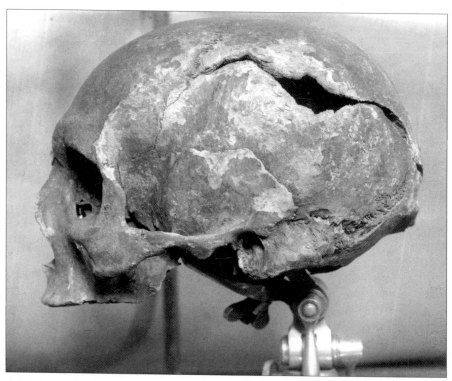

26. *The Skull of St Magnus. Relics presumed to be those of St Magnus were found in 1919 in the south pier of the choir of St Magnus Cathedral. The damage to the skull is consistent with* Orkneyinga saga's *account of how Magnus was killed. 'Stand in front of me', Magnus said, 'and hit me hard on the head, for it is not fitting for a chief to be beheaded like a thief'.*

years later was abducted, imprisoned in Atholl, and reputedly maimed and blinded, whereupon even his closest friends abandoned all thought of restoring him to the earldom.[42]

The saga-writer had some difficulty in portraying Hakon and felt the need to treat his part in the martyrdom with delicacy, no doubt because at the time of writing Hakon's grandson, Harald Maddadsson, was Earl of Orkney. The assembly is invented, or its role is given prominence, in order to divert some of the blame from Hakon. He is represented as willing to accept Magnus's final offer, and the ultimate responsibility is put on the assembled chiefs. The neutral party had vanished; 'We will kill one of the two of you now', the chiefs declared, and thus we are led to believe that Hakon agreed to Magnus's execution only when the alternative was his own death. Hakon ordered Ofeig, his standard-bearer, to kill the earl, but he indignantly refused, so Lifolf, his cook, was reluctantly compelled to be executioner. Magnus instructed the tearful and trembling servant how it should be done. 'Stand in front of me', he said, 'and hit me hard on the head, for it is not fitting for a chief to be beheaded like a thief'. The skull of St Magnus, discovered within a pillar in the cathedral, bears the evidence of this fatal blow.[43]

Hakon had been prevailed upon to allow Magnus's body to be buried within Christchurch in Birsay. Soon afterwards stories began to be told of heavenly lights and a strange fragrance which surrounded his grave. When the Shetlander Bergfinn Skatisson miraculously recovered his sight, and a further 24 men who kept vigil with him were restored to health, a popular cult of the murdered earl rapidly developed despite the opposition, first of Hakon, and then his son Paul II. The *Magnus sagas* catalogue the many miracles attributed to the saint—the cure of lepers, the blind, the crippled and the insane.

Bishop William initially discouraged the cult, declaring 'it heresy to go about with such tales',[44] but he was finally convinced of Magnus's sainthood when, having been struck blind within his cathedral of Christchurch, his sight was miraculously restored by the intervention of the saint. He agreed to the exhumation of Magnus's bones which he tested in fire. Magnus's sainthood was proclaimed, and a triumphal procession conveyed his relics from Birsay to Kirkwall, reputedly by the route which was later marked by the 'Magnus Stones'.[45] Magnus's relics were placed in a reliquary above the altar in 'the church that was there'.[46] This was St Olaf's church; the cathedral had not yet been built.

There were also some rather far-fetched miracles of doubtful religious significance. Two gamblers bet on a throw of two dice; one was a rich merchant who had lost everything except his last ship. When his opponent threw two sixes it was obvious that more than normal luck was required; making a vow to St Magnus, the gambler made his throw; one dice came up a six and the other split in two with one half showing a six and the other a one, thirteen in all, so the gambler won back all his property.[47] Confidence in the miracle is somewhat shaken when you discover that the same story of the split dice is told of St Olaf—and that is not the only miracle which they have in common.[48] We probably regard these miracles as unscrupulous borrowings in the worst traditions of hagiography, but there is another way of looking at it: if Magnus and Olaf share the same miracles, it just goes to prove that they are the same kind of saints—as indeed they are.

It is easy to see that Magnus fits precisely into the pattern of the Scandinavian patron-saints, St Olaf of Norway, St Cnut of Denmark and St Erik of Sweden, all of whom came to represent a growing sense of national identity.[49] These royal patron-saints, like Magnus, met violent deaths at the hands of their own people. The creation of an Orkney saint in this fashionable

97

27. *Altarpiece from Andenes, Norway. The figures from left to right are St Thomas, God the Father holding the dead Christ, St Olaf, and St Magnus. Magnus, despite his somewhat gaudy and unathletic appearance, is intended to portray a martial saint: he holds the pommel of a sword in his left hand (the blade is missing).*

mould can be seen as an assertion of the quasi-royal status of the earls of Orkney. Perhaps it tells us more about the nature of the earldom than about the actual life and character of Magnus. Early visionary appearances were related to the transfer of Magnus's relics to Kirkwall and to miraculous cures, but later Magnus appeared at times of national crisis. It was as a martial patron-saint, rather than a miracle-worker or pacifist-saint, that Magnus had an enduring appeal. When Orkney faced invasion from Caithness, Magnus appeared at Summerdale (1529) and 'faucht for the libertie of this cuntrie, quha was its patroune'.[50] It was as 'ane knycht with schynand armour' that he brought news of Bannockburn first to Aberdeen and then across the Pentland Firth to Orkney.[51] When he appeared in 1249 to warn Alexander II not to invade the Norwegian territory of the Western Isles, he was accompanied by Columba and Olaf. Whereas the figure of Columba was large and menacing and Olaf was rather stout and ill-tempered, Magnus was tall, slender, youthful and the fairest of men.[52] It is a description which is rather difficult to reconcile with the gaudy and unathletic figure which we find in Norwegian statues, although they too were intended to depict Magnus as a garlanded earl, sword in hand, in his role as patron-saint.[53]

Most of what we know about Magnus originally comes from a Latin *Vita* (Saint's Life) which is lost. However, a great part of the *Vita*, or perhaps all of it, was translated and incorporated in *Orkneyinga saga* (c.1200). The saga also makes use of another source which it describes as the *Jarteinabók* or 'Book of Miracles', which presumably was compiled at the saint's shrine in Kirkwall.[54] *The Shorter Magnus Saga* is a revision of all this material dating from c.1250, and *The Longer Magnus Saga* is an even later version from about 1300. There is also a short Latin summary of late date known as the *Legenda de Sancto Magno*. *The Longer Magnus Saga* incorporates not only the *Vita* and the miracle list, but it includes what purports to be a sermon by a certain 'Master Robert' which he delivered on St Magnus's Day 20 years after the death of the saint.[55] Master Robert, we are told, was also the author of the Latin *Vita* and, if true, it must have been composed when eye-witnesses to the martyrdom were still readily available. Since we do not hear of Master Robert in earlier sources, it is possible that he is a literary invention, designed to give *The Longer Magnus Saga* an appearance of authenticity. On the other hand the sermon is combined rather crudely with the other sources, giving the impression that it was a separate document which the author inserted, rather than a literary creation woven into his account.[56]

If the sermon was genuinely preached 20 years after Magnus's death, it takes us right back to the period when he was raised to sainthood by Bishop William and, in fulfilment of Rognvald's vow, work began on the building of the cathedral which was to house the saint's relics. When the sermon refers to how 'God raises up and makes sons to Abraham out of stones',[57] Master Robert was quoting a text which is associated with St Olaf's forgiveness of his enemies on the eve of his death at the Battle of Stiklestad, and which may have been included in an early version of Olaf's liturgy.[58] We are therefore led to believe that from the very beginning there was a deliberate comparison of Magnus to Olaf. Master Robert then goes on to describe these stones as:

> ...smoothed and polished and four-cornered, with four main virtues[59] that they may fit into the heavenly edifice, as strong and steadfast cornerstones in Jesus Christ, our head of the corner... For the Lord Jesus is the son of the great builder who made and makes the world, and all that is therein.[60]

His words suggest that his sermon marked the laying of the foundation stones of St Magnus Cathedral. We know that when work started at Durham

*28. **St Magnus Cathedral from Broad Street.***

Cathedral, individual stones were laid by a number of prominent people including Malcolm III, King of Scots.[61] Master Robert's scholarly sermon may have marked a similar event in Kirkwall when no doubt Earl Rognvald played the leading role in the ceremony. If we accept Master Robert and his sermon at face value, we can picture that, among those listening to the preacher, there were those who knew Magnus, and indeed some who had been present on Egilsay on the day he died.

Although the *Vita* and Master Robert's sermon take us very near in time to the martyrdom, it would be a mistake to accept these accounts as telling a simple story which preserves a straightforward record of events. We would be wrong to suppose that all we need to do is to make due allowance for the credulity of medieval authors and to discount their unfortunate tendency to introduce the miraculous. Sainthood is seldom straightforward; often it has a political dimension which is unlikely to be made explicit in a 'Saint's Life'. The next chapter returns to some of these same events, but it does so from the standpoint of Earl Rognvald. It looks at the political aspect of Magnus's sainthood, and how the cult was manipulated by Rognvald and Bishop William for their mutual advantage.

7

St Rognvald and the Twelfth Century Renaissance

The greatest extent of Orkney's military power was in the reign of Thorfinn the Mighty (1014–c.1065) when he reputedly ruled 'nine earldoms in Scotland' (see Chapter 5). A century later, the reign of Earl Rognvald Kali Kolsson (c.1135–1158) marked the cultural high-point. Rognvald presided over the flowering of Orkney's twelfth century Renaissance;[1] he promoted Magnus's sainthood, he initiated and financed the building of St Magnus Cathedral, and he supervised the creation of a more powerful episcopate; he was the patron of Icelandic poets who were attracted to his court, and he was himself an accomplished poet; he was a crusader and eventually, somewhat incongruously, he was made a saint. Thorfinn's rule was built on military might, but Rognvald's winning of the earldom, and his success in retaining it, owed more to his skill as a politician. There is, however, a continuous line of development from Thorfinn to Rognvald: Thorfinn in his later peaceful years began to open Orkney to the outside world by making contact with the Norwegian and Danish kings, the Emperor and the Pope, and he established Orkney's first Norse bishopric, albeit on a modest scale. In the reign of Rognvald the process was completed, and Orkney emerged with fully developed secular and religious institutions which made it part of the mainstream of European society. Orkney ceased to be 'Viking'.

Orkney's twelfth century Renaissance, however, was achieved against a background of political instability and recurring violence (as indeed was the Italian Renaissance 200 years later). Rognvald's reign was a period of shifts of alliance of bewildering complexity, and his survival required all his political skills. Constant low level warfare, as epitomised by Sweyn Asleifsson, was a way of life and an end in itself. The first part of the twelfth century was marked by the violent deaths of Magnus Erlendsson (martyred c.1115), Harald Hakonsson (poisoned c.1130), Paul Hakonsson (murdered 1136), Erlend Haraldsson (killed 1154) and of Rognvald himself (assassinated c.1158). Rognvald's reign corresponds almost exactly with 'the Anarchy' in England, when local magnates with little attachment to either Stephen or Matilda took advantage of civil war to plunder their neighbours and engage

101

in purely private feuds—it was the time 'when God slept'. God can hardly be said to have slept in Orkney when the earldom was ruled by a future saint and work began on St Magnus Cathedral, but the achievements of Orkney's twelfth century Renaissance took place against the same background of disorder and casual violence.

The saga describes how Hakon, after the killing of Magnus, visited Rome where he received absolution from the Pope. He journeyed to Jerusalem where he bathed in the Jordan, and then returned to Orkney where he proved to be a good and popular ruler.[2] The saga's verdict on the murderer of Orkney's patron saint is surprisingly favourable, and no doubt its sympathetic portrayal of Hakon reflects the fact that at the time the saga was written (c.1200) Harald Maddadsson, a grandson of Hakon, was Earl of Orkney, and so much of the saga-writer's information was derived from this side of the family.

Hakon died c.1023 and was succeeded by his sons, the half-brothers Harald and Paul (see Fig.24). Harald's mother was Helga, a member of the powerful dynasty in Dale (possibly Helmsdale)[3] who, for want of a better term, are sometimes known as 'Clan Moddan'. Harald had the backing of this family in disputes with his brother which caused the earldom once again to be divided. Harald, however, was shortly removed from the scene in spectacular fashion when he insisted on trying on an embroidered shirt made by his mother and aunt for his brother, the golden threads of which carried poison which had been intended to cause Paul's death, but which unfortunately caused the death of Harald.[4] The poisoned shirt is probably no more than a story which owes its origin to rumours which surrounded Harald's sudden death. Paul II, however, having escaped this unusual death, was left in the position of sole earl. The saga represents Paul as peace-loving and no great speaker at *things*, but capable, high-principled and popular. He stood in the way of Rognvald's succession to Orkney, and it was obvious that he would not be easy to dislodge. However, the enmity between Earl Paul and Clan Moddan provided Rognvald with an opportunity. The family was ruled by the sinister Frakok, aunt of Harald of the Poisoned-Shirt, and military leadership was provided by her grandson, Oliver *rósti* ('the Unruly'). It was an important part of Rognvald's strategy to draw this family into his plans.

Rognvald needed all the allies he could muster, for his chances of succeeding to the earldom must have seemed remote. He was a grandson of Kali, a Norwegian nobleman who had served with King Magnus Barelegs and had received wounds at Menai from which he later died. In recompense Kali's son, Kol, was given Gunnhild in marriage.[5] Gunnhild was sister to Earl Magnus, and it was as a son of this marriage that Rognvald inherited a claim to the half of the earldom which had belonged to his murdered uncle (see Fig.24). But not everyone who inherited a share succeeded in making

29. **St Rognvald.** *This statue, probably of St Rognvald, was inserted in the 'Moosie Tower' of Bishop Reid's episcopal palace. It may have been removed from the cathedral at the Reformation.*

good their claim. Rognvald belonged to the branch of the earldom family which had been defeated and replaced, he inherited through the female line, he was brought up in Norway and was little known to Orcadians. He also faced the opposition of Earl Paul who was firmly entrenched and had no intention of conceding Rognvald's claim to half the earldom.

The way in which Rognvald prepared the ground demonstrated his formidable political talents. First, royal recognition was needed and this was obtained in 1129 from King Sigurd *Jórsalafari* ('the Crusader').[6] An interesting feature was that the new earl, hitherto Kali Kolsson, assumed the name 'Rognvald' in memory of Earl Rognvald Brusisson (see Chapter 5). The saga tells us that the new name was adopted at the wish of King Sigurd, but Rognvald probably saw advantages in taking the identity of an earl who had been closely associated with Norwegian kings and had always enjoyed their support. The name 'Rognvald' may also have had political advantages in Shetland where Rognvald Brusisson had been 'Lord of the Shetlanders'. However, the image-making change of name and the royal grant were not by themselves enough; five years later we again find half of the earldom being given to Rognvald by King Harald Gilli (1134 or 1135)[7] because the initial grant had been ineffective.

Having received this second grant, Rognvald set about building a network of alliances which united the northern world in his favour and left Earl

Paul isolated. These alliances are best understood in conjunction with the family relationships shown in Fig.24. Envoys were sent to Orkney to meet with Paul whose refusal was anticipated, so they had instructions to proceed to Sutherland to open discussions with Frakok and Oliver *rósti*. The inducement was that, if Paul could be displaced, his half of the earldom would be available for Harald, son of Maddad Earl of Atholl, grandson of Earl Hakon and a nephew of Frakok. Since Harald Maddadsson was an infant, this half of the earldom could meantime be possessed by Oliver. It was an arrangement which met with the approval of King David of Scotland to whom Maddad of Atholl was a cousin.[8] The king presumably saw the promotion of Maddad's son to the earldom of Orkney as offering long term prospects of strengthening Scottish influence in the north. From Rognvald's standpoint, the deal not only brought him valuable allies, but Scottish approval also opened up prospects of his eventual acceptance as earl in Caithness which might otherwise have been difficult. Frakok set about mustering forces from Scotland and sought further allies in the Hebrides where Olaf *bitling*, King of Man, was her son-in-law.[9]

A key element in Rognvald's network of alliances was the winning-over of William the Old (Bishop of Orkney 1102-1168). The way in which the bishop was persuaded to support Rognvald is glossed over in *Orkneyinga saga* which avoids attributing political motives to Magnus's elevation to sainthood. We are told that it was Rognvald's father, Kol, who counselled Rognvald to seek the heavenly assistance of his martyred uncle and advised him to promise to build a 'stone minster' in Kirkwall and to dedicate it to Magnus.[10] The saga places this advice after Rognvald's first attack had been repelled by Earl Paul (1135) and immediately before his successful invasion (1136). We are led to understand that earthly means fail but heavenly assistance brings victory. It is possible, however, that the chronology has been altered to avoid the incongruity of the vow being followed by an unsuccessful expedition. The story belongs some twelve chapters earlier where the saga tells us that Bishop William initially had done his best to damp down enthusiasm for the cult of Magnus but, following a voyage to Norway, his attitude abruptly changed.[11] The bishop's voyage is undated, but it was before Rognvald launched his invasion so, given the circumstances and the bishop's sudden change of heart, it appears that a bargain had been struck. This, we may assume, was the occasion when promises were made to build the cathedral, endow the bishopric and promote Magnus's sainthood.

The events which immediately followed depended on the bishop taking the initiative. On his return from Norway he was detained in Shetland by contrary winds, and we are told that he was persuaded not to resist the exhumation of Magnus's relics provided he was home in Birsay to say mass on Sunday but, when the wind changed and he returned safely, he was still not entirely convinced. A second miracle was required: one day when Bishop William was alone within Christchurch he was struck blind; falling on Magnus's grave he prayed in tears to the dead earl, and his sight was miraculously restored.[12] Nowadays the creation of a new saint is a lengthy process, but at that time it was controlled by the local bishop and so there was no need for delay. Magnus's canonisation involved, first, local enthusiasm for his cult, part spontaneous and part carefully fostered by those who hoped to benefit; second, there were miracles at his grave, and finally came the taking up of his bones and the proclamation of his sainthood. The elevation of Magnus to sainthood evoked popular enthusiasm, but it met with the disapproval of Earl Paul who was not likely to take kindly to the idea that his father had murdered a saint, and was even less pleased that Magnus's sainthood was being used to undermine his own position. When the Westray man, Gunni, recounted how Magnus had revealed to him in a dream that his relics should be removed from Birsay to Kirkwall, the saga tells that Paul listened in silence 'as if he had water in his mouth, and turned as red as blood'.[13]

The alliance between Rognvald and Bishop William is a good example of how the medieval church and state could co-operate for their mutual benefit. The bishop was not only provided with a magnificent new cathedral but, according to the fifteenth century *Diploma* or genealogy of the earls, Rognvald 'dotat (endowed) the same with great possessions, riches and rents'[14]—Bishop William received landed estates which transformed him into a prince of the church. This strengthening of the episcopate was a feature of church organisation in north-west Europe at this time and, as in Orkney, it was often associated with the building of cathedrals. Rognvald's cathedral was not a unique gesture—it was entirely typical of what was happening elsewhere. Kirkwall (founded c.1137) was later than Durham, it was contemporary with work at Dunfermline, Glasgow and Trondheim, and rather earlier than the great cathedral at St Andrews. For Bishop William there was the additional advantage that a cathedral which housed the relics of a popular saint could grow in wealth and prestige. The many miracles involving Shetlanders show that visitors were drawn from outside Orkney, and we also know that a pilgrim-route developed through Caithness. The *Magnus sagas* record the rich gifts from those who were cured by the saint's intervention.

While Bishop William benefited from Rognvald's patronage, Rognvald hoped to gain at least as much from the bishop's support. The bishop was a diplomat of considerable skill, and potentially he was a dangerous enemy who was never entirely committed to Rognvald. He had an agenda of his own and already he had links with Scotland and with the Atholl family who also had claims on the earldom. But the real importance of the bishop was that he was needed if the canonisation of Magnus was to be achieved. He was the key to unlocking the full potential of the Magnus cult as a means of recruiting popular support for Rognvald as heir to his saintly uncle. In the same way that St Olaf was 'perpetual king of Norway', the martyred Magnus was described by Rognvald's father as 'the true owner of the realm' who would bestow it on his successor.[15] Rognvald no doubt found it useful to base his rule on a feudal grant which emanated directly from heaven—it provided a legitimacy which it was difficult to dispute. It was propaganda at its most imaginative; modern attempts to manipulate public opinion are crude by comparison.

Although Rognvald had constructed a network of alliances, won the bishop's support and enlisted the aid of heaven, Paul's position within Orkney was not easy to undermine. The earl depended on his *godings* ('good men') who formed a sub-aristocracy second only to the earl in status.[16] They owed their rank, however, to personal ties with the earl rather than to an independent position. Typically godings were closely related to the earl by kinship or by marriage, and they were bound to him by personal friendship and loyalty. The earl depended on his godings for advice and for military assistance, and in return he placed them in positions of power and rewarded them with land. Paul's leading goding was Sigurd of Westness; Sigurd was married to Ingibjorg, a great-granddaughter of Earl Thorfinn and a first cousin of Earl Paul. Paul was described as *a veizlu* when he was in Rousay staying with Sigurd, *veizla* involving the obligation to accommodate, feed and entertain the lord when he was travelling round his possessions. Thus Westness was not Sigurd's private property, but was a large earldom estate on which Paul had installed a reliable supporter—indeed as late as 1503 there was still land in Westness which was described as 'auld earldom'.[17] Kugi of Rapness was another important goding; he occupied the huge manor farm in the southern part of Westray (Fig.47),[18] not as private property, but on behalf of the earl who regularly took up residence in Rapness when collecting his rent in the North Isles.[19] Another leading supporter was Olaf Hrofsson (Sweyn Asleifsson's father) who had an estate of his own based on Gairsay, but occupied the more important estate of Duncansby in Caithness on Paul's behalf.[20] The earl's position therefore depended on placing competent and reliable supporters on strategically-located estates, and he needed to take care to cultivate their friendship and reward their loyalty. Thus the earl's military power was more personal and less systematic than the *leidang* (territorial naval levy) which was at one time proposed by Clouston and Marwick without much evidence that any such levy really existed.[21]

Rognvald made two expeditions against Orkney; his first attack in 1135 failed, but he was successful in 1136.[22] Both expeditions sailed via Shetland. This was the part of the earldom which had belonged to Rognvald Brusisson and to the earls of the Erlend line (see Chapter 5), so Rognvald,

30. ***Langskaill, Gairsay.*** *The handsome seventeenth century mansion house, the home of the Craigies of Gairsay, stands on the presumed site of Sweyn Asleifsson's viking hall.*

who represented this branch of the family, was readily accepted. The ease of conquest may also reflect the fact that, although Paul had *godings* in Orkney and in Caithness, we know of no reliable allies of a similar kind in Shetland. Support for the Erlend line in Shetland is shown by the enthusiasm for the Magnus cult as demonstrated by the high proportion of miracles which involved Shetlanders.[23] A remarkable number of miracles involve Bergfinn Skatisson, his relatives and his servants, which suggests that this otherwise unknown Shetlander was actively involved in the promotion of the cult from which Rognvald expected to benefit.

In the summer of 1135 Paul had to deal not only with Rognvald's invasion via Shetland, but also with an attack by Oliver *rósti* and his Hebridean allies. It was Oliver who arrived first, crossing the Pentland Firth and sailing east round Deerness, presumably with the intention of joining forces with Rognvald. Paul was victorious in a sea engagement, the Battle of Tankerness,[24] at which we find godings such as Olaf Rolfsson and Kugi of Rapness acting in their military capacity as captains of ships. Five of Oliver's ships were captured, and he retreated in confusion to Caithness. Paul immediately sailed for Shetland where he surprised and captured Rognvald's ships in Yell Sound. Although Rognvald remained in Shetland for the remainder of the summer, his attempt on the earldom had failed and he was forced to return to Norway in the autumn.

In the following summer (1136) Rognvald made a second attempt. Again he had no difficulty in securing Shetland and, by surreptitiously sabotaging the beacon on Fair Isle, he was able to enter the North Isles of Orkney and land in Westray where Kugi of Rapness was captured. At that moment when the success of his invasion was in the balance, the crisis was resolved in typically ruthless fashion by Sweyn Asleifsson. Paul was staying with Sigurd of Westness, presumably to be in a position to repel Rognvald's advance, and he had risen early to hunt otters along the shore. Sweyn disguised his ship as a merchant-vessel and, before anyone was aware that he was back in Orkney, he plucked Paul from the rocks and delivered him to the less-than-sisterly care of Margaret, Countess of Atholl. Rumours of his imprisonment filtered back to Orkney but, according to *Orkneyinga saga*, 'the truth was a lot uglier'.[25] Paul was never seen again.

Even in the confusion which followed the unexplained disappearance of Earl Paul, there was a reluctance to acknowledge Rognvald as earl, but he eventually won grudging acceptance in a series of district *things*. Then he began the work of building St Magnus Cathedral in fulfilment of his vow (c.1137). The saga tells how the foundations were marked out and builders engaged, probably masons who had recently completed their work at Durham.[26] For the first few years building work went ahead rapidly under the supervision of Kol, Rognvald's father, then construction began to slow down because of the high cost. Kol advised that money should be raised by levying special taxation. The claim was to be made (or revived) that the earls had in the past acquired 'odal rights' (see pp.34-5) and that it was consequently necessary for heirs to private property to secure their inheritance by means of some kind of payment. Rognvald seems at first to have contemplated the imposition of the usual feudal obligation whereby, each time an heir succeeded to a property, an entry fine or 'relief' had to be paid to the feudal superior. However, in Orkney where udal tenure prevailed, the imposition of this feudal payment was regarded as 'rather hard', and Rognvald was persuaded to forego the recurring 'relief' in favour of a one-off 'aid'.[27] It was an arrangement which the financially threatened landowners evidently regarded as the lesser of two evils.

By 1151 Rognvald was secure enough to go off on a crusade to the Holy Land, leaving his young co-earl, Harald Maddadson, to rule in his absence. Rognvald visited England and Spain, he was beguiled by the beautiful Queen Ermingarde at Narbonne, and he visited the Holy Land and bathed in the Jordan before returning via Constantinople.[28] The saga's story of his care-free voyage and the adventures along the way are largely reconstructed from Rognvald's own light-hearted verses.[29] The problems he had to face when he returned in 1153 after an absence for over two years are described in the next chapter.

If Rognvald personifies 'Renaissance' in twelfth century Orkney, 'Anarchy' is represented by Sweyn Asleifsson whose violent and unpredictable behaviour dominates some 40 chapters of *Orkneyinga saga*.[30] Sweyn was son of Olaf Hrofsson who had family estates in Gairsay and Stronsay, and also held Duncansby on behalf of Earl Paul. Sweyn, however, took his name from his mother, Asleif, which suggests that she may have been of even higher standing, perhaps being related to the earls. However, the saga chooses its words carefully when, in a rather backhanded fashion, it describes the limits to Sweyn's status:

> He was the biggest man in every way in the lands of the west, both in days present and in days past, among men who were not of higher rank than he.[31]

The saga makes much of Sweyn's loyalty to Rognvald, and puts in his mouth the dying words that he lived and died as a faithful soldier of the Holy Earl Rognvald[32]—but that was not strictly true. He had originally supported Earl Paul and then transferred his services to Rognvald, then he advanced the claims of Harald Maddadsson, and later he opposed both of them when Erlend aspired to the earldom. In the War of the Three Earls (1152-1154) he at one time supported each of the protagonists. It seemed to matter little to him which earl he served.

At first it appeared that Sweyn was closely bound to Earl Paul. His father had fought for Paul at the Battle of Tankerness, but at the end of the same year (1136) he was killed at Duncansby when Oliver *rósti* surrounded the house and set fire to it. It was natural for Sweyn to take refuge with Earl Paul in Orphir and, since his father had been killed by Paul's enemies, Sweyn's attachment ought to have been even stronger. Within a matter of days, however, he had quarrelled with the earl's champion, Sweyn *brjóstreip* ('Breastrope'), and killed him in a drunken brawl. The incident was typical of the casual, even accidental way in which Sweyn was liable to change sides. He made a hurried escape from Orphir and was well received by Bishop William who described the murder of Sweyn Breastrope as 'a good riddance' and recruited Sweyn to Rognvald's cause. It would, however, be truer to say that Sweyn became the bishop's man. Bishop William was deeply involved in promoting Harald Maddadsson's claim to half of the earldom, and Sweyn was employed as an emissary in dealings with Atholl and with King David. He could also undertake more dubious tasks when it was advisable that the bishop should not seem to be too openly involved.

The saga describes Sweyn's annual routine. During the winter he was

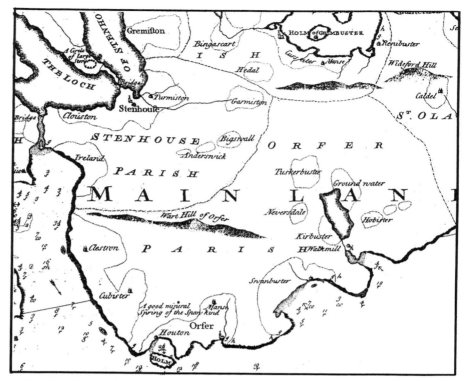

31. **Orphir.** *Mackenzie's 1750 charts show pre-Improvement township boundaries, and his abbreviations ('h' = heather and 'g' = grass) help to determine land use. The earl's seat was beside the church, shown in the extreme east of 'Orfer'. The settlement takes its name from ON, ørfiri, tidal island, now Houton. Many of the surrounding townships have bólstaðr-names ending in -bister. (Mackenzie, Orcades).*

usually at home in Gairsay where he had the largest drinking hall in Orkney, and where he kept 80 men at his own expense. He was busy in spring when there was seed to be sown, attending to the work himself, but when the spring work was finished he went on a viking cruise to the Hebrides and Ireland. He returned after mid-summer and stayed at home until the harvest was secured, then he made an autumn cruise until the onset of winter forced him to return. Warfare became a way of life and an end in itself. The heroic lifestyle required constant success in order to hold the war-band together. Sweyn needed a regular income from plunder and from mercenary activity to bind his followers with generous gifts, and on a more basic level it was essential to have the means to support a large following, to accommodate them over the winter, and to provide them with abundant supplies of meat and drink. Drinking was the main activity on winter nights, and was a frequent cause of violence. For young men, the opportunity to gain a reputation for

110

32. **The Bu of Orphir.** *The present Bu of Orphir is situated on good farmland near the shore. To the left lies the churchyard with the remains of the Round Church. Between the Bu and the churchyard lies the foundations of a building which often has been interpreted as Earl Paul's hall within which Sweyn Asleifsson killed Sweyn brjóstreip.*

feats of bravery was also an important consideration, so they would attach themselves to a successful leader, whereas even an earl, if less successful, might find himself with no greater a following.

Sweyn is depicted as the master of sudden attack and equally he had to be constantly vigilant that he was not himself taken by surprise. Until midway through the twelfth century military success could still be achieved with small numbers. The 80 men wintering in Sweyn's drinking hall might represent two ships' companies, and the biggest fleet which Sweyn ever commanded was five ships which he took on a raid on the Hebrides[33]—they might have carried about 200 men. Even Earl Rognvald's first invasion consisted of only five or six ships,[34] and the biggest recorded fleet was the 12 ships which Oliver and his Hebridean allies brought to the Battle of Tankerness. Twelfth century Orcadians might build cathedrals, but there was an absence of stone-built castles, or at least they seem to have appeared at a late date and even then they were small and few in number. The principal Norse building was the *skáli* (skaill, hall). Its lack of defence and its low thatched roof made it vulnerable to sudden attack when it could easily be

111

destroyed by fire. Killings of individuals were frequent, but in the kind of warfare waged by Sweyn Asleifsson casualties were usually light; we often hear of six or nine deaths at a burning, but it was only at the Battle of Tankerness and at the burning of Frakok that deaths were significantly more numerous.

When Sweyn killed Sweyn Breastrope and deserted Earl Paul for Rognvald he was in the awkward position that he was now on the same side as Frakok and Oliver who had killed his father only a few weeks earlier. Blood-feud and revenge were important to Sweyn, but for the moment he had to compromise. The change in his circumstances came, not with accession of Rognvald, but only when the infant Harald Maddadsson was installed as joint-earl—an indication that Atholl, King David and Bishop William were at that stage his paymasters. Then he had his reward: he was able to recover all the lands which his father and brother had possessed and he became 'a great chief'.[35] He immediately used his new power to launch a raid which utterly destroyed 'Clan Moddan'. Oliver *rósti* had many men around him, but he expected Sweyn to come from the sea, so when Sweyn gathered men in Atholl and made his way through the Sutherland hills, he took Oliver by surprise. Among the dead was Frakok; Oliver escaped to the Hebrides and, we are told, 'he was out of the saga'.[36]

The next chapter describes how Harald Maddadsson's Orkney came under pressure from kings in both Norway and Scotland. Sweyn Asleifsson's military methods were becoming obsolete—he was the last of the Vikings. The great armies which William the Lion brought into the north of Scotland and his stone castles brought an end to the days when a few ships' companies resolutely led could win famous victories.

8
Harald Maddadsson

The long reign of Harald Maddadsson[1] (1138-1206) marks the transition from the semi-autonomous Orkney of the sagas to the medieval earldoms of Orkney and Caithness whose rulers stood in a regular feudal relationship with the kings of Norway and Scotland. Harald was one of the earls who made an impact beyond the bounds of his earldom, yet he was not exactly a simple saga-hero. As he himself said, he had 'drawn near to the knees of many kings, often in difficult circumstances'.[2] His dealings with Kings Eystein, Magnus and Sverre of Norway, and with David I, Malcolm IV and William the Lion of Scotland were seldom easy, and it was with an ill-grace that he was forced to bend and submit. He was above all a survivor; he succeeded to the earldom at the age of five, and was earl for 68 years, the first 20 as co-earl with Rognvald. Harald was continuously threatened by rivals from the time of his birth until the time of his death and, in a century which saw the violent death of six earls,[3] his survival was no mean achievement.

The problem which Harald had to face was the growth of royal power in Scotland and Norway, both endeavouring to extend their control into peripheral areas, and to convert the loose ties of the saga-period into a more binding feudal relationship. Earls of Orkney had never actually aspired to independence, mainly because there was no need to do so. They had ruled what might be described as a client chiefdom rather than a feudal fief, and they were free within very broad limits to manage its internal affairs and external relationships. In the latter part of the twelfth century, as Norway emerged from civil war, it became increasingly difficult for the earls to serve two masters, paying homage to the King of Scots for Caithness and to the King of Norway for Orkney. Both kings attempted to undermine Earl Harald by the well-tried expedient of recognising the claims of other members of his family, and exploiting the fact that the earldom was divisible among heirs. When faced with these tactics, it is difficult to see how Harald could have avoided eventually aligning himself with rebel elements, especially in Scotland. It was, however, a reversal of a 200-year-old policy stretching back to Sigurd and Thorfinn whereby Scottish kings and Orkney earls had usually co-operated for their mutual benefit. As the twelfth century drew to a close it also became less easy to rebel with impunity. What was new was the ability of kings to intervene directly: all accounts testify to the great size of the armies which William the Lion could bring to bear on the north of Scotland, rendering obsolete traditional Norse warfare as had been practised so successfully by Sweyn Asleifsson.

The way in which Harald Maddadsson himself represented Scottish penetration into the Norse earldoms is best seen with reference to Fig.24. His father was Maddad, son of Maelmuire who was a brother of Malcolm III ('Canmore'); Maddad had been placed in the Earldom of Atholl as a means of strengthening royal authority, and it was natural to use his son to extend the same process. It was through his mother that Harald inherited a claim to Orkney; she was Margaret, daughter of Earl Hakon and a half-sister to Earl Paul II, but on her mother's side she was also part-Scots with many relatives in the Norwego-Celtic 'Clan Moddan' which dominated the southern frontiers of Caithness. Yet Harald's Scottishness should not be over-emphasised. In Caithness and the Hebrides there were many who were of mixed families, and were equally at home in the Norse and Gaelic-speaking worlds. People looked to individual leaders and were not familiar with abstract concepts of nationality. Moreover Harald, although Scots by birth, was Orcadian by upbringing, having been fostered in Orkney from the age of five. His mother also reverted to her Orkney roots: after the death of the Earl of Atholl, Margaret returned to Orkney where her love affairs complicated the internal politics of the earldom.[4]

The system of alliances which laid the groundwork for Rognvald's conquest of Orkney had included the promise of half of the earldom for Harald in return for the support of 'Clan Moddan' and their allies in Atholl and Scotland (see Chapter 7). Two years later a diplomatic mission visited Orkney headed by Bishop John whom the saga describes as 'of Atholl', although there was never a bishopric of Atholl nor at this date was there a bishop John of Dunkeld. This Scottish bishop is usually identified as John, Bishop of Glasgow and a former tutor of King David, who is known to have been regularly used to undertake royal business.[5] On his arrival Bishop John worked in close collaboration with Bishop William of Orkney to implement the arrangements made prior to Rognvald's invasion. It was confirmed that the five-year-old Harald was to be brought to Orkney as co-earl, but Rognvald was to have charge of the government of the islands even after Harald attained manhood. For Rognvald it was not an unattractive package: he had claimed only half the earldom in the first place, he had no son to succeed him and, because of the difference in age, Harald might be regarded as an heir rather than a rival. The acceptance of Harald was also a price worth paying for Scottish recognition of Rognvald's position as earl in Caithness. For David I the arrangement provided an opportunity to advance a near relative; in the long term Earl Harald might be expected to be sympathetic to Scottish interests and to be a useful ally who would help to counter the dangers which the Canmore dynasty still faced from Moray. More immediately Scottish influence could be brought to bear through Thorbjorn Clerk. Thorbjorn, like Harald, was a grandson of Frakok; he accompanied Harald when he was brought to Orkney, he fostered his cousin and for many years and was Harald's chief counsellor.[6] Thorbjorn was 'shrewd and forceful', and was 'very much the master' of the young earl. Over the next twenty years Thorbjorn divided his time between Orkney and Scotland. An immediate result of the Scottish-Orkney accord was the presence of an Orkney contingent fighting for David I at the Battle of the Standard that same year (1138).[7] A meeting in Caithness in the following year (1139) ratified the terms which Bishop John had negotiated, sealing them with the oaths of 'the best men from Orkney and Scotland'.[8]

If Rognvald's position had been properly established in relation to Scotland, the same cannot be said for Harald's position with regard to Norway. He had been intruded into Orkney as a Scottish-backed candidate, and there is no indication that Norwegians had been a party to the meetings in Orkney and Caithness which negotiated his acceptance as co-earl. When Harald was about fifteen and the question of his status as earl was becoming more urgent, he visited Norway where he was well received by King Ingi (1148).[9] However, Ingi ruled jointly with his brothers, yet Harald made peace with Ingi alone. In 1151 one of the other brothers, King Eystein (whom Kolbein Hruga or 'Cubbie Roo' helped to promote to kingship alongside Ingi[10]), appeared in South Ronaldsay with a large fleet. Harald was now 18 years of age and had been left in charge while Rognvald went off to the Holy Land. Hearing that Harald was in Thurso, King Eystein crossed the Pentland Firth with three small ships and was able to capture Harald before the young earl was aware of his presence. Harald had to ransom himself with three gold marks (or seven gold marks according to another account)[11] and yield his realm into King Eystein's hands from whom he received it again, binding himself by oaths to become Eystein's man. Eystein then left on a voyage of plunder which took him down the east coat to Aberdeen, Hartlepool and Whitby. It has been suggested that the main thrust of the expedition was intended to be against Orkney, and having achieved Harald's submission with unexpected ease, Eystein diverted his followers with a little piracy at the expense of the Scots and English.[12] It seems that this raid was devoid of political purposes, but Eystein's dealings with Harald are obvious—what is described is the act of feudal homage. It is possible that the three (or seven) gold marks for which Harald had to ransom himself were not an arbitrary fine, but a feudal 'relief' or entry fee which the heir had to pay his superior in order to be confirmed in the property he inherited. We know that the

Kings of Man and the Isles paid a lump sum to each new king of Norway, so Harald's payment might have been of a similar kind.[13]

If Harald had originally been advanced as the pro-Scots candidate, he was eventually to prove a disappointment, in the end aligning himself with the very rebels whom he was intended to counter. Eystein had advanced no claim to kingship over the Norse inhabitants of Caithness, but Harald's homage to Eystein—an oath made on Scottish soil to a foreign king during the course of an attack on Scotland—is bound to have been viewed with alarm, and was probably the first step in the breakdown of relations between Harald and the Scottish kings. It can hardly be coincidental that David I that same year saw fit to introduce a new claimant for a share in the earldom.[14] He was Erlend, son of Harald of the Poisoned Shirt, and a grandson of Earl Hakon. He was the last direct descendant of Torf Einar in the male line, and so he had as good a claim as his cousin, Harald Maddadsson (see Fig.24). Erlend was now given half of Caithness, thanks to 'powerful friends' at the Scottish court. One of these friends was Sweyn Asleifsson whose association with Harald Maddadsson had recently been broken. Sweyn's change of allegiance was as usual the result of fortuitous circumstances rather than any real political purpose. When Maddad of Atholl died, his widow Margaret returned to Orkney and some time later she had a child by Gunni Olafsson, Sweyn Asleifsson's brother.[15] Earl Harald, now a young adult, was highly displeased; he outlawed Gunni who had to be shipped off to safety in the Hebrides. The resulting breach between Earl Harald and Sweyn Asleifsson provided Erlend both with a powerful champion and with useful contacts with the court of King David.[16] Sweyn proceeded to wage a lightning war against Harald in his own inimitable manner. He captured a ship off the Caithness coast which was bringing Harald's *skat* from Shetland, then a week later he took a second ship on its arrival from Lewis, and he also captured Harald's steward, robbing him of twelve ounces of gold. Sweyn then took refuge with the King of Scots at Aberdeen and as usual he received a warm welcome.[17] Clearly King David had ceased to trust Harald, and was attempting to advance Scottish interests in other ways.

The ensuing War of the Three Earls (1152-4) illustrates how easy it was for distant kings to make trouble in Orkney by encouraging the claims of competing co-earls. The grant to Erlend of half Caithness from the King of Scots was followed by the grant of half Orkney from the King of Norway who similarly recognised Erlend to the exclusion of Harald.[18] Scotland and Norway set the contest in motion, but left it to the participants to fight it out. Three claimants, Rognvald, Harald and Erlend, for two halves was likely to result in the expulsion or violent death of one of them. The war saw all possible combinations—Harald and Erlend scheming to dispossess Rognvald when he was on crusade, then, on his return from the Holy Land ahead of most of his ships, Rognvald had little option but to combine with Erlend to the exclusion of Harald, then finally the 'natural' alliance of Rognvald and Harald was restored. The incidents in this war are recounted in graphic detail (and with a good deal of imaginative reconstruction) in *Orkneyinga saga*.[19] Highlights included Harald's mid-winter raid when he was forced to seek shelter within Maeshowe from a driving snow storm—an experience which drove two of his men mad—and his pursuit of his mother who took refuge within the Broch of Mousa with her new lover.[20] Sweyn Asleifsson constantly outmanoeuvred Rognvald and Harald, but had increasing difficulty in looking after Erlend. Erlend was dead drunk in the stern of his ship when Rognvald and Harald surprised him off the little island of Damsay. Two days later a spear was seen sticking out of a pile of seaweed, marking the resting place of Erlend Haraldsson.[21]

Another killing in 1158 left Harald in the position of sole earl.[22] When he and Rognvald crossed to Caithness to hunt deer in the Caithness dales, as was their annual custom, news reached them that Thorbjorn Clerk was hiding somewhere in the interior. The pursuit of deer was put aside for the hunting of men. Thorbjorn's position in Orkney had become increasingly difficult when he became embroiled in a feud with Sweyn Asleifsson as a result of the burning of Frakok (Thorbjorn's grandmother), then disputes between Thorbjorn's followers and those of Earl Rognvald resulted in killings for which Thorbjorn was outlawed. Thorbjorn, at one time Harald's foster-father and chief mentor, was latterly regarded as a violent and dangerous troublemaker. Thorbjorn was hiding on the farm of Forsie, and as Rognvald led his men through the yard, he was struck down as he attempted to dismount from his horse.[23] In the ensuing confrontation, Thorbjorn was killed.

Harald could hardly be held responsible for the killing of Rognvald, although his attitude was somewhat ambivalent because of his long association with Thorbjorn Clerk. The removal of Thorbjorn's pro-Scottish influence may have been a factor in Harald's drift into rebel politics. After the defeat of Angus, Earl of Moray, at Stracathro in 1130, the danger to the Scottish kings of the Canmore dynasty for a time came from the strange figure of Bishop Wimund who claimed to be the Earl of Moray's son. Wimund, who began his career in the Sauviniac abbey of Furness, transferred to Rushen and was elected Bishop of Sodor and Man, invaded Scotland c.1142 but was defeated, blinded and castrated.[24] After Wimund's defeat, the mantle of rebellion fell on the MacWilliams whom, as seen from Orkney, 'all Scots wished to have as their king'.[25] The MacWilliams united the claims of Moray which had once put Macbeth on the throne with descent from Malcolm Canmore's first marriage to Ingibjorg, widow or more probably the daughter of Earl Thorfinn (see Chapter 5).[26] Malcolm's first family had been set aside in favour of the kings, Edgar, Alexander and David, the sons of Malcolm's second marriage to Queen (Saint) Margaret, possibly on the pretext that Malcolm and Ingibjorg had been related within a forbidden degree.[27] The MacWilliams became the symbol of the resistance of the native Gaelic aristocracy to Norman kings. Behind the meagre surviving records it is possible to glimpse the belief of the MacWilliams in the justice of their cause, and the fierce loyalty which they commanded in the north.

The course of events is by no means clear in Scottish sources, and the MacWilliam years are a major gap in *Orkneyinga saga* which becomes fragmentary and disjointed in its closing chapters. The symbol of Harald Maddadsson's alignment with rebel Scots was his repudiation of his first wife, Afreka, daughter of the Earl of Fife, and his marriage to Hvarfloð, daughter of the arch-rebel, Malcolm MacHeth.[28] Malcolm had been one of the rebels at Stracathro and had persisted in rebellion until 1134 when David I captured him with the aid of barons brought in from the north of England,[29] and thereafter he was imprisoned for 23 years. His sons joined Somerled in rebellion in 1153, then in 1157 Malcolm was released and allowed to assume the title of Earl of Ross.[30] Any rapprochement was short-lived, since Malcolm IV attempted to give Ross to his sister on the occasion of her marriage in 1162.[31] Evidently Malcolm MacHeth successfully resisted attempts to depose him since he still held Ross at the time of his death in 1168.[32] His descendants, however, were prevented from inheriting. According to the historian Fordun, the king 'removed them all from the land of their birth, as of old Nebuchadnezzar, King of Babylon, had dealt with the Jews'.[33]

We do not know the date of Harald Maddadsson's second marriage, but since Thorfinn, the son of this marriage, was old enough to be in command of Orkney forces in 1197,[34] Harald's marriage to Hvarfloð can be pushed back at least to the 1170s. According to Fordun, Harald was 'a good and trusty man' until he was 'goaded on' by his wife.[35] However, it is possible that Harald's new marriage was not so much the cause of his links with the rebels as a means of gaining their friendship. His relationship with Scotland had been deteriorating ever since King David tried to exclude him by backing the claims of Erlend Haraldsson. A new claimant to a share in the earldoms now appeared; he was Harald *ungi* ('the Younger'), grandson and heir to Earl Rognvald (see Fig.24). Harald was the son of Rognvald's only daughter Ingirid and the Sutherland chief Erik *stagbrellr* ('Staybraills'). He was probably born c.1155,[36] and by the 1170s the question of his succession to Rognvald's patrimony must have been increasingly urgent. We know that Harald the Younger had received recognition from King Magnus Erlingsson at an unknown date prior to 1184 (the year of the king's death) but his acceptance by Scotland might have been earlier. By 1179, when the MacWilliam rebellion broke out, Harald the Younger was a young adult and was probably already favourably regarded by King William because Harald Maddadsson's marriage to Hvarfloð had by then committed him to the rebel cause.

In the MacWilliam rebellions during the period 1179-1187 Harald seems to have remained safely out of reach, protected by a broad band of rebel territory. His part in these events, if any, is unknown, yet it seems likely that he was in some measure implicated. William the Lion's opening moves suggest that he feared Orkney involvement. In 1179 he established, or perhaps strengthened, royal castles at Dunskeath on the north shore of the Cromarty Firth, and at 'Etherdouer' or Redcastle near Beauly.[37] As well as consolidating royal power in Ross, both make sense as defending the land and sea approaches to Moray from attack from the north, as well as providing bases from which campaigns into Sutherland and Caithness might be launched. In 1181 Donald MacWilliam, who had previously made a number of incursions, arrived in Scotland with a large army.[38] Although he had come from outwith the Scottish kingdom, there is no reason to suppose that he was using an Orkney base, since later MacWilliam invasions came from Ireland. This first MacWilliam rebellion was brought to an end only in 1187 when a raiding party from the king's camp at Inverness foraging north into Ross surprised and killed Donald MacWilliam at an unidentified place known as Mam Garbh ('Rough Hill').[39]

The reign of Harald Maddadsson also saw the end of Orkney's ability to interfere in Irish affairs. In 1170 a force of Orkneymen killed Dirmait, King of Ui-Meith, on a fortified artificial island on the boundaries of Monaghan and Louth,[40] and in the following year Irish sources recount how a memorable Scandinavian, 'Eoan Lochlandach' or 'John the Wode' ('wode', mad, furious) met his death in circumstances which suggest that he was one and the same person as Sweyn Asleifsson. Despite *Orkneyinga saga's* fascination for Sweyn and the many stories about him which the saga-writer collected in Orkney, this uncertain identification is the only mention of Sweyn in non-Norse sources. The absence of confirmation for his adventures casts doubts on the whole corpus of stories about Sweyn Asleifsson. Although much of the saga's account of Sweyn is fiction, it takes into account the reality that the English invasion of Ireland no longer left much place for small scale Orcadian operations. The largest fleet which Sweyn ever commanded consisted of five ships, whereas the army which Henry II took to Ireland in 1171 consisted of 400 ships and 500 knights.[41] In *Orkneyinga saga* Earl Harald warns Sweyn against further Irish adventures; Sweyn was determined to make one last voyage before he settled down, but from the way the story is told, we know that there is to be no peaceful old age. Perhaps we have a last glimpse of Sweyn in a description of the men whom 'John the Wode' brought to Dublin:

...warlike men clothed round with iron, after the Danish custom; some with long coats of mail; some with iron plates skilfully sewn together; also with round red shields strengthened in circles with iron; men of iron minds as well as iron arms.[42]

Both the saga and Irish sources describe how the islanders were caught between two hostile forces inside the gates, the saga adding that Sweyn and his men met their death in concealed pits which the Dublin people had constructed to trap them.[43]

The saga's account of Sweyn ends when his sons divide his estate between them, and also partition the great drinking hall on Gairsay where Sweyn had entertained his retinue in such inimitable style. Wars were no longer fought by a band of companions bonded together by winter feasting, by famous reputations and the giving of extravagant gifts, so there was no longer a need for large open halls designed for the feasting of military retinues. With the dividing of Sweyn's hall we probably reach the end of the *Orkneyinga saga* as it was originally written. The saga uses the building of the partition across the Sweyn's hall as a symbol of the end of the Viking age.

In the last dozen years of his reign, Harald's relations with both Scotland and Norway reached crisis point. Although Harald was described as a 'excellent friend' of King Magnus Erlingsson,[44] this had not prevented the Norwegian king from recognising the claims of Harald the Younger as heir to Rognvald's half of the earldom, and this right was subsequently confirmed by King Sverre.[45] Harald the Younger, however, seems as yet to have taken no steps to secure actual possession of his entitlement.

So Harald Maddadsson, when faced with this threat to his earldom, drifted into involvement in Norway's civil wars as part of the aristocratic opposition to King Sverre.[46] In Norway a plot was hatched to put Sigurd, youthful son of the late King Magnus Erlingsson, on the throne. One of the leading proponents was Olaf *jarlsmágr*, whose name indicates a relationship with the earl by marriage. The prospective boy-king was placed in Olaf's care, and in 1192 Olaf brought him across to Shetland. In the following spring they both visited Orkney where Harald received them kindly; Sigurd was presented with a good longship and the earl allowed him to be proclaimed king. We are led to believe that Harald was swept along by the enthusiasm of others, as indeed he was to claim when the enterprise ended in disaster.

The *Eyjarskeggjar* ('Island-beards'), as the Orkney-Shetland invaders were known, crossed to Norway where they seized Tonsberg and held an assembly at which Sigurd was accepted as king. That winter they were in control of large parts of southern Norway, but just before Easter 1194 Sverre attacked. He found the *Eyjarskeggjar* in disarray, many still being dispersed in winter quarters. In a pre-dawn attack at Florevåg just north of Bergen, Sverre's ships completely annihilated the Orkney fleet. Olaf *jarlsmågr* and the boy-king Sigurd were both killed, as was the greater part of the Orkney-Shetland contingent.[47] News rapidly reached Harald that the *Eyjarskeggjar* were defeated and that King Sverre was planning to sail west to punish the islands for their rebellion. Sverre was Faroese, and he was apparently no stranger to Orkney which he had reputedly visited in 1168 in circumstances important enough for the visit to be recorded in *Icelandic Annals.*[48] There was nothing that Harald could do but submit, and the sooner the better. The following year (1195) he sailed for Bergen accompanied by Bishop Bjarni. Sverre had assembled all the bishops and magnates and received Harald in an intimidating *hirðstefna* (assembly of liegemen) in the yard of Christchurch, with his famous *birkbein* guard drawn up around him. Although the assembly was technically a court, the earl did not plead his case, but made abject submission and referred the outcome to the king's judgement.[49]

The post-Florevåg settlement imposed severe terms which had a lasting effect on the way that Orkney and Shetland were governed—it was the single most important event which shaped Orkney in the later Middle Ages. A scroll rental was drawn up recording the lands of those killed; the heirs (and probably also the survivors of Florevåg) were given three years to buy back their land, failing which it was to become the property of the crown. Shetland, which had been the main recruiting ground for the *Eyjarskeggjar,* was detached from the Earldom of Orkney and was placed under direct control of the king on the same basis as his native Faroe. In Orkney the king was to receive half of all fines and a *sysselman* (royal officer) was appointed to collect the revenue, administer the forfeited estates and look after the interests of the crown. On these terms the earldom was restored to Harald, and he was allowed to renew his oath of fealty. Sverre's conditions at one time existed in more detailed form: *Hirdskrå* (a document dating from c.1274 setting out the laws and customs relating to the nobility) states that when appointing earls in tributary provinces the king should observe 'the letter of conciliation between King Sverre and Earl Harald'.[50] Thus the letter must have still existed at that time, but it has unfortunately been lost, although *Sverre's saga* provides a summary of its contents.

Florevåg was one of the turning points of Orkney history. Orkney and Shetland remained separate for the rest of the Middle Ages, with the result that the island groups developed in different ways. The loss of Shetland diminished the political power of Orkney earls, and royal control by a *sysselman* was a check on their independence. The stipulation that heirs had to buy back their land within three years no doubt led to Sverre acquiring a good deal of property from those who failed to redeem their estates. Just how

121

much land he took over in this way is uncertain. It seems clear, however, that this so-called *kingsland* was not so extensive a feature, or at least not so permanent as was at one time supposed. Storer Clouston and his contemporaries were mistaken when they envisaged that for the remainder of the medieval period there were large royal estates which were approximately equal to, or even greater than, the earldom lands.[51] Strangely Harald the Younger was not a beneficiary of Harald Maddadsson's misfortunes; Harald could count himself lucky that he was allowed to continue as sole earl, and indeed it must have seemed that his exclusive right had been confirmed. The success of his peacemaking owed much to the mediation and diplomatic skills of Bishop Bjarni.

During Harald's reign the work of building St Magnus cathedral continued.[52] After its founding c.1137 work progressed rapidly, and we know it was roofed by 1155 when we hear of ship's sails being stored in the building.[53] It is possible that this first part of the church had been completed a few years earlier in time to allow its consecration and the installation of Magnus's relics before Rognvald departed for the Holy Land in 1151. This first church consisted of the choir and the eastern end of the nave. A failure of the crossing, or perhaps its total collapse, occurred c.1170-80, requiring extensive rebuilding. Thereafter the work continued with a renewed impetus with the election of Bjarni Kolbeinsson (Bishop of Orkney, 1188-1223).[54] Bjarni's father, Kolbein Hruga, was Norwegian but his mother was the earl's second cousin, so the bishop, like Earl Harald, was a scion of the 'Paul Line' and he was 'a near friend'.[55] Bjarni was one of the most distinguished figures of Orkney's twelfth century renaissance; not only was he active in cathedral building and diplomacy, but he was a famous skald[56] and author of the poem *Jómsvíkingadrápa*, which recounts the deeds of the legendary Jomsborg vikings. During his episcopate the original apse which had terminated the eastern end of the cathedral was removed and an eastwards extension was built to accommodate an enlarged cathedral chapter.

Such extensive work on the cathedral must have required the support of the earl, and Harald was also a benefactor of the church in other ways. He is believed to have issued a charter protecting the unidentified monastic establishment of 'Benkoren' which, it has been suggested, might have been in Ireland.[57] There is also a record of an annual gift to the canons of Scone of one mark of silver in return for prayers for the souls of his forebears, himself and his wife.[58] In addition he attempted to enforce the collection of the papal tax of Peter's Pence in Caithness (discussed below). It is therefore ironic that someone with as good a record as a supporter of the church should become involved in a bitter quarrel with the bishops in Caithness which was to lead to the wounding of one bishop and the murder of his successor.

From the time of King David, kings had attempted to extend their influence in Moray by introducing non-native feudal settlers, but in Caithness they relied on pro-Scottish bishops who acted as royal agents. Whereas Harald could count of the support of Bishop Bjarni in Orkney, his relations with the bishops in his Caithness earldom were always difficult. The problem was not just that they acted on behalf of the King of Scots, but they were trespassing on an area which previously had been regarded as part of the bishopric of Orkney. Originally the Orkney bishopric had been coterminous with the earldom and, although its boundaries were not defined, it probably was regarded as stretching south to the Dornoch Firth. A residual feature of its once greater extent was that the Orkney bishopric, right up to the time of the Reformation and beyond, owned scattered estates in Caithness as well as the right to the skats of the parishes of Dunnet and Canisby.[59] The first encroachment was at a date prior to 1153 when Scottish monks, apparently from Dunfermline,[60] were established at Dornoch on the very edge of the Caithness earldom. A letter from King David addressed to Rognvald as earl of Orkney and to the 'good men' of Caithness and Orkney required them to protect the monks 'whenever they come among you', which suggests that their field of operation was north into Caithness and perhaps as far as Orkney.[61]

The first Caithness bishop, Bishop Andrew (c.1153-1185), was appointed soon after. He also was a monk of Dunfermline,[62] so he may have been initially a member of this Dornoch community, but his impact was probably minimal since he was frequently found at the Scottish court rather than in his diocese.[63] The second bishop, Bishop John (1185-1213) was more active, and he took exception to a household tax which Harald Maddadsson had allowed to be levied for the benefit of the Papacy. The tax was almost certainly Peter's Pence, then recently introduced into Norway and therefore into the Orkney diocese, but which was not levied in Scotland.[64] To pay or not pay became the test of the relative strength of Norwegian and Scottish influence, but it put Bishop John in the invidious position of opposing a payment to the church which the earl was keen to enforce. The dispute was eventually referred to Pope Innocent III, who wrote to the neighbouring bishops, Bjarni of Orkney and Reginald of Ross, ordering them to compel Bishop John to accept the tax.[65] Harald's hostility was directed specifically at Bishop John, whom he regarded as responsible for his deteriorating relationship with William the Lion; he regarded the bishop as 'an informer and the instigator of the misunderstanding between him and the lord king.'[66] In the long term Peter's Pence was not paid from Caithness—the secular balance of power was radically altered in Scotland's favour by a series of massive military incursions led by the king in person.

Since Harald Maddadsson occupied (or perhaps continued to occupy) large parts of Ross and Moray, King William came north in 1196, crossed the Oykell, and 'bowed to his will both provinces of the Caithness men'[67] (Caithness and Sutherland), capturing and destroying the castle at Ormlie in Thurso.[68] It seems likely that the campaign was precipitated by Scotland's desire to take advantage of Harald Maddadsson's defeat at Florevåg by re-activating the claim that lands which he still occupied had previously been adjudged to be Harald the Younger's share of the earldom. This explanation seems more likely rather than that Harald Maddadsson so soon after Florevåg should have undertaken an invasion of large parts of Moray and Ross which would inevitably have brought him into conflict with William the Lion. Never before had a Scottish king penetrated so far north. Harald retreated before him, but bad weather prevented him escaping across the Pentland Firth into Orkney,[69] so for the second time in two years Harald had to throw himself on the mercy of a king and await his terms. He had to agree to hand over 'the king's enemies' when next the king came north, and on that condition he was allowed to hold half of Caithness, which seems to imply that the other half was given to Harald the Younger.

In the following year (1197) there is a record of a battle fought near the castle of Inverness between Thorfinn, son of Harald Maddadsson, in alliance with an unidentified Roderic against 'the king's vassals', presumably the feudal settlers who had been introduced into Moray.[70] According to Roger of Howden, this brought King William hurrying north to the royal castle at Nairn where Earl Harald arrived, apparently intending to honour his pledge to surrender 'the king's enemies', who were presumably MacHeth relatives of his wife or MacWilliam adherents. At the last moment, however, hearing of the king's intransigent attitude, he allowed them to escape, but then went on to meet the king.[71] If that account is true, he showed a naive faith in what might be achieved by a personal appearance. Fordun has the rather different story that Harald was fortuitously captured somewhere in the north of Scotland.[72] The outcome, however, was that Harald was deemed to have forfeited all the lands which he held from the Scottish crown, and he was taken in chains to Edinburgh (or perhaps Roxburgh) where he was imprisoned until William's men went to Orkney to fetch Thorfinn to take his place as a hostage.[73]

On Harald's release he had to cope with a full-scale invasion of his earldoms from Harald the Younger. The invasion came from Norway via Shetland where, like other members of the Erlend line, Harald could probably expect to draw adherents. He seems also to have been well supported in Caithness, so he was able to take advantage of the absence of both Harald and Thorfinn to gain control of Caithness and invade Orkney. Roger of Howden's account describes how Harald Maddadsson visited the Isle of Man in search of assistance.[74] With or without the help of his Manx relatives Harald Maddadsson defeated and killed Harald the Younger in 1198 in a decisive battle fought near Wick.[75]

It is interesting to speculate if the canonisation of St Rognvald played a part in Harald the Younger's bid for the earldom. After Rognvald had been killed in Caithness, he was interred in St Magnus Cathedral[76] 'until the time that God revealed his merit with many great miracles'. Bishop Bjarni then took up his relics and proclaimed his sainthood 'by leave of the Pope'.[77] *Orkneyinga saga* provides no information about Rognvald's miracles or about his cult. The saga's account of Rognvald is reconstructed from various none-too-satisfactory secular sources such as the earl's own poetry, some light-hearted tales from his youth, and adventure stories from his crusade. Because of the saga's reliance on these sources we gain an impression of Rognvald's character as carefree and even irresponsible—and there is no *Saint's Life* to strike a more sober note. We have exactly the opposite problem with Magnus for whom the saga-account is entirely based on a *Saint's Life* while the heroic poetry about Magnus's deeds which at one time existed has been lost.[78] However, the canonisation of Rognvald is likely to have worked in favour of Harald the Younger (his grandson) in exactly the same way that Rognvald exploited his kinship with Magnus (his uncle). And in the same way that Earl Paul and Bishop William the Old declared it heresy to go about with stories of Magnus's sainthood, Harald Maddadsson and Bishop Bjarni must have seen dangers in a cult which reflected favourably on a rival from the Erlend line. There is no doubt that Bjarni was hostile to Harald the Younger, since the bishop's kinsmen played a prominent part in his defeat at Wick.[79] Presumably, like Earl Paul and Bishop William, Harald and Bjarni were powerless to stand in the way of a cult which commanded popular enthusiasm.

Sainthood ran in the family of the earls of the Erlend line, and Harald the Younger very nearly became their third saint. A great light was seen on the spot where his blood fell, and 'countless miracles' testified to his merit; he was called a 'very saint' by the Caithness men, and a church was built where he was killed.[80] The combination of noble birth and violent death had again worked its magic but, in the same way as Harald failed to win the earldom, he fell a little short of recognition as a saint. In fact, Harald the Younger's abilities seem to have been limited: despite royal recognition and enthusiastic support for his cause, he had been slow to press his claim and had been unable to take advantage of Harald Maddadsson's problems. The saga was written within a few years of Rognvald's canonisation and Harald the Younger's death, and at that time further members of the Erlend line still posed a threat. We may suppose that talk of Harald the Younger's sainthood was discouraged and aspects of Rognvald's cult were quietly suppressed.

Having killed his rival, Harald Maddadsson still had to make his peace with William the Lion, and this proved difficult. He travelled south to meet the king under the safe conduct of the bishops of St Andrews and Rosemarkie, but failed to obtain the settlement he needed.[81] As well as demanding the surrender of further hostages, the king required that Harald should put away Hvarflǫð to whom he had been married for many years and should reinstate his first wife, Afreka.[82] These terms were unacceptable, but they make it very clear that William the Lion's main concern was to break Harald's rebel links and bastardise Thorfinn who embodied the dangerous links with the MacHeths. But the king achieved the destruction of the heir by more direct and brutal means: he still held Thorfinn as hostage, and he now gave orders for him to be blinded and castrated because of his father's bad faith.[83] The king then sold Caithness to Rognvald Gudrodsson of Man, a cousin of Harald Maddadsson, on terms which allowed the Scots to draw an annual income. The Manx king occupied Caithness for a summer (apparently 1201) with a mixed army drawn from the Hebrides, Kintyre and Ireland, but as winter approached he withdrew most of his men, leaving Caithness in the hands of stewards. One of the stewards, Hlifolf, was assassinated by orders of Earl Harald, and the others fled to the Scottish court.[84]

If Harald was in trouble with his immediate feudal lord he could seek help elsewhere. On 6 January 1201 King John of England issued a safe conduct to allow his 'dear cousin' to come and visit him. It is unlikely that Harald went to England, but the payment of 10 marks to Adam, chaplain of Orkney, and his companions who were on the king's business shows that some kind of joint action was being explored.[85] These treasonable dealings came to the notice of Bishop John of Caithness who immediately informed King William. Hearing of the bishop's treachery Earl Harald crossed to Caithness in a decidedly ill-humour. He landed not far from the bishop's castle at Scrabster, and when the bishop tried to placate him, the earl's men seized the bishop, cut out his tongue and blinded him—a punishment, it has been observed, specifically designed to emphasise that the bishop was a spy and an informer. But since the bishop subsequently recovered his speech and the sight of one eye through the intervention of St Tredwell, his injuries were perhaps not as serious as were first reported.[86] From the subsequent judgement of Pope Innocent III it seems that Harald was not personally responsible. Punishment fell on a man by the name of Lombard; he was sentenced to walk through Caithness for fifteen days, bare-footed and stripped to the waist, with his tongue tied so that it projected from his mouth, and he was beaten with rods outside Caithness churches. On the completion of his penance he was to depart for Jerusalem to labour for three years in the service of the Cross.[87]

When King William heard of the assassination of the steward and the maiming of the bishop, he assembled a large army and marched north to 'Eysteinsdalr' on the border of Caithness (probably Ausdale[88]). The saga, still accustomed to small scale Norse warfare, spoke in awe of the size of the royal army, remarking that its tents stretched the whole length of the valley—'and that is a long way'. Despite the size of his army William advanced no farther. Earl Harald also commanded a large force, 6,000 men according to the saga, and the diplomatic activity between Orkney and England made it inadvisable for William to become too deeply committed in the far north. Accordingly Harald was able to secure not unfavourable terms: he was compelled to pay 'every fourth penny' in Caithness—a payment likely to represent a quarter of his revenue from rent and skat. However, he now regained undisputed control over all Caithness,[89] so he may have considered himself fortunate to come out of the Scottish wars as well as he did.

Harald's long reign was drawing to a close. While Sverre was alive Harald risked no further trouble from Norway, but on the death of the king in 1202 he freed himself from royal control by murdering the *sysselman*, Arne Lorja,[90] and when he died in 1206 he was again in a state of rebellion. The *Orkneyinga saga* lists Harald as one of the three greatest Orkney earls,[91] a verdict with which historians have not always agreed. There is something less than heroic about Harald's losing struggle with Norwegian and Scottish kings and his submission to both. Sometimes he allowed himself to drift into dangerous situations which with greater foresight he might have avoided. Yet there was an inevitability about the advancing power of Norway and Scotland—although Harald Maddadsson might resist the idea, the days of a semi-independent Orkney were over.

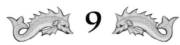

9

Earl John and His Successors

After the death of Harald Maddadsson the earldom was ruled jointly by his two sons, John (Earl of Orkney 1206–1231) and David (Earl of Orkney 1206–1214). The issues they had to face were those which had confronted their father: the inevitability of submission to Norway and Scotland, involvement in MacWilliam rebellions, the hostility of the Bishop of Caithness, and the competing claims of members of the Erlend line.

The earldom to which John and David succeeded had been in a state of rebellion in their father's final years following the killing of the sysselman (royal bailiff), and John and David initially continued to retain revenues which ought to have been paid to the Crown. However, news that peace was restored in Norway and that *birkbeins* ('birch-legs') and *crosiermen* were to bury their differences and make a joint expedition to the west persuaded the earls that there was an urgent necessity to make peace. Bishop Bjarni was sent to Norway to negotiate a reconciliation (1209) and, when the expedition arrived in Orkney in 1210, the earls had made their peace and a sysselman had already been restored, so the expedition directed its attention to the Hebrides.[1] The earls, however, were required to make a personal appearance in Norway in the following year (1210). As well as accepting the restoration of the sysselman, they were forced to pay a large fine, hostages and other pledges were required, and they were then allowed to swear faithfulness and obedience 'with such conditions as were afterwards kept to their death-day'.[2] Later, when kings were appointing Orkney earls, the *Hirdskrå* enjoined them to have regard for the conditions imposed on the earls in 1195 and 1267, but it did not mention this settlement of 1210.[3] The likelihood is that the 1210 settlement largely reimposed the terms which Sverre had dictated to Harald Maddadsson. The statement in *Inga saga* that John and David were then restored as earls in Shetland as well as in Orkney is unlikely to be correct.[4] The 1210 settlement was no doubt at least as severe as the conditions imposed after Florevåg fifteen years earlier when Shetland was detached from the earldom.

During Earl John's reign (David having died in 1214)[5] he visited Norway on an unprecedented number of occasions, demonstrating the closer relationship which was now expected. John seems to have played no major part in the conflict between King Hakon and Earl Skuli, or in the question of Hakon's right to kingship but, as a leading nobleman, he could not altogether escape involvement. In 1217 when letters bearing the royal seal were sent to John by Earl Skuli without the king's knowledge, there was a natural suspicion that John was involved in treasonable dealings.[6] It seems likely that the letters related to proposals then under discussion to give Skuli, not only a share of Norway, but also a third, a half, or even all of the *skattlands* (the overseas territories which included Orkney).[7] In the following year (1218) John was present in Norway when the ordeal was administered to Hakon's mother to prove the truth of Hakon's royal parentage,[8] and he was again present in 1223 when Hakon's rights were solemnly debated in Bergen.[9] Although John did not play a significant role in these discussions, his association with the king's opponents led to a further visit to Norway in the following year (1224) when he was required to make atonement to the king 'for those quarrels which were between them'. He remained at court all that summer and, when he left, his son Harald stayed behind as a hostage.[10]

That was John's final visit to Norway, but in 1228 he demonstrated that he intended to keep on friendly terms by sending messengers to Hakon 'with many good offerings'. The king reciprocated by sending John 'a good long-ship and many other gifts'. The cementing of their friendship by gift-exchange was related to the 'great strife' in the Southern Isles and the activities of 'the very unfaithful' Hebridean kings which *Hakonar saga* mentions in the same chapter.[11] The king was anxious to retain John's loyalty, and John was equally intent on distancing himself from the Hebridean rebels. In 1230, the year before John was killed, he provided substantial assistance to the Norwegian expedition to the Hebrides. John did not himself take part, but nine of the twenty ships were drawn from Orkney including John's personal contribution of a large and handsome vessel named the *Ox*.[12] Although it had not always been easy to keep out of trouble while Hakon's succession was disputed, John had shown that in the main he was willing to accept the role of a loyal vassal.

Earl John was also caught up in Scottish affairs as a result of continuing MacWilliam rebellions. In the summer of 1211 Guthred MacWilliam rose in rebellion 'by the advice of the thanes of Ross'.[13] It is possible that one of these 'thanes' was John's half-brother, Henry, who had inherited land in Ross from their father.[14] It was only the following year and with the help of Brabantine mercenaries supplied by King John of England that order was restored. After the capture and execution of Guthred, leadership of this desperate family devolved on Donald Bán MacWilliam who, with Irish assistance, descended on Moray in 1215 where he was in turn defeated, captured and beheaded.[15] There is no direct evidence of Earl John's involvement in these rebellions—unlike his father, he was careful to avoid a major campaign against

Scotland—but between these two MacWilliam rebellions and shortly before his death the aged William the Lion made his last expedition into the north of Scotland. Evidently John had been to some degree implicated, since the king's main business in the north was to conclude 'a treaty of peace' with Earl John. A unnamed daughter of John was handed over to the king as a hostage.[16] Her name and her fate are unknown, but the king might be expected to have bestowed her in marriage in Scotland, and so one possibility is that she was mother of the Angus earls who succeeded after John's death and whose relationship to the previous earls is unexplained (but see below p.135).

The dealings between the earls and the bishops of Caithness which had caused such difficulty in the reign of Harald Maddadsson continued to be a major problem. At issue was not just the relationship between Norse and Scots in Caithness, but the whole question of lay resistance to strengthened episcopal structures, and in particular opposition to more effective tithe-raising powers. We have seen how Harald Maddadsson had been involved in the wounding of Bishop John of Caithness in 1201—Earl John now found himself similarly caught up in the killing of his successor.[17] Adam (Bishop of Caithness 1213-1222) was a Cistercian and formerly abbot of Melrose[18] who returned from the Fourth Lateran Council and set about collecting tiends (tithes) 'with more zeal than discretion'.[19] The Icelandic *Flateyjarbók* states that the dispute involved the butter tithe which the bishop increased from a *span* of butter from every 20 cows to a span from only ten cows.[20] Since the tithe was being collected using the ancient Norse measure, the span or pail, the butter tithe was probably not a new introduction by Scots bishops; it was probably the doubling of the rate rather than its imposition which was resented. Butter was technically a 'small tithe' but, according to the *Annals of Dunstable,* the 'great tithe' of hay was also involved.[21] The resistance to the hay tithe had been protracted, and the question of its payment was so contentious that it was heard in the king's presence. The bishop resorted to obtaining the royal seal in confirmation of the payment, and Earl John had also been obliged to appended his seal, although he had apparently done so with some reluctance.[22] There may also have been other areas of dispute: Fordun states that, in addition to the tithes, there were 'other church rights' which the bishop was claiming from his subjects.[23] Matters came to a head when the Bishop Adam was on his manor farm at Halkirk, and the earl was nearby at Braal. The increased payments were bitterly resented by the Caithness farmers, and the earl who was no friend of the pro-Scots bishops refused to intervene, leaving it to Rafn, the Lawman, to do his best to mediate. The outcome was that an angry crowd confronted the bishop, killed his priest, thrust him into an outside kitchen and set fire to the building with the result that the bishop perished.

Alexander II was on his way to England and had reached Jedburgh when the news reached him. He turned about, intent on punishing the murderers with the utmost rigour. When the previous bishop was attacked, punishment had fallen on a single individual, the unfortunate Lombard, but on this occasion there was widespread retribution. Icelandic Annals tell how Alexander II caused 80 men who had been present at the burning to have their hands and feet cut off,[24] while the *Annals of Duisk* recount the killing of the Caithness men, the castration of their sons, and the expulsion of their wives from their property.[25] While the king was in Caithness he was present in person when Gilbert of Moray was chosen as the next bishop. Gilbert (1223—1244/5) was no doubt the king's nominee and was intended to strengthen royal power. He was a member of the powerful 'de Moravia' family which dominated Sutherland, and his father had already granted him an extensive personal estate consisting of Skelbo, Fernebuchlyn, Invershin and lands to the west.[26] Bishop Gilbert abandoned Halkirk as the seat of the bishopric because of 'the poverty of the place and frequent invasions', and built his cathedral at Dornoch in Sutherland where he could rely on family protection and was less vulnerable to the hostility of the Orkney earls.[27]

Alexander II's brutal punishment of the Caithness men won the unqualified approval of Pope Honorius, who wrote to the Scottish bishops praising the king's prompt actions and allowing them, if appropriate, to place the lands of the culprits under ecclesiastical interdict until suitable satisfaction was given.[28] It was uncertain to what extent John would be held personally accountable. According to *Flateyjarbók* his sin seems to have been one of omission—a failure to render assistance when the bishop was in danger.[29] The *Annals of Dunstable*, on the other hand, attribute to him a more direct part in the killing, and tell us that:

> …he fled from the king's realm and, in the manner of Cain, roamed about among the islands of the sea.[30]

No doubt this colourful description reflects the reality that Earl John found it prudent to remain within his Orkney earldom when Alexander II was in Caithness and his own part in the killing was unresolved. As punishment, half his Caithness earldom was forfeited, but the following year (1223) Earl John was able to visit the king in Forfar, where a short stay at court enabled him to prove his loyalty, and he was then allowed to buy back the forfeited land.[31] It seems that John was probably not held primarily responsible for the attack on the bishop, but he emerged weakened from the affair, whereas the power of the king had been asserted in a way which Caithness people were unlikely to forget.

The reign of Earl John saw the final round of the conflict between the Paul and Erlend Lines which had bedevilled the earldom for over a century and a half. The question of John's successor probably became urgent after

1226 with the drowning of Harald, his only son who had remained hostage in Norway.[32] The latest rival was Snaekoll Gunnisson who was a great-grandson of Earl Rognvald and a nephew of Harald the Younger (Fig.24). Snaekoll at least initially did not aspire to a share in the earldom, but he had a long-standing claim to certain farms which had belonged to Rognvald's side of the family yet which were in the possession of Earl John. The question at issue seems to have been whether Snaekoll as the Erlend-line heir had a right to these farms even when he was not himself an earl, or whether the farms were an unalienable part of the earldom estate, what would later be termed 'bordland' (see Chapter 16). When Snaekoll failed to obtain redress from the earl, he sought the assistance of Hanef *ungi* ('the Younger) who was the current sysselman representing King Hakon. In a legal dispute of this kind where the earl's interests were involved, it is by no means clear what were the respective roles of the Lawman, sysselman and earl. Their relative powers were as yet untested, and indeed the dispute ultimately proved to be incapable of being settled in Orkney and had to be remitted to King Hakon.

The presence of a *sysselman,* a royal bailiff representing the king's interests and acting as a curb on the earl's independence, had been part of the post-Florevåg settlement. His relationship with the earl was bound to be difficult, and had already led to the killing of the first sysselman in Harald Maddadsson's latter years. The problem was compounded in Hanef *ungi's* case because of his local connections. His family links are not quite certain, but he was apparently a nephew or great-nephew of Bishop Bjarni, and was the heir to Kolbein Hruga's property in Wyre. He seems also to have had close relatives in Rendall and if, as has been suggested, he was a great-grandson of Sweyn Asliefsson, he was probably a cousin of Snaekoll Gunnisson.[33] Hanef also had important Norwegian connections: Kolbein Hruga and Bishop Bjarni had owned estates in Norway,[34] and Hanef himself held the rank of *skutilsvein* in King Hakon's *hird.*

The appointment of a sysselman with partisan connections was a potential source of trouble. When Snaekoll failed to regain the disputed farms, he attached himself to Hanef, whose faction was further augmented by some troublesome members of the 1230 Norwegian expedition to the Western Isles who remained in Orkney on the homeward voyage; one of them was Oliver *ilteitt* ('All-ill') who was a ship's captain and, like Hanef, a member of King Hakon's *hird.*[35] The dispute came to a head when both Earl John and Hanef were in Thurso, each with a large following (1231).[36] During the course of a bout of heavy drinking, Hanef's men got it into their heads that they were about to be attacked, so they decided to strike first. As *Hakonar saga* puts it, 'they were all so drunk that they thought what they intended to do was a good plan'. They caught up with Earl John and killed him as he hid among the barrels in a Thurso cellar.[37] The murderers fled to Orkney where

33. ***Cubbie Roo's Castle, Wyre.*** *This little twelfth century stone keep was described in* Hakonar saga *as 'a very unhandy place to attack'.*

they made themselves secure within the Castle of Wyre. This little stone keep, built in the previous century by Kolbein Hruga, was a mere 26 feet square, but it was 'a very unhandy place to attack'.[38] Cattle were brought within the confines of the surrounding earthworks, and Snaekoll and Hanef prepared for a long siege. When Earl John's unnamed kinsmen failed to take the castle, a truce was arranged. It was agreed that both parties should allow King Hakon to settle the dispute. Accordingly in 1231 they made their way to Norway, Hanef and his party in one ship, and 'all the best men' (the godings) in another.

It proved no easier to settle the dispute by peaceful means in Norway than it had in Orkney. When the horn was sounded to bring the case to trial, Hanef's friends in the *hird* spirited him away along with some others accused of the earl's murder, whereupon the late earl's kinsmen led by Sigvaldi Skjalgsson seized the five who remained and took them out to a holm where they were summarily beheaded.[39] We are not told how all this was resolved but, whatever the king's decision, it was overtaken by events. In the rough weather of the autumn of 1232 when the earl's kinsmen were returning to Orkney, all of them in one ship, they were drowned when the vessel was lost.

133

The sinking of the 'Godings Ship' wiped out at a stroke the late earl's kindred and the heads of Orkney's main families. The account of these events in *Hakonar saga* ends with the ambiguous comment: 'and many men have had to atone for this afterwards'.[40] This has been taken to mean that the loss of the godings ushered in a period of misfortune and alien rule. It is true that the Norse line of earls came to an end, and the earldom passed into the hands of the Angus family, but no very obvious misfortune followed. The phrase probably relates to the atonement for the killing of Earl John, and to fines imposed on the godings for the way in which they had taken the law into their own hands. Hanef, however, was soon forgiven his part in the killing of Earl John. In the spring of 1233 he was given permission to return to Orkney, but he was driven back by bad weather and died in Norway shortly afterwards.

Although many of the earl's kinsmen were lost on the goding ship it seems unlikely that John's immediate heir was among them. The Orkney party appears to have been a group of leaderless godings, rather than a potential earl and his entourage, and there is no indication in *Hakonar saga* that the succession to the earldom was discussed during that visit. However, John's son had been drowned in 1226 and the fate of his daughter, taken hostage by William the Lion in 1214, is unknown, so the question of the succession was probably already a matter of concern. After John's death there was a five-year interregnum during which the succession remained unresolved. The succession then passed to earls of the Angus line for reasons which are difficult to unravel. The fifteenth-century *Diploma* or genealogy of the Orkney earls states that the title passed to Magnus II, but fails to explain his relationship to Earl John; Magnus II was succeeded by Gilbert I whose relation to Magnus II is also unspecified, then Gilbert I was in turn succeeded by his son Gilbert II.[41] However, it is only in the *Diploma* that we hear of two distinct Gilberts, so the very existence of a second Gilbert is dubious.

The first move following the death of Earl John was by Malcolm, Earl of Angus, who on 7 October 1232 witnessed a charter in which he described himself as 'M.comite de Angus et Katanie' ('Malcolm, earl of Angus and Caithness').[42] He was probably using the Caithness title as soon as he heard of the murder of Earl John, and even before the news of the loss of the goding ship, which suggests that he believed that he was Earl John's nearest heir. Malcolm, however, did not actually succeed to the earldom, although the next earls were other members of the Angus family. Presumably either Alexander II was not willing to see Caithness and Orkney united to the Earldom of Angus, or else Hakon may have objected to a candidate with such a strong Scottish base. The eventual solution seems to have been to find an alternative member of the Angus family. This was an important change: kings were no longer obliged to accept whoever was the nearest heir; they were able to delay recognition of a new earl, and could decide which member of the ruling family was acceptable.

It is not clear what was the family connection which allowed the Angus earls to claim the title. It seems unlikely that Malcolm could be descended from Earl John's hostage daughter (although if she survived she might be expected to have made a Scottish marriage). The connection is more likely to be a generation farther back—the result of the marriage of Helena or Margaret, daughters of Harald Maddadsson's marriage to Afreka or, less probably, the daughters of his subsequent marriage to Hvarfoð: Gunnhild, Herborga or Langlif.[43] It is even possible that the Angus connection was with the Erlend line: Magnus II's christian name suggests a family connection with the branch of the family which had included St Magnus, but the remoteness of the relationship of an Erlend-line candidate to the late earl makes such a descent unlikely. In any case the Erlend line seems to have been represented by Snaekoll Gunnison. Snaekoll escaped the summary executions in Bergen and remained in Norway for many years in the service of King Hakon and Earl Skuli.[44] There is no indication that Snaekoll was considered to be a possible candidate or that he had ever seriously advanced any such claim. The fact that the new earl was named Magnus cannot be taken as proof that he was a member of the Erlend line. The name of Orkney's patron saint had probably ceased to belong to a faction and, a century after the martyrdom, 'Magnus' was likely to have been used by anyone who wished to emphasise an Orkney connection.

In the years before Magnus II became earl, in addition to Malcolm, Earl of Angus, we find Walter Comyn, Earl of Menteith, describing himself as 'Earl of Caithness'—he used the title in a charter which he witnessed in July 1235.[45] Comyn was a leading supporter of Alexander II, and he seems to have been entrusted with achieving a more permanent solution to the problem of royal authority in northern Scotland, but his tenure of the earldom was probably never intended to be more than temporary. The following year (1236) Alexander II was in Inverness, and this was probably the occasion when the new settlement was finalised. It was there that Magnus II first appears, witnessing a charter in which he is described as 'Earl of Caithness' along with Malcolm who is now only 'Earl of Angus'.[46] The area Magnus II controlled was much diminished; Sutherland was detached from Caithness and was created a separate earldom for the de Moravia family.[47] The remainder of Caithness appears to have been granted to Magnus in two separate charters, one for North Caithness and another for South Caithness.[48] Magnus's reign, however, was brief and in 1239 he died.[49]

There is a fragment of a Latin document which sheds some light on the confused inheritance at this time. The first part is missing and the surviving portion begins in mid-sentence:

...for a year and a half, and died a virgin without issue, and so the earldom reverted to the older sisters, Joanna and Matilda, of which the elder sister was married to Freskin [de Moravia] as above noted.[50]

The missing portion must have named an earl who ruled Caithness for a year-and-a-half. Since the earl described in the document died childless, he cannot be Earl Gilbert I if the *Diploma* is correct in naming Gilbert I as father of Gilbert II. Thus it seems likely that the reference is to Magnus II, although his actual reign was slightly longer (1236-9). Barbara Crawford identified Matilda as the daughter of Malcolm, Earl of Angus, and suggests that these important heiresses inherited both the Earldom of Angus from their father and the Earldom of Caithness from their brother.

All our information comes from Scotland so the part which the King Hakon played in the establishment of the early Angus earls is unknown, although he must have taken a keen interest in the succession. Whereas Matilda was found a Comyn husband and became Countess of Angus in her own right, Hakon probably prevented the parallel scheme of settling Joanna and her husband, Freskin de Moravia, in Caithness, although it might have suited Alexander II's purposes to make Freskin earl.[51] It was probably the Orkney connection which prevented Joanna receiving the Caithness title; a female could not succeed to the Orkney earldom, and could only transmit the right to her sons, but Joanna had no sons—she only had two daughters. Freskin, because of his commitment to Scotland, was in any case unlikely to be acceptable as an earl ruling by right of his wife. Thus the title of earl and half of Caithness passed, not to these heiresses, but to another member of the Angus line, Earl Gilbert. Further fragmentation of the former earldom lands in Caithness took place on Joanna's death when her lands were divided between her daughters.

It is difficult to avoid the conclusion that, with the accession of the Angus earls, the great days of medieval Orkney had come to an end. This impression is partly due to a change in the sources from which Orkney's history is written. The closing chapters of *Orkneyinga saga* provide a disjointed account of the latter years of Harald Maddadsson's reign and, with the accession of John and David, the curtain descends on the world of the saga. For a further sixty years some degree of continuity is provided by other sagas, notably *Hakonar saga,* although the focus has shifted away from Orkney. Thereafter it is a case of piecing together such scraps of information as can be extracted from the few documents which have survived. These have an accuracy and reliability previously lacking, but there is none of the wealth of detail, vivid characterisation and swift-moving action which made *Orkneyinga saga* such an attractive source.

The changes, however, were real—it was not just that the sources become more prosaic. The earldom was now much reduced in political power:

the ability to extend Orkney's authority into the Hebrides and the Irish Sea was long gone (before 1098), Shetland had been lost (1195), as had Sutherland (c.1235) and half of Caithness (c.1240). The whole nature of the north of Scotland was also altered by the final defeat of the MacWilliams and the establishment of earldoms in Sutherland and Ross which were supportive of royal authority. Initially kings had exercised authority by punitive expeditions and by the exaction of the large fines paid to Norway in 1195, 1210, 1224 and 1232, and to Scotland in 1202, 1214 and 1223. Fines of that size and frequency no doubt weakened the earls, but latterly the ability to withhold recognition from potential claimants and to manage the marriages of heiresses had been even more effective. We do not know whether there was still a sysselman acting as a curb on the earl's powers, but a more regular relationship continued to develop. The presence of Orkneymen in Bergen among those who swore oaths of loyalty to Hakon *ungi* when he received the title of king and was designated successor in the spring of 1240 showed that Orkney continued to be represented in Norway on important occasions.[52]

The first Angus earls seem to have made little impact; perhaps Magnus II was still quite young (although old enough at the beginning of his reign to witness a charter), and it is possible that Gilbert was a minor at the time when he became earl.[53] It is not, however, necessary to assume that they were absentees; the Orkney earls of the Angus line were not Earls of Angus but a distinct branch and, as far as we know, they did not have major interests outside their earldom. Within Orkney it is possible only to guess at the implications of the loss of so many of the godings—perhaps Orkney was a more peaceful place without them. The new earls, however, being incomers, may have lacked a supporting network of kinsmen. If the earls were largely inactive, the same was true of the bishop: Bjarni's successor was the Norwegian Jofrey (Bishop of Orkney 1223–1246) who for many years was ill and bedridden to the extent that Pope Gregory IX sought his resignation because of 'the grave damage in spiritual and temporal matters' caused by his incapacity.[54]

In 1256 *Icelandic Annals* record the death of Earl Gilbert.[55] He was succeeded by his son, Magnus III (Earl of Orkney 1256–1273), who also maintained a low profile. It was, however, less easy to do so in 1263 when he was caught up in King Hakon's great expedition to the Hebrides which culminated in the Battle of Largs.

10
King Hakon's Expedition and the Loss of the Hebrides

King Hakon's 1263 expedition which culminated in the Battle of Largs and the loss of the Hebrides can be seen as a struggle against the hard facts of geography. There is a sense of inevitability about the Scottish advance into islands which were easily visible from the mainland and were separated by hundreds of miles of stormy seas from the Norwegian homeland. In the long run the frontier which Magnus Barelegs and King Edgar had established between the Norse islands and the Scottish mainland might serve as a rough-and-ready demarcation of their respective spheres of influence, but as a boundary between states it was bound to fail.

Yet the 'hard facts of geography' are not so unchanging as they seem. There had been a time when the whole ragged sea-fringe of Europe from the north of Norway to Ireland had a unity for a sea-going people. The North Sea itself was not a much greater barrier than Stadlandet which separated Bergen from the Trondheim area, or Ardnamurchan which divided the northern and southern Hebrides. In the same way as coastal Norway was distinct from inland Sweden, the western seaboard of Scotland with its Norse-Gaelic culture was separated by mountains from lowland eastern Scotland. If Norway found it difficult to retain the Hebrides, Scotland was to find them equally difficult to assimilate. By the thirteenth century this Viking Age geography was changing. The seaways through the Hebrides were no longer the golden road which led to Norse Dublin. As the north-south Ireland-Norway axis decayed, a whole series of new east-west links were developing. As the English pushed westwards into Ireland, Scotland and its fringing principalities of Galloway and Argyll expanded into the Hebrides, while the Kings of Man developed ambiguous links with England. These events had an important bearing on Orkney: at one time Orkney had occupied a pivotal position on the Ireland-Norway axis; when that axis was destroyed we can see with hindsight that Orkney's future was with Scotland rather than with Norway. That, however, was not so obvious at the time, and indeed the relationship with Norway seemed to be growing stronger.

Since the death of Magnus Barelegs in Ulster in 1102, no Norwegian king had visited the Hebrides. The creation of the archbishopric of Trondheim in 1154 brought the bishoprics both of Orkney and Sodor (Man and the Isles) within the framework of Norwegian ecclesiastical control, and Sverre's victory at Florevåg had imposed on Orkney a more regular relationship with Norway, but the Hebrides had been largely neglected during the period of Norway's civil wars (1161-1208). Scotland under William the Lion had showed equally little interest. Although he fought a series of major campaigns in the north of Scotland and was a consistent enemy of Harald Maddadsson's Orkney, he had little involvement in the west. Collision between Scotland and Norway became more likely in the changed conditions of the thirteenth century. In the same way as the Scots fondly remembered the reigns of Alexander II and III as their 'Golden Age', Norwegians regarded the contemporary reign of Hakon IV as their 'Storhetstid' (Period of Greatness).[1] An outward-looking Norway made new contacts with popes, emperors and kings and adopted the pageantry and display of contemporary European rulers. Hakon also took a new interest in the overseas *skattlands* (tributary provinces); in the early 1260s on the eve of the Largs campaign, he finally succeeded in persuading Greenland and Iceland to acknowledge his kingship. Far from losing the Hebrides from neglect, Hakon took a keen personal interest; by 1263 he was Hakon 'the Old', and he had a lifetime's experience of the intricacies of Hebridean politics.

Politically as well as physically the Hebrides was a difficult area to control. Ever since Somerled's invasion of insular Argyll in the previous century the Kingdom of Man and the Isles (the Sudreys) was split into two widely separate parts, the Isle of Man to the south and Skye and Lewis to the north, sometimes ruled by mutually hostile members of the Manx dynasty.[2] Between these two regions lay the territories of the descendants of Somerled, by the mid-thirteenth century represented by two branches of the family, King Ewen Duncansson MacDougal of Lorn, and King Dougal MacRuahri of Garmoran whose territories lay to the north. For the Norwegians the promotion of these Somerledian kings was an alternative to the more usual policy of bolstering up the Manx kings. However, Ewen and Dougal, being in an ill-defined way subservient to the Kings of Man, were suspicious of favours shown to the Manx rulers, and they were constrained by the fact that, in addition to the islands which they held from Norway, they also held mainland territories from Scotland. In practice Norway could do little more than react to whatever was the latest crisis in the Hebrides. Orkney had frequent contacts with the Hebrides, but was no longer a major player. The Orkney-based Hebridean empire of Sigurd and Thorfinn had disintegrated after Thorfinn's death (c.1065) and in the twelfth century, although Orcadians were active in the Hebrides as pirates and mercenaries and as allies of native rulers, the restoration of Orkney rule was never an objective.

Long before 1263 the great expedition to daunt the isles was a well-established tradition. In 1209–1210 the contending factions in Norway's civil wars had celebrated their new-found unity by combining to send an expedition to counter Somerledian threats to Skye.[3] It was the threat from this expedition which had led the joint earls of Orkney, David and John, to end the rebellion of their father's later years (see Chapter 9). They were closely followed to Norway by Reginald III of Man who arrived to pay arrears and do homage.[4] A second expedition in 1229–1230, when nearly half of the ships were drawn from Orkney, had attempted to replace disloyal Hebridean kings by Uspak, a member of the Somerled family long resident in Norway.[5] The untimely death of Uspak foiled the primary purpose of the expedition, but the presence of the force was sufficient to cause the collapse of opposition, and to put to an end threats to the Isle of Man from Alan of Galloway. The success of these expeditions led to the dangerous conclusion that it was only necessary for a Norwegian fleet to appear in strength for opposition to melt away.

Possibly from as early as 1244 Scottish embassies had visited Norway proposing various solutions to the Hebridean problem. At first Scots had questioned the validity of Magnus Barelegs' 1098 treaty by which Norwegian dominion over the isles had been recognised; then, when they found the Norwegians unyielding, they had offered to buy the Hebrides. Hakon replied that 'he was aware of no such urgent need of silver that he needed to sell these lands', but the Scots continued to press their offer.[6] The drowning of the young king of Man, Harald II, plunged Hebridean affairs into crisis (1248); his ship foundered in Sumburgh Roost south of Shetland when he was returning from Norway with his newly-wed bride, Cecilia, daughter of Hakon IV.[7] Seeing that the moment was opportune for a military solution and 'very greedy for the realm of the Southern Isles', Alexander II declared that he would not rest until he planted his standard on 'Thursa Skerry' (perhaps Muckle Flugga, the northernmost point of Shetland).[8] He moved into Lorn demanding that King Ewen hand over his island fortresses. However, the time had not yet come for King Ewen to abandon his Norwegian allegiance, and he fled to Lewis. At this point, when Alexander II was in Kerrara near Oban, St Olaf, St Columba and St Magnus appeared to him in a dream, representing Norway, the Hebrides and Orkney. Whereas Columba was large and menacing, and Olaf was stout and short tempered, Magnus was 'slim-built and young, of all men the fairest'.[9] Undeterred by this ghostly delegation, Alexander was still apparently intending to advance into the isles when he suddenly took ill and died. With his death the immediate crisis was over.

As soon as Alexander III came of age, the Scots embassy to Norway was renewed. Negotiations in Bergen in 1262 were conducted in a strained atmosphere, and when the Scots attempted to slip away without taking formal leave, they were captured and detained over the winter.[10] They must still have been at court when news was received of an attack on Skye in 1262 by the Earl of Ross. The Somerledian Kings of the Isles told of a massacre, the destruction of a 'town', and they reported atrocity stories of infants impaled on the spears of advancing Scots.[11]

In the spring of 1263 the levy was called out and King Hakon, although he was in his sixtieth year, announced that he intended to take personal charge of the expedition to the west. The first Orkney reaction seems to have been loyal. John Langlifsson (possibly a grandson of Earl Harald Maddadsson)[12] was sent ahead from Bergen to find pilots in Shetland. He met King Dougal who was already in Orkney, and he sailed into the Hebrides where he made contact with King Magnus of Man, and heard rumours of King Ewen's impending defection to the Scots. Earl Magnus III of Orkney joined the expedition, not in Orkney but in Bergen, so presumably when John Langlifsson sailed west he had carried a summons to the king's presence which the earl had been prompt to obey. Magnus III was presented with a good longship, so he appears to have been in favour.[13] Also accompanying the expedition from Bergen were Bishop Henry of Orkney and Bishop Gilbert of Hamar. Bishop Gilbert had previously been Archdeacon of Shetland, then he was King Hakon's personal chaplain, and had recently been elevated to the bishopric of Hamar at the king's insistence.[14] His name, Gilbert, and his connections with the Orkney diocese suggest that he may have been a relative of the Angus earls. The presence of these bishops underlines the importance of Orkney involvement, and it also indicates that the purpose of the expedition was only partly military. King Hakon expected that a display of naval power would lead to negotiations in which the bishops would play an important part.

There were difficulties in assembling so large a levy, so it was late before the expedition set sail and there was a lack of urgency about its advance. Nearly two weeks were spent in Bressay Sound in Shetland, and it was only towards the end of July that the fleet arrived in Orkney and anchored at Elwick in Shapinsay, a harbour conveniently close to Kirkwall. There were disagreements about future tactics. King Hakon wished to remain in Orkney while a raiding party was sent into the Moray Firth. Others with Hebridean interests urged the west coast route, while the levy-men declared that 'they would go nowhere unless with the king himself'.[15]

On St Olaf's eve King Hakon heard mass ashore and he feasted the common people aboard his ship. They must have marvelled at the *Krossuden*, for Hakon's flagship had no equal in Europe.[16] She was of oak construction throughout, she had 37 pairs of oars, and the great dragon heads at stem and stern were overlaid with gold. She carried nearly 300 men, including the king himself, and the immediate members of his government. The fleet then moved round to St Margaret's Hope where they witnessed an eclipse of the sun which can be dated to 5 August. Delays were caused by the necessity of securing Caithness which was granted a separate peace in return for the payment of a fine. Earl Magnus III was left behind when the fleet sailed west on 10 August, and the likelihood is that he had been entrusted with uplifting the Caithness payments. But, having escaped from the king's presence, Magnus III was in no hurry to join him again, and took no further part in the campaign.

The Largs campaign lies beyond the scope of Orkney history, so it is sufficient to describe it only in outline. The size and magnificence of the fleet was sufficient to restore most Hebrideans to their allegiance. King Ewen, however, defected to the Scots, but at first it seemed that his change of side was neither crucial or irreversible. Hakon's fleet received enlargement from King Magnus of Man and from the levy of Argyll before entering the Firth of Clyde and making its base on Arran. Negotiations were opened with the Scots, and at first it seemed that little separated the two sides, merely the question of the Clyde islands, Arran, Bute and the Cumbraes. However, it soon became apparent that the Scots were dragging out discussions, relying on the lateness of the season to force King Hakon's departure. King Hakon brought his fleet to Cumbrae nearer the Scottish mainland, but at the beginning of October it was struck by a severe south-west gale, and a merchant ship was blown ashore. When the Norwegians were trying to retrieve the cargo, they were attacked by the Scots and retreated in some confusion, while the fleet was unable to render much assistance. The Battle of Largs was hardly the great set-piece battle which Scots later imagined it to have been, but it was nevertheless decisive. It put an end to discussion, and King Hakon, refusing an invitation to winter in Ireland, began the long voyage back to Orkney.

On the voyage northwards Hakon allocated castles and lands to his loyal Hebridean followers, and *Hakonar saga* could claim that 'he had won back those realms which Magnus Barelegs had won from Scotland'.[17] The extent of the expedition's failure may not have been immediately apparent, but those who received these lands soon discovered that they would need more than a title from King Hakon once he had gone. The *Chronicle of Man* was more realistic when it described the expedition as 'effecting nothing'[18] and, in the opinion of the *Chronicle of Melrose*, the Norwegians were forced 'to go back to their land less honourably than they came'.[19] If Hakon had not been defeated, neither had he achieved the diplomatic settlement on which success depended.

It had originally been Hakon's intention to return to Norway, but the onset of winter and the state of his own health made him decide to remain in

34. *The Bishop's Palace, Kirkwall, from St Magnus Churchyard. Only the lower level of the palace within which King Hakon died in 1263 remains. The palace was reconstructed by Bishop Reid who added the Moosie Tower. He also developed Broad Street as a cathedral precinct and accommodated the Grammar School on a site now occupied by the buildings below the palace.*

Orkney. The 20 ships which stayed behind with him were laid up, some at Houton and some at Scapa, and arrangements were made to billet crews in country areas in proportion to the number of *urislands* in each district,[20] while King Hakon himself took up residence in the Bishop's Palace. The palace in which he spent the last few weeks of his life was later much altered by Bishop Reid, but the original foundations are still visible. It was an elegant building, probably dating from the time of Bishop William the Old (1102–1168), and the whole upper story consisted of a great hall.[21] It was here that King Hakon died in the depths of an Orkney winter. The saga tells us that, tiring of Latin books, the king ordered the sagas of the kings of Norway to be read to him beginning with Halfdan the Black. In the early hours of 18 December the king died, just after *Sverre's saga* had been completed and the story of Norway had been brought down to the beginning of his own long life. His body was temporarily interred in St Magnus Cathedral, then in spring it was taken back to Bergen for permanent burial.

Early in 1264 those leaders who had remained in Orkney attempted to open negotiations in which Henry, Bishop of Orkney, played an important part, but the mission was not well received by the Scots. Meanwhile Ogmond *krakadanz* ('Crow-dance') was sent from Norway to take charge in Orkney, bringing with him instructions for the defence of the Hebrides. He discovered, however, that there was a Scots army in Caithness exacting punishment for the separate peace which had been made with Hakon, and there were rumours that the Scots intended to invade Orkney.[22] So Ogmond refused to let help be sent to the Hebrides where the advancing Scots met little resistance. The Manx were also ready to surrender. The Scots were preparing to invade the Isle of Man when King Magnus of Man arrived in Dumfries, prepared to do homage to Alexander III on condition that he was given refuge in Scotland if the Norwegians ever returned.[23] It was only in the north that resistance was successful; King Dougal of Garmoran defeated the Scots in Caithness, killing their sheriff and seizing goods which the Scots were carrying off.[24]

By the time that the Treaty of Perth was concluded in 1266,[25] those who once had held land from King Hakon had mostly submitted. The settlement recognised the inevitable: Norway resigned the Isle of Man and all of the Hebrides, but on the express condition that Scotland recognised that Orkney and Shetland remained Norwegian—the treaty stated 'the King of Norway has specially reserved them for his own dominion'.[26] The terms of the transfer of the Hebrides involved the purchase of the islands, as first suggested by the Scots in 1244. A lump sum of 4,000 marks was to be paid in four yearly instalments, and thereafter the annual sum of 100 marks was to be paid in perpetuity—a payment which came to be known as the 'Annual of Norway'. The Annual was to be handed over in St Magnus Cathedral, either to the Bishop of Orkney or to bailiffs appointed by the Norwegian king. Two hundred years later it was the non-payment of the Annual which provoked further tensions and ultimately led to the pawning of Orkney and Shetland (Chapter 14).

Earl Magnus III had initially answered King Hakon's summons and had travelled to Bergen to join the expedition, but in Orkney he disappeared as if into thin air. He was left behind to collect the fine which was levied on Caithness, but he had instructions to follow as soon as possible. Earl Magnus was important enough to be named first among those sailing from Bergen,[27] and *Hakonar saga*, being an official record of the voyage, often contains lists of names of those taking part at different stages in the campaign. Yet there is no mention of Earl Magnus at the Battle of Largs, he took no part in the arrangements for wintering in Orkney in 1263-4, he was not present at King Hakon's death, and he did not accompany the king's corpse back to Bergen. The defence of Orkney in 1264 was entrusted to Ogmond *krakadanz,* and

Earl Magnus, whose function as earl was to defend the islands when invasion threatened, is not mentioned, so he was presumably still absent. Clearly Earl Magnus had been at some pains to distance himself from the whole campaign.[28]

As the holder of two earldoms, owing allegiance to King Hakon for Orkney and to Alexander III for Caithness, Earl Magnus was in a peculiarly difficult position when his lords were at war. His initial reaction appears to have been pro-Norwegian but, in view of King Hakon's imminent arrival in Orkney, it could hardly have been otherwise. A clue to his behaviour is contained in the *Exchequer Rolls* for the sheriffdom of Inverness, where in 1263 and 1264 there are records of expenses in connection with 21 hostages from Caithness, and of fines imposed on Earl Magnus.[29] Since the Scots had plenty of warning of Hakon's coming, these hostages may have included Earl Magnus's immediate relatives, thus effectively neutralising him. Magnus's whereabouts between 1263 and 1267 remain a mystery: apparently he was not in Orkney, nor had he committed himself to the Scots. He may have been somewhere in his Caithness earldom, although it offered no safe refuge. His main concern was not to jeopardise his relationship with either king so that he could resume both earldoms when the trouble was over.

King Hakon was succeeded by his son, Magnus *lagebøte* ('the Lawmender') who was anxious to repair the breach, not only with Scotland, but with Earl Magnus. *Hakonar saga*, completed in 1265, was very much an official record of recent events likely to reflect the views of the new king,[30] and it is significant that it tactfully avoids mention of Earl Magnus's failure of allegiance. But it was equally natural that, as soon as possible after the Treaty of Perth, Earl Magnus should wish to return to a proper relationship with Norway, so we find him visiting Norway in 1267. The settlement between king and earl may have been based on the terms which King Sverre had imposed on Earl Harald Maddadsson some 72 years earlier when there had also been a failure of allegiance. Although the precise details are not known, it appears that Earl Magnus was allowed to renew his homage and received a new grant of Orkney, possibly subject to certain restrictions and the payment of a fine.[31] King Magnus must have been as keen as Earl Magnus to restore normal relations; to have had the Earl of Orkney go over permanently to Scotland as others had done would be a disaster.

After the loss of the Hebrides, Orkney's links with Norway, far from weakening, were probably at their closest ever. It is unfortunate that so little information has survived from the period 1267–1330. We may suspect that this was a time of considerable prosperity when the population reached its medieval maximum. It would be good to know more about how Magnus the Lawmender's Landlaw affected Orkney. The earls, the brothers Magnus

145

IV (1273–1284) and John II (1284–c.1300) seem, as far as we can see, to have had uneventful reigns as loyal vassals. Magnus IV visited Norway three years after he succeeded his father and was installed as earl in Tønsberg.[32]

High though the social standing of the Orkney earls might be, their usefulness was mainly confined to ceremonial occasions, especially those where their dual allegiance to Norway and Scotland could symbolise the improvement in relations between the two countries. The Treaty of Perth (1266) had been followed by the marriage of Alexander III's daughter, Margaret, to King Erik of Norway (1281) and, following the death of Margaret and her two brothers, Erik and Margaret's infant daughter was Alexander III's sole surviving descendant. Magnus IV's only recorded appearance in the Scottish parliament was in 1281 to seal a declaration that Margaret, the Maid of Norway, was the nearest heir to Alexander III.[33] Similarly Magnus V appended his seal on behalf of both his sovereigns when the Treaty of Perth was renewed in 1312. On the other hand his father had been absent on the more contentious occasion when arrears of the Annual of Norway were under discussion.[34]

The reception of the Maid of Norway was another occasion when John II's dual allegiance was of symbolic value. Alexander III was killed in 1286 when his horse stumbled on a Kinghorn cliff-top, and only the fragile life of his three-year old Norwegian granddaughter delayed the horrors of a disputed succession and the Scottish Wars of Independence. The four years before the infant-queen was brought to her new kingdom was a time of intense diplomatic activity, centring on proposals that she should marry Edward, Prince of Wales (the future Edward II of England) and so pave the way for a dynastic union of Scotland and England. Edward I did his best to ensure that the Maid was sent to England, and a ship was despatched from Yarmouth complete with such luxuries as rice, sturgeon, ginger and whale-meat which might tempt the appetite of the young queen.[35] Her father, however, insisted that she should be handed over the Scots in his own territory of Orkney. There were reports that King Erik intended personally to accompany his daughter, but in the event she was entrusted to Bishop Narve of Bergen. A succession of English messengers sent north to glean news of her coming were the first to hear alarming news of her serious illness or death. She appears to have died on or about 26 September 1290, either at sea, or shortly after her arrival in Orkney.[36]

Various entirely erroneous stories have gathered round the death of the Maid of Norway. A slab of grey marble near the south-east pier of the choir of St Magnus Cathedral was popularly believed to mark her place of burial,[37] and a cap and ribbons contained in a small wooden box discovered in a nearby pillar were once thought to have belonged to the Maid.[38] Yet, unlike King Hakon, Margaret was not even temporarily interred in the cathedral but was taken straight back to Bergen for burial.[39] There is also an unshakeable conviction among South Ronaldsay people that Margaret was brought ashore at St Margaret's Hope, although the story arises from nothing more than a coincidence of the name 'Margaret'. Curiously, the Maid later was regarded as a saint or at least a cult figure in Norway. In 1300 a suspiciously elderly woman turned up in Bergen claiming to be the queen and telling how she had been kidnapped during the voyage. This 'False Margaret' was declared an impostor and was burned at Nordnes in Bergen but, after her death, she was widely regarded as a martyr, and pilgrimages were made to her place of execution.[40]

The death of the Maid of Norway plunged Scotland into all the troubles of the Scottish Wars of Independence. Eventually Orkney was pro-Bruce in its sympathies, but initially Earl John II was one of the few magnates to back neither Bruce nor Balliol, probably because King Erik was also one of the claimants to kingship of Scotland, although he had little chance of success. Then in 1292 when King Erik remarried, his second wife was Isabella, sister of Robert the Bruce. In 1300 Earl John, himself a widower, was betrothed to the daughter of this marriage, the two-year-old princess Ingibjorg. Norway's Bruce connections were responsible for John's failure to do homage to John Balliol, and for being the very last to append his seal to the Ragman's Roll which he did, not at Berwick, but at Murkle in Caithness.[41] It appears that in the Balliol years he found it convenient to rely on the remoteness of his earldom and emphasise his Norwegian loyalties.

Angus and Strathearn

When Earl John died at an unknown date between 1300 and 1303 his heir, Magnus V, was a minor. Wardship both in Caithness and in Orkney was granted to Weland de Stiklaw, a Scot whose career made him equally acceptable to both Scotland and Norway.[1] Weland was a career administrator; he was first found in the employment of the Bishop of Dunkeld, and he also served Robert Bruce, King Robert I's father. His initial link with Norway was as one of the Scots who accompanied the Maid of Norway, and he later took part in the arrangements for the marriage of Isabella Bruce and King Erik. Thereafter he seems to have remained in Norway with the queen; he took part in a Norwegian embassy to Scotland in 1297, and in 1305 he was to be found as a royal councillor.

Welland de Stiklaw was eventually replaced in Orkney, possibly as a result of English complaints about the harbouring of Bruce fugitives during the Scottish War of Independence. The pro-Bruce Bishop of Moray was certainly in Orkney in the winter of 1306-7, and there is a tradition that King Robert himself was in the islands where he was hospitably entertained by the laird of Halcro.[2] That was the time when, according to legend, Bruce was in Rathlin Island drawing moral conclusions from the perseverance of spiders. In fact his whereabouts that winter are unknown, except that he was in an island refuge. Orkney would have been a natural retreat, but modern opinion is dubious of the theory that the spider he was observing was Orcadian.[3] Even more doubtful are stories of the laird of Halcro distinguishing himself at Bannockburn with 300 Orkney men, and of the ghostly figure of St Magnus as a knight in shining armour galloping through the streets of Aberdeen, then miraculously crossing the Pentland Firth to bring news of the victory to Orkney.[4] These stories nevertheless correctly reflect the pro-Bruce sympathies of both Norway and Orkney during the Scottish Wars of Independence.

Weland de Stiklaw's successor as Governor was Sir Bernard Peche, who was caught up in the Scottish wars in a way which remains unclear. In 1312 when the Treaty of Perth was renewed, it was necessary to sort out a series of outstanding problems between Scotland and Norway resulting from an invasion of Orkney by unnamed 'malefactors'. A meeting in Inverness, at which

King Robert was present, dealt with the question of compensation. Sir Bernard had himself been captured, his goods stolen, and he was forced to redeem his life with the rents he was collecting on behalf of the King of Norway. The depredations of the Scots had extended to Shetland, but the question of compensation for damage done there was left pending further enquiries.[5] In retaliation Patrick Mowat, an esquire of King Robert, had been seized in Orkney; he was beaten and imprisoned in chains, his property was destroyed and he had to purchase his liberty for a ransom of 40 marks sterling. King Robert was not personally responsible for the attack on Orkney, but agreed to pay 600 marks in settlement, a sum which suggests that the damage was extensive. As a further goodwill gesture Robert confirmed the payment to St Magnus Cathedral of £5 a year from the customs of Aberdeen to provide bread and wine for use as mass elements.[6] This gift, perhaps originally made by Alexander III at the time of the Treaty of Perth, (1266), regularly appears in the *Exchequer Rolls* for the remainder of the Middle Ages.

Magnus V was still a minor during the attack on Orkney, but he must have come of age by 1312 when he was a witness to the renewal of the Treaty of Perth and the agreement about compensation.[7] His rule as an adult earl may have lasted about ten years. His final act was to append his seal to the Declaration of Arbroath (October 1320),[8] but the likelihood is that he was dead by August of the following year when Robert I complained that a Scottish traitor, Alexander Brown, had been given refuge in Orkney. Sir Henry Sinclair, the Scottish baillie in Caithness, had demanded Brown's surrender in accordance with the 1312 agreement, but his request was refused. King Robert directed his complaint about this unfriendly action, not to Magnus V, but to 'the baillies [plural] appointed by the King of Norway'. The probability is that Magnus V was dead, and Orkney was once again ruled by royal officials. It is possible that these officials were governing Orkney during another minority; it has been suggested that Magnus V may have left an heir who died c.1330 while still a minor, since the question of the succession appears to have become an issue only around that date; in December 1330 we find Margaret, Simon Fraser's wife, described as one of the heirs to the earldom of Caithness.[9]

Magnus V's widow, Countess Katherine, was involved in interesting land transactions in South Ronaldsay which are the subject of letters of 27 March and 4 April 1329.[10] The properties were in two groups. The first consisted of land to the value of £45 which had been adjudged to Earl Magnus for a debt owed by 'Herra Hoskull' to the earl's father, and which Magnus then bestowed on his wife. The transaction illustrates the apparently quite common practice whereby earls acquired land as a result of money owing to them, often for the non-payment of skat. The second group of properties consisted of Stews, Cleat, Thurrigair, Brough, Lykquoy, Hoxa, 'Kvikobba' and the Pentland Skerries.[11] This estate had belonged to no less a person than the Norwegian regent, Erling Vidkunnsson, who had inherited the land from his deceased Orcadian wife. This is one of the few examples of an estate owned by a Norwegian landowner, and it contrasts with Shetland where much land was owned by absentee Norwegians ('the Lords of Norway'). The sale of the regent's Orkney property was conducted by Herra Sigurd Jatgeirson who had some kind of official position—probably he was the sysselman then governing Orkney. A feature of both groups of property was that their extent was described in terms of their purchase value in *marks* rather than in pennylands (1 mark = £⅔). These 1329 letters are the first indication of the later ubiquitous land unit, the 'mark of land', and clearly illustrate its origin. In most cases the 1329 purchase value of the land in marks was the same as the number of marks of land which the property was described as 'containing' in the 1492 and 1500 rentals—a mark of land was originally the amount of land which might be purchased for one mark of money. The appearance of these new land units is generally taken as evidence that the growth of population and the expansion of arable land had been so great that the older ouncelands and pennylands had become variable in size and value, and therefore they were unsatisfactory for the purpose of buying land (see Chapter 15).[12]

With the extinction of the Angus line, the earldom eventually passed to Malise, Earl of Strathearn, whose great-grandmother was Matilda, daughter of Earl Gilbert. The Sinclair *Diploma*, a fifteenth-century document which traces the genealogy of the earls, describes Malise as:

> …lineally succeeding …as lawful heir by the law of heritage to both the earldoms of Orkney and Caithness as the records, evidence and charters of confirmation of the kingdoms of both Scotland and Norway most clearly show.[13]

The *Diploma* has no comparable statement about a search for documents when other earls succeed, so it seems that a lengthy investigation was needed because of the remoteness of Malise's relationship to the previous earl. Such a thorough examination suggests that Malise was not the only candidate. One of the other claimants may have been Simon Fraser, whose wife, Margaret, in 1330 claimed to be one of the heirs to yet another partition of the Caithness inheritance resulting from the division of the property among female heiresses.[14] In the light of the complexity of the enquiry and the need to find an earl acceptable to both Scotland and Norway, there was probably a gap of several years before Malise was officially installed.

Malise was earl not only of Orkney, but also of Caithness and Strathearn. In Caithness, however, his share of the earldom lands was much reduced by their division among heiresses, with the result that the Caithness earldom

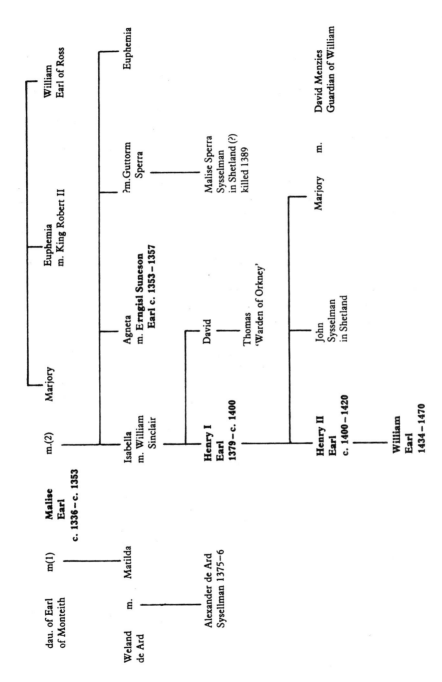

35. *Stratthearn and Sinclair Earls, c.1336-1470.*

ceased to be an effective political unit. Then in 1343 Malise's position was further weakened when his Strathearn earldom was forfeited. Malise had been tried for treason in 1338-41 because of his dealings with Edward Balliol and Sir John de Warenne and, although he was acquitted, he was deprived of Strathearn which was granted to Maurice Moray.[15] When Moray was killed at Neville's Cross in 1346, effective control, and eventually the title of earl, passed to Robert the Steward (the future Robert II).

As Malise's prospects of regaining Strathearn receded, his interests became increasingly identified with the north. His second marriage was to Marjory, sister of William 5th Earl of Ross, and this brought him into a political group linked by intermarriage, which included William of Ross, Robert the Steward and John, Lord of the Isles. The result was that Malise was a junior member of a 'Highland Party' which David II found troublesome when he was released from captivity in England.[16] Malise found a powerful ally in the Earl of Ross, whose own succession was delayed by an absence in Norway—perhaps at that time he was actively engaged in promoting Malise's candidature for the Orkney earldom.[17] Malise had five daughters but no sons, and a year after the loss of Strathearn he entered into an agreement with William of Ross whereby Isabella, the eldest daughter of his second marriage and William's niece, was designated heir in Caithness in preference to his daughter from his first marriage (1344). At the same time William of Ross was given the right to dispose of Isabella in marriage, in return promising to defend Caithness as faithfully as he would defend his own earldom.[18] A little over a week later the Earl of Ross spoke before parliament in favour of Malise's claim to Strathearn.[19] It seems that Malise's main aim was to recover Strathearn, although there was little either he or the Earl of Ross could do to reverse the grant to Moray. Strathearn was a lost cause, but Ross's support in Caithness may have been of real value. William exercised his right over Isabella by giving her in marriage to William Sinclair, and so it is as protégés of the Earl of Ross that the Sinclairs were introduced to Orkney. It is a proof of the importance of Malise's island earldom that two of his remaining daughters made Scandinavian marriages: Agneta (or Annot) married the Norwegian-Swedish nobleman, Erngisl Suneson, and another daughter married Guttorm Sperra who was a member of a Swedish family with landed interests in Shetland.[20]

The death of Malise c.1350 resulted in a complicated succession dispute which was not resolved for nearly 30 years. The dispute can best be followed with reference to Fig.35. Malise's was survived by five daughters but no sons. A male heir would have inherited all his father's lands and could expect to be recognised as earl both in Orkney and in Caithness, but when there were only females the lands and possessions had to be divided between them, and it was not clear what rights any of their husbands had to be recognised as earl. Malise's lands in Caithness and Orkney were consequently divided into five parts, but neither Alexander de Ard, the son of Malise's eldest daughter, nor Henry Sinclair, son of his second daughter and designated heiress, received the title of earl, which went instead to his son-in-law, Erngisl Suneson. Both Alexander de Ard and Henry Sinclair were probably minors at this time, and in any case Norway may have preferred an earl whose Scandinavian origins made him less open to Scottish influences. However, the brief rule of Erngisl Suneson (c.1353-7) is likely to have been fraught with difficulties: unlike all previous earls, he ruled merely by right of his wife, and her landed estates comprised only a part of Malise's property;[21] in addition Erngisl had been intruded contrary to the intentions of the late Earl Malise who had designated Isabella as his heiress, and therefore must have expected that her son, Henry Sinclair, would eventually be given the title. In 1357 Erngisl was deprived of the earldom, earning the distinction of being the first earl to be dismissed.[22] It has been suggested that his Swedish origins may have led him into opposition to King Magnus Ericsson;[23] on the other hand, it is possible that his reign was terminated on the death of his wife (we know that she died at a date prior to 1360),[24] or simply that his tenure of Orkney had become impossible. As late as 1388 Erngisl was still describing himself as 'comes Orchadensis' ('Earl of Orkney'), but by then his connection with the islands had long since been terminated.[25]

Following the removal of Erngisl Suneson, Duncan Anderson, a Scot who held the guardianship of Alexander de Ard, informed Orcadians that his ward was 'the true and legitimate heir of Lord Malise' (1357). As the son of Malise's eldest daughter, Alexander had a strong claim which he pursued for nearly 20 years, although he ended up with nothing. His guardian warned Orcadians that the Orkney revenues, which in the absence of an earl had been sequestrated by the King of Norway, should not be sent out of Orkney until he had the opportunity to present the heir, which he hoped to do very soon.[26] The dismissal of Earl Erngisl and the proclaiming of Alexander de Ard's rights was accompanied by real or threatened disorder in Orkney. In December 1358 David II issued instructions to the Sheriff in Inverness and to the Coroner in Caithness prohibiting travel to Orkney except for purposes of pilgrimage and commerce.[27] It appears that hostile intervention in Orkney's affairs was feared, presumably from Duncan Anderson on behalf of Alexander de Ard, but perhaps equally from the Earl of Ross on behalf of his niece and her son, Henry Sinclair. It is likely that Orcadians when faced with these threats had appealed to Norway, which in turn had asked David II to intervene in the interests of peace.

In the same way as there was increasing direct control of secular matters, the Norwegian church in the first half of the fourteenth century was also more

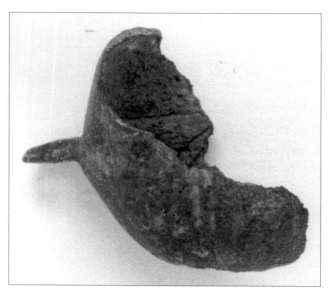

36. *Hawk's Bell. This tiny hawk-bell from Cubbie Roo's castle in Wyre is a reminder of the importance of falcons. William III (Bishop of Orkney) was one of those who enjoyed 'the boisterous pastime of hunting' and, at a later date, royal falconers were constantly employed in the islands to capture and train young hawks.*

frequently involved in Orkney affairs. At a provincial council held in Bergen in 1320 a series of complaints was made against William III (Bishop of Orkney 1310–c.1328). Kormak, an archdeacon in Sodor, and Grim Ormson, a priest in Trondheim, had been sent to Orkney by the archbishop. They reported that Bishop William had squandered the property of the see, and had bestowed the offices of the church on foreigners and apostates; he had compromised the dignity of the church by participation in the boisterous pastime of hunting; he had been careless in the exercise of his spiritual office, and had not sought out those who practised idolatry, witchcraft and heresy. Bishop William had also imprisoned Ingilbert Lyning, an Orkney canon whom the archbishop had authorised to enquire into the collection of Peter's Pence, and he had deprived him of his prebend. The bishop was also accused of misappropriating 53 marks sterling, and of refusing permission for the corpse of an Orkney woman to be buried in Trondheim.[28] In 1321 Bishop William was suspended, after which we find the archbishop directly appointing priests in Shetland,[29] but he was soon reinstated and in 1324 he was in Norway assisting at the consecration of a Norwegian bishop. Then in 1327 Bishop William promised the archbishop of Trondheim 186 marks in sextennial papal tithes, to be paid in instalments over three years.[30] In the same year he was informed that Bishop Audfinn of Bergen had appointed an agent to collect 'Sunnifumiol' (Sunniva's meal), a small grain payment which Shetlanders paid to St Sunniva's shrine in Bergen 'on account of the fertility of their soil'.[31]

It is not obvious what lies behind such omnibus complaints against the bishop or to what extent charges of laxness ought to be taken at face value. The accusation that offices were bestowed on foreigners indicates that there was a desire to counter Scottish influence within the Orkney church and to exercise a greater degree of direct control. It is significant that the two priests appointed by the Archbishop of Trondheim to Shetland churches while the bishop was suspended were both Norwegians from the diocese of Bergen, rather than Scots who were beginning to dominate the Orkney church.[32] The failure to pay Peter's Pence, a papal tax which was collected in Norway but not in Scotland, may also be a symptom of Scottish affiliations; Peter's Pence had been a cause of dispute in Caithness at the close of the twelfth century when it became a test of the relative strength of Scottish and Norwegian influence (see Chapter 8). The other point to emerge even more clearly is the desire of the archbishop, and the Norwegian church generally, to maximise their income from the islands.

Bishop William IV was involved in a bitter dispute with the king and his officials which lasted for a dozen years or more, and which resulted in a complete breakdown of their relationship. The breach had still not been resolved at the time of the bishop's death in 1382. In 1369 we first find Bishop William embroiled in a complicated feud with Hakon Jonsson, the Norwegian sysselman. Evidently the quarrel continued, since a subsequent sysselman, Alexander de Ard (1375-6), was required to report how the contest between himself and the bishop was turning out. Finally when Henry Sinclair was installed as earl in 1379, one of his installation promises was an undertaking that he would make no alliance with the Bishop William. The dispute throws a good deal of light on the workings of Orkney society, and the part played by the bishop, the sysselman and the Lawting. Unfortunately, although a legal decision of a Commission of the Lawting has survived,[33] this document only partly describes the circumstances, and so we cannot entirely understand the issues which were at stake.

The bishop's opponent, Hakon Jonsson, was a formidable official: he was related to the old Norwegian royal house (Sverrætten) and was also King Hakon VI's closest relative. During his long career he was often to be found as an effective collector of money on behalf of the Crown.[34] The settlement which was made between Bishop William and Hakon in 1369 illustrates how, even in a case involving people as important as the bishop and sysselman, a Commission acting under the authority of the Lawman and Lawting could achieve a negotiated solution, or at least attempt to do so. Both sides appear to have nominated 12 arbiters, and bound themselves to accept their decision. The commissioners were not entirely drawn from the 'goodmen' who were the actual members of the Lawting, but included a number of clerics, no doubt representing the bishop, and there were also some relatively obscure people. Interestingly, at least two of the commissioners, Sira Christian of Tain and John of Dounreay, were from outside Orkney.

The Commission's main judgement was that the bishop was to pay Hakon Jonsson 141 true gold nobles and also the butter which he had impounded in his store. Since Hakon was then to be held accountable to the king for this payment, it obviously represents rent or other revenue which in the absence of an earl were due to be paid to the king. The mention of butter makes it likely that the disputed payment included the *butter skat*, detailed records of which appear in later rentals (see Chapter 15). We do not know why these royal rents were in the hands of the bishop: perhaps they were arrears due from the bishopric estate in the aftermath of the Black Death, or the bishop himself may have been the royal rent collector before the arrival of Hakon Jonsson. Barbara Crawford has further suggested that the debt might be an instalment of the 'Annual of Norway' which Scotland was obliged to pay in St Magnus Cathedral and which the bishop might have misappropriated.[35] We do not know whether the 141 nobles represented the total sum which Hakon claimed—the settlement was on the whole hostile to Hakon, so very likely he had to settle for less than he considered to be due to him.

The dispute had resulted in violence between the supporters of the bishop and the sysselman. Some of Hakon Jonsson's men were arrested by the bishop and their property seized. The arbiters did not altogether condemn the bishop's arrest of these men which they described as 'a lawful investigation of their crimes', suggesting that the bishop intended to prosecute them in a church court. Hakon reacted in like manner, prosecuting the bishop's men including clerics, and the violence spilled over into Shetland where Hakon (or more probably his wife) had property.[36] The negotiated settlement involved the unconditional release of all those who had been arrested by both parties, and the restoration of their property. The Commission recognised that the bishop and his men might continue to have recourse to church courts in purely church matters, but it was made clear that in disputes between the bishop and sysselman, or between their tenants, each side should make atonement 'after the law and custom of the country'. The Commission was asserting the authority of the Lawman and Lawting to settle disputes, however powerful the parties might be.

The Commission's decision reveals a desire to limit the power of the sysselman. It was agreed that henceforth the bishop and 'rikest men' of the country in Orkney and Shetland should be 'first and foremost in all councils according to the laws and customs of the country'. The 'rikest men' were the 'goodmen', the members of the leading families who by tradition composed the Lawting. The statement that they should be 'foremost' is a Home Rule declaration, hostile to the control which Hakon had exercised on behalf of remote central government. It is interesting to see that the bishop, despite the church's Scottish links, was regarded as an ally of the Lawting and as a supporter of Orkney interests. However, arbitration has to appear even-handed, and the warning that the bishop should have 'good native men about him' is an indication of the continuing unpopularity of Scottish clerics. The decision of the 1369 Commission may not have been the end of the story. An endorsement on the back of the 1369 document thought to be in a fifteenth hand refers to 200 nobles owing by the cathedral to Hakon Jonsson.[37] Then again, on the day that Henry I was installed as earl (2 August 1379), he promised to pay Hakon Jonsson two instalments of 100 nobles,[38] and in 1389 Henry promised to pay him £140 sterling in three instalments, payment to be made at St Magnus church, Tingwall, and he used the revenues and escheats from Sanday and Ronaldsay to guarantee payment.[39] These financial dealings cannot be properly understood and, if these further payments refer to the same debt, Hakon had a long wait for what was due to him.

The Orkney earldom had been abeyance ever since the death of Earl Malise c.1350, apart from the brief period when it was entrusted to Erngisl Suneson (1353-7). Erngisl's rule had not been a success, but rule by a Norwegian sysselman had also created tensions in the local community which the attempted arbitration between Hakon Jonsson and Bishop William did not permanently resolve. The restoration of the earldom in the person of Alexander de Ard was apparently seen as a possible solution, and the long traditions of the Orkney earldom probably made it difficult to resist his claim as son of Malise's eldest daughter (see Fig.35). However, the appointment which Alexander received in June 1375 was for one year only, and it was made clear that he was given Orkney, not as earl, but as an official. At the end of the year Alexander was to appear in Norway to assert by what right he claimed 'the lordship or earldom'.

Part of the difficulty about accepting Alexander as earl seems to have involved his Scottish interests. He might claim a right to the earldoms of Strathearn and Caithness, although Strathearn had been forfeited in his grandfather's time and was not likely to be restored, and his lands in Caithness were not extensive. It was not so much that Norway feared Alexander's Scottish interests which in practice amounted to very little, but that Robert II intended to take advantage of Alexander's Orkney ambitions by withholding his support until he had stripped Alexander of his Scottish possessions. Thus four months before his appointment as sysselman, Alexander was at

Scone where he surrendered the Castle of 'Brathwell' (Braal) and all the lands in Caithness which he had inherited from his mother.[40] A few weeks later, also at Scone, Alexander resigned his 'entire right and rightful claim to Strathearn', an earldom which he did not actually possess but to which he had a hereditary claim.[41] In both cases David Stewart, the king's son, was the beneficiary. Then during his year as sysselman Alexander surrendered three *davachs* of land in Banff,[42] and a further three davachs of Garthyes in Sutherland, both of which were probably inherited from his father. The beneficiary on this occasion was another son of Robert II, Alexander Stewart ('the Wolf of Badenoch').[43] It seems that Alexander de Ard had voluntarily surrendered all or most of the Scottish property which he owned or might claim on the understanding that he would then be allowed to inherit the Orkney earldom. The delay in appointing Alexander as earl may have been because Scottish approval was withheld until these transactions were complete. However, it is also possible that King Hakon was not particularly keen to resurrect the earldom, and at the very least he may have insisted on the same detailed investigation of Alexander's claim as had been undertaken when Malise had inherited.

Although Alexander de Ard, being a potential earl, was an unusual sysselman, the terms of his appointment are the best description we possess of what, in the absence of an earl, the office of sysselman entailed.[44] He was to be head of the country and its guardian, acting on behalf of the king, and was given everything which pertained to the kingdom and earldom, 'nothing excepted'. He had custody of all the earldom lands and all the revenues which belonged to the earldom. One half of this income was to be sent to Bergen where his accounts were audited. He was allowed to retain the other half, but this was not clear profit since he had to meet the expenses of his administration, including the payment of the officials whom he was authorised to appoint and dismiss. He was also allowed all money derived from fines with the exception of *ubotamal,* serious offences which were in theory irredeemable and which were reserved to the central authorities. He was entrusted with dispensing law and justice; this involved apprehending criminals and bringing them to trial before the Lawman and the lawrightmen who in lesser cases acted as lay judges.

Alexander's commission as sysselman consisted of a brief Latin document, but it was accompanied by a letter in Norwegian addressed to 'all men in Orkney' which set out the terms of Alexander's appointment in more detail.[45] The expectation was that the Lawman would read the letter at a meeting of the Lawting, or make its contents known in other ways. Besides describing Alexander's authority (and emphasising its limitations) the letter also set out the role of the community: if either foreigners or natives threaten the rights committed to Alexander, the Lawman and people were enjoined to be obedient and helpful in matters regarding the security of the country; the bishop and royal liegemen were particularly enjoined to assist. An enigmatic clause informed the Community that at the end of Alexander's year as sysselman he was to report to king and council 'how the contest between the Bishop of Orkney and him is turning out'. It seems that the struggle between local interests and central government was continuing. Tensions of this kind, and the time-limited nature of Alexander's office, no doubt made his trial year a difficult one, while the mention of threats from 'foreigners' suggests that the opposition of Henry Sinclair as son of Earl Malise's designated heiress was expected. There is no indication what went wrong, but Alexander's rule was not regarded as a success. His appointment was terminated, probably at the end of the trial year, and at the latest by August 1379 when his cousin, Henry Sinclair, was installed as earl. Alexander de Ard had been heir to three earldoms, Orkney, Caithness and Strathearn, but ended up by losing all of them.

12

The Sinclair Earldom

Henry Sinclair belonged to a family of landowners whose main property was the barony of Roslin some eight miles south of Edinburgh.[1] Although they remained rooted in the Lothians, the Sinclairs had over the previous half century been developing interests in the north. In 1321 Sir Henry Sinclair was the Scots baillie in Caithness whom we met in the previous chapter, vainly demanding the return of the traitor, Alexander Brown.[2] Perhaps he was then managing the earldom of Caithness in the absence of an adult earl. Then in 1364 we find Thomas Sinclair similarly employed in Orkney where he was 'Baillie of the King of Norway', again at a time when there was no earl.[3] Apart from their careers as stewards, the Sinclairs owed their advancement to the patronage of the Earl of Ross.[4] We have seen that Earl Malise had entrusted the marriage of his daughter, Isabella, to her uncle, William, Earl of Ross, at the same time designating her as his heiress (1344). Isabella was married off to William Sinclair whose son, Henry Sinclair, was the future earl.[5]

On 2 August 1379 Henry Sinclair was at Marstrand, a Norwegian town near the present-day Göteborg, from where he announced that he had been installed as Earl of Orkney and acknowledged the terms on which he had been appointed.[6] He had rendered fealty to Hakon, king of Norway and Sweden, kissing him on the hand and mouth, and he had been admitted as a royal councillor after which the king appointed him to rule over Orkney. If Alexander de Ard's appointment is the best account of the role of a sysselman, the installation of his cousin, Henry Sinclair, describes in considerable detail what was required of an earl in the final century of Norwegian rule.

Prominence, at least in theory, was given to Henry's military function. He promised to defend Orkney from hostile attack, not only by commanding Orkney forces, but by mobilising the whole strength of his kin, friends and servants—he was expected to call on his Scottish followers if need be. Interestingly, he was required to defend 'even the land of Shetland' which was a Norwegian possession, but not actually a part of Henry's earldom. His military duties were not confined to Orkney and Shetland but, if he was given three months notice, he was obliged to appear in person with 100 well-armed men for service outside the islands in order to take part in offensive as

37. **Kirkwall and the Peedie Sea.** *The Oyce or 'Peedie Sea' formed Kirkwall's medieval harbour and extended almost to the west door of the cathedral. It is now much shrunk in size, and the part of the town west of the main street is built on reclaimed land.*

well as defensive operations. His duties were carefully defined, but so were the limits to his authority: despite his role as defender of Orkney, his terms of appointment forbade him to build castles or construct fortifications without express permission. He was forbidden to begin any war, litigation or quarrel which might damage the Kingdom of Norway, and he promised not to violate treaties which had been entered into by the king.

A further set of clauses described the way in which Henry was to govern the inhabitants and the conditions on which his tenure of the land depended. He promised to 'cherish' the people, both lay and cleric, rich and poor, according to their rights, and to govern them according to national law and local customs. If the earl was responsible for any offence against any of the inhabitants involving loss of life or serious injury or the confiscation of property, he was to be answerable to the king and council. It was also made clear that the earldom was held in trust: Henry was forbidden to sell any part of it or to alienate any of the lands or rights he had received, nor was he allowed to mortgage its lands without the permission of the king.

Henry's installation document contains no mention of annual payments to the Crown, and in view of the detailed nature of his promises and the Crown's urgent need for money, it seems certain that *skat* (tax) would have been mentioned if annual payments were to be made. It therefore seems likely that Henry as an earl retained the entire amount and also kept the profits from fines. We have already seen that, when Duncan Anderson was earlier advancing the claim of Alexander de Ard to the earldom, he had tried to prevent the rents being sent out of Orkney.[7] The implication is that, had Alexander been earl, the rents would have remained in Orkney for his use, but when the earldom was vacant the revenue was sent to the king. Henry made no promises about annual payments but he undertook to hand over a lump sum of 1,000 gold nobles, the payment to be made at Tønsberg before the feast of St Martin (11 November) of the same year. Perhaps because of the reduced state of the islands following the ravages of the Black Death, Henry had been able to purchase his installation by this large one-off payment. If Hakon Jonsson, Alexander de Ard and perhaps other recent sysselmen had failed to deliver the proper annual revenue because of abandoned land, reduced population, disruption of trade and local opposition, it may have become attractive to the Crown to agree to the restoration of the earldom in return for a lump-sum payment.

Henry's installation provides one of the few direct pieces of evidence that, in addition to the earldom estate, there were other lands in Orkney belonging to the Norwegian Crown. The extent of this *kingsland* is an unresolved problem: the view of Storer Clouston was that very extensive royal estates had existed in Orkney ever since King Sverre had confiscated the land of those who fought against him at Florevåg (1194), whereas modern opinion is inclined to believe that kingsland, whatever its original size, was not of great extent in the late medieval period (see Chapter 16). The royal lands were given into Henry's keeping, but the king wanted to ensure that they were not simply absorbed into the earldom; Henry was required to promise that he would not 'assume' the lands which 'the king and his progenitors had reserved for themselves'. He also had to promise that he would have regard for any 'special letters' which he might receive concerning their management. Despite the clear instruction that these royal lands were to remain distinct, they were in fact merged with the lands of the earldom and by the time of the 1492 and 1500 rentals they can no longer be distinguished.

The terms of Henry's installation show how much the earldom had changed since the twelfth century. The right to claim the earldom still remained hereditary, but actual possession depended on installation by the king who attached conditions to the earl's appointment. The expectation was that Henry was appointed for life, but it was made clear that he might be removed if he breached any of his pledges. On the death of the earl there was a requirement that the lands were to be returned intact to the king— great stress was placed on the integrity of the earldom, no doubt because of the problems which had recently been created by its division among Malise's daughters. Only a male heir had a right to inherit, but it was not an automatic right. If Henry had one or more sons then one of them (apparently not necessarily the eldest) had a right to claim the earldom, but the king equally had a right to delay his installation, or perhaps even to veto it.

One of the clauses in the installation charter was a promise Henry made with regard to his relations with the bishop who, being still on bad terms with the king, was not present at the installation ceremony:

> We promise we shall make no league with the Bishop of Orkney nor enter into or establish any friendship with him unless with the good pleasure and consent of our said lord the king, but shall assist him against the said bishop until he shall do what of right or deservedly he ought to do in those things in which our said lord the king desires, or may reasonably desire of the said bishop.[8]

It would have been helpful if the installation promise had been more explicit—we do not know what it was that the king required Bishop William IV to do. It seems that the long-running dispute between royal authority as represented by the king and sysselman and local interests as represented by the bishop, Lawman and Lawting had not been resolved. There was a fear that Henry might side with local interests against the king. However, Henry's relationship with the bishop was overtaken by events; only three years later (1382) *Icelandic Annals* record 'mournful tidings that Bishop William was slain in the Orkneys'.[9] It is unlikely that Henry was responsible, and indeed the fact that we are never told who was to blame suggests that the bishop met his death in an isolated act of violence rather than as the result of his long feud with the Norwegian authorities. The appointment of a successor was complicated by the Great Schism. Pope Clement VII in Avignon 'provided' Robert Sinclair ('de Santoclaro'), Dean of Moray and no doubt a near relative of Earl Henry I, who was 'unanimously elected' as bishop by the canons.[10] Scotland supported Avignon, but Norway's allegiance was to the Roman popes, and it was Norwegian influence which apparently prevailed, at least in the short term. There is evidence that the authority of the Clement VII of Avignon did not at that time extent to Orkney since he made no other provisions to parishes, vicarages, canonries or prebends in Orkney, nor does Robert Sinclair appear to have gained possession, since we find that he was first allowed to remain Dean of Moray and then was appointed Bishop of Dunkeld.[11] The bishopric went, not to Robert Sinclair, but to John, Rector of Fetlar, who was probably a Norwegian, but who seems to have failed to establish himself in Orkney because of local opposition (see Chapter 13).

It was also necessary to extinguish the claims of Malise Sperra and Alexander de Ard, who, like Henry Sinclair, had shares of Earl Malise's inheritance

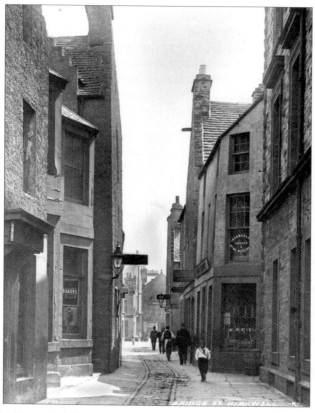

38. **Bridge Street.** *Kirkwall's narrow main thoroughfare, Bridge Street, Albert Street, Victoria Street and Main Street, was once a shore road skirting the Oyce or Peedie Sea.*

as a result of its partition among female heirs. It was made clear that Henry had an obligation to ensure that his cousins abandoned their claims: he was required to promise that Malise Sperra would 'altogether demit his rights, if he is known to have any to the said lands and islands.' Henry also had to promise that, if he made any compact or understanding with his cousin Alexander de Ard, he would similarly ensure that Alexander gave up his claim. The mention of a possible compact strongly suggests that such a compact actually existed and that Henry had bought out Alexander by some private arrangement. The king, however, was anxious to ensure that competing claims did not disturb the peace of the earldom, and that secret deals did not result in its division. Interestingly, Hakon Jonsson, who had been sysselman when arbitration had been attempted in 1369, was one of those who witnessed Henry's installation on behalf of the king.

Henry's installation was witnessed by nine friends and kinsmen who swore to uphold these conditions. Malise Sperra was one of the witnesses and he was also one of three hostages who remained behind until the conditions of Henry's grant were fulfilled (principally the payment of 1,000 nobles). Since Malise was a rival, it was desirable to obtain his oath to abide by the terms of the charter and, by detaining him as hostage for nearly a year, it was probably intended to allow Henry an opportunity to consolidate his position in his new earldom. Alexander de Ard, however, was not a witness and therefore cannot have been present. As a failed sysselman, he probably had few expectations of future patronage and he may no longer have been regarded as a threat. A further provision required Henry to obtain guarantees from the earls of Douglas and March, from the bishops of St Andrews and Glasgow and from a group of his Lothian neighbours and kinsmen.[12] These people were expected to ensure that Henry would not alienate or mortgage either the earldom or the crown possessions in Orkney. On 1 September 1379, one month after his installation, Henry had returned to Scotland and had already obtained the seals of the guarantors—he had been in a hurry to complete all the formalities well in advance of the St Martin's day deadline.[13]

Nothing further is heard of Alexander de Ard, but there was continuing hostility between Earl Henry and Malise Sperra.[14] In November 1387 Malise entered into an agreement with Earl Henry whereby he made his peace on very unfavourable terms. The agreement was drawn up in the presence of the Earl of Douglas (who was one of the guarantors to Henry's installation promises and so was acting in the way in which King Hakon had intended). Malise had to undertake to make payment for injuries to Henry's property while at the same time he abandoned any counter-claims which he might have against Henry.[15] Meantime Malise was involved in a quite different dispute about land in Shetland in which Henry is unlikely to have had an immediate interest. In 1386 the Bailie in Shetland reported to the authorities in Bergen that Malise, without legal judgement, had seized lands which once were the property of Herdis Thorvaldsdatter and now belonged to the rich and powerful Norwegians, Jon and Sigurd Haftorsson. Jon was the father of the former Orkney sysselman, Hakon Jonsson. Presumably Malise believed he had a hereditary claim on this estate as a result of some unknown family connection.

Although it might appear that Malise was losing out to his cousin, we find that two years later his situation was remarkably improved. In September 1389 Malise and Earl Henry were together in Norway where they both signed the accession document of King Eric the Pomeranian.[16] On a formal occasion of this kind, the presence of the Earl of Orkney was expected, but it is surprising to find Malise among the group of eleven signatories. His inclusion indicates that he had become a royal councillor and had probably been given some kind of official position. One possibility is that Malise was now Governor of Shetland. It seems likely that some new animosity between the cousins arose during this visit; immediately afterwards, apparently on the homeward voyage, Malise and seven of his followers were killed in Shetland by Earl Henry. The very presence of an Orkney earl in Shetland is surprising since it had been long separated from the Orkney earldom. The *Icelandic Annals* state that 'he had been previously captured by him', but it is uncertain whether Henry had captured Malise, or Malise had captured Henry.[17] A standing stone midway between Scalloway and the site of the Lawting in Tingwall marks the traditional site of the killing, and the location suggests the possibility that the incident was somehow connected with a legal dispute. According to *Icelandic Annals* one follower of Malise escaped to Norway in a six-oared boat. Henry's installation promise to defend 'even the Shetland islands' can hardly have been a basis for this kind of intervention, although we never hear of Henry being blamed for the incident.

The killing of Malise Sperra is part of Henry's 'Viking-image'—an apparent reversion to saga days when the feuds between competing earls ended in bloodshed. It has sometimes been supposed that Henry, having gained the earldom, ruled Orkney with little regard for his installation promises. This is suggested by the building of Kirkwall Castle: his charter forbade the building of castles and the construction of fortifications unless he had obtained permission, but it later transpires that the immensely strong castle was built without royal consent.[18] The reality or otherwise of this Viking-image is, however, only part of the problem: it has been Earl Henry's singular fate to enjoy an ever-expanding posthumous reputation which has little to do with anything he achieved in his lifetime. As a result of the fabulous inventions of van Bassan (charitably described as 'a very confident genealogist')[19] and the credulous work of Father Hay,[20] Henry became a 'Prince' and was credited with titles and honours which he never possessed and with a royal marriage which never took place. Van Bassan's exaggerated account of his authority also tells us that:

> ...he had power to stamp his own coine within his dominions, to make laws, to remit crimes: he had his sword carried before him wheresoever he went, he had a crown in his armes, bore a crowne on his head when he constituted laws, and in a word was subject to none save only he held his lands from the King of Noraway, Sweden and Danemarke...[21]

Roland Saint-Clair, author of *The Saint-Clairs of the Isles* (1898), was sceptical about some of these tales, but he combined his thorough knowledge of the documentary sources with a reluctance to abandon stories

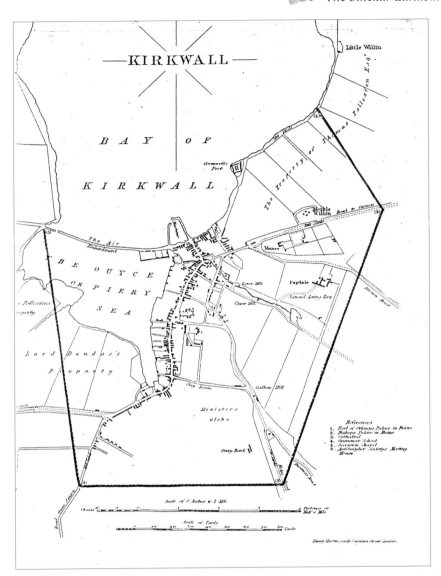

39. **Kirkwall.** *In the first half of the nineteenth century Kirkwall still exhibited all the components of the medieval burgh when a single shore road had linked the old nucleus around St Olaf's Church to the twelfth century developments around the cathedral and the fourteenth century Sinclair castle. Seven hundred years of reclamation had advanced the shoreline some 50-60 metres into the Oyce, and the prosperity of the Kelp Boom financed new harbour works and a certain amount of building outside the traditional limits of the town. Feus of the burgh commons led to much of the land in the vicinity of the town being enclosed. Leading out through the new fields was a radiating pattern of loans—grassy roads in some cases 100 metres in width.*

which reflected so well on his Sinclair ancestors. Another set of stories origi-
nating in the late nineteenth century credits Henry with a voyage to America
a century before its discovery by Columbus.[22] There is nothing in contemporary records to suggest that such a voyage took place, and the Atlantic
crossing does not even appear among the fabulous narratives of Van Bassan
and Father Hay.

Transatlantic contacts were not, of course, intrinsically impossible. The
Norse colony in Greenland was affected by the same climatic and economic
conditions which brought about the decline of medieval Orkney, but it did
not actually become extinct until c.1450. Known contacts with the British
Isles include the *Inventio Fortunata,* the record of the travels of an English
Minorite friar who visited Norse Greenland c.1360. What appears to be a
c.1330 version of the Campbell coat-of-arms has been found in Greenland
in association with fragments of chain-mail, and there are also items of adornment which are unmistakably English.[23] One possibility is that these objects
reached Greenland via Orkney, or perhaps they were transported by English
fishing expeditions which might have called at Orkney on the voyage north.[24]
There were even contacts of a kind at an official level: in 1389 we find
Hakon Jonsson, the former Orkney sysselman, taking action against traders
who had contravened the royal monopoly by going to Greenland,[25] and by
1394 Orkney had acquired a Greenland bishop. Bishop Henry, a Dane who
was absentee bishop of Gardar, exchanged sees with John of Orkney, although John like his predecessor never actually made the voyage to
Greenland. By the end of the fourteenth century Greenland was visited less
frequently, but it was still a well-known part of the Norse world.

It is not, however, valid to argue from these real contacts that we ought
to take seriously the fabulous voyages of the Venetian brothers, Nicolo and
Antonio Zeno. Those who believe in Henry's transatlantic voyage not only
accept the imaginary places and non-existent islands which appear in the
dubious Zeno narrative and the even more dubious Zeno map,[26] but modern elaboration of the tale supposes contacts with Nova Scotia which even
Zeno does not support. Furthermore any Orkney connection depends entirely on believing that a chief by the name of 'Zichmni' was none other
than Henry Sinclair, the name 'Zichmni' being optimistically interpreted as
a rendering either of 'Sinclair' or 'D'Orkney'. If Earl Henry was actually
Zichmni who plays a central part in the story, it is somewhat surprising that
Orkney is neither mentioned in the narrative nor shown on the Zeno map,
although the name 'Orcades' had been universally known ever since Roman
times. As well as the voyage to America, the narrative credits Zichmni with
campaigns supposedly fought in islands which have been identified as Shetland and/or Faroe, and this adds an entirely fictional element to Henry's
Viking image. The adventures of Zichmni are not consistent with what we

know about Earl Henry. Henry's fictitious trip to America continues to receive a good deal of unfortunate publicity, but it belongs to fantasy rather than real history.

The counter-view is that Henry was a Lothian gentleman of middling rank who was mainly an absentee from Orkney and was content to draw a modest income from his impoverished island estates. His earldom was certainly much reduced from the lands of the saga-earls; Henry was not earl in Caithness and Sutherland, nor was Shetland included in his Orkney earldom, and within Orkney the divided inheritance of Earl Malise meant that Henry's possessions were less extensive than those of any previous earl. Even before the Black Death ravaged the islands in 1349,[27] the economy was probably on a downward course and, with a declining population, worsening climate and a depressed economy, it is likely that Henry enjoyed a smaller income than his predecessors. We have also seen that, far from being an independent 'Prince' (an entirely spurious title), Henry was bound by an installation charter which placed all sorts of constraints on his authority.

Nevertheless it is possible to see how the legend of Henry as a magnificent 'Prince' originated: the Earl of Orkney occupied a unique position in Norway, and on ceremonial occasions he was second in precedence only to the Archbishop of Nidaros. In Scotland Henry was of middling importance—he is quite well documented as one of a group of gentlemen associated with the Earl of Douglas who played an active part in Lothian and Border politics—but he occupied a much grander position in Norway. In 1308 Hakon V had abolished the title of earl with the exception of the royal princes and the Earl of Orkney. As the only person entitled to the dignity of earl outside the immediate royal family, the Earl of Orkney occupied a unique if somewhat anomalous position. His role, however, was confined to ceremonial occasions and brought him no extra wealth or power. In the main Henry fulfilled this limited role in a conscientious way, and was quite frequently to be found in Scandinavia. He was present at Marstrand in 1379 for his installation as earl, and the gaining of the earldom had probably required previous visits to argue his case and to demonstrate his suitability. He may have been again in Norway the following year (1380), he was certainly present in 1388 when he acknowledged Eric of Pomerania as king,[28] and in July 1389 we know that he was at Helsingborg.[29] While he continued to be mainly concerned with his Lothian estates, he was not entirely an absentee from Orkney, and attended fairly regularly both to his Norwegian duties and to the affairs of his earldom.

The importance which Henry attached to his Orkney property can be seen by the way he was willing to trade outlying portions of his Scottish lands in order to gain advantages in Orkney. In 1391 he was in Kirkwall from where he issued a charter vesting his brother David Sinclair with the lands of Newburgh and Auchdale in Aberdeenshire in return 'for any right or claim in the parts of Orkney or Shetland falling to him by reason of Isabella of St Clair, his mother, or in any other way'.[30] Similarly in 1396 Henry obtained from his daughter, Elizabeth, and her husband Sir John Drummond a renunciation of any claim to a sister-share of property within the kingdom of Norway in favour of himself and his male heirs.[31] He may have been keen to prevent division such as had followed the death of Earl Malise, but his objective was probably more specific. He had no need to be concerned about the division of the earldom, since on his death it was to be returned intact and, if all went well, it would be granted to a single male heir. The fact that his brother gave up his rights in Shetland as well as in Orkney suggests that the lands Henry was trying to secure included the estates of the late Malise Sperra, and the presence of Shetland witnesses to the charter tends to confirm this interpretation. Over a century after the death of Malise, the 1503 Orkney rental, which seldom recorded the names even of contemporary landowners, considered it necessary to note that property in Enstabillie in North Sandwick and in Quham and Quandale in Rousay had at one time belonged to Malise.[32] Similarly in the *Exchequer Rolls* of 1438 there is a mention that certain lands in Banff had belonged to 'the former Lord Malise Speir'.[33] These references to Malise long after his death point to a particular interest in his property. Malise Sperra had died childless and, his parents being dead, his heir was his aunt Isabella, the mother of both Earl Henry and David Sinclair (see Fig.48). Henry was drawing a distinction between the earldom proper which he hoped his son would be given, and acquired land which was not part of the earldom, and would be subject to udal division if precautions were not taken to secure it for his son. This is the beginning of the distinction between the *bordlands* (earldom estates) and the *conquest lands* (acquired lands) which is given so much prominence in later rentals (see Chapter 16).

At an unknown date between 1396 and 1402 Henry was killed. According to the *Diploma*:

> ...he retirit to the parts of Orchadie, and josit [possessed] them to the later part of his lyfe, and deit [died] Erile of Orchadie, and for the defence of his country was slain there cruellie by his enemiis.[34]

The *Diploma* is at pains to stress that Henry was Earl of Orkney when he died and was in full possession of his earldom; it emphasises that he was then living in Orkney (but perhaps not permanently) and that it was in Orkney that he met his death.[35] The whole tenor of the entry is to stress the completeness of Henry's connection with his earldom, and therefore the undeniable right of his son to claim the title. Henry's death as a patriotic earl fighting 'for the defence of his country' is a further part of his image as an earl in the saga-mould. His death has been linked to an incident described by Holinshed when an English fleet fishing off Aberdeen was attacked by Scots and, in retaliation, raided some of the Orkney islands.[36] It is a reflection on his Viking-image that Henry may have met his death when his Norwegian earldom was mistaken for a part of Scotland.

13
Orkney at the End of the Middle Ages

When Henry I was killed and his son succeeded it was the first time in over a century when there was no interregnum or a disputed succession—or at least so it seems. There is, however, no record that Henry II (Earl of Orkney c.1400–c.1420)[1] was ever officially installed as earl, and indeed no certain record that he ever visited his earldom. His reign therefore marks a further stage in the development of a Scottish-orientated society. Henry II married Egidia Douglas, heiress of Lord William Douglas of Nithsdale and a granddaughter of King Robert II. He was a grander nobleman than his father, and more closely involved with Scottish court circles, with the result that his remote earldom was lower in his priorities. Given that Queen Margaret was then at the height of her power it seems unlikely that so important a matter as his installation as earl would have been allowed to go by default, but in the early years of his reign he would have found it difficult to visit Scandinavia: he was captured by the English at Homildon Hill in 1402,[2] then on his release he was briefly one of Robert III's key supporters when, along with Bishop Wardlaw of St Andrews and David Fleming, he was entrusted with the youthful Prince James (soon to be James I). The young prince was in Henry's keeping when on the voyage to France they were intercepted by the English off Flamborough and held in captivity (1406).[3] In the years which followed Henry was in and out of England on business connected with the James' imprisonment, then in common with several other members of the Scottish nobility, he spent some time in the service of the Duke of Burgundy.[4]

Yet there is no evidence that Henry was considered to be in breach of his proper allegiance or that he was blamed for neglecting his duties as earl. The way in which Shetland was entrusted to Henry II's brother, John Sinclair, indicates approval of Sinclair rule. In 1418 John was in Helsingborg where swore an oath of fealty to King Eric as liegeman and in return received a feudal grant of Shetland for life. His charter stated that the grant was 'in consideration of the fealty and obedience shown by his father and the rest of his kindred'.[5] The confidence expressed in the fealty and obedience of the Sinclairs was not just a form of words: the fact that John Sinclair received Shetland on terms which mirrored the life-grant by which the Sinclair earls

172

held Orkney, shows that the Crown was not dissatisfied with how Sinclair rule had hitherto operated, and regarded the arrangement as preferable to management by short-term officials.

Henry II had the good fortune to reunite the inheritance which in the absence of a male heir had been divided among Earl Malise's daughters. The remarkable chain of circumstances can be best be followed from Fig.48. The Sinclair *Diploma* describes how Isabella of Strathearn returned to Orkney and lived there continually after Henry I was killed. By the early fifteenth century Isabella must have been a great age, since her marriage had been entrusted to the Earl of Ross as far back as 1344.[6] She not only outlived her son Henry I, but she also outlived all her sisters, and her sisters' children. Thus the divided inheritance, which included the property of Alexander de Ard and Malise Sperra, reverted to Isabella as their nearest living heir. On her death Henry II consequently inherited everything from his grandmother except the title of earl in Caithness and those Scottish lands which Alexander de Ard had alienated.[7]

During Henry II's latter years the management of his Orkney property was entrusted to David Menzies of Weem. Menzies is one of the villains of Orkney history with an evil reputation which he probably deserved, although he suffers from the fact that most of what we know about him comes from his enemies. In his old age he became a monk at Melrose and was known to his descendants as 'Saint David', so there may have been a side to his character which was not obvious in Orkney.[8] David Menzies was Henry II's brother-in-law, being married to Marjory, daughter of Henry I. His family lands were in Atholl and Breadalbane but he seems to have made a career of estate management—after his connection with Orkney was ended he is found acting as Queen Joan's 'welbelufit' bailie' for the Appin of Dull and for lands around Loch Tay.[9] In Orkney, however, Menzies was never 'well beloved': he was a rapacious steward who had little regard for the limitations which Orkney and Norwegian law placed on his management of the earldom.

Trouble broke out towards the end of Henry II's life and involved the competing spheres of influence of David Menzies and Thomas Sinclair. Menzies was the earl's Orkney manager and business partner, but the position of Thomas Sinclair is less clear. He was Henry II's cousin,[10] and he held some kind of official appointment from the Crown.[11] Clearly Thomas Sinclair's appointment, whatever its nature, was deeply resented. While Thomas was absent in Scotland, one of his men was attacked on his farm by Menzies's men, beaten 'blue and bloody' and imprisoned in irons in the castle. On Thomas's return the *goodmen* (members of the Lawting) arranged a truce, on the expiry of which Thomas sought sanctuary within St Magnus Cathedral. Threatened even there, Thomas managed to slip out, and he convened a meeting at which he produced documents proving that the king had taken him under royal protection. He then rescued his followers from the cathedral, but not without bloodshed, and in the ensuing mêlée one of his nephews was killed. Much as in 1369 when the sysselman Hakon Jonsson had quarrelled with the bishop, the Lawman and *goodmen* endeavoured to resolve the quarrels of competing officials through arbitration: both David Menzies and Thomas Sinclair were 'to enjoy as much as they were respectively entitled to' (they were to adhere strictly to the terms of their appointments), and they were each to find twelve men to provide security that they would keep the peace.[12] Thomas Sinclair appealed, not to the king as might have been expected in view of his royal appointment, but to Henry II. On his arrival in Scotland, however, he discovered that Henry had recently died (probably 1 February 1420)[13] and that David Menzies had been appointed guardian of William Sinclair, his son and heir, who at the time of his father's death was not far short of his majority. In the meantime Menzies was to be 'speceall governor of said William's lands, rents, possessions and moveable guds in Orkynnay till he comis of age'.[14] When the news of the earl's death reached Orkney, Menzies completed his triumph by putting heavy fines on all his opponents—the twelve men who had stood security for Thomas Sinclair, those who had been with Sinclair in sanctuary, and also on those who had corroborated the terms of his appointment from the king.

The way in which David Menzies disregarded the arbitration of the Lawman and goodmen, and the high-handed way he meted out illegal punishments on his enemies, inevitably brought him into conflict with the Lawman and Lawting. Thomas Sinclair emphasised his Orcadian origins, so the dispute became a contest between the native community and an unpopular Scots steward who had exceeded his powers. The flashpoint was an incident when a kinsman of David Menzies was prevented from riding off on a horse which did not belong to him. The outcome was that the Lawman, William Thorgilsson, was seized on the street of Kirkwall and was briefly imprisoned in the Castle. On his release a party of Caithnessmen was sent to plunder, not only his farm, but also his private chapel, apparently with a view to forcing his resignation. Menzies was determined to gain possession of the Lawman's seal—the 'Sigillum Communitatis Orcadie'—which was used to authenticate the decisions of the Lawting and was the emblem of the Lawman's authority.[15] Several people whom he suspected of having hidden the seal were imprisoned, and William Thorgilsson himself was again arrested and kept in custody. Eventually his wife, rather than yield the Lawbook and seal directly to Menzies, placed them on the altar of St Magnus Cathedral. David Menzies took possession of these symbols of power, and used them to appoint a new Lawman, who apparently accepted the post with some reluctance.[16] It need hardly be said that Menzies' action was entirely illegal; his position as William Sinclair's guardian gave him no authority to appoint a

Lawman or indeed to interfere in the business of the Lawting. It is, however, as a result of his quarrel with the Lawting that we have such full record of his misdeeds.

Menzies continued to collect the Orkney rents for at least a further two years on the grounds that he had a right to do so as the guardian of the young earl.[17] He also retained possession of the Castle of Kirkwall, no doubt regarding it as Sinclair private property, although it had been built contrary to the condition of Henry I's installation which prohibited the construction of castles and other fortifications without royal permission. Menzies was ostensibly acting in the interests of his ward, but he also had an eye to his own profits. His management of the Orkney lands was, however, in breach of the requirement that, on the death of an earl, the earldom was to be returned to the king who would expect to appoint officials to administer the islands and collect the rents during a minority. That is what had actually been done as soon as the news of Henry II's death was known: Bishop Thomas Tulloch (Bishop of Orkney 1418–c.1461) was appointed governor. We find the bishop in Laaland, Denmark, in June 1420 from where he announced that he had received 'all the Orkneys with all royal rights' from King Erik, promising to give up the islands when the king required.[18] Although the terms of Thomas Tulloch's appointment appear comprehensive, and he had been appointed with due formality, Menzies did his best to evade the bishop's authority, continuing to occupy the Castle of Kirkwall and apparently claiming that, whereas the bishop had royal rights, the management of the earldom was not included in his grant. Two years later (1422) Bishop Thomas Tulloch received a further grant which was intended to clarify the position and strengthen his powers. He was given the Castle of Kirkwall in *slotsloven* (the tenure of a castle in trust for a liege-lord) and it was expressly stated that his grant comprised both the country of Orkney and also the earldom.[19]

The tensions between David Menzies as guardian of William Sinclair and Bishop Thomas Tulloch as the king's representative were further complicated by a breach between William and his guardian. That same year (1422) William arrived in Orkney to prepare for a visit to Copenhagen to establish his claim to the earldom. The visit was opposed by David Menzies who may merely have judged the approach premature, but who is usually suspected of wishing to prolong his own management for financial gain. Menzies did not prevent the voyage, but he ensured its failure. Since he now controlled the Community seal, he was able to prevent its use to authenticate a written statement of William's birth-right. A prospective earl on a visit to court also needed to be accompanied by a retinue of the *goodmen*, but Menzies' menaces appear to have prevented their attendance. So William sailed for Denmark lacking the documentary proof which was traditionally required and accompanied only by the Archdeacon of Shetland and by his uncle, Thomas Sinclair.[20] It is not surprising that he returned without having been installed as earl. William was later noted for his love of display and formal court etiquette, so he was probably acutely conscious of his failure to make a good impression—perhaps his youthful disappointment soured his relations with Denmark for the rest of his life. In the light of this unsuccessful visit there may even have talk that the earldom might be given to another member of the family. Later that same year (1422) James Craigie obtained a formal certificate from the Lawman testifying to his wife's descent from Earl Malise; the document also bore witness to his own reliability as a royal liegeman, and it described how he had 'endured many troubles' as a result of his support for Bishop John Pak (John of Colchester).[21] Bishop John was one of three Roman bishops during the Great Schism who had the support of Norway, whereas the bishop's adversaries probably included the earl and the local clergy who favoured the rival Avignon bishops. Although Craigie cannot have been a serious contender, he apparently thought that something might be gained by advertising his descent and making known his proven record of loyal service.

Menzies must have wondered what seeds of distrust had been sown in Copenhagen, so he hurried there the following year (1423) to put matters right. Like his nephew, he found it difficult to obtain convincing credentials. He asked for a letter sealed by members of the Lawting testifying to his good rule, which they were only willing to give if 24 of their number were allowed to accompany him.[22] Not trusting the evidence they might give, Menzies was nevertheless successful in obtaining the letter he needed while avoiding the threatened delegation. Menzies' mission was entirely successful: from Copenhagen he announced that he had received 'the earldom and country of Orkney, as much as there justly belongs to the kingdom of Norway, to manage, administer and preserve', on condition that he suffers no injury in the right and agreement he has with the father of 'the young lord, Junker William'.[23] 'Junker' William was William Sinclair, Menzies' ward. Menzies' reservation, however, was probably not only concerned with William's interests but also with ensuring that he himself continued to benefit from the profitable arrangement he had entered into with Henry II regarding the management of the earldom estates. Menzies' appointment was endorsed by Bishop Thomas Tulloch, 'so promise we too', and this has led historians into supposing that the bishop and Menzies had different spheres of authority and were acting in concert.[24] It is clear, however, that this interpretation is wrong: Menzies had replaced Thomas Tulloch as governor of the islands, and the bishop's seal was required as an acknowledgement that his appointment had been terminated. In similar circumstances Malise Sperra's seal had been appended when the earldom had been granted to

Henry I in 1379 in recognition that Orkney had been given to his rival. Since officials were often given charge of Orkney for relatively short periods, too much ought not to be read into the termination of the bishop's appointment after a three-year term. However, his replacement one year after it had been necessary to strengthen his powers by a second charter suggests that his rule had not been a success. It seems that Menzies had come out best in a power-struggle, and that the government had decided to back the winner.

It has been assumed that Menzies' period of misrule followed this royal grant. In fact his rule was over, and he never had the opportunity personally to exercise the power which he now legally possessed. On the return voyage from Copenhagen he forced the Orkney skipper, Thomas Brown, to take him to Scotland where the cargo belonging to Brown and his fellow merchants was illegally sold and the ship was detained so long that it was winter before she sailed for home. Menzies was not aboard when, on the voyage back to Orkney, the ship was wrecked and lives lost.[25] A few months later Menzies and William were both members of a Scottish delegation which visited the imprisoned James I at Durham. William had been with the king during the previous year when Menzies was in Copenhagen, and there had been talk of him as a possible hostage. However, it was Menzies who remained in captivity with the king from March 1424 until July 1425, part of that time being spent in the Tower of London.[26] It seems not improbable that David Menzies' selection as a one of the Scottish hostages was deliberately contrived by William to remove his obstructive guardian. While Menzies was imprisoned, William returned to Orkney (1424). He was favourably received by the Lawting, but met with a certain amount of opposition from Bishop Thomas Tulloch. Soon after we find the bishop pursuing his studies at the infant university of St Andrews, so he may have bowed to pressure to remove himself from Orkney while William consolidated his position.

News of the conflict reached Denmark, and the following year (1425) Queen Philippa sent her chaplain with a letter enquiring who was to blame for the recent trouble between William Sinclair and the bishop, and on what authority William had interfered in the government of the islands. The reply was sent on behalf of 'the canons, clerks, gentlemen and all others of your community of Orkney', under the Community seal which apparently was once again in the possession of the Lawman. The queen received a bland assurance that all disputes had been resolved through the good offices of the Lawman and Lawting, and she was told that 'the earl' had assumed power at the unanimous desire of the Lawting and with its consent. The royal summons to William and Thomas Tulloch to appear in person was met with the rather specious excuses that William was fully occupied with his Scottish affairs, and Bishop Thomas Tulloch was immersed in his studies at St Andrews.

The Community requested that the earl should be officially appointed as their governor. David Menzies was not mentioned directly, although in theory he was still entrusted with the government of Orkney and the management of the earldom. In practice he had been outmanoeuvred and replaced. The Community informed the queen that:

> ...we have been very often unjustly overborne by strangers who have been appointed governors in our affairs, sustaining innumerable losses, indignities and shame, wherefore... we earnestly entreat... that no judge or governor among us presume to introduce any new laws, customs or novel constitutions.[27]

What in fact was a coup by William Sinclair in which he outwitted his guardian and assumed the title of earl was presented as a return to legality. Perhaps William now controlled the seal as thoroughly as David Menzies once had done. Members of the Lawting, however, probably approved of William's assumption of power since they had a conservative and traditional view of how Orkney ought to be governed. Their ideal system of government was an earl who paid due regard to the local gentry, so that they could rule the islands together subject to royal approval.

The Lawman's reply referred to certain enclosures and this presumably included the famous 'Complaint of the People of Orkney' against David Menzies.[28] In 1424 investigations were being made into misrule by local officials in the Oslofjord region, and into peasant unrest in Vestfold and Borgarsysla, and it suited the Lawting to take the opportunity to cast similar doubts on the rule of David Menzies.[29] It suited Earl William to encourage such testimony: he had seized power illegally from Menzies who held Orkney by royal grant, so allegations of misrule by Menzies could be used to justify, or at least excuse his actions. So the complaints came pouring out. Evidence was produced relating to Menzies's attacks on Thomas Sinclair's servants, of how he had ignored Sinclair's royal accreditation, and the arbitrary fines he had imposed on his enemies. The 'Complaint' told how the Lawman was kept in prison until his wife had laid the Lawbook and seal on the cathedral altar, and how Menzies had used his possession of the seal to prevent William communicating with Copenhagen. The meal, tar, iron, kettles, pans and hemp which had comprised skipper Thomas Brown's lost cargo were enumerated to the value of £26 sterling. Evidence was produced of how Menzies had manipulated the rate of exchange for his own advantage. The story was also told how in a famine year Menzies had allowed nine shiploads of grain to be exported contrary to an agreement made at the Lawting that corn should be reserved for the local market. The 'Complaint' also repeated gossip about Menzies's heartless remarks when the inhabitants of South Ronaldsay were plundered by 'wild Scots'; when they complained that they would rather die than continue to suffer these attacks, Menzies had told them that 'they would die every day' as long as he had power over them. The raids were probably serious: the following year (1426) the Bishop of Oslo inspected David II's prohibition on Scots going to Orkney except for purposes of commerce or pilgrimage, which suggests that the re-enactment of this legislation may have been contemplated as part of the renewal of the treaties between Scotland and Norway.[30]

William continued to have difficulty in obtaining the title of earl despite the evidence of the 'Complaint' and the support of the Lawting. The way that William had seized power and was using the title of earl no doubt met with disapproval, particularly if, as seems possible, his father had also as-sumed the title without official installation. The next year (1426) Bishop Thomas Tulloch was in Norway, his studies at St Andrews apparently con-cluded, to take part in negotiations for the reissuing of the Treaty of Perth.[31] He may have given a more impartial account of recent events in Orkney than the version contained in the 'Complaint'. William was not present at these negotiations; his position was as yet unrecognised, and in any case Orkney earls traditionally avoided occasions when their dual allegiance might complicate diplomacy between Scotland and Norway. The Crown's official representative in the years before William's installation was apparently his uncle, Thomas Sinclair, whom we find described as 'Warden of Orkney'.[32]

It seems that it was at the request of James I that King Eric in 1434 eventually granted the earldom to William. His installation was preceded by a great search for charters and other documentary evidence, much of which, it was claimed, had been consumed by fire or destroyed in time of hostility through the lack of 'a sure house'—a none-too-subtle hint that William should be allowed to retain the castle. The investigation was conducted by Bishop Thomas Tulloch possibly as early as c.1425 following William's visit to Copenhagen when he lacked the credentials he needed to prove his right to the earldom. The resulting *Diploma* or genealogy was a careful piece of work, showing familiarity with sagas then preserved in Denmark, and trac-ing with considerable scholarship William's descent from the first Norse earls.[33] William's installation charter was modelled on that given to his grandfather Henry I in 1379, with the exception that the clause hostile to the Bishop of Orkney was removed. The castle which had been built without permission was to be returned to the king on the earl's death along with the rest of Orkney. In the event of the earl failing to fulfil his promises—and this was relevant for the future—William undertook to appear before king and coun-cil, failing which his earldom was to be forfeit.[34] In addition to the Scots guarantors which, like his grandfather, he had to provide, William was re-quired to try to persuade James I to affix his seal to the installation charter although, if the king was unwilling, he was absolved from this requirement.

That the seal of a foreign king was thought necessary to secure the future of Orkney was an indication of the extent to which Orkney had been drawn into the ambit of Scotland.

The point at which Orkney and Shetland were about to come under Scottish rule is a good time to review the way the government of Orkney had evolved in the post-saga period. The terms imposed on Harald Maddadsson by King Sverre following the Battle of Florevåg (1194) proved to be a turning point: Sverre's intention was that the semi-independent saga-earldom, which had previously been controlled only intermittently and mainly by divide-and-rule tactics, should become a regular part of the Norwegian state, and in this aim he was largely successful. Sverre's settlement was re-enforced but perhaps not greatly altered when in 1210 John and David ended the rebellion of their father's latter years, and when in 1267 Magnus III regularised his relationship following his failure fully to support Norway during King Hakon's Hebridean expedition. The importance of these treaties is confirmed by *Hirdskrå*, a document dating from c.1274 which sets out the customs and statutes governing the Norwegian nobility. It states that, when kings were appointing earls to the tributary provinces, they should have regard for the conditions imposed on Harald Maddadsson and Magnus III.[35]

The *Hirdskrå* also describes the oath which earls were required to take at their installation. The earl received a sword as the symbol of his duty to support the king, to defend the honour of the realm and punish injustice. He also received a banner which symbolised his title to the earldom and the delegation of 'dominium' by the king; he swore to be faithful and obedient, and to govern his earldom in accordance with the terms on which it was entrusted to him.[36] The *Hirdskrå* also describes the role of the earl in the government of the islands: he had a right rule over the part of the country which was entrusted to him; he had a right to the income from all royal property, but was not given ownership of it, so he was not permitted to sell land or to alienate it in any other way. Nevertheless there appears to have been a certain tension between theory and practice: although kings might claim that the earldom lands were merely entrusted to the earls for their lifetime, the division among the daughters of Earl Malise shows that in some respects the pre-Sinclair earls and their family were still able to treat the earldom lands as heritable property.

Defence and the administration of justice were the earl's main functions. The conditions described in *Hirdskrå* are essentially those on which Henry Sinclair received the earldom in 1379, so we may suppose that other thirteenth and fourteenth century earls were given Orkney on similar terms. The military role of the earl received prominence: when the earl and his men went to war in company of the king, they were all to be part of the same war-band of which the king was to be the leader. This, however, had become a chivalric fiction: the military assistance which Earl John provided to the 1230 expedition to the Hebrides was the last occasion when whole-hearted support was forthcoming, and even then neither the king nor the earl took a personal part in the campaign (see Chapter 9). In King Hakon's 1263 Largs campaign Magnus III had been less than fully committed, and in the last 200 years of Norse rule, the military role of the earls was limited to the defence of Orkney against occasional Hebridean raids. In addition to the rents, the earl had a right to the income from all penal fines provided he dispensed justice according to the law and with mercy. In the same way that large fines were imposed by Scots and Norwegian kings on the earls, it seems likely that fines imposed by the earls on those over whom they had jurisdiction may have been an important source of income.

During the 134-year period between the accession of Magnus V (c.1300) and the installation of William Sinclair (1434) the islands were without an adult earl for the greater part of the time. The minority of Magnus V and of his infant successor (if indeed he had one), and the brief minority of William Sinclair accounted for about 20% of the period, but there were even longer gaps when the earldom had been left vacant (approximately a further 43% of the time). In addition there were other periods of unknown duration when the earls had been absentees, apparently including the entire reign of Henry II. Between 1300 and 1434 an adult resident earl was very much the exception. It took time to install a new earl, especially if Scottish agreement was needed for a candidate who was also to be earl in Caithness, but there was also a distinct lack of urgency. Government could function quite effectively without an earl and there was also a financial incentive to perpetuate direct rule: a letter which was catalogued in Akershus in 1494 makes it clear that kings collected all the rents until the rightful heir appeared and received Orkney from the king.[37] Delays preceded the first earls of the Angus, Strathearn and Sinclair lines, and on each of these occasions the position of the Crown was further strengthened by its ability to select a candidate which suited its interests. As far back as 1236 Magnus II was chosen as a politically acceptable member of the Angus family, although he was perhaps not the nearest heir, and more recently it had been possible to pick and choose from among Malise's family. The undermining of the strict hereditary principle weakened the position of potential earls; it resulted in Alexander de Ard bartering land in the hope of Scottish support which failed to materialise, and Henry Sinclair apparently having to purchase the succession by a large lump-sum payment. And yet the hereditary nature of the earldom was respected to the extent that it was never granted to complete outsiders, in contrast to the Scottish earldom of Caithness which passed into the hands of Comyns and Stewarts who had no link whatsoever with the former earls.

The integrity of the Orkney earldom was considered important; had it been allowed to fragment like Caithness, it would inevitably have passed piecemeal to owners whose interests were predominantly Scots.

In addition to the earl, we find a variety of officials under titles such as sysselman, baillie, custos (guardian), höfudzmanne, ombudsman, foud and ministrii. There must have been a distinction between the role of officials who ruled the islands in the absence of an earl or during a minority, and those who had more limited powers when there was an adult earl. In Norway the office of sysselman dated from c.1160-1170,[38] so when Sverre imposed a sysselman on Orkney as part of the post-Florevåg settlement (1195) the office was still quite new. The appointment of sysselmen represented a step away from rule by the feudal nobility in favour of government by royal officials, which exactly suited Sverre's plans for Orkney. The *sysla* was an office rather than a fief: the sysselman could be dismissed, he was frequently moved, he operated under the control of central government, and his accounts were audited. In Norway the sysselman had responsibility for collecting royal revenue, organising defence, prosecuting criminals and implementing government decisions, but it was difficult for him to operate in exactly this way in Orkney where there was also an earl who had similar functions.[39] These tensions led to the killing of the sysselman, Arne Lorja, by Harald Maddadsson in 1202 or soon after, and to the murder in 1231 of Earl John by Hanef *ungi*. Thereafter it is only during the minority of an earl or when there was no earl that he hear of a sysselman, although in view of the scarcity of records we cannot altogether rule out the possibility that a sysselman was sometimes present alongside an earl.[40] Latterly the powers which Henry Sinclair received as earl were not greatly different from those which Alexander de Ard had exercised as sysselman, so by that date it is clear that earls and sysselmen no longer co-existed. Earl and sysselman had much the same function: admittedly the earl had a grander title and a more permanent appointment and he was not so immediately accountable, but ultimately he might be dismissed just like an official, as indeed was the fate of Earl Erngisl Suneson.

In the fourteenth century bishops had sided with local interests against the Crown and its representatives. We have seen that in 1369 Bishop William IV was involved in a bitter dispute with the sysselman, Hakon Jonsson, and that when Henry I was installed as earl in 1379 he was required to promise that 'he would make no league with the bishop... nor enter into any friendship with him'. Norway had been able to take advantage of the Great Schism to try to appoint a more amenable bishop. It foiled an attempt to install a Sinclair bishop in the person of the Scottish-backed Avignon candidate, Robert Sinclair, Dean of Moray, but whether Norwegian-backed Roman bishops were any more successful in gaining possession is less clear.[41] The

40. **Sigillum Communitatis Orcadie.** *The seal of the Orkney Community was used by the Lawman as a symbol of his authority and to authenticate decisions of the Lawting.*

fact that Robert Sinclair's Roman rival, Bishop John (Rector of Fetlar) was willing to give up the bishopric of Orkney in order to become absentee Bishop of Gardar in Greenland suggests that he had not established himself in Orkney,[42] and the 'many troubles' which John Pak suffered from 'his adversaries' suggest that he too met with local opposition.[43] It seems that during the Schism Orkney was often without a resident bishop of either persuasion. After the Schism bishops were Scots in origin, but they were nevertheless the most reliable supporters of the Norwegian Crown, and were consistent upholders of legality. The government had turned to Bishop Thomas Tulloch when faced with the disorder resulting from local opposition to David Menzies, and for a time the bishop had been given charge of the islands (1420-3). We find Thomas Tulloch acting with scrupulous correctness: he opposed the illegal seizure of power by William Sinclair, but when William made a legal attempt to claim his inheritance, the bishop helpfully researched the *Diploma* which set out William's genealogy. Thomas Tulloch was succeeded by William Tulloch (Bishop of Orkney c.1461-78) who was also a skilful and trustworthy servant, first, of Christian I and thereafter of James III. William Tulloch was also entrusted with the government of the islands when William Sinclair's loyalty was in doubt (1466-8), he assisted the smooth transfer of the islands to Scottish rule (1468), after which he managed the earldom estate on behalf of James III (1471-8).

Another key figure in the government of the islands was the Lawman.

The Lawman had a dual function. First, he acted as a royal judge, and in this capacity he had custody of the Lawbook, and he was adviser to the *lawrightmen,* the lay judges who dealt with routine cases. Second, the Lawman presided over the *Lawting,* the Orkney assembly, and he had custody of the Orkney seal, the 'Sigillum Communitatis Orcadie', which he used to confirm the Lawting's decisions and to authenticate documents issued on its behalf. As presiding officer of the Lawting he had the additional role of acting as spokesman for the community. The Lawman was recruited from the local gentry, probably being elected by the lawrightmen,[44] but his salary was paid by the Norwegian king and continued to be paid by the King of Scots: in 1476 the Scottish Exchequer accounts allowed the Lawman £48 for that year and the three preceding years, the payment being made by Bishop William Tulloch from the rents he was collecting on behalf of the Scottish king.[45] The Lawman was essentially a judge rather than an administrator but, because he was a paid official, he was occasionally used in an administrative capacity. The earliest Lawman known to us is Rafn, who was Lawman in Caithness c.1198–1222, and even at that early date he acted both as an administrator and as community spokesman. He was appointed one of three stewards briefly governing Caithness on behalf of King Rognvald Gudrodsson of Man, and he only narrowly escaped assassination at the instigation of Harald Maddadsson. Later Rafn was present at the burning of Bishop Adam and did his best to mediate between the bishop and the angry farmers. Rafn had Orkney relatives, so he was probably himself an Orcadian. His son, Andreas, later settled in Iceland and has sometimes been regarded as a source for some of the information which appears in the latter part of *Orkneyinga saga.*[46]

The Lawman operated in conjunction with the *goodmen* ('gentry').[47] The terms 'goodmen', 'best men' and 'rikest men' emphasise their social position, but they were also known as *roithmen* (*raðmen,* 'councillors') which reflects their role as members of the Lawting, and as *lawrightmen* from their function as lay judges.[48] The goodmen originally derived from the members of the earl's *hird,* and the January meeting of the Lawting even as late as 1574 was still known as the *Hirdmanstein* (*hirdmannsstevne,* 'hird court').[49] In Earl Paul's time (c.1135) *godings* such as Sigurd and Westness and Kugi of Rapness were related to the earls by blood or by marriage, and were placed in strategically-located bordland farms. These godings were primarily a warrior class, bound by ties of personal loyalty and by a strict code of behaviour; they were responsible for defence when invasion threatened, but they also had functions in connection with local administration and rent collecting. The earl's godings were still an active force in 1232, when as a group they sought revenge for the murder of their *hird*-patron, Earl John. The *Hirdskrá* set limits to the size of an earl's *hird,* and it was treason to exceed the stipulated number, but, after so many of them were lost in the Goding ship, the earl's kindred had already ceased to be of much consequence. It seems that the Angus and Strathearn earls had few relatives resident in the islands, and it was only towards the end of Norwegian rule that a numerous Sinclair gentry began to appear.

To a large extent the role of the earl's godings was overtaken by membership of the king's hird. Originally the hird was the king's personal war-band, comprising the royal bodyguard and household servants with ceremonial court functions. The earl's hird had been similar but, whereas it ceased to be effective after 1232, the king's hird had developed into something rather different. All royal offices were reserved for hird members ('håndgange menn', 'liegemen') who formed a political network and were organised as a brotherhood or guild with the king as patron, and so the hird became the basis for national and local government. The hird extended to the tributary provinces, and indeed even when it declined in importance in Norway in the early fourteenth century, the hird continued to be fully functional, not just in Orkney, but also in the other *skattlands* (Iceland, Faroe, Shetland, and Jemtland).[50] Membership of the hird was attractive to local gentry: it brought social prestige as well as positions of power. The gentry's first loyalties were therefore often to the king, rather than to the earl, and this was one of the reasons why Orkney could function effectively during the long periods when there was no resident earl.

After about 1300 Orkney emerges as a typical Norwegian provincial commune—the 'Communitas Orcadensis' (Orkney community).[51] For most purposes Orkney was managed by the Lawting consisting of 'the 24 best men in the country' presided over by the Lawman. The strongest efforts to integrate Orkney and the other tributary provinces were made about this time, but the system also devolved a good deal of communal self-rule with the result that the Lawting resented interference from officials in its conduct of public affairs. The members of the Lawting also functioned as lay judges, and they were frequently included in the commissions which attempted to arbitrate between disputing parties. Since membership of the Lawting conferred both power and social position, the *roithmen* tended to be selected from a limited number of influential families, and so the position became almost hereditary. The Lawting was not exactly a peasant democracy—it was a small self-selected group—but in Orkney udal estates were of only middling size, and since the Lawting provided a high degree of self-rule, it was as near to being a democratic system as one was likely to find in the late Middle Ages.

Although the Lawbook has not survived, some insight into the law is provided by the complaint about David Menzies's illegal acts. The Lawting petitioned that:

...their governors ...should be bound to observe the ancient laws approved by his Highness, King Olaf, and the ancient constitutions and customs, as well as the royal letters sent to us which are commonly called letters of law or rectitude, or corrective letters.[52]

Apparently the law was regarded as consisting of three elements: first, there were the 'ancient laws' which the Lawting believed had been sanctioned by St Olaf himself, but which actually were the Norwegian Landslaw dating from the reforms of Magnus *lagabote* ('the Lawmender', King of Norway 1263–1280). This formed the main body of the law. Second, there were 'ancient constitutions and customs' which related to the adaptation of Norwegian law to meet local circumstances in the same way as the 1298 Faroese *Seyðabrævið* ('Sheep Letter') had permitted the continuation of certain agricultural practices in Faroe despite King Magnus's law reforms.[53] Norway fully recognised this local element to the law; when Bishop Thomas Tulloch was appointed governor he promised 'to keep law and justice as the Norse Lawbook mentions and the old obligatory custom of the country hereto has been'.[54] The third element to the law was the 'letters of law or rectitude', also known as 'corrective letters'. The decisions of the Lawting were liable to correction and amendment on appeal, and these letters created precedents to which the Lawting would have regard in future cases.

We must suppose that the Lawting originally met in the open air as in Shetland and the Isle of Man—the place-name 'Tingwall' ('assembly field') in Rendall suggests a possible location.[55] But even in saga-times we hear of assemblies in Kirkwall, and latterly the Lawting met within St Magnus Cathedral. The main meeting, the Lawting proper, took place for one full week in June, the *Allhallow court* was held in November, and the *Hirdmanstein* in January. In addition the Lawman heard criminal cases at other times and in other places, and the members of the Lawting in their capacity as lay judges dealt with lesser offences. Latterly its legislative functions were limited, perhaps being restricted to imposing agricultural regulations and similar local measures rather than law-making as such. In saga-times the earl had used the assembly as a means of obtaining approval for his plans but, because later earls were frequently absent, they were not greatly involved in the Lawting, although they continued to have the responsibility of bringing criminals to trial. The earl, if he was in Orkney, might attend the more formal part of proceedings: for example, we find Earl William present at the Hirdmanstein in 1438/9 while oaths were being taken.[56] It was the business of the Lawting to take decisions which were binding on the community, and to receive and publicise royal letters. In addition there was a great deal of business of a minor nature, often connected with the sale of land,[57] disputes about run-rig, and the division of udal inheritance among heirs.[58] Since these matters might require on-the-spot inspection, much of the work was conducted through Commissions which reported back to the Lawting.

The last three chapters have been written using the pitifully few documents which have survived from the later Middle Ages out of the large number of charters, legal decisions and letters which once existed. They permit us to reconstruct an outline picture of the political history of Orkney and the way the islands were governed, but there is much else we would like to know about which written sources are silent. We know from a brief entry in *Icelandic Annals* that Orkney was 'ravaged' by the Black Death in 1349, but it is only from indirect evidence that we can guess at the scale of the disaster. It later is clear a good deal of land went out of cultivation, and that there was a shift from arable crops to more pastoral farming (Chapters 15 and 16). The Black Death was probably also a political turning point, marking the end of the integration of Orkney into the Norwegian state, and the acceleration of the process which led to the Scottish takeover of the islands.

In contrast to Orkney's rich archaeology from other periods, the late Middle Ages is comparatively blank. Medieval farms are difficult to investigate because most of them lie under present-day farm-buildings, but one relevant site is Tuquoy in Westray where the medieval site was abandoned because of coastal erosion. The most visible surviving monument is the twelfth century Cross Kirk, a superior building with a nave and chancel, and a dedication which perhaps became fashionable after Orkney's involvement in the Crusades (c.1151-3). Separated from the church only by a little stream which has now been diverted, a rectilinear hall has been found, with adjacent domestic and farm buildings including what was probably a smithy. The same close association of a church and hall is found at other sites, for example at the earl's residence in Orphir. A runic inscription similar to those from Maeshowe suggests a twelfth century date, but the site continued to be occupied into the fourteenth or fifteenth century, so it may be typical of the homes of Orkney's late medieval *goodmen*. The hall was built of mortared stonework, and is not particularly typical of Norway; the varied pottery assemblage from Scotland and northern Europe including the Low Countries shows that links were not exclusively Scandinavian, and that the Scottish connection was becoming more important.[59]

Whereas agriculture continued to be the mainstay of the economy, a number of places show the importance of fishing. Large fish middens have been investigated at Quoygrew, Westray, and at the St Boniface site in Papa Westray, and similar sites are found at Robert's Haven and Freswick Links in Caithness and at Sandwick in Unst. They reveal that cod, ling and related species were caught and beach-dried in quantities which may be comparable to the production of post-medieval commercial fishing stations in Shetland.

At the St Boniface site it appears that extraction of valuable fish-liver oil was also undertaken. The fish could have been for an Orkney market but the probability is that Orkney, like Norway, was engaged in a wider trade in stockfish.[60]

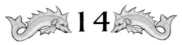

The Marriage Treaty and the Pawning of the Islands

The pawning of the islands in 1468 by Christian I of Norway and Denmark, who was short of the ready money to provide an adequate dowry for his daughter on the occasion of her marriage to James III of Scotland, marks a decisive point in the history of Orkney.[1] Yet the 'impignoration' (pledging) to Scotland was not a sudden event, brought about simply by a dynastic alliance. It was one step in a very lengthy process of Scottish penetration which had begun long before 1468. This chapter begins by looking at the broad picture of the changes to the North Sea world which the Norse had once dominated, before looking in detail at the politics of the pledging of the islands.

From the founding of the Orkney earldom its rulers had been inextricably involved in Scottish affairs. Some, like Earl Thorfinn, had extended Orkney rule over large parts of Scotland, and others, like St Magnus, had risen to power as Scottish-backed candidates for a divided earldom. When the earldom passed first to the Angus earls, then to Strathearn, and eventually to the Sinclair family, Scottish influence steadily increased. The fact that Earls of Orkney, until the mid-fourteenth century, had been vassals of the King of Scots for Caithness, encouraged Scottish connections and, ever since Norway lost the Hebrides, the position of Orkney had been potentially vulnerable. The possibility of transfer had been implicitly recognised as early as 1281 when it was stipulated that the islands would be ceded to Scotland if King Erik failed to fulfil his contract to marry Margaret, daughter of Alexander III.[2] The marriage took place, and Orkney's status was unaffected, but the use of the islands as a pledge served as a precedent in the somewhat different circumstances of another marriage treaty in 1468.

While the earldom itself was one channel of Scottish influence, the church was another. Although the bishopric of Orkney was still subject to Nidaros (Trondheim), bishops had shown a tendency to be influenced by Scottish practice from as early as the Peter's Pence controversy of 1320. At the time of the Great Schism (1378-1417), when Norway adhered to Rome and

Scotland to Avignon, the local Scots clergy seem to have created insuperable difficulties for Roman bishops.[3] By the fifteenth century the clergy seem to have been entirely Scottish, a situation which probably reflected the great scarcity of priests in post-Black Death Norway.[4] Since churchmen formed the bulk of the literate population, other symptoms of Scottish influence included the adoption of the Scottish calendar as early as 1312,[5] and the appearance in 1425 of the last official document written in Norwegian—43 years *before* the Impignoration.[6]

The transfer of the islands was thus a political expression of the growth of Scottish influences, but it also reflected changes in Norway's relationship to its overseas territories. In 1186 King Sverre had specifically mentioned Orkney merchants as being among those welcome in Norway since they brought 'such things as we cannot do without'.[7] The main cargo was grain which was increasingly in deficit from the twelfth century onwards. Two hundred years later Orkney traders were less assured of a friendly reception. With the founding of the Bergen *kontor*, the Hanseatic League, and particularly the merchants of Lübeck, established a stranglehold on Norway's external trade. The League shipped German grain northwards, to be exchanged for Norwegian stockfish. There was a prohibition on German merchants sailing beyond Bergen, the intention being to channel the trade of North Norway and the Atlantic Islands through the Bergen *kontor*.[8] Prohibitions on direct trade with Orkney and Shetland were frequently repeated, and continued to be issued even after the Impignoration, but they were increasingly ignored. A Lübeck merchant, Hinrich Sparke, was said to be the first to trade directly with Orkney at a date prior to 1423,[9] but regular contact failed to develop, in marked contrast to Shetland where there was the beginning of a long association with the German merchants. Shetland fitted easily into the trading pattern of the Hanse, having fish to sell and a need to make good a grain deficit just as in Norway. On the other hand, Orkney's grain surpluses are likely to have been seen as a disruptive influence and to have met the same obstructions as the League placed in the way of other competitors.

Hanseatic domination was compounded by the effects of the Black Death which struck both Orkney and Norway in 1349. There is no direct evidence of its effects in Orkney, apart from the statement in *Icelandic Annals* that Orkney was one of the areas ravaged by the plague,[10] but there is reason to believe that the reduction in population may have been substantial.[11] In Norway the consequences of the plague were catastrophic, resulting in demographic and economic collapse, and the loss of between one-third and half the population.[12] Then, at the end of the century, the union of the Scandinavian kingdoms shifted the centre of gravity southwards and eastwards to Copenhagen. With Norway itself becoming more peripheral within the new power structure, Orkney was increasingly remote, not just in physical terms, but also in terms of political priorities. In the years which followed, there was a reduction in trade with Iceland, and all contact with the Norse settlement in Greenland was eventually lost and the colony perished. In Orkney a good deal of land passed out of cultivation, and economic conditions possibly reached their low-point in the 1460s when the islands were pawned. As Scottish-orientated patterns of trade developed, it is not too much to say that the whole medieval structure of North Atlantic society was in a state of disintegration.

Yet the degree to which Scandinavian links were broken and Orkney subjected to a process of 'Scottification' should not be over-emphasised. There was at work an equally powerful process of 'Orkneyfication' whereby incomers not only conformed in an outward way, but were completely assimilated. The Scottish Sinclairs, Spences, Cromarties and Irvines were totally indistinguishable from those who bore Orcadian surnames such as the Fletts, Linklaters, Inksters and Rendalls. 'Orknification' was a process which affected even the ruling classes; earls as thoroughly Scots in their origins as Harald Maddadsson were easily absorbed. The clergy too, despite their Scots origins, remained in close contact with Norway and Denmark and, in the last half century of Scandinavian rule, they were the king's most loyal supporters. Nationality was not much of an issue, and race even less so. Whereas A.W. Johnston attempted to estimate the proportion of Norse blood in various earls, it is unlikely that the earls themselves would have seen much point to his calculations (according to Johnston St Magnus was $^{51}/_{64}$ Norse and $^{13}/_{64}$ Gael).[13] Johnston's absurd fractions are unlikely to be right but, even if they were correct, they would tell us little about the complex interaction between Norse and Scottish culture.

There is also the problem of knowing to what extent the upper strata in society—the people visible in the historical record—were typical of the population as a whole. The last official document in Norwegian may have appeared in 1443, but 300 years later a form of Norn still survived as a spoken language in country districts,[14] and even in the twentieth century significant remnants of its rich vocabulary were recorded by Hugh Marwick in his *Orkney Norn*. Even stronger evidence of continuity is to be found in the whole technology of rural life, recorded in detail in Alexander Fenton's *Northern Isles*. Likewise Ernest Marwick's *Folklore of Orkney and Shetland* shows how old habits of thought, superstition and story formed the continuing basis for the Orcadian's mental world. At the time of the Impignoration it is possible that the rural population was relatively immune from the Scottish influences which affected the upper classes.

By the fifteenth century earls had become decidedly alien figures. It is true that Earl William Sinclair's first entry into public life had been in Orkney where he had outmanoeuvred his ex-guardian, David Menzies of Weem, seized control of the islands, and bought pressure to bear on the Danish-Norwegian king to recognise him as earl. But thereafter William, like his father, was first and foremost a Scottish magnate, becoming thoroughly immersed in Scottish affairs, and one of the most consistent supporters of James I and James II. Despite his loyalty to the Crown, his Scottish interests were often delicately poised, and sometimes did not coincide with the aims of the king. In 1432 James I had sanctioned William's marriage to the rich heiress, Elizabeth Douglas, whose two former marriages had left her well provided with land. From her second husband Elizabeth held tierce lands in the Earldom of Mar (tierce, a widow's right to a life-rent of one-third of her former husband's estate). In addition she had the whole of Garioch, and there were also lands in central Scotland from her first marriage. James I's intention was to reward Earl William and at the same time to provide himself with an ally in the Earldom of Mar. However, William eventually was not able, or was not permitted, to establish himself in Mar in which James II took a personal interest. Legal proceedings were necessary in the 1450s to establish his wife's rights.[15]

William's marriage to Elizabeth Douglas, and the Scottish marriages of his father and grandfather, provided him with a host of Scottish relatives, including several branches of the Sinclair family established on landed estates in lowland Scotland. The important connection, however, was with the family of Douglas. William's mother Egidia, granddaughter of Robert II, was a Douglas, and his marriage to Elizabeth reinforced the alliance: she was a granddaughter of Robert III and sister of the all-powerful Earl of Douglas who dominated the kingdom during the minority of James II. The Douglas connection also brought an interest in Nithsdale and in the Sheriff-dom of Dumfries. This was another potential area of conflict since James II wanted to keep these lands in his personal control because of their strategic location in relation to English invasion. When dealing with these delicate Scottish matters, Earl William's Norwegian allegiance was no advantage and might easily cause suspicion. Earl William played down his Norwegian links and committed himself entirely to Scotland. It was, however, a policy which left him friendless when he fell from power during the minority of James III.

In the meantime Earl William was much in favour. He accompanied James I's daughter to France for her marriage to the Dauphin, and he represented the Scots king at the ceremony. The mission which he commanded had about 1,200 men, and the princess's personal attendants included 140 servants in royal liveries.[16] The lavish display on this occasion was a precedent for the extravagant dowry for which Orkney and Shetland were later pledged. Thereafter William was regarded as an expert on such fashionable occasions, and he acted as steward at the marriage of James II and Mary of Guelders.[17] His keen interest in chivalry was typical of the age, and he commissioned

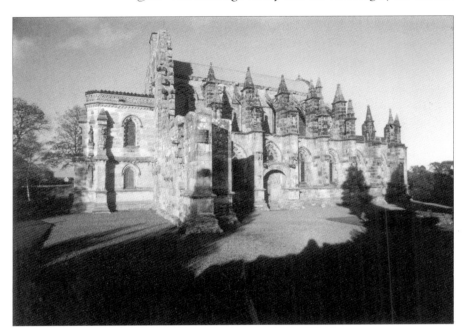

41. ***Rosslyn Chapel, Roslin.*** *Earl William's collegiate church founded in 1446 and decorated with 'a prodigality of enrichment'.*

translations of French treatises which were rendered into Scots as *The Buke of the Law of Armys* and *The Buke of the Ordre of Knychthede.*[18] Although Father Hay's eulogy of the Sinclair earls blatantly exaggerates the numbers in Earl William's train of followers,[19] Annie Dunlop remarked that it was 'essentially true as a description of the composition and etiquette of a great fifteenth century household'.[20] According to Hay the Countess Elizabeth had 75 gentlewomen serving her, all clothed in velvets and silk and with chains of gold, and she was accompanied by 200 gentlemen in all her journeys; at Roslin the earl had chambers richly hung with tapestries, and was attended in princely style by an elaborate household. The same love of the ornate is to be found in Earl William's collegiate church which he founded in Roslin in 1446, and which he decorated with such 'a prodigality of enrichment'[21] that it inspires the fanciful belief that it contains treasures as diverse as the Holy Grail, the secrets of the Knights Templar and evidence of the discovery of America. There were further signs of royal favour: in 1449, the same year as the king's marriage celebrations, William received a concession to import hides from Orkney without paying customs dues, and there were further privileges for his burgh of Dysart. The affairs of Roslin also prospered with the town's erection as a burgh of barony in 1456.[22]

The death of his first wife enabled Earl William to extricate himself from the potentially dangerous Douglas connection before James II set about the destruction of a family which had been over-mighty during his minority. By cutting his ties at the right moment, William emerged strengthened rather than weakened by the fall of the Douglases. He was entrusted with escorting 'the great bumbard' (perhaps Mons Meg) to lay siege to the Douglas stronghold of Threave.[23] In the next few years he and Bishop Kennedy of St Andrews were recognised as James II's principal counsellors.

In 1454 Earl William reached the height of his power when he was appointed Chancellor of Scotland. In the following year he received a grant of the Earldom of Caithness which had remained detached from Orkney ever since the death of Earl Malise a century earlier. In return William gave up claims to Nithsdale and the Marches which James intended to keep in his own hands. The Caithness grant was partly the rewards of office, but it is interesting to speculate what other reasons there may have been. James II's plans to acquire Orkney were already taking shape, so the move was probably intended to strengthen the king's position in the north by placing a reliable ally in Caithness and at the same time further binding Earl William to Scotland. Royal policy was eventually rather different: after the impignoration the personal control which the Scots king wished to exert over his new territories required the removal of William from Orkney. It has been suggested that the earl knew of the king's intention, and that Caithness was intended as compensation for the eventual loss of Orkney. However, it seems doubtful that the grant of Caithness in 1455 was expressly compensation for Orkney which William did not lose until 1470. Besides, had James II wanted William out of Orkney, it would have been advisable to remove him entirely from the region, rather than establishing him only a few miles away on the other side of the Pentland Firth. It seems that in 1455 Earl William was regarded as an asset rather than a liability. In the meantime Earl William's position in the north was strengthened by his second marriage; about this time he married Marjory Sutherland, daughter of the wealthy Alexander Sutherland of Dunbeath and a kinswoman of the Earl of Ross (Lord of the Isles).

The origin of the increasing tension between Scotland and Denmark, which must have been already apparent during William's time as Chancellor, lay in the payment for the Hebrides known as the 'Annual of Norway'. The 1266 Treaty of Perth by which the Hebrides were ceded to Scotland involved an initial lump sum and the yearly payment of 100 marks but, even before the end of the century, the Annual had fallen into arrears. In 1312 payment briefly resumed, and in 1426 the Treaty of Perth was reissued,[24] although there is no evidence that the Annual was subsequently paid.[25] Christian I 'of the leaking purse' saw the collection of these outstanding debts as a way out of his financial troubles, but his demands were strongly resisted by James II. It was against that pugnacious monarch's instincts to pay tribute to a foreign power; he particularly resented that he should be asked to continue to pay for the Isle of Man, an island he no longer possessed. Nevertheless it was a considerable sleight of hand to turn Scottish indebtedness into a successful bid to acquire Orkney and Shetland.

In this dispute Earl William, like so many of his predecessors, was trapped by his dual allegiance. He ceased to be Chancellor at some point during the winter of 1456-7. His loss of office was no doubt because his Scandinavian links were incompatible with the policy which James II intended to pursue. Arrangements were made through the agency of the French king to discuss the question of the Annual in Paris at 1457, but these talks were wrecked by a diplomatic incident in Orkney in the autumn of 1456. Björn Thorleifsson, Governor of Iceland, was on the homeward voyage to Denmark, accompanied by his wife and family and transporting royal and ecclesiastical rents. When a storm forced him to take shelter in Orkney his ship was seized, the Governor was imprisoned and his goods were stolen.[26]

The incident was hardly in the interests of diplomacy, and one possibility is that the capture of the Governor was deliberate mischief-making by Earl William with a view to souring relations between Scotland and Denmark, thus sabotaging any agreement which might affect his earldom. If this was the motive, the move was entirely successful since the opening of the talks on the question of the Annual were delayed for a further two years. Yet it was hardly in William's interests to wreck negotiations; he may have been aggrieved by the recent loss of the Chancellorship and by the frustration of his ambition in Mar and Buchan, yet in the long run he would be more secure if he could be rid of his dual allegiance. It has also been suggested that the entire incident was 'a bizarre hoax' concocted by Christian I with a view to influencing diplomatic relations with Scotland and France.[27] Perhaps all that had happened was that the storm-stayed vessel had been threatened by local people who were always on the look-out for plunder. Perhaps the whole incident was deliberately blown out of proportion.

The postponed meeting about the arrears of the Annual eventually took place in July 1459 under the supervision of Charles VII of France. Nothing was settled, but it was probably at these talks that the suggestion was first made that a solution might be found in a marriage of Prince James of Scotland and Princess Margaret, daughter of Christian I. When the two parties met at Bourges in 1460 both had already informed Charles VII that a marriage settlement offered the best hope of resolving their differences. The Scots, however, adopted an unexpectedly hard-line position: they demanded not only the cancellation of all arrears of the Annual, but also that Orkney and Shetland should be ceded and that Margaret should bring 100,000 crowns for 'her personal adornment'.[28] The Danes were taken aback by these outrageous demands since, not unnaturally, they had assumed that they were the aggrieved party as a result of Scotland's failure to pay the Annual. Then news came of the death of James II, killed by the bursting of a gun while he was besieging the English in Roxburgh. Although this did not bring an immediate end to the talks, all sense of urgency went out of the crisis.

It was apparent that Earl William was not directly blamed for the incident involving the Icelandic governor. Soon after he was a member of a diplomatic mission to England (1459),[29] and he now became one of an inner circle entrusted with the care of the eight-year-old James III. Whereas Earl William remained closely involved in Scottish affairs, his relations with Norway and Denmark became ever more tenuous. Homage to King Erik was a condition of his installation promise in 1434, and this homage ought to have been renewed to each successive king. Bishop Thomas Tulloch attended the coronation of King Christopher in 1440, but Earl William was not present although, as the senior vassal, he would normally have been expected to attend. Tentative arrangements were made for a meeting between king and earl in Bergen in 1447, but the likelihood is that the meeting never took place.[30] Homage was never renewed to Christian I and over the next dozen years there was a remarkable lack of contact. The tenuous relationship was symptomatic of the distancing of Orkney and Scandinavia in the changed political and economic conditions of the fifteenth century, but Earl William no doubt was positioning himself in preparation for the impending takeover by Scotland.

The negotiations at Bourges and Scottish demands for the transfer of the islands to Scottish rule awakened Christian I to the weakness of his position, and he now made repeated attempts to secure the allegiance of Earl William. Early in 1460[31] John Nory, a royal chaplain, was despatched to Orkney with letters requiring the earl's presence. William may have been keen to avoid such an obvious display of his Norwegian allegiance, but it would genuinely have been difficult for him to visit Copenhagen at that particular time. He did not reply directly, but Thomas of Kyrkness and John Mager, bailies of Kirkwall, excused the earl on the grounds that he was in his Caithness earldom repelling the attacks of 'our old great enemy', John MacDonald, Earl of Ross and Lord of the Isles.[32] The bailies' letter seems to indicate that attacks had been continuing for some time, perhaps ever since William had received his Caithness earldom five years earlier.

A MacDonald history attributes Earl William's feud with the Lord of the Isles to a dispute about the magnificence of their respective households. It tells of the splendid breakfast which was intended to impress Earl William and how, in order to thwart MacDonald's pretensions, the Earl of Orkney sent his servants through the streets of Edinburgh to prevent anyone selling food and fuel to him.[33] While personal animosity may have been a factor, the way in which William represented royal power on the boundaries of the Earldom of Ross was the real cause of friction. Following the death of James II in August 1460, the situation became a good deal more serious and Orkney itself came under attack. The Lord of the Isles seized royal revenues in Inverness and embarked on the policy which was to lead to dangerous links with England and with the disgraced Douglases, culminating in the treasonable Treaty of Westminster-Ardtornish (1462). Earl William, on the other hand, 'was personally residing with the most serene Prince James for the purpose of keeping his royal person during his tender age',[34] so he represented the government which the Lord of the Isles was conspiring against. Perhaps Orkney was regarded as an easy target, especially if the earl was absent. The Islemen believed that 'the common people are no great warriors, whatever their gentry are'.[35]

The attack which was launched on the Orkney Mainland in June 1461 was led by Hugh of Sleat,[36] a brother of the Lord of the Isles. MacDonald sources describe how the Orkneymen were waiting on a headland, but the Islemen were able to land without opposition on the other side of a long inlet (perhaps farther into Scapa Flow). The outcome was that the Orcadians were defeated amid great slaughter.[37] The MacDonald account, however, tells of the death of the Earl of Orkney (who manifestly was not killed and indeed was not then in Orkney)[38] so the details of the invasion have to be treated with some scepticism. However, a letter which the newly-elected Bishop William Tulloch wrote to Christian I later in the same month reported the attack in broadly similar terms; he told the king how the Islemen had:

> ...entered in great numbers with their fleets and boats in warlike manner... and burned your lands, towns, houses and buildings to the ground, and most cruelly destroyed your people of both sexes and all ages with the sword, and carried away with them their goods, animals, plenishings, jewels, money and everything they could for their own use; leaving little or nothing but the burnt soil of the ground, empty and useless.[39]

It seems that the bishop's letter, besides reporting the raid and how it had 'emptied his diocese', was in answer to a second summons to Earl William to appear in the royal presence. The bishop conveyed the earl's excuses, but promised that he would himself visit the king as soon as possible, which he did in the following year. Both the bishop and John Nory, the Danish royal chaplain, could report the genuineness of Earl William's problems in 1460 and early in 1461, but by September 1461 when he served on an embassy to England seeking better relations with Edward IV,[40] a visit to Copenhagen would have been equally possible. And yet there was no final breach; the earl made his excuses and he expected these excuses to be accepted.[41] Earl William chose not to attend in person, but he did not entirely neglect his Scandinavian interests. An entry in the 1503 rental records that Sir Hugh of Rendall had been given four pennylands in Avelshay, Rousay, as a reward for going to Norway on Earl William's behalf.[42] The payment was a generous one, and suggests that at some stage Sir Hugh had been involved in a lengthy and important mission.

In December 1461 there was a third demand from Christian I that William should appear in person. A date was set, St John's day 1462, and if the earl still failed to attend, it was stated that the penalties of Norwegian law were to apply.[43] The exact nature of these penalties remained vague, but William's installation charter contained a clause that his earldom was to be forfeited if he failed to honour its conditions, one of which was to attend the king when required to do so. The earl yet again ignored a royal summons and, although the evidence is indirect, it seems that he was deposed and his earldom was forfeited. It is known that about this time a copy of William's installation charter was made, suggesting that his legal status was under investigation.[44] Then, one month after the St John's day deadline, Bishop William Tulloch swore an oath of fealty to King Christian and promised to be the king's loyal councillor.[45] He promised to report any 'hidden designs', and henceforth he was described as the king's *iuratus* (sworn-man) with respect to Orkney.[46] It looks as if he was given the powers which would be exercised by a sysselman in the absence of an earl. The gift of certain skats provided him with an appropriate income, and at the same time deprived Earl William of his Orkney revenue.[47]

The king's other ally was the Lawman whose function was strictly speaking that of the chief legal officer, but whom the king in his search for supporters tended to use in an administrative capacity. It is evidence of the strength of local institutions that some semblance of normality and good government was preserved by the bishop and Lawman despite all their problems—the hostility of the earl, threats from Scotland, the increasingly distant relations with Denmark, the depressed economic conditions, and the damage caused by the recent raids. In 1466 Christian was again in contact with the Lawman, who was still evidently struggling to maintain the king's rights in the islands; the king wrote:

> We well note your good heart and mind towards us, that our annual rent from Orkney could be enjoyed yearly as is befitting, and that your goodwill is in no manner lacking, but you meet encroachment and opposition.[48]

The king's letter summoned the Lawman to Copenhagen in connection with matters which 'should be discussed by word of mouth rather than in writing'; the Lawman was required to consult with the bishop to whom a separate letter was sent. Originally the bishop had also been summoned to Copenhagen, but was excused the journey because of the expense. The 'encroachment and opposition' no doubt came from Earl William who was able to prevent the rents being sent out of the islands.

The matters which were so secret that they could not be committed to writing probably concerned new proposals for the marriage of James III and Princess Margaret. There are indications of Scottish interest that same year (1466) when Parliament debated the perennial question of the Annual.[49] Earl William played no part in the promotion of Scottish claims. He had been central to the Scottish government at the very beginning of James III's minority, but he was now out of public life and had no connections with the ruling Boyd family. Having committed himself to Scotland, he found he had no Scottish friends just when he most needed them.

In early 1467 a further violent incident in Orkney threatened to upset the delicate diplomacy between Scotland and Norway-Denmark. Bishop William Tulloch was taken from his church, put in prison, bound in chains and forced to take certain oaths,[50] presumably to renounce the office he had received from Christian I. This was said to be the work of William, only son of Earl William by his first marriage. Young William ('The Waster') was of doubtful sanity; in 1482 he was officially declared to be 'incompus mentis et fatuus' and to have been in that state for sixteen years, that is from the year before the imprisonment of the bishop.[51] The incident may have been the work of a mentally unbalanced young man, but another possibility is that it was a repeat of the tactics of 1456 when the imprisonment of the Icelandic Governor had interrupted the marriage negotiations. However, it seems that Earl William had nothing to gain by postponing a final settlement. The cause of young William's outburst is more likely to have been animosity resulting from the way the bishop had supplanted his father. With the gate of the Sinclair-held castle barely a hundred yards from the west door of the cathedral, a sudden angry confrontation was a distinct possibility.

On this occasion violence in Orkney did not interrupt the negotiations. In January 1468 the Scots parliament agreed to the sending of an embassy to choose a bride for James III, while in May Christian I staked out his negotiating position with strongly worded demands that the arrears of the Annual should be paid. The embassy included Bishop William Tulloch whose attitude to Christian had been entirely correct. He was, however, equally acceptable to Scotland and, when a settlement was reached, Christian I commended him to James III and asked that the bishop should remain with his daughter until she learned the language of her new country. Earl William was not part of the delegation, and would not have been welcome. Earlier in the year, when a final attempt had been made to summon him to Copenhagen,

199

a Scottish messenger had been sent by James III to present the earl's excuses.[52] William was probably discouraged from interfering.

The marriage treaty was concluded on 8 September 1468 with Christian I agreeing to provide his daughter with a dowry of 60,000 Rhenish florins.[53] Prestige demanded that the dowry be handsome, but it was a sum which both sides realised could not be raised by the impoverished king. Agreement was reached that Orkney should be mortgaged to Scotland for 50,000 florins, but could be redeemed when the king was in a position to pay cash. The Scots were well satisfied with the outcome: from a crisis precipitated by Scotland's debts, they emerged with all arrears of the Annual cancelled, and with at least temporary control of Orkney and Shetland. But Christian I could also be reasonably content: he had succeeded in providing a magnificent dowry for his daughter at little cost in terms of real money, and he had conceded less than the Scots had asked in 1460 when the demand had been that the absolute sovereignty of both Orkney and Shetland should be ceded. Since he had signally failed to exercise meaningful control of Orkney for the last twenty years, Christian was giving away little that he actually possessed. Similarly, by abandoning his claim to the arrears of the Annual, he was renouncing a debt which he had no chance of collecting.

The 1468 treaty left Christian with a balance of 10,000 florins to be paid in cash. There is evidence that he made some attempt to raise the money, and 2,000 florins may actually have been paid. At the last moment a further treaty pledged Shetland for the remaining 8,000 florins.[54] There is no reason to suppose that the 50,000 florins for Orkney and the 8,000 for Shetland reflected the comparative value of the islands, as has sometimes been stated.[55] The price put on Shetland was merely the balance of the debt which Christian I was anxiously seeking means to pay as the date of his daughter's marriage approached.

Was there any serious intention that Christian I or his successors would ever redeem the pledge, or was the mortgage simply a device to disguise a transfer which both sides recognised would be permanent?[56] Pledging land was a common way of coping with debt, and Christian I's complex financial dealings involved the similar pledging of land in Denmark, so in one sense his pawning of Orkney and Shetland was no different from many other temporary transactions.[57] Yet he must have realised that transfer to a foreign power which for many years had coveted the islands could not so easily be reversed. It has been argued that impignoration was a face-saving exercise: Danish-Norwegian kings including Christian I gave an undertaking not to alienate Norwegian fiefs and revenues—they were not supposed to pledge them either, but perhaps pledging was seen as a less serious breach of their coronation oath. It has also been pointed out that the pledge contained no stipulation about how long the islands were to remain mortgaged, no details of the currency in which repayment was to be made, nor did it state where payment was to be offered and received. Since contemporary pledges did not always include these details, their absence is not conclusive proof that the arrangement was intended to be permanent. Whatever the intention at the time, Danish-Norwegian kings made repeated, if somewhat half-hearted efforts to redeem the pledge during the next 200 years (see p.240). Scotland, on the other hand, took immediate steps to ensure that it would be difficult, if not impossible, to regain control of the islands. In view of the diplomacy of the past dozen years, that is an eventuality which must have been foreseen. For the islanders themselves, the impignoration marked a low point in their history; with their economy in ruins, their wishes, whatever they may have been, counted for nothing. Their future was decided by kings who had never set foot in Orkney, but who had power to settle matters in whatever way they pleased.

There has been quite unnecessary confusion surrounding exactly what was transferred to Scotland by the impignoration. John Mooney advanced the view that James III acquired only the Crown estates,[58] which he erroneously believed to have been much bigger than they actually were.[59] Mooney believed that the earls held their earldom in their own right and not by royal grant—a surprising conclusion since Norwegian kings at least from the time of Sverre had continuously and successfully maintained that the earldom was in their gift, and earls had accepted it on these terms without demur. Mooney, however, convinced himself that the earldom was unaffected by the impignoration. He was also confused about the position of udallers: the king was not their feudal superior (a udaller had no feudal superior) and so, it was argued, he could not give away their property. Mooney's conclusions stem from a failure to distinguish between ordinary 'property' and the 'dominion' which a king exercises over lands which may be other people's property. His theories were also coloured by the regret which he shared with many of his contemporaries at the severing of Orkney's Norwegian links. His belief that only the Crown estates were pledged reflected a desire to deny the completeness of the Scottish takeover. His interpretation was clearly wrong, but for a time his theory was widely accepted,[60] and it still finds the occasional adherent.

The most relevant passage in the marriage agreement states that Christian I handed over:

> All and sundry our lands of the islands of Orkney with all and sundry rights... pertaining to us and our predecessors, Kings of Norway.[61]

It is clear that royal estates in Orkney were transferred to Scotland, as Mooney supposed, but when a king speaks of 'our lands' he refers to more than the farms which happen to be under the management of his stewards. As well as land, the treaty refers to 'all and sundry rights'; these rights included superiority over the earl whose claim was hereditary but whose entry into his earldom was in the gift of the king. Similarly, although the king was not the feudal superior of udallers, he certainly had rights over them, principal of which were the rights to collect skat, administer justice and to impose fines. When Christian I in his farewell message to his Orkney and Shetland subjects in May 1469 told them to be dutiful and obedient and to pay their skat to King James,[62] he was addressing not just his own tenants, but the entire community. The obvious intention was that the King of Scots should enjoy exactly the same lands and rights as had previously been possessed by Christian I as successor to the Kings of Norway.[63] While ultimate sovereignty remained with the Norway, all exercise of that sovereignty was in abeyance until the islands were redeemed. James III certainly acted on the assumption that he had acquired full royal rights, and that it was not necessary to keep the administration of the islands in a state of suspended animation until the pledge was redeemed. Bishop William Tulloch immediately took his seat in the Scottish parliament, and in the next few years the king made fundamental changes to the earldom (1470 and 1472) and granted a royal charter to Kirkwall (1486).

Clearly ultimate sovereignty was not transferred in 1468 since the islands might be redeemed. Even today, when people are frustrated with Westminster government, a means of seeking publicity is to call for the pledge to be paid and the Norwegian link to be restored. However, it is generally held that in the course of time Orkney and Shetland have become Scottish by use and wont, and that Norwegian sovereignty has lapsed.[64] As Gordon Donaldson remarked, the link with Scotland 'may resemble a marriage by habit and repute, but a legal marriage nonetheless'.[65]

Since Earl William had identified so thoroughly with Scotland, he ought to have been more secure after the impignoration but, if his relationship with James III was now to be that in which he formerly stood in relation to Christian I, it was actually a very dubious one. Earl William had failed to do homage to Christian I; he had been deposed, his earldom had been forfeited, and its management had been put into the hands of William Tulloch. Earl William by this time was detached from the Scottish government, and the marriage treaty did nothing to clarify his position. James III needed to establish his authority in the islands as quickly as possible, and he intended to do so by direct rule rather than through Earl William. The best way to strengthen royal authority was to gain personal possession of the earldom. This would have the advantage that, even if Christian I or his successors redeemed the isles, it was the Scots king rather than William Sinclair who possessed the right to claim the earldom—a prospect which made redemption less attractive to the Norwegian-Danish king.

Accordingly James III bought out Earl William and united the earldom with the Crown. It has often been said that William received poor compensation for the loss of Orkney, and yet it was hardly a hostile takeover. James seems to have been willing to make all sorts of minor concessions, and indeed to indulge William by agreeing to the earl's detailed requests. William received no less than seven charters from the king, all issued under the Great Seal on the same day (17 September 1470). He was given the modern castle of Ravenscraig, built only a few years earlier for James II's queen, Mary of Guelders. It has been described as 'possibly the earliest structure in Scotland designed specifically for use with guns',[66] and it provided him with a prestigious residence conveniently close to his burgh of Dysart. He also received a pension from the customs of Edinburgh,[67] and he was freed of the obligation to attend parliament and take part in other official duties.[68] He might reside wherever he wished (so long as it was not in England) and he had a right to transport his rents to his residence without let or hindrance.[69] The king guaranteed him against any claim which Christian I might have against him, presumably for the skat and rent which William had continued to collect after he was officially deposed.[70] The king not only confirmed William's rights in his Caithness earldom which he retained when Orkney was lost, but offered to confirm his right to his other lands.[71]

One reason why William received so little compensation was that, strictly speaking, he had little left to resign to the king. The wording of the charters is important. William was addressed as 'Earl of Caithness and Lord Sinclair' but he was not described as 'Earl of Orkney'. What he gave up was 'the Castle of Kirkwall and his entire *right* to the earldom of Orkney',[72] but there was no mention of him resigning the actual title of earl or handing over the lands of the earldom. James III apparently took the view that, since William had been deprived of the earldom by Christian I, his lands had already reverted to the Norwegian crown before the impignoration. If that were the case, James III already possessed the earldom estate, and it was only the question of the Sinclair family's future claim to the earldom which needed to be tidied up.

William, however, may not have come out of the agreement quite so badly as is sometimes supposed. He was able to make a distinction between the lands of the earldom proper, which were now in the hands of the King of Scots, and his personal property in Orkney which he had acquired, for example by purchase. This personal estate, the so-called 'conquest lands' consisted of a very large collection of fragmented and dispersed properties which he was allowed to keep. Since nearly all of this land had previously been udal, his right to these properties must in many cases have been poorly documented. One of William's charters allowed him to resign lands and to receive them back with a charter and sasine from the king.[73] He gained even more explicit confirmation when, a few months later in February 1471, James III acknowledged that he had no claim to William's conquest estate.[74] Although the earldom had been lost, the extent of the conquest lands was so great that he still held an estate of equivalent size, and he passed on to his grandson lands which allowed the Sinclairs to retain a foothold in the north which was independent of the former earldom. A further concession which William Sinclair received in this remarkable series of charters was a guarantee that he might transport his rents to his residence without let or hindrance. It is hardly likely that this provision was made with his Fife and Lothian estates in mind, but rent-collecting in Orkney was unusually diffi-cult. The conquest lands often lay run-rig with the former earldom lands, with the result two or more sets of rent collectors were operating in the same townships in circumstances where the inter-mixture of the lands made disagreement almost inevitable—indeed there ultimately proved to be insu-perable difficulties in keeping the conquest lands distinct (see p.240). The concession cannot have been of much practical significance, but the charter was apparently intended to strengthen William's powers in disputes with Bishop William Tulloch's agents who were collecting the rent of the former earldom.[75]

The Ravenscraig exchange and the accompanying concessions were rather more than a 'retirement package' which left William in comfortable circum-stances in his old age. It is clear that William intended to maintain a presence in Orkney, and his charters shows that his Orkney interests were uppermost in his mind. Nevertheless James III seems to have been entirely relaxed about William's conquest estate, even allowing him to retain as 'conquest' a good deal of property which the Crown could probably have claimed to be part of the earldom. Evidently the king did not regard William's Orkney interests as posing a threat. James may have come to recognise that a family with a long history of loyalty to the Crown had suffered as a result of the impignoration and deserved to be placated.

The consolidation of the king's position was completed when in the par-liament of 1472 it was enacted that:

> ...our souverain lorde, with deliverance of his thre estatis annext an united the erledome of Orkney and the lordship of Scheteland to the croune, nocht to be gevin away in tyme to cum to na persoune nor personis except anerly [only] til ane of the kingis sonnis of lachtfull [lawful] bed.[76]

The Act did not alter the fact that Scotland held Orkney and Shetland in pledge rather than by sovereign right—it dealt with the earldom rather than with sovereignty. It entrenched the King of Scots' hold over the earldom in a way which was intended to be irreversible. The earldom continued to be united to the Scottish crown for a further century until it was given to Robert Stewart, a king's son as the Act required, although not 'of lawful bed'.

15

Taxing and Renting Land in Norse Orkney

The point at which Orkney passed into Scottish hands is a good place at which to interrupt the chronological history of the islands to look at the more general issues of assessing, taxing and renting land. Orkney is fortunate to have a detailed series of skat rentals, the earliest dating from 1492 and 1500,[1] but these were based on an even earlier 'auld parchment rental' which has now been lost.[2] The next chapter makes use of the extant rentals in order to shed light on Lord Henry Sinclair's management of the islands in the early years of Scottish rule, but the rentals embody much that was older, and have been used to construct theories about Norse society and even Viking-age settlement. One such theory, Clouston and Steiness's division of the earldom into 'halves and thirds', was discussed in Chapter 5. Skat and rent, however, did not come down unchanged from the days of King Harald Fairhair as at one time was supposed. Some of the more ambitious reconstructions have been based on an over-confident assumption about the antiquity of the taxation system and an optimistic belief in its unchanging nature.

Land in Orkney was valued in *urislands* (ouncelands), each of which consisted of 18 *pennylands*. Urislands are rather shadowy units, but pennylands were ubiquitous and were in everyday use. There were about 3,670 pennylands in Orkney, and at the height of nineteenth century expansion there were about 3,373 agricultural holdings, so it is useful as a rough guide to think of the pennyland as more or less equivalent to a croft or small farm. Medieval households, however, must have been a good deal less numerous than nineteenth century agricultural holdings, and so too much ought not to be made of the equivalence of the pennyland and the house. The urisland cannot so easily be equated with the township. Some very large townships were valued at a whole urisland, but the great majority of townships were in the 2-6 pennyland range, so the urisland commonly consisted of a grouping of several small farming communities.

Urislands and pennylands were never defined in terms of standard area. By the eighteenth century when acreages can be calculated, pennylands were

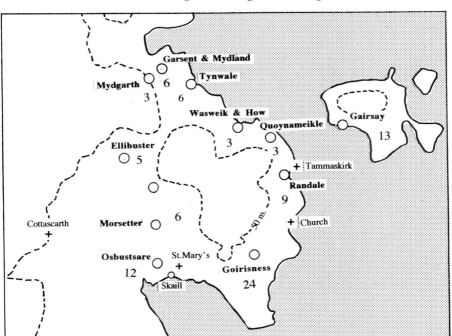

42. **Urislands in Rendall.** *Garsent & Mydland (6 pennylands) Mydgarth (3)
Tynwale (6) and Wasweik & How (3) make up the first urisland (= 18 pennylands).
Quoynameikle (3) Randale (9) and Goirsness (24) make two urislands (= 36
pennylands). The fourth urisland is Osbustare (12) and Halkland (6), leaving the
final artificial grouping of Ellibuster (5) and Gairsay (13). Chapels include a
further unlocated 'Kirkabreck' in Tynwale, so there is a distribution of a type which
gave rise to the term 'urisland chapel'.*

highly variable in size, and even adjacent districts might show wide variation. Thus pennylands in the Southside of Birsay were only 5 acres (2 ha.),
whereas they were 10 acres in the Northside; in neighbouring districts
pennylands were 11 acres in Marwick, 29 acres in Isbister, and 68 acres (28
ha.) in Sabiston.[3] Land inside the hill dyke was a complicated mixture of
arable rigs and grazing sections, so some pennylands were big simply because they contained a high proportion of poor grassland. Some districts
like the North and Southside of Birsay were highly valued because of their
early importance as part of an earl's farm, and pennylands generally remained
small on the sandy soils of the North Isles because opportunities for further
reclamation were limited. Where the growth of population had been combined with opportunities to break out new land, pennylands could become
very large. We might guess that the period of expansion in many townships
was in the twelfth and thirteenth centuries.

Urislands can often, but not always, be plotted with reasonable accuracy and, wherever it was possible, they had been made to correspond to natural subdivisions of parishes (or perhaps of districts which subsequently became parishes). However, this was sometimes difficult, and since urislands did not normally cross parish boundaries, there could be a degree of artificiality in making urislands fit the parishes. Thus the five urislands of the parish of Rendall consist of four natural districts, but the final urisland can only be discovered by adding the 5 pennylands of Ellibister to the 13 pennylands of the island of Gairsay which lay some four miles away (Fig.42). The result was a highly artificial urisland—indeed Ellibister and Gairsay can never have been intended to have had any unity for practical purposes. However, the way the assessment was made to fit suggests that a round-figure assessment was placed on parishes, then sub-partitioned on individual urislands, and further allocated to individual townships in terms of their pennylands, and finally shared among individual farmers. We need not think of all this being done on a single occasion; perhaps early rough-and-ready assessments on parishes and urislands were later refined by the creation of pennylands. Unlike the urisland, the pennyland only occasionally existed as a single block of land—it was essentially a measure of a share. If a farmer held a pennyland in a three-pennyland township, he was entitled to a third of the arable land which was probably dispersed in run-rig, and indeed he had a right to a third of all the resources available to the community, while at the same time he was responsible for one-third of the community's obligations, the most obvious of which was to pay taxes. Since pennylands were mainly used to define a share within a township rather than to compare townships, the variation in their size and value from one township to another was not as great a disadvantage as it might seem.

Lord Henry Sinclair's 1492 and 1500 rentals record the skat due from each farm and township in the form of *butter skat, malt skat* and *forcop*, and at the end of the rental of each parish he noted the further payments of *wattle, skat merts* and *hawk hens*. These skats were taxes payable by udallers and tenants alike; those who were tenants had the additional burden of *landmale* or rent.

The rentals provide evidence of how butter skat payments had evolved. In 1490 Lord Henry Sinclair personally conducted an enquiry into the butter skat payments of the North Isles.[4] Witnesses came to Sanday from other North Isles and gave evidence that in 'auld tymes' butter skat had consisted of half a lispund of butter from every newly calved cow (see 'Weights and Measures', p.451). Although butter skat was eventually to become even more onerous, the 'auld tymes' rate was not a light one; it was exactly the same rate which provoked the Caithness men to murder Bishop Adam in 1222,[5] although the payment on that occasion had been tithe rather than skat. It is difficult to estimate medieval milk yields, but the butter skat must have represented a large part of the produce of the cow. The development of medieval taxation often involved a transition from payments on men or cows, which were both mobile and variable in number, into an assessment on land which provided a more secure basis for taxation.[6] Thus butter skat came to be assessed at a rate of six spans from every urisland (a span from 3 pennylands). The span or pail of butter was equivalent to about five lispunds, but it was a unit which by the fifteenth century was no longer used in commercial transactions, but was confined to the assessment of the butter skat. Because the assessment was made using this obsolete measure it is likely to be of considerable antiquity, although the witnesses at the enquiry apparently had knowledge of an even older system in what they described as 'auld tymes' when butter skat had been a direct tax on cows. The fact that they had knowledge of this older system is a clear indication that skat-payments did not come down unchanged from the remote Viking Age, as was at one time supposed. However, the witnesses were harking back to a time when butter skat had been much less, so 'auld tymes' might well have been a century or two before the 1490 enquiry.

Lord Henry's enquiry led to an agreement that, for his time as tacksman, the total value of the butter skat was to be paid in full, but only a lispund in every span (about 20%) need actually be paid in butter, the value of the remainder being acceptable in 'pennyworths' of other produce such as grain. The record of the enquiry tells us that Lord Henry made this concession because he 'understood their poverty'. By allowing people to pay in grain, he was encouraging the re-occupation of land which had gone out of cultivation. The part of the butter skat actually paid in butter was the *stent*, and the following equation underlies the butter skat payments in the 1492 and 1500 rentals:

A Span	**=**	**Stent Butter**	**+**	**Pennyworths**
A span (tub) was paid by three pennylands.		1 lispund was paid in real butter for every span that was due.		The remainder could be paid in products such as grain.
A span was valued at 21 pennyworths.		A lispund was valued at 4 pennyworths.		So the remainder was 21 – 4 = 17 pennyworths.

The division of the butter skat into two parts, the stent butter and the remainder paid in 'pennyworths' of other produce, became a permanent feature. During the course of the sixteenth century the pennyworths came to be paid in money (skat silver), the value of which was greatly eroded by the high rate of inflation in the later part of the century.

The second main tax was *malt skat,* and while it may have its origins in supplying the earl's household with ale, it came to be regarded simply as a tax on arable land. Malt skat was remitted when land passed out of cultivation and so reductions in malt skat can be used to identify the land variously described as ley, waste or 'untane' ('not taken', untenanted) which was a common feature of the 1492 rental. Whereas butter skat was paid at one uniform rate, malt skat was charged at a variety of rates, the commonest being 4 settens of malt (c.50 kg.) on the pennyland. The additional rates of 4½ and 4⅔ settens were frequently found, while a further series of rates, 6, 8, 9 and 9⅔ settens were described as 'high malt skat' or 'double malt skat'. The variety of rates seems to be an attempt to cope with pennylands which had become very variable in size and worth as a result of new land being brought into cultivation. Since so much land was abandoned in 1492, we must suppose that the expansion which required the variable malt skat was not recent but dated from the period before the Black Death (1349).

A third skat known as *forcop* was the most variable element in the whole system. Entire districts paid no forcop and while 1⅔ 'pennies' (pennyworths of produce) per pennyland was the commonest rate, a variety of other rates up to 6 pennyworths per pennyland can be identified. The derivation of the term 'forcop' causes problems. It has often been identified as *fararkaup,* the tax Icelanders had to pay to meet the expenses of those travelling to the Althing.[7] However, the fact that neighbouring townships might pay forcop at quite different rates, and many places were entirely exempt, makes this derivation unlikely. But, when taken in conjunction with malt skat to which forcop is closely related, it was much less random. Perhaps the payments reflect the structure of Orkney townships where the malt skat originally was payable on the arable heartland, and either extra malt skat or forcop was levied on outward expansion. It is possible that the term *forcop* is derived from the Scots *furr* (furrow) and *kaup* (payment) in which case it might be a tax with the meaning 'cultivation payment'. What seems to be the same skat occurs in Caithness under the name of *Plough Silver.*[8] The fact that farmers did not have an unrestricted right to reclaim land without an extra payment can be seen from a court decision of 1584 which records that land in Deerness and St Andrews was escheated from Magnus Sinclair because he had built houses on land which was 'brokin furth upoun the kingis balk' ('back', rough grassland on the margin of the township).[9] While this particular forfeiture is usually regarded as sharp practice by Earl Robert Stewart, his court may have based its decision on Norwegian Landlaw according to which all members of the community had a right to make use of the *allmenninger* ('common land') but any new settlers automatically became the tenants of the king, or in this case tenants of the earl.[10] Thus forcop was a variable payment which took account of the new arable land which was added to a township. Like the variable malt skat rates, the outward expansion of arable land and the imposition of the charge is likely to date from the pre-Black Death period, although the actual term 'forcop', if it is Scots, might not be quite so old.

Butter skat, malt skat and forcop were collected from each individual farm or township, but the further skat of *wattle* had come to be a payment used as the fee for the parish baillie who made his own arrangements to uplift it.[11] The term *wattle* derives from the Old Norse *veizla;* the payment originally stemmed from the obligation to provide food and hospitality for the lord, equivalent to Scots *conveth.* Wattle can be seen in its original sense in *Orkneyinga saga* when Harald Maddadsson 'boarded out his men at various places over Easter',[12] and perhaps in the extended feasting of earls by their *godings* such as Sigurd of Westness.[13] The billeting of King Hakon's forces on the Orkney urislands in the winter of 1263-4 after the Battle of Largs was also in keeping with the practice of wattle, although it strained hospitality beyond its accustomed limits.[14]

Wattle was charged at the uniform rate of one 'penny' (pennyworth of produce) per pennyland, so there are at first sight attractions in the idea that it is the key to understanding the whole system: perhaps the penny of wattle might be the original tax of one penny which gave the pennyland its name,[15] and since enforced hospitality is a primitive form of taxation, it might seem that it is the kind of payment in which we might find the origins of skat. Unfortunately there are fundamental objections to this attractive theory. The term 'pennyland' could only have arisen when the obligation to provide hospitality had been converted into a money payment, or at least into a fixed food render valued at one pennyworth. However, there is ample evidence that, long after pennylands appeared as land units, wattle continued to take the form of night quarters for the earl, his retinue and officials. In Shetland, where wattle continued to be calculated in 'nights', it was only in the middle of the sixteenth century that it was converted into a money payment; until then it was paid in actual accommodation 'for the mainteinance of the schireff yeirly as he cam to do justice, meit for men and hors'.[16] In Orkney the change came earlier, and wattle was already being paid in pennyworths when the 1492 rental was compiled, but its conversion may then have been recent. It may have been during the time of the largely absentee Earl Henry II and Earl William (c.1400–1470) that night quarters for a numerous following were no longer required, or else wattle might have been converted into money only after the earldom was abolished in 1470. An earl on his travels always needed enforced hospitality; when Lord Robert Stewart was in Shetland and demanding 'bankettis and great cheer',[17] he was only behaving in the traditional manner of earls enjoying their wattle. When the Shetlanders objected in 1575, the nub of their complaint was the

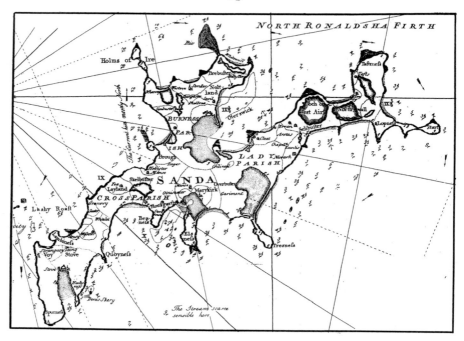

43. **Sanday.** (*Mackenzie,* Orcades). *In Sanday townships were often whole urislands. In the flat landscape they were separated one from another by turf dykes and, because there was little opportunity for outward expansion, urislands and their constituent pennylands were unusually small.*

arbitrary nature of these 'banquets', but they no doubt resented that they were being made to pay twice: they were still having to provide real hospitality although wattle had been commuted to a money payment some twenty years earlier.

Hawk hens were poultry collected by the royal falconers from udallers and tenants alike, not just as a food supply for the hawks, but probably to train young birds.[18] The hens must have amounted to about 550 birds in total, but it is difficult to discover any rational basis for the charge. Wallace describes how in the seventeenth century the king's falconer was entitled to 'a hen or a dog out of every house, except some houses which are priveledged'.[19] The payment resembles the Scots 'reek-hen', the payment of a bird from every building which had a hearth, although many houses for no very obvious reason seem to have escaped the payment of the hawk-hen.

The last of the skats involved the collection of the *skat merts* which was one of the more onerous of the skats. The 'merts' were cattle, killed and salted at Martinmas, and were levied at the rate of one per urisland.[20] For most purposes urislands had become obsolete because obligations had been sub-partitioned to individual places in proportion to their pennylands, but it was less easy to apportion a mert. The skat mert was the only payment which continued to be made on an urisland basis, and it seems to have been left to the inhabitants to sort out how the mert was to be paid. Districts which were less than an urisland in size were sometimes grouped in pairs, and were liable for the skat mert year-about.

When malt skat was discussed earlier in this chapter it was shown that it provides evidence of an expansion of arable land in the High Middle Ages. As land was reclaimed and townships grew in size, new pennylands were seldom created—existing pennylands simply became bigger—probably because the creation of extra pennylands would have destroyed the 18-pennyland urislands. However, the opportunities for expansion were variable; the sandy soils of the North Isles were attractive to early settlement and little further expansion was possible with the result that pennylands remained small in comparison to the Mainland, where there was a greater reservoir of reclaimable land. In the eighteenth century it was a common rule of thumb that a pennyland in the North Isles was equivalent to a farthingland on the Orkney Mainland (one-quarter of a pennyland). Since skat was levied on pennylands in a way which took only a limited account of their variable worth, it follows that taxation was far from equitable. The situation was further compounded by the fact that skat had become an inflexible traditional payment, and in consequence some of the more recently reclaimed arable land, the *quoyland*, escaped taxation altogether.

Although these highly variable pennylands remained the basis for taxation, they were unsatisfactory for ordinary business transactions involving buying, selling, renting, exchanging, inheriting and mortgaging property. For these everyday purposes a different unit, the *mark*, was used. The mark was in origin a valuation based on purchase price, so one mark of land was the amount of land which might be bought for one mark of money (£⅔).[21] We have already seen the earliest recorded use of the mark in 1329 in Countess Katherine's South Ronaldsay land deals (see p.150). It was possible to describe the variable pennylands in terms of the number of marks of land they contained. Pennylands worth 3 or 4 marks were commonest (and hence were said to 'contain' 3 or 4 marks of land) but the rate of 6 marks in the pennyland was often found, and on the sandy soils of the North Isles, the small pennylands might contain only 1½ or 1 mark or even less. Although there is no reason to suppose that pennylands had ever been strictly equal, they had clearly become increasingly variable, and the number of marks to the pennyland is a rough guide to medieval expansion. However, a further complication is that the mark, like the pennyland, also became fossilised, and by 1492 marks had ceased to be strictly comparable, with the result that these supposedly equal-value units were actually rented at slightly variable rates.[22]

213

Those who have sought to discover the origins of ouncelands and pennylands have naturally looked for the penny which was paid by the pennyland, and the ounce, presumably of silver, which was levied on the ounceland. The search has proved elusive: no record of these payments has been discovered or indeed is likely ever to be found.

Captain Thomas's paper 'What is a Pennyland?' (1884) initiated the discussion about the origin of ouncelands and pennylands. He wrote: 'The origin of this valuation is, of course, Norse'.[23] His reasons were obvious: the system is common to Orkney, Caithness and the west of Scotland where the *tir unga* ('land of an ounce') and the *unciata terra* are direct translations into Gaelic and Latin of the Norse *eyrisland* ('ounceland', urisland), hence the terminology is found throughout the region in which the Norse were active. It is less easy to agree with Thomas when he assumed that they were taxation districts imposed by Norwegian royal authority: be believed that 'it is very probable that the assessment was made by King Harold Fairhair on his conquest of the isles',[24] although he conceded that the division of ouncelands into pennylands might be later. Nowadays it would no longer be thought possible that a sophisticated system of annual taxation could have been imposed at anything like such an early date, nor indeed would it be assumed that pennylands were first created for purposes of national taxation. Thomas was also interested in the *davach*, a land unit commonly found in northern Scotland, and he thought that the Norse might have adapted preexisting *davachs* in order to levy an annual payment of one ounce of silver from each ounceland.[25] However, he offered no direct evidence that there had ever been payments of ounces from ouncelands, or pennies from pennylands. It seemed obvious to him that the names implied the payments.

The idea that the assessment was created during the course of King Harald's voyage to the West was enthusiastically espoused by Hugh Marwick.[26] He also regarded the Pictish *davach* as a likely ancestor of the Orcadian ounceland, although there is no indication that davachs ever existed in Orkney, and clear evidence from Caithness that davachs and ouncelands are not actually identical (in Caithness ouncelands can often be shown to be composed of three davachs).[27] However, Marwick's main contribution to the debate was his theory that ouncelands were connected with the Norse naval levy.[28] 'Leidang', the system whereby fully manned and provisioned ships were made available for the use of the king, was the basis of Norwegian taxation, and leidang was raised on a territorial basis from districts known as *shipreides*. Marwick focused on the Orkney unit known as the *skatland* which was one-quarter of an urisland (4½ pennylands). The term 'skatland' suggested to him that the unit was important in some fundamental way for the payment of skat, and he came to the conclusion that the *skatland* was the unit which had been obliged to provide one man and his sustenance when the levy was called out. These skatlands are in fact found much less frequently than readers of Marwick's papers might suppose. Modern opinion is sceptical about leidang in Orkney: it is one of those theoretical constructions about what might have been, rather than a description based on any real evidence that the Norse in Orkney raised ships on a territorial basis. Such evidence as *Orkneyinga saga* provides suggests that Orkney earls exercised power through kinship and personal ties with their *godings* rather than through the formal structures of a community levy.[29]

Another theory finds a possible origin of ouncelands and pennylands in the early house groupings which are recorded in the seventh century *Senchus Fer nAlban*.[30] The *Senchus* is a survey of the military capabilities of the three *cenéls* (tribes) which composed the kingdom of Dál Riata (mainly Argyll), and it states that two-seven benched ships were required for galley service

44. *The Hall of Tankerness. Tankerness was the home of Erling and his sons who provided crucial assistance to Earl Paul at the Battle of Tankerness (a sea battle fought somewhere in the vicinity). The little churchyard in which St Andrew's church was once located is typical of the close association between chief's hall and parish church. From the seventeenth century the Hall was the residence of the Baikie family, and the centre of their extensive estate. The sequence of development on this ancient site is completed by the large modern farm buildings to the right.*

from every 20 houses. There are attractions in connecting these 20-house groupings to ouncelands which in the west of Scotland contained 20 pennylands (unlike the 18-penny ouncelands of Orkney and Caithness). Many people searching for the origin of ouncelands look no further, and simply assume that the Norse took over and renamed existing 20-house-groups,[31] yet on closer inspection it is difficult to find continuity, or even much evidence that 20-house groupings in Dál Riata ever existed. Equally unsatisfactory are theories that this ancient obligation is the same as the galley service often found in Scottish charters in the medieval and early modern period; these are feudal obligations required of individual vassals (the naval equivalent of knight-service) rather than obligations placed on the community as a whole, and they seldom, if ever, bear any relationship to ouncelands.

Another attempt to discover the origins of pennylands connects them Peter's Pence. We have already seen that in the late twelfth century Harald Maddadsson made a gift to the papacy of one penny from each house in Caithness, a payment usually identified as Peter's Pence, a papal tax levied in Norway but not in Scotland (see p.123). At much the same time, we find a similar grant to Paisley Abbey by Rognvald, son of Somerled, of one penny 'from every house from which smoke issues'.[32] Since the pennyland can be approximately equated to a house, there are attractions in this theory. Yet in practice most households were usually exempt, and only wealthy people paid Peter's Pence. In 1327 the payment from the Orkney diocese for two years amounted to only £6:5s.[33] and, since Orkney contained about 3,670 pennylands and the diocese included Shetland, the total which was collected was only a small fraction of what one penny per pennyland would have yielded. It is difficult to imagine that the terminology could have arisen if the great majority of people lived on pennylands that did not actually pay pennies of Peter's Pence, and those who paid one penny actually possessed several pennylands. Furthermore, Scots clergy in the Orkney diocese collected Peter's Pence with such little enthusiasm that it is difficult to imagine that its collection could have given rise to a universal system of land valuation.

It is quite possible that there never was a penny-payment made by pennylands. People who did not have decimals and percentages regularly had recourse to the terminology of weight and money when they needed to express complicated fractions. Renting land and apportioning obligations in terms of shares was the usual method in a country where resources were unevenly distributed, and a terminology based on proportionate shares also provided a framework within which the inhabitants could sort out their rights and obligations with a minimum recourse to outside authority. The terminology of the 18-pennyland ouncelands of Orkney and Caithness and the 20-pennyland ouncelands of the west were both used to describe shares, but they were based on different currencies. The eleventh and twelfth centuries saw the development of a monetary system using the mark, a unit of weight which was Scandinavian in origin, and equal to 8 ounces. Until the mid-eleventh century the Scandinavians exchanged coin by weight, and so they used the mark and ora (ounce) as money values. By end of the eleventh century the mark (c.216 gms.) was a standard weight in England, Normandy, Scandinavia, Flanders and the Rhineland. Although the mark was standard, the number of pennies coined from a mark of silver varied. After the dissolution of Cnut's empire, Denmark and Norway coined the mark into 240 pennies, in contrast to the English sterling mark of 160 pennies (£⅔) which was also adopted in Scotland. From about the middle of the eleventh century onwards the prolific mint of Cologne coined a slightly heavier penny, with 144 to the mark. These German pennies are very commonly found in Scandinavia, being second only to Arabic coins and about twice as common as Anglo-Saxon pennies.[34]

It can be seen that the 20-pennyland ouncelands of the Hebrides and western Scotland were based on the familiar sterling mark. A mark was 160 pennies and contained 8 ounces, so 20 pennies could be made from one ounce of silver. When money-terminology was used to describe land there were therefore 20 pennylands to an ounceland. In contrast, the 18-pennyland ouncelands of the Northern Isles and Caithness seem to be based on the Cologne mark which was in common use in Scandinavia.[35] Since the mark was 8 ounces but was coined into 144 Cologne pennies, 18 pennies were coined from the ounce, and so one ounceland was 18 pennylands. When Orkney and Shetland were pawned in 1468-9, the dowry for which they were pledged was expressed in *rhinegulden*, or 'florins of the Rhine' which were part of the same currency. In Shetland, but not in Orkney, the Cologne penny lived on even longer as a unit of accounting. A judgement relating to land in Yell in 1538 described a payment as:

…marks burnt [of refined silver]… 12 Shetland shillings in every mark, in Shetland wares.[36]

This document is stating that there are 12 Shetland shillings (= 144 pennies) to the mark, in contrast to the 160 pennies in the sterling mark. However, these shillings and pennies were 'money of account' rather than coins, since the actual payment was to be made in 'Shetland wares' (fish and agricultural products at standard conversion rates expressed as 'pennyworths').

Although skat is usually described as 'taxation' because it was paid by udallers as well as those who were tenants, its origins lie, not so much in annual national taxation which in most countries is a fairly late development,[37] but in the kind of payments which had always been necessary to support lordship in early society. The lifestyle depicted in *Orkneyinga saga* required the bonding together of the chief and his military retinue, and feasting in the *skali* over the winter months was an important element in their relationship. It was essential to have generous quantities of ale and beef, and to have the means to uplift these commodities from farmers in the surrounding district. At the same time travel around the islands by the earl, his followers and officials required a scale of hospitality which reflected well on both the guest and on the host. The saga praises successful leaders who were able to maintain this heroic lifestyle: the great Earl Thorfinn 'furnished all his bodyguard and many other men of rank with meat and ale through the whole winter',[38] and we find his nephew Rognvald going in person to Papa Stronsay to supervise the collection of the malt for the Yule ale.[39]

Given the complete absence of early documents which relate to taxation and land, and *Orkneyinga saga's* lack of interest in such matters, it is difficult to date the point at which the payments which an early society had always required were formalised into a system of payments raised on ouncelands and pennylands. If, as suggested, the pennyland relates to the Cologne penny, it is impossible that the pennyland could be earlier than the mid-eleventh century, and it is more likely to date from the twelfth century when the circulation of money was commoner. That is also the time when we have the earliest hints in Orkney of taxation based on an assessment of land. Soon after 1137, when Earl Rognvald had difficulty in raising money to finance the building of St Magnus Cathedral (see Chapter 7), we are told he levied a special tax raised at the rate of one silver mark per *plógsland* ('piece of ploughed land'), a unit never otherwise recorded in Orkney.[40] It is, however, doubtful if the saga uses *plógsland* in a precise sense. It is more likely that the Icelandic saga-writer was unfamiliar with Orkney land units, but had heard of *ploughgates* and *carucates* in the Danish districts of England. Rognvald's tax was a one-off payment, a feudal 'aid' raised for a specific purpose, rather than the annual payment of skat. Nevertheless it was similar to later taxation insofar as it involved a payment based on some kind of land assessment, and was therefore probably a step towards more regular payments raised on ouncelands and pennylands.

The first actual records of pennylands are from outside Orkney, when in 1222 Roderick, a grandson of Somerled, gave three pennylands to the church of St John and two pennylands to church of St Mary, both in Kintyre. Another early mention is Ewen of Argyll's grant of 14 pennylands in Lismore to the impoverished Bishop of Argyll in 1240.[41] We can be reasonably sure that ouncelands and pennylands already existed in Orkney by this date, although no documents survive and so we have no record of them. Shetland pennylands were first recorded in 1299 in Papa Stour.[42] By then Shetland had been detached from the Orkney earldom for more than a hundred years, and eventually its ouncelands and pennylands were entirely forgotten as the islands went their separate ways. It seems likely that the Orkney-Shetland pennylands have a common origin prior to Harald Maddadsson's defeat at Florevåg in 1194 when Shetland was lost to the Earls of Orkney. Countess Katherine's land transactions in 1329 are also relevant (see p.150). It seems that pennylands then had existed long enough for them to become so variable in value that the introduction of the new unit was required—the mark of land.

The balance of probability is that pennylands originate in the period 1137–1194, although they may have been a refinement of an older method of tribute collection which was based on districts which came to be standardised as ouncelands. Perhaps the growth of population in the twelfth century resulted in a more complex and fragmented pattern of landholding which needed a vocabulary better able to cope with shares and fractions. We ought to think of pennylands as supplying a terminology which was suited to the parcelling out of shares of land to small tenants and defining the obligations to which they were subject, rather than as a unified system of taxation imposed by a single authority. The fact that Orkney ouncelands contain 18 pennylands and those in the west have 20 pennylands points to diversity rather than anything so regular as 'a system'.

Although we can see that the methods of assessing, taxing and renting land which have been described in this chapter do not date back to the time of King Harald Fairhair, assessment and skat-paying had probably not greatly changed at least in the last century and a half before the 1492 rental. Stewards administering the islands either for absentee earls, or on behalf of the Norwegian Crown, lacked the authority and confidence to make radical alterations. The impression is that they tended to perpetuate increasingly inflexible traditional payments. In the next chapter it is possible to describe the business of gathering the rents in some detail. The payments were unaltered: all that had changed was that collection was now managed by Lord Henry Sinclair on behalf of the King of Scots.

16
Under Scottish Rule, 1468-1513

The political transfer of the islands (1468) and the acquisition of the earldom by James III (1470) were followed by the annexation of the earldom of Orkney and the Lordship of Shetland to the crown (1472). That same year the bishopric was transferred from the jurisdiction of Nidaros (Trondheim) to that of St Andrews. The marriage contract had made no mention of the future of the bishopric, nor had it defined the respective roles of the kings of Norway-Denmark and Scotland in ecclesiastical matters, so the transfer of the see had every appearance of being yet another step in a rapid consolidation of Scottish control.

The assumption that this was deliberate Scottish policy may be incorrect. In 1472 Patrick Graham of St Andrews, a somewhat unpredictable bishop often at odds with James III, visited Rome on his own initiative and persuaded the newly elected Sixtus IV to issue a bull erecting St Andrews into an archbishopric with metropolitan authority over the other Scottish bishoprics to which were added Orkney and Sodor (Man and the Hebrides).[1] Just how much attention was paid to the arrangement following the overthrow and imprisonment of Archbishop Graham is open to question. As late as 1520 it appears that Orkney still adhered to some of its old Norwegian connections. In that year Pope Leo X complained that money was being sent to Nidaros which ought to have gone to Rome for the building of St Peter's.[2] Apparently the 1472 bull was unknown in Norway, or had somehow been forgotten. In 1525 Nidaros employed a representative, Zutpheldus Wardenburg, to visit Rome to investigate by what authority St Andrews claimed jurisdiction over Orkney. This led to the rediscovery of the 1472 bull, but the whole affair was overtaken by the Scandinavian Reformation.[3] The same uncertainty had already caused a dispute between Scotland and Denmark regarding the right of presentation to the Archdeaconry of Shetland, an office second in importance only to that of the bishop. First, a certain Magnus Herwood (or possibly 'Harrold') was presented by the King of Norway-Denmark, but this was contested by James IV who in 1502 successfully presented Henry Phankouth, an illegitimate son of Bishop Andrew. The contest, however, although apparently between the respective kings, had more to do with the long-running dispute between the Sinclairs and

Bishop Andrew. It seems that Lord Henry Sinclair used the Scandinavian influence of his uncle, David Sinclair of Sumburgh, in an unsuccessful attempt to thwart the bishop's intention to provide his son with a valuable benefice.[4]

Disputes of this kind were the exception, and at a local level the transfer to Scottish rule involved no immediate break with the past. Continuity was provided by Bishop William Tulloch who had formerly been Christian I's *iuratus* (sworn man) with respect to Orkney with powers to administer the islands when the king could no longer trust Earl William. James III continued to use the bishop in the same way, so it is likely that many of the inhabitants were hardly conscious that they were under Scottish rule. William Tulloch proved to be just as loyal to James III as he had been to Christian I. Management of Orkney was entrusted to him in a series of short tacks, whereby for a stipulated payment he was given the right to the king's revenues. In 1472 he was given the tack for the payment of 50 chalders of bere (barley), 120 salt marts (cattle slaughtered and salted) and £120 in money.[5] Later when the tack was renewed it remained the same in real terms, but the bere was valued at only five marks per chalder instead of the previous eight marks, with the result that the nominal value of the total payment was reduced from £466⅔ to £366⅔.[6] In 1478 William Tulloch was translated to the Bishopric of Moray and he was succeeded in Orkney by Bishop Andrew Pictoris. Bishop Andrew was a very odd bishop—he was a German who had arrived in Scotland via Denmark and whose medical and astrological skills had won him favour with James III.[7] He continued to hold the tack for a further eleven years, when management was entrusted to Lord Henry Sinclair, grandson of the old earl.[8] He too provided continuity—he would have been Earl Henry III if the earldom had not been abolished.

As far as the king was concerned, the management of his new property was an easy matter. The produce of the tack was delivered by the tacksman to Leith where the bere was malted and loaded on the king's ships, presumably for export.[9] For the tacksman it was not so simple. He had to collect a very large number of small payments, partly in money, but mostly in butter, malt, grain, meal and 'flesh'. For flesh there was a complicated scale of equivalents for accepting cattle, sheep, pigs and geese. All produce was uplifted using traditional Orkney weights and measures—lasts, meils, settens, lispunds and marks—but it had to be paid in Scottish units such as the chalder. To add to the problem, all calculations involving money were based on 'money of account', which had at one time been real money but which by this date had become a coinless currency defined by 'pennyworths' of produce. Not only were these pennyworths quite divorced from any real currency, but in the course of time pennyworths of grain had ceased to be genuinely equivalent to pennyworths of butter and meat.[10] In practice the bishop delegated his business affairs to factors such as Thomas Inglis and Robert Yorkstoune.[11]

They in turn dealt with a network of sub-tacksmen whose transactions were scrutinised by district weigh-masters appointed with the approval of the populace to act as referees in case of dispute.[12] No doubt there were profits in these subordinate posts, but there were also risks as John Yensta discovered; he was tacksman of St Andrews parish in 1542–1543 when, failing to raise the sum required, he had nearly three marks of land confiscated to make good the deficit in his accounts.[13]

Despite the difficulties of collection, the tack was capable of raising a handsome profit provided it was managed efficiently. The tacksman paid £366⅔ for both Orkney and Shetland, but in theory he might raise £700 from Orkney alone, and even more when income from fines and escheats is taken into account. In practice his profits are likely to have been more modest since a good deal of land was still out of cultivation; payments of skat were proportionately reduced, and concessions in rent had to be made in order to attract tenants. On the other hand, whatever the tacksman's problems, it was rare for the crown to settle for less than its full income. In 1475 an outbreak of the plague at Leith delayed the arrival of the Orkney rents, with the result that 46 of the salt marts were unfit for consumption,[14] and in other years when they were of doubtful quality they were distributed to the Edinburgh poor or gifted to the Friars Observatine.[15] In 1484 an abatement of £64 was allowed because disorders in Shetland caused by 'the Lords of Norway', the absentee Norwegian landowners with large estates in Shetland.[16] Otherwise the Orkney rents arrived year after year with great regularity, and there was no need for direct government interference. But, if the crown never showed much interest in the human inhabitants, it was keenly interested in the islands as a source of falcons and sparrow-hawks. From the earliest years of Scottish rule there were usually three to five royal falconers at work, and one of the tacksman's functions was to collect six hundred poultry to feed and train the birds in their care.[17]

It is possible to build up a picture of landownership at the end of the Norse era and in the early days of Scottish rule from rentals dating from 1492 and 1500.[18] The most prestigious properties were the former earldom *bordlands*, recognisable by their exemption from skat. Whereas the Castle of Kirkwall was now the centre of power, the Norse earls had formerly based their rule on a dozen or so huge manor farms strategically located throughout the islands. These farms had an administrative function at a time when peripatetic earls still travelled round the islands dispensing justice and seeing to their affairs. In the days before the appearance of an urban community in Kirkwall, these farms must also have functioned as the centres of craft industries and trade.

By far the largest of the bordlands was Birsay, which is well attested in

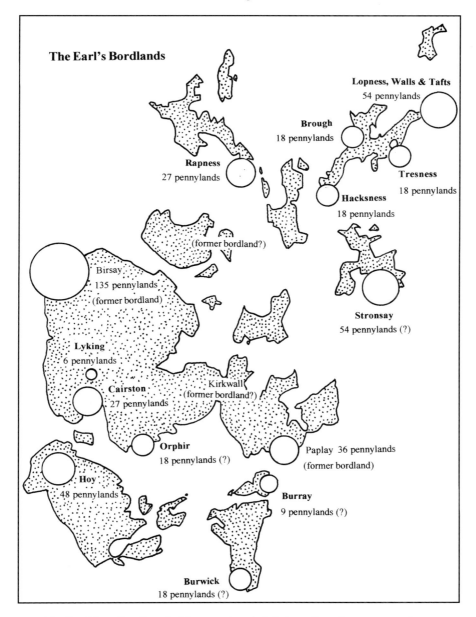

The Earl's Bordlands

Lopness, Walls & Tafts
54 pennylands

Brough
18 pennylands

Rapness
27 pennylands

Tresness
18 pennylands

Hacksness
18 pennylands

(former bordland?)

Birsay
135 pennylands
(former bordland)

Stronsay
54 pennylands (?)

Lyking
6 pennylands

Cairston
27 pennylands

Kirkwall
(former bordland?)

Orphir
18 pennylands (?)

Paplay 36 pennylands
(former bordland)

Hoy
48 pennylands

Burray
9 pennylands (?)

Burwick
18 pennylands (?)

45. *Earldom Bordlands. Norse earls ruled Orkney from large manor farms strategically located throughout the islands. These farms had an administrative function when earls travelled round the islands collecting rent, dispensing justice and seeing to their affairs.*

saga as the residence from which the great earl Thorfinn ruled his empire.[19] The property had passed into the hands of the church at an unknown date, but it still retained its skat-free status, and exhibited the structure of an enormous manor farm. The core was the Barony where there were 135 pennylands of skat-free land; this bordland had once comprised both the earl's desmene, today still represented by large farms in the centre of the district, and also numerous satellite farms located in peripheral locations. One of the satellite communities can be seen particularly clearly in Fig.62 where Birsay-be-south exhibits a linear pattern of settlement along the upper margin of cultivation following the 50 metre contour on the slopes of Ravie Hill, with the houses so close together that their yards were often built one on to the next. We can imagine that the inhabitants of this kind of community were obliged to divide their labour between their own holdings and the earl's desmene, and no doubt they had once provided the oarsmen for the earl's longships. Outside the Barony we find an extensive estate consisting of about 55 pennylands in Marwick, 18 pennylands in Abune-the-Hill in Birsay, and a further 101 pennylands in Evie and Costa. All these districts were latterly part of the bishopric but, like the Barony, they must previously have been part of the earl's Birsay estate. It was, however, only the Barony which was bordland; the distinction seems to be that the manor farm in the Barony was regarded as the principal residence, and so was exempt from skat, whereas the surrounding districts, although part of the same estate, were occupied by tenants and so were liable to pay tax.[20]

Other bordlands included the Bu of Orphir, which is frequently mentioned in saga as the residence of the earls, but which at 18 pennylands was much smaller than Birsay. Several times the saga also tells us that earls would take up residence at Rapness in Westray when collecting their rents in the North Isles.[21] The locations of the earl's bordland farms are shown in Fig.45 from which it can be seen that they were on coastal sites commanding the northern approaches from Norway via Shetland, controlling the crossing of the Pentland Firth, and guarding the sounds between the islands including the entrances to Scapa Flow. Hoy (originally 48 pennylands) was biggest in terms of its area, and second only to Birsay in value. Hunting may have been the attraction in Hoy; we know that the earls shared medieval nobility's universal passion of hunting,[22] and we also know that deer flourished in Hoy when they were reintroduced in the nineteenth century.

By the time we have information from fifteenth century rentals some of the bordland, including Birsay itself, had passed into the hands of the bishop. We have no knowledge of the date of the transfer, but Birsay may not, as is sometimes suggested, have been gifted to the church quite as early as the building and endowment of St Magnus Cathedral.[23] Another large bishopric estate which must also have been gifted by the earls comprised the whole of the island of Egilsay and the extensive districts of Sourin and Scockness in the east of Rousay. This estate is associated with one of the interesting *huseby*-names which, it has been suggested, were power centres of the early earls.[24]

The King of Scots had acquired the earldom, so these great bordland farms now belonged to James III and were entrusted to Lord Henry Sinclair as part of the tack. Lord Henry in turn often placed his immediate relatives in these farms in much the same way as earls had always done in the past. Thus Lord Henry Sinclair's brother, Sir William Sinclair of Warsetter, held a good deal of bordland on advantageous terms, and another group of relatives were installed in Cairston.[25] The bordland farms, however, had been shrinking ever since the thirteenth century, as indeed had manor farms throughout Europe. They were much reduced in size and most of the former bordland was now divided up and rented to tenants. Thus Rapness, which was over 5 miles from north to south, was no longer a single manor farm but consisted of a large number of properties, most of them only one-sixth of a pennyland, their small size reflecting the low status of those who had at one time cultivated the earl's desmene (Fig.47).[26]

Besides the skat-free bordlands there was a good deal of other land which had been acquired over the years. A small proportion of this additional land was skat-paying and was described as 'Auld Earldom', so it evidently was part of the earldom estate which Earl William Sinclair received when he was installed in 1434. The *bordland* and other *auld earldom* land had to be returned intact to the king of Norway-Denmark on the death of an earl. In addition, however, there was other land which the earls had acquired on their own account and which did not require to be returned to the Crown. These were the so-called conquest lands. The term 'conquest' carries no connotations of forcible or illegal possession, but is a Scots legal term for land which had been acquired in the owner's lifetime, for example by purchase or gift, as opposed to land which had been inherited. However, it is likely that this personal estate had not all been acquired by Earl William, but included his father and grandfather's acquired lands, and there might even have been acquisitions from the even more distant past including lands inherited from Malise Sperra. When James III acquired the earldom in 1470 Earl William was therefore able to differentiate between the earldom, the right to which he resigned to the king, and the 'conquest' lands which it was acknowledged he had a right to retain as private property (see p.203).

Thus Lord Henry Sinclair, in addition to the lands he held in tack, also owned the 'conquest' estate which he inherited from Earl William. This included the substantial 'grange' of Paplay in Holm which had been earldom property in the distant past. It had passed into private hands in the twelfth century and Earl William had been able to buy it back after a lapse of 350 years.[27] But Paplay was not typical; the conquest land mainly consisted of tiny scraps of land and fractions of townships scattered throughout nearly every district in Orkney including many places in which earls had not previously owned property. Since some of the acquisitions can be dated to 1460–1468, it has been suggested that, in the years immediately before the impignoration, Earl William was borrowing money deliberately to build up an estate which he would retain in the event of the earldom lands being lost.[28] If this was his motive, he was entirely successful, since the conquest lands (about 12% of Orkney) were about the same in total extent as the former earldom. With economic conditions at their worst, and much land out of cultivation, it seems likely that property could be bought fairly readily, but cash transactions were by no means the only method. Earl William found various ingenious ways of converting earldom income, which he feared he might lose, into conquest property, which he hoped to retain.[29] For example, it was possible to give away earldom land in exchange for private property which could then be claimed as conquest, or he might accept land in return for reducing or abolishing the obligation to pay skat. The remission of skat at Sebay as part-payment for the purchase of the 'grange' of Paplay is an example of this means of increasing the conquest estate at no real cost. He also benefited from the difficulty which udallers experienced in paying skat in the years of depression; small parcels of land could be accepted in lieu of skat or, failing such informal arrangements, skat debt ultimately resulted in *skatfaa*, the confiscation of property to pay arrears.[30] The fragmented nature of the conquest land suggests that this may be how much of it was acquired.

The Norwegian crown had possessed lands in Orkney which, as we have seen, were entrusted to Earl Henry I in 1379 (page 162). On the impignoration of the islands in 1468 these lands had also passed into the possession of the King of Scots and they were included in Lord Henry Sinclair's tack. It is often supposed that the bulk of this *kingsland* consisted of estates sequestrated from the rebels after their defeat at Florevåg in 1194.[31] Although these estates were originally administered separately on behalf of the crown, royal land had latterly been entrusted to the Sinclair earls as part of their installation grant. Over the years *kingsland* had been absorbed into the earldom lands, despite undertakings to keep it distinct. Since both categories now belonged to the King of Scots, and since Lord Henry collected payments from both as part of his tack, he had no practical need to distinguish between them. Insofar as Henry may have had ambitions to be reinstated in the earldom, he may actually have been quite willing to blur the distinction between earldom and kingsland in the hope that he might some day acquire the ownership of both.

The extent of this former kingsland is an unsolved problem. Throughout the rental the term 'pro rege' (belonging to the king) is frequently found.

Storer Clouston, interpreted 'pro rege' as 'belonging to the King of Norway'. He produced figures suggesting that the Norwegian Crown estates had included about 20% of all the land in the islands.[32] He is unlikely to be right: it seems clear that the terms 'pro rege' and 'kingsland' were often used to mean 'belonging to the King of Scots' and were used to describe the former earldom lands which the Scots king now possessed.[33] It appears that the Norwegian crown lands were not very extensive, at least by the end of the Middle Ages, and the fact that we have no information about how they were managed, or the name of any steward, seems to confirm that they were not very important.

It was under the capable and energetic management of Lord Henry Sinclair that a remarkable revival of family fortune restored the essential substance of power, although a Sinclair never again attained the title of earl. Earl William died at a date prior to July 1480, having disposed of his principal Scottish properties to the sons of his second marriage, Oliver who received Ravenscraig and Roslin, and William who became Earl of Caithness. Although Henry's father was the eldest son, he was virtually disinherited, receiving only the barony of Newburgh in Aberdeenshire.[34] He was another William ('the Waster') and was of doubtful sanity but, as principal heir-at-law, he was able to contest his exclusion and eventually received Ravenscraig and its adjacent lands.[35] Henry Sinclair's appearance in Orkney can be dated to about the time of his grandfather's death, and he seems to have been entrusted with the conquest property. By 1484, when he first appears in *Exchequer Rolls* delivering the rents, he had succeeded in obtaining a sub-tack from the bishop of all or part of Orkney. The death of his eccentric father in 1487 brought a rapid improvement in his position: he inherited Ravenscraig for which he received a charter of confirmation in 1488,[36] and in the following year he was recognised as Lord Sinclair, 'chief of that blood'.[37] Then in 1489 he was given the tack of Orkney and Shetland in his own name and with it the custody of the castle and powers of 'justiciary, folderie and balliatus' which conferred authority to govern the islands and collect the rents.[38]

Although Henry Sinclair received this recognition, the king was careful to set restrictions on his authority. Henry had risen at the expense of Bishop Andrew, the previous holder of the tack, and their relationship became increasingly difficult. Although there was no real reason to doubt Henry's loyalty, the king found it prudent to balance his growing power with charters to Kirkwall (1486)[39] and to Bishop Andrew (1490).[40] The latter charter vested the bishop with judicial powers and, since the bishopric was not a distinct territory but lay interspersed with other lands throughout every parish of Orkney and Shetland, it created what was in effect an alternative jurisdiction. Later the Lords of Council commented that the bishop's charter 'is of na avale in the self', having been granted without the advice of parliament.[41] The charter apparently conferred powers intended to be held in reserve should they be needed, rather than for immediate use.

With every intention of establishing himself on a permanent basis, Lord Henry Sinclair could afford to take a long-term view of Orkney's economic problems. When he took over the tack, a great deal of former arable land was abandoned and tenantless, and the position was particularly serious on the highly taxed lands in the West Mainland and in the North Isles.[42] Abandoned land was not unique to Orkney but was part of a European phenomenon, the ultimate cause of which was the slowness of population recovery following the Black Death and other outbreaks of the plague. Fewer mouths to feed brought a drop in grain prices which reached a low point in the decade 1460–1470. With grain sometimes barely saleable even in the more favoured parts of Europe, a marginal grain-growing area like Orkney was particularly badly affected, and this situation was compounded by climatic deterioration and the loss of Scandinavian markets.[43] The worst of the abandoned lands, the badly eroded sandy soils in parts of the North Isles were simply written off, sometimes with the wry comment that the land was 'blawin to Birrowne' (Bergen) or to 'Issland' (Iceland).[44] Elsewhere Lord Henry encouraged the reoccupation of ley land by a variety of concessions, and a comparison of the 1492 and 1500 rentals reveals his considerable success both in reducing ley land and augmenting his income. Generally his aim was to have skat paid in full since it was paid by everyone, udallers as well as his own people, and to make any necessary concessions in rent. Whereas poor tenants might be allowed to pay in grain, he expected more substantial people to pay as much as possible in the more valuable pennyworths of animal products. Quite often traditional skat and rent were entirely set aside, and land was 'set for a soume'; these new rents involved large reductions but were paid in barrels of butter, illustrating the greater emphasis on pastoral farming.[45]

Another of Henry's preoccupations was the task of identifying the conquest lands which were his own property, but lay so hopelessly intermixed with the lands he held in tack from the Scottish king that his 1492 rental rarely attempted to distinguish them. The task of establishing ownership involved research, including an investigation of the property of Malise Sperra who had died a century earlier.[46] Where ownership was disputed, the case had to be taken to law. Between 1497 and 1503 Henry compiled a second rental, a main purpose of which was to list the conquest lands and record the payments which were due from them.

The main issue in Henry's embittered relations with Bishop Andrew was a dispute about the skat of the bishopric which the bishop collected, but which Henry claimed was rightfully his. Henry gathered what information he could about the payments, and his rental makes the claim that Bishop William Tulloch:

46. **Land Blown to Bergen.** *Lord Henry Sinclair was forced to remit butter skat on the Westray links when farmers told him that their land was 'blawn til Bergen'.*

...quhen he had our Soverane Lordis landis in tak wes the first that evir began to tak ony of the Kingis scattis contenit in this buik'.[47]

Ever since David Balfour's *Odal Rights and Feudal Wrongs* (1860) it has been customary to blame the Bishop William Tulloch for surreptitiously misappropriating the king's property or, more charitably, confusing it with his own as a result of mismanagement during the period he was entrusted with the tack of the former earldom,[48] but it is not necessary to accuse the bishop of dishonesty or incompetence. The skat of the bishopric estate seems indeed originally to have been payable to the earl, at least in theory, but it had been granted to William Tulloch in the latter days of Danish-Norwegian rule when Christian I had given the bishop the management of the islands.[49] In Bishop Andrew's 1490 charter the rights conferred on him included the skat of his bishopric, and so the bishop's claim to the bishopric skat was explicitly recognised by Scotland. However, the issue took on international implications when, as a response to this charter, King Hans attempted to reassert his right to grant 'royal revenues and rights' ('koninglige renttæ oc rettigheed') from Orkney church land. Within months of Bishop Andrew receiving these rights from Scotland, King Hans on his personal initiative bestowed the revenues and rights once held by Bishop Tulloch on Sir David Sinclair of Sumburgh. Sir David was Henry's uncle, and he served both the King of Scots as Foud of Shetland and also the Norwegian-Danish king as governor of the Castle of Bergen and as a member of the Norwegian royal administration.[50] Uncle and nephew usually co-operated closely, so King Hans' grant to Sir David was no doubt a Sinclair attempt to subvert the bishop's Scottish charter.

In 1501 Henry Sinclair's tack was renewed, this time for a lease of 19 years with a modest augmentation of 'hams for the king's use' which brought the total amount payable to £433⅓.[51] Early in the following year Bishop Andrew received confirmation of his alternative jurisdiction, so it was apparently still the intention to use the bishop as a potential check to Henry's power.[52] The bishop's confirmation was accompanied by letters directed by the Lords of Council to Henry warning him not to interfere with the bishopric skats, but despite the warning Lord Henry and his brother soon after took forcible possession of a whole series of bishopric properties, or so it was claimed. But the Scottish king seemed to follow no consistent policy. In 1503, perhaps on the death of Bishop Andrew, Sir David Sinclair of Sumburgh received the disputed skats in a Scottish grant which was closely modelled on the gift he had received in 1491 from King Hans, except that the somewhat vague 'koninglige rentæ' ('royal revenues') was translated in more specific terms to include a gift of 'all the skattis'.[53] And yet in the long term this grant was inoperative, or perhaps it lapsed with Sir David's death. Bishopric property continued to pay skat to the bishop, and indeed even after the abolition of episcopacy, skat from the former bishopric continued to be paid to his lay successors. Thus, despite his best efforts, it was only in exceptional cases that Lord Henry was able to recover any income from bishopric property.[54]

In the last eight or ten years of his life Henry was increasingly absent from Orkney. He may have seen prospects for further advancement at court if the recovery of the title of earl was his aim, or there may no longer have been the need for the close supervision of business affairs which had characterised his Orkney years. In his absence his brother, Sir William Sinclair of Warsetter, acted on his behalf. Warsetter in Sanday was a new creation, apparently an amalgamation of conquest property, and was only a part of the extensive estate which Sir William accumulated. He had other land in Sanday including the Bu of Brough, and probably the bordland farms of Tafts, Walls and Lopness; in Westray he held Rapness and Tuquoy, and for a time he seems to have occupied Westray bishopric property; possibly he held the bordland in Stronsay; he owned Newark in Deerness, and was later to acquire extensive property in St Andrews.[55] The huge Orkney estate built up by the Warsetter

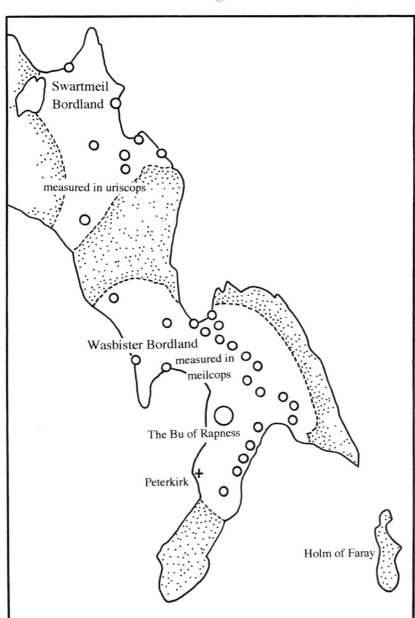

47. Rapness and its Bordlands. *The Bu of Rapness was surrounded by low-status satellite places (the Wasbister bordland). The farms of the Swartmeil Bordland were also very small, but rather bigger than those nearer the Bu suggesting greater independence. Meilcops and uriscops were renting units of one-sixth of a pennyland.*

231

Sinclairs was a base from which they eventually disputed control of Orkney with Lord Henry's descendants whose interests were divided between the islands and lowland Scotland. However, as long as Lord Henry was alive, Sir William was a partner rather than a rival.

Lord Henry Sinclair was a hard-headed and meticulous businessman, well able to ensure that his tack yielded him a good profit, but he was also a soldier, a courtier, a lover of literature and owner of an extensive library. Perhaps it was the same quiet humour and appreciation of the apt turn of phrase which led him both to note down the protests of the Westray farmers who told him that their land was 'blown to Bergen' and to enjoy the poetry of his kinsman, Gavin Douglas. As Douglas acknowledged it was at Henry's insistence that he undertook his translation of the Aeneid into Scots:

> At the request of ane lorde of renowne
> Of ancestrie maist nobill, an illustir baroun,
> Fadir of bukis, protector of science and lair
> My special gude lord, Henry lord Sinclare
> Quhilk with great instance, diverse times sere
> Prayit me translate Virgil or Homere.[56]

But the 'father of books' was drawn into matters of another kind as relations with England worsened. In 1512 he was reputed to have served as captain of James IV's flagship, the *Great Michael,* and in March of the following year he was appointed 'Master of all our Machines and Artyleris' with £100 a year and a place in the royal household.[57] He did not live long to enjoy his new post. At Flodden he was among the first to fall, killed in the initial artillery exchange as he vainly tried to bring his guns to bear on the English ranks. His uncle, William Earl of Caithness, and the bishop of Caithness were among the many others who died that day. In Orkney Lord Henry was long remembered as 'my lord Sinclaris that deit at Flowdin', and in Caithness it was long considered unlucky to travel south across the Ord on a Monday.[58] His widow, Lady Margaret Sinclair, received £100 for the eight machines called 'serpentynis' which Henry had supplied to the king, and she also received the tack of Orkney in her own name.[59] Up to this point Scottish rule had not proved bad for Orkney; indeed Henry's rule can largely be seen as a continuation of the kind of society which had existed in Earl William's day, but with fewer political pressures and a greater degree of order and efficiency. The first half century of Scottish rule had been a period of peace, in marked contrast to other places in the north of Scotland. Now that Margaret Sinclair had the tack it was to be a different story.

17

The Summerdale Years

Ever since the pawning of the islands the Sinclair empire had been in a state of progressive disintegration. Earl William had lost both the title of Earl of Orkney and the possession of the earldom estate and, after his death, his remaining property was partitioned between three main families: Roslin was left to his son, Oliver; the earldom of Caithness went to William (the younger son of that name), and Ravenscraig was with some difficulty secured by the other William ('the Waster') who passed it to his son, Lord Henry, who had also been left the Orkney conquest lands. In addition, a dozen or so lesser Sinclair lines were emerging as Orkney gentry in their own right, principal of which was the branch headed by Lord Henry's brother, Sir William Sinclair of Warsetter (see p.230). When Lord Henry was killed at Flodden, disintegration was carried a stage further as Sinclair struggled against Sinclair in the most serious breakdown of civil government since saga-times. In James Sinclair of Brecks, son of Sir William Sinclair of Warsetter, there was a figure of saga-proportions. Like the earls of old he pursued a murderous feud against his own kinsmen, overcame his enemies in battle, and briefly enjoyed the same kind of independence and power. His defeated cousin complained that James was 'kingis-like, as he war ane king in thai partis'.[1]

When Lord Henry was killed at Flodden his tack still had many years to run, and his widow, Lady Margaret Sinclair, continued to collect the rents. Their son, Lord William Sinclair, may still have been quite young in 1513 but he, rather than his mother, might have been expected to receive the tack when it was renewed in 1528 and again in 1536. William never seems to have had much success in anything he attempted. Perhaps he had more in common with his half-mad grandfather, William the Waster, than with his businesslike father, and it may be that he was regarded as incapable of managing such an important enterprise as the Orkney tack. During the latter part of Lord Henry's lifetime, Orkney affairs had been largely in the hands of his brother, Sir William Sinclair of Warsetter, who acted as 'Justice'.[2] This arrangement was allowed to continue,[3] but it was inevitable that there should be friction between the absentee holder of the tack—a female, and that was a novelty—and her ambitious brother-in-law who had grown accustomed to managing Orkney. The first sign of trouble was revealed by irregularities in Margaret's payments to the Exchequer: in 1515 there were arrears of £100; in 1518 the royal falconer complained that Margaret had not paid him;[4] no payment for the tack was made to the Exchequer in 1519 and 1520, then the debt was cleared in 1521; no payment was made in 1522, and arrears of £275 were still outstanding in 1524.[5] The death of Sir William Sinclair of Warsetter c.1523 and the transfer of power to his sons, James Sinclair of Brecks and Edward Sinclair of Strom, brought matters to a head. In 1525 the Exchequer allowed a remission of £80 because in the previous year the islands had been 'completely laid waste' by the Sinclair brothers, and in the same year there was an English attack on Shetland with the result that 'the said lessee never got a single penny from the said lordship during that time'.[6]

Matters were further complicated by Lord William Sinclair's difficult relationship both with the Warsetter Sinclairs and with his mother. In 1524 he had received a charter confirming his rights to the Barony of Newburgh in Aberdeenshire which had belonged to his father and grandfather,[7] but in 1527 he lost part of the barony in settlement of a debt of 550 marks due to Helen Gordon, Sir William Sinclair of Warsetter's widow.[8] Thus on the eve of Summerdale it was no longer the case that the Warsetter Sinclairs owed money to their Ravenscraig relatives for arrears of rent which they had collected but failed to deliver; on the contrary they were taking legal action to recover debts owed to them by Lord William Sinclair. But we cannot assume that William's interests were identical with those of his mother, and that she always approved of his conduct. For example in 1542 Lady Sinclair made a complaint against her son who, when she was ill and in peril of her life, had forcibly seized Ravenscraig with a band of accomplices and taken possession of the keys with the intention of stealing her goods.[9] Thus in the years immediately before Summerdale, the three parties—Lady Margaret Sinclair, her son William, and the Warsetter Sinclairs—all had their individual interests, but all to some degree were compelled to co-operate in managing the tack. Meanwhile another Sinclair, John, Earl of Caithness, was waiting to take advantage of their quarrels.

Given these difficulties it seems inconceivable that Margaret could have collected rent and skat during the Summerdale crisis (1528-9) when James Sinclair was waging war against her son. Yet after 1526 all irregularities in payments to the Exchequer ceased, and even when Orkney was in a state of rebellion there were no further interruptions or arrears.[10] Part of the explanation was probably that much of the extensive estates of the Warsetter Sinclairs derived from lands which Margaret held in tack, so no matter how they might quarrel with her, they could not afford to let her default on payments, particularly when the 19-year tack was due for renewal in 1528.[11] Thus the Orkney rents continued to be delivered to Leith, and the Exchequer

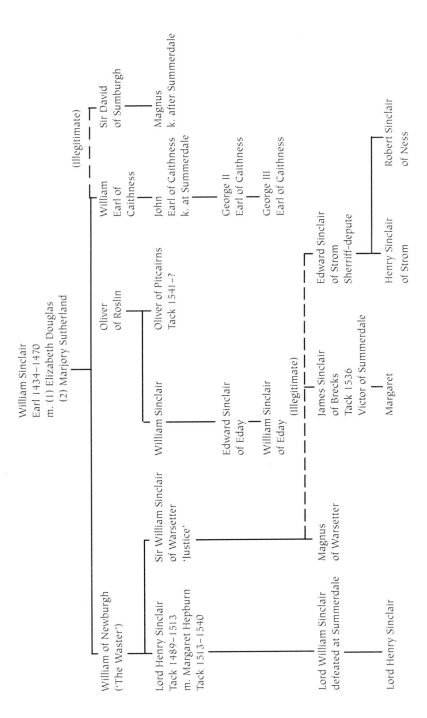

48. *The Sinclairs, c.1434-1560.*

was paid in full, although it seems quite likely that during this period James Sinclair may have appropriated the surplus which ought to have gone to Margaret.[12]

The dispute also involved the 'conquest lands'. These, it will be remembered, were the 'acquired lands' which Earl William was allowed to keep as private property when James III took over the earldom. By letters issued under the Privy Seal in 1471 Earl William's ownership of the conquest estate was explicitly recognised very soon after he abandoned his right to the earldom.[13] From the start he had realised that it would be difficult to maintain his rights to land which often lay run-rig with earldom land (see p.204). His son, Lord Henry Sinclair, made two attempts to produce rentals which identified the payments due from these lands, but it is a reflection on the unsettled nature of the times that this large estate was eventually absorbed into the Crown lands. According to Lord Henry's grandson who was still vainly trying to establish his rights in 1581, the conquest lands had been taken over illegally by 'officers' who were administering Orkney following Lord Henry's death at Flodden.[14] These 'officers' were Sir William Sinclair of Warsetter and his sons, acting on behalf of Margaret Sinclair. The Crown had little practical interest in the conquest lands since, whatever their ownership, the Crown's income was fixed, being restricted to the lump sum it received from the tack. Both Margaret Sinclair and the Warsetter Sinclairs stood to benefit if the rents of the conquest lands augmented their income from the tack. Lord William Sinclair was the only person who had an interest in keeping the conquest property distinct; he ought to have inherited these lands from his father but, despite his undoubted rights, his repeated pleas met with no success. On at least two occasions a commission was granted requiring the Sheriff to take evidence, but investigations were 'stoppit and debarrit throwe occasioun and trubill in thai parts'.[15] Those in actual possession of the conquest lands found it easy to block enquiries.

Meantime Margaret Sinclair received the estate of Sir David Sinclair of Sumburgh which provided a very large addition to her property. Sir David was an illegitimate son of Earl William, and he followed a successful career in the service both of the King of Denmark and the King of Scots, at different times commanding the Castle of Bergen, acting as Foud (chief magistrate) in Shetland, Chamberlain of Ross and keeper of the castles of Redcastle and Dingwall.[16] He had used his very considerable wealth to buy out the udal rights in Shetland of his thirteen brothers and sisters, as well as making many land purchases on his own account, both in Orkney and Shetland.[17] Sir David's will has survived,[18] and his numerous bequests testify both to his wealth and to his good relations with his many Sinclair relatives including Lord Henry. Nevertheless when David died in 1507, Lord Henry had been quick to seize his uncle's estate; he went to Shetland 'in haste' from where he wrote an obsequious letter to King John of Denmark in which he reminded the king that Orkney and Shetland had been granted to his family by the Kings of Norway 'even before the birth of Christ'. With a similar disregard for the truth he described how he had granted lands to Sir David (and so had a right to recover them) although in reality most of David's lands had been purchased. It is interesting that, 38 years after the impignoration, it still was important for Lord Henry to try to enlist the support of 'the councillors of the King of Norway'.[19] In fact Sir David's property was forfeited to the Scottish Crown on grounds of bastardy, and it was only in 1524 that his estate was granted to Lady Margaret Sinclair.[20] The fact that Sir David's estate was given, not to Lord William Sinclair who was ostensibly the head of the family, but to William's mother, is another indication of a lack of confidence in his abilities.

In February 1526 William Sinclair, now a young adult, appeared before the Lords of Council and had to find security that he would remain in Edinburgh until his followers handed over the Bishop's Palace to Robert Maxwell, the newly appointed Bishop of Orkney. Storer Clouston in his *History* regarded the seizure of the palace to which William Sinclair 'had no right whatsoever' as evidence that he was a young man 'rash and violently inclined'.[21] More recently Peter Anderson has pointed out that there is little else in William Sinclair's career which would support such a judgement—in later life he was an ineffectual litigant rather than a warrior; perhaps the Council's order was a formality to ensure that the secular authorities holding the palace during the vacancy yielded it up to the new bishop.[22] A further possibility is that the 'followers' who were ordered to quit the palace were Warsetter Sinclairs, technically Margaret's agents in Orkney and for whose conduct she and her son were held responsible although they were in a state of virtual rebellion against her. This is further suggested by a grant two weeks later by which Margaret gave her son custody of the Castle of Kirkwall with powers to administer justice, while reserving the *bordland bus* (the main farms of the former earldom) for her own use.[23] These measures were designed to deprive James Sinclair of the authority to manage Orkney on her behalf, and at the same time to evict him from the bordland farms which had been held by his father.

Although armed with this authority from his mother, which received confirmation from the Lords of Council, it is not clear whether Lord William was immediately successful in making good his appointment. However, by Easter week 1528 if not earlier he was installed in the Castle of Kirkwall. Initially his credentials were perhaps sufficient to prevent overt opposition from James Sinclair, but violence was to follow. In a night attack outside the walls of the castle James and Edward Sinclair set on their cousin and captured him. It is an indication of the bitterness of the feud that seven of

William Sinclair's gentlemen followers were allegedly killed in cold blood after they had been disarmed, including three Sinclairs who were related to all the protagonists.[24]

There was a surprising delay before William reported his misfortunes to the Council. In the meantime he was ejected from Orkney and found refuge in Caithness where he and his relative, John, Earl of Caithness, together planned an invasion of Orkney. In the previous year John had received a royal mandate to wage war against 'the kin of Clanquhattane'[25] (which he chosen to ignore) but, if similar authority could be obtained, an attack on Orkney was a more attractive proposition. The Earl of Caithness would be helping a relative who had a legal right to establish himself in Orkney, and he might earn the gratitude of the king by defeating the rebels. He also had more personal motives for becoming involved: he could hark back to the days when his grandfather had ruled the two earldoms of Caithness and Orkney (see Fig.48); if James Sinclair was defeated, and if William Sinclair was unacceptable as tacksman, the Earl of Caithness was a likely alternative, and securing the tack might even open the way to regaining the Orkney earldom. The invasion was launched within a few days of authority being received, so it is clear that everything was ready in advance. William received the necessary letters from the king 'in the first, second, third and fourth forms' charging the rebels to deliver up the Castle of Kirkwall to him and, in the event of them refusing to do so, commissioning the Earl of Caithness to recover the castle and punish the offenders. When David Lawrie, the messenger entrusted with serving the royal letters, was deforced and imprisoned, the invasion was launched with full royal authority. The attack was expected; James Sinclair had a large force already assembled from both Orkney and Shetland when the invaders landed on the Orphir coast 'with spears, darts, arrows and the sound of trumpets'.[26]

Although Summerdale was a civil war within the Sinclair family, the cause of James Sinclair seems to have commanded such widespread support that his followers were identified as 'the Orkneymen'. He had the backing of most of the Sinclair kindred, although there were important exceptions.[27] The visionary appearance of St Magnus during the battle, at which 'he faucht for the libertie of this cuntrie, quha was its patroune',[28] is another indication that Summerdale was widely regarded as patriotic resistance to an outside threat. The Summerdale campaign was fought with quite unaccustomed bloodshed and with little mercy for defeated opponents. There is a well-established tradition that Orcadians were afraid that William intended 'to extinguish the udal rights of the ancient inhabitants'.[29] Fear of the feuing of udal land, however, seems premature: in 60 years of Scottish rule there had been no hint of interference with the traditional system of land tenure, and indeed there had been very little change to the way in which Orkney was governed. William Sinclair's intention was to regain the management of the tack, and there is no evidence that he intended to grant feus. During his short time in Orkney, however, he had certainly antagonised most people and united Orcadians against him.

The battle between the invaders and 'the Orkneymen' took place, not on the Orphir shore or under the walls of Kirkwall Castle, but at Summerdale,[30] which lies more than three miles inland just under the crest of the pass which leads through the Orphir hills. It may be that the Earl of Caithness had found the way to Kirkwall defended against him and had turned inland, only to be caught on open moorland. Most of what we know about Summerdale comes from William Sinclair's subsequent complaint to the king which is no doubt a somewhat one-sided account.[31] He described how 30 men including the earl were killed in the first onslaught,[32] and tells of horrifying violence in the aftermath of the battle: a further 100 perished as they tried to reach the safety of their ships; 22 'poor carriage men' (sailors in a transport vessel) were brought ashore, killed on the beach, and their naked bodies 'turfitt' into the sea. Some sought refuge in churches, but three weeks later, and with a disregard for the right of sanctuary, 30 men were executed when they were brought out from St Magnus Cathedral, St Lawrence (probably in Burray) and from an unidentified church of Our Lady. A month later James Sinclair went to Shetland where he executed the Lawman and hanged a number of others; his victims were said to include three boys whom he killed simply for malice against their masters. Altogether William estimated that over 300 had been killed, and other accounts put the death toll even higher.[33] William Sinclair was himself taken prisoner along with his son (also William), and young William died after spending some time in captivity.

Even in saga-times there had been few battles on this scale and nothing of the sort had disturbed Orkney in the later Middle Ages. It is not surprising that all sorts of stories came to surround the battle. One tale tells of the fatal consequences of the rhyme:

> Which spills the foremost foeman's life
> That party conquers in the strife.

When the invaders landed in Orphir, they caught and killed a herd lad, only to discover that he was a Caithness boy who had emigrated to Orkney.[34] Last to die was an Orkneyman who lived at Tuskerbister near the battlefield; he had stripped the corpse of a Caithness man, and went home dressed in his new finery; his mother, seeing this strange figure approaching, waited behind the door with a large stone in the toe of a sock and killed him with a single blow.[35]

The government was at a loss to know how to react effectively to these events. Lord William Sinclair demanded that the rebels should be 'haistely punist with all rigour',[36] but he does not appear to have been keen to undertake the task himself, or even to be restored as Justice. Having twice been captured, and twice expelled from Orkney, he confined his future attempts to recover his property to legal means. In 1541, 1548, 1567 and 1581—that is every time there was a change of regime in the islands—he or his son petitioned the government regarding the lost conquest lands. William, however, was discredited by his defeat at Summerdale and the whole question of the conquest lands was of such complexity that his opponents were able to hinder investigations which threatened to diminish their income.

Then, in a sudden shift of policy in 1534, James V began to look with favour on the unrepentant rebels. Perhaps there was little else he could do. In 1530 the islands had been given in feu to the Earl of Moray, the king's half-brother.[37] It was a grant which looks as if it was intended to place Orkney in the hands of someone with sufficient authority to restore the islands to obedience, but it turned out to be one of those strange charters which appear to be important but which in fact turn out to have been totally inoperative. With James Sinclair firmly in control it was difficult for an outsider, whatever his birth, to rule Orkney by paper rights alone. The rehabilitation of James Sinclair marked a realisation that it would be easier to come to an accommodation with him than to impose anyone else by force, and the decision was no doubt influenced by the regularity with which the royal rents continued to be delivered to Leith. The king's dealings with the rebels were a typical example of how James V's ferocious pursuit of justice was often combined with respites which tended to negate his good intentions. There were also people at court who may have been ready to urge a settlement: the change in James V's attitude coincided with the growing ascendancy of Oliver Sinclair of Pitcairn. An even more direct line of communication was provided by James Sinclair's wife, Barbara Stewart, since her brother was the latest husband of Margaret Tudor, the king's mother.

In his *History* Storer Clouston suggested that, if Scotland had failed to come to terms with James Stewart, he might have turned to Denmark.[38] After 1468 the Norwegian Council of the Realm had time and time again urged the king to redeem the islands, and Christian III seems to have made a serious attempt to do so, levying a special tax to raise the money and requesting a meeting in Orkney in 1550 at which payment was to be made.[39] The question of redemption was later raised in 1560, 1564, 1570, 1589, 1660, 1667 and 1749, and so the possibility of a return to Norway remained a live issue.[40] Regular contact on legal matters still continued between Shetland and Norway (but not Orkney). For example, there are a number of sixteenth century legal documents written in Norwegian (and occasionally in Danish) which record transactions involving land in Shetland made by Shetland people who were resident in Bergen.[41] Orkney and Shetland vessels were still allowed to enter the port of Bergen without paying a toll, and there was a steady stream of young folk from the islands whom the governor of the castle placed in employment. Several rose to be city councillors, one Orkney immigrant attained the position of burgomaster,[42] and James Sinclair's great-uncle, Sir David Sinclair of Sumburgh, had once been governor of the castle. Another danger was that England might become involved; in 1535 when the Danes were anxious that England should cease aiding Lübeck against her, Henry VIII was offered the right to Orkney and Shetland if he was willing to pay the redemption price.[43] While there is no indication that the victors of Summerdale intended to revert to their Scandinavian roots, or that the Danish-Norwegian king was ready to treat with the rebels, there were all sorts of reasons for seeking a solution to James Sinclair's rebellion rather than allowing the situation to drift.

The first sign of approval for James Sinclair was in June 1534 when he is recorded as acting as 'Justice of Orkney for the time'.[44] This was a phrase which his father had used both when deputising for Lord Henry and again when he was acting on behalf of Lady Margaret Sinclair, and it probably indicates that James had received a commission from Margaret (rather than seizing power illegally). In June 1535 James and Edward Sinclair received precepts of legitimisation as the next step towards their rehabilitation.[45] Although they were described as bastards, the investigation of the legitimacy of a half-sister, the child of Sir William Sinclair of Warsetter's known marriage to Helen Gordon, suggests that James and Edward may have been sons of an earlier marriage which had been annulled.[46] That same month we find that James Sinclair had been knighted and was given a feudal grant of 'the lands and island (sic) of Sanda and Stronsay' along with the 'holms' of 'Rynitsay' (North Ronaldsay), Papa Stronsay and Auskerry for the annual payment of 200 marks.[47] This is the first instance in Orkney of the granting of a feu, an arrangement by which the recipient was given heritable possession in return for an annual payment (the feu duty). It was stipulated that, unlike udal property, James Sinclair's feu was to pass to a single heir. Feuing was generally disliked in Orkney where udal tenure prevailed, and this first feu must have caused immediate suspicion because of its slipshod drafting. Although the King of Scots held a good deal of former earldom land in Sanday and Stronsay which he might legally feu, both islands contained extensive bishopric lands, and there were also many udal landowners in Sanday. By claiming to include the whole islands, the charter purports to grant land which the king did not actually own. According to the historian, Barry, there was a tradition that Sir James obtained his feu by falsely representing the islands to be mere holms, fit only for grazing.[48] Although in the case of North Ronaldsay the charter does somewhat surprisingly describe the island as a 'holm', the term is not used for Sanday or Stronsay. The annual payment of 200 marks and the requirement that Sir James should build a mansion house on the property make it unlikely that Sanday and Stronsay were thought to be islands of insignificant size. Probably James's intention had been to secure Warsetter in Sanday and the bordland farms in both islands which his father had occupied for many years. He may have been given more than he had originally asked as a result of careless drafting by Scots lawyers unfamiliar with Orkney. The grant of these new powers to Sir James Sinclair was balanced by the confirmation of Kirkwall's charter (1536)[49] in exactly the same way as Lord Henry Sinclair's first appearance as tacksman had been accompanied by the burgh charter of 1486.

Although it can hardly have been regarded as satisfactory that James Sinclair's violent conduct was rewarded, his rehabilitation at least offered a solution acceptable to the majority of the Sinclair gentry. However, the prospects of a permanent settlement were frustrated by his death in the following year (1536). Adam Abell, an Observantine friar who knew him well, described Sir James's sudden breakdown and the bizarre circumstances of his suicide.[50] In Abell's opinion it would have been better if Sir James had been hanged for his wicked life rather than made a knight; he was holding court 'with great gloriatioun and arrogance' when a writ from the king was produced which called for an investigation of some aspect of his conduct —Orkney people later believed that King James had discovered the true worth of the feu he had been tricked into granting.[51] The next morning, at his home in Linksness in Tankerness, Sir James rose at first light, put the king's writ and his signet ring under his wife's side as she lay sleeping; he then ran out of the house 'castand gamuntis' (gamunt, a leaping dancing step), he pulled peats out of the peat-stack, and jumped into 'a foul deep dub', then, casting off his clothes and his bonnet, he ran to a high crag from which he leapt into the sea and drowned himself. According to Abell it was rumoured that that 'the evil spirit led him by the oxter into the sea and drowned him'. The place of his suicide is identified as the nearby Gloup of Linksness.

Sir James Sinclair's property was escheated to the Crown on the grounds that 'he had wilfully slain himself',[52] and Margaret Sinclair's tack was confirmed for a further seven years.[53] In 1537 James Sinclair's widow and 12 others were ordered to appear before the Council 'for art and part the *stoutreif* [theft with violence] from Lady Margaret Sinclair of the rents of her lands...and for art and part the stoutreif from the tenants of the Lordship of Shetland and Orkney of their marts, hides, sheep, meal, butter, oil and malt'.[54] The rents were probably those illegally collected by Sir James Sinclair during his period in power. When the accused failed to appear, they were denounced as rebels and their goods escheated. The setback, however, was temporary, and in 1539 a number of measures show that that the king was trying to bring about a reconciliation between the rival Sinclair factions. In April Sir James Sinclair's widow received a grant of the estate which had been forfeited on the grounds of his suicide.[55] Then in September both Lord William Sinclair and Edward Sinclair, brother of the late Sir James, were at Falkland where, at the king's insistence, they entered into a *band of manrent* (a legal contract of alliance between the two parties) whereby all actions stemming from 'the deadly feud and enmity' between them were set aside and they agreed to co-operate as a means of pacifying the islands and restoring good government.[56] Security of £2000 was required that both parties abide by the terms of the band. Among the witnesses were Oliver Sinclair of Pitcairn, and this is an indication that he was becoming involved in the affairs of the islands. Two weeks later Edward Sinclair and thirty other named gentlemen along with their kinsmen and servants obtained a formal respite under the Privy Seal, not only for their part in the slaughter at Summerdale ten years earlier, but also for any crimes they had subsequently committed.[57] As far as we can see the king's intention was to put an end to the feuds resulting from Summerdale, and to resolve matters in such a way that Lady Margaret's tack continued, while at the same time regularising the position of the capable Edward Sinclair, with the hope that he might manage the islands on her behalf. This solution, however, was overtaken by events when, in the following year, James V visited the islands in person.

James V had good reason to be dissatisfied with the situation which had pertained in Orkney for the last quarter of a century. In view of the his interest in law, he may also have considered that one cause of disorder was the way the tacksman or her representative acting as 'Justice' was superimposed on the traditional system of Norwegian law rather than the normal laws of his kingdom. Furthermore, although Margaret's payments for Orkney arrived with commendable regularity, the king's income from the tack was not large and with different management it might be significantly increased.

In the early summer of 1540 the king embarked on a voyage which took him round the north of Scotland. English spies reported that he intended to visit Orkney, and the rumour was that he would create one of his bastard sons 'Lord of the Isles'.[58] Orkney, however, was only one of his concerns, and his main purpose was the pacification of parts of the West Highlands which had recently been in a state of rebellion. The fleet consisted of about 16 ships including the king's ship, *The Salamander*, which was fitted out at such expense that the 'the expedition was something of a luxury cruise'.[59] There were merchant vessels for the lords and gentlemen, three ships with victuals, a baggage hulk, and a well-trimmed barque which sailed ahead of the fleet acting as 'scurior'. The king was accompanied by the Earls of Huntly and Arran and by Cardinal Beaton, and some estimates put the total force as high as 3000-4000 men. Alexander Lindsay's 'rutter' (a navigational manual drawn up during the course of the voyage)[60] suggests that, after leaving the Forth on 12 June, the fleet followed the coast northwards, possibly landing at Scapa rather than Kirkwall. The king stayed for several weeks in Kirkwall, being hospitably entertained by Bishop Maxwell.[61] The discussions he held during his time in Orkney gave rise to the story that he had convened a 'thing' or even a 'parliament' which met in what was later known as Parliament Close.[62] When he sailed onwards from Orkney the king carried certain hostages with him and, although we do not know their names, Lord William Sinclair may have been one of them.

An Act of Parliament which followed the king's return listed the many lordships which were to be annexed to the Crown. The list included Orkney and Shetland: the islands were to remain permanently united to the Crown and were not to be given in feu except with the consent of parliament; even if they were feued with parliamentary consent, the king reserved the right to take them back into his own hands at any time without process of law.[63] The Act disposed of any claims which might stem from the Earl of Moray's inoperative feu of 1530, and so the way was clear for a new tacksman and a new beginning.

Margaret Sinclair's tack was cancelled although it still had three years to run, and she received generous compensation in the form of an annuity of 500 merks. The king's new tacksman was Oliver Sinclair of Pitcairn, younger son of Oliver Sinclair of Roslin. His appointment was from August 1540 and so the decision to give him the tack was probably made during James V's stay in Kirkwall, although it was April of the following year before he received a retrospective commission.[64] From one point of view it was a conservative appointment since Oliver was yet another descendant of the last earl (see Fig.48), and so the management of the islands was kept within the Sinclair family. However, Oliver was very much the king's man; he was James V's confidant and 'the most secret man living'; in 1540 he was rapidly rising to power and had recently been given the keepership of Tantallon and other rich gifts. One of his functions was to extract a much larger income from the islands than the king had hitherto received. In contrast to the £433⅓ which Lord Henry Sinclair's tack had yielded, Oliver was to make an annual payment of 3,000 merks (£2000),[65] but he had not been long in his tack when he somewhat optimistically reported that the Crown's annual income from Orkney might be £9750 with a further £4210 from Shetland.[66]

Oliver Sinclair's commission made important changes to Orkney's legal system, abolishing the office of Lawman and replacing it with the Scottish post of Sheriff, and so it marks an important stage in the integration of the islands with Scotland. Oliver Sinclair was empowered to act as Justice, Sheriff, Admiral and Baillie, to hold courts for these purposes and to appoint deputies who would attend to day-to-day business. Scottish courts replaced the native Norwegian courts, and instead of the Lawman and the roithmen ('council men') we now find the Sheriff and the suitors of court. To some extent these changes were superficial since the courts continued to use the Lawbook and its system of Norwegian law, and the families which had traditionally provided the roithmen continued to supply the suitors of court. We even find that from time to time the main sessions of the Sheriff Court were still described as the Lawthing, Allhallow Court and Hirdmansein. The tacksman in his capacity as Justice also performed a familiar role—essentially he had a similar function to the former Norse earls and sysselmen. However, there were two important changes: since the courts were Scottish in form, there was a tendency to use Scottish law as well as Norwegian law, and so as the sixteenth century progressed there was increasing confusion and corruption resulting from people seeking whichever system was likely to provide the most favourable outcome. Nor was the change from Lawman to Sheriff a mere change of name: the Lawman was elected by the Lawting, rather than being appointed by the earl, sysselman or tacksman, with the result that he could act as an independent spokesman on behalf of the community. The tacksman, on the other hand, now was the Sheriff; he combined legal and executive powers and derived his authority from the Crown, with the result that the role of community spokesman was lost. How much difference this made in practice is difficult to say, since the Lawman's function as independent community leader had not been very prominent ever since the Scottish takeover of the islands.

Lord William Sinclair was apparently in Kirkwall during the king's visit in 1540,[67] and the band he had entered into with Edward Sinclair in the previous year demonstrated his continuing interest in Orkney. However, he was not regarded by James V as part of the solution to Orkney's problems, and he drifted into ineffectual opposition to Oliver Sinclair. In May 1544 he seized a ship carrying Oliver's rents from Orkney to Leith when it put in at his burgh of Dysart.[68] No doubt William might try to justify the seizure of the ship on the grounds that he was entitled to compensation for the loss of his rights. The Queen-regent, however, ordered Sheriff-officers to distrain part of William's Ravenscraig estate in order to recover the value of the stolen property. Her letter provides a good illustration of the rents which the tacksman collected, since it lists the cargo—the number and prices of the barrels of butter, beef, tallow and oil, the chalders of bere and the 'dakers' of hides (daker, a unit of 10 hides). As late as 1548 William was still pressing for an investigation of the lands which 45 years earlier he ought to have inherited from his father.[69]

Oliver Sinclair's credibility in Orkney must have taken a severe blow when he led a disaffected Scottish army to humiliating defeat at Solway Moss

(1542). The death of James V a few weeks later further undermined his position, particularly as the widowed queen was left the income from Orkney as part of her tierce. Oliver Sinclair, whose tack conflicted with Mary of Lorraine's rights to her widow's portion, was involved in legal proceedings regarding the custody of the Castle which the queen granted to one of her French followers,[70] a certain M.Bonot about whom little is known, although he is found holding a court in Orkney as late as 1558.[71]

At local level some measure of continuity was provided by Edward Sinclair of Strom who in 1542/3 was created Oliver's Sheriff-depute.[72] Although conducting himself in a more circumspect manner than in the heady days after Summerdale when his brother had ruled 'king-like' in Orkney, Edward Sinclair's redoubtable military career was not yet at an end. In his old age he commanded the islanders at Orkney's forgotten battle, the Battle of Papdale which rivals Summerdale, both in the scale of the engagement and in the comprehensive nature of the victory. During the course of the century there were increasingly hostile relations with English shipping, especially with the fishermen whose voyages to Iceland were conducted along the lines of armed expeditions. In 1535 James V complained that English fishermen were in the habit of raiding the North Isles of Orkney and carrying off the inhabitants as 'slaves'.[73] The islanders likewise attacked English ships whenever they had an opportunity: in 1533 James Sinclair ignored a summons to appear before the English Council in connection with the rich cargo of the *Andro and Graith* of King's Lynn which he seized in North Ronaldsay.[74] The 1557 attack was more serious, and may have been motivated by the part which Bishop Reid played in Scottish diplomacy. An English fleet of 13 ships commanded by Sir John Clere, Vice-admiral of Queen Mary of England, was sent north to protect the homeward-bound fishing fleet and at the same time to annoy the Scots. On 11 and 12 August they landed at Kirkwall, burning part of the town, capturing the cathedral and bringing ashore artillery which was used bombard the castle. When the English landed again on Friday 13 August intent on capturing Bishop Reid's palace, they were confronted by a force which they estimated to be about 3000 strong. A sudden storm trapped the English on shore; ninety-seven were killed including three ships' captains, and Sir John Clere was drowned when his boat capsized as he attempted to return to his ship. The English guns were all captured, and many prisoners were held to ransom.[75]

The Reformation

The Reformation in Orkney was less traumatic than in many parts of Scotland thanks to the influence of two bishops, Robert Reid (Bishop of Orkney 1541–1558)[1] and Adam Bothwell (1559–1593).[2] Reid was a great Catholic churchman in the medieval tradition, noted for his building activities and for his reorganisation of the cathedral chapter. His successor, Adam Bothwell, was one of the few Scottish bishops to side with the reformers, and his moderate leadership guided Orkney through the period of transition. Both Reid and Bothwell concentrated on church organisation rather than doctrine, and the community at large was similarly not greatly concerned with religious disputes—as far as we can see there was little dissatisfaction with Catholicism and only isolated instances of much enthusiasm for Protestantism. There is an distinct impression that for many people religion was a secondary issue—it was church land rather than faith which caused passions to run high. Large new secular estates were carved from the bishopric, and they dwarfed the lands of the traditional gentry. Most of these new estates were possessed by outsiders, typically with an Edinburgh legal background and with the skills and contacts to secure feus of church land. The Bothwells, Bellendens and Balfours were a new inter-related kindred whose arrival signalled a major influx into positions of power. These feudal landowners formed a new class, superimposed on native landowners with whom initially they had few family ties. The tensions thus created threw Orkney into half a century of turmoil which was compounded by the rule of the notorious Stewart earls, Robert and Patrick. It was only with the execution of Earl Patrick in 1615, and with the eventual merging of the feuars and the traditional gentry, that these tensions were finally resolved.

The building work on the cathedral which had made such good initial progress seems to have 'gone to sleep' about the middle of the thirteenth century. After a gap of a century or more, work began again on the construction of the western part of the nave and the completion of the west gable overlooking Broad Street. The chronology of this final period is uncertain: the re-start has been attributed either to Bishop William Tulloch (c.1461–77) or to Bishop Andrew (1477–c.1505);[3] it was continued by Edward Stewart (c.1505–c.1524) and Robert Maxwell (c.1524–1541) and completed by Robert Reid, but how much of the work should be attributed to each is uncertain. Maxwell provided elaborate new stalls for the cathedral clergy and a peal of three new bells, cast in Edinburgh by Robert Borthwick who had been Lord Henry Sinclair's master gunner at Flodden.[4] Reid also repaired St Ola's Church and rebuilt the Bishop's Palace to which he added the round 'Moosie Tower'.[5] The period immediately before the Reformation saw more building work than any period since the days of Bishop Bjarni.

The inside of the cathedral was very different from the mellow sandstone of the present day. Walls were covered with a thin coat of plaster and decorated in brilliant colour. The centrepiece was the internationally famous shrine of St Magnus to which pilgrimages continued to be made; in 1441 Bishop Thomas Tulloch had petitioned the pope to grant indulgences to pilgrims visiting the shrine on certain feast days.[6] In addition there was a proliferation of side altars dedicated to numerous saints including St Ninian, St Catherine, St Barbara, St Andrew, St Lawrence, St Olaf, St John, St Peter, St Augustine, St Nicholas, St Christopher, St Columba, St Salvador, St Matthew and the Holy Trinity, while altars of Our Lady in St Ola's Church and of St Duthac at Pickaquoy were served from the cathedral.[7] Some altars were endowed with the rent of a single house in Kirkwall which provided for occasional masses for the souls of the founder, but the richest were served by their own priest and were so well provided with land that their chaplains ('prebendaries') were wealthy landowners. Several of the altars had originally been endowed by the earls themselves. For example, the altar of St Augustine was supported by half a pennyland detached from each of the Sanday bordland farms of How, Walls and Lopness and a further pennyland from the neighbouring earldom farm of Langta.[8] The rents of these lands provided the endowment of the Sang School, supporting 'ane persone meit and abill to instruct the youth in musick'.[9] The date of the endowment is unknown, but there is no reason why Clouston might not be right when he suggested that the original gift dated back to the twelfth century.[10] Many other endowments, however, can be dated to the late medieval period, and provision for masses to be said at favourite altars continued to be a popular form of piety: St Duthac's *Stouk* (prebend) and its chapel at Pickaquoy had been endowed by Earl William Sinclair, no doubt in imitation of the fashionable St Duthac's shrine at Tain which received royal patronage.

St Catherine's Stouk illustrates the large, scattered estates which some altars were still accumulating. The dedication was to St Catherine of Alexandria, one of the 14 'auxiliary saints' whose cult was among the most popular in medieval Europe. Much of its land was in Sanday where the altar owned 8 pennylands in Housgarth, 2 pennylands in Levisgarth, and a further 4½ pennylands at various places in Burness,[11] and there was in addition the Karny Kirk ('Catherine's Church'), a chapel now preserved only as a field-name near

Bressigarth.[12] St Catherine's Stouk also had 3½ pennylands at Tuquoy, and further land in Midbea in Westray;[13] there were 2 pennylands in Rothiesholm in Stronsay, and a scattering of land in Shapinsay in Sound, Elwick, How, Skennistoft and Horroldisgarth;[14] there were 2 pennylands in Birsay-be-South,[15] and some further land in Deerness lying in the township of Skea.[16] Finally it owned the two St Catherine's quoys (fields) which were situated on the outskirts of Kirkwall.[17] It appears that in the pre-Reformation period the stouk was still adding new endowments, since the 1500 rental tells us that the 8 pennylands at Housgarth had been bought from udal men, apparently recently.[18] The greater part of the stouk, however, was probably donated at various times by members of the Sinclair family who were particularly devoted to the cult of St Catherine. The father of Earl Henry I built a church dedicated to St Catherine at the Hopes near Roslin, and the location of some of the more important Orkney endowments such as the land in Burness and Tuquoy shows that these gifts were portions which had been detached from earldom properties.[19] These endowments illustrate how on the eve of the Reformation the building work of the bishops was paralleled by continuing support for the cathedral from the Sinclair earls and their relatives.

When James V wrote to the pope in 1541 seeking Robert Reid's appointment as bishop, his letter included some background information about Orkney. The king explained that the diocese consisted of scattered islands situated not far from the North Pole and lying near Norway, Denmark and Germany.[20] The king's geography seems rather suspect considering that he had visited Orkney in the previous year, but his description was true of Orkney's relative position in terms of its links with the continent, and these contacts were becoming increasingly Protestant. The beginning of Lutheranism in Germany (1517) was already a generation in the past, and it was now several years since Norway and Denmark had also opted for the reformed church (1536). Bishop Reid was typical of a strong strand of Catholicism in Scotland which sought to counter Protestantism by the reform of the organisation of the church. As Abbot of Kinloss and Commendator (manager) of the Priory of Beauly he had already earned a reputation as a scholar with an interest in the new humanist learning, but he was not so much a theologian or spiritual leader as an organiser who aimed at putting structures in place to ensure that the services of the church were conducted with dignity and indeed with splendour. It was particularly necessary to put the organisation of the cathedral on a good footing since Reid was usually absent from his diocese. A bishop, and especially an able one, was liable to find that his national role took precedence over his local responsibilities. Reid was a lawyer, busily engaged in the Court of Session of which he became president (c.1548), he was involved in the affairs of the Exchequer, and from time to time he was called on to take part in diplomatic missions to

49. *Kirkwall, Centres of Power.* St Magnus Cathedral is in the centre of the photograph with Broad Street below. The round Moosie Tower of the Bishop's Palace can be seen immediately to the right with the Earl's Palace above. The Sinclair castle, of which nothing remains, was located over Castle Street (bottom left). The East Church, at one time the powerful and influential Secession Church is top left, adjacent to the former Grammar School, now the Council Offices.

England and France. As a result he seems to have made only five visits to Orkney, the first in 1541 shortly after his consecration and the last in 1554. It is unlikely that he ever visited Shetland.[21]

Although Bishop Reid's visits were brief, his impact on his diocese was considerable. The new constitution which he devised for St Magnus (1544) enlarged and strengthened the cathedral chapter,[22] and indeed it aimed at providing an organisation which could function efficiently without his close supervision. Formerly the cathedral had six canons and six chaplains, but now there was to be a provost,[23] chancellor, archdeacon, precentor, treasurer, subdean and succentor (seven canons) assisted by 13 chaplains and six choristers. The duties of the cathedral clergy were carefully set out, and chaplains were assigned to prebends (the service of altars) or were nominated to act as stallholders, deputising for the canons in their absence. Bishop Reid's scheme placed emphasis on education: one of the Chancellor's functions was to give a public lecture each week on canon law; the chaplain of St Augustine had charge of the Sang School, and the chaplain of St Peter acted as master of the Grammar School for which a new block of buildings was built. As well as setting out the qualifications for each post, Reid took steps to ensure that the holders did not absent themselves unnecessarily, and he required the principal clergy to build manses adjacent to the cathedral within a period of three years. The completion of the western part of the cathedral, the rebuilding of the bishop's palace and the construction of the canons' residences created a distinctive cathedral precinct, the remains of which still form the centre of Kirkwall. In addition to the clerics, there were also numerous lay servants; one of these was Bishop Reid's French gardener who had lost a foot in an engagement with the Spanish at Marseilles and, with little call for his horticultural skills, he combined the pruning of fruit trees with the practice of surgery.[24]

Bishop Reid described the previous financial provision for the cathedral canons as confused, and he attributed this confusion partly to carelessness and partly to 'the wetness of the country whereby everything is easily destroyed'.[25] His new scheme carefully assigned incomes from individual parishes to provide for the new posts. The unfortunate consequence was that the reform of the cathedral was financed by stripping the parishes of much of their revenue and, although 'appropriation' of parishes in this way was not new, a higher proportion of the income was diverted than in any other Scottish

50. *Tankerness House.* In pre-Reformation times the building was occupied by the Archdeacon and another part by the Sub-chantor and the choir boys. The property was acquired in 1642 by the Baikies of Tankerness. It now houses Tankerness House Museum.

diocese. The original provision for the bishopric had consisted of large blocks of land in Egilsay and Sourin, Flotta, Midbea in Westray, Birsay, Evie and a large part of St Ola. Some of these endowments might date back to the founding of the cathedral, but others, we might suspect, were the price which an aspiring earl had been prepared to pay when he needed episcopal support, and one large endowment was quite recent: James IV in 1494/5 granted Bishop Andrew the entire island of Burray which had been one of the earldom bordlands.[26] In addition to the major endowments there were many smaller farms and portions of townships which had been added to the bishopric either as pious gifts or as penalties for ecclesiastical offences. As Bishop Graham later remarked, the pre-Reformation church 'grew daylie as adulteries and incests increased in the countrey'.[27] It appears that further land was probably bought from time to time as a financial investment.[28] From the early thirteenth century the systematic collection of tiends (tithes) provided further income.

The cathedral's increasing revenue was reflected in the growth in the number of its clergy, the first evidence for which can probably be found in Bishop Bjarni's eastward extension of the choir to provide a *presbytery* for use by secular canons.[29] The earliest surviving record of a proper chapter, however, dates from 1247.[30] A Vatican tax roll of 1327-8 shows that by that time a number of prebends had been added, including the 'prebenda de Sconsay' (Stronsay), the Prebenda de Sandwik, and the 'prebenda ecclesie sancte crucis de Be' ('the prebend of the church of the Holy Cross in Bea', i.e. Cross parish, Sanday). Thus parish income was already being diverted to provide for a priest within the cathedral.[31] Altogether 23 parishes were even-tually appropriated, but since the corn tiend was probably divided equally between the bishop and the vicar who looked after the parish, there initially continued to be a reasonably satisfactory provision for the parish clergy. Bishop Reid's reforms carried the diverting of parish incomes a stage farther, and the appropriation of the vicarages in Orkney (but not in Shetland) left the parishes in the hands of 'vicars pensionary' or curates who survived on a very inadequate stipend.[32] Thus Reid's ambitious reforms were built on unsatisfactory financial foundations, and the situation was made a good deal worse by the way, in the period 1541 to 1560, the bishopric became increas-ingly burdened with pensions to royal nominees granted from its revenue which, in his desire to placate James V and prevent his lapse from the Catho-lic faith, the pope could not easily refuse. John Stewart, bastard son of James V, received £400 and, after Reid's death, there was another £400 payable to Sir John Bellenden and £200 to the son of Lord Ruthven, with the result that, when Adam Bothwell succeeded in 1559 on the eve of the Reforma-tion, the income of the bishopric was largely being drawn off by other people.[33]

Bishop Reid did not actually sell any of the bishopric land in Orkney, although he did feu lands in Caithness which his predecessors had long possessed (see p.123).[34] In Orkney, however, it had become common to lease out large parts of the bishopric so that an income could be received without much involvement in day-to-day management. Flotta and a large part of Evie had been given out in long leases with papal consent from at least as early as 1484,[35] and in 1550 Reid similarly rented out Burray and Flotta on a 19-year lease.[36] Secular affairs were in the hands of Thomas Tulloch of Fluris who was continually at odds with the tenants. It may have been Bishop Reid's appointment as a commissioner to establish a uniform system of weights and measures throughout Scotland which suggested to the tenants the possibility of attacking the inefficient and oppressive chamberlain on the grounds that he was using fraudulent weights to uplift the produce which the bishop received in rent from his own estate. Complaints about false weights, now made for the first time, were regularly repeated over the next 200 years. William Moodie received a commission to examine the complaints, and Tulloch was obliged to produce the weights he used, but he was eventually absolved by a decree of M.Bonot, the Queen-regent's French sheriff.[37]

In 1558, when returning from negotiations regarding Queen Mary's marriage to the Dauphin, Bishop Reid died suddenly in Dieppe. It was rumoured that he had been poisoned.[38] His successor, Adam Bothwell, was like Reid both a Renaissance scholar and an eminent lawyer but, whereas Reid never deviated from Catholicism, Bothwell's sympathies were with the Reformers. Bothwell's enormous and apparently well used library shows the breadth of his interests:[39] he was one of the first Hebrew scholars in Scotland, and owned works by German and Swiss Protestant theologians; his library also contained the Latin and Greek classics, and books on law, medicine, architecture, the natural sciences and demonology. His scientific interests aroused suspicion, and he had a reputation as 'a sorcerer and an execrable magician'.[40] A bishop appointed on the eve of the 1560 Scottish Reformation was not likely to have an easy episcopate. Bothwell was young, perpetually in poor health, and he was surrounded by a band of predatory relatives who intended to enrich themselves at the expense of his bishopric.

Bishop Adam Bothwell sprang from a prominent legal family.[41] His father, Francis Bothwell, had been Lord Provost of Edinburgh and had served with Bishop Reid in the Court of Session. The bishop's mother, Katherine Bellenden, was from an even more powerful family which held the post of Justice Clerk for three generations. The bishop's cousin, the Justice Clerk Sir John Bellenden of Auchnoull, was the power-behind-the-scenes during Adam Bothwell's time in Orkney and also in the early years of Robert Stewart's rule. Bothwell's mother was married three times, her final husband being Oliver Sinclair of Pitcairn, who thus was the bishop's stepfather, and, although

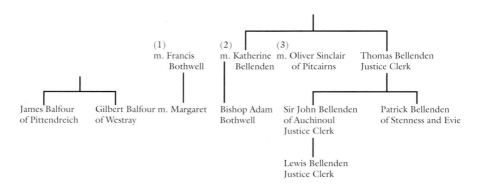

51. **Bothwell, Balfour and Bellenden.** *This new inter-related kindred signalled a major influx into positions of power.*

Oliver Sinclair no longer had the influence that he had once possessed as James V's 'minion', it seems possible that he was the means by which Bothwells and Bellendens were introduced to Orkney. Sir John had control over the temporalities of the bishopric during the vacancy following the death of Bishop Reid,[42] and he had already secured a pension from the bishopric before his cousin was appointed, and he was anxious for more. He worked in partnership with his brother, Patrick Bellenden, who eventually secured estates in Stenness and Evie. While Patrick looked after affairs in Orkney, Sir John managed the vital contacts in Edinburgh.

A similar partnership existed between Gilbert and James Balfour. Although Gilbert was a merely a grim and dangerous adventurer, James Balfour of Pittendreich was an eminent lawyer whose *Practicks* are a well known compendium of Scots law. He was one of Queen Mary's inner circle of advisers and, like Gilbert, he was deeply implicated in the Darnley murder. Gilbert married Margaret Bothwell, the bishop's sister. He had been involved in the murder of Cardinal Beaton in 1546 although John Knox, with whom he was imprisoned on the French galleys, observed that Gilbert was motivated by 'neither the fear of God, nor love of virtue, further than his present commodity persuades him'.[43] On his return from France, Gilbert became Master of the Queen's household, but he was at the heart of the conspiracy which led to the killing of her husband. It was Gilbert Balfour who went to Rome to obtain the papal bull appointing Adam Bothwell. Becoming a bishop in the pre-Reformation church was an expensive business, involving heavy payments in Rome which were often met by borrowing from Italian bankers. It is not entirely clear how Bothwell's appointment was financed, but it appears that the arrangements were handled by John Bellenden of Auchnoull and Gilbert Balfour, both of whom intended to be recompensed from the lands of the bishopric. On the Westray property which Gilbert Balfour acquired, he built the sternly functional fortress of Noltland Castle as a safe retreat. It has been described as 'built by a man with a bad conscience, a man with fear in his heart'.[44] The household goods, valued after his death at a mere £67,[45] suggest that the interior was as spartan as the exterior was forbidding. Yet even Noltland was not a sufficient refuge when the Queen's party collapsed. In 1571 Gilbert Balfour escaped to Sweden where, as an inveterate plotter, he was executed in 1576 for an attempt on the life of the Swedish king.

The Reformation not only brought a new class of landowners, but it also introduced a new form of tenure since the estates carved from the bishopric were held by feudal charters. By this time the feuing of land was common in Scotland, but there had been little alteration to the traditional system of udal tenure in Orkney. Examples of feuing, however, were not entirely unknown. We have seen that Sir James Sinclair of Brecks had in 1535 received a feudal charter which purported to grant him Sanday, Stronsay and North Ronaldsay (see p.241).[46] There had also been occasional instances of udallers seeking the greater security of a charter issued in feudal in form. James Irving

52. **Noltland Castle, Westray.** *The sternly functional fortress was built by Gilbert Balfour, 'a man with a bad conscience, a man with fear in his heart'.*

had received a charter which confirmed his right to Sebay,[47] then in 1545 (on the same day that a charter confirmed Bishop's Reid's new constitution) the cathedral Provost, Malcolm Halcro, and his brother Hugh Halcro (a canon) similarly received a charter for the family lands of Halcro in South Ronaldsay.[48]

The introduction of feudal tenure in Orkney has usually been regarded as an unmitigated evil. Early historians in both Orkney and Shetland were quite uncritical and sometimes a little hysterical in their condemnation of the feu which they saw as subverting the udal freedom of Norse society—the title of David Balfour's book, *Odal Rights and Feudal Wrongs* (1860), encapsulates that simplistic attitude. In retrospect the feuing of the bishopric estate can indeed be seen as the despoiling and dispersing of the estate—little more than legalised theft. That was not the original intention. A feu was not the same as selling-off, far less giving away. It was an arrangement which involved an annual payment, the feu duty, which in Orkney was normally equal to the full rent formerly charged. Orkney feu charters usually make it clear that the payment was 'to conform to the rental'. The intention was to dispose of land in what was in effect a perpetual lease which gave security to the occupier and an undiminished income to the former owner (the feudal superior). It was only inflation, which was rapid in the second half of the sixteenth century, which eroded the value of the original rent. The feu also had the advantage of securing ownership by a formal charter, rather than by unwritten right, and a further attraction was that land could pass to heirs without udal division among brothers and sisters which was required under island law. Primogeniture was described as 'more Scotiae' ('according to Scots custom') and charters explicitly stated it was to apply 'notwithstanding the laws and customs of the country of Orkney to the contrary'.[49] Not only were bishopric feus large but, because they were not subject to udal division, they stayed large. Margaret Sanderson's study of the feuing of church land in Scotland describes how much of the land passed into the hands of sitting tenants 'without a revolution'.[50] Orkney, however, was different—feuing did involve a revolution: the feus were of unprecedented size and were given, not to sitting tenants or even local gentry, but to powerful incomers who had the ability to circumvent the restrictions imposed by the native system of landownership and law.

Bothwell's troubles began even before he arrived in Orkney. It was late autumn when he received the papal bull confirming his appointment, and with commendable haste he set off in February 1560 to visit his diocese. The English had a fleet in the Forth to aid the Protestant faction in their struggle against Mary of Guise and, somewhere near Fife Ness, Bothwell was captured and taken to St Andrews where he was detained for six weeks.[51] When

256

he arrived in Orkney he found the islands little touched by divisions in religion. The only known instance of pre-Reformation Protestantism involved James Skea, described as a native of Orkney, who in 1448 was obliged to flee to England 'for fear of burning for the word of God'.[52] He is probably the same person as James Ka,[53] a chaplain in Robert Reid's cathedral chapter, who two years later sought a respite for his 'tenascite and pertinessitie' in heresy and was ordered to return to Scotland (presumably from England).[54] On the other hand, if there were not many early adherents to Protestantism in Orkney, the attitude of the clergy cannot have been entirely hostile, given the high proportion of pre-Reformation clergy who eventually conformed to the new regime.

Within a year of his arrival Bothwell was complaining that Gilbert Balfour was 'continuallie at debait...because I wald not geiff him all that I hald'.[55] In June 1560 Balfour obtained the huge feu of the church lands in Westray and Papa Westray.[56] Clouston calculated that the largest of the udal estates, that of the Irvings of Sebay, extended to about 38 pennylands.[57] In contrast, Balfour's feu amounted to 164½ pennylands to which he added a further 211¾ pennylands in a separate feu of Birsay and Marwick.[58] When the bishop visited Birsay a month later he found the community in uproar and he was attacked by an angry mob which seized his Birsay residence and threatened to kill him.[59] The leaders of conservative Catholic opinion were Henry and Robert Sinclair, the sons of Edward Sinclair of Strom who was himself rather more cautious in his opposition but, behind the unrest, Bothwell detected the hand of Justice-clerk Bellenden who was jealous of the grants made to Balfour and seems to have calculated that a little terrorism might speed the feuing process. The bishop was genuinely frightened for his life and he reported that 'thair uttir purpose was to haiff either slaine me, or taiken me'.[60] Bellenden was accused of having 'put them (the tenants) in belief to live freely and know no superiors in times coming'.[61] This ambiguous statement allows a rare glimpse of the opinions of ordinary folk: their attitude seems to be partly a reluctance to have religious change imposed on them, partly a fear of what feudalism under Gilbert Balfour might mean, and partly a desire to salvage something for themselves out of the break-up of the bishopric—presumably feus of their own which people of similar status could often obtain in Scotland. Meantime Gilbert Balfour took cynical advantage of the situation to withhold the feu duty, not only of Birsay and Marwick where he may have had difficulty in collecting the rents, but also of Westray and Papa Westray.

By January 1561 Bothwell had decided to reform his diocese, and he referred his decision to 'the first head court after Yule'. This was the court still known as the Hirdmanstein ('hirdmanstevne', the court of the earl's *hird*). It is interesting to see that even after the abolition of the Lawting it could still function as a forum of public opinion, although this is probably the last important occasion it did so. A great multitude of people were present and they refused to assent to the bishop's 'mutation of religion'. The bishop's own account describes how he closed the door of his church and, despite repeated requests, refused to allow mass to be said. Matters seem to have come to a head over the resulting delay to a number of marriages. When the people were debarred from the cathedral they crowded into a little chapel adjacent to the bedchamber where the bishop was lying sick, and a priest conducted mass within earshot and celebrated marriages in the old way. Despite popular opposition Bothwell persisted, and by March it was known in Edinburgh that 'the Bishop of Orkney beginneth to reform his diocese and preacheth himself'.[62] Because the Reformation was managed by Bishop Bothwell, his cathedral survived both the destructive zeal of the reformers and the subsequent neglect of the great medieval churches. Inevitably the shrines of St Magnus and St Rognvald were demolished; their relics, however, were not cast out but were decently interred within neighbouring pillars. What appears to be a statue of St Rognvald was similarly removed from the cathedral and was inserted high in the walls of the Bishop's Palace where it was out of the reach of all but the most agile of reformers.[63]

Shortly after Easter 1561 Bishop Bothwell sailed for France to lay his troubles before Queen Mary. In the past year he had been pressurised into granting large feus from his estate, yet this had failed to satisfy Gilbert Balfour, it had aroused the jealousy of Sir John Bellenden and alienated both the Sinclair gentry and the majority of the population. The bishop was also enmeshed in lawsuits with Thomas Tulloch of Fluris, Bishop Reid's former chamberlain, while the Earl of Caithness, latently hostile ever since Summerdale, was actively seeking the Orkney tack, and was finding support within the bishop's own chapter. In these circumstances it is easy to understand why the next large feu, the grant of the island of Eday to Edward Sinclair, nephew of Oliver Sinclair of Pitcairn, contained an obligation on Sinclair to defend the bishop 'against whatsoever invaders'.[64] The bishop's departure for France did not bring disorder to an end: in the autumn of 1561 there was a riot, the cause of which is obscure, in which a mob led by Francis Bothwell (the bishop's nephew), Magnus Halcro (Cathedral Precentor) and Edward Sinclair (feuar of Eday) searched the town with the intention of killing Henry Sinclair and William Moodie.[65]

In the years which followed, Bishop Bothwell was usually in his diocese in the summer and autumn months.[66] He was a more regular visitor than Bishop Reid had been, but like Reid he was diverted from church matters by his involvement with the Court of Session. The Birsay dispute was resolved by a formal treaty with the Balfours and Bellendens. The resulting arrangements have been described as 'labyrinthine'.[67] The contentious feu of Birsay to Gilbert Balfour was cancelled, but the bishop had to pay 1,000 marks for its surrender as well as waiving all claims to arrears of feu duty. Birsay was now granted in feu to Sir John Bellenden, but he then leased it back to Bishop Bothwell, his own feudal superior. The net result of these over-ingenious manoeuvres was that Gilbert Balfour received a lump sum, and Sir John Bellenden was able to draw an annual income from the property.

This arrangement was supposed to end any claims which Sir John Bellenden or his brother had on the bishopric, but further feus to Patrick Bellenden followed in the next few years. In 1563 Patrick received the Stenness lands which had provided the endowments of the Precentor (Magnus Halcro).[68] On this property the Bellendens had their principal residence, the Palace of Stenness, which according to popular tradition stood so high that it was possible to see ships in Hoy Sound from the upper windows.[69] This grant opened the floodgates and over the next five years most of the cathedral dignitaries similarly disposed of their livings. Patrick Bellenden received a second and much larger grant of 72½ pennylands in Evie from the bishop himself (1566),[70] to which he added the 40½ pennylands of St Duthac's Stouk, and four pennylands in Walls belonging to the prebend of St Columba.[71] There were also further spoils for Gilbert Balfour who received the Provost's lands in South Ronaldsay,[72] while a feu of St Catherine's Stouk was obtained in the name of his son.[73]

For the cathedral clergy the steady income from a feu was not the only way to rise in the world. Some like the Provost, Alexander Dick, a reluctant convert to Protestantism, used Edinburgh connections to make a new career for his family outside the islands. In the following century the wealth of Sir William Dick was legendary and his family returned to the islands to hold the tack.[74] Of the other clergy the most immediately successful—and the most notorious—was Magnus Halcro. The Halcros were a landed family and, as we have already seen, they had been among the first to confirm their udal ownership of their South Ronaldsay property by obtaining a charter under the Great Seal. Magnus's father, also Magnus, was Provost of the Cathedral and other Halcros included Sir Nicolas who was Precentor and Sir Hugh who was second prebendary. In due course Magnus succeeded as Precentor, in which capacity he was in charge of church music and supervising the roll of prebendaries who said mass, drawing his income from the prebend of Orphir and the vicarage of Stenness.[75] In 1556, four years before the Reformation, he bought the substantial udal property of Brough in Rousay,[76] and in 1560 he obtained a lease (not a feu) of the extensive bishopric land in the island.[77] Summerdale politics were not yet dead, and in that same year he entered into a band with the Earl of Caithness 'to rise, flock and fuir with the said noble lord' when the earl had entry to the tack of Orkney.[78] Then, in a remarkable *volte face*, he took advantage of the Reformation to marry Margaret Sinclair, daughter of James Sinclair of Brecks, who had killed the Earl of Caithness's father at Summerdale. Three years later he was able to obtain a feu of Burray and Flotta in the name of his wife and her mother (1566).[79] In keeping with the family's landed status, a suitable genealogy was at some point invented, tracing the Halcro descent from an otherwise unknown Prince Halcro of Denmark.[80]

Under Adam Bothwell's leadership good progress was made in providing for reformed worship. A major difficulty was the poverty of the parishes resulting from the way that Bishop Reid had annexed their incomes to cathedral dignitaries. Bothwell's answer was to reverse Reid's reforms by the simple expedient of requiring the cathedral clergy to act as ministers in the parishes from which they drew their stipends. Some embraced Protestantism with enthusiasm, notably James Annand who was Prebendary of St John and Gilbert Foulsie who succeeded to the prebend when Annand was promoted to Chancellor; some took time to make up their minds, and a minority never accepted the ministry of the reformed church.[81] Bothwell brought in new ministers to replace them, and by 1567 Orkney had at least seven and possibly nine ministers and about 13 readers, so that nearly every parish had provision of some kind.

Since the reformed church initially lacked a formal structure, and Bishop Bothwell was willing to reform his diocese, he was given a free hand for the first year or so. In 1562 he received a commission to plant kirks and to oversee Orkney and Shetland parishes in the way a Superintendent did in most parts of Scotland. However, he was viewed with suspicion since he had originally accepted the office of bishop in the Catholic church, and there was also criticism of the way he combined his duties with his work in the Court of Session.[82] Bothwell was closely associated with Queen Mary's court, and in 1567 he found himself in trouble for officiating at her hasty marriage to the Earl of Bothwell (no relation). The bishop was quick to dissociate himself when the queen was deposed and, along with two superintendents, he crowned the infant James VI. He was active too in pursuing the queen's husband. The Earl of Bothwell, created Duke of Orkney, fled north, apparently hoping to find refuge in his new dukedom, but he was to discover that it was a mere paper dominion. The bishop joined Kirkcaldy of Grange in hot pursuit with 400 men in four ships. The 'duke' had counted on help from Gilbert Balfour, but Balfour refused him entry to Kirkwall and to Noltland Castle, and he probably assisted the pursuers. Continuing his flight northwards to Shetland, Bothwell was able to make his escape to Denmark when Kirkcaldy's ship, the *Unicorn,* was wrecked on a sunken rock just north of Lerwick harbour.[83]

Bishop Adam Bothwell's final appearance in his diocese was as an armour-clad figure clinging desperately to the wreck of the *Unicorn* from which he leapt into an already overcrowded boat—the bishop's *loup* was long remembered. In December of that year he appeared before the General Assembly accused both of his part in the queen's marriage and of neglect of his diocese. According to his critics the consequences of this neglect were formidable:

> …not only ignorance is increased, but also most abundantly all vice, and horrible crimes are committed as the number of 600 persons convicted of incest, adultery and fornication in Zetland beareth witness.[84]

Perhaps most of these 'incests' were marriages within a closer degree than the church permitted. Bishop Bothwell protested that he had visited every church throughout Orkney and Shetland at least twice despite 'the hazard to his life in dangerous storms on the seas'; it was only 'the evil air' which prevented his regular residence. Although he had indeed attended to the affairs of the reformed church in Orkney in a conscientious way, it was becoming less easy to leave a former Catholic bishop in his diocese. Bothwell was suspended, and although he remained bishop in name until his death in 1593, he never visited Orkney again. The next chapter describes how he exchanged what was left of the temporalities of his bishopric for the income of the Abbey of Holyrood (1568). Later he was to claim that the exchange was forced on him, and indeed it was hardly to his advantage, yet he was probably glad to be rid of the islands which had caused him nothing but trouble.

19
Earl Robert Stewart

The upheavals of the Reformation years (1560-8) altered the balance of Orkney society. Sinclair families, the traditional leaders, found themselves outclassed by the huge estates of incomers like the Balfours and Bellendens with whom initially they had few, if any, ties of kinship. That tough old veteran of the Battles of Summerdale and Papdale, Edward Sinclair of Strom who acted as Sheriff-depute and *de facto* ruler on behalf of absentee superiors, disliked the changes, but he was growing old and died in the 1560s. His sons did not inherit his political leadership: Henry, despite heading grass-roots Catholic opposition to Bishop Adam Bothwell, was regarded as little more than Sir John Bellenden's chief mischief-maker.[1] The Sinclairs, already a declining gentry, were left leaderless. They profited little from the dismemberment of the bishopric, having neither the family connections, political influence or legal expertise to share in the first round of feus.[2]

On this unhappy and divided society Robert Stewart, bastard son of James V, was imposed as a royal outsider. His lofty parentage and his possession of the ancient earldom estate, to which he soon added the carcase of the bishopric, put him in a different class from even the Balfours and Bellendens. Yet, despite his apparent power, Robert's position was isolated. The feuars of church land were not dependent on him and owed him nothing; they did were not in any sense his 'subjects', but on the contrary he might easily threaten their future pickings. Robert's opponents could count on expert lawyers and well-connected politicians among their Edinburgh relatives, whereas apart from brief periods, Robert had little influence at court and, despite having a reputation for having introduced a train of greedy Scots followers, Robert had few supporters with estates to compare to the bishopric feus of his opponents.

Robert was born in 1533, son of James V and Euphemia Elphinstone. As a royal bastard he was at the age of six created Commendator of Holyrood Abbey.[3] He never showed any inclination to make a career in the Church and, while still in his teens, he won the approval of John Knox as 'one of those who had renounced papistry and professed Jesus Christ'.[4] It was an optimistic assessment: Robert's attachment to reformed principles, or indeed to any principles, was always tenuous. English spies reported that he was 'dissolute in lyef, lyttle sure to any faction, of small zeal in religion'; he was 'vain and nothing worth, a man full of evil'.[5] For a time Robert was under the influence of his older and more able brother, the Earl of Moray, later regent and leader of the Protestant party, but with the return of Queen Mary from France, Robert's interest in Protestantism waned. He was active in the more frivolous aspects of court life, and exerted a malign influence on the queen's weak-minded husband. Ultimately he appears to have played a double role in his relations with Darnley. Robert was on the fringes of the plot to murder him at Kirk o' Field (property of James Balfour), yet tried to drop hints to Darnley about the danger he faced.

In 1565 Robert received a grant of Orkney and Shetland along with possession of the Castle of Kirkwall and the offices of Sheriff of Orkney and Foud of Shetland.[6] Oliver Sinclair had previously paid the Crown 3000 marks a year, and Robert was to have the islands at the same rate plus a nominal augmentation of 10 marks. Robert's position, however, was quite different from that of Oliver Sinclair, and indeed from all the Crown's previous representatives who had been tacksmen empowered to collect the rents for a fixed term. Robert's grant was a not a tack but a feu which gave him permanent possession of the islands, and allowed his heirs to succeed him. The obvious expectation was that the gift of the islands would be a prelude to Robert becoming Earl of Orkney, although in the event it was another 16 years before he obtained the coveted title. Peter Anderson has suggested that, behind Robert's good fortune, was the moving spirit of the Justice-clerk, Sir John Bellenden of Auchnoull, who was on the look-out for a new front man for his money-making schemes.[7]

Much has been made of the illegality of Robert's charter on the grounds that it contravened the 1472 Act of Parliament when, following the pawning of the islands, it had been enacted that Orkney and Shetland were annexed to the Crown, not to be given to anyone except a king's son 'of lawful bed' (see p.204).[8] Clearly Robert was not of lawful bed, but the grant was not altogether surprising: in 1530 the islands had been given in feu to the Earl of Moray, bastard son of James IV,[9] although that grant turned out to be entirely inoperative (see p.240), and again at the time of James V's visit to Orkney in 1540, there had been talk that the earldom might be given to one of his illegitimate sons, perhaps to Robert (see p.243).

Other questions, however, have been raised about the legality of Robert's charter. In the opinion of Sheriff Alexander Peterkin writing in 1822 it was *null* on the grounds that the Crown had no right to feu 'all the haill the lands of Orkney and Zetland' since its property was confined to the former earldom and the lands once possessed by the kings of Norway.[10] Peterkin was always hypersensitive to encroachment on udal freedom, but he was quite correct to point out that the 'free tenants' over whom Robert was given superiority were not tenants at all, but udallers who by definition could have no feudal superior. Scots lawyers frequently had a poor understanding of land tenure in Orkney, and attempts to draft charters which make reference to udallers were usually awkward and clumsy. Perhaps the intention was to convey to Robert the Crown's right to collect the skat and to act as a judge over them, but the phraseology suggests that the Crown was none too clear what privileges it might confer, and Robert's subsequent actions suggest that he sometimes had inflated ideas about the powers he had received.

Later it appears that Robert's feu of 1565 was considered to be defective in some way, and he was accused of trying to take possession of Orkney 'under prentense of a pretendit heritabill infeftment'.[11] It is difficult to see what was wrong—his feu was approved by Parliament[12] and was issued under the Privy Seal,[13] yet it seems that at the last moment the government had second thoughts. A charter of this importance might have been expected to have been issued under the Great Seal although the absence of that formality did not render it invalid, so perhaps the granting of sasine (the ceremony of taking possession) had been withheld. Nevertheless immediately afterwards Robert is found acting on the authority of his charter, dealing with Orkney pirates[14] and feuing land,[15] although he had not yet visited the islands. The upheavals of the Reformation were paralleled by confusion in civil government. George Bellenden acted as Sheriff-depute in 1563;[16] despite Robert's grant Patrick Bellenden appears as Sheriff in 1565 with James Redpath as his depute,[17] while early in 1566 Robert was deprived of the office and Gilbert Balfour was created Sheriff with John Balfour as his depute.[18]

Whatever rights Robert was given were swept away when the islands were created 'a haill and free dukry' for the Earl of Bothwell on the occasion of his marriage to Queen Mary.[19] As has been seen, the new duke's acquaintance with his domain was brief—a mere episode—but within a few weeks of the duke's flight, Robert arrived in Orkney with the obvious intention of establishing himself in power. By a combination of bribes and promises he induced Gilbert Balfour to surrender the Sheriffship and the custody of the castle,[20] and early in November 1567 Robert was found for the first time acting in person in the capacity of Sheriff Principal.[21] Although Gilbert Balfour had been successfully placated, Robert failed to come to terms with Patrick Bellenden who for many years remained his implacable enemy. Bellenden complained to the Regent Moray that Robert's occupation of Orkney was illegal,[22] and the Regent discharged tenants and occupiers from paying rent and skat until Robert's title had been investigated.

While Robert had gained possession of the Castle of Kirkwall, the cathedral remained in possession of the bishop's men. Its steeple overlooking the walls of the castle was of strategic importance, later demonstrated in the siege of 1614. Accordingly in March 1568 Robert's followers seized the cathedral, and in the affray two of the bishop's men were killed. Robert was embarrassed by these deaths which further discredited his Orkney adventure. The regent refused to accept any payments for the feu which would have recognised the legality of Robert's tenure of Orkney.[23]

While the success of his attempt to impose himself on Orkney hung in the balance, Robert suddenly found a solution to his problems. Perhaps Justice-clerk Bellenden was again at work behind the scenes, won over by the prospect of further profits.[24] The brilliantly simple plan was that Robert should receive a feu from Bishop Bothwell of everything that was left of the temporalities of the bishopric, and in return he would give Bothwell the Abbey of Holyrood. At a stroke this exchange of properties gave Robert a secure legal basis for his presence in Orkney, it removed his most influential rival, and simplified administration since the earldom and bishopric lands often lay run-rig with each other. Bishop Bothwell was later to claim that he was a reluctant party to the exchange, and indeed the violent seizure of the cathedral may have been part of a softening-up process designed frighten the bishop and secure his agreement. Bothwell later complained that Robert had 'violently intruded himself on his living, with bloodshed and hurt to his servants',[25] and when he sought 'the very eye of justice' in Edinburgh his servants' lives were in danger. One such was William Lawder, the bishop's chamberlain, who was forced to leave Orkney so hurriedly that he could take neither clothes or papers with him. However, since he had failed to render accounts for 1564 and all subsequent years, Lawder found himself in equal danger from the bishop. On his arrival in Edinburgh he was imprisoned in the bishop's newly-acquired property of Holyrood until he undertook to pay 306½ angels and 21 zopindales.[26] Despite Adam Bothwell's insuperable difficulties in collecting the arrears of rent which were due to him, he may have been a less reluctant party to the exchange than he pretended: as the Reformation progressed his position in Orkney was becoming increasingly difficult, whereas in Edinburgh he could pursue a safe, busy and useful career as a Court of Session judge and a Privy Councillor. He may also have taken into consideration that Holyrood, being monastic rather than episcopal property, offered better prospects of conversion into a hereditary estate. The culmination of this process was attained in 1607 when his son was elevated to the peerage as Lord Holyroodhouse.

For the next seven years until his disgrace in 1575 Robert was intent on consolidating his position in Orkney. In 1569 he is reputed to have seized the town's charter chest and destroyed its contents with the intention of limiting Kirkwall's independence as a royal burgh.[27] The exile of Gilbert Balfour to Sweden removed a rival with whom Robert must surely have clashed had he remained in Orkney. Robert took advantage of Gilbert's departure to occupy Noltland Castle and appropriate the Westray rents, paid mainly in bere, which were sent secretly to Flanders with express instructions that the two ships should not enter the Forth even in the case of bad weather. As a result one of the ships, the *Marie Blith* of Dundee, was lost.[28]

Work began on the building of the Palace of Birsay, a symbol of Robert's intention that his stay in Orkney should be permanent. It was a prospect which alarmed the church feudatories who found him arbitrary and overbearing. Robert's position became more precarious after 1570 when his brother, the Regent Moray, was assassinated. Complaints received a readier hearing as the Earl of Morton climbed to power in the minority of James VI and eventually succeeded to the regency. Robert found himself in serious trouble over his seizure of Gilbert Balfour's Westray lands, and he was eventually forced to abandon Noltland Castle.[29] His most implacable opponent continued to be Patrick Bellenden, who entered into a potentially dangerous alliance with the Earl of Caithness and gathered 300 men for a proposed repeat of the Summerdale invasion. Within the islands opposition was led by Magnus Halcro and William Moodie. Moodie was variously described as parson of South Ronaldsay, Walls and Hoy; at the time of the Reformation he was sub-dean,[30] and thereafter he rose to be Treasurer, then cathedral Provost (c.1571-4).[31] Yet, despite these benefices, Moodie's interests were essentially secular: he had acted as Mary of Guise's Chamberlain in Orkney,[32] and he was intent on building up a South Isles estate centred on his Castle of Snelsetter which, with considerable exaggeration, he claimed his ancestors had occupied as udal property from time immemorial.[33] In 1563-4 he acquired a charter for Snelsetter,[34] and the following year he bought the mansion house of Breckness,[35] and acquired parts of Magnus Halcro's benefice.[36]

For many years while Robert's right to the islands remained unclear and complaints about his rule began to accumulate, he remained safely out of reach in Orkney, but in 1575 he was induced or compelled to travel south and was warded in Edinburgh castle. The many complaints which reached the Privy Council found their fullest expression in *The Complaint anent Usurpations by Lord Robert Stewart* (1575).[37] It sought to discredit Robert and spread alarm about his pretensions to sovereignty by repeating an injudicious remark that he was 'as free a lord …as the King of Scots in his own realm'. Stories of his treasonable dealings with Denmark were even more damaging. According to the *Complaint*, Robert had in 1572 sent Gavin Elphinstone, the Master of his Household, and Henry Sinclair, his 'chalmerchild' or page, to Copenhagen with an offer to restore 'the supremacy and dominion' of Orkney and Shetland to Norway-Denmark. In return his tenure of the islands was said to have been confirmed in a document which was reputedly hidden in a bolt of cloth and brought back to

Orkney by Yanis Corsmay, a Bremen merchant. At the same time the King of Denmark had allegedly appointed a new Lawman, Lawrence Carness, who from his name was apparently an Orcadian, but about whom nothing other is known. Danish sources confirm that there was some substance in these stories: it seems that when Robert was threatened with invasion by the Earl of Caithness and Patrick Bellenden, and when his relations with Scotland were distinctly cool, he had explored the possibility of Danish support. Gavin Elphinstone who conducted the negotiations was no doubt a close relative on Robert's mother's side, but his mission was treated with suspicion by the Danes. A marginal note in a Danish royal letter book describes Elphinstone as 'scurra et praestigiator improbissimus'—a thoroughly untrustworthy scoundrel. Frederick II was careful to keep his distance and perhaps was not even aware of the contact, but officials seem to have been sufficiently interested to allow the discussions to continue for a year or two.[38]

It was also easy for the authors of the *Complaint* to show that Robert had acted beyond his authority. Perhaps they regarded him as having no authority apart from his commission as an ordinary sheriff but, even if the disputed feu of 1565 was valid, it had not been very specific about his legal powers. The document he received was described as 'a charter... over the lands of Orkney and Shetland... with superiority over the free tenants... along with the office of Sheriff of Orkney and Foud of Shetland',[39] but whether by design or omission his authority was less comprehensive than the powers of 'justiciary, sheriffship, admiralty and bailliary' which had been expressly included in Oliver Sinclair's tack.[40] It was easy to show that Robert had regularly 'usurped the office of Admiral', for example, when he apprehended nine English pirate ships and confiscated their cargoes, optimistically valued at £100,000. Again, although he had not been created Justice, he had arraigned a number of people on capital charges, including William Moodie and Magnus Halcro, and therefore had exceeded the competence of an ordinary sheriff. When Robert was on good terms with the government it had no doubt been readily assumed that his feu of Orkney and Shetland gave him the powers which previous tacksmen had exercised over the legal system in the islands, and indeed there was no one else who could act in that capacity.

The whole question of Orkney law and Robert's relationship to it was bound to cause problems. When the Hebrides were transferred to Scotland by the 1266 Treaty of Perth it had specifically been stated that they were in future to be subject to Scots law, but no similar stipulation was made in the 1468 marriage treaty, no doubt because the pawning of Orkney and Shetland was ostensibly a temporary measure. On the other hand, contrary to popular belief, the marriage treaty included no guarantees for the future, although the implicit assumption was that Orkney law would remain unchanged. This was apparently recognised when an Act on its passage through

Parliament in 1504 was altered to exclude Orkney and Shetland from the requirement that all the king's subjects should be ruled 'by the common laws of the realm and by no other laws'.[41] The earliest innovation was the appointment of Lord Henry Sinclair to act as 'Justice',[42] but this function was so similar to the role of the former Norse earls and sysselmen that it brought about no discernible alteration. More important changes came in 1541 when, with the arrival of Oliver Sinclair as tacksman, the Lawman was transformed into the Sheriff, and the Lawting became the Sheriff Court (see pp.244-5). Although the courts were thereafter Scottish in form, the law they administered remained the traditional island law based on Norwegian Landlaw. Despite these changes the Sheriff Court in 1560 was still capable of fulfilling the same role as the former Lawting when it acted as a forum of public opinion and refused to sanction Adam Bothwell's reform of religion. Then in 1567 a decision of Parliament again recognised the validity of Orkney law, although it was so briefly recorded that it is difficult to know what was at issue. The question before Parliament was 'whether Orkney and Shetland shall be subject to the common law of the realm, or whether they shall use their own laws'.[43] Only the decision was recorded—that the islands should be subject to their own law. From that same year, when the validity of Robert's rule was in question, William Sinclair made his oft-repeated demand that the lost conquest lands should be returned to him (see p.236). He was successful in obtaining an order that evidence regarding these lands should be gathered by 'an inqueist of the cuntrie *according to the old order observit in thai partis*'.[44] All this shows is that for the moment the government was acting with unexpected sensitivity to Orkney law.

As late as 1587 the Privy Council decided a case explicitly on the basis of Orkney law.[45] Nicol Oliverson in infancy had been deprived of his udal rights in Gairsay and had spent the last 40 years in Norway but, hearing that he could now expect better justice in Orkney (a surprising rumour), he returned to claim his inheritance. He was successful in obtaining a decreet against the widow and heirs of Magnus Halcro, but Robert, having dispossessed the Halcro family, then gave the lands to Isobel Brown, a former mistress and mother of his son Robert.[46] The surviving records suggest that Nicol Oliverson, 'wearied and beggared in the pursuit of his just heritage', was accused of 'stealing' the land, perhaps by taking possession before the legal process was completed, and for that reason the property may have been escheated to Robert. When Nicol took the case to the Privy Council, Robert's lawyer claimed that the matter had been properly settled by 'the laws and practice observed within the country of Orkney in times past'. The Council, however, ordered the law books to be produced and, having examined them, decided in Nicol's favour. This case shows that the Privy Council could act as a court of appeal and was prepared to base its decision on Orkney law.

The examples which have been quoted show that in the period 1468–1587 there were a number of occasions when Scotland showed due regard for the existence of distinctive laws in Orkney, but it was not always so scrupulous. Gordon Donaldson's 'Sovereignty and Law in Orkney and Shetland' traces how Scotland gradually assumed supremacy in civil and criminal jurisdiction. If cases were few in early years, this owed more to Orkney's remoteness rather than to any feeling that Orkney was beyond the competence of Parliament, the Privy Council and the laws of Scotland. At worst Orkney and Scots law became competing systems: many of Robert's enemies had considerable legal expertise, and those dissatisfied with decisions in Orkney courts tended to take their case to Scottish courts in the hope of a different outcome, or they might initiate proceedings in Scottish courts where a poor defendant could not afford to appear. A situation which allowed a choice of law and enabled cases to be tried twice by different legal systems was a recipe for chaos, yet Robert's decree forbidding complaints to be carried to courts outside Orkney was bound to be interpreted as an attempt to muzzle genuine grievances and to prevent appeal from his misrule.[47]

Although it was ultimately Robert's misrule and the corruption of his courts which discredited Orkney law, his opponents found it just as easy to attack Robert for using Orkney law as for infringing it. It was not difficult to cast suspicion on an over-mighty subject who had the 'princely' power to make new laws and revoke old ones. The 'new laws' which Robert was accused of making were actually fairly minor, little more than the kind of regulations which the Sheriff Court continued to enact long after island law was abolished. The authors of the *Complaint* cited a new law against 'swine rutting'—a profitable law since it was alleged that fines for allowing pigs to destroy crops brought Robert no less than 1500 dollars from Shetland alone. Robert was also accused of altering the law regarding the sister-part in udal inheritance, and of revoking old laws, although no example of the latter was given. A strange accusation was that Robert gave license to men to fight in single combat.[48] He seems to have done so on at least four occasions, and one of the combatants was Gavin Elphinstone, the kinsman whom he had employed on the secret mission to Denmark. Peter Anderson speculates that the archaic custom of *holmganga,* whereby disputants took part in trial by combat on a little island, might still have been theoretically sanctioned by the Lawbook, although it was long obsolete in Norway and unlikely to have been allowed in late medieval Orkney.[49] Robert's bizarre legal proceedings also involved the trial for capital crimes of men long dead, such as Sir James Sinclair of Brecks and Sir David Sinclair of Sumburgh, who were tried in effigy with the aim of escheating their lands and possessions.[50]

Other complaints concerned Robert's arbitrary and high-handed conduct. His train of Highland followers, described as 'broken men', despoiled and oppressed the country and were involved in a particularly violent affray in Graemsay. In Shetland Robert travelled with six or seven score followers, exacting enforced hospitality and demanding 'banquets and great cheer'. He was accused of equipping pirate ships and receiving the profits of piracy, of banishing people, 'stopping the ferries' and forbidding people to leave Orkney without permission. While Robert remained warded in Edinburgh Castle other complaints were received including detailed accusations from Shetland regarding the oppressive rule of Robert's half-brother, Laurence Bruce of Cultmalindie.[51] Towards the end of the following year (1576) a commission was granted to William Moodie and William Henderson, the Dingwall Herald, to visit Orkney and Shetland and take evidence from witnesses.[52] It was hardly an impartial commission since Moodie had long been in dispute with Robert, and Henderson had arrived in Orkney as an associate of Patrick Bellenden.

None of the commission's Orkney evidence has survived, if indeed any was taken, but there is a mass of detailed statements from Shetland where public meetings were held of the heads of households from each parish. The way in which ordinary people in Shetland were ready to voice their complaints reveals a community in which Norse peasant democracy was less touched by Scots influence than in Orkney where the presence of earls and bishops created a more hierarchical society. The universal complaint was that the Shetland *lawrightmen* had been replaced by Bruce's bailiffs. Since the lawrightmen had supervised the measurement of the *wadmell,* the coarse cloth in which the Shetlanders (but not the Orcadians) paid their skat, there were frequent complaints that people were given short measure. When the inhabitants of Nesting protested, they were told that their wadmell was 'no velvet'. Other complaints related to false *bismars* (weigh-bars). There is no doubt that Bruce was manipulating weights and measures to his own advantage, and was accepting bribes to permit Hanseatic merchants, on whom the inhabitants depended for trade, to perpetuate similar corrupt practices. Other accusations stemmed from monetary chaos. A century after the impignoration Scots currency was not in normal use in either Orkney or Shetland. Often transactions were in 'pennyworths', the traditional 'money of account' defined by small quantities of 'wares' (butter, meal, meat, fish etc), but the actual coins came from all over northern Europe—zopindales, gullions, angels, nobles, bawbees, dollars and reals. Inflation was high during and after Morton's regency, and it was easy for Robert and Laurence Bruce to set exchange rates to their own advantage.

With his enemies amassing evidence of his misrule, it may seem surprising that Robert was able to take advantage of his enforced stay in Edinburgh to recover his position. The power of Regent Morton was crumbling, and Robert was able to make himself agreeable to the young James VI (his

53. ***Birsay Village.*** *Near the top of the picture is the palace, built by Earl Robert Stewart. Below and to the left is St Magnus Church, one of the possible sites of Earl Thorfinn's cathedral of Christchurch. In the cluster of buildings immediately below the church lay Mons Bellus, the 'lower palace', which was one of the residences of the Bishops of Orkney.*

nephew) and to his inner circle of friends. Within weeks of the collection of the damning Shetland evidence, Robert's fortunes were on the mend. In 1578 he received permission to return to Orkney,[53] although for the moment he continued to spend the greater part of the time in the south. In 1580 he was admitted to the Privy Council and he attended its meetings fairly regularly.[54] In January 1581 he was described as 'feuar of Orkney and Zetland', showing that his disputed feu was apparently once again recognised.[55] Later that year he had the satisfaction of being one of a group of nobles who escorted the Earl of Morton to imprisonment in Dumbarton,

54. *Palace of Birsay. The fisherman is Robert Rendall (1898–1967), poet, artist, preacher, archaeologist and a writer of many learned papers on sea-shells.*

and the regent's fall signalled Robert's advancement. In August he was created Earl of Orkney. His dubious feu of 1565 was confirmed, to which were added powers of justiciary which, his charter explained, were needed because of attacks by pirates and vagabonds from the northern and western parts of Scotland.[56] The authors of the 1575 *Complaint* must have been dismayed that he was now given the very powers they had accused him of usurping, and they no doubt worried that these powers might not necessarily be directed solely against pirates and wild Scots, who indeed had often been in Robert's pay. Four years later Robert received confirmation of his tenure of the bishopric.[57] He was now secure in his possession of both the earldom and the bishopric, and he was armed with the powers which he needed to govern the islands.

The year 1584 was described by Storer Clouston as Robert's 'vintage year' for oppression.[58] There were three important cases in which he used his corrupt courts to confiscate property and to advance his supporters. In January the brothers Magnus, Gilbert and Edward Irving were dispossessed of the lands of Sebay, and another brother, William Irving, a follower of the earl, was installed in their place.[59] Another case involved the Rousay estate which had formerly belonged to Magnus Halcro, now deceased. It seems that Magnus had taken advantage of Robert's confinement in Edinburgh to withhold skat for the years 1575-8. Robert was not quick to foreclose on his old enemy's family but in 1584 he demanded arrears amounting to £1009. In October a search was made for moveable goods which might be sold off, but 'none were found'. A month later an assize declared the property forfeited and it was offered for sale but, since no bids were received, it became the property of the earl in lieu of skat debt.[60] Robert was careful to obtain permission from the Lords of Council to recover the debt, but the way he used this authorisation in order to take possession of the estate is a good example of his use of his courts for his own profit. The assize was packed with the earl's own followers, and the escheat of the property appears to have taken place on the same day that it was offered for sale.[61]

Confiscation of land from lesser proprietors and petty udallers was achieved through the earl's Court of Perambulation and Ogang.[62] Perambulations were nothing new, and throughout the sixteenth, seventeenth and eighteenth centuries there are frequent records of this inquest by 'honest men' who descended on a township with measuring rod and line to reallocate land whenever there were complaints that inequalities had developed in the runrig system. One of these inequalities was the way in which the rigs of resident proprietors tended to grow in size and to be situated on good land whereas the shares of absentees including the earl and bishop suffered in comparison. It was a long time since a superior had been regularly resident in Orkney, with the result that Robert probably had good grounds for insisting on redistribution. However, the work of Robert's commissioners was not likely to be popular. They were authorised to visit the lands so that the lands of the earldom and bishopric might be made equal with pennylands of udal land.[63]

Robert's perambulations, however, were not just about reallocation, but had the more sinister purpose of confiscating udal land wherever it could be proved that *kingsland* had been illegally occupied. Kingsland, according to Robert's interpretation, was not only the cultivated lands which had once been held by the king, and for which he now had a feu, but any outbreaks which had been made from the common. Townships had expanded by means of intakes from the common from time immemorial, but the lost Lawbook probably contained the provision found in Norwegian Landlaw that, although everyone had a right to use common hill land, any new settlers on the common automatically became the tenants of the king.[64] It is interesting that the 1567 charter to Earl of Bothwell on the occasion of his marriage to Queen Mary conveyed to him the 'quylandis' and 'outbrekkis'.[65] The fact that so important a charter makes mention of such minor features indicates that there had recently been disputes about the Crown's rights to the commons. It therefore seems probable that Robert from his earliest time in Orkney had been confiscating reclaimed land. The 1575 *Complaint* accused Robert of:

...appropriating the common moors and pastures of Orkney, common before to the whole country, now to himself in property, whereby he means to oppress the country... and to escheat the whole udal lands.[66]

A notorious example from 1584 involved Magnus Sinclair of Braebister who appeared in court accused of making outbreaks of cultivation on the 'backs' (the grassland on the edges of the township) and building houses on the land he reclaimed.[67] Magnus Sinclair's punishment involved more than just the loss of the new land: Robert's court confiscated 5¾ pennylands in Braebister (Deerness), 3 pennylands in Havell and 2 pennylands in Swartabrek (both in Toab). The confiscated land was immediately given to Robert's niece, Marie Stewart, who was married to Magnus Sinclair's son so, as with the Irvings of Sebay, the property was transferred to a branch of the family which Robert wished to favour. However, four years earlier Magnus Sinclair had entered into a contract to resign these lands in favour of his son and daughter-in-law.[68] Apparently the contract had not been fully honoured, and so Robert was probably using the new outbreaks as a pretext to obtain these lands which had been promised to his niece.

It was ostensibly complaints from the dispossessed Irvings of Sebay which led to a second period of disgrace, but more fundamentally James VI's increasing maturity enabled him to come to a truer estimate of his uncle's character. In 1587 the king was taking an interest in matters which Robert had no desire to see examined too closely. A proclamation from the High Court of Justiciary announced that cases of maladministration by sheriffs were to be tried in the king's presence and, somewhat ominously, three days were set aside for Orkney cases.[69] The king was also investigating the damage the church had sustained by the secularisation of bishopric land, and this ultimately led to an Act of Annexation whereby bishoprics were appropriated to the Crown. As Orkney benefices fell vacant Robert had been filling them with his own candidates, as indeed his 1581 charter gave him authority to do.[70] Nevertheless Parliament decided that Robert's appointments were *ultra vires*,[71] and by December he was described as 'lait Erle of Orknay' and had apparently been deposed. A commission to try him was granted to Lewis Bellenden, Justice-clerk in succession to his father, and to the Chancellor, John Maitland of Thirlestane. They also jointly received the management of the former earldom.[72]

Foreseeing the possibility of a second term of imprisonment, Robert had already returned to Orkney in search of all the support he could muster, and he was willing to make concessions to those he had wronged. In September 1587 he made a general re-grant to the 'gentlemen udallers' whose lands had been forfeited by his Court of Perambulation and Ogang. There was, however, a catch: the land confiscated from udallers was to be restored to them in return for 'trew, thankfull and auefald (honest) service' by the owners, their kinsmen, friends and allies in times to come and, should they not prove true 'vassals', the re-grant might be withdrawn.[73] While Robert was offering to return the land he had corruptly acquired and was anxious to gain the support of the udallers, he was not restoring their land as udal property, but proposed to return it in the form of a feudal grant with himself as superior.

A further cause of Robert's disgrace may be found in the negotiations which led to the marriage of James VI and Anne of Denmark. The diplomacy revived the whole question of the status of the islands and brought renewed demands that they should be returned. Since Robert was known to have had treasonable dealings with the Danes in the past, his interference might prove an embarrassment; it was better to keep him out of harm's way until the negotiations were finalised. The Danish match was suggested as early as 1582. Three years later a magnificent Danish embassy visited the Scottish court at Dunfermline where a certain Dr Nicolaus Theophilus gave 'a brilliant oration' on the history of the Orkney-Shetland impignoration and the continuing right of redemption; he argued that matters could be settled either by Norway-Denmark redeeming the islands, which she was able and willing to do, or else by a new marriage agreement. Scotland initially demanded that Norway-Denmark renounce all claim to the islands but, when the marriage agreement was finalised in 1589, the whole issue was sidestepped and the status of the islands remained unchanged.[74]

Within weeks of Robert's concession to the 'Gentlemen Udallers', news was received that his old enemy, Patrick Bellenden, had been given command of three ships being fitted out at Leith which were to 'fetch' Robert from Orkney.[75] For his part Robert sent money south to procure a rival fleet of three ships from Dundee which were to be sent north on the pretence of protecting fishing vessels from pirates. When Patrick Bellenden arrived in the Northern Isles and attempted to collect rents and skat, he was met with a blank refusal. He was forced to withdraw when confronted by an army of Orcadians and Shetlanders bearing arms, displaying banners and led by Robert in person.[76] Resistance to taxation was an understandably popular cause, but it is nevertheless interesting that, at least on this occasion, Robert was capable of rallying grass-roots support. Probably Orcadians supported Earl Robert's resistance to Patrick Bellenden's invasion for much the same patriotic reasons as when they sided with James Sinclair of Brecks at Summerdale and when they later supported Earl Patrick and his son in the face of the Caithness invasion of 1614. Despite defiance which verged on rebellion, Robert's troubles were again ended by political means without his misrule being properly investigated.

In his final years Robert was seldom out of Orkney. He dabbled in pro-Spanish politics along with the Catholic earls of Huntly and Errol, but he was not actively involved as the remnants of the Armada struggled to return north-about to Spain in the terrible gales of August and September 1588. The most famous of the Armada wrecks was *El Gran Grifon* which perished on Fair Isle, and at least one other ship foundered in stormy seas off North Ronaldsay. Certain Westray families noted for their swarthy appearance and volatile temperament are 'the Dons', and are held to be descendants of the few Spaniards who reached the safety of the shore.[77]

When Earl Robert died in 1593 he had ruled Orkney for 28 years. On the basis of his dubious and ill-drafted 1565 charter, he had managed to establish himself in the islands, and he had been resident for long periods, sometimes because he dared not leave. He survived two periods of disgrace, and avoided any real investigation of his misrule. Eventually he seemed to be in a stronger position than the Sinclair earls had ever been: Robert's feu included Shetland as well as Orkney, and he had been able to add the temporalities of the bishopric to the lands of the earldom. Furthermore his title as earl was hereditary, and was not hedged around by the restrictions which had been designed to limit the power of the Sinclairs. Robert's position, however, was never secure: his personal limitations and the corruption of his rule made it impossible for him to find a satisfactory solution to his problems. At the time of his death the power-struggle with the Orkney landowners, the question of Orkney law, and the relationship between his earldom and central government remained unresolved. In terms of character, his son was no better equipped, and these same problems ultimately led to Patrick's execution, and to the downfall of the Stewart earldom.

20
Earl Patrick Stewart

In the entire history of Orkney there is no one with such an evil reputation as Patrick Stewart (Earl of Orkney 1593-1615).[1] His father's misdeeds have faded from popular memory, but Patrick's tyranny became part of folklore.[2] Posterity has been uniformly hostile in its verdict: the name 'Black Pate Stewart' has always been 'a synonym for oppression', he has been universally regarded as 'an oriental despot' whose exactions were 'openly outrageous'.[3] The ruins of his castles and palaces still serve as a reminder of an extravagant lifestyle financed by his Orkney subjects. Yet it has been Patrick's misfortune that the accepted version of Orkney history has largely been written by his enemies[4]—perhaps it could hardly have been otherwise when there were so many of them. The over-simple view of Orkney history which regards the Norse period as a 'Golden Age', and all subsequent history as a decline from greatness, casts Patrick in the role of caricature villain, principally responsible for Scottish oppression and the destruction of Norse institutions. Besides tyranny, murder, rape and the expropriation of property, popular tradition accuses him of the destruction of the Norse Lawbook. Of all the stories about him, the most absurd is that he forced people to adopt patronymics ('Patrick-names') in order to prevent them knowing their family descent.[5] In the case of Earl Patrick there is more than ordinary difficulty in separating myth from reality. Nevertheless there is no denying the violence and lawlessness of his reign, and it began with a horrifying story of torture, attempted murder and witchcraft.

When Patrick succeeded to the earldom he was already in dispute about land which Earl Robert had left to Patrick's brothers, John, Master of Orkney (Master = heir) and James Stewart of Graemsay. At one stage Patrick imprisoned both of them, and he also pulled down James Stewart's house.[6] As a consequence Patrick faced a plot which, in addition to John and James, involved a third brother, William Stewart. It is difficult to know what credence to give to their schemes since the evidence against them was obtained under torture. The conspirators seem to have indulged in unguarded talk of murder; perhaps Patrick could be killed as he slept in his bed at the Palace of Birsay, or it might be possible to poison him, or else to make away with him when he attended a banquet to be given in Kirkwall by David Moncrieff.

Suspicion fell on Thomas Paplay, who was a servant of the Master. Paplay was imprisoned, kept for eleven days in the *caschielawis*,[7] and he was scourged with ropes so that 'they left neither flesh nor hide upon him'. Not only did he implicate his fellow conspirators, but his pain-crazed revelations led to startling accusations of attempted murder by witchcraft.[8]

The witch named by him was Alison Balfour who seems to have been a servant or a friend of Patrick Bellenden and his wife at Stenness. In the witch-hunts of 1590-7 elderly females were principally at risk but, as is common in these cases, 'the accusation of witchcraft was a prop to the main political purpose'.[9] Not only could damaging 'evidence' be obtained to implicate the Master, but witchcraft smears might be used with effect against Patrick Bellenden, particularly since it was common knowledge that his nephew had raised the Devil in the yard of his Edinburgh house.[10] So Alison Balfour was tortured under the direction of Henry Colville, parson of Orphir and Patrick's chamberlain, and when she proved resistant she was forced to watch as her elderly husband was put in the *buits* and her daughter's fingers were crushed in the *pilliewinkies*. Colville's line of questioning was directed to establishing Bellenden's involvement. A piece of wax found in her purse was considered particularly incriminating, since it was assumed that it was that it was intended for making images of her intended victims. In vain she explained that it had been given to her by Lady Bellenden to make an 'implaister' because she suffered from colic. Alison Balfour was executed on the 'heding hill' in Kirkwall on 16 December 1594, but before she died she dictated a clear statement in which she withdrew the confession she made under torture.[11]

John, Master of Orkney, was charged in June 1596 with plotting the death of Patrick by witchcraft and by other means. At his trial in Edinburgh the presence of Lawrence of Cultmalindie as a member of the assize probably aided his chances since Bruce was no friend of Earl Patrick. In any case, the witchcraft scare was for the moment on the wane, and the evidence against the Master was rejected on the grounds that it had been obtained under torture. But the decision that evidence obtained under torture was unreliable came too late for Thomas Paplay and Alison Balfour, both of whom had already been executed on the basis of exactly the same 'evidence'.[12]

Henry Colville's assiduous questioning of Alison Balfour with the express purpose of implicating the Master made him a target for immediate revenge now that the Master had been cleared. John Stewart, accompanied by his friends and servants, instantly embarked from Montrose and sailed for Orkney where he learned that Colville was in Shetland, having taken refuge at Neap in Nesting. The pursuers took aboard stores and munitions at Gairsay, then sailed for Shetland where they caught up with Colville and killed him, a mere 18 days after the Master's acquittal in Edinburgh.[13] A later legend surrounds the killing with gruesome but entirely fictitious circumstances:

Brand and Hibbert describe how Colville was pursued by four remorseless 'Sinclair brethren' whom he had deprived of their lands; in an Odin-like sacrifice worthy of Torf Einar, they laid open his breast, tore out his heart, and drank his heart's blood.[14] Gilbert Pacock, a relatively minor figure, was eventually executed for his part in the murder, and several others were found not guilty, but John, Master of Orkney, escaped punishment by ignoring a summons to appear in Edinburgh for trial.[15]

Despite the violence and disregard for law which characterised Patrick's reign, and of which the Alison Balfour affair and the murder of Colville is a sample, it was also a period of considerable prosperity, and indeed only a buoyant economy could have supported the semi-regal splendour with which Patrick surrounded himself. He inherited the Castle of Kirkwall, still a strong-hold of great strength, and also his father's palace in Birsay which Earl Robert began in 1569 and which was largely complete by 1574.[16] The former bish-op's palace, which had been thoroughly reconstructed 50 years earlier by Bishop Reid, provided Patrick with a commodious town house. To these he added Noltland Castle which he captured from Michael Balfour, Gilbert Balfour's successor in Westray.[17] In Shetland he owned the House of Sumburgh (built c.1591),[18] and ten years later the building of Scalloway Castle provided him with a fortified tower-house[19]—'by far the largest struc-ture built in Shetland since the Iron Age'.[20] As at Birsay, the building of Scalloway left the same bitter complaint of the use of forced labour,[21] and the same stories of the eggs which people were compelled to provide to mix with the mortar.[22]

Patrick's most ambitious building project, however, was the Palace of the Yards, the new Earl's Palace in Kirkwall.[23] It is described in the *Inventory of Ancient Monuments* as 'one of the most accomplished Renaissance buildings in Scotland'.[24] It was designed for comfort rather than defence—the castle a mere 200 yards away provided a refuge if one was needed—yet in Patrick's day there was a great display of force and such a collection of guns that 'no house in Scotland was furnished with the like'.[25] Its great first-floor hall with bay windows and magnificent fireplaces provided a setting appropriate for the grandson of James V and the cousin of James VI. At the same time alterations were made to the adjoining Bishop's Palace, converting it into a forecourt to provide living quarters for Patrick's numerous retinue.[26] The ambitious building programme reveals Patrick as a man with a cultivated taste, but these fine new castles and palaces hugely overtaxed the earl's fi-nances and were largely responsible for his eventual bankruptcy.

In his heyday Patrick gave little thought to money, and he suffered from an overwhelming compulsion to maintain a lifestyle which proclaimed his royal ancestry. His two pages, four lackeys and three trumpeters were clothed in a red and yellow livery, and when he left his palace he was commonly

55. *The Earl's Palace, Kirkwall.*

accompanied by fifty musketeers and a train of gentlemen. The trumpets would sound before dinner, and similar fanfares announced the arrival of the second course,[27] while music of a less martial nature was provided by Archibald Graven, the earl's fiddler.[28] Patrick's seat in the cathedral, elevated above the seats of the magistrates, was surrounded by an elaborately carved oak screen, bearing the royal coat-of-arms without any mark of bastardy.[29] It aroused the same suspicions as his father's inscription at the Palace of Birsay— ROBERTUS STEUARDUS FILIUS JACOBI 5[ti] REX SCOTTORUM HOC AEDIFICIUM INSTRUXIT—where an elementary grammatical error makes the inscription appear to claim that Robert, rather than James, was King of Scots.[30] James VI is reputed to have been annoyed, but that pedantic monarch was likely to have been as displeased by the bad Latin as he was by the absurdity of the claim. For a time Patrick was considered to be sufficiently grand for a diplomatic marriage to Emilia, sister of Count Maurice of the United Provinces (the Netherlands) but Orkney was too remote for her taste, and she had heard talk that Patrick might lose the islands since the queen was keen to bestow them on her second son, the future Charles I.[31] If Charles had been given Orkney, it is interesting to speculate whether history would have been much different: both Charles I and Earl Patrick were men with a cultivated taste, but with a stubborn pride which made them unwilling to compromise with opponents; both were beset by money problems, and both ended their lives on the executioner's block.

Patrick's despotic power and his princely lifestyle were less secure than appeared. At the start of his reign he was bitterly opposed by his brothers and his mother, while opposition in Shetland was led by his uncle, Lawrence Bruce of Cultmalindie. Possession of the earldom and the bishopric estate put Patrick in a different class from other landowners, yet he was their superior only in the limited sense that he held the office of chief magistrate and had the right to collect skat. Lairds were seldom bound to him by ties of kinship, or even a feudal relationship, and there was nothing resembling a 'clan' to unite them in a common purpose.

In 1597 the Privy Council required all major landowners in Orkney and Shetland to enter into a General Band whereby they had to find surety for their peaceable behaviour.[32] It was a requirement resented by Patrick who argued somewhat disingenuously that the band might be appropriate for Highland chiefs, but it ought not to be used in a peaceful and law-abiding place like Orkney. The amount of surety which was demanded is a useful guide to the relative strength of three groups within the community—the Stewarts, the feuars of bishopric land and the native gentry—although, given the complicated relationships within Orkney society, these were never homogeneous groups, nor indeed were they entirely distinct in their interests. Clouston, who printed the list in his *History*, commented that it makes astonishing reading when compared to the lists of 'the best men' at the beginning of the century; a revolution in landownership had taken place and many old families had disappeared.[33] Yet, contrary to their reputation, Robert and Patrick had not created big estates for their relatives and henchmen. It is true that not far short of half the total surety had to be found by Patrick (£20,000) and the Master (£6,666), but none of Patrick's other brothers, legitimate and illegitimate, with the exception of James Stewart of Graemsay, appeared on the list. Of those owing their position to the Stewart earls, only Lawrence Bruce of Cultmalindie (£3,333) figured prominently. However, his lands lay in Shetland and he did not hold them as a feu from the earl and, although he was Patrick's uncle, he was certainly not an ally but an implacable opponent. Families owing their origins to Bishop Bothwell's feus in the immediate post-Reformation years were a more numerous class accounting in total for nearly £20,000 of the surety. Foremost among them were Michael Balfour who had inherited Gilbert Balfour's Westray property, Patrick Bellenden of Stenness and Evie, and the Sinclairs of Eday, all of whom were at odds with the earl. Only £15,000 had to be found by representatives of the old landowning families, and many of the Sinclair gentry were in such reduced circumstances that no surety was demanded of them. Traditional gentry may have been a declining class, but time had done little to reconcile them to political eclipse. When Richard James, the English traveller and antiquary, visited the islands (c.1615) he was forced to listen to tales of the once-important Sinclair connections with Norway and Denmark, and he was reminded that their proud family had 'until late years' been earls of Orkney. It was actually 145 years since the Sinclair earldom ended. Declining gentry had long memories.

What all these groups had in common, the earl's kin, bishopric feuars and native gentry, was a quite extraordinary degree of quarrelsomeness, a readiness to pursue each other at law, and to take all complaints to Edinburgh. Richard James described a society where swords and firearms were everywhere in evidence, and violence was never far below the surface:

> Generally all the gentlemen keep their guard, so that many times they have deadly fewds, all in general given excessively to drink in which they cut and stab with their durkes and swoardes.[34]

Richard James was probably right to attribute many of the feuds to drunken quarrels. The strength of Orkney ale was famous: according to Hector Boece it was 'the starkest ale in Albion', although he added somewhat optimistically that Orcadians had a remarkable capacity for consuming great quantities without becoming 'wod, daft or drunkin'.[35] Heavy drinking was common among the clergy as well as the laity: Gilbert Body, minister of Holm, was a 'drunken Orkney ass',[36] and even Bishop Law learned to be wary of 'the power of our Scapa aill'.[37]

In this atmosphere of suspicion and violence Patrick's feuds took on the character of private warfare. Michael Balfour of Westray had secured an exemption from the earl's jurisdiction, but in September 1597 Patrick invaded Westray with 60 armed men, in order to recover a debt of £8,000. Nearly 4,000 thraves of grain were removed, and he stripped Noltland so thoroughly that some of the arable land went out of cultivation. Over the next two years Patrick uplifted the rents, held courts, and profited from the fortuitous stranding of 29 whales. Balfour's protests were met with a threat to hang him from his own roof-tree. Since Patrick had taken possession of Balfour's ship, it was with some difficulty that he escaped in a little yoal and took his complaints to the Privy Council. Characteristically Patrick ignored the Privy Council's oft-repeated summonses, arguing that these frivolous complaints were intended to compel himself and his friends to leave the country at harvest time.[38] Patrick had right on his side, and in the end he received the £8,000 that was owed him, yet his violent conduct, his arrogant and obstructive attitude to the courts, and the way he ignored well-intended advice were typical of the conduct which eventually caused his downfall.

Another protracted feud involved Lawrence Bruce of Cultmalindie, his father's half-brother, whose base was in Muness castle in Unst, and about whose nefarious conduct a mass of evidence had been gathered in 1576.[39] At the very start of Patrick's reign Bruce had been the leading figure among a group of landowners, mainly from Shetland, who had organised a plea to Parliament alleging that Patrick was trying to have himself recognised as feudal superior of the udallers. Bruce claimed that Patrick had attacked him with 600 men at Laxfirth in Shetland,[40] forcing him to flee to Out Skerries, and had subsequently compelled him to renounce his tack.[41] There was another violent confrontation in 1604 when Bruce was captured by Patrick's warship, the *Dunkirk*, while taking a cargo of butter and fish to Sumburgh. When Bruce attempted to leave Shetland on a merchant ship, he was brought ashore and forced to march, booted and spurred, all the way from Maywick to Scalloway Castle, following a route on the steep and rough ground along the shores of Clift Sound.[42] Then in 1608 Bruce incurred Patrick's wrath by giving refuge to Thomas Black, ex-chamberlain and yet another adherent with whom Patrick had quarrelled. The earl arrived in Unst with a retinue of 36 followers including his trumpeters and fiddler, but he was also accompanied by his master-gunner who had brought 'a number of great brazen and iron pieces'. The earl's intention had been to attack Muness Castle, but at the last moment he was diverted by 'some news'.[43] It was typical of Patrick that the only result of his expedition was to alarm the government which was already highly suspicious of his actions.

But who paid the trumpeters? And who was it who built the castles and the palaces? Who paid the bills for the fine French wines, and the lavish entertainment?

Skat and rent formed the basis of Patrick's income, and the whole system was essentially parasitic, extracting from the udaller and tenant a large part of any surplus over and above what was needed for mere subsistence, and in a bad year not leaving even that. Those who paid customary medieval rents and taxes seldom expected any investment by the landowner, or indeed any discernible return. Yet, having said that, there was little that was new in the payments which Patrick collected. A new rental was drawn up in 1595,[44] probably as part of a general survey of the Crown's finances. It was compiled by John Dishington, Patrick's Sheriff-depute, and was a careful piece of work which reveals few innovations. Despite the transfer of the islands from Denmark to Scotland, the abolition of the earldom, the break-up of the bishopric estate, the introduction of the feu, and all the turmoil of Stewart rule, many of the payments remained exactly as they had been a century earlier in the days of Lord Henry Sinclair. It is true that the basis for calculating the rates of payment were no longer very well understood, and all sorts of payments tended to be lumped together under the heading of *skat silver*. In monetary terms *skat silver* had shown a considerable increase, yet the payments had probably not increased by more than the rate of inflation. It may be doubted that Patrick was an easy landlord, but his property was well managed, at least in his early years, and the payments he collected were in the main in accordance with tradition. Similarly there was nothing to compare to his father's unscrupulous use of escheats as a means of amassing property; in Shetland the lands Patrick held at his death were, with certain well-documented exceptions, identical to the estate he had inherited.[45]

Patrick's profits from fishing involved the same levying of tribute on the industry of others. Not only were there licenses to be obtained and bribes to be paid for permission to land and dry fish, but there were tolls to be paid for the right to fish in Orkney and Shetland waters. Patrick used his warship, the *Dunkirk,* in order to enforce the collection of these dues. He was later to maintain that these were 'accustomed payments',[46] and this was probably correct. His father had collected an *angel* (10 shillings sterling), 100 fish and 2 bolls of salt from each dogger boat. The 1575 *Complaint* against Earl Robert had protested that these rates were higher than 'auld use and wont', but had objected to their collection only on the grounds that he lacked the powers of Admiralty, not on the grounds that tolls were illegal.[47] What was new, however, was the increased scale of the fishing, and the profits which Patrick could grasp.

The Dutch Grand Fishery developed very quickly after 1580 and by the end of the century a huge fleet gathered for its midsummer rendezvous in Bressay Sound, giving rise to the town of Lerwick.[48] In Orkney activities were on a lesser scale, but in 1619 the revenue from Dutch rights in Stronsay alone amounted to £800 per annum.[49] East Fife fishermen were also present in great numbers but, unlike the Dutch who fished for herring, the men from Craill, Anstruther and Pittenweem were line fishermen who needed a shore base to build lodges and dry fish.[50] In 1594 Patrick entered into an agreement which allowed them to fish around Orkney except in the vicinity of Westray, but they were forbidden to set great lines 'within the headlands' or to catch small fish in the sounds between the islands except for bait; they also had to undertake not to oppress the islanders, not to carry them off as servants, nor to kill their sheep, and they were to keep the peace with English fishermen. In return every great line boat was to pay 50 ling and a barrel of salt, while hand-line boats were subject to a payment of 100 cod.[51] While the agreement brought handsome profits for the earl, it also shows that Patrick did not neglect the interests of the native population for whom inshore subsistence fishing was an important part of their livelihood. The east Fife fishery continued until the middle of the seventeenth century when, according to popular belief, so many of the fishermen were killed at the Battle of Kilsyth that the fleet rotted in port and the Orkney fishery never recovered.[52] Orkney boats were also involved in commercial fishing, at least to a limited extent; they were to be found in Shetland where they probably sold their catch to Hanseatic merchants, and they too were liable to pay the earl's landing charges.[53]

The sea brought another harvest in the form of wreck, and this became increasingly lucrative as the Dutch made more use of the north-about route on their voyages to the Indies. Wrecks were an irresistible temptation to gentry and peasantry alike, the successful plundering of a wreck being more than enough to set up a family in prosperity. Early charters had given tacksmen 'wrak and waith',[54] but Patrick's charter of 1600 was even more explicit: he was now vested with powers of Admiralty and given the right to 'whatever is left from shipwrecks and whatever is thrown up by the sea'.[55] It was a profitable privilege which he had no intention of sharing with anyone. One of the charges against Patrick which is best remembered is the accusation that he forbade the inhabitants to give help to shipwrecked seamen. Patrick did not deny that he had made a new law about this, but he explained his difficulties: this law was to prevent people 'invading' ships under pretext of rendering assistance; he complained that, no matter how careful his enquiries, he seldom recovered much from shipwrecked cargoes, and only a few of the poorest and most miserable culprits were ever produced for punishment; his new law required the baillie of the parish to be present, and to account for all the property removed from a wreck.[56] Both Patrick and his enemies claimed to be guided by humanitarian motives, but in reality both were more concerned with salvage than with saving lives.

Patrick was also capable of 'invading' ships. In July 1592 the *Ark of Noy* ('Noah's Ark') en route from Danzig to Spain put into Burrafirth in Shetland when she was badly damaged in a storm. In October, when the crew had failed to carry out repairs, William Manson, the Under-foud (Sheriff-depute) seized her. Her cargo of 'knappald, wainscoitt, pype wood and lead' was unloaded and the vessel was stripped of her sails, anchor and artillery, all of which was sold to Scots merchants for a total of £3,000. Patrick had to answer to the Privy Council for the 'wrangeous, violent and maisterfull spoilation' of the ship, but the Council decided that the Danzig owners had failed to prove the charges and Patrick was allowed to keep the proceeds.[57]

The affair of the Danzig ship lies on a thin dividing line which separates salvage from piracy. Other instances were more blatant, since the northern seas continued to be a hunting-ground for pirates, and sometimes Patrick was the victim rather than the offender. In 1590, when he sailed south from Orkney to visit the Scottish court, his ship was captured by the brutal English pirate, David Gwynn. Gwynn was later arrested and was imprisoned in England but, despite agents working on Patrick's behalf, the stolen property was not returned.[58] His losses were huge since he claimed 'his whole furnishing in money, jewels and moveables' to the value of £36,000 had been stolen. The value of the loss is extraordinary—it was about three times the annual income from the earldom—and it demonstrates both Patrick's psychological need to impress when he visited the Scottish court, and also his foolhardiness in venturing on pirate-infested seas with such treasure. As a reprisal, Patrick seized an English ship, the *Hoip Weill* of Dunwich, carrying a cargo of wheat from Danzig to London. The Privy Council ordered him to return her, but James VI had some sympathy with Patrick's predicament and wrote a personal letter to Queen Elizabeth seeking redress for Patrick's losses although, as far as is known, without result.[59] Patrick, however, might reflect that, in the business of piracy, there were profits and losses: the value of the cargo of the *Ark of Noy* which he had commandeered went a little way towards recompensing him for his losses at the hands of the English pirates. He must also have been well aware of the activities of Orkney-based pirates who were sometimes to be found in seas far from home: in 1590, for example, the *Elizabeth* belonging to James and Robert Brown was captured in Wales and the crew committed to prison.

The Stewart earldom had never properly taken root in the Northern Isles and, although of comparatively recent origin, it belonged to a kind of aristocracy which was becoming outmoded. Patrick's princely pretensions, his unruly earldom, and his disdain for the courts were less likely to be tolerated in the more law-abiding Scotland of the early seventeenth century. He would have been well-advised to heed warnings that James VI was of a different disposition now that he had succeeded to the English throne (1603).[60] To survive Patrick needed to adapt, but his irascible and unbending temper made that impossible. He was also trapped by his debts and enmeshed in feuds from which it was impossible to extricate himself.

21

The End of the Earldom

Orkney had seen no resident bishop since the armour-clad Bishop Adam Bothwell was rescued from the wreck of the *Unicorn* (see pp.260-1). After 1568 Bothwell's connection with his diocese was effectively severed. He remained bishop in name until his death in 1593, but he was not replaced since bishops were then in abeyance. Not only had the religious functions of the bishop been superseded, but the landed estates had passed out of church control when Robert Stewart acquired the temporalities of the bishopric in exchange for Holyrood. In 1600 Patrick received two charters under the Great Seal: the first, issued on the same day that Patrick was hunting with James VI in the Borders,[1] was for the earldom estate, and the second charter a few weeks later confirmed his right to the bishopric.[2] The uncertainties of Patrick's earlier years were swept away, and his position now seemed secure. His rights extended to the 'advocation, donation and patronage of bishoprics, rectories, vicarages, prebendary churches, chapels and other ecclesiastical benefices'.[3] Not only was his ownership of the bishopric land assured, but he seemed to have been given a free hand to dispose of the income from former benefices to his own nominees.

Bishops, however, were essential to James VI's future plans for the government of his kingdom, and in 1606 an Act of Parliament was passed which led step by step to the restoration of bishops. At first this was to be a civil measure only, which was needed, the king argued, because bishops were an essential part of the constitution, but almost immediately they were appointed 'constant moderators' of synods, and in 1610 a fully consecrated episcopate was restored. James Law, minister of Kirkliston, was James VI's appointment to Orkney (Bishop of Orkney 1606–1615). He was one of a small group of ministers entrusted with the management of the unruly Scots kirk. He was to be found playing an important role in Parliament, and was at the centre of the king's plans to impose bishops on a somewhat reluctant church. There is little sign that Orkney had much interest whether or not the church was ruled by bishops, but Law's presence, and his need to derive an income from the bishopric estate, was bound to cause conflict with Patrick's recent charter. Law has generally had a good write-up from posterity: he was 'a man of consummate ability, tact and resolution',[4] who brought to an end two generations of misrule by the Stewart earls. The over-simple view of Orkney history which regards the Stewart earldom as melodrama and casts Patrick in the role of caricature villain, requires the presence of the hero who appears in the final act to defeat tyranny and restore sanity. Law was certainly able, and he outmanoeuvred Patrick at every turn, but he also was a highly political bishop with his own objectives. He also had what Patrick was rapidly losing—a ready hearing at court.

Law could only establish himself in Orkney by deriving an income from the bishopric, but Patrick was so deep in debt that he could ill-afford any diminution of his rents. Patrick's principal creditor was the wealthy Sir John Arnot, Lord Provost of Edinburgh and Treasurer-depute of Scotland. The earl's dealings with Arnot dated at least as far back as 1594 when Arnot provided 5,000 merks surety (1 merk = £⅔) that Patrick would appear before the Privy Council to answer complaints from his brother, James Stewart of Graemsay.[5] Arnot was also in the business of lending money to the king, some of it for the lavish entertainment which marked the baptism of Prince Henry[6] at which Patrick acted as server,[7] and as a means of repayment, the king granted Arnot £2,000 from the bishopric for each of the years 1594, 1595 and 1596.[8] On the whole Arnot did his best to help Patrick by offering good advice, and the king may even have been responsible for placing him at Patrick's side as a financial adviser,[9] yet it was beyond the power of Arnot or anyone else to control Patrick's spiralling debts. By 1601 Patrick's debts amounted to nearly 80,000 merks, mainly as a result of his building works. Two years later when he visited England, he borrowed 73,700 merks from Arnot, and a whole series of further loans followed. By 1605 he was pursued by a host of creditors, of whom Robert Monteith of Egilsay claimed to be due £40,000.[10] Patrick's confused financial affairs were well beyond the point of no return, and his debts were so complex that they can no longer be unravelled. Peter Anderson estimates that his total liabilities eventually amounted to more than a quarter of a million merks[11]—he was 'drownit in debt'. In July 1606 Patrick was forced to grant Arnot the greater part of his Orkney lands because of failure to repay his debts—Birsay, Sandwick, Hoy, Walls, South Ronaldsay, Shapinsay, Deerness, Sanday, Stronsay, Egilsay, Rousay and North Ronaldsay. The terms of the grant allowed Patrick to regain possession when he was in a position to repay 200,000 merks,[12] but this was an impossibly large sum, and there was no likelihood that Patrick would ever clear the debt.

It was eventually the Earl of Caithness who brought about Patrick's downfall (George III, Earl of Caithness 1582–1643). The Caithness Sinclairs were the branch of the family which retained the title of 'earl' and they did not readily forget that their ancestors had also been earls in Orkney. Relations had remained strained ever since Earl John was killed at Summerdale (1528).

We have seen that George II (Earl of Caithness 1528–1582) had hopes of regaining the Orkney tack in 1560, and was actively recruiting allies within Orkney (see p.258). No doubt the Caithness Sinclairs resented Robert and Patrick Stewart as quasi-royal interlopers into a Sinclair domain. Patrick Bellenden found a willing ally in Caithness when he was pursuing his feud with Earl Robert, and at one point had gathered 300 men for a threatened re-run of the Summerdale invasion (see p.275). Then there had been talk that Earl George's half-brother, Francis Bothwell, whose madcap attacks thoroughly alarmed James VI in the years 1591-4, had plans to bring 300 men from France who, with Caithness help, were to seize Orkney. Bothwell believed that this might easily be done since 'the inhabitants dislike their natural lord'.[13] In 1597 Earl George had cast doubts on the legality of Patrick's title, and had aspirations to be appointed chamberlain in Orkney. Relations were so bad that George and Patrick each accused the other of homicide and perjury, and George went as far as to have swords and daggers made in order to challenge Patrick to a duel.[14] In 1599 both earls had to find surety that they would suspend their quarrels.[15]

The threat from Earl George became much more dangerous when he found an ally in Orkney in the person of William Sinclair of Eday. To some extent it was a natural alliance since William's father, Edward Sinclair, was from the Roslin branch of the family and was therefore closely related to Earl George (see Fig.48). Edward's feu of Eday from Bishop Adam Bothwell was one of the few instances of a member of the Sinclair family benefiting directly from a major feu of bishopric land. Edward was still alive, but he was now a great age, being described as 'an auld decrepit man...aged 100 or thereby',[16] and affairs were largely in the hands of his son. The Eday Sinclairs were deep in debt to Edinburgh merchants, and this provided Earl George with his opportunity. In 1601 there were reports that George was 'buying an isle in Orkney'. The deal involved clearing the debts of the Eday Sinclairs, in return for which they not only became Earl George's tenants, but also recognised him as 'their chief'.[17] Patrick was alarmed that his enemy had gained a foothold in Orkney, and he had even more to worry about when six or seven boatloads of 'vagabondis, broken Highland men of Caithness' arrived in Eday. He was at pains to emphasise the aggressive intentions of the Caithness invaders and to hark back to the days of patriotic resistance at Summerdale: 'of the cuntrie men of Caithness thair barbarous interpryssis lang of befoir against the countrey of Orknay thair remaineis yit experience'.[18]

Although William Sinclair's deal with Earl George had ostensibly been reached with the agreement of his father, Patrick was able to take advantage of the bad relations between father and son. According to Patrick's own version of events, he received a complaint from the old man that his son was treating him badly, firing *hagbuts* (a type of musket) at him, and gripping him by the neck as if he was a dog. Patrick was to claim that the old man sold him Eday and all his other lands in return for protection. On the pretext of restoring order, Patrick dispatched Henry Black, Captain of the Castle, who seized the house of Holland, emptied it of its contents, and ejected William Sinclair to the accompaniment of his wife's loud threats that, if Patrick had two heads, she would 'gar him want ane of them'.[19] In the years which followed Patrick gathered the Eday rents, and extracted great quantities of valuable building stone from the Towback quarry.[20]

If Earl George's relations with Patrick were bad, his dealings with his southern neighbour, the Earl of Sutherland, were even more difficult, erupting periodically into open violence.[21] The result was a much publicised alliance between Orkney and Sutherland who made common cause against Caithness. In 1602 Patrick's warship, the *Dunkirk,* was dispatched to Cromarty to fetch the Earl of Sutherland who was entertained in great style in Birsay and at Kirkwall, and a band of friendship was signed between them. Two years later Patrick visited Dornoch and stood as godfather for Sutherland's infant son.[22]

In 1606 Patrick was first pursued on the charges of treason from which he never entirely escaped. His enemies alleged that he possessed a forged Commission of Lieutenancy complete with signet and royal signature which he used to usurp the royal prerogative: he was also accused of illegal taxation, the use of forced labour, contravening laws relating to the carrying of arms, and forbidding appeal to Scottish courts.[23] Whereas Patrick might disregard summonses for debt, it was not possible to ignore treason charges. He appeared in Edinburgh on several occasions before being called to England in September. His troubles followed him, first, to Windsor and then to Hampton Court where, at the instigation of Robert Monteith of Egilsay, there were *executions of horning,* a judicial pronouncement of outlawry, in this case as a means of recovering debt.

At Hampton Court Patrick witnessed the acrimonious debate about the restoration of bishops to the Scottish church. Patrick probably did not share his cousin's keen interest in the institutions of the church, and he cannot have been well pleased that the king rewarded two of his supporters with pensions which were to be paid from the revenue of the Orkney bishopric.[24] An even more pressing problem was how Bishop Law was to derive an income. Those parts of the bishopric which had not been feued by Bishop Adam Bothwell were now in the hands of Patrick, and his rights had been confirmed by charter as recently as 1600. Patrick, however, was not in a good position to negotiate since he still faced treason charges, and his many creditors had claims on his lands. Complicated dealings by Sir John Arnot resolved the question of the bishop's income, but hardly to Patrick's satisfaction: in January 1607 it was agreed that Patrick was to pay Law 4,000 merks a year from the revenues of the bishopric, and he was also to pay the stipends of the Orkney ministers with Sir John Arnot acting as guarantor.[25] A particularly galling part of the deal was that Patrick was forced to hand over his fine new palace of the Yards. Although known as 'the Earl's Palace', Patrick lived in it for a very short time. Perhaps the palace was not entirely completed when he undertook to make good, doors, windows, roofs, slates, glass, iron and timber work before the bishop's entry in October 1608.[26]

In return for these concessions Patrick received a promise that Law would intercede with the king on his behalf. James VI generally took a kindly and indulgent interest in his lesser relatives, and Patrick and the king had been hunting companions in their youth. Patrick always had the absurdly optimistic notion that all his problems would melt away if only he could meet the king face to face. Wiser counsels advised against another visit to court, but Patrick must have been frustrated by the way the king's view of Orkney affairs was henceforth filtered by Bishop Law. The bishop's fulsome letters were larded with flattery and literary allusions designed to appeal to James's pedantic self-importance, but they were uniformly hostile to Patrick. Late in 1608 the bishop wrote to the king drawing attention to 'the great and continual complaints of your Majesty's poor subjects in these islands' who were 'manifestly and grievously oppressed'.[27]

The bishop's letter was in support of a new tactic by Lawrence Bruce and Robert Monteith. Since Patrick usually ignored summonses to appear in court to face charges, they now sought a commission which would give them authority to levy men and use whatever force was needed in order to compel his attendance. The king was rather unwilling to grant such powers in a civil case, and Patrick was given one final chance. Even then he played for time, but in May 1608 he was finally obliged to appeared before the Council. George, Earl of Caithness, was also present: his conduct was also under investigation, and so were the complaints made by the earls against each other. In an absurd incident some of Patrick's servants had been captured when they put ashore in Caithness in a gale; they had been filled with drink, half their hair and beards were shaved off, then they were sent out into the Pentland Firth in the same bad weather which had forced them to take shelter.[28] Both earls were required to appear before the Privy Council to answer for their conduct, but mutual friends persuaded them to settle their differences in private 'lest they should reveal too much of the other's doings'.[29]

Although the settlement with Earl George brought an end to their quarrel for the time being, the treason charges against Patrick remained. In 1609 he was warded in Edinburgh Castle. A cat-and-mouse game of alternate close confinement and relaxation of the terms of his imprisonment was to be the pattern of the remaining six years of his life—he was never again entirely free. In 1610 he was formally indicted on seven counts of treason, some of which were charges which had also been made against his father (see pp.268-70). 1. Patrick was accused of passing sentence against a number of landowners according to laws treasonably made by himself 'contrary and repugnant to the laws of the kingdom'. 2. He induced many gentlemen to subscribe to a *band mutuus* whereby they promised to reveal anything which threatened the earl's interest, and to settle claims in local courts rather than have recourse to the Privy Council and the Court of Session. 3. He caused Adam Moodie and others to be tried before 'pretended deputes and judges', as a result of which they had been sentenced to banishment and forfeiture of goods. 4. He 'stopped the ferries' and forbade anyone to leave Orkney without his passport. 5. He compelled people who were not his own tenants to work for him. 6. He levied 'great and exorbitant taxes', although he had no right to levy any taxation. 7. He issued licences for buying and selling goods and exacted penalties for the contravention of his regulations.[30] Before Patrick had an opportunity of answering, he had to face a number of additional charges including the allegation that he exacted tolls from Dutch and English fishing vessels, and the well-known accusation that he had forbidden people to aid ships in distress.

Although the charges against Patrick had at last been made in some detail, he was never brought to trial for these offences. On seven occasions between August 1610 and May 1611 the case was adjourned with Patrick protesting his innocence and apparently confident that he could clear himself. The likelihood is that a reasonable defence could have been offered, since he could only be found guilty on the main charges if it was proved that he had no right to operate Orkney's distinctive legal system. In the absence of the Lawbook it is not always possible to know the extent of Patrick's powers and whether the decisions of his courts were arbitrary or properly based on traditional practice. There is no doubt that he sometimes used his courts for his own ends, although perhaps not so blatantly as his father had done. For ordinary purposes, however, island law remained fully operational. Gordon Donaldson's study of the many everyday cases recorded in the Shetland Court Book for 1602-4 reveals a legal system which was still vigorous and effective.[31] There is no sense that island law was in decay or that it was inadequate, or that the populace at large had lost confidence in the ability of the courts to mete out justice. Patrick's position as earl placed him in at the head of a legal system which was different from the law of Scotland, but which was undoubtedly valid. Patrick was accused of using Orkney law rather than breaching it; his enemies had little difficulty in creating the impression that a subject who controlled his own legal system was dangerously overmighty, but it was personal enmity, rather than much real substance, which lay behind the treason charges. If Patrick had been content with a less extravagant lifestyle, if he had stayed out of debt, if he had listened to good advice, and if he had kept on better terms with his neighbours, these charges would never have been made. However, with his case still unheard, the Privy Council on 22 March 1611 passed a comprehensive series of measures designed to dismantle his regime: all who held commissions from the earl for the offices of Justiciary, Sheriffship and Bailiary were discharged, and others were warned not to accept such offices from Patrick in future; all 'foreign laws' within Orkney and Shetland were abolished, and magistrates were ordered to use 'the proper laws of the kingdom'.[32] The Privy Council found it convenient to represent the ancient system of Norse law as merely part of Patrick's arbitrary regime.

Meanwhile there had been fluctuations in the terms of Patrick's imprisonment. In March 1610 conditions were relaxed after he was forced to abandon any claim to the lands of the bishopric and to church income. Bishop Law and Sir John Arnot were then armed with powers of sheriffs and were sent to Orkney with a commission to investigate complaints. A commission which included Bishop Law was not likely to be impartial, yet its terms of reference were surprisingly neutral in tone: it was to determine whether the complaints against Patrick were justified, or whether they were made 'upon the distemperit humour and disposition of people without good ground and warrant'.[33] Having dismantled Patrick's regime, King James' natural inclination was to be merciful to his cousin, and alarming rumours reached Law that Patrick might now be allowed to return to Orkney. There may even have been a popular demand for his restoration. Patrick was described as 'feeding the poor and simple people with hopes that he will soon return, armed with His Majesty's power and authority'.[34] To counteract any such possibility Law wrote to the king urging him to remember that Patrick's natural disposition was such that he could not return to Orkney without prejudicing Law's own position and that of Sir John Arnot; justice in a remote part of the kingdom ought to be more important than showing favours. Despite Law's efforts to the contrary, the relaxation of Patrick's conditions continued, although for the moment he was forbidden to travel more than four miles from Edinburgh.

A few weeks later Patrick's conditions abruptly changed and he was placed in close confinement in Dumbarton Castle when it was discovered that he had sent his son to Orkney. Robert Stewart was a bastard son; he was a tall, handsome young man, popular in Orkney,[35] but barely 20 years of age and out of his depth when he attempted to act on his father's behalf. Patrick was to claim that Robert was merely authorised to collect arrears of rent and skat, and indeed the earl's circumstances were now so straitened that he was in desperate need of even a small income, but in truth Robert seems secretly to have been given wider powers to act as Patrick's depute.

What made Robert's mission to Orkney even more alarming were the movements of a group of mercenaries known as 'the Sinclair Expedition'. These mercenaries consisted of three companies of Scots, one commanded by a certain George Sinclair, who were recruited in the Netherlands to be used by Gustavus Adolphus of Sweden in the war against Denmark. The plan was that the mercenaries should rendezvous in Orkney or Shetland, cross the North Sea, then travel through Norway to Sweden. For a time the government was alarmed that this force might be used in Orkney, and perhaps that was a real possibility. Early in 1612 Patrick's warship, the *Dunkirk*, was involved in attacks on shipping in Norwegian waters,[36] but whether this was merely to relieve Patrick's hard-pressed finances with a little piracy, or whether the operations were in some way connected with the impending Sinclair expedition is not known. The Scottish government tried to prevent the expedition sailing, but in the event two of the companies embarked from Caithness (which the Danes apparently believed was one of the islands of Orkney). The expedition, however, sailed directly to Norway, landed in Romsdal, and was almost totally annihilated by Norwegian farmers as it attempted to cross the mountains into Sweden.[37]

To counteract these threats Sir John Arnot was authorised to obtain some warships,[38] and Bishop Law prepared to visit the islands. The state of affairs which Law found on his arrival fell a little short of open rebellion. Robert had broken open the Girnel and seized its store of grain, and he had gained possession of the Castle and the palaces, but Law was not openly resisted and, much to Patrick's fury, Robert negotiated the surrender of the fortified places. Law was not prevented from reconstituting the Burgh of Kirkwall, nor from holding his courts of justice, but he did not use his courts to pursue Robert and his followers. Anyone reading the printed *Court Book* for 1612-3[39] might easily fail to appreciate that the islands were on the brink of rebellion. Law was content to deal with routine crime and to pass a number of Acts dealing with such uncontroversial matters as the control of beggars, the regulation of servants, the *rooing* of sheep, theft, slander, the depredations of pigs, riding other people's horses and stealing hair from horses' tails.[40] It is difficult to see how these Acts differed from the laws which Patrick was accused of having treasonably made, and indeed Law's 'Act for Swyne' may well have been a re-enactment of Earl Robert's 'law' against 'swine rutting' which had caused such a fuss 40 years earlier (see p.269). Meanwhile the Privy Council decreed that no one was to be transported out of Orkney without licence,[41] thus 'stopping the ferries' just like the Stewart earls. Bishop Law also received a blank commission which he could use to require anyone to remove from Orkney on ten day's notice,[42] banishing people in the same way as Patrick was accused of doing when he had controlled the courts.

Although the earl was imprisoned, disgraced and deprived of his authority to rule Orkney, he still remained in possession of his lands, although they were pledged to others because of his debts. In October 1612 the king bought out Sir John Arnot's interest for £300,000, and Orkney was annexed to the Crown as it had been before the arrival of the Stewarts. The Crown acquired the earldom estate, the offices of Justiciary and Sheriffship, the superiority over the udallers and the keepership of Kirkwall Castle, and the whole estate was erected into a *stewartry* (a territory under the direct rule of the Crown and administered by a steward). The new tacksman was Sir James Stewart of Killeith, later Lord Ochiltree, whose brother-in-law John Finlayson was made Steward-depute. Finlayson, who lived at Papdale on the outskirts of Kirkwall, set about the enormous task of enforcing the collection of arrears of rent and skat, in the process making himself thoroughly unpopular: he was 'of an evil demeanour...hated to the death by all sorts of men'.[43] Finlayson's oppressive rule resulted in many Orcadians seeing the prospects of Patrick's restoration as a return to some kind of normality, and his unpopularity added to the support which Patrick might hope to command.

Ever since 1612 Patrick had been playing a double game. On the one hand it seemed that he might be restored to favour, while, on the other, his impatience with his long imprisonment without trial led him to contemplate a violent seizure of power. When James VI felt that he had acted decisively, he was always inclined to be lenient and, although Patrick continued to be warded in Dumbarton Castle, the terms of his imprisonment were easier. Early in 1614 Patrick was brought before the Privy Council to discuss proposals that he should resign his rights in Orkney in return for 'honourable and good conditions'.[44] Attempts were made to persuade him to accept the keepership of one of the Scottish royal palaces and a payment of £10,000 if he would give up Orkney.[45] Patrick would have been well advised to accept these terms, but he still clung to the absurd hope that a personal meeting with the king might lead to the restoration of his fortunes.

Robert Stewart visited his father at Dumbarton, and listening servants later described how the earl launched into an impassioned attack on his son's simplicity in handing over the fortified places to Bishop Law in 1612. The earl was highly excited and called his son 'a feeble beast'. Robert protested that, if he ever held the castle again, he would not let it go so easily. Patrick was not to be pacified—'he trowed he would do no better'.[46] Robert was a young man, much in awe of his irascible father, and his determination not to let him down a second time was to be fatal to both of them. The motives for sending Robert back to Orkney were muddled. Although Patrick was now dispossessed of the earldom estate, he still had a right to arrears due to him before the annexation of Orkney to the Crown. Robert received a commission to collect all debts from crop 1611 and earlier,[47] but he was also furnished with two documents which might prove useful—a commission to hold the Castle of Kirkwall and a list of friends who might assist him. The plot also involved Patrick's escape from Dumbarton, but attempts to bribe his gaolers failed. However, rumours that he was free reached Orkney and induced a number of people to join the rebellion.

Failure to raise money resulted in Robert having only five followers when he arrived in Orkney in May 1614. He was hospitably received by Bernard Stewart at the Palace of Birsay, and apparently Robert hoped that Bernard would be persuaded to hand over the palace. Bernard Stewart was a long-serving supporter of Patrick and was on the fringes of the plot; he had visited Patrick in Dumbarton, and had been responsible for bringing Robert to Orkney, mistakenly believing that Patrick was about to be restored to favour. He was now better informed and refused to act in a way which might be construed to be rebellion.[48] However, he was not expecting violence when two weeks later he was expelled from the palace at sword-point and his wife held hostage. Country people from round about were hastily recruited, and they brought in muskets, powder and shot.[49] When the news reached Kirkwall, Steward-depute John Finlayson gathered between 60 and 80 men, many of whom were later to side with Robert, and marched on Birsay. He offered to give Robert 14 days to uplift his rents, but the offer was met with a volley of musket shot, and Finlayson beat a hasty retreat.

Soon Robert had a sizeable following mainly drawn from the Birsay estate. He held musters and 'waponne-shawis' (inspection of weapons) and drew up a band by which 17 of the leaders undertook to follow him 'to the death'. The band was to play a crucial role at the trial of those who signed it, for it made the intention to rebel unnecessarily explicit. The preamble set out the justification for the rebellion: it argued that the way so many outsiders were appointed to official posts put the whole community at jeopardy, with the result that it was in danger of perishing from the corruption of the laws, the oppression and venality of the magistrates and the greed of officers; these officials consumed the king's rent without contributing anything, and poor people laboured under a yoke of servitude.[50] A manifesto attacking incomers and officials might command a good deal of support even in the twenty-first century, but it is ironic that the final act of the Stewart earls was capable of being represented as a patriotic resistance to incomers who threatened native institutions—the very charge usually levelled against the Stewarts themselves. In the previous year Finlayson had issued no less than 2,400 handwritten rent-demands,[51] and his rapacious gathering of arrears no doubt did much to revive the fortunes of Patrick and his son. Robert's advance on Kirkwall met with only a little resistance, easily scattered by a volley of musket shot at the Bu of Corse, then with the sounding of trumpets, the 'touking' of drums, and with ensigns displayed, the rebels entered Kirkwall. Over the next few days they occupied the Castle, the cathedral, the

Palace of the Yards and the Girnel. John Finlayson and Bernard Stewart were both captured and sent south, and a ship was dispatched to Norway to purchase supplies of gunpowder.[52]

News of the capture of Kirkwall Castle reached James VI at an inopportune moment when he was coping with an unwelcome visit from his brother-in-law, Christian IV of Denmark, who had appeared unexpectedly in England.[53] Since Danish redemption of Orkney was still theoretically possible, the rebellion was a potential embarrassment. Its suppression was properly the task of James Stewart of Killeith as tacksman and Steward but, as news trickled south, it became clear that this would be no easy matter. Killeith was unpopular in Orkney due to the oppressive rule he had exercised through John Finlayson, and he was reluctant to lead the proposed expedition. A commission was then granted to Patrick's old enemy, Robert Monteith of Egilsay, but three days later he stepped down in favour of George, Earl of Caithness. The expedition offered Earl George an opportunity to divert attention from his own misdeeds which were again under investigation, and to gain credit by aiding the government, while at the same time he was provided with the men, money and equipment which he needed to bring his long feud with Earl Patrick to a successful conclusion. That was the limit of his ambitions, and he seems to have accepted that there was no chance that he would be left in charge of Orkney after the rebellion was defeated. His offer was gratefully accepted and, over the next two weeks, he assembled ships and took on board artillery from Edinburgh Castle including the one-and-half-ton cannon known as *Thrawn Mou* ('obstinate mouth').[54] His first call was in Caithness where he embarked a further 30 men and gave orders to others to follow. Then on 23 August he landed at Carness, some two miles from Kirkwall. Letters were sent throughout Orkney requiring gentlemen to assist him, but the response was poor; even the gentry who had pursued long feuds with the Stewart earls were conspicuous by their absence.[55] Orcadians, whatever their feelings towards Earl Patrick, had no enthusiasm for a Caithness invasion.

Over the next few days the invaders struggled to manoeuvre the heavy guns over the soft ground so that they could bring their fire to bear on the walls of the Castle. They were met with a show of defiance, first at Carness, and then at the Ba' Lea on the outskirts of the town. The surrender of the cathedral, whose steeple towered above the walls of the Castle, provided a vantage point for musket fire, but the Castle proved resistant to artillery. The Earl of Caithness described how cannon balls split like wooden golf balls against the massive walls of the ancient Sinclair fortress: 'I protest to God the house has never been biggit by [without] the consent of the Devil, for it is one of the strongest houlds in Britain'.[56] Three weeks later a breach was made in one of the walls, but an attempt to storm it with a timber engine failed when the defenders set fire to the contraption. As the rains of a wet and stormy autumn set in, and as the besiegers exhausted their supplies of gunpowder, hopes of taking the castle began to fade, but the morale of the defenders was also low. Robert was an irresolute leader; he was terrified by the gunfire, and lacked any real plan. There was talk of the 'many alterations' which might occur: it was possible that the Spanish would come, or else the papists might make trouble, or the king's attention might be diverted by the Count Palatine's affairs. Robert was reluctant to surrender, fearing that under torture he would reveal his father's part in the rebellion.[57] In parallel to the siege, however, there were constant discussions. Patrick Halcro and perhaps Robert himself slipped out of the Castle to discuss the terms on which they might yield the Castle. Patrick Halcro, although second only to Robert among the rebels, later escaped execution, so it is likely that he negotiated the terms of surrender.

Bishop Law had been persuaded somewhat reluctantly to join the Earl of Caithness's expedition, but he enjoyed the campaign. He relished the victory, carousing 'after the Orkney fashion' when the king's colours were broken out over the Castle and *Thrawn Mou* was dragged along the street with the keys of the Castle displayed from its muzzle. Robert Stewart and Patrick Halcro were sent south for trial, lesser people were hanged, and labourers were put to work demolishing the Castle. It was only with difficulty that Law prevented the earl from pulling down the cathedral whose steeple had been of such strategic importance during the siege. Robert's trial in Edinburgh led to an inevitable conviction and he was hanged on 1 January 1615. His father did not long survive him. Patrick tried to disown his son's actions, and he concealed his own part in the plot quite skilfully, but there was sufficient evidence to prove his complicity. When Patrick was beheaded, it was for his part in the rebellion, not for the many charges which over two generations had been made against the Stewart earls, and for which he had so long been imprisoned. A last minute delay, ostensibly so that he could learn the Lord's Prayer, may have been a final stratagem in the hope that there might yet be a royal pardon. However, open rebellion had put him beyond King James' mercy, and he was executed on 6 February 1615.

Bishop Law had double cause to celebrate when four days after the surrender of the Castle, the arrangements for his new bishopric were finally approved.[58] Previously the bishop's land had been scattered throughout every parish of Orkney and Shetland, often lying run-rig with earldom lands and with the lands of udallers. For the past two years Law had been working on a scheme whereby the bishopric and earldom lands were to be separated out. Now, by means of a major exchange, Orkney was divided into earldom and bishopric parishes. The bishop's lands were to lie in the parishes of

Holm, Orphir, Stromness, Sandwick, Shapinsay, Walls, Hoy and parts of St Ola, and he was to be superior of the feued lands in Evie, Burray, Flotta and Caithness. Other parishes were designated 'earldom parishes' and, in the absence of an earl, these lands were in the hands of the king and his tacksman. What was conveyed to the bishop was not absolute ownership of entire bishopric parishes: he now owned the land in these parishes which in the past had belonged to the bishop and to the earl, and he was superior of any land in bishopric parishes which had been feued by either estate; udal lands, however, remained the property of the udallers, and from these lands the bishop's rights were confined to the collection of skat.

The last two chapters, although trying to look beyond Patrick as a mere caricature tyrant, hardly amount to a rehabilitation of his reputation. He had an unhealthy and compulsive need to sustain a lifestyle which proclaimed his royal origins, whatever the cost to himself and to others. His reign was from first to last a catalogue of disorder, he was ruined by his extravagance, and he was finally destroyed by instigating a rebellion at the very time when James VI could easily have been persuaded to be merciful. As Robert said of his father, 'Thair was never thing lookit weill yet whilk he devysit'.[59]

The real question is not the justice of Patrick's execution, but the value of the institutions he brought down with him. One of these institutions was the earldom itself which had a long but not unbroken 700-year history stretching back to Viking times. Orkney was undoubtedly better off without the earldom as it had existed under the Stewarts, but the new regime was not an improvement: earls were replaced by short-term and often corrupt absentee tacksmen who were no more interested than Earl Patrick in the wellbeing of the islanders. A second institution brought down by Earl Patrick was Norse law. Perhaps its demise was inevitable: its abolition was the natural sequel to the introduction of Scottish courts in 1541 when the Lawman and Lawting had been replaced by the Sheriff and Sheriff Court (see pp.244-5). Because the Lawbook no longer exists, we hardly know enough about island law to regret its passing, although it seems to have operated effectively and with general approval right up to its abolition. However, having been cut off from its Scandinavian roots for 144 years, it retained some undesirably archaic features and, after the abolition of the office of Lawman, it lacked the independence necessary to resist unscrupulous manipulation by the earls who were able to dominate the courts when their interests were involved. The conflict between Orkney and Scottish law also created a good deal of confusion in cases involving people rich enough to appeal to Scottish courts. On the other hand the difficulties which small udallers faced in the seventeenth century in maintaining their unwritten rights to their property would have been less under a legal system which took better cognisance of these rights.

The value of Orkney law is also bound up with the question of cultural identity. There is something very attractive about the medieval Lawting as an independent forum for public opinion, although we actually know so little about its workings that it is difficult to assess its potential as a democratic institution. One possibility is that Orkney might have retained home-rule status like other Norse outposts in the Isle of Man and the Faroe Islands. That might have led to greater linguistic and cultural distinctiveness, and perhaps to greater economic success. On the other hand very small sub-nations sometimes have difficulty in maintaining forward-looking institutions, and there might be drawbacks as well as benefits had twenty-first century Orkney become an offshore tax-haven. There is little point in speculating about alternative 'might-have-been' histories, and indeed the Lawting and much of the structure of Norse law had already been irretrievably destroyed before Patrick's time. Nevertheless we can see that the downfall of Earl Patrick was one of those decisive moments when Orkney lurched in the direction of closer integration with Scotland.

There is another sense in which the fall of Earl Patrick marks the end of an era. Storer Clouston in his *History* wrote that, with the beheading of Patrick Stewart and the hanging of his son, 'the history of the *country* of Orkney comes to an end and the annals of a remote Scottish *county* begin'.[60] He and his fellow-historian, Hugh Marwick, lived at a time when history was still political history, so Clouston was able to end his book with a ten-page chapter entitled 'The Last Two Centuries', and Marwick disposed of 'Orkney in the Last Three Centuries' in even less space.[61] Yet, as the story of kings, earls and bishops comes to an end, documentary sources begin to be much richer—there is a sense in which Orkney history is just beginning. Clouston himself was a pioneer in the use of these sources, for example in his splendid papers on the structure and organisation of Orkney townships, while Marwick's linguistic and place-name studies demonstrate that a rich cultural identity does not entirely depend on the survival of a distinctive political system.

22
Tacksmen, Lairds and Udallers, 1615-1707

It was easier to bring down the regime of Earl Patrick than to find anything very satisfactory to replace him, since there was an understandable reluctance on the part of government to trust any individual with the same dangerous monopoly of power as had been enjoyed by the Stewart earls. By the seventeenth century those twin institutions of medieval Orkney, the earldom and the bishopric, had only an intermittent existence. In the period 1615–1707 earldom rule totalled only 26 years and was provided by the 7th, 8th and 9th Earls of Morton (1643–1669), while two periods of episcopacy amounted to 50 years (Bishops Law and Graham up to 1638, and Sydserff, Honyman and Mackenzie from 1662 to 1689). For most of the period both estates were Crown property and were entrusted to short-term tacksmen who paid a lump sum for a right to uplift rent and skat.

Orkney did not emerge from the chaos of Earl Patrick's misrule into a tranquil age of settled government, as Bishop Law's propaganda would have us believe. James VI and Charles I were chronically short of money, and the islands were treated simply as a source of income from which to satisfy whoever was for the moment the most pressing creditor. Government ministers with Edinburgh mercantile connections who lent money to the king were frequently given a tack as a means of paying off debts to them, and so Earl Patrick's creditor, Sir John Arnot, may be regarded as the prototype for this new breed of tacksmen. Sometimes several creditors could be placated simultaneously, since the tack could be held by someone who profited from the actual collection of the rents, while the lump sum properly payable to the king could be assigned to another creditor, or several people might hold conflicting grants which spilled over into disputes between rival groups of officials within the islands.[1] By 1629 the Privy Council was seriously worried, and it reminded the king of 'the many pressing burdens' on his royal lands as a result of these various grants and assignations.[2]

So the early seventeenth century is a period of great complexity, and its political history has never been studied in detail. It is not always easy to distinguish those who held real power from those who held grants and feus as mere paper transactions resulting from temporary financial deals. It was a hand-to-mouth form of government, efficient only in its exploitation of the islands. Earl Patrick's lavish spending, although ultimately ruinous to himself, had at least recirculated much of his income within the Orkney economy (and also recirculated a good deal of money borrowed from other people). From 1615 onwards, the greater part of skat and rent was simply drawn off by faceless financiers to be spent elsewhere.

The first tacksman, James Stewart of Killeith, Lord Ochiltree, was already entrusted with the collection of the Orkney rents before Patrick's execution. He had previously been used to extend royal authority to remote areas. In 1607 he had led a military expedition to reduce the chiefs of the Western Isles and to ensure the payment of royal rents, and thereafter he was regarded as something of an expert in island regions. In Orkney, however, he was associated with the oppressive rule of his deputy, John Finlayson, and he soon became embroiled in disputes about a separate tack of the customs given to Robert Monteith. There were also complaints that he collected skat and rent with greater rigour than ever before,[3] and that he tampered with weights and measures to his own advantage.[4] These hostile charges may well have had some foundation, in view of the desperate state of his own finances. He was called to account by the Treasury for falling behind with payments;[5] in 1622 his tack was terminated, and he fled abroad to avoid his creditors.[6]

Following Patrick's execution, his heir was his brother John Stewart, the former 'Master of Orkney', now Lord Kinclaven and later Earl of Carrick. Despite his violent opposition to Patrick at the time of the Alison Balfour witchcraft trial, John had latterly been reconciled with his brother and did everything he could to secure his own succession. In 1616 the government was worried about the possibility of another rebellion, this time led by John Stewart. Ochiltree's difficulties were mainly due to continuing Orkney support for the Stewart family which made it difficult for anyone else to collect the rents.[7] John Stewart was James VI's first cousin, and despite his unruly and arrogant behaviour, the king treated him generously. In 1621 he was granted a pension of £3,600, and he was eventually created an earl by Charles I. The king had no intention of reviving Patrick's earldom of Orkney, but John had acquired land in Ayrshire from his Kennedy relatives,[8] including Greenan which lay three miles south of Ayr. Since this land lay within the ancient earldom of Carrick, he hoped to acquire this prestigious title which had once been held by the Bruce family, and so emphasised a near relationship to royalty. The king, however, was reluctant to advance John Stewart quite so far but, as a sop to John's vanity, he was allowed to rename his Eday property, and so it was from 'Carrick', Eday, that he took his title. In 1632 he received a grant of extensive lands in the North Isles and in Deerness, once the property of the Eday Sinclairs and Sir William Sinclair of Warsetter. At the same time Calfsound became 'the town and port' of Carrick; it was erected into a burgh, the only one in Orkney apart from Kirkwall, and it had the right to appoint bailies, create burgesses, and hold regular markets.[9] For a time the new Earl of Carrick engaged in the extraction of salt from sea-water. In northern Europe fuel is needed for making salt, and the great advantage of Eday was its plentiful supply of peat. In 1634 the earl entered into a contract to set up six salt pans on the Calf of Eday and supply peats to keep the pans continuously fired for three years,[10] and by 1636 he had a salt girnel from which merchants were collecting salt.[11] However, there was never much prospect that the burgh of Carrick would flourish; the king was care-ful to deny John Stewart any real power, and with his death the title of Earl of Carrick became extinct.

Following Ochiltree's departure, Orkney and Shetland were then given in a five-year tack to Sir John Buchanan of Scotscraig and his spouse[12]—a decidedly odd appointment in view of their past. John and his wife, Margaret Hartsyde, had served at the English court of King James, and in 1608 they had been involved in a very public scandal in connection with the disappear-ance of jewels belonging to the queen.[13] Buchanan was cleared, and his wife was found guilty only on a modified charge, but the king was displeased with the Buchanans who were banished to Orkney where Margaret's father was a Kirkwall merchant.[14] They prospered during their exile and, even after restrictions on their movements were relaxed, they showed no desire to make their home elsewhere. By 1620 John Buchanan was sufficiently restored to receive a sub-tack to collect the rents of Shetland,[15] and he was one of those commissioned to investigate Ochiltree's misdeeds.[16] Even so it is surprising to find him knighted and given the tack in 1622. Perhaps by then the king had realised that the queen knew more about the disappearance of her jew-els than she cared to admit.

Sir John Buchanan was essentially a front-man, and the 45,000 marks scots which he ostensibly paid to the king were in fact assigned to creditors in deals of impenetrable complexity. In 1623 this income was in the hands of William Dick who passed on all or part of it to John Stewart of Coldinghame, who in turn transferred his rights to Sir Robert Douglas of Blackerstoune.[17] But hardly had Buchanan been given the tack than the king wrote to the Privy Council ordering it to investigate whether more money might be raised from Orkney and Shetland; if that were not possible, would it be better to grant the islands in feu rather than in tack?[18] Margaret Buchanan was asked to negotiate with her husband for the surrender of the tack, but refused to do so.[19] A complicated solution was eventually found whereby Buchanan retained his tack and the actual management of the islands, but a feu was simultaneously granted to the Chancellor, Sir George Hay of Kinfauns (later 1st Earl of Kinnoul) for the payment of 40,000 marks.[20] Like Ochiltree, Hay had previously been employed to suppress disorder in the Hebrides,[21] but his connection with Orkney was to be purely nominal. He could pocket the difference between the 45,000 marks he received from Buchanan and the 40,000 marks which he passed on to the king. The feu was a temporary device to give him security for the repayment of money owed to him by the king.

Fortunately it is not necessary to trace other similar deals, since these nominal superiors have no place in the history of Orkney except insofar as they drew off up to one-third of the income of farmers without providing any discernible benefit. One notable tacksman, Sir William Dick of Braid who received an eight-year tack in 1629,[22] was a descendant of Alexander Dick, the pre-Reformation provost of St Magnus Cathedral. After they left Orkney the Dicks had risen in the world; Sir William's banking activities financed trade with Holland, and he had shipping interests in the Baltic and Mediterranean. He was reputedly the wealthiest man in Scotland, so rich that it was said that he had discovered the Philosopher's Stone which transmutes base metals into gold. Sir Walter Scott's *Heart of Midlothian* made use of folk-memories of the cartloads of silver dollars sent by Dick to finance the Covenanting army. Indeed he impoverished himself by lending money to the cause of the Covenant, and he also lent money to Charles II. He died in an English prison, perhaps as the result of starvation.[23] From 1632 his payments to the king were assigned as a life pension to William Douglas, 7th Earl of Morton and Treasurer of Scotland.[24] This began a long-term connection with the islands which eventually culminated in the Earls of Morton acquiring ownership of the earldom estate.

In 1615 Bishop Law was promoted to the Archbishopric of Glasgow and so he remained in Orkney for only a short time after the suppression of Robert Stewart's rebellion. But during this brief period in his newly re-organised bishopric (1614–1615) he granted at least 14 feus, and this policy was continued by his successor Bishop Graham (1615–1638) who also sold the right to collect teinds (tithes).[25] Thus the bishopric became not so much a landed estate in any normal sense as a complex assemblage of feu duties, tacks, teinds, rents and skats. After something of a moratorium during the Stewart earldom, the feuing movement was again in full swing.

The new round of feuing produced a new set of landed families, principal of which were the descendants of Bishop Graham. At the Glasgow Assembly when relations between the Scots kirk and King Charles worsened and episcopacy was abolished, Bishop Graham had the wisdom to send his resignation and express contrition for having accepted the office of bishop.[26] Consequently he was neither excommunicated nor deposed, and was able to live out his life as a country gentleman, dividing his time between his Perthshire property and his estate of Skaill in Sandwick which he had previously feued to his son-in-law and business partner, Patrick Smyth of Braco.[27] Smyth also obtained feus of bishopric land in Holm where his property of Meall eventually passed to Patrick Graham, the bishop's third son, and was renamed Graemeshall.[28] The estate of Breckness was obtained for another son, John Graham; it came into the bishop's possession as a result of a bond which the bishop held from Francis Moodie, backed up, it was popularly believed, by threats of ecclesiastical censure on the dissolute and spendthrift owner.[29]

The outbreak of the Civil War provided the Earl of Morton with the opportunity to turn his pension from Orkney into something more substantial. Morton advanced large sums of money to Charles I, disposing of his Dalkeith estates in order to do so, and in common with many of the older Scottish nobility, his family was impoverished by his support for the Royalist cause.[30] As security for his loan to the king, Morton received a *wadset* (mortgage) of the Orkney earldom lands in 1643. He was entitled to hold them until the Crown redeemed them for £30,000 sterling.[31] The islands were in pawn again, and Morton might reflect that, if the precedent of the Impignoration of 1468-9 held good, a temporary mortgage might become permanent possession. In 1646 Morton received a further grant of the bishopric estate,[32] which conflicted with the rights held by the City of Edinburgh. Two years later Edinburgh gave a seven-year tack to one of its merchants, James Butter, who was prevented by Morton from uplifting the rents.[33]

Morton's acquisition of Orkney secured a potential Royalist base in the far north, well away from the pervading influence of the Marquis of Argyll. Following the execution of Charles I, Orkney was used by the Marquis of Montrose to launch his final ill-fated expedition. Preparations were made by the Earl of Kinnoul who arrived in September 1649 with a small force of Danish mercenaries. He was well received by his uncle, Robert 8th Earl of Morton who was in residence in Birsay, but uncle and nephew died within in a few days of each other, and the expedition was left leaderless. Montrose's departure from Göteburg was delayed when his ships were beset by ice in the harbour, then the greater part of his fleet was lost in the North Sea. Orkney farmers and fishermen were hastily recruited by royalist gentry and ministers, but it was a small and inadequate army which embarked from Holm on 9 April 1650. Less than three weeks later it was annihilated at Carbisdale on the shores of the Kyle of Sutherland. This last Orkney invasion of the Scottish mainland ended in inglorious defeat only a few miles away from where Sigurd the Mighty had fought the first recorded battle of Orkney history (see p.28). It was a long time since Orcadians had been called on to fight, and the days were long gone when a Viking expedition inspired terror in the north of Scotland. Lads from Orkney farms had never seen anything so fearsome as a charge of dragoons, and they streamed away from the battlefield at the first encounter. About 400 were killed including many drowned in the Kyle, and a similar number were captured including two over-enthusiastic Orkney ministers.[34]

In the aftermath of Carbisdale Orkney was in the grip of what was described as 'a vigamorish insurrection amongst the clowns and commons of this countrie, headed by one Currey'. Rebels prevented meetings of the Royalist gentry and imprisoned some of them. The rebels were described as 'whiggamore' and they 'soundly banged' forces sent north to recruit for the Scots army's Worcester campaign.[35] Presumably these 'clowns and commons' were the remnants of Montrose's Carbisdale army, still retaining their arms and having no intention of ever again being recruited by anybody. It was only when Sir James Douglas of Smithfield (later the 10th Earl of Morton) arrived in April 1651 that Currey was captured and order restored.[36]

From January 1652 a body of Cromwellian soldiers were quartered in Kirkwall,[37] and they proceeded to strengthen the town's defences by building batteries on either side of the anchorage in the bay. The other achievements of the Cromwellians have been succinctly described as the introduction of cabbages and venereal disease.[38] Like soldiers in later wars many had bleak memories of their Orkney posting, and they had a less friendly reception than their twentieth century counterparts. The Cromwellian author of *The Poetical Description of Orkney* had nothing good to say about the islands; in a flood of bad verse he waxed eloquent on the subject of lice, dirt, and the slovenly habits and loose morals of his Orkney landlady.[39] As far as Orcadians were concerned the only support for the English occupation came from a minority of the clergy and one or two enthusiasts within the burgh of Kirkwall.[40] The majority of Orkney folk were less concerned with the great issues of church and state than with the interruption of the Norway trade which made it difficult to obtain timber to build boats and make ploughs.[41] The 1653 land valuation imposed new taxation over and above the ancient land tax of skat, and this was resented. There were tensions too between the burgh of Kirkwall and the largely Royalist Justices of the Peace who put the expense of quartering the occupying forces on the burgh. This was a dispute which after the Restoration led to the Earl of Morton suppressing Kirkwall's privileges on the pretext that the town owed these privileges to a grant from Cromwell.[42]

William Douglas, 9th Earl of Morton, resumed control after the Restoration. The renewed grant which he received in 1662 again took the form of a mortgage redeemable by the Crown for the same payment of £30,000, but because of the reduced state of the earl's finances and to protect him from his creditors, the grant was in the name of Viscount Grandison, his uncle. But Grandison held Orkney in name only, and a trust for Morton's benefit was administered by the Earl of Middleton, the Duke of Hamilton, Sir Andrew Ramsay (Lord Provost of Edinburgh) and by Morton himself.[43] The trust delegated the business of managing the islands to its chamberlain, the infamous Alexander Douglas of Spynie.[44]

The 9th earl's tenure of Orkney was dominated by the *Kennermerland* affair.[45] This rich Dutch East Indiaman was sailing 'achter om' (north about) en route for Batavia when in December 1664 she was wrecked on Out Skerries in Shetland. The arrival of such amazing riches on these tiny islands passed into folklore; it was long remembered how:

> The Carmelan from Amsterdam
> Cam on a Maunsmas day.[46]
> On Staura Stack she broke her back
> And Skerry folk got a prey.

A traditional story tells how so many of her 60 barrels of wines and spirits were washed ashore that the entire population was drunk for 'three weeks and a day'; it was only when the islanders failed to collect their Christmas supplies from Whalsay that the outside world was alerted to the fate of the *Kennermerland*. The Earl of Morton sent Robert Hunter to conduct salvage; five iron guns and some general cargo were recovered and also three money chests, the contents of which were counted out in Scalloway Castle. But, as Earl Patrick had found on similar occasions, the loot passed into many hands. Sheriff-depute Patrick Blair made some minor finds, but reported that nothing else could be recovered. Meanwhile Charles II laid claim to the wreck, and he clearly believed that Morton had not handed over everything he had found. Lengthy investigations in the Court of Exchequer (1667-8) led to a verdict that Morton owed the king 24 bags of gold, each containing 900 ducats, and also two brass cannons which had reportedly been seen at the Palace of Birsay. Modern research in Dutch archives suggests that Morton had in fact declared most of what he recovered, and that the missing bullion had in fact been consigned aboard another ship.[47] However, Morton was in disgrace, and in 1669 his Orkney and Shetland property was once again annexed to the Crown.

The extractive rule of the tacksmen was one of the reasons for Orkney's failure to cope with the terrible famine periods which characterised the seventeenth century. Orkney was always able to survive a single bad harvest, which was so common an occurrence that it passed unnoticed outside the islands, but a run of bad harvests, liable to occur about twice a century, brought total disaster and many deaths from sheer starvation. Orkney's cool and moist conditions made it particularly vulnerable to small changes in climate. In the seventeenth century the climatic deterioration known as 'the Little Ice Age' shortened the growing season and increased the frequency with which summer gales and early snowfalls destroyed the crop.

It is from this period that we have strange stories of Eskimos in kayaks arriving in Orkney waters. Wallace reports that a 'Finn-man' was seen off Eday in 1682, but rowed swiftly away when people tried to apprehend him, and that another was seen off Westray in 1684; the second edition of Wallace's book in 1700 contains a note that a Finn-man's boat was preserved in the Burray Church.[48] That same year Brand recorded that a Finn-man had been seen off Westray, and the previous year one had visited Stronsay.[49] Their appearance was regarded as a bad omen, and presaged poor fishing. It has to be said that Finns are part of Orkney folklore, and that they were magical creatures who could row to Norway with seven strokes of the oar.[50] The sceptical might also observe that kayaks could be brought back from the Davis Straits aboard fishing vessels and whalers, but it is interesting that their appearances date from 1684–1700, rather than the eighteenth century when contacts with the Arctic were commoner. In the period immediately before 1700 there was a dramatic fall in sea temperature between Faroe and Iceland; the water was probably as much as 5°C colder than today,[51] and sometimes Arctic ice came south of Iceland. Even in 1921 a warning was posted in Kirkwall harbour office when icebergs had been sighted in the same latitude as Orkney but 200 miles to the west.[52] For these reasons the possibility that the Finn-men really were Eskimos has sometimes been taken seriously.[53]

In 1628 the Head Court was to be found dealing with the perennial problem that poor harvests and 'the frequent death of the labourers of the ground these years bygone' were resulting in land going out of cultivation with a consequent loss of revenue to the tacksman. Measures were also taken to control the movement of nomadic hordes of beggars, many of them small farmers fleeing from destitution.[54] The following year Orkney was visited by the plague, apparently introduced from Scandinavia, and Orkney's trade was halted to prevent the spread of infection to the Scottish mainland.[55] Worse was to follow. The famine of 1631 so impressed itself on people's memory that even at the end of the century dates were still being calculated from that grim year.[56] Yet the rule of the tacksmen was so inflexible that, even in a famine of these proportions, a hundred *lasts* of malt and 250 *lasts* of bere were still exported as part of the earldom rents.[57]

The harvest of 1633 was no better, and a petition to the Privy Council from the bishops of Orkney and Caithness graphically described what harvest failure entailed in the days before mass relief. Bitterly cold gales sweeping in from the sea had destroyed the corn before it ripened; people died in the open fields, and the minister going out with his servant buried them wherever he found them; people were reduced to stealing, eating dogs, or attempting to live off seaweed, and some were so desperate that they threw themselves in the sea.[58] It was a famine of a kind still seen in third-world countries. The Privy Council was sympathetic, but there was little it could do beyond commending the plight of the islanders to 'charitable consideration' and appointing the minister of Holyrood to pass contributions to Bishop Graham.[59] The next harvest was also a disaster; many people had consumed their seed corn and eaten their cattle; such corn as had been sown was 'utterly broken and blasted'; people were fleeing the country and a 'plain supplantation of population' was taking place.[60] It was later believed that between 3,000 and 4,000 had perished.[61]

Famine returned in the closing years of the century and, although less severe than in some parts of Scotland,[62] people died in hundreds, and land again went out of cultivation. The worst year was probably 1696 when the harvest was said to have yielded not one-twentieth of the normal crop,[63] and in July of the following year when food was exhausted we find the church in Stromness ordering people to bury their dead and attempting to fine those who failed to do so.[64] Distress was compounded by the activities of the notorious tacksmen, Colonel Robert Elphinstone of Lopness and Sir Alexander Brand. The period known in Scotland as 'King William's Ill Years' was remembered in Orkney as 'Brand's Years'.[65]

The Revolution of 1688 put a Dutch king on the throne, and when Elphinstone arrived with his Dutch wife, it was widely assumed that it was to her that he owed his good fortune in obtaining a tack of both the earldom and the bishopric.[66] Orkney was Jacobite in its sympathies—a good deal more so than it was by the time of the 1745 uprising—so Elphinstone, although an Orcadian, was entering hostile territory. He immediately tried to use his position as chief magistrate to escape from his debts. His principal property of Lopness, Walls, Tafts and How in Sanday had been mortgaged to the Baikies of Tankerness, but had been rented back to him. However, Elphinstone fell seriously in arrears with the rent and in 1687, just before the Revolution, James Baikie had taken possession of the farms. The Revolution suddenly placed Elphinstone in a position of power; he sent a crowd of his relatives accompanied by court officers who violently seized the property, casting out Baikie's household furnishings and taking possession of the farm stock. Rennibister in Firth had also been mortgaged to the Baikies for many years, and it was seized by the same methods. Elphinstone had to answer charges of 'hamesucken and bangstrie'[67] and he had the trouble and expense defending himself before the Privy Council.[68] His rule in Orkney met widespread opposition; the previous tacksman of the earldom estate, William Craigie of Gairsay, and Bishop Mackenzie's sons who had managed the bishopric estate, were deliberately obstructive, and found excuses to avoid handing over the rentals which were needed for estate management.[69] Problems were compounded by French privateers which attacked shipping on a 'daily' basis, taking their prizes into Shetland where the ships were ransomed and their cargoes sold.[70] The activities of the French disrupted the trade of the Hamburg merchants, with the result that Shetlanders were deprived of the money income on which they depended to pay their rent. Elphinstone was commissioned to enlist landowners, both to defend the islands from the French and to deal with local disaffection.[71] However, he was eventually overwhelmed by his troubles and was believed to have fled the country without accounting for one farthing.[72]

Elphinstone had hoped to recoup his losses by renewing his tack for future years for which he was willing to pay £1,500 per annum, and the Treasury had already recommended acceptance when another bid was received. The government owed £1,500 to the arms dealer, Sir Alexander Brand, for military equipment he had supplied and, in settlement of the debt, Brand was willing to take Orkney and Shetland on Elphinstone's terms. Elphinstone increased his bid, but he was bettered by Brand who eventually paid £2,150 for the tack. It was Brand's misfortune to have paid an inflated price for the years 1693-5 when harvests were desperately poor. Starving tenants had no surplus from which to pay rent, and a good deal of land was tenantless. In addition privateers continued to plunder places in both Orkney and Shetland. One target was Lamb Holm which the French occupied for a week in 1694, ransacking the single farm on the island, killing animals to replenish their supplies, and crossing to the Mainland to break open the storehouse which still stands on the seaward side of the road in the village of St Mary's. Brand was forced to visit Orkney in person, and on his return his ship was captured by the French. They eventually put him ashore in Unst, but the money he had collected was stolen, his ship burned and the island plundered. To add to his troubles, another ship carrying the butter and oil payments from Shetland was wrecked at Aberdeen. As late as 1707 Brand was still petitioning the Exchequer about his debts and the losses he had incurred.[73]

Recovery from Brand's Years was slow. A list of about 220 rigs of earldom land in Skeatown, Deerness, recorded land which were still ley in 1707,[74] and as late as 1713 about half the bishopric land in Walls remained tenantless.[75] At the upper end of the social scale Nicol Johnston gave up Langskaill, one of Birsay's largest farms, having failed to pay his rent for five consecutive years (1716–1720) while, at the bottom end of the scale, his neighbour, Janet Olsone, abandoned her half share of the little croft of Cooperhouse 'to go a-begging'.[76] Even a hundred years later 'miserable skeletons' of rigs abandoned at this time were still visible.[77] The University of Aberdeen, which held the tack of the Bishopric from 1699 to 1704, had to resort to the use of troops to exact payment from James Moodie of Melsetter.[78] He was one of 60 leading landowners 'put to the horn' for debts still owing on the expiry of the University's tack.[79]

Orkney's trade was thoroughly geared to the export of agricultural surpluses, and in time of famine there were no surpluses, so Kirkwall merchants were reduced to poverty, and sometimes to bankruptcy. Formerly there had been five or six ships belonging to merchants in the burgh, but by 1696 they had all been lost or sold, and trade with Norway and Leith had virtually ceased. By 1703 there were again three small ships, then one was captured by French privateers, two of Kirkwall's Bailies and four of the Councillors being carried off to Dunkirk. Most merchants were reduced to freighting small part-cargoes in other people's vessels.[80] The result was that the population of the burgh was much reduced from the estimated 3,000 there had been in 1661.[81]

The failure of the system to yield proper revenue, and complaints about the 'rigiditie and oppressione' of the tacksmen,[82] led to renewed support for the Earl of Morton's claims. The impoverished state of the 9th earl soon demonstrated that he did not have the 20,000 ducats allegedly missing from the wreck of the *Kennermerland,* and as early as 1673 he had been discharged of any debt owing to the king. Members of the family had never entirely severed their Orkney connections,[83] and after the Revolution of 1688 their fortunes improved. James (11th Earl) was allowed to petition for a reversal of the 1669 annexation of Orkney to the Crown, and he made much of his intention to re-occupy abandoned land, drain lakes and marshes, divide commons and encourage fisheries.[84] In 1706 he unsuccessfully invested £2,000 in floating a joint-stock company in London to encourage fishing and whaling, and to trade in the produce of Orkney and Shetland.[85] Other voices forthright in support included the Rev John Brand[86] (not to be confused with Sir Alexander Brand, the former tacksman). John Brand was the General Assembly's Commissioner to Orkney and Shetland, and his *Brief Description,* published in 1701, roundly condemned the system of short tacks, arguing that a permanent master would result in better management.[87] In 1703 the earl himself was the last of the tacksmen, and in then in 1707, perhaps as a reward for having voted for the Union of the Parliaments,[88] Morton was at last restored. Initially the terms were exactly as they had been before—*wadset* redeemable by the Crown for £30,000—but in 1742 this was converted to an irredeemable grant. The bishopric continued to be held in short tacks until 1737 when it was obtained on a long-term lease by Andrew Ross, Morton's Steward (Sheriff-depute).[89]

Ever since Earl William Sinclair had acquired almost one-third of the udal land which existed in the fifteenth century,[90] the proportion of owner-occupied land had been in decline. The process accelerated in the seventeenth century, and between 1660 and 1750 the number of landowners fell from 776 to 245.[91] This startling reduction reflected the difficulty which udallers had in maintaining an unwritten right to their land. These 'petty udallers' were a very decayed class. By the seventeenth century 'petty' was the inevitable adjective, but that had not always been their status. At one time the udaller had been able to claim his rights by means of six generations of continuous occupation, and he had been the aristocrat among freemen with a blood-price twice that of other men. His rights were firmly embedded in the Landlaw which King Magnus *Lagabøte* (Lawmender) had introduced to Orkney c.1280.[92] Udal tenure was an absolute form of ownership; the owner held his land outright, with no duties or services apart from the universal obligation to pay skat. It was a system which it was impossible to reconcile with the Scottish legal fiction that all land had once belonged to the king, and that ownership devolved on his subjects by written charters, sasines and feudal obligations. Scots lawyers were apt to regard skat as a payment which recognised a feudal superior; they were inclined to treat udallers as 'vassals', or even as squatters who had no right to the land they occupied. We have seen that Earl Robert Stewart tended to regard udallers in this way, and further examples of the same attitude are to be found in Earl Patrick's Uthel Buik.[93]

The other feature which contributed to the reduced circumstances of seventeenth century udallers was the system of inheritance. Unlike Scottish property which passed to a single heir, udal land was divisible among all children, with daughters receiving half the share allocated to sons, and the eldest son's rights being confined to the *heid buile* or principal residence. It was a system which spread ownership through a wide sector of the community, but it led to fragmentation and, if there were large families in successive generations, udal inheritance might be reduced to mere scraps of land. Since this inherited land was supplemented by new land which a bride might bring into the family, the pattern of landholding was not only fragmented, but it was often highly dispersed. At its simplest, the process of division is illustrated by a Bailie Court decision regarding the co-heirs James, Robert and John Corrigal. The *toft* and *tunmal* (the house site and adjacent ground) was to be split between them, with James and Robert having entry, house freedoms and corn-yard on the west side of the original house, while John enjoyed the same rights on the east side.[94] Carried to an extreme, the process could result in theoretical fractions which had no practical use. In 1679 James Beaton was successful in establishing a 113-year-old claim to the twelfth part of Clouk; he succeeded in obtaining a right to a fraction of a ruinous building, and was given vague directions as to where the remains of a former kail yard dyke might be found.[95]

Yet the original purpose of udal law had not been to disperse land but to

56. *Kirbister Farm, Birsay. Now Kirbister Farm Museum.*

keep it within the kindred. At an early date these divisive tendencies had been counteracted by restrictions on the sale of land outside the family, by the right of kinsmen to have first refusal of land offered for sale, and indeed a right to redeem land which had been sold out of the family. The splitting of property as a result of udal inheritance had been largely counteracted by one member of the family acquiring the rights of other heirs and compensating them with moveable goods. The abolition of Norse law in 1611 did not, and could not, abolish udal tenure, and udal division continued, but all legal restriction on fragmentation was removed.

Under tacksmen who knew little about Orkney land tenure and whose interest was profit, udallers felt that their unwritten right to their land was increasingly at risk. In 1633 they petitioned Parliament that no one should be interposed between themselves and the king until 'His Majestie conforme their rights to the lawes of this kingdom'.[96] Behind this somewhat ambiguous request lay a desire for greater protection than udal tenure could provide in the seventeenth century. The general desire, however, was not that udal law should be abolished. On the contrary, udal law, although not always properly understood, came to be regarded as the very essence of the freedoms which were under threat.[97]

After the Earl of Morton was restored in 1662, the trustees administering his estate were authorised, not only to feu Crown land, but also to offer feus to udallers because, as the king's authorisation stated, 'this udal right is meerlie possessione and no kind of fundamental right or tytell by chartour'.[98] Some of the earliest feus in Orkney, such as the feu of the Halcro lands in 1545, had been of this kind, involving the voluntary surrender of udal land to the Crown, with the owner receiving it back with the additional security of a charter.[99] Now the chamberlain, Alexander Douglas of Spynie, put considerable pressure on udallers to purchase his charters. However, as well as continuing to pay skat in full, they had to pay an 'augmentation', so there was considerable hostility to his charters. Various lands in Westray held under Spynie's charters were repossessed by the earl as feudal superior when owners failed to keep up the heavy annual payments.[100] The fact that a number of owners of middling and larger udal properties, including James Baikie of Tankerness,[101] fell for Spynie's money-making schemes, reflects their real need for 'a more perfect right' to their land.[102]

But a meek acceptance was not the only possible reaction to oppression. About 1670 the militia had to be sent to enforce payments of taxes in Harray, the udal heartland of Orkney. An imperfectly preserved contemporary ballad records the defeat of the soldiers at the hands of the country folk:

> So the Harra-men upon them fell
> Wi' flail and staves and stones;
> Some women wi' the kettle cruick
> And others wi' the tongs.

Tax-gatherers spoke in hushed tones of Harray as 'a place where devils dwelt'.[103]

It is unlikely that the archetypal peasant society of sturdy udallers pictured by nineteenth century romantics had ever existed—a primitive democracy of equals—but by the seventeenth century it had certainly gone. Many Orcadians rented rather than owned the land they farmed and, because of the extremely fragmented nature of property, another common form of tenure combined ownership of scattered property with the renting of other portions. Frances Shaw's investigations of property transfers reveals that, despite the many pressures on petty udallers, at least some 50-60% of properties remained less than one pennyland in size, although at the other end of the scale, the proportion exceeding 18 pennylands more than doubled in the course of the century.[104] Estates were growing. Orkney was far from a classless peasant society, but it is true to say that distinctions were somewhat blurred. Unlike the Western Isles where clan chief, tackman and crofter occupied well defined places in a stratified society, there was in Orkney a gradation of property sizes with no absolute dichotomy between petty udallers and the owners of larger properties, nor any obvious social distinction between those who owned land and those who rented it.

23
Old-style Farming

Orkney's fertile soils derive from Old Red Sandstone smoothed by the action of ice which deposited great sweeps of glacial clay over much of the lower land. It is an undulating landscape of long unbroken skylines and distant views and, before Orkney's mid-nineteenth century Agricultural Revolution, the absence of field boundaries further contributed to the bareness of the countryside. It was a browner landscape than the Orkney of today, with much more moorland and much less lush green grass. Instead of square fields, the arable land lay in a bewildering strip-patchwork of hundreds of corn rigs, yellow with charlock and purple with valerian, intermixed with sections of rough grassland on which animals might be tethered in summer. To outside observers the world of run-rig was an incomprehensible maze-like landscape, and usually outsiders made no real attempt to understand it. Even Storer Clouston, whose careful research unravelled many of the complexities of the system,[1] regarded run-rig as 'absurd'; it was, he thought, 'clean daft'. But run-rig was not imposed on reluctant tenants by their lairds: on the contrary the people keenest to abolish run-rig were always landowners, ministers, surveyors and visiting agricultural experts, whereas those who had devised the system and wanted to retain it were the farmers themselves. It was only when run-rig clashed with 'Improvement' that it became 'absurd'. This chapter explores how run-rig reflected, first, the diversity of the landscape and, second, the nature of Orkney society, particularly the landlord-tenant relationship.

The boundaries of Orkney's townships as they existed in the early nineteenth century had not greatly changed from the pattern revealed in Murdoch Mackenzie's charts (1750)[2] or indeed from the first record of townships in Lord Henry Sinclair's 1492 rental.[3] The evidence of place-names suggests that the essential features of the settlement pattern were even older and can be traced back to Viking times—perhaps the basic pattern was already established when the Vikings arrived. Townships were of very variable size; in 1492 about half of them appear to have been in the 2-pennyland to 6-pennyland range, but quite a number were much bigger, especially in the North Isles, in which case they might contain upwards of 20 households. Although most of the land lay in these multiple-occupancy townships, there

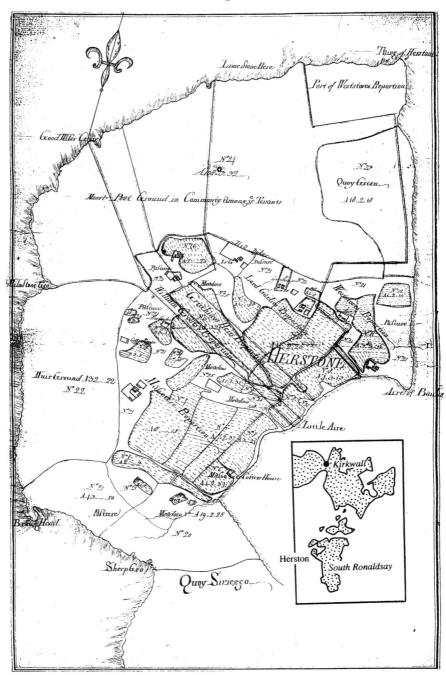

57. *The Township of Herston, 1768-9. From a survey by David Aitken (OA D13/ Addl./9/1).*

were also many farms with a single owner or tenant, and the biggest of these farms were of township-size. As well as the farmer and his regular farm servants, these large farms supported a numerous cottar population, summoned when their labour was needed and paid in land which was intermingled with the rigs of the main farm. Although the social structure of the township and big farm were different, the outward appearance of the landscape was much the same. The great majority of Orcadians lived either within the framework of the township or of the big farm.

The South Ronaldsay township of Herston which is shown opposite was 3 pennylands, so may be regarded as fairly typical. In 1768 when the map was drawn there were within the hill-dyke some 59 acres of very good arable land, 27 acres of ill-drained meadow suitable for making bog-hay, and 64 acres of pasture. This in-bye pasture was mainly located on 'the backs', the outer margins of the township near the hill-dyke. The inhabitants also had access to a further 141 acres of common outside the hill-dyke. Herston's common land was not as extensive as in many other townships because of its restricted headland position, but the quality of the grazing was better than average. At this date there was no village (the future village of Herston was along the shore below Quoygreen), and it is unlikely that there was any commercial fishing at this time, although fishing for home consumption was always important. Sometimes there was an opportunity to trade in a small way with ships which took shelter in Widewall when bound for America. In 1696 there had been 11 households,[4] and in 1768 the number of houses was probably unchanged. The earliest censes gave a population of about fifty.[5]

Herston illustrates how landownership had over the course of time become extremely complicated (Fig.58). The place has a *staðir*-name, (*Harðar-staðir*, Horðr's farm) so it had presumably at some point been a single farm owned or occupied by someone of that name. Hugh Marwick speculated it might have been in the time of Earl Thorfinn (1014–c.1065) that the original Horðr was installed in this strategically-located farm commanding the entrance to Scapa Flow through Hoxa Sound.[6] In our earliest record, however, 1½ pennylands of this three-pennyland township was bishopric property and was rented to tenants (1492),[7] so the single owner seems to have disposed of half of his land to the church, either as a sale, a gift or as a forfeit for an offence. The remainder of the township did not remain in single ownership but, as a result of udal division among heirs, it came to be shared among proprietors who held increasingly complex fractions. An example of these complicated shares is the 1⅙ farthing of udal land in 'Hairstane' which William Stewart of Maynes passed on to his son in 1654, along with a collection of other lands in South Ronaldsay.[8] Since 1⅙ of a farthing in a 3-pennyland township entitled the son to 7/72 of the resources of the entire township, it can be appreciated that the complexity of the fractions challenged the ability of those who attempted to measure them out on the ground. The landholding pattern became even more complicated when the bishopric half of Herston became earldom property as a result of the exchange in 1615 when South Ronaldsay became an 'earldom parish' (see pp.298-9). The next step came shortly before 1653 when the Earl of Morton sold most of what had formerly been bishopric, sometimes to the owners of adjacent udal land.[9] Thus in Herston, although it was no great size, there were people who were udallers, others held their land by a feu, and some owned land by more than one kind of tenure; some farmers were owner-occupiers, others were tenants of lairds whose residence was elsewhere, and in addition there were two or more households of cottar sub-tenants. However, by the date of the 1768 map, landownership had become a little simpler: the landowners had been reduced to five, and the one remaining udaller was the only resident proprietor. Yet landownership remained complicated by Scottish standards since it would have been most unusual to find a single township with so many proprietors. In Scotland land was usually allocated to tenants in simple fractions. In Orkney the fractions were far from simple, but a more fundamental difference was that, in addition to tenant run-rig, the actual ownership of land was in run-rig because property was defined in terms of a share rather than by fixed boundaries. Proprietorial run-rig of this kind was not very common in Scotland where whole townships were generally in the hands of a single laird.

Ownership of land expressed as a run-rig share frequently appears in documents. A typical example from 1560-1 involved udal land in Grimbister in Firth which Anne Grimbister and her brothers, Alexander and Magnus, had inherited from their father. As was not uncommon, Anne sold her 'sister's share' to her brothers. It consisted of:

> Twa merk land with houssis, toftis, and towmellis and all other rychteous pertinentis tharto pertinand, lyand within the town of Grymbuster...[10]

Grimbister was 4½ pennylands, and we know that each pennyland contained 6 marks of land,[11] so the two marks which Anne sold represented only a small proportion of the township. The document transferred the ownership of the buildings, apparently more than one, and also the land immediately associated with them (the tofts and tunmals). The arable land, however, was not defined by fixed boundaries, but was included in the 'pertinents' which rightly pertained to the two marks. This share of the *townsland* was probably laid out in run-rig. Sometimes these pertinents were set out in rather more detail; it might be stated that they included a proportionate share of outpasture and inpasture (common hill land and the grassland within the

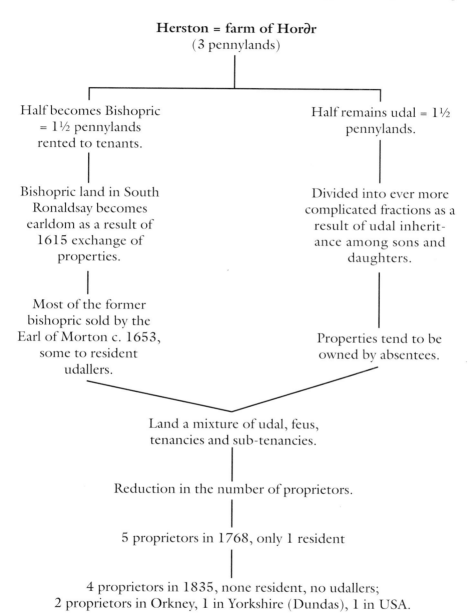

Herston = farm of Horðr
(3 pennylands)

Half becomes Bishopric
= 1½ pennylands
rented to tenants.

Half remains udal = 1½
pennylands.

Bishopric land in South
Ronaldsay becomes
earldom as a result of
1615 exchange of
properties.

Divided into ever more
complicated fractions as a
result of udal inherit-
ance among sons and
daughters.

Most of the former
bishopric sold by the
Earl of Morton c. 1653,
some to resident
udallers.

Properties tend to be
owned by absentees.

Land a mixture of udal, feus,
tenancies and sub-tenancies.

Reduction in the number of proprietors.

5 proprietors in 1768, only 1 resident

4 proprietors in 1835, none resident, no udallers;
2 proprietors in Orkney, 1 in Yorkshire (Dundas), 1 in USA.

58. *Landownership in Herston, 1000 AD to 1850.*

59. *Herston Village.* The village which owes its origins to herring fishing lies along the shore below Quoygreen.

hill-dyke). Sometimes, in the same way as a Norwegian farm extended from 'fjord to fjell', rights were expressly said to extend from the highest point in the hill to the lowest point in the ebb,[12] thus asserting a claim to a share, not just of every different quality of land, but of whatever other resources were available.

The fact that land was in the hands of so many proprietors and their tenants made it difficult for the community to co-operate effectively, although co-operation was regularly needed. In Scotland the ordering of agricultural matters was usually in hands of a single laird, and he might manage his tenants by means of his Barony Court. Barony courts of this kind did exist in Orkney: the bishop had possessed a legal jurisdiction and, as the bishopric was sold off in portions, each new owner usually acquired, not just the land, but the right to administer justice within his new property.[13] Such powers were seldom used; it can be seen at Herston, for example, that the complicated pattern of landownership made it out of the question for any one person to exercise powers of Barony, even if they possessed such a right. So, alongside these moribund jurisdictions, there were parish and island Bailie Courts with powers which were delegated by the earl or tacksman in his capacity as chief magistrate[14]—they were sub-courts of the Sheriff Court, and operated under its supervision. These courts were presided over by the parish Bailie appointed from among the leading landowners, who was assisted by *lawrightmen* or *ranselmen* chosen from each district. In 1696 Herston had two lawrightmen, Henry Groat who came from the township's leading udal family, and Robert Omond. They were both members of the Bailie Court of South Ronaldsay.[15]

Bailie Courts were empowered to deal with petty crime and to administer the body of laws known as the Country Acts. The earliest version of these Acts dates from 1615 when they were codified by Bishop Law,[16] presumably because the recent abolition of Norse Law cast doubts on the validity of traditional agricultural regulations. From time to time the Head Court continued to enact whatever measures it thought necessary. Bishop Law had been instrumental in destroying Earl Patrick's 'foreign laws', so there is a certain irony that he is now found creating new local laws. No doubt it had quickly become apparent that the 'foreign laws' included local regulations necessary for the day-to-day management of agriculture. We may suppose that Law's Country Acts were not new, but largely re-enacted measures which had formerly been in force, including Earl Robert's controversial law on 'swine rutting' (see p.269). However, Orkney's seventeenth and eighteenth century Bailie Courts were also influenced by Scottish Birlay Courts. The older system is most clearly seen in Shetland where, even into the seventeenth century, suspected persons had to declare their innocence on oath in the presence of their neighbours (the *larycht oath*) or, in more serious cases, they had to find six members of the community willing to vouch for them by taking the *saxter oath*.[17] Periodic *Commissions of Granderie* had at one time investigated 'good neighbourhood', for breaches of which the whole township was held collectively accountable. Older concepts of communal responsibility for breaches of the law were, however, on the wane and a rural police-force of ranselmen searched from house to house when theft was suspected. A typical case involved James Meason of Toab: in 1668 he was brought before the Bailie Court of St Andrews where ranselmen gave evidence that they had found four pieces of mutton hidden in the *oddler* of his byre (the channel which collected the manure).[18] Considering where he had hidden the mutton, he was fortunate to be caught before he could eat it.

Bailie Courts also had certain administrative functions such as inspecting weights and measures, and they were called on to maintain the beacons on the ward hills during the seventeenth and eighteenth century wars against the Dutch and the French. The bulk of their work, however, was concerned with agricultural management. Their first task was the maintenance of the hill dykes. A hill-dyke might encircle an individual township as at Herston, defining the community and binding it together, or else it might be a great crumbling rampart of turf snaking across an entire parish, separating the farm land from the moorland. Since the landscape was otherwise unenclosed apart from the actual farmyards, the hill dyke was a line of fundamental importance. Animals had to be kept separate from corn, and so they were banished to the common grazing beyond the dyke while crops were growing. Then, after the harvest, the *grinds* and *slaps* (gates and gaps in the hill dyke) were opened, and the hungry horde returned, not just to graze the arable land of their owners, but to roam over the entire in-bye land which might be open from one end of the parish to the other. Communal stubble grazing was much prized by poor people who had little land of their own, and it worked well enough as long as grain was virtually the only crop. However, the indiscriminate grazing of township land after harvest made it difficult or impossible to experiment with turnips and sown grass, and for this reason there was a divergence of interest between progressive farmers and small tenants.

Since the hill dyke was largely turf, it required annual repair. Typically the Bailie Court would set a date in March by which dykes had to be 'put up'. People generally paid no attention to the order, and so the instruction would be repeated, and in exasperation the Court would eventually threaten to poind the stock of those who still had not obeyed, releasing the animals to their owners only on payment of a fine. Similarly, the Court set dates by which sheep, cattle, geese, pigs and horses had to be put to the hill, after which any animals still inside the dykes were to be tethered. The owners of animals were obliged to keep their neighbours 'skaithless' (free from harm),

bigger than the planks which were common later in the eighteenth century. These early Birsay planks were about 23 acres (c.9 ha.) whereas the plank later became standardised as a unit of area 40 fathoms square (1.3 acres, 0.52 ha.) which was a close approximation to the Scots acre. Thus the term 'plank' went through a series of meanings: planks evolved from being 'blocks of land' to being 'blocks of land of equal area' to being squares of one Scots acre in extent.

Whereas the early Birsay planks were large and were run-rig within themselves, the acre-size planks which were characteristic of the later eighteenth century were designed to be held by individual farmers. The *Old Statistical Account* of Evie and Rendall provides an example of how the term was then used. The *Account* first uses 'plank' as a measure of area equivalent to the Scots acre: it tells us that the cultivated land in Evie and Rendall extends to about 1200 planks, and individual farms are described being 6, 10 or 12 planks. The account then goes on to say that 'the whole of the arable land of these parishes lay formerly in run-rig, as a small part of it still does', but about 30 years earlier (c.1766) a division had taken place. Evidently the author thought of planking as having largely abolished run-rig, but he goes on to comment that the division was so 'injudicious' that, even where there were large and compact fields, 'each farmer possesses perhaps twelve patches of ground of a plank each, scattered over the whole'.[2] The same system was described by the Sanday crofter, David Wallace, in his evidence to the Napier Commission: he told the Commission that prior to the creation of modern fields, 'one had an acre and another had an acre'.[3] Planking might be described as a greatly simplified form of run-rig with land held in blocks which were bigger than individual rigs, but still with a degree of dispersal and intermixture. Extensive planking also occurred in Holm in the 1750s, and indeed where farming has been studied in detail, evidence of planking is usually found. The system was widespread but not universal. Attempts have been made to find the origins of planks in traditional farming.[4] It seems more likely that planking was an innovation based on the Scottish system of *acre-dale,* which is its exact equivalent, being designed to allocate land in acre-sized blocks and thus achieve a measure of consolidation of run-rig.[5] The non-Norse root of the term 'plank' (French *planche*) is another indication of its non-indigenous origins.

Some long-term changes had taken place in the pre-Improvement period, such as the development of a more pastoral economy in the late Middle Ages, and the introduction of new crops. Flax had been cultivated since Norse times,[6] but its cultivation greatly increased in the eighteenth century in response to the development of the linen industry. The revolutionary change was, however, the introduction of the potato which provided a valuable protection against famine. According to Barry's *History,* potatoes were first grown as a field crop about 1750,[7] but their cultivation only became widespread after the hurricane which blasted the corn crop in August 1756.[8] The next spring, with meal in short supply, William Balfour sent nearly a ton to Westray with instructions to his wife to 'cry them at the kirk on Sunday to be sold on Monday'.[9] In 1766 Patrick Fea, who was no great believer in Improvement, was growing potatoes on his farm of Stove in Sanday,[10] but even then their cultivation appears to have been localised. It is said that in places such as Stronsay, Eday and Evie no potatoes were grown until about 1780.[11] Other innovations included the use of marl, first revealed as 'marl-pit pows' (water-filled hollows) in a seventeenth century ballad,[12] and occasional experiments with lime.[13] Liming, however, was also achieved by traditional practices, being an indirect benefit of the use of seaweed to manure the land, since shell-sand usually adhered to the wet weed.[14]

While much was achieved at this fairly basic level, more grandiose ventures had a chequered history. There was a general wave of interest in all sorts of trading schemes around 1630, several of which involved ambitious plans for the development of Orkney and Shetland.[15] In 1633 the Privy Council had before it a document entitled 'Ane Overture for the Improvement of Orkney and Shetland' of which nothing is known except its title.[16] Perhaps it involved proposals modelled on the attempted plantation of Fife settlers in Lewis. Later in the seventeenth century James, 11th Earl of Morton, expressed ambitious intentions to re-occupy abandoned land, drain marshes and divide commons as an inducement to the government to reinstate him as tacksman (see p.311). The earliest improvements actually to exist on the ground, as opposed to mere paper schemes, involved dyke-building by a number of lairds, not so much to enclose arable land as to create grazing enclosures. Typically this involved the enclosure of a headland as a means of shutting off a large area with a short section of dyke. The purpose of these enclosures was the control of stock since, if improved breeds were to be introduced, it was necessary to prevent indiscriminate breeding with the native animals which roamed the common grazings. In 1703 James Moodie of Melsetter enclosed land at Snelsetter and Cantick Head which was to be stocked with sheep sent home by his naval uncle, Captain James Moodie RN. The experiment was a failure; the sheep 'never recovered after the sea, but dyed all in Fyfe', while the grazing on the exposed headland proved so poor that it was devoid of pasture from December to June.[17]

Moodie's political rival, Sir James Stewart, the laird of Burray, Flotta and parts of South Ronaldsay, was responsible for the huge enclosure known as the Park of Cara. The park was only part of the quite astonishing evidence for agricultural improvement on his estate, evidence which would be remarkable in any part of Scotland, but which one hardly expects to find in a place as remote as the South Isles of Orkney. Unfortunately the exact nature of Sir James' farming enterprise is not easy to understand. The park itself was a great rectangular grazing enclosure of about 420 acres[18] surrounded by stone dykes and containing rough pasture which seems to have been grazed by cattle rather than sheep. Sir James was an irascible and belligerent Jacobite who in 1725 was responsible for the murder of Captain James Moodie in Broad Street in Kirkwall.[19] He was related to, and was eventually succeeded by, the Earl of Galloway, and it is tempting to see similarities between the Park of Cara and those enclosures built in Galloway to serve the needs of the droving trade.[20] The park seems to make best sense as a place where cattle purchased from South Ronaldsay tenants might be grazed before being exported through St Margaret's Hope.

By 1700 drovers were active in Caithness,[21] where Sir James had business and family connections, and a few years later dealers were buying cattle in Orkney, for example at the Kirkwall Lammas fair. The trade was sufficiently lucrative for Captain James Moodie, who owned the public ferry operating across the Pentland Firth from Brims in Walls to Rattar in Caithness, to obtain a legal injunction against dealers shipping cattle from unauthorised 'creeks' such as Houton and Holm.[22] The supply of the droving trade continued well into the nineteenth century, when Caithness dealers regularly bought Orkney cattle in the spring, grazed them in Caithness over the summer, and then drove them south to be sold at Bonar Bridge. The drovers hired fleets of boats, each capable of carrying ten or a dozen animals, uplifting the cattle from a number of collecting points.[23] But Orkney was too remote and the crossing of the Pentland Firth too difficult for the droving trade to have much impact on the economy. Perhaps that was the reason why the Park of Cara was a failure. Even before Sir James Stewart died as a Jacobite prisoner in a Hanoverian gaol, he was deep in debt and the park was mismanaged and neglected by factors who had no knowledge of agricultural improvement.[24]

After Sir James Stewart's death an inventory of his property revealed an amazing collection of broken bits and pieces of improved agricultural implements scattered through various buildings, and much of it described as 'old'.[25] These seem to add up to at least seven English ploughs, and this at a time when few examples were to be found anywhere in Scotland.[26] He owned various two-wheeled carts and four-wheeled wagons, although most Orkney parishes were then devoid of any form of wheeled transport and, most surprising of all, a hundred years before turnips were commonly grown as field crop, he possessed a turnip-drill plough.

Despite the failure of his schemes, there was a continuous line of development from these early improvements. Sir James was succeeded in the Bu of Burray by the Earl of Galloway who tried in vain to bring about a division

63. *Ox cart.*

64. *Singling turnips.*

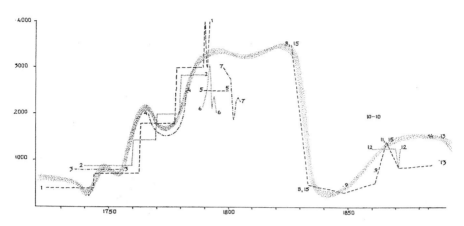

69. **Kelp Production (tons).** *The graph is constructed from a number of contemporary estimates (Thomson, Kelp-making, App.II). The stippled line shows the general trend.*

could exercise a degree of compulsion—kelp always required 'a good deal of pushing'—yet it was a compulsion which fitted easily into existing landlord-tenant-cottar relationships. Cottar sub-tenants on big farms traditionally held land, not for a money rent, but in return for their services. They were *on ca'* ('on call'), expected to turn out for whatever work was required, and this often included carrying up enormous quantities of seaweed to be spread on the land as manure. It was necessary only to redirect seaweed-gathering into new and more profitable channels. Penurious Orkney lairds might have had difficulty in finding capital for a new industry which required significant investment, but kelp-making needed little outlay; it was labour intensive, and for little more than the cost of a few long-shafted rakes and shovels, fortunes could be made by lairds who could set their tenants to work. Since Orkney lairds were already merchants and ship-owners, they were able to take part in the whole process of making and marketing kelp, in contrast to the more aristocratic landowners of the Hebrides who were generally content to rent out their shores to incoming kelp-manufacturers.

The *New Statistical Account of Deerness* (1841), written at a time when kelp-making was already on the decline, contains a good description of what kelp-making involved:

> The number of hours per day that they work is uncertain and those that cut the weed from which it is made are almost unremittingly occupied while the tide allows them to reach it, whether that time be day or night. They often rise at one or two o'clock a.m. to prosecute their toil and may sometimes be seen until eleven p.m. But they refresh themselves with sleep during part of the intervening period when

353

70. **Burning Kelp.** *Acrid smoke drifting to leeward yellowed corn growing in the vicinity of the kelp kiln and was commonly blamed for crop failure.*

71. **Burning Kelp using a Flaikie.** *The kelp-makers are using a straw* flaikie *to direct the fire to parts of the kiln where the seaweed is not yet burned.*

80. ***John Rae and his wife.*** *John Rae (1813-1893) was a pioneer of light travel in the Arctic. He led expeditions which discovered the fate of the 1845 Franklin expedition to the North-west Passage.*

on stores before the voyage north.[73] In 1841, when whaling was already past its peak, 292 men were recruited in Orkney for Greenland and the Davis Straits.[74] For a short time Orkney was more directly involved when a group of Kirkwall businessmen purchased the barque, *Ellen,* and operated her fairly successfully in the Davis Straits, bringing blubber to Kirkwall where the firm erected the 'Oily House' and storage sheds.[75] At least another 200 seamen were employed in Orkney-owned trading vessels,[76] and to those who earned a living outside the islands must be added the large number of seamen who either volunteered or were pressed into the navy in time of war. Barry, who had examined the Navy Books, may have over-estimated when he reckoned that 2,000 men served in the American War of Independence; his figure probably involves double-counting of those who served aboard more than one ship.[77] In the 1790s several hundred men were also serving in Thomas Balfour's fencible regiment in Ireland, and others had joined the regular army, contributing to the shortage of able-bodied men in the islands.

Much of the booming trade of eighteenth century Orkney bypassed the ancient city of Kirkwall. In some respects Kirkwall and Stromness stood in the same relationship to each other as the east and west coast ports of Scotland where older centres looked eastwards across the North Sea, whereas the new and developing ports lay on the west coast and engaged in Atlantic trade. But Kirkwall was a royal burgh, and as such its privileges included a monopoly of foreign trade—strictly speaking it was the only place through which goods could be exported or imported. In the past it had sometimes been necessary to issue warnings to 'idle persons who... play the merchant... by going on board ship under cloud of night or privallie under colour of buying or selling merchandise',[78] but Kirkwall was to find it was one thing to warn off itinerant pedlars and quite another to attempt to restrain the growing trade of Stromness.

At the beginning of the eighteenth century Stromness hardly existed. In 1700 there were only five houses with slate roofs, and a few scattered huts along the shore of Hamnavoe, and the valued rent of the whole place was estimated to have been only about £30.[79] The growth of transatlantic trade brought about a transformation. It was not only the Hudson's Bay Company ships and the whalers which made use of its sheltered harbour with its easy access to the open sea, but also merchant ships which sailed north-about to the Americas, especially in time of war. The quarrel between Kirkwall and Stromness hinged on the rights of the royal burgh to pass on some of its taxation to the 'unfree traders' of Stromness, who paid no tax on their activities. Matters came to a head in 1742 when Alexander Graham and a number of fellow Stromness merchants received an assessment from the Kirkwall magistrates. Graham was required to pay a mere £16 scots, but Kirkwall was to find him a stubborn, single-minded and litigious opponent, ultimately willing to ruin himself and his family for principle, or perhaps just for sheer obstinancy. The case was a lawyers' paradise, since constitutional issues were at stake. Kirkwall based its claim on a clause in the 1707 Act of Union which guaranteed the continuation of the privileges of the Scottish Royal Burghs, while Stromness argued that a conflicting clause in the Act promised Scots the same trading rights as other citizens of the United Kingdom. The case dragged on for 16 years through local courts, to the Court of Session, and eventually to the House of Lords where Alexander Graham was ultimately victorious. He found Stromnessians ready enough to encourage him to go to law, but much less willing to bear a share of the expenses. Graham was involved in a further law suit in an unsuccessful attempt to recover a proportion of his costs.[80]

While fishing, whaling and service with the Hudson's Bay Company brought in a much needed income, the ministers in their *Statistical Accounts* often viewed these developments with a somewhat jaundiced eye. Their opinion of the Hudson's Bay men strangely contrasts with the high value which the Company put on the sobriety and industry of its servants. The Rev. Francis Liddell, minister of Orphir, launched into an impassioned attack on those who abandoned wives, children and parents to enter the service of the Company, eventually returning home with enough money to outbid honest farmers; they brought home none of the virtues of the savage, but all the vices—indolence, dissipation and irreligion. 'My God!', he declaimed, 'Shall man, formed in the image of his Creator, desert the human species, and for the paltry sum of £6 a-year, assume the manners and habits of the beasts that perish?'.[81] Fishing attracted equally hostile comment from other ministers, although usually less colourfully expressed; George Barry in Kirkwall complained that the wages of Iceland fishermen were 'almost always spent on idleness, and sometimes in dissipation',[82] while James Watson in South Ronaldsay condemned 'drunkenness, idleness and extravagance';[83] fifty years later his successor was still bemoaning 'the universal appetite for spirits'.[84]

It is not difficult to see that the opinions of the ministers were essentially the views of employers of labour in a society where manpower was in chronically short supply.[85] In the second half of the eighteenth century the population was static, but the demand for labour had never been greater. It was labour, rather than the supply of seaweed, which limited the rich profits which might be made from kelp, and at the same time it was increasingly difficult to find servants at former rates of pay. Local competition for labour was compounded by the wars against revolutionary France, and at the same time the circulation of money resulted in the economy becoming less purely local and more responsive to national trends. After only a gradual increase during most of the eighteenth century, prices and wages in the final decade were rising at an alarming rate. The Rev William Clouston in Stromness and Sandwick, who was one of the more perceptive ministers, realised that there was no single cause for shortage of labour, but he remarked that blame was principally directed against the Hudson's Bay Company because its recruiting was so visible. Yet the Company's calls on labour were quite modest compared with the numbers serving in the Royal Navy and the army. Of course, it was not easy to criticise the army and navy in time of war without appearing unpatriotic, hence the rich and powerful Company was singled out as the symbol of competition for labour and all the inflationary ills which went with it.

But there were more fundamental objections to the Hudson's Bay Company than mere complaints about rising prices and shortage of labour.

Ministers and lairds had an uneasy feeling that the natural order of society was somehow under threat. For most of the eighteenth century social control had been firmly in their hands, and indeed their combined power had been increasing rather than diminishing as estates grew bigger and ministers came increasingly to identify with the interests of the landowner. As the eighteenth century drew to a close the relationship between master and servant now seemed under threat, and the *Statistical Account* is full of examples. Servants were often able to set their own terms: it was complained that it was not possible to keep a man servant or even a boy without allowing him a month or two in the summer to go to the fishing. Another symptom was the abandonment of certificates of good character which servants had previously obtained from the Kirk Session. As the Rev George Low remarked, 'Everyone now, it seems, takes servants just as they get them'.[86]

Labour shortage was compounded by the fact that for the first time there was significant emigration from the islands, resulting from Orkney's many contacts with Scottish and English seaports. In contrast to the rapidly increasing population in Shetland and in the Hebrides, Orkney's population was static at around the 23,381 recorded in Webster's unofficial census of 1755.[87] Contrary to the opinion of Malthusian-minded ministers who were constantly worried by early marriages and the improvident breeding of the poor, marriages were actually delayed until money could be saved, and the birth rate, insofar as it can be determined from the *Statistical Account,* was quite low at around 27 per 1000 of population.[88] But the death rate (perhaps 19 per 1000) was still lower and had probably fallen dramatically during the eighteenth century. Hence it was only emigration of young men to Newcastle, London, Edinburgh and America which prevented population growth. This was a selective emigration which left Orkney with 25% more females than males, a highly undesirable state of affairs according to the outrageously male-chauvinistic James Fea:

> By reason of the constant drain on the male part of our inhabitants, we must necessarily have a greater number of women than men among us, who being destitute of any kind of employment, must ly as a useless burden on the country; and what is still worse, many of them must likewise be destitute of husbands, by which means they degenerate into that wretched species of being called Old Maids, so that to all our other evils, that of being pestered with these female *Grimalkins* is likewise added.[89]

But women left to fend for themselves were not necessarily destitute as James Fea implied. Margaret Vedder lived in the township of Easterbister in Holm and, when she was deserted by her husband, she had a small income from a tack of the estate's bere mulctures (the payment for the use of the laird's mill). After the storm of 1778, when the crop was totally destroyed by an August gale and no one had bere to take to the mill, she was plunged into debt, but a year later she was able to pay off her arrears in linen cloth. Although she was probably no better-off than her neighbours, linen spinning eventually left her in comfortable circumstances. When she died in 1788 her property was auctioned, including the astonishing contents of her wardrobe: she had a large collection of gowns, petticoats and plaids which were sold for a sum which was equivalent to 25 times the annual rent of her house.[90]

Whereas ministers and lairds might complain about the social consequences of the new pattern of employment, ordinary folk can have had no doubts about the advantages. An analysis by Sheena Wenham of the accounts of tenants of the Graemeshall estate reveals the beneficial effect of industries such as linen and kelp-making.[91] No less than 87 tenants traded linen with the estate in the period 1780-6 and, while it brought only a modest profit to the laird, the money income was of real benefit to the tenants who also enjoyed an income from the manufacture of about 35-50 tons of kelp per annum. The most direct result of this income was that it provided some protection from harvest failure. After the 1778 storm Patrick Graeme was able to import four shipments of grain which he sold at cost price. Hardly had the community recovered from this disaster than there was a run of bad harvests in the cool, wet seasons of 1782-5. In earlier times there would have been many deaths, but the estate was able to organise supplies of seed corn, meal and potatoes. Tenants did not receive this famine relief as charity; they were often able to pay in cash or in linen and, if they were unable to do so, they were given food, the cost of which was simply added to their rent account as arrears. The debt seldom seems to have been a serious burden, and arrears were usually cleared quite quickly. From the study of these accounts 'the general impression is that many people in Holm survived these years remarkably well'.

The verdict that people came out of these years remarkably well applies to the whole period of proto-industrial activity. Lairds, and the employers of labour, might complain that their traditional relationship with their tenants and employees was undermined, but they had made substantial profits particularly from kelp. Ordinary folk might be of the opinion that they had received a disproportionately small share of the new wealth, but at least they had gained protection from harvest failure, and there was something left over to produce a better standard of living.

27

The Nineteenth Century Agricultural Revolution

The booming economy of the period 1770–1830 was less secure than it seemed. There had always been a few prophets of doom who forecast that industries like kelp-making and straw-plaiting could not last,[1] the one inflated by artificially high war-time prices, and the other dependent on the whims of fashion; Arctic whaling was destined to ultimate self-destruction by over-fishing, and there were clear signs that the industrialisation of the textile industry spelled the end of the domestic manufacture of linen in places like Orkney. The islanders escaped the worst effects of the Industrial Revolution and knew little to compare to the degradation to be found in coal mines and textile mills. Their lives were hard, but they worked on the land, sea and shore in small communities where relationships remained at a personal level. Yet it was a far from satisfactory state of affairs that many occupations—kelp, linen, bonnet-making, the Hudson's Bay Company and whaling—were partly based on, and in some cases solely attracted to Orkney by cheap labour, or else by the possibility of coercing agricultural tenants.

There was a drastic narrowing of the economy in the first half of the nineteenth century. In 1821 the merger of the Hudson's Bay Company with the rival Northwest Company led to a decline in Orcadian recruiting since the combined company adopted a policy of finding most of its servants in Canada.[2] Ten years later kelp collapsed in spectacular fashion, and linen came to an equally sudden end. The demise of kelp and linen, which had been Orkney's main money earners, resulted in a crisis the severity of which was mitigated only by an expansion of herring and cod-fishing. Yet before 1840 cod-fishing was also in decline with the fleet more than halved, herring fishing had passed its peak, and there was a series of poor fishing seasons.[3] Paradoxically, as its ancillary industries declined, Orkney entered a period of sustained population growth. Whereas numbers had been virtually static between 1755 and 1811, in the next fifty years there was a 39% increase from 23,238 in 1811 to a maximum population of 32,225 in 1861.[4] The rise in population, combined with the disappearance of alternative employ-

378

ment, encouraged the reclamation of new land, both by big farmers with their plough-teams of heavy horses and by crofters who set about trenching the heather-covered hill-side with the spade. Large reserves of casual labour were also available for ditching, dyke-building and picking stones from newly reclaimed fields. Elsewhere in Britain improved farming has often been blamed for displacing surplus labour, but in Orkney it is not too much to say that it was the surplus of rural labour which made rapid improvement possible.

Old-style Orkney farms had employed a great deal of labour. These people were *on ca'* (on call), summoned whenever they were needed for ploughing, sowing, harvesting, threshing, carrying up seaweed and the thousand-and-one other tasks about the farm. For example, Patrick Fea who for 30 years kept a diary recording the day-to-day work on his farm of Stove in Sanday, noted that on Saturday 9 September 1769 he had eight people working in the hay, while others were boating his peats from Eday and leading the 24 horses needed to carry the peats home; on Monday he had nine 'hooks' and eight 'bansters' harvesting bere, while the rest of his people were busy plaiting bent to make ropes.[5] This cottar labour force was paid in land rather than money, and their holdings were not distinct from the main farm but consisted of rigs which were to some extent intermingled with those of the farmer.

Robert Scarth, who was factor on several estates and more than any other individual was the architect of agricultural improvement, was in 1842 managing the Westove (Scar) estate after Thomas Traill went bankrupt due to the kelp collapse. It was Scarth, not the parish minister, who wrote the account of the parish of Cross and Burness in the *New Statistical Account,* and he was scathing in his comments on the inefficiency of *on ca'* labour:

The cottar system, which formerly prevailed universally, and still does prevail to a small extent, is perhaps the most degrading to the labouring

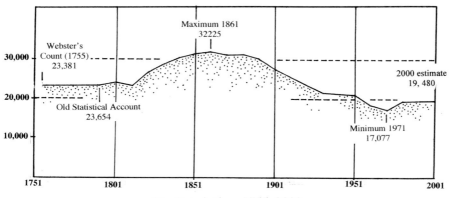

81. *Population, 1755–2000.*

class, the most discouraging to industry and exertion, and consequently the most injurious to morals, which can be conceived. A youngster, when he has hardly attained to manhood, and before he can have saved as much as will purchase a bed and blankets, makes an improvident marriage, and only then thinks of looking for a hut to shelter him and his fast-increasing family. Having got the hut, and a small piece of land, he has to go in debt for the purchase of a wretched cow and a still more wretched pony, and paying his rent in small but never-ending and ill-defined personal services, or, as it is expressively called in the country language *on ca' work,* he becomes the slave of the principal tenant, who is so blind to his own interests, as to prefer the slovenly half-executed work of this hopeless, ill-fed and inert being to the willing and active services of a well-paid and well-fed farm servant.[6]

Scarth went on to comment that Sanday farmers were generally kind to their cottars, and hardly a day passed but they would grant some favour or supply some need. He pointed out that farmers failed to calculate the cost of these little gifts which in the course of a year might amount to the wages of a good ploughman. Progressive Victorians like Scarth deplored enforced services, and they saw the money relationship as bringing dignity to the labourer and profit to his master. It had been no great disadvantage that a farm was in 'a state of cottarage' as long as the farmer and cottar used the same methods of cultivation; *on ca'* labour had distinct advantages over regular farm-servants because of the seasonal labour demands of old-style farming. New crops and better breeds of animals, however, required that the cottar and his 'wretched cow' were kept well clear of the farmer's squared fields and improved stock. The need for ploughmen permanently employed to look after their plough-teams and for skilled stockmen who could care for increased numbers of cattle swung the balance in favour of regular farm servants rather than casual labour.

The same system of holding land in return for ill-defined services had at one time been common in Aberdeenshire and throughout the north-east of Scotland, but in these areas cottarage had usually been abolished in the period 1760–1780, and in the nineteenth century it was rarely found.[7] Its continuation in Orkney was a consequence of kelp-making, and was symptomatic of the increasingly backward state of Orkney farming relative to the rest of the country. The first move to abolish cottarage was made by Samuel Laing at Stove. The farm's twelve cottars were removed and were resettled on little satellite holdings of about three acres of arable land and the same amount of pasture for which they each paid a rent of five guineas. All obligations to perform labour services were abolished. In theory the crofters were free to accept or reject employment on Stove, but the small size of their crofts and the high rent were designed to ensure that Laing 'never lacked good and efficient workmen'.[8] Laing's scheme was widely copied, notably in the 1828 squaring of Holm,[9] and other estates also resettled cottars, in the process converting them from subtenants of the farmer into direct tenants of the laird. Thus nineteenth century crofting was hardly an age-old system as is sometimes supposed—to a large extent it evolved after 1820.

Crofters' reactions to these changes were mixed. The demands of *on ca'* work had always been irksome, and they could now earn more from kelp since they sold directly to the laird rather than through the principal tenant. Crofting, however, involved a parting of the ways for large and small tenants, and a diverging of their interests. Crofters were increasingly pushed to the margins. They particularly resented the abolition of common pasturing in winter whereby animals were no longer free to range over the entire arable land in the district after the harvest was secured. Where sheep farms were created, crofters were also liable to find that restrictions were imposed on 'wild or Orkney sheep' on hill grazings.[10] The intention that crofters should become 'good and efficient workmen', employed for a money wage, turned out to be wildly optimistic. Whereas the small size of crofts and the high rent ensured that crofters had to seek ancillary employment, little was available except casual agricultural work. On Stove, as late as 1861 when cottarage had been long since abolished, there were 13 fulltime farm servants, but there were another 21 men employed as casual labourers, as well as a further 8 men and 24 women classed as field workers—in all 66 people were employed in one capacity or another.[11] Those who were skilled at dyke-building and draining might find fairly steady employment, but the great majority were under-employed for most of the year, and found regular work only at harvest.[12] And while they were free of the obligation to provide *bummacks* of strong ale and their best food to set before their master on such occasions as Easter, Lammas and Yule, the fact that they no longer sat down together on these festive occasions was symptomatic of the social distancing of laird, farmer and cottar.[13]

Agricultural improvement in Orkney did not usually involve the dispossession of crofters by capitalistic farmers as often happened elsewhere. On the contrary new crofts continued to be created throughout the period of improvement and the number of agricultural holdings reached a maximum of 3,373 in 1883, when the process was halted by a combination of agricultural depression and the landowners' fear of crofting legislation. Later generations have concentrated their criticism on the abolition of these crofts and on the policy of clearance, but in the mid-nineteenth century, lairds attracted hostile comment for allowing too many over-small crofts to be created on their property. In 1855 an early edition of *The Orcadian* argued that the division of common land, the disappearance of ancillary employment and the easing of population pressure through emigration left no place for small crofts; such places were a drag on agricultural improvement and a source of weakness to their occupants and, for the sake of all concerned, they ought to be abolished.[14] But the demand for land was such that estates found it profitable to rent to small tenants. When Captain William Balfour was asked by the Poor Law Enquiry (1843) why he did not favour large farms, he replied bluntly, 'My objection to farms being large is that I derive greater profit from farms being small'.[15] The Enquiry's evidence from Eday illustrates the point: whereas large farms were rented at seven shillings an acre, a rent of £1 per acre could be obtained from crofts.[16]

The resettlement of cottar subtenants removed them from the heartland of the farm—they were on the fringes of the community both physically and psychologically. As population increased, new tenants might be given permission to settle on a tract of hillside on which they could build a house, while others merely settled as squatters. The use of small tenants to break out new land was not new: a 1743 lease of Durcadale from Nicol Spence obliged his tenant to 'build some cotthouses on the extream parts of the said grounds and oblidge the cottar possessors thereof to break and burn some ground yearly'.[17] Occasional place-names such as 'Bruntland' originate from this practice of burning the heather and shallow peat in order to facilitate the breaking out of new land. However, as new crofts multiplied in the nineteenth century, the process was accelerated; arable districts were surrounded by a zone of tiny crofts, forming a 'Pioneer Fringe' advancing on the hill.[18]

This process gave rise to place-names quite as worthy of study as the ancient *bus, bisters, garths and skaills* of the Norse period. Many names such as Heather House, Mossbank and Stonefield describe the marginal nature of the ground; Hillcrest, Berryhill and Braehead reflect the relatively higher altitude of many of these places; Inkerman, Balaclava, and Lucknow commemorate the military exploits of nineteenth century Orcadians; Ballarat, Bendigo and Klondyke are gold rush names, but perhaps they are also a rueful comment that digging up an Orkney hillside was no goldmine. Galilee and Pisgah illustrate a fondness for biblical names, and Orkney folk took great delight in names such as Hell and Purgatory; members of the Secession and Free Church enjoyed the story, apocryphal or otherwise, that Hell, which was located on the Birsay glebe, was sold off by their lax brethren in the Established Church as 'surplus to requirements'. These reclamation-names are frequently 'humorous and radiant with high spirits':[19] the Ark was so called because it was high on a hill and surrounded by animals, while Jericho and Fa' Doon (Fall Down) preserve the comments of sharp-tongued neighbours who forecast the imminent collapse of these ill-built huts. Fa' Doon also belongs to a tradition of 'imperative naming', other examples of which include Rattle Up! and Blow High! But the most common names incorporate the Scots *Ha'* (hall) applied in an ironic sense to the smallest of cottages. Thus Plover Ha' was situated out on the moorland among the plovers; Feelie Ha' (Scots, *fail*, turf) indicates that the original 'hall' was built of turf, while Tarry Ha' is also a comment on its rudimentary construction. Wrangle Ha' was an ale-house, and Crab Ha' was the home of a Harray man—Harray is Orkney's only inland parish, and improbable stories of its inhabitants' ignorance of the sea were a perpetual source of amusement.

Since encroachments were regarded as remaining part of the common until forty years had elapsed, the maps and papers relating to divisions of commons sometimes provide very full details of this debatable zone, and illustrate the piece-meal nature of reclamation by crofters. In Shapinsay, even after Thomas Balfour's appropriation of the West Hill, the remaining common, most of it eminently reclaimable, extended to a total of 2,956 acres, and of this 167 acres were taken over between 1791 and 1831 (5.6%). Yet these encroachments consisted of no less than 221 parcels of land of which 155 were arable with an average size of only about one-third of an acre; a further 48 were tiny grazing enclosures, and the remainder were house-sites, *plantie-crøs* (for raising cabbage plants), sheep pens and pig-houses.[20] In the vicinity of Greenwall the hill-dykes had been 'flitted out' on three occasions between 1791 and 1831. Since the dykes were of turf, and often the land was badly cut up in the shelter of the dyke, it was often easier to build a new dyke rather than repair an old one. Abandoned turf dykes were sometimes brought into cultivation since the collapsed and outward-spreading remains of a turf dyke provided a ridge of deep organic soil. At Greenwall a series of cultivated rigs, five to ten yards in width and upwards of a quarter of a mile in length, ran through the grassland and marked the former boundaries.[21] Similar 'fossil dykes' which map the advancing tide of cultivation have been found in other parts of Shapinsay (Fig.83) and also in Birsay.[22]

The evidence which crofters gave to the Crofters' Commission in 1889 (much of it printed in *The Orkney Crofters*) records the painfully slow and truly heroic process by which new land was won. The best of these places grew to be little farms in their own right. Myrtle Lane in Sanday is an example: John Grieve had been given leave to settle on 18 acres of hill land in 1847, nearly all of which he reclaimed through his own efforts over the next 42 years; he carted in some 3,000 loads of earth to deepen the soil, he built the house, put in 946 yards of deep stone drains and constructed 638 yards of dry-stone dyke; by 1889 his stock consisted of four cows, two calves, one horse and three sheep.[23]

The increasing value of these crofts inevitably led to successive rent rises which were bitterly resented by crofters who had reclaimed by their own efforts. They had little option but to pay whatever the laird asked. Should they refuse, there were plenty of others clamouring for land, and the outgoing tenant was likely to receive little or no compensation for his improvements. Crofters were usually tenants-at-will, or held only short leases, so they had no real security and were frequently alarmed by rumours that they were to lose their land and that it would be given to a neighbouring farm. Thus John Grieve of Myrtle Lane had originally paid 10 shillings a year for the uncultivated site of his future farm, and he had seen this rise by three stages to the £7 he paid in 1889. During that time he had lost some of his hard-won land, and in its place he had been given what he described as 'heather and rocks'.[24] But he was more fortunate than some of those evicted from Quandale in Rousay who twice in a lifetime had to start from scratch on a bare hillside.[25]

The first passenger paddle steamer to reach Orkney was the *Velocity*, which operated a service from Aberdeen to Inverness and Wick. In 1833 its August runs were extended to Kirkwall, and after 1836 a regular summer service was provided by the 378 ton paddle steamer, the *Sovereign*.[26] The benefits which a reliable outlet could bring to cattle sales had already been recognised in Sheriff Peterkin's *Orkney & Shetland Chronicle*, and in 1833 James Baikie canvassed landowners by means of a printed circular, urging them to support the planned steamer service.[27] It took a little time for the benefits to be apparent, but ten years later Aberdeenshire cattle dealers were regularly visiting the islands with ready money to offer for their purchases. Under the stimulus of greatly improved cattle prices, Orkney entered a period of sustained growth (c.1846 to c.1875) which entirely transformed not only the Orkney economy but also the landscape and the way of life of its inhabitants.

Reclamation by crofters had been mere nibbling at the edges of the commons, but that was all that was possible as long as common land remained undivided, since capital could not be invested in a scheme without first securing a proper title to the ground. A legal division of common was a precondition of large scale reclamation, and by mid-century this process was well advanced.[28] Equally crucial was access to capital at reasonable rates of interest. In 1840 parliament passed a measure which allowed money to be borrowed for improvement using the land as security for a debt which might be passed on to heirs as a heritable burden on the estate. Then in 1846 a further measure, the Public Money Drainage Act, made government loans available at low rates of interest.[29] Orkney, more than other areas, was quick to take advantage of this scheme which provided finance just when the rapidly improving outlets for Orkney cattle created confidence in a prosperous future. The Balfour estate with £6,000 was the biggest borrower, and other loans went to Heddle of Melsetter (£3,000), Traill of Wyre (£3,000), the Earl of Zetland (£2,000) and Fortesque of Swanbister (£1,000).[30] Drainage loans were the very key to improvement since humped-backed rigs were no longer required to provide surface run-off, and so the land could be levelled, squared and enclosed, enabling new crops to be grown and new agricultural machinery to be used. The loans were not, however, for drainage alone but might be used for dyke-building and the construction of new steadings and farm-workers' cottages. Throughout the period of improvement, loans were administered through bodies such as the Scottish Drainage and Improvement Company. Typically money might be available over a 25 year period at about 6½% per annum which covered both interest and the repayment of capital. The company encouraged landowners to borrow with the advice that instant profit could be achieved: an average 10% increase in the value of the improved property might be expected, so more than the actual 6½% interest rate might be passed on to tenants in the form of a rent increase. There was the further advantage that the cost could be partly set against tax once the work had been inspected and approved by the Inclosure Commissioners.[31] The ease of borrowing encouraged rapid progress, but often resulted in estates being encumbered with over-large debts when the period of agricultural prosperity came to an end.

82. *The Squared Landscape, Shapinsay. David Balfour was reluctant to modify his rectilinear field pattern even when ditches of inordinate depth had to be dug or, as in this photograph, a new straight road had to be cut through the middle of a glacial mound.*

Shapinsay, described as the 'fountain and origin' of Orkney improvement,[32] was a model of what might be achieved with drainage money, and it illustrates the essential difference between crofting and capitalistic reclamation. David Balfour aimed at nothing less than the comprehensive development of the whole island. Marcus Calder, his bagpipe-playing factor, superimposed a grid of ten-acre squares whose straight-line boundaries ran for three miles or more and paid no regard to existing arable land. It was a grid which Balfour was reluctant to modify even when the lie of the land required exceptionally deep ditches (see Fig.82). These squares were used as a basis for letting, and deep open ditches driven through arable land and hill marked their boundaries. Such a rigidly planned landscape could only have come into existence in that generation; in earlier times when estates were smaller and more fragmented, and later when Orkney became a land of owner-occupiers, such geometric regularity could never have been achieved—it was *par excellence* the landscape of the big estate. A condition of letting was that tenants should put in stone drains and build stone dykes, for which they were to receive compensation at the termination of their lease. If they were unwilling or unable to undertake this work, it was done by the estate and charged to the tenant in the form of a rent increase. Previous to improvement there had been only 748 acres of arable land in Shapinsay, but Calder's grid provided a framework within which a further 1,500 acres were soon added. While on the one hand the former North Hill Common, the 'fossil dykes' and crofters encroachments all disappeared under the plough, the once prestigious eighteenth century improvements of Thomas Balfour at Sound were treated no differently, being swept away in their entirety when the new pattern of field boundaries was imposed.[33]

Archer Fortesque, a Devon man who bought Swanbister in 1845, also made special use of drainage loans. He was a flamboyant character who startled Orkney folk by hunting in the Orphir hills with a pack of hounds. Like all improvers, he forbade the grazing of tenants' animals over his arable land in winter, much against the interests of small farmers and crofters who paid little attention to his regulations regarding herding. The 'Devil of the Hills' was determined to have his own way; he waged war on straying animals, impounding cattle and fining their owners. A feature of his reclamation was deep ploughing combined with heavy applications of manure. In addition to bone meal and Peruvian guano, 'night soil' from Stromness was carried aboard his sloop, and he employed people to catch dogfish and sillocks which were composted to form an evil-smelling manure. Fortesque also owned the farm of Kincausie in Kincardineshire and his sloop transported sheep to be wintered there.[34]

While there might be strong initial opposition to the kind of improvement carried out by Balfour and Fortesque, tenants quickly discovered that

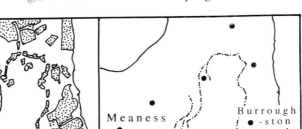

83. *'Fossil Dykes', Shapinsay. The collapsed remains of abandoned turf dykes formed
ridges of deeper soil easily brought into cultivation. These 'fossil dykes' plot the retreat
of the North Hill Common and the disappearance of the 'spine' of common land
between the townships of Meoness and Burroughston (OA Map of Shapinsay, 1846).*

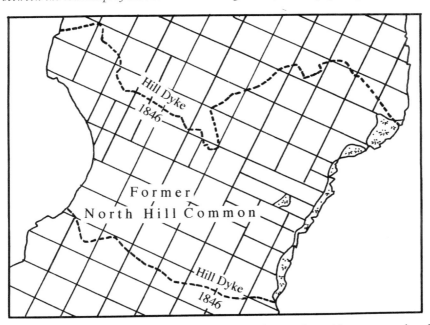

84. **Former North Hill Common, Shapinsay.** *This regular grid pattern replaced
the rigs and 'fossil dykes' shown in Fig.83. By 1861 the former common was entirely
cultivated except for insignificant portions mainly along the cliff-edge (OA Maps of
Shapinsay, 1831, 1846 and 1861).*

there were profits for themselves in the new methods of farming. Improvement was generally a success story in which most people benefited. But those who once tenanted George William Traill's Rousay property were not so easily reconciled. Traill had made his money with the East India Company, and in India he is still remembered as an enlightened administrator who championed the grazing rights of the existing population in Himalayan pastures which prospective settlers regarded as 'empty'.[35] Paradoxically Traill used his drainage loan to clear the impoverished crofting community of Quandale and attach the land to the big farm Westness as a sheep-run. Where there had once been 80 people, there was now a solitary shepherd. It is the only major example in Orkney of the policy of total clearance so common in the Highlands, and it left a legacy of bitterness which contributed to the notoriously bad relationship between General F.W.T.Burroughs and his crofting tenants.[36]

The Orkney economy had shown substantial if spasmodic growth ever since 1746.[37] Initially this was due to linen and kelp, and in 1800 kelp had accounted for about two-thirds of the total value of exports.[38] At that time agricultural exports had been of lesser importance since farming was mainly a subsistence base or served an internal market within the islands; a grain surplus was available for export in most years, but the export of live animals on which Orkney's future depended was then insignificant. By 1833 the economy had shown some further modest growth, but there was a radical alteration in the composition of trade. Linen had ended, kelp had declined to a very low level, and fish accounted for more than half of Orkney's earnings.[39] In the depressed conditions after 1833 the value of Orkney trade was at best static, or showed a slight decline, but at the same time there was an increasing emphasis on the agricultural sector. By 1848 Orkney was already exporting 8,000 live cattle a year and thereafter, under the stimulus of the drainage loans, the economy for a time grew at the astonishing rate of more than 10% per annum.[40] Soaring cattle exports masked the continuing importance of arable crops in the initial period of expansion. Although now relatively less important than cattle, corn exports grew in absolute terms as a result of higher yielding grains and the reclamation of new arable land, and there was also a substantial trade in potatoes.[41] After 1870 there was less emphasis on cash crops as government policy, steamships and American railroads combined to flood the country with cheap grain. The acreage of cereals was little affected, but there was a tendency to feed oats to poultry, and egg exports began to take off. Orkney remained prosperous for a further decade, but in the early 1880s the price of store cattle slumped disastrously, being down on average by about one-third, and the price of wool and dairy produce fell by nearly as much. The years of expansion were over, and thereafter Orkney farming remained remarkably static until the

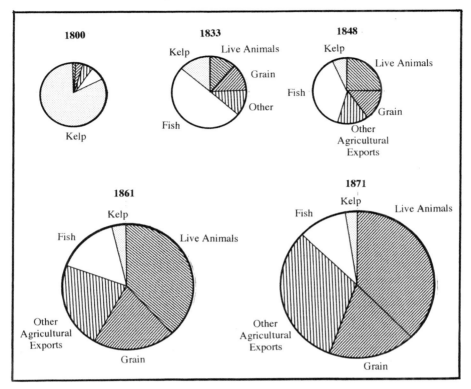

85. **Exports.** *These contemporary estimates are not entirely reliable, but they are good enough to illustrate the growth of trade and changes in its composition. Kelp dominated the economy in 1800 when agriculture was little more than the subsistence base to the economy. There was not much growth before 1848, although agricultural exports became increasingly significant. The economy took off in the 1850s and 1860s when steamships made it easier to export live animals.*

1914–1918 war. Developments in transport are the key to understanding the changes: there had been a mid-century window of opportunity after transport links had opened new markets for Orkney, and before the further improvement in communications in the form of Atlantic steamers, American railroads and refrigerated ships resulted in imports of grain, beef, mutton, wool and dairy produce with which Orkney, like the rest of British farming, found it difficult to compete.

A comparison of the agricultural returns of 1866 with such figures as appeared 24 years earlier in the *New Statistical Account* (1842) reveals an increase of at least 75% in the arable acreage. Reclamation by crofters was already proceeding apace before 1842, so a doubling of the arable acreage in the course of the nineteenth century seems a possibility. Expansion continued into the decade 1870–1880 which saw an increase of 200 in the number of agricultural holdings, but in 1883 the process ceased abruptly. It was not just that Orkney had entered a new era of agricultural depression and that emigration was easing the pressure of population on the land. The depressed state of the crofting community led to the investigations of the Napier Commission (1883) and the subsequent Crofters' Act (1886), with the result that landlords were wary of creating new holdings which would be subject to the restrictions of Crofting legislation.

The Napier Commission was appointed by Gladstone's government as a response to popular disturbances in Skye and other places in the West Highlands where crofters were threatening to repossess land which had been engrossed in sheep farms.[42] Crofters aimed to secure concessions similar to those which had been won from Irish landlords, and they were ready to copy the Irish tactics of rent strike and rural outrage. But there was little common feeling between small Orkney farmers and the Gaelic-speaking crofters of the West Highlands. When the Commission visited Orkney it found the community singularly ill-prepared. Only in Sanday where the Rev. Matthew Armour had mobilised crofting opinion,[43] and in Rousay where memories of the Quandale evictions remained fresh, was much done to organise meetings and elect spokesmen.[44] The Commissioners' visit to Orkney was brief: on Friday 20 July they took evidence in Sanday where they investigated the compulsion involved in kelp-making and the iniquities of *on ca'* labour. The following day was spent in Harray where the high proportion of owner-occupiers was of interest, since a land purchase scheme was one possible solution to the crofting problem. Then on Monday in Kirkwall Sheriff Court the Commission listened to highly charged evidence from General Burroughs' Rousay estate. Old men recalled the Quandale clearance, and the delegates bitterly complained that rents were rising faster than ever, although incomes were falling. The hearing culminated in the moment of high drama when General Burroughs refused to give an assurance that there would be no victimisation of those who gave evidence to the Commission.[45] Lord Napier pointed out that a Royal Commission was hampered in its task if witnesses were not free to give evidence without intimidation, but Burroughs remained adamant:

> Is the property mine, or is it not mine? If it is mine, surely I can do what I consider best for it? If these people are not contented and happy, they can go away.

This confrontation between the laird and his crofters was followed a few days later by the eviction of the crofters' delegates, threats to shoot the General, the sending of a gun-boat to Rousay, and the beginning of a very public ten-year war of attrition between Burroughs and his crofting tenants.[46]

86. ***General Burroughs and his Medals.*** *General F.W.T.Burroughs was recommended for, but did not receive, the Victoria Cross during the Indian Mutiny. He was involved in a bitter struggle with the crofters on his Rousay estate following his eviction of tenants who gave evidence to the Napier Commission.*

The report of the Napier Commission and continuing unrest in the Highlands led to the passing of the 1886 Crofters' Act, the main provisions of which protected crofters from eviction and arbitrary rack-renting. Not only were crofters given security of tenure, but they might assign their croft to a member of the family or other successor. The Act established the Crofters' Commission, a Land Court with powers to fix judicially-determined rents and, if it saw fit, to order the cancellation of arrears. On its first visit to Orkney in 1888 the Commission heard no less than 443 cases; rent was reduced by nearly one-third on average and about half crofters' rent arrears were cancelled.[47] The Act also made provision for the enlargement of crofters' holdings at the expense of big farms, but this was largely inoperative since the granting of enlargements was subject to many restrictions, principally that the land should not already be held on a lease.[48] Sanday crofters applied for extensions to their holdings at the expense of Lopness, Elsness, Backaskaill, Cleat, Newark, West Brough, Warsetter and Stove but it was only in the case of Elsness that some minor enlargements were allowed. In Papa Westray, where Holland was not leased but managed by a trust which administered the bankrupt estate, concessions were also possible. The Crofters'

87. **Digro, Rousay.** *Digro was the home of James Leonard, leader of the Rousay crofters who were evicted for giving evidence to a Royal Commission. This 8-acre croft was high on the margins of cultivation and had been reclaimed from the common. In 1884 it was home to 15 people.*

Act, however, did little to satisfy land-hunger and may indeed have aggravated the situation since landowners were now reluctant to create new holdings. A fresh enquiry, the Deer Forest Commission (1894), scheduled large areas to be returned to crofting use, including the vanished township of Quandale, but the government lacked the political will to embark on an expensive scheme of buying out existing landlords.[49] It was only when crofts were created for returning ex-servicemen after the 1914-1918 war that any real concession was made to the crofters' need for more land. The farm of Stove in Sanday was purchased and divided, but by that time a declining population had removed many of the pressures, and the scheme was not a success.

It is difficult to see how crofters could have survived on estates such as General Burroughs' Rousay property without the protection provided by the Crofters' Act. Yet the Act provided only a partial solution since it failed to release more land for crofting or restore land which had been cleared. Ultimately the crofting problem was left to solve itself by the slow process of

	The Villein Bodo A villein on the Abbey of St Germain-des-Pres c.820 AD.	**The Orkney Tenant** Tenant farmer in the Parish of Sandwick, Orkney, 1834.
Farm Size	30 acres not all arable	30 acres not all arable
Money Payment	2 silver *solidii*	£2 rent
Payments in kind	20 gallons of wine 100 planks every third year	14 lbs of butter 2 bolls of bere
Poultry Payments	3 hens 15 eggs	3 hens 36 eggs 2 geese
Services	Maintain section of boundary fence Winter and spring ploughing; 2 days corvée per week Carrying services as required	Maintain hill-dyke of undivided common On ca' work, ploughing, barn work, harvesting Carrying services as required
Handicrafts	1 day per week	Required to spin 6 hanks of linen
Mill	Payment of 2 *solidii* for use of mill	Mill mulcture
Legal Status	Unfree	'Free'

The Medieval Villein and the Orkney Crofter. The Orkney crofter is loosely based on James Linklater, Sandwick, whose circumstances were described to the Crofters' Commission. Bodo is from Eileen Power, Medieval People, *1937. Despite being separated by over 1,000 years, there is a remarkable similarity between the ninth century French villein and the nineteenth century Orkney crofter.*

population decline, continuous from 1861 to 1971, and the piecemeal absorption of crofts into neighbouring farms. The number of crofts declined from 2,843 in 1890 to only 390 in 1986, and in Rousay, once the stronghold of the Crofters' Movement, only nine crofts remain.[50] The life of crofters, scraping a living among the heather and rocks on the fringes of the common, had never been easy but, with the loss of so much of the crofting community, there was a fundamental alteration in the nature of rural society, and a vital element was lost from the Orkney way of life. Twentieth century Orkney became a more staid place, and much less radical in its opinions.

The disputes between lairds and their crofters were symptomatic of the harsher economic climate after 1883. Both mid-century high farming and reclamation by crofters were at an end. Yet the achievements of these years were immense. Those who lived through the nineteenth century farming revolution had begun life as children in the cold, lonely work of herding animals on the undivided commons;[51] they had come to manhood and womanhood amid the vanished world of run-rig in a landscape which was positively medieval. In Ernest Marwick's phrase, the nineteenth century was a 'journey from serfdom'[52]—and this is no exaggeration: the comparison in the table on the preceding page between Bodo, a *villein* on the Abbey of St Germain des Prés near Paris about the year 820 AD[53] and a small tenant farmer in Sandwick, Orkney, in the year 1834[54] shows that the nature of the payments and the obligations of service were remarkably similar. The difference was in legal status only: whereas Bodo was 'unfree' and tied to the estate (which may have provided him with welcome security), the Orkney tenant was 'free' and might abandon irksome *on ca'* work for the freedom of the frozen seas of Greenland or the wastes of northern Canada.

These same people in old age lived surrounded by square fields which were neatly enclosed and well cultivated according to the five-shift rotation. The very landscape of their youth had vanished, and few of the old field and rig-names, many of them Norse, have survived. The people of Stove would no longer remember Volyar, Inglea, the West Sheed, Gosslea, the Tumel of Gorn, Cloen and Sinnaspels, each a familiar piece of ground with its distinctive character, but all swallowed up by universal improvement.[55] When the way of life in the old days was described to the Crofters' Commission in 1889, the record of the proceedings often records 'laughter'. Young folk always think of their parents and grandparents as old-fashioned, but few can have thought of them quite so absurdly old-fashioned as did those who were young in 1889. For the older generation there may have been nostalgia for a vanished world, but the more successful had the consolation of a healthy balance deposited in one of the Kirkwall banks. No generation before or since had to adapt so quickly, or had achieved so much.

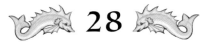

28
Orkney Society in the Eighteenth and Nineteenth Centuries

Orkney landowners shared the universal appetite to acquire land for financial gain, political power and social prestige. These ambitions were worked out, not solely in a local context, but within the ever-changing framework of British society. The result was a remarkable series of changes in the nature of landownership. The Stewart earls, Robert and Patrick, were the last to regard Orkney as a power-base from which to assert their authority as feudal magnates in the medieval manner. Even in their day such pretensions were anachronistic, and their attempt to resurrect 'an ancient and moribund body politic' was doomed to ultimate failure.[1] Ever since the Impignoration (1468) an alternative system had been developing whereby the collection of rent and skat was managed on strictly business lines. After the removal of Earl Patrick the earldom estate was again managed by tacksmen who paid a lump sum for the right to collect the rents and, when there was no bishop, the bishopric estate was managed by the same methods.

The natural instinct of Orkney lairds was to oppose their superior whether he was a feudal Stewart earl or a post-feudal rent-collector. The Morton earls, and their successors the Dundases, were even less integrated into Orkney society than the Stewarts. They were absentees who only occasionally visited the islands; they founded few landed families and did not marry into the tight-knit kindred of Orkney lairds. Opposition culminated in the protracted and complex legal battle known as the Pundlar Process (1733–1759).[2] The case had its origins in a dispute between Sir James Stewart of Burray and John Hay of Balbithan, Morton's chamberlain, leading to allegations that Morton had surreptitiously increased the traditional Orkney weights and had thus fraudulently increased the value of the produce which he collected as rent and skat. Complicated antiquarian arguments to back up these claims were advanced by James Mackenzie.[3] Few lairds could understand his arguments, but they were attracted to his conclusion that the rent, skat and feu duties which they paid to Morton ought to be reduced by at least one-third. After the death of Sir James Stewart as a Jacobite prisoner in a London gaol,

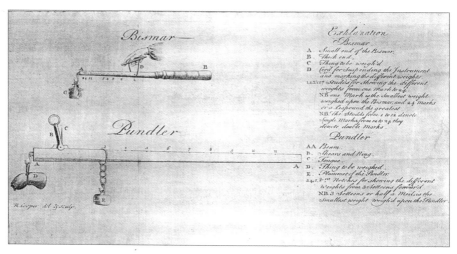

88. *A Pundlar.* This drawing of a pundlar (weigh-beam) comes from the celebrated eighteenth century 'Pundlar Process' when Orkney lairds accused the Earl of Morton of uplifting skat using corrupt weights and measures.

leadership of the anti-Mortonians passed to his heir, the Earl of Galloway. A second and more fundamental argument was added: landowners in Orkney as elsewhere in Scotland paid *cess* (land-tax) and so, it was maintained, they ought no longer to be required to pay *skat* to Morton (*skat*, the ancient Norse land-tax), since this resulted in them being double-taxed.

There is no doubt that the *bismars* and *pundlars* (weigh-beams) which were used to weigh produce were easily falsified. Some lairds notoriously kept two weigh-beams, one for use when they were buying, and the other when they selling. The weights kept by the Deacon of Hammermen for the standardising of new *bismars* and *pundlars* were also highly suspect. The standard for the smallest weight, the *mark*, was a boar's tooth filled with lead, and other so-called standards consisted of a motley collection of beach stones, to which lumps of lead had been attached at an unknown date.[4] There was the justifiable suspicion that extra lead had been added, either by Morton's Chamberlains or their predecessors and, since one beach stone is very like another, perhaps heavier stones had been substituted for the originals. This kind of confusion was not unusual; modern opinion believes that throughout Scotland weights and measures probably increased by a factor of about two-and-a-half times between the twelfth and eighteenth centuries,[5] and it is quite likely that changes to Orkney weights were of that order. Mackenzie's abstruse arguments about the origin of skat made little impression. To eighteenth century minds it was simply a traditional payment, the origins of which were lost in antiquity. Morton's right to collect skat was confirmed, and he was awarded substantial legal costs.

Although ultimately victorious, Morton was left disillusioned by the difficulty of controlling quarrelsome Orkney lairds. He was increasingly immersed in the affairs of the Royal Society of which was an active president, and in the preparation for Captain James Cook's voyage to Tahiti to observe the transit of Venus.[6] So, when in 1766 Sir Laurence Dundas offered to buy his Orkney and Shetland estates, Morton was glad to be rid of the islands.

Laurence Dundas was an Edinburgh merchant, originally dealing in wine and coal, whose upward career began when he supplied bread and forage to the Duke of Cumberland's army during and after the 1745 rebellion. He was elected MP for Linlithgow in 1747, but was unseated for electoral corruption. Contracts for the supply of the army in Germany during the Seven Years War (1756–1763) brought him enormous wealth: James Boswell greatly underestimated the profits when he reported in his *London Journal* that Dundas would 'bring home a couple of hundred thousand pounds'; others believed that he had acquired a fortune of between £600,000 and £800,000. The 'Nabob of the North' used his wealth to acquire a baronetcy and a seat in Parliament, and he set about buying land on a grand scale. Between 1759

89. *Sir Laurence Dundas. Sir Laurence in the library of his London residence in the company of his grandson, later 1st Earl of Zetland (from a 1769 painting by Johann Zoffany).*

90. Sir Laurence Dundas's Edinburgh Townhouse. Sir Laurence's Edinburgh residence occupied the finest site in Edinburgh's New Town, now the Royal Bank of Scotland, St Andrew's Square.

and 1762 he paid £63,000 for an estate in Sligo and Roscommon and £31,000 for lands in Fife; in 1762 he acquired the Yorkshire property which eventually became the family seat, and in the same year he paid £22,000 for land in Clackmannan; in 1763 he bought the palatial Moor Park in Herefordshire, and an elegant house in London; in 1764 he added Loftus in Yorkshire with its alum works; in 1766 he paid £63,000 for the Earldom estate in Orkney and the Lordship of Shetland, and two years later he acquired Burray and the Earl of Galloway's other Orkney property at a cost of £16,000. In addition he purchased two slave estates in the West Indies. He had a preponderant interest in the Forth and Clyde canal, he was a Governor of the Royal Bank of Scotland, and he had shares in the British Plate Glass Manufactory. He was much involved in developing the New Town of Edinburgh, where by devious means he acquired the best site for himself on which he built his magnificent town-house, now the Royal Bank of Scotland in St Andrews Square.[7]

As an enormously wealthy self-made capitalist, Dundas was a new kind of superior. His primary interest was not to screw the last penny from rent and skat (the Dundases always had the reputation for being relatively easy landlords) but rather to achieve aristocratic respectability through the exercise of political power. It was an ambition neatly encapsulated in Sir Laurence's instructions to his wife not to leave London until his son, 'Thomie', was presented at court. 'Order him.' Dundas wrote, 'to have his teeth put in and to dress as an Englishman'.[8] In his heyday Dundas controlled a group of eight or nine MPs, with his man-of-business, Colonel James Masterton, acting as whip to the group. The main advantage from the purchase of Orkney was control of the parliamentary seat. In 1768 his brother, Thomas Dundas, was duly elected by the unanimous decision of all eight assembled voters.[9]

At a more modest level eighteenth century merchant-lairds also reflected growing capitalism, yet there were limits to the heights to which Orkney lairds could grow through trade alone. For them too the next upward step depended on politics and patronage. Even more pressing was the need to provide for younger sons if they were not simply to sink back into the ranks of the peasantry. Hence the natural instinct to oppose their superior was tempered by careful calculation of the benefits which friendship with the great man might bring. Minor posts as clerks and assistants in estate management, administration of justice, admiralty and customs could usually be obtained through his influence. The presentation of parish ministers was in his gift and, since the families of lairds and ministers frequently inter-married,[10] the church provided comfortable livings for the sons and sons-in-law of landowners. At a more ambitious level, Dundas's great influence in Edinburgh could be used to secure entry to the legal profession and, depending on his standing with the government, he could often obtain army and navy commissions and posts with the East India Company.

Best able to tap the patronage system were the actual voters. They were few in number since the vote depended on the possession of the superiority of land to the value of £400 scots. As elections were more regularly contested, factions scrambled to increase their vote by splitting the 'superiority' into a number of fictitious parcels, each of £400 scots, which were given to members of the family and other reliable dependants, while the real owner retained the 'property' or actual possession of the land. By 1780 the electorate numbered 27, of whom about half were these 'faggot' voters. There were four Dundases, two extra Honyman voters and one extra Graeme.[11]

It was necessary not just to placate voters when an election was imminent, but constantly to use the expectation of patronage to prevent the formation of an opposition group. For the lucky recipients the opportunities were immense. William Honyman (1756–1825) was started on a legal career in which he rose with remarkable swiftness to become a judge, Lord Armadale, carrying his family upwards and right out of the Orkney scene.[12] Alexander Graeme (1741–1818) entered the navy and ended up as a one-armed admiral,[13] while John Balfour (1750–1842) followed a highly profitable career in the East India Company which laid the basis of the fortune which enabled him to buy the Honyman estate (1827) and which later allowed his grand-nephew to live in baronial splendour in Balfour Castle.[14]

Yet there were limits to patronage. By its nature it created demands which could never be fully satisfied, and disappointed voters might revert to their natural instincts of opposition and seek favours from Dundas's political enemies. Elections, when they could not be avoided by compromise, were characterised by 'perjury, villainy, drunkenness and deceit'.[15] Both the county election, and the contest for the Northern Burghs which included Kirkwall, were contested with quite unusual bitterness. The election of 1833 was the first at which the franchise was extended to Shetlanders. Orkney votes had secured the apparent victory of Samuel Laing, Kirkwall's popular provost and benefactor, but the arrival of the Shetland votes was delayed by bad weather. The Kirkwall populace (few of whom possessed a vote) spent the time parading Laing through the streets, demanding that the Sheriff declare their candidate the winner without further delay. The Shetland votes, however, tipped the balance in favour of George Traill of Hobbister. The Sheriff, had to be escorted to the declaration 'by a lot of prominent Conservatives'. They were pelted with peats, Captain Balfour fell into an open drain, and a Tory supporter, John Traill-Urquhart suffered a blow from which he later died.[16] The importance of the 1833 election was, however, not the violence, but the increase in the electorate brought about by the Reform Act of 1832. It was no longer possible for voters to hold out for favours, although some still tried to do so. The result was that, at the same time as kelp collapsed and the linen industry finally expired, Orkney lairds discovered that the doors of patronage were closing.

From foundations laid by kelp profits and opportunities of patronage, a new breed of Orkney laird arose in the nineteenth century. Typically they had spent much of their life outside the islands. For example, George William Traill of Rousay (1792–1847) was 30 years in the Bengal Civil Service as 'uncrowned King of Kumaon', while his successor, General Burroughs (1831–1905) commanded the 93rd Highlanders in India.[17] The education of lairds shows the same divergence from the Orkney community and is well illustrated by three generations of Balfours. William Balfour (1718–1786) was educated at the Grammar School in Kirkwall, as was his son, Thomas Balfour (1752–1799) who also received a university education in Aberdeen, but in the next generation John (1780–1799) and William (1781–1846) were sent to Harrow.[18] Nineteenth century Orkney lairds might bear familiar surnames, but they were increasingly distanced from their tenants by their anglicised speech, empire careers and upper-class habits of thought.

The distancing of the landlord and tenant was also the result of larger

91. ***David Balfour (1811–1887).*** *David Balfour's extensive squaring, enclosing and reclaiming of his Shapinsay estate was described as 'fons et origo' (the fountain and source) of Orkney Improvement.*

estates. In Orkney owner-occupied land had been declining ever since the medieval period but, because a good deal of land had at one time been held by udal tenure, owner-occupancy was still well above the national average. Estate growth was greatly accelerated in the nineteenth century when affluent lairds found it easy to acquire bankrupt kelp properties and to buy out small udal owner-occupiers, many of whom were in reduced circumstances.[19] The degree of consolidation which this achieved was important since improvement could not easily have been undertaken on the fragmented and scattered properties of previous centuries. By 1880 about 84% of Orkney land was tenanted, although the owner-occupancy rate of 16% was still twice the Scottish average. Continuing estate growth resulted in owner-occupancy being further reduced and by 1919, when tenanted estates were at their greatest extent, only 9% of the land was owner-occupied.[20]

The growth and consolidation of estates had social as well as economic consequences. Where lairds such as Balfour in Shapinsay and Burroughs in Rousay acquired ownership of an entire island, they achieved not only a monopoly of land, but also an unhealthy dominance over an entire island community. It was a power seen at its most unpleasant in Burroughs' eviction of crofters who dared to give hostile evidence to a Royal Commission (see pp.389-90)[21] and Balfour's eviction of Secession Church elders who

92. *Balfour Castle* and 93. *Margaret Brown. Two ends of the social scale, Balfour Castle, David Balfour's baronial mansion house and Margaret Brown, South Ronaldsay, 'the last of the cottars'.*

had the audacity to criticise the 'promiscuous dancing' (men dancing with women) which was permitted at the laird's Muckle Supper or Harvest Home.[22]

The inauguration of the steamship service (1836) and the building of the Highland Railway to Thurso (1874) left Orkney a degree of remoteness which lent a certain romantic charm without the stifling isolation which made contact with polite society impossible. From a secure social position the landed classes viewed a picturesque landscape and its equally picturesque inhabitants, made fashionable by the Georgian and Victorian cult of the Highlands, and more particularly by Daniel's landscapes, Vedder's poetry and the popularity of Sir Walter Scott's novel, *The Pirate*. Romanticism was fashionable, but there was a certain incongruity in David Balfour's destruction of the real Middle Ages by his ruthless squaring of the landscape while at the same time he was creating his own medieval dream-world. He built a mock-baronial castle; he decorated his private gasworks with fake fortifications, incorporating a stone with the date '1725' which he obtained from Noltland Castle in Westray;[23] he printed historical documents[24] and collected ancient music to which he set abominable verses,[25] and he commissioned a genealogy which set out to prove his claim to be head of the senior branch of the Balfour family. His grandfather's village of Shoreside was renamed 'Balfour', and when he persuaded the Post Office to change the name of its office from Shapinsay to Balfour, he possessed the most imposing of addresses: David Balfour of Balfour, Balfour Castle, Balfour.[26] Like other nineteenth century lairds he used landownership as a means of aspiring to an aristocratic lifestyle which had been beyond the reach of the ship-owning and shopkeeping lairds of the previous century.

Lairds had never been surer of the future than when they entered the second half of the nineteenth century. They were investing heavily in their estates, playing a key role in agricultural improvement, and were supremely confident in the exercise of their social responsibilities. But the leaner times after 1880 proved that many had over-capitalised, and that investment had not always been wisely directed. As purely landed gentry without trading and shipping interests, lairds were less versatile than their forebears. Faced with hard times, they ceased to invest as they struggled to maintain a lifestyle which they were reluctant to modify. By the end of the nineteenth and the beginning of the twentieth century, a quite different style of landownership had developed: several of the bigger estates were bankrupt and were administered by trusts, while others were managed by absentees who had failed to sell and were content to draw whatever income they could from rents without involving themselves in active estate management.[27]

After the Revolution of 1688 and the abolition of bishops, Orkney was slow to conform to the Presbyterian mould, and indeed only four of the 18 ministers eventually made their peace with the new regime.[28] In terms of the clergy who refused to be reconciled, 1688 was a more complete break with the past than was the Reformation (1560). The presentation of their successors was in the gift of the Earl of Morton, and his appointees were staunchly Presbyterian. As long as Jacobitism remained an active force, relations between Presbyterian ministers and the predominantly Episcopalian gentry were strained.

As Jacobitism faded and Presbyterianism mellowed, lairds and ministers settled down in comfortable harmony. Their detractors might dismiss the Orkney clergy as 'a troop of poor ragged students from the College of Aberdeen who, after being shin-burned and smoke dried for twelve or fourteen years in a country school, are at length introduced to a living in Orkney'.[29] Schoolmastering was indeed often a prelude to the ministry, but schools were few and at least as many were engaged by estates such as Burray, Gairsay, Brugh, Tankerness, Graemeshall and Breckness to act as private chaplains— 'Levites' as they were nicknamed—whose principal function was to tutor the laird's children. Because Orkney estates were of modest size, and because lairds were in trade rather than in an aristocratic landowning tradition, ministers and lairds were on terms of greater equality than in many parts of Scotland. Since their Orkney ministry often began with a period of apprenticeship in a laird's household, it is not surprising that they shared the same outlook and prejudices. Ministers were usually non-Orcadian, often from a small-town or rural background in the north-east of Scotland but, by making the kind of marriage society expected of them to a daughter of one of the landed families, they instantly achieved a place in a ministerial-landed network, and they reinforced these relationships in the next generation by a further series of marriages of their daughters and sons (who might also be ministers).[30] Ministers often spent a lifetime in a single parish; on average ministries were twice as long as they had been in the previous century. Many ministers were men of considerable accomplishments. George Low (Birsay 1774–1796)[31] was a gentle, studious naturalist, blind in old age and tragically bereaved; he was the author of *Fauna Orcadensis,* and he also wrote a *Tour* which provides the best account of eighteenth century Orkney and Shetland, and a scholarly *History of Orkney* which was not published until 205 years after his death.[32] George Barry (Kirkwall 1782–1793 and Shapinsay 1793–1805) was the celebrated author of the *History of the Orkney Islands.* The best Statistical Accounts were written by William Clouston (Cross and Burness 1773–1793; Stromness and Sandwick 1793–1832), whose accounts combine a breadth of learning with a thorough knowledge of the economy of his parishes.

In the eighteenth century central government had little direct impact on the lives of individual Orcadians for whom 'Authority' was likely to take the form of the parish minister and Kirk Session. The clergy had its share of drunkards, adulterers and eccentrics, but the majority of ministers served the church well. In addition to their parochial duties, ministers took on many of the functions now performed by local government: they established and supervised schools, they managed poor relief, and they were called out to provide medical help in cases of illness and injury. Some ministers undertook programmes of smallpox inoculation, apparently with some measure of success.[33] Many ministers were products of the Scottish Enlightenment and they combined a comfortable living with a busy and useful life in their parishes. They saw their role as working for the good of society rather than whipping up religious enthusiasm, although it would not have occurred to them that there was any conflict between these aims since moral betterment was inseparable from religious instruction.

An interesting series of sermons has been preserved, preached by Thomas Baikie, minister of St Magnus from 1698 to 1740.[34] What remains is the second of two manuscript volumes, suggesting that the series might have extended to about 40 sermons on about 900 pages of closely written text. His broad theme was the Commandments, but each sermon had a title, 'Against Slander', 'Against Cheating', 'Against Rash Anger', and so on. Some had exciting subtitles; for example 'Against Murder' was subtitled 'The Cry of Blood', but those in search of excitement are likely to be disappointed. The sermons were prepared with great care; little marginal notes testify to Baikie's knowledge of Latin, Greek, Hebrew and French, and he illustrated his sermons with example after example drawn from the Bible. These sermons are, in fact, early instances of the moral preaching of eighteenth century Moderate ministers which was so much criticised by their nineteenth century evangelical successors.

It must have come as some relief from the tedium of Mr Baikie's worthy sermons when each Sunday delinquents were brought forward dressed in sackcloth to stand on 'the White Stone' in front of the pulpit to be rebuked by the minister. Sabbath breach was treated seriously, as was slander resulting from verbal abuse between neighbours, but the great majority of cases involved sexual offences—fornication, adultery and disputed paternity. Ministers and elders certainly showed an unhealthy interest in sexual indiscretions, but private morals could also be a public matter. It was necessary to ensure that children were born into the supporting framework of a family. Endless trouble was caused by the need to take up public collections and make arrangements to board out the occasional fatherless child.

It cannot be said that an appearance on 'the White Stone' was regarded as a great disgrace. Typically the minister or one of the elders would hear gossip that a servant-girl was pregnant. She would receive a summons to appear before the weekly meeting of the Session when she would readily confess her condition, and would name the father who was already waiting outside. He would be called in, cheerfully admit paternity, and announce their intended marriage. For more well-to-do members of society, a public appearance on 'the White Stone' could be commuted to a rebuke within the privacy of the Session in return for a money penalty. A desire to avoid publicity does not always seem to have been a prime concern: William Brodie, in addition to paying one guinea, volunteered to repair the dial of the clock. Suspended high on the tower of the cathedral in full view of Broad Street, he could hardly have performed a more public penance.[35]

The combination of laird and minister working through the Kirk Session transformed the character of the people. At the beginning of the eighteenth century Orkney society was at all levels turbulent, drunken and often violent. At the end of the century the Statistical Accounts in parish after parish describe a 'regular and industrious' society where drunkenness was rare. In the parish of Holm no person had been criminally prosecuted 'in the annals of time',[36] and no doubt the same might have been said of other places. It was the combined influence of the minister and laird which produced the 'sober and tractable' qualities so much admired by the Hudson's Bay Company.[37]

But human nature does not take easily to that degree of heavy-handed paternalism. People develop defence mechanisms. When they cannot openly assert their independence, they react in ways which appear obstructive and devious. This side of the Orkney character was described by the historian George Barry whose relations with the lower orders were frequently strained:

> They are in a high degree indolent, wedded to old customs, averse to every improvement, dark, artful, interested, respectful to their superiors from fear, sometimes endeavouring to slander and undermine one another.[38]

It is not an attractive picture, yet perhaps a common enough reaction to social control. This description allows us to recognise some of the less desirable traits which the Hudson's Bay Company identified in its servants such as 'clannishness' and 'closeness'. You can see why they had the reputation of being 'the slyest of men' and you can understand their 'universal propensity for clandestine dealings'. You can well believe the comment that it was 'beyond the power of any one Englishman to detect them'.[39] Probably they saw little difference between an English officer of the Hudson's Bay Company in Canada and an anglified laird in Orkney, and they had plenty of experience of the latter.

In the last decade of the eighteenth century the old system of social control was breaking down, and the *Statistical Account* is full of examples of the changing relationship between laird and tenant, master and servant. In conditions of inflation and labour shortage, servants were often able to set their own terms. It was complained that it was scarcely possible for a farmer to keep a man servant, or even a boy, without allowing him a month or two to go to the kelp or to the summer fishing. Another symptom was the abandonment of certificates of good character which servants had formerly obtained from the Kirk Session when they moved from one parish to another. As the Rev. George Low commented, 'everyone now, it seems, takes servants just as they get them'.[40]

No doubt independence in the lower orders was seen as particularly threatening because of contemporary events in revolutionary France, yet changes in the master-servant relationship owed little to radical ideas which percolated into Orkney to only a limited extent. Lairds might complain about the weakness of the arm of the law, and pretend to be worried about revolutionary violence, but in reality they knew that there was no such danger. In Stronsay, where the collection of teinds in 1670 and the making of kelp in 1742 had provoked riots,[41] the minister reported, apparently with satisfaction, that his parishioners were more likely to believe in fairies than in revolution.[42] The real concern of lairds was their inability to monopolise the labour of their tenants when there were enormous profits to be made from kelp.

At the same time as the authority of the laird was weakened by economic diversity, religious diversity undermined the position of the parish minister. The ministers who appear such secure and commanding figures from the pages of their Statistical Accounts were soon to find themselves deserted by two-thirds of their flock. Ministers and lairds had been a powerful combination, but the Established Church had been too closely associated with landowners for its own good. One of the attractions of the evangelicalism which swept Orkney at the turn of the century was that religious dissent could be an indirect expression of anti-landlordism. In their Statistical Accounts ministers took credit for the absence of the dissent and schisms which in mainland Scotland had produced the Secession (1733) and Relief Churches (1761). Yet, despite the slowness of organised dissent to penetrate the north of Scotland, there was enormous interest in evangelical forms of worship. The Quaker, John Pemberton of Philadelphia, visited the islands in 1785 and again in 1786, preaching to packed congregations which included 1,500 people who crammed into the cathedral.[43] There was a similar response to the Haldanes who in 1797 swept Orkney in an emotional crusade. The fact that these evangelists were offered the use of churches and were hospitably entertained in manses did not prevent them from attacking their hosts in the most forthright terms for their erroneous doctrine and lax routine.[44]

Although the authors of the earnest histories of the Secession Churches saw dissent purely in terms of religious revival, it had in fact rather more complicated origins.[45] Society was changing, and dissent was one of the ways in which change found expression. Dissent had its origins in conflicts between the dominant merchant-laird burgesses of Kirkwall and the Incorporated Trades. The Trades,[46] the weavers, shoemakers, tailors and hammermen, were becoming more important as a result of economic growth, but they were excluded by the burgh's traditional power structure. The Incorporated Trades were given a sense both of the extent and the limits of their power as a result of a series of bitterly contested parliamentary elections. In addition to the member for the county seat, an MP was also returned from the Northern Burghs (Kirkwall, Wick, Tain, Dornoch and Dingwall) and in 1784 there were a hotly contested election and a subsequent by-election involving such high-profile candidates as Charles James Fox and Sir John Sinclair of Ulbster, later the editor of the Statistical Account. Since the MP was elected by one delegate from each burgh, the choice of this representative was of crucial importance. The Incorporated Trades had a say in the choice of delegate, and they found themselves in a position of unaccustomed power as they were courted by rival candidates.[47] A visit by Prince William, the future William IV, aboard HMS *Hebe* in 1785 added to the Trades' sense of importance, when he snubbed the whiggish Kirkwall merchants by refusing the freedom of the burgh, but accepted the freedom of the Trades Incorporations.[48] In furtherance of their dispute with the merchants, the Trades refused their contribution to *cess* (tax), and when their deacons were imprisoned, the prison was broken open (which was not a difficult undertaking) and the prisoners were set free.

The dispute took on a religious dimension over the hiring out of the cathedral's mortcloth which was used to cover the coffin during funerals. The hire of the best mortcloth was 10 shillings for those living in the parish, and £1 for use outside the parish. When the Incorporated Trades acquired their own mortcloth and hired it out at cheaper rates, they undermined an important part of the church's income. Legal proceedings generated a good deal of ill-feeling between the Trades and the Rev. George Barry, at that time the minister of the cathedral's second charge.[49] The dispute spilled over into the Masonic Lodge where Barry was chaplain, and as a result several aspiring members from the Trades were blackballed by the merchant-laird majority. The lodge split, with Trades members hiving-off to form the rival St Paul's Lodge.

The impetus for the formation of a Secession congregation seems to have come from within the new Masonic lodge. A Praying Society was formed in 1790, the same year as the mortcloth dispute, and in 1793 Malcolm Laing donated a site for the proposed church. Laing also provided advice about which branch of the much-fragmented Secession Church they should join, telling the incipient congregation that they might obtain an Anti-Burgher minister at half the cost of one from the Relief Church. A solemn procession

94. ***Rev. George Ritchie.*** *When George William Traill cleared the district of Quandale in Rousay, the minister challenged him with the text, 'The earth is the Lord's and the fullness thereof'. Ritchie was one of the ministers who 'came out' at the time of the Disruption, bringing the greater part of his congregation with him into the Free Church.*

from St Paul's Lodge marked the beginning of the work on the new church, and the foundation stone was laid with Masonic rituals or, as a hostile observer described it, with 'a great many antique tricks'.[50] Incredibly, the members of the new congregation were entirely unaware that the Anti-Burgher church did not approve of freemasons, and the first church discipline cases dealt with those who had taken the Masonic oath. The arrival of a regular minister broke the Masonic connection, splitting St Paul's Lodge between those who remained Masons and those who adhered to the new church.

The Anti-burgher church (later the United Secession Church and then the United Presbyterians) quickly outgrew its origins among the 'turbulent mechanics' of Kirkwall and achieved a mass following in all sections of society. During the expansionist ministry of Dr Robert Paterson (1820-69), it spoke with great earnestness and authority, and with a profound sense of its own moral leadership of the community. The Secession Church was associated with progress and with liberal ideas; it championed causes such as Education and Temperance, it encouraged a respectable and responsible lifestyle, and expanded outwards from its urban roots to found congregations in most islands and country districts. The church had an enormous appeal, and its members had a great sense of achievement.[51]

A generation later a further wave of dissidents left the Established Church in the Disruption of 1843 to form the Free Church. They were led by the ministers of the Kirkwall second charge, and of the parishes of Stromness, Rousay, North Ronaldsay, St Andrews, Firth and Stenness, and Evie and Rendall, as well as a number of influential assistant ministers. Whereas the Secession Church (United Presbyterians) owed its origins to the tradesmen and craftsmen of Kirkwall, the Free Church was associated with rural radicalism. Combative Free Church ministers provided leadership in the struggle of small tenants against their lairds. They included Matthew Armour in Sanday, who famously was imprisoned for disrupting a Tory election meeting, and the Rev. Archibald MacCallum who organised the Rousay crofters when they gave evidence to the Napier Commission (1883).[52] By 1892 the United Presbyterians with 4,301 communicants was the largest, the Established Church with 4,279 was only slightly smaller, and the Free Church with 3,743 communicants was the smallest of the main denominations.[53]

Country congregations measured their attendance in hundreds, while the United Presbyterians in Kirkwall claimed an average attendance of 1,250 on a Sunday morning. These vigorous churches proliferated a whole range of weekday activities—Bible classes, prayer meetings, mission collections, temperance societies, and separate guilds for young men and women—so that for many people social life revolved round the church. But paradoxically there was also a secularisation of other aspects of community life. Seceders were initially strict in their enforcement of church discipline, but those taken to task could transfer their allegiance to another denomination and so the ability of all churches to discipline their members was undermined. Similarly the division of the churches into Established, United Presbyterians and Free led to secular bodies such as Parochial Boards and School Boards undertaking the functions of Poor Relief and Education which once had been the province of the united church. Elections to School Boards were often keenly contested by rival ministers and groups of elders who used their religious denomination as a 'party label'.

Religious convictions, although deeply held, were never the suffocating blanket of negative Presbyterianism which descended on some Hebridean islands with such mournful effects. Respect for ministers was not automatic; sharp-tongued parishioners were always ready to retail the latest clerical foibles. On the other hand these people were capable of being moved by a powerful sermon, the details of which were sometimes recounted a generation later. It was long remembered how, one summer evening, the Rev David Calderwood arrived back in Sanday in a small boat from pastoral duties in North Ronaldsay, having had little time to prepare his service; his congregation was gathered in a barn at Galilee on flowery shores of the North Loch; as he approached he was suddenly struck by the words 'Ye men of Galilee, why stand ye gazing idly into the Heavens?'[54] and from this text he preached one of his most moving sermons.[55] Spontaneity in preaching was much admired.

It is easy to exaggerate the isolation of Orkney at the beginning of the nineteenth century. In every part of the islands there were people who had spent a year or two in Canada, others who knew the kelp-ports of the eastern seaboard of Scotland and England, those who had carried grain to Norway, Holland and the Baltic, or had sailed the seas with Nelson's navy. But many others lived out their lives with few contacts outside the islands. This was to become less easy as Orkney was drawn into a closer relationship with mainland Britain.

News from the outside world found avid readers. From 1824 to 1826 the *Orkney & Zetland Chronicle* was published in Edinburgh by Alexander Peterkin, largely to further his campaign to win the parliamentary vote for Shetlanders, and to attack the Orkney gentry who had brought about his dismissal from the post of Sheriff-substitute. Then Arthur Anderson's *Shetland Journal* (founded 1836) was, with Samuel Laing's assistance, briefly transformed into the *Orkney & Shetland Journal* before it ceased publication in 1839. As well as these short-lived ventures, the Caithness-based *John o' Groat Journal* carried some Orkney news and, although only more affluent Orcadians were actual subscribers, second-hand copies were greatly prized and were passed from house to house.[56] *The Orcadian,* founded in 1854 and still flourishing, was the first newspaper to be published within the islands, and it was followed by *The Orkney Herald* (1860–1961) and *The Orkney and Zetland Telegraph* (1878–1885). There was also *The Stromness News,* founded in 1884 to defend the burgh from 'hostile and unfriendly attack' but, when it ceased publication a few months later, no such attack had yet been made.[57] The front pages of these papers proclaimed the virtues of patent medicines and miraculous home-cures, they announced the sailing of emigrant ships to America and Australia, they advertised seeds, guano and the latest farm machinery, and offered everything that was needed to furnish a polite Victorian home. These papers carried a good deal of national news; pungent editorials and a correspondence column which made few concessions to the laws of libel made for compulsive reading. Local newspapers acted as a forum of public opinion on such matters as the crofters' struggle against their landlords.

Improvement in postal services also brought Orkney into closer contact with other places. From at least as early as 1741 bags of mail were being made up in Edinburgh for dispatch to Orkney, and a post office was established in Kirkwall in 1747. For a hundred years mail was sent overland to Thurso, thence to Huna and by open boat across the Pentland Firth to Burwick in South Ronaldsay from where it was taken by foot and by ferry across Burray to Kirkwall, The crossing of the Pentland Firth was dangerous, and in 1815 and again in 1817 mail boats were lost with all hands. Nor was that the only hazard: in 1797 Thomas Urquhart, postmaster in Kirkwall, was hanged for complicity in the theft of banknotes from the mail.[58] From 1845 mail was carried aboard the Aberdeen steamer, and after 1846 a small wooden paddle steamer, the *Royal Mail,* operated on the Stromness-Scrabster route.[59] The introduction of the penny post greatly increased the volume of mail, and from mid-century sub-post offices opened in all country districts.

Of even greater importance to the integrating of Orkney to British culture was the advent of a national system of education. Kirkwall had its ancient Grammar School which was already in existence in 1486 when a royal charter of James III granted it and the Sang School to Kirkwall as part of the cathedral establishment.[60] In all probability the Grammar School is much older. Since part of the master's salary was drawn from the island of Wyre, it has been suggested that the school might owe its origins to Bishop Bjarni (Bishop of Orkney 1188–1223), son of Kolbein Hruga of Wyre.[61] On the eve of the Education Act (1872) the Grammar School was very run down, the building was in poor repair, and attendance was lax.[62]

A school had also existed in South Ronaldsay in Earl Patrick's time, but closed in 1615 when the teacher's salary was withheld by Ochiltree's chamberlain.[63] Parish reports dating from 1627 reveal a complete absence of schools outside Kirkwall, although the need for education as an aid to religious instruction was stressed by most parish ministers.[64] By the early eighteenth century some progress had been made, and in many parishes there was a schoolmaster who, whatever his musical ability, was expected to act as precentor, leading the singing of a few familiar psalms, and he might also act as a reader in parishes with more than one church. These schools tended to have an intermittent existence, and the education was usually elementary. There were, however, occasional attempts to provide a more ambitious education: in 1698 Birsay had a 'Grammar School' which was still in existence in 1709,[65] and in 1719 John Clow opened a school of 'humanity and philosophy' in Stromness which abruptly closed when the Presbytery summoned him in order to examine his qualifications.[66]

Even at the end of the eighteenth century only a few properly constituted parochial schools had been established, but by 1841 there had been what can only be described as an explosion of educational provision. Not only did every parish have its Parochial School, but there were other schools operating under the auspices of the three churches; the Society for the Propagation of Christian Knowledge had a number of schools in districts or islands where access to the parish school was difficult; endowed schools had been gifted by Magnus Twatt and James Tait (both in Orphir) and by William

95. *The* **Lizzie Burroughs.** *Between 1879 and 1892 General Burroughs' little steamer provided a slow and erratic service from Sourin in Rousay to Egilsay, Trumland, Wyre, Hullion, Evie, Tingwall, Gairsay and Rendall and to Kirkwall.*

Tomison in South Ronaldsay, all of whom had made their money with the Hudson's Bay Company.[67] Tomison's Academy had a good reputation for teaching Navigation, and attracted prospective mariners from as far away as Caithness and Westray. In addition many 'adventure' schools were run as private concerns by individuals whose school-teaching ability was often very doubtful. Thirty years before the Education Act made attendance compulsory, Orkney had about 80 schools—three times as many as exist at the present day. The parish of Sandwick which nowadays buses out all its Primary and Secondary pupils, had in 1841 no less than nine schools.[68]

Although the standard of instruction was variable and the buildings often pitifully inadequate, these schools achieved significant progress towards a universal basic literacy. In 1841 ministers reported that only a few of the older people were unable to read and write, and an examination of the register of births, deaths and marriages confirms that all but a few tinkers could at least sign their name.[69] On the eve of the Education Act about 80% of school-age children were enrolled, although attendance was markedly seasonal, depending on the child-labour requirements of herding, working peats and gathering tangles.[70]

413

The 1872 Education Act established School Boards on a parish basis, each dealing directly with the London-based Scotch Education Department. Boards set about their work with enthusiasm; they undertook ambitious building programmes and convinced the Department of the need for schools, even on the smaller islands. Schools saw their task as the assimilation of their pupils to a national culture as a means of bringing Orkney into the modern world and of creating opportunities for employment outside the islands. This involved the deliberate destruction of much that was regionally distinctive. Teachers, many of them non-Orcadians, seldom stayed long, and they had little understanding of, or sympathy with, Orcadian culture. Universally their attitude to dialect was that of the teacher at Cross Primary School in Sanday who noted in his log: 'the old pronunciation still lingering notwithstanding continuing efforts to eradicate it'. It was only with the publication of *The Orkney Book* (1909), inspired by a group of young students in Edinburgh University's Orcadian Society and edited by John Gunn, that the Orkney identity began to receive some recognition in schools. Even then toleration did not extend to speaking Orcadian in the classroom.

In the depressed conditions of the late nineteenth century, education was valued as a means of escaping from the treadmill of poverty on the small farm. The string of professors produced by the Grammar School testifies to the efficiency of the system and to the determination of young Orcadians to succeed. But respect for education for its own sake was better epitomised by the activities of the Young Men's Mutual Improvement Societies. Small groups of these earnest young men, and some not so young, met on cold winter's nights in comfortless country schoolrooms to recite Victorian poetry and to read to each other their essays on such abstract subjects as 'Perseverance', 'Politeness' and 'Promptitude and Punctuality'. The minute books of the group which met in the Sellibister School in Sanday reveals that they rarely discussed current issues such as crofting legislation, and they had no interest whatsoever in local history and folklore.[71] Walter Traill Dennison, the great folklore collector, was then living in the same island; Ernest Marwick commented that Dennison:

> ...saved from extinction, single-handed, a whole corpus of myth, legend and historical tradition which educated Orcadians of his time ignored, *even deplored.*[72]

The phrase 'even deplored' is interesting: it shows that regional culture was baggage to be shed by those who wished to appear modern and progressive. The activities of the members of the Young Men's Mutual Improvement Society was self-improvement in its purest form, with no thought to qualifying themselves for a different way of life, but the lack of concern with local issues was symptomatic of a changing society which had not much confidence in its own identity. Improvement in agriculture had involved the acceptance of outside ideas as superior to traditional practices; self-improvement in the same way involved a rejection of the language, folk-beliefs and habits of thought of an earlier age. Contrary to the experience of the people of Faroe who began to recover their language and identity at about the same time, Orkney experienced cultural loss. Orkney's circumstances were, of course, different from Faroe. The first generation of modern Orcadians had to come to terms with the wider world within the context of imperial Great Britain where subtle distinctions of class and accent encouraged conformity, and a regional identity was regarded as a handicap.

29
Farming in the Twentieth Century

The rapid expansion of agriculture in the period c.1846 to c.1875 brought Orkney farming into the modern age. Growth slowed down in the late 1870s and came to a complete standstill as prices fell back in the 1880s. Orkney then entered a period when farming incomes declined, new holdings ceased to be created, new land was no longer being reclaimed and new farm buildings were no longer being erected. In the early twentieth century few farmers under the age of 45 had practical experience of draining. Those who had worked the land in the mid-nineteenth century had needed to adapt to change, but their sons and daughters inherited a farming economy which was stagnant. In the period between 1880 and the outbreak of war in 1914 crop acreages, animal numbers and farming methods were largely static.

Following the 1914-18 war a second revolution took place when big estates were broken up and a society of owner-occupiers was created.[1] It is doubtful if even the arrival of the Vikings brought about such a rapid change in landownership as occurred in the 1920s. Yet this 'Owner-occupier Revolution' has somewhat faded from the memory of later generations which simply assume that it is natural for farmers to own their own land. Owner-occupancy had actually been on the decline ever since the medieval period: Earl William Sinclair had acquired almost one-third of the privately-owned land which existed in the fifteenth century,[2] there had been further contraction in the sixteenth, seventeenth and eighteenth centuries when udallers experienced difficulty in maintaining their unwritten rights, and then in the nineteenth century small landowners were often bought out by lairds like Burroughs in Rousay and Balfour in Shapinsay who had independent incomes which they used to enlarge their properties and build up cohesive estates. Because so much of land had once been udal, owner-occupancy in 1880 was still nearly twice the Scottish average. The decline, however, continued, and in 1919 only 9.4% of the land was owner-occupied, bringing Orkney close to the Scottish average. On the eve of the owner-occupier revolution estates had never been bigger. The year 1919 was a watershed:

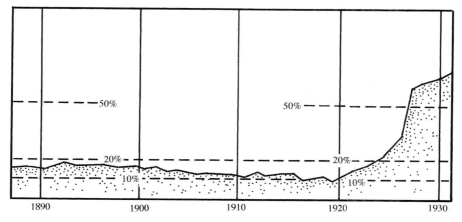

96. **Owner-occupancy.** *The graph shows the steady decline in owner-occupancy to 1919 and the reversal of the trend in the 'owner-occupancy revolution' of the 1920s.*

this was the year when rented land was at its most extensive, but it was also the year of the first sales. The scale of what happened in Orkney over the next few years can be measured against national trends. In Scotland as a whole owner-occupancy increased from 8.2% of agricultural land in 1919 to 21.2% by 1930. That was certainly a large increase, but much less than the change in Orkney from 9.4% to 65.8% owner-occupancy over the same period. After 1930 the trend towards owner-occupancy continued, but at a slower pace, reaching 86% at the close of the twentieth century. Estate ownership entirely disappeared in most parts of Orkney.

Rents had risen steadily during the period of mid-nineteenth century agricultural improvement, reflecting the buoyant farming economy and the improved price of cattle, but, after a peak c.1880, there was a downward trend. The Crofters' Commission ordered an average reduction of 30% in the rent of Orkney crofts in 1888,[3] but rent was reduced on bigger farms by a comparable amount without the need for government intervention. By 1900, despite lower rents and less labour-intensive methods, the majority of big farms were in arrears. Family farms which employed less paid labour, and where modest improvements had been undertaken without borrowing, were better able to survive depression, and even better placed were crofts where there were outside incomes, for example from fishing. In 1900 on the Earldom estate one-third of tenants were in arrears and the total indebtedness amounted to about half the annual rental. The father of the poet Edwin Muir (1887–1959) was one of the casualties of the crisis. Edwin remembered the island of Wyre as a childhood Eden, and sunlit memories of its rural stability provided him with a store of images which he used for the rest

417

*97. **Thomas Traill of Holland.** Thomas Traill was an agricultural improver who built some of the finest nineteenth century farm steadings. He went bankrupt in spectacular style, and his former estate was one of many administered by trusts in the early years of the twentieth century.*

of his life, but in reality Wyre was in turmoil—the island was the property of General Burroughs, and all six of its farms changed hands between 1893 and 1898 as a result of the tenants' inability to pay their rent.[4] By 1900 the worst was over, and the immediate pre-war years were relatively prosperous. Farming did well during the 1914-18 war, and continued to flourish in the immediate postwar years until c.1923 when government subsidies were dismantled.

The landowner's income from rent, however, did not follow the upturn in prices, but remained virtually static at 1900 levels. While tenants began to prosper once again, landlordism decayed. Many estates had opted out of active management. Prior to the sales there had been a period of 30 years when the estates which had been offered for sale had often failed to find a buyer, with the result that they might be managed by trusts which preferred to derive an income from the property rather than sell for less than what was optimistically believed to be the true value. Of the top dozen estates in 1919, five were administered by trusts,[5] four others including the earldom were owned by absentees, and several had been rescued from bankruptcy. The result was a cautious, tight-fisted style of management where the main concern was to collect the rent rather than to invest or innovate. A typical case was Orkney's third largest estate, once the property of the Traills of

Rattar, much of whose lands lay in Sanday and Stronsay. This Caithness branch of the Traill family had bought land in the 1820s with the money which they made from their Castletown flagstone quarries.[6] By 1880 the fortune had gone, the estate went bankrupt and it was thereafter in the hands of a trust managed by Thurso lawyers. The trust tried unsuccessfully to find a buyer in 1904 and again in 1912, before taking the decision in 1921 to divide the estate into lots and sell to sitting tenants. In contrast to lairds like David Balfour who had made massive investments in draining and enclosing in the previous generation, the Thurso lawyers, it was said, never expended as much as would have bought a lock for a single door.

Andrew Gold, the Chamberlain of the Earldom Estate, retired in 1898 after 58 years in the service of the estate, but even at the age of 78 he felt he had to make excuses for leaving a post, the duties of which, he explained, were now very light because 'the management of the estate is reduced to a minimum'.[7] As early as 1887 he had forecast that landlords were no longer likely to be much involved with crofts because the Crofters' Act of the previous year had given crofters a status almost equal to proprietors.[8] Another reason why estates tended to withdraw from active management was the way they handled compensation for improvements. Prior to 1883 estates had not been obliged to compensate tenants for the work done during the tenancy, and Andrew Gold in his evidence to the Napier Commission could not recall a single instance in his long career when compensation had even been discussed with small tenants.[9] However, the Agricultural Holdings (Scotland) Act of 1883, and the Small Landholders' Act of 1911 strengthened the position of tenant farmers. Tenants usually put up houses at their own expense, and they could claim compensation for draining, liming, fencing, building new roads and other work of this kind. The estate had the ultimate responsibility to provide compensation, but since the amount was based on an estimate of the value of the work to the new tenant, it was common practice to require the incoming tenant to make the payment to his predecessor. Compensation could be high, and in extreme cases it might actually exceed the price for which the holding was eventually sold. One Burray crofter, who had reclaimed his croft from hill land and had built the house himself, received £63 at his way-going in 1921, whereas his successor was able to buy the entire property for £50 only three years later when the Earldom Estate was broken up. The practice whereby incoming tenants 'bought' the improvements relieved the estate of its immediate responsibilities, but at the cost of limiting its future income, since the tenant who paid for the improvements naturally expected to occupy the farm at its unimproved rent. The way compensation was handled caused the fossilisation of the rents with the result that rent failed to rise in response to the better economic conditions of the early twentieth century.

From this static income from rent, estates were having to meet increased expenditure in the post-war years. Death duties, which had been progressively increased in the period 1894-1919, are often blamed for estate sales but few, if any, Orkney estates were sold specifically for this reason. It was rather that these new death duties, along with national taxation and local rates, were costs which estates had to set against their static income. Throughout Scotland tax on land had risen from about 1.5% of the rental in 1870-1 to about 15% in 1919, while Parish rates for education and poor relief and County rates, which included roads, police and water, had risen five-fold during the same period.[10] Landowning did not actually become unprofitable, but it was the common wisdom of the period that land offered a lower return on capital than other forms of investment. At the same time the activities of Lenin abroad and Lloyd George at home created an uneasy feeling that the days of the landed estate might be numbered. Government interference and even the possibility of land nationalisation were taken more seriously than we might imagine.

The first sales were in 1919 when much of the Sanday estate which had belonged to the late Captain Horwood was sold, then two years later the trusts which had for so long administered the Traill of Rattar estate and the Rousay estate which had once belonged to General Burroughs both decided to sell. The pace accelerated in 1923-4 when 548 Earldom Estate properties were sold, and then between 1924 and 1928 the Balfour estate sold, first, its properties on the Mainland, and then its Shapinsay farms. The whole exercise was completed swiftly: for example in Burray where the Earldom had owned the whole island, every scrap of agricultural land had been sold by 1926, and the estate was left with only a few houses in the village and some moribund kelp-rights. Prices were generally in the region of '20 years purchase' (20 times the rent), but might sometimes be a good deal lower where the occupier would have been entitled to a large amount of compensation had he given up the tenancy. About 70% of holdings were sold to the sitting tenant, and in the remainder of cases the buyer was often a son or son-in-law. However, in about 10% of sales the holding was bought as additional land by a neighbour already buying his or her farm. These places were nearly all very small, and a typical arrangement allowed the former tenant to continue to occupy the house when the land was incorporated in the adjacent farm. Occasionally a member of the family in the United States or in Australia might become the nominal owner, but land was seldom, if ever, sold to people with no Orkney connection.

Although some tenants were eager to buy their farms, another strand of opinion was dubious of the benefits of owner-occupancy. It was generally held that capital was better invested in stock and equipment for a farm, rather than buying the land. But when the moment of decision arrived, sitting tenants generally bought their farms. They recognised that the price represented a good bargain, the asking-price was usually within their reach, and ownership offered long-term security. They were also motivated by the fear that they might lose their home and livelihood if they failed to buy. The new owners, however, were entering a hard world: the year 1923 was the worst in living memory with a cold spring, a wet summer, damaging autumn gales and a disastrous harvest.[11] These were the conditions which in earlier centuries would have resulted in famine, and indeed in the spring of 1924 government supplies of oats and potatoes were distributed in North Ronaldsay. It was even more worrying that farmers were buying against a background of deteriorating economic conditions. They had done well during the war, and when peace was restored, prices were still supported. Then, with the dismantling of government subsidies, the index of agricultural prices fell by 46% between 1920 and 1923, although beef prices held up better than grain, at least until the 1930s.[12]

The investment in farm purchase had been made in such difficult circumstances that contemporary surveys of Orkney agriculture literally mention no benefits from ownership.[13] Instead they concentrate on the difficulties of farmers who had all their capital tied up and were paying interest on loans; they were worried that farm servants and crofters who had saved a little money no longer found it easy to gain an entry into farming; there was also concern that farmers who were no longer bound by a lease to follow a specified crop rotation 'might take all the good out of the land',[14] and how could major improvements ever be possible in the future without the capital which landowners had once provided? From a perspective 80 years after the sales, this pessimism seems absurd—the Owner-Occupier Revolution was a great step forward. In the same way as crofters began improving their crofts after they gained security of tenure from the 1886 Crofters' Act, the buying of farms released a burst of energy. This was the period when a good deal of shallow 'breck land' was broken into cultivation; cattle numbers increased from 36,000 in 1920 to 39,700 in 1930 (a 10% increase over the period of the sales); egg production soared to new heights and played a significant part in financing farm purchase. All this was achieved in difficult times when agriculture was contracting in many other parts of Britain.

In social terms the disappearance of landowners had a less sudden impact than the rapidity of the sales might suggest. Because so much of Orkney was in the hands of absentees or was administered by trusts, the lifestyle of the Victorian landed estate had already disappeared. The big house with its staff of indoor and outdoor servants had already gone, or at least was run on more modest lines. In many parishes there was no longer a resident laird to assume automatic precedence at every public event and social occasion. Landowners had been in the forefront of nineteenth century improvement but, even before the break-up of the estates, new ideas were being disseminated through channels independent of the lairds. Leadership was provided by progressive farmers and enterprising College of Agriculture advisers. The papers they wrote for the early volumes of the *Proceedings of the Orkney Agricultural Discussion Society* reflect a lively and very attractive rural community. The writers show an openness to new ideas, a pride in their farms, and a confidence in the long-term future of farming despite all the immediate difficulties.

In the early years of the century the five-shift rotation was still standard practice on most farms, and quite often it was a requirement written into the lease. The five-shift rotation was: (Year 1) turnips or potatoes (Year 2) bere or oats under-sown with rye grass (Year 3) grass cut for hay (Year 4) grass for grazing (Year 5) oats. Often the second year of grass was not very successful, and pasture laid down for longer periods rapidly deteriorated. All this was changed by the introduction of Wild White Clover. It was sown at Balfour Mains, Shapinsay, as early as 1906, and was listed in Garden's seed catalogue in 1909,[15] but it was only in the post-war years that its use became universal. Farmers regarded Wild White Clover as a miracle crop, since its nitrogen-fixing nodules built up fertility, and it was particularly effective in creating good pasture on poor land. Its use enabled more flexible crop rotations to be introduced: in the 1920s it was common to follow a six-shift rotation (the five-shift plus an extra year of grass), and in the next decade six or seven years of grass became common. On these improved pastures it was possible to carry many more cattle, and there was less need for such a large turnip crop with its heavy demands on labour. The turnip acreage declined from 14,544 acres in 1900 to 8,089 acres in 1950 and, by the end of the century the feeding of silage to cattle had reduced the turnip crop to almost insignificant proportions.

There had been occasional rather unsuccessful attempts to make silage around 1880, and there was renewed interest after the First World War. Even then it was reckoned that 10-12 men were needed for the work of cutting, carting and packing, and so the labour involved put silage beyond the reach of most farmers.[16] It was only about 1950 that the first forage harvesters came to Orkney, but progress thereafter was swift: silage completed the 'greening' of the landscape, replacing the brown of newly turned earth and the gold of ripening corn. But cereals did not always turn golden in Orkney's uncertain climate. Agricultural contractors whose machinery can strip a field of silage in a matter of hours have replaced the never-ending struggle to salvage a grain crop amid the rain and mud of a late season. Today some 116,664 acres are under grass (90% of the farmland excluding rough grazing) and of that 40,668 acres are cut for hay or silage.

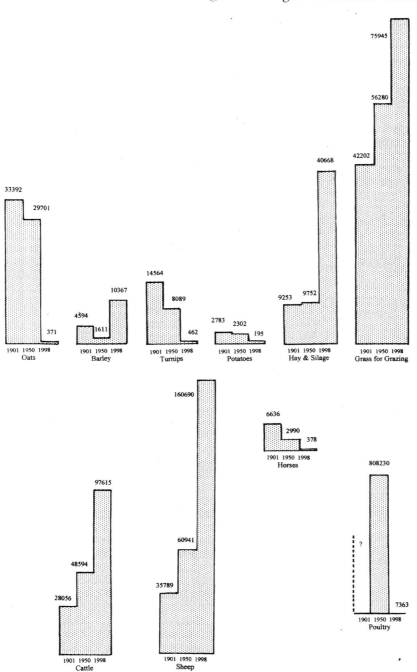

98. *Crops and Animals, 1900, 1950 and 1998.*

423

The increase in grass has been accompanied by a decline in grain-growing. By the end of the century the 10,738 acres under grain represented a mere 28% of the 37,986 acres which was grown in 1900. At the beginning of the century the grain crop was predominantly oats (wheat has never been important) and a good deal of the barley was still the old-fashioned bere. By 1977 barley had overtaken oats, and the oat crop is now quite small. Orkney barley is fed to cattle, but is normally unsuitable for use in the local distilleries.

Orkney's mid-nineteenth century Agricultural Revolution was based on beef cattle, but the numbers were then much smaller than they were to become in the twentieth century when beef production was a continuing success story. Cattle numbers had trebled during the period of nineteenth century expansion,[17] and in 1900 there were 28,056 cattle; the number rose to 48,594 in 1950 and to 97,615 by the end of the century. The introduction of artificial insemination improved the quality, and it also resulted in a greater variety of breeds. In addition to the once near-universal Aberdeen-Angus and Shorthorn, Herefords appeared in the 1960s and Charolais in the 1970s, and they were followed by Simmental and Limousin. In the last part of the twentieth century the dam-breed began to change: instead of cows which were largely Aberdeen-Angus and Shorthorn, there was a move towards bigger breeds where Simmental predominates. The result has been bigger cows, and thus increased profitability, but the downside is the more frequent calving problems which occur in the new breeds. In 1960 the industry had to cope with an outbreak of foot-and-mouth disease which devastated the affected farms.[18] Later there were successful programmes for the eradication of tuberculosis and brucellosis.

This improvement both in the number and the quality of cattle has been achieved by a much reduced agricultural labour force. The old routine was labour-intensive: cattle housed indoors in winter were usually fed three times in the day, and the 'suppering' of cattle made for long working hours. In addition the byre had to be mucked out using a four-pronged fork and a wheel barrow, and the large quantities of turnips which were an essential part of the cattle's diet involved a laborious routine of lifting, tailing, carting and slicing. On farms which lacked a bore-hole or other private water supply, cattle also had to be let out once a day and driven to a burn. A piped water supply became available from the 1950s onwards, and grid electricity had reached the great majority of farms by the 1970s. Modern cattle management makes much reduced demands on labour: cattle are housed in large, well-ventilated buildings where the slurry collects under the slatted floors, and they are now usually fed *ad lib* on silage and twice a day on concentrates. An alternative to slats is the 'Orkney sloping floor' where cattle are fed and bedded at the top of a 1:16 slope, the lower part of which is easily cleaned with a tractor-scrapper.

Butter-making was an important activity on Orkney farms as far back as the Norse period, since a substantial part of taxation was paid in butter (see pp.208-9). The first reference to a dairy herd dates from the time of Earl Robert Stewart, when an inventory made at the time of his death (1593) reveals that he had possessed a herd of 24 dairy cattle which were grazed at the Bu of Corse just outside Kirkwall.[19] However, dairying was on a limited scale up to the 1939-45 war, and was mainly localised in a number of small dairies near to its market in the towns.[20] In the inter-war years Sir Robert Hamilton, the Liberal Member of Parliament, urged Orkney farmers to copy the Danish system of co-operatives and its concentration on dairy produce, pigs and poultry.[21] Pig-numbers fluctuated according to a boom-and-burst 'pig-cycle', but many farms which did not specialise in pigs nevertheless kept one to sell and another to eat. It was a common rule of thumb that the pig which was sold paid for the feeding of both of them.

A rapid growth of dairying was encouraged during the 1939-45 war to meet the needs of the large service population, and by 1942 some 40% of cattle were dairy animals. To Orkney folk accustomed to the beef breeds the presence of 120 dairy herds scattered throughout the Mainland seemed 'very peculiar'.[22] When the war ended, and the demand for fresh milk declined as service personnel were withdrawn, a small cheese factory was established in disused RAF huts at Hatston on the outskirts of Kirkwall with the assistance of the Milk Marketing Board. In 1958 it moved to larger premises (the present Claymore Dairies Ltd.) concentrating on dried milk and butter-making before eventually reverting to cheese.[23] In 2000 work commenced on a new creamery which will again be located in Hatston. Orkney butter enjoyed a good reputation in marked contrast to previous centuries, when the butter paid in rent was often so foul that it was fit only to grease wagon wheels, or else was mixed with tar to be used by Scottish farmers to smear sheep—according to rumour butter sold in Edinburgh in previous centuries was advertised specifically as '*not* made in Orkney'.[24] After 1970 the EEC 'butter mountain' and incentives to move out of dairying resulted in a gradual reduction in the number of dairy cattle but, due to an increase in productivity, milk production continued to increase. In the 1990s, despite the fact that only about 7% of Orkney cattle were in dairy herds, annual production rose to around 16,400,000 litres.[25] The setting of milk quotas in 1994 stabilised production; these quotas are saleable, but the scheme whereby they may not be sold outside of Orkney provides protection for the continuing future of cheese-making.

A feature of Orkney farming between 1880 and 1960 was its remarkable concentration on egg production.[26] This first developed as a response to nineteenth century depression when, as grain prices fell, there was a tendency to feed oats to poultry rather than sell it off the farm. Egg prices,

99. **Travelling Shop.** *As egg production grew many eggs were bartered to horse-drawn vans in exchange for groceries.*

100. **Hens.** *As poultry became ever more numerous in the first half of the twentieth century, portable wooden hen-houses were introduced and became a familiar feature dotted across the landscape.*

around eight pence per dozen, later fell back a little, but tended to hold up better than other farm produce. Eggs had already reached the million mark in the 1880s, when they were sufficiently important for landlords to accuse their tenants of having a secret income from which they could very well afford to pay proper rents for their farms. Egg-money was the subject of several sharp exchanges between lairds and crofters at early hearings of the Crofters' Commission. The Commission's chairman tried to draw James Craigie of Braes in Rousay on the subject of hens, but Craigie, who had been very exact in his evidence up to that point, suddenly became vague: he admitted to owning poultry, but was unsure of their number and would express no opinion when asked whether the sale of eggs helped him to pay his rent.[27] According to the minutes of other hearings, questions about eggs generally provoked 'laughter' and elicited absolutely no information—hens were women's work, and men were not supposed to know anything about them. Egg production, however, was to become much more than a sideline: initially many eggs were bartered with Garden's horse-drawn vans for groceries, then in the early years of the twentieth century there was a growth of parish co-operatives. Latterly most of the eggs were handled by three grading stations, Orkney Egg Producers Ltd based at Ayre Mills in Kirkwall and in Stromness, and Pomona Egg Packers. The industry grew in spectacular fashion: by 1914 when exports reached 19 million eggs, portable hen-houses became a familiar feature dotted across the landscape. After 1945 production increased still further, rising to over 50 million and making Orkney one of Britain's leading egg-producing regions, although Orkney had no very obvious natural advantage for poultry. The accounts of one 50-acre farm from this post-war period show that egg sales grossed £600 in the year while cattle sales at £577 were rather less.[28] The industry received a setback in the gales of 1952 and 1953 when many hen-houses were destroyed, some being blown right out to sea.[29] After the gales it became commoner to keep hens in deep-litter houses, but the industry suddenly collapsed in the early 1960s. The demise of the Egg Marketing Board and the growth of large battery units in mainland Britain brought an end to egg production in Orkney where the transport costs on feeding stuffs swallowed up what was by then a small margin of profit. Agricultural returns recorded 808,230 poultry in 1950, but in 1998 the number had fallen to only 7,363 (less than 1% of the 1950 number).

In 1900 there were 6,636 horses in Orkney and as late as the Second World War there was at least one farmer still ploughing with oxen. One of the first tractors, if not the very first, was an American-built Mogul tractor which was acquired in 1917 by the farm of Stove in Sanday,[30] but there was only a modest reduction in horse numbers in the period up to the 1939-45 war. Early tractors made a good job of ploughing, but they were temperamental

101. *Early Tractor.* This Fordson tractor probably dates from the early
1920s. It is photographed in front of W.R.Tullock's Cycle and Motor Depot,
Kirkwall. Note the metal bands which were attached over the lugs on the rear
wheels when the tractor was to operate on roads.

and often not well maintained. Their narrow wheels with metal 'lugs' had
difficulty in coping with soft ground and were liable to destroy roads, so
there were tasks around the farm which were better done with horses. Farmers also complained about the high cost of tractors; a common witticism was
that, unlike horses, tractors did not breed and so they were expensive to
replace—an argument which tractor-enthusiasts countered with the observation that tractors did not eat when they were not working. Some
mechanically-minded farmers made their own tractors by adapting small
second-hand cars.[31] During the 1939-45 war farmers were required to plough
as much land as possible, and in the immediate post-war period food remained scarce. Some of the technology which had been devoted to armaments
was diverted into making agricultural machinery, and the numbers of tractors steadily grew. In the post-war years there was consequently a rapid
reduction in the number of horses; already by 1950 there were only 2,990
(45% of the 1900 figure) and at the end of the century the small numbers
which appear in Agricultural Returns are hardly ever used for agricultural
work. In 1942 there were only 316 tractors, but the numbers increased very

rapidly during and immediately after the war, reaching 2,337 in 1967. A ploughman with a pair of horses might plough an acre in a day, whereas nowadays a tractorman with an 80-100 hp tractor and a four-furrow revers-ible plough can plough an acre or even more in an hour. As tractors increased in number, they also became more powerful and more versatile; early trac-tors were mechanical horses which could only pull, but the next generation of tractors replaced the man as well as his horse. The hydraulic lift and power-drive took much of the manual labour out of tasks such as loading and spreading dung. There was no longer a need for the poorly paid farm serv-ant who had been compelled to work into old age, bowed by a lifetime of unremitting toil.

In the middle of the century most farmers owned factory-made reapers, binders and possibly potato-diggers, but many other implements such as harrows, grubbers and rollers were relatively simple and were usually made by the local blacksmith. A symbol of what was to come was the arrival of combine harvesters. Combines had been occasionally used in Orkney ever since the war years, but as late as 1951 there were none at all. The combin-ing of grain became the norm with the introduction of Golden Promise barley, an early ripening variety with an ability to withstand windy condi-tions. The arrival of Golden Promise coincided with the introduction of tanker combines and the use of propcorn as a treatment for the moist stor-age of barley. Forage-harvesters, pick-up balers and dung-spreaders continued the trend towards bigger and more complex machinery. Fertiliser-spreaders were common in the 1960s and encouraged heavier applications of artificial manures. Large round bales of hay and straw appeared in the 1980s, and were followed in the 1990s by plastic-wrapped bales of silage. Plastic bales have the advantage that they cut down on silage-effluent, which is a prob-lem for farms near lochs and water-courses, although the plastic contributes to the wind-blown debris which festoons many barbed-wire fences.

Hitherto farmers had owned the implements they needed, but that was not so easy as machinery became more expensive. The belief that the only way to compete was to keep up with the latest developments led many farmers on average-sized farms to over-invest in machinery. Sometimes they might hire out under-used machinery to neighbours, and those who did so with a realistic assessment of costs found a profitable business as agri-cultural contractors. Contracting was not altogether new: tractors had been hired out to reclaim the brecks in the 1930s, but it was the combining of barley from the early 1970s onwards which increased the scale of contract-ing. In the last two decades of the twentieth century there was a great increase in the use of contractors for ploughing, sowing and cutting silage as well as for combining. The work is done quickly and well, and it fits in with the need to cut back on labour and with the increasing tendency for farming to be part-time. Farmers, however, are often no longer personally involved in the whole production process. Their predecessors in 1900 would have been astonished that farmers a century later might not own a plough.

The whole tendency of twentieth century farming was to employ fewer people. Old-style farming was incredibly labour intensive. In 1861 no less that 2,114 farm servants were employed, and many more under-employed casual workers—men, women and children—congregated around big farms looking for work. The more difficult conditions from the 1880s onwards caused farmers to economise, and the number of paid workers had already been halved by 1914. During the 1914-18 war labour was scarce, yet at the same time farmers were exhorted to produce more food, and this acted as a spur to adopt labour-saving machinery such as binders, double-furrow ploughs and even tractors.[32] After 1918 most farmers regarded farm servants at six shillings a day as prohibitively expensive, and even at these wages they were difficult to find.[33] As the century progressed the sons of farm servants seldom followed their fathers into agriculture; instead they migrated to towns and found better wages in non-agricultural employment. This encouraged a trend towards family farms independent of outside labour, and this was reflected in farm size. While there was a steady decline in the number of small crofts, there was also a reduction in the number of really large farms. However, mechanisation and a move away from the arable crops greatly increased the size of farm which could be managed without paid labour. As a result of piecemeal amalgamations, sometimes with government 'golden handshakes', the number of agricultural holdings has declined from a maximum of 3,373 in the 1880s to a present figure of around 600,[34] and is likely to decline still farther. Once farms had been busy places: there had been big families, two or three farm servants had been employed and there had been cottar neighbours close by, but by the end of the century agriculture had become a rather solitary occupation.

One of the favourite sayings of public speakers from 1850 onwards was that 'the man who makes two blades of grass grow where only one grew before is a benefactor to the whole human race'. This self-congratulatory remark was repeated so frequently that farming audiences can hardly have thought it very original, but it probably never occurred to them to doubt its truth. These attitudes were reinforced in the post-1945 period when the experience of wartime shortages encouraged a drive for national self-sufficiency, and at the same time the country's balance of payment problems made it desirable to cut back on imports of foodstuffs and animal feed. Until the 1980s there was never any thought to produce less: successive governments controlled farming by subsidies which were designed to encourage heavier applications of fertilisers and to maximise production. A large part of the farmer's income came to depend on attending promptly to the ever-growing paperwork which accompanies these schemes. Grants for drainage encouraged the reclamation of some very marginal land which in retrospect would have been better left as grass and heather. The way subsidies are structured also influences farming practice: for example the Hill Livestock Compensatory Allowance, which is designed to assist farming in areas of difficult climatic and environmental conditions, went some way to countering the transport costs which Orkney farmers have to meet. The way it has been paid, however, encourages the breeding of cattle, whereas changes in the method of payment could make it more profitable for farmers to carry cattle through to the finishing stages. For a long time government policy showed little awareness that agricultural policy needed to address environmental issues, but a host of new factors now affect land management—over-production, environmental concerns, public access, the demand for organic food, animal welfare, diversification, global warming and energy considerations. These result in a range of new policies such as Sites of Special Scientific Interest and Set-aside Schemes. The largest landholder in Orkney is now the Royal Society for the Protection of Birds.

On Balfour Mains in Shapinsay where Thomas Balfour in the eighteenth century created some of Orkney's earliest improvements, and where David Balfour squared and drained the land with ruthless efficiency in the nineteenth century, the process was being reversed as the twentieth century drew to a close. The owner, Richard Zawadski, disposed of his breeding herd and, although he still kept store cattle and sheep and grew barley, parts of his farm were managed under habitat-creation schemes. This involves limiting grazing and managing the land without the use of fertilisers, with a view to developing a more natural vegetation and encouraging nesting birds and wild flowers. Other areas are managed as wetland by reversing the effects of drainage and encouraging flooding.[35] Orkney was one of the areas most quick to take up these schemes: already by 1995 some 33 habitat-creation schemes had been approved, and the take-up continues. Farmers accustomed to using land to produce food sometimes doubt the wisdom of these schemes—there is an uneasy feeling that taking good land out of cultivation is 'morally wrong'.[36] However, managing farmland in ways which meet environmental concerns and which enhance tourism is likely to be of increasing importance.

Despite the many successes of Orkney farming, the twentieth century ended with general pessimism about the immediate future. The BSE crisis ('mad cow disease') undermined the market for beef, and this also affected the demand for Orkney's largely grass-fed product. Cattle prices fell, and the total value of agricultural output was down from £23.3 million in 1993 to £16.2 million in 1998 (a reduction of over 30%) while at the same time

102. *Harvesting in Stenness. Large round bales of barley straw became common in the 1980s. The internationally-famous chambered cairn of Maeshowe is in the background.*

costs, especially the cost of fuel, was rising. As a result there was a drastic decline in farming incomes, and the number of people engaged in agriculture was also down.[37] A second income was increasingly necessary, and although farmers are always secretly pleased to see their sons follow them into farming, they express doubts about the wisdom of such a career move. Orcadians were bemused by the attitudes of the Countryside Alliance as represented by the English fox-hunting counties, but they also were deeply worried about farming incomes, fuel costs and the decline of rural services.

People have usually been not very good at seeing into the future. In the first half of the nineteenth century it was obvious to everyone that steamships and railways were going to have a beneficial effect on the prices of Orkney cattle—what was not foreseen was that better prices would bring about the total destruction and replacement of the familiar landscape and of old-style farming. As prices fell in the 1880s it was obvious that difficult times were ahead—what was not foreseen was that depression would result in the disappearance of Victorian 'High Farming' and that it would never return. In the early 1920s it became clear that farmers might have a chance to buy their farms—what was not foreseen was that within a decade the big estate would disappear as an economic and social institution. Throughout the twentieth century everyone has known that machinery would become more sophisticated and would take much of the physical labour out of farming—what was not foreseen was that increased efficiency would result in over-production, and that the capital cost of machinery would lead to much of the work being undertaken by contractors rather than by the farmers themselves. Despite the present pessimism about future prospects, few people contemplate a 'post-agricultural countryside', although clearly food production will in future be combined with other uses. Even when the futurologist is correct in his predictions, he is bound to be wrong about the details: the member of the Orkney Agricultural Discussion Society who in 1933 foresaw the day when 'the farmer may sit at the fireside, smoke his pipe, and press a button'[38] was right about computerised technology—but wrong about sitting around, and probably wrong about smoking a pipe!

The lesson from the past seems to be that, when trying to see into the future, the thing to do is to identify the present trends and imagine them carried farther than most people would think likely. At present 16% of Orkney's gross domestic product comes from agriculture, and this is a greater proportion than in any other Scottish county. The place which farming plays in the economy is a source of pride, but it may also be a source of vulnerability, and in future farming is likely to be relatively less important. Although the number of farms is much reduced, it seems inevitable that there will be further reduction. As Orkney competes within the increased productivity of a global market, it is important to maintain quality and to cultivate Orkney's 'clean and green' image, but other places will also strive for quality, and only so much can be achieved by image-building. We have seen in the last half century that many decisions have been taken out of the control of individual farmers, and are made in Edinburgh, London and Brussels. These policies in the future are likely to take account, not just of food production, but also of environmental and wildlife concerns. The future, however, as well as being the continuation of present trends, is certain to contain elements which will surprise us. There may, for example, be new crops which we cannot foresee, in the same way that at the beginning of the twentieth century Orkney's present reliance on silage was unimaginable. Crops as a source of fuel as well as for food may become important in the long term. There are also some hopeful signs that farming may be conducted within the context of policies which begin to take better account of the social structure of rural society. In terms of land use, it seems likely that the advance of arable land will be reversed and that pasture will be managed in a way which allows a proportion of the poorer land to revert to a more natural type of vegetation.

The Twentieth Century: War and Peace

In two World Wars the even tenor of island life has been interrupted by incidents which captured the headlines and which belong, not just to Orkney history, but to a wider stage. The circumstances surrounding Orkney's involvement with the ships of the British and German navies have generated their own extensive literature, and for a fuller account the reader is referred to other works of which W.S.Hewison's *This Great Harbour, Scapa Flow* is the most comprehensive.

It was during the war of 1812 that Longhope was first used as an assembly point for shipping bound for the Baltic and liable to attack by American privateers. Martello towers were built on either side of the entrance, and in 1866 they were reconstructed and used as Volunteer batteries.[1] But the Flow, although identified as a possible naval base, was otherwise undefended when war broke out. From 1914 to 1918 it served as the main base for the Grand Fleet and played a crucial role in blockading the northern entrances to the North Sea. It was from the Flow that the greater part of the Grand Fleet sailed out to take part in the major naval engagement of the war, the Battle of Jutland.

Less than a week after Jutland, on 5 June 1916, the cruiser *HMS Hampshire* left the Flow to convey the Minister of War, Lord Kitchener, on a mission to Russia to bolster the crumbling eastern front. A north-west gale was blowing when she struck a mine off Marwick Head, and there were only 12 survivors, although many others got ashore between Birsay and the Bay of Skaill only to perish of cold or to be dashed against the rocks of this forbidding coastline. Orkney folk were highly critical of the delay in informing local people of the disaster, and of the way in which civilians were prevented from taking part in the rescue.[2]

The sinking of the *Hampshire* was the first of a series of naval disasters involving appalling loss of life. The following year the battleship, the *Vanguard*, blew up at her moorings with the loss of all but two of her crew.[3] At the time there were rumours of sabotage, but the likely cause of the explosion was unstable cordite ammunition. Over 1,000 men were lost, a larger

103. *The* **Bayern.** *The final plunge of the* Bayern, *scuttled in Scapa Flow in June 1919.*

number than perished in the better-remembered sinking of the *Royal Oak*. Then on the night of 12-13 January 1918 when the destroyers *Narborough* and *Opal* were returning to the Flow in darkness and blizzard conditions, they ran full-tilt on to the cliffs of South Ronaldsay.[4] The sole survivor of the 180 crew members clung to a rocky ledge until he was rescued 36 hours later. Sailors in the age of the dreadnought had a poor chance of survival when their ship was lost.

When the war ended Scapa Flow served as the place of internment for the German High Seas Fleet consisting of 74 vessels, including 11 battleships and five battle-cruisers. For many British servicemen 'Bloody Orkney'[5] seemed a bleak posting, but for the disaffected and mutinous crews confined aboard German ships over the winter, Scapa was 'a place where wolves said good-night to themselves'.[6] On 21 June 1919 a party of school children out for a day excursion aboard the little steamer, the *Flying Kestrel*, witnessed the final act: that morning Admiral Ludwig von Reuter gave the order to scuttle the fleet, and the youngsters watched in amazement as one by one the great ships settled in the water, or overturned and sank with great spouts of water marking their resting places.[7] There was a good deal of self-righteous indignation about German treachery, but the world was a safer place with these ships on the sea bed. Salvage work, initially undertaken by Cox and Danks, provided a source of employment in the inter-war years,[8]

435

but many ships were never raised including the *Kronprintz Wilhelm, Markgraf* and *König*. In recent years the sunken wrecks have become an asset to a specialist branch of the tourist industry, with a number of boats catering for recreational divers.

The outbreak of the 1939-45 war once more found Scapa Flow inadequately protected, allowing the German submarine U-47 to slip past sunken blockships in Kirk Sound and to sink the battleship, the *Royal Oak*, on the night of 13-14 October 1939 with the loss of 833 lives.[9] To protect the Flow from future attack, work commenced on sealing-off its eastern entrances by the construction of the Churchill Barriers—causeways linking the islands of South Ronaldsay, Burray, Glims Holm and Lamb Holm. Overhead cableways strung across the sounds transported mesh containers filled with rubble, and these foundations were topped with massive concrete blocks and a roadway.[10] The Italian Chapel on Lamb Holm, adapted from an ordinary Nissen hut by the Italian prisoners-of-war engaged in the construction work, remains as a reminder of the time when the tiny island had a population of over 1000, and it forged a bond of friendship between Italy and Orkney which triumphed over enmity and imprisonment.[11] One result was that the once-busy fishing ports of St Mary's and Burray village were cut off from the open sea. Burray and South Ronaldsay also provide a case study of what happens to islands when they cease to be insular. Road links to the Mainland bring both islands within easy commuting distance of Kirkwall, so there are opportunities for employment and for a more varied social life. On

104. **The Derfflinger.** *Salvage work in Scapa Flow. The* Derfflinger *is brought to the surface after 20 years on the sea-bed.*

105. ***The Building of the Barriers, 1943.*** *A close-up of the tide pouring over the almost closed barrier in Kirk Sound. The bolsters filled with rubble are clearly seen minus their final cladding of concrete blocks.*

the other hand local shops, trades and services contracted in the face of more direct competition from the Mainland.[12]

Between 1914 and 1918 when the Grand Fleet was in Scapa Flow, the population was at times boosted by as many as 100,000, a number about four times greater than the resident population. Extra numbers created an insatiable demand for milk, eggs, meat and fish at prices well above what Orkney farmers and fishermen had earned in peacetime. Profits accumulated during the war were an important factor in the ability of farmers to buy their holdings when they were offered for sale in the immediate post-war years. Relations between Orkney folk and the navy were sometimes rather strained in the First World War, when high-handed naval officers were sometimes rather tactless in their dealings with civilians. However, most servicemen were aboard ship, and there were fewer contacts than in the Second World War when, in addition to the fleet, there was a huge land-based presence. The massive Scapa defences included airfields at Hatston, Skeabrae, Twatt and Grimsetter for the R.A.F. and Fleet Air Arm,[13] as well as numerous searchlight positions, anti-aircraft guns and coastal batteries.[14]

The naval base at Scapa Flow was rapidly run down after the war, and it closed entirely in 1957 as a result of naval economies.[15] Today the Flow is as empty of dreadnoughts as it is of Viking longships, yet many reminders of the wartime years are still visible. Where derelict buildings remained on a

437

106. **No.2 Barrier.** *The causeways built to shut off the eastern end of Scapa Flow following the sinking of the* Royal Oak *provide a road link to Lamb Holm, Glims Holm, Burray and South Ronaldsay. Note the remains of the 2,338 ton* MV Lycia, *built in Port Glasgow in 1924 and sunk in 1940 as a blockship.*

farmer's land he was given the choice of their removal, or else a small money payment in compensation—almost invariably farmers took the money. Temporary buildings were sometimes converted into houses by the addition of a concrete-block cladding, and even more frequently they were turned into deep-litter houses for hens. Concrete foundations and the debris of wartime structures still disfigure parts of the landscape, although half a century later, those that are left become increasingly interesting as a new generation of ancient monuments.

A portrait of life as it returned to normal after 1945 is to be found in the *Third Statistical Account.* The parish descriptions in the *Old Statistical Account*

438

(1791–8) and the *New Statistical Account* (1845) are invaluable sources, much used in previous chapters. The *Third Statistical Account* was less of a landmark, since it had to compete with the much wider range of information available in the twentieth century in official and unofficial sources. It also had a chequered history, since much of it was written in the early 1950s but published only in 1985. By then it had matured into a period piece revealing changes of attitude which come as a surprise even to people who lived through these years. The account was fortunate in its authors, such as Hugh Marwick writing about his native Rousay, John D. MacKay, the polymathic Sanday schoolmaster, and Harald Mooney, then half-way through his 50-year ministry in the parishes of St Andrews and Deerness. The picture of the post-war years which emerges is of a people who were conscious that they were more prosperous than their forebears, thanks to the encouragement which agriculture received in the post-war years, but who were also confident that a better society was emerging. It was an optimistic outlook seen at its most smug in the account of the parish if Sandwick:

> One cannot fail to note the great difference in the conversation of the folk in this parish compared to that of say forty years ago. The people are more refined and consequently adhere to that which is good and despise the base and vulgar things of life and seem ever striving to lead better lives.[16]

It is a surprising attitude: it has always been a common belief that the younger generation has an easy time and has forgotten how hard the struggle was in the old days, but there can have been few other periods which regarded the present day as morally better than the recent past. It is a view not so likely to be found at the end of the twentieth century. Yet this self-satisfied attitude was found in parish after parish. In South Ronaldsay the douce and respectable behaviour of its inhabitants was contrasted with market nights in the old days;[17] in former times great 'brousts' of ale were made ready to be retailed from neighbouring houses; feelings ran high between men from neighbouring parishes and 'hid waas a puir market if hid was no' bluid for supper that night'.[18] It was not the Victorian Age with its moral rectitude and stern values, but the more relaxed middle years of the twentieth century which saw the emergence of Orcadians as a quiet people. Most parishes commented on the rarity of drunkenness and the almost total absence of violence and crime.

This new-found respectability was a characteristic of a farming community conscious of its rising status. As owner-occupiers farmers had moved up in the world, they had struggled to pay for their farms, but postwar incomes, mechanisation and the spread of electricity into rural areas opened prospects of better living and working conditions. They were also aware of a social levelling, and the emergence of what was often described as a 'classless society'.[19] The parish was no longer dominated by land-owning gentry who expected tenants to touch their cap when the laird's gig went by, but the poorer elements of society were also much less in evidence. Tinkers and beggars were less frequently encountered, farm-labourers were few, and many of the smallest crofts had disappeared. There was a decline in fishing which farming folk at that time tended to equate with idleness and drunkenness. The rural community was becoming much more homogeneous and, although after 1950 it was consistently loyal to Liberalism, first in the person of Jo Grimond (MP 1950–83) and then of Jim Wallace (MP 1983–2001, Deputy First Minister 1998 onwards), its attitudes became distinctly less radical.

The afterglow of the Victorian evangelical and temperance movements was another influence on the character of the community. Local polls to decide whether licensed premises were to be permitted were contested with enthusiasm, but 'Dry' parishes consistently voted 'Wet'—Kirkwall in 1929, Stromness in 1947 and the last parish (Holm) in 1975.[20] In the second and third generation Victorian values had become more a matter of social conformity than personal conviction. Although 'God-fearing and law-abiding',[21] post-war Orkney gradually became less of a church-going community. The *Third Statistical Account* reported that 'the popular feeling seems to be that good Christian living is not necessarily the same thing as regular church attendance'. Whereas nineteenth century evangelicals had blamed the poor state of religion on the philosophical preaching and want of fire of eighteenth century Moderates, there was now a reversal of attitudes: the 'emotional excesses' of nineteenth century ministers were seen as the cause of a wary attitude to organised religion—'by nature the Orcadian abhors a strong display of emotional fervour' and prefers 'reason'. [22] St Magnus Cathedral remains well attended, but country congregations are usually very small, and new sects such as Jehovah's Witnesses have a growing following.

Despite the general satisfaction at rising standards in the early 1950s, the quality of rural housing was often poor. Financially-pressed estates had spent nothing on tenants' houses, and after 1918 it was no longer possible to build cottages for profitable renting. When tenants bought their farms there were loans to be repaid and investment was required in new barns, byres and stables. The popular saying, 'it's the outside which keeps the inside going', was used to excuse the poor state of housing. The unsatisfactory state of housing, however, was relative. A decline in family size had alleviated overcrowding, and people were no longer living in the incredible conditions described by Walter Traill Dennison, who gave evidence to the Napier Commission about the family consisting of a married couple and their six children who inhabited a one-roomed cottage measuring fourteen feet by ten and,

107. ***Shore Street, Kirkwall.*** *Damage to the Kirkwall water-front after the great gale of February 1953. The picturesque houses of Shore Street were demolished before urban renewal became fashionable.*

by a feat of organisational ingenuity, all contrived to sleep in a single box-bed.[23] Generally the traditional linear house with inter-connecting dwelling house and byre had been somewhat modified.[24] As early as 1870 the fire in the middle of the floor had virtually disappeared, often by retaining the hearth and building a chimney and partition dividing the *but-house* into two parts, the *in-bye,* or kitchen-living room, and the *oot-bye* or scullery, while the cattle, if still housed in the same building, at least entered by a separate door. By 1870 plastered walls and wallpaper were common, even in quite humble cottages,[25] and the *ben-end,* when not required for extra sleeping accommodation, became a musty haven of respectability with sombre, heavy furniture, a few books, and perhaps pictures of royalty. It was little-used except on special occasions and when the minister visited.

Despite these improvements houses more often than not lacked basic amenities. Just after the First World War, when Ernest Marwick's father erected a sentry-box-like earth closet, neighbours considered it to be a some-what fanciful and unnecessary extravagance.[26] Even in 1951 one-third of the rural population still lived in one or two-roomed houses, 55% of houses were without a piped water supply, 77% lacked a flush toilet, and 82% were without a bath.[27] Dampness was a common problem, often resulting from earth which had accumulated against the outer walls to a depth of several feet. Houses in Kirkwall and Stromness were better provided with ameni-ties, but many of them were unsatisfactory in other ways. The Medical Officer of Health was scathing in his comments on housing in Shore Street, Main Street and Burgar's Bay, 'an unsavoury recess'[28] off Wellington Street; such housing ought to be 'absolutely condemned and wiped out'.[29] Unfortunately in the case of the picturesque houses of Shore Street, this advice was followed to the letter, and the whole area was demolished before urban renewal became fashionable.

In the immediate post-1945 period government grants and profits from agriculture were used to improve houses, many of them now built from concrete blocks rather than from traditional materials. The advent of oil stimulated another round of house-building in the 1970s. The increasing tendency to live in the country and commute to Kirkwall resulted in the appearance in the 1980s and 1990s of large suburban-type houses in the countryside, while traditional buildings which blended better with the landscape were allowed to fall derelict. House-building peaked in 1994, then declined significantly in the less prosperous final years of the century.[30] Rural communities were quick to take advantage of electrification, many houses already using generators in advance of a mains supply. Housewives soon purchased cookers, irons and vacuum cleaners; later they acquired immersion heaters, washing machines and eventually deep-freezes. Enchantress and Victoress stoves, which had been the height of sophistication in the 1870s, were consigned to the past, as were Tilley and Aladdin lamps. But housing shortages remained, especially in Kirkwall where the Council was slow to appreciate the scale of house building which was required. Twenty-five years after the war had ended a large population remained housed in temporary wartime huts at the former Hatston airfield. It was only with the building of Alcatraz-like housing schemes at Papdale and Meadowbank in the 1970s that the housing shortage was alleviated.

For much of the twentieth century the constant background was a depressing sense of the inevitability of depopulation (Fig.81). Perversely a melancholy nostalgia for older and busier days became one of the attractions of island communities, not so much for the inhabitants themselves, but for those who viewed them from far off. The population reached a peak of 32,225 in 1861 and thereafter followed a downward trend for the next 110 years, reaching a low-point of 17,077 in 1971. The 'Great Emigration' had more to do with the 'pull' of new lands overseas than with the 'push' of a hard life at home. Indeed the rate of emigration seemed to be scarcely affected by the state of the Orkney economy: there was net emigration of 4,190 between 1861 and 1871, a decade of unprecedented prosperity when new crofts were still being created and employment could readily be found, whereas an almost identical number (4,260) left between 1881 and 1891 when agriculture had entered a period of depression.[31] Much of the early emigration was

108. *The* **St Ola I.** *The* St Ola *was built in 1892 and served on the Pentland Firth run between Stromness and Scrabster for nearly 60 years including the two wars.*

to the United States, where emigrants were sufficiently numerous to have their own newspaper, the *Orkney & Shetland American*. In 1889 the editor conducted a survey of emigrants, collecting 3,000 names, and he estimated that as many again had not replied to his questionnaire.[32] The great nineteenth century diaspora left families scattered throughout the world. For example, when the tenant of Ronaldsvoe, South Ronaldsay, died in 1914, his eldest son was in America, a second son was in Australia, a third son was in South Africa, and a fourth son was in Glasgow, and none of them were interested in succeeding to the South Ronaldsay croft. Even after 1945 when rural incomes were improving, the perception of city life was still of 'easy work and short hours'; it was 'relatively easy to earn a living in towns without fear of unemployment or want'.[33] The drain was also the result of large numbers of young people entering Further and Higher Education and qualifying themselves for careers which were scarce or non-existent in Orkney. In the latter part of the twentieth century the situation was rather different: unemployment rates in Orkney were a good deal lower than in the cities, and the quality of life was generally perceived to be better.

The long decline of the 'Great Emigration' bottomed out in 1971. Numbers have subsequently increased to 19,480 in the year 2000 and, with the stemming of depopulation, the sense of inevitable decay has been lifted. Yet depopulation continues unabated in many of the North Isles: Papa Westray contains only 22% of the population which existed at its nineteenth century maximum, and in Eday a mere 18% remain.[34] Sustaining a viable level of

443

population is vital to island communities. An island population of less than 50 is unlikely to have much in the way of a structured community; numbers around 200 can sustain the basic provision of a primary school, doctor, nurse, shop, community hall, church and minister, and can provide occasional opportunities for wage employment. Above a population of 200, secondary education becomes a possibility, as on Westray, Stronsay, Sanday and Hoy, and numbers are sufficient for a greater range of trades and services. Island life benefited from the replacement of the ancient *Earl Sigurd* and *Earl Thorfinn* by the *Orcadia* and *Islander*,[35] but an even greater improvement came in the 1990s when the Orkney Islands Shipping Company introduced roll-on roll-off services. Islanders had easier contact with the Mainland, it was easier to provide services to islands, schoolchildren could travel home at weekends, and people even began to commute to work from the more accessible islands (Shapinsay, Longhope, Flotta and Rousay).

An important factor in the halting of population decline was the discovery of large reserves of oil in the Piper Field in 1973 and the Claymore Field in 1974. Oil from these, and eight smaller associated fields, is brought ashore by means of a 135-mile pipeline. Occidental Oil Company's preferred landfall was Scapa Flow, although the island of Flotta was not their first choice as the site for a terminal. While Orkney struggled to comprehend the scale of the development, there was a good deal of concern about the effect which such a large and rich industry might have on the Orkney economy and way of life, and this played a part in the choice of the Flotta site.[36] Flotta wages were legendary (as were the quality and quantity of its canteen food), but 25 years later the terminal no longer employs so many people or pays them so much. There has been a modest decline in the amount of crude oil which passes through the terminal (about 10 million metric tonnes in 1998). In addition, shuttle-tankers handling Foinaven oil account for a further 2.7 million tonnes.[37]

Another reason for the reversing of population decline was that losses from emigration came to be balanced by inward migration. Hitherto the flow of population was predominantly outwards, although it was never entirely one way. At the time when common land was divided, some Aberdeenshire crofters bought blocks of cheap land which they reclaimed as a means of making the first step up the farming ladder. Immigrants were more often professional people—ministers in the eighteenth century, schoolteachers in the nineteenth, and doctors and civil servants in the twentieth century. Orkney was accustomed to this type of immigrant, and they were fairly readily accepted provided they did not try to apply the standards of middle class city life and consider themselves to be a cut above ordinary folk. But most Orcadians had an instinctive ability to switch from dialect to standard English when addressing incomers, showing that at a subconscious level the distinction between *ferrylouper* and native-born was never forgotten.

In the 1970s immigrants of a different type began to arrive in considerable numbers. Sometimes they were looking for an entry into farming, of which they seldom had much experience, and when they were deterred by land prices farther south, they took on rundown crofts from which Orcadians would hesitate to attempt to earn a living. Even more families were 'urban refugees' in search of a country environment which they perceived to be 'peaceful, quiet, friendly and safe'.[38] By the 1981 census there were 1,500 people born in England and Wales, about six times as many as there had been 50 years earlier. Immigration of this kind has been particularly marked in the North Isles, and in Egilsay the replacement of the small native population has been complete.

The society which these immigrants entered was remarkably stable. In 1931 over 90% of the population had been born in Orkney. Most people lived in little communities whose members knew each other from childhood and were often related by ties of kinship resulting, not necessarily in amicable relations, but at least in a comprehension of each other's idiosyncrasies. It is interesting to note how the *Third Statistical Account* of Eday (1957) used the term 'incomer': the term was not restricted to non-Orcadians but was applied to those farmers who had moved from other places in the North Isles. There was no memory of Scots immigration into Eday, and the inhabitants imagined themselves to be 'of real old Norse stock'. The writer was unable to find a single instance of an islander who had brought a Scots bride back home—marriage to an outsider inevitably led to emigration.[39] Even on the Mainland and not far from Kirkwall something of the same stability prevailed: in Orphir in 1952 only one-third of the families had originated from other Orkney parishes in the previous 50 years.[40] Perhaps some of these communities were more self-contained than they had been 200 years earlier when shipping and fishing interests had resulted in greater mobility.

The result was a society where new immigrants were courteously received, but where proper integration was difficult. A visiting Canadian sociologist who arrived in Rousay to study the problems of depopulation quickly discovered that the really interesting problem was not emigration but immigration. She found 'a reservoir of mutual misunderstanding'; incomers often failed to appreciate the harsher realities of island life, while the very quality of life which had attracted them in the first place was seen by the islanders to be under threat from their presence. Despite an apparent desire for a country life, immigrants brought with them urban expectations and values. The native population regarded incomers as feckless, pushing and quarrelsome, while in turn the new settlers failed to understand the informal and leisurely process of leadership and decision-making in a traditional society, and so they regarded the natives as backward and unenterprising.[41] Some

20 years later the two groups have settled into a more comfortable relationship. While there is still an ever-changing population of incomers who become disillusioned by island life and leave Orkney after a short time, there are others who have settled permanently in the islands. Eventually their English accents are no longer even noticed, and they become thoroughly accepted as part of the Orkney scene.

There had never been a time when Orkney had been immune from outside influence. Girls who wore mini-skirts in the 1960s despite the rigours of Orkney winters, or who adopt styles appropriate to southern California when a north wind is blowing up Bridge Street, are no different in their adherence to fashion from the eighteenth century gentlemen who wore wigs even when travelling in the North Isles.[42] In the twentieth century, however, outside influences became much more all-pervasive through the influence of newspapers, the telegraph and telephone, then radio, the cinema and television, with the result that once-isolated communities are becoming internationalised.

Links with the Scottish mainland were provided for more than a century by the North of Scotland, Orkney and Shetland Steam Navigation Company whose 'north boats', latterly the *St Magnus* and *St Ninian*, provided weekly round trips from Leith to Aberdeen, Kirkwall and Lerwick.[43] In the 1960s there was a sharp decline in passenger traffic as a result of what for a time were relatively cheap air fares. The steamers were filled with tourists in summer but empty in winter and the service was withdrawn, leaving Kirkwall harbour a deserted place, and for a time severing links with Shetland. With the ending of the Aberdeen link, external communications were channelled through the other route, the crossing of the Pentland Firth from Stromness to Scrabster. Improvements to the A9 and the acquisition of a third and fourth *St Ola*, both roll-on roll-off vessels much larger than their uncomfortable predecessors, brought about an increase of traffic on this route. Any delay in the daily arrival of large container lorries carried aboard the *Ola* now causes immediate shortages on the shelves of Kirkwall's supermarkets. The numbers of passengers and the number of cars showed a 50% increase between 1990 and 1998, and yet the number of tourists has not shown the same increase.[44] High fuel costs, exorbitant air fares, and an unfavourable rate of exchange for foreign visitors, all create difficulties for hotels and bed and breakfast establishments. At the beginning of the twenty-first century there is also a freight link with Invergordon, and plans for the transfer of the main shipping services from P & O to Northlink offers prospects of an improved service on the Scrabster, Aberdeen and Shetland routes.

Air services commenced in 1931 with Captain Fresson's Highland Airways' Rapides. In 1933 he obtained a contract to deliver the *Scotsman* on the day of publication, and in 1934 he secured the mail contract.[45] In postwar years British Airways and more recently Loganair have provided links with Aberdeen, Edinburgh, Wick, Inverness and Glasgow, but at fares which cost more than flying the Atlantic. Captain Fresson also pioneered inter-island services in pre-war years, and in 1967 this service was revived by Loganair. It is a service which thrives on carrying businessmen and officials who need to make a quick visit, and the specialist teachers who fly to island schools.

Throughout much of the nineteenth century certain parts of the Mainland were just as isolated as islands and relied just as much on sea transport. For example, the little Rousay steamer, the *Lizzie Burroughs,* from 1876 onwards served, not only the islands of Rousay, Egilsay, Wyre and Gairsay, but also called at Aikerness, Evie, Tingwall and Rendall en route for Kirkwall.[46] Following Acts of Parliament in 1857 and 1867 rapid progress was made in the construction of a road network. The coming of horse-drawn vans, coaches, bus services and private cars did much to break down the distinction between town and country. At the same time the concept of the parish as a self-contained community began to disappear. Most parishes at one time had their own market with a frequency varying from two meetings a year to one a month, but increasing mobility led to the abandonment of these local markets between 1920 and 1930.[47] Older people who remembered sending 12 miles or more to fetch a doctor by horse, or chartering a steamer in an emergency, were very conscious of the advantages of telephones, cars and the air ambulance service, but they still found it strange that young people sought their social life outside the parish and could take off in cars and buses to attend concerts and dances at the other end of the island.

Orkney at the end of the twentieth century enjoyed a vigorous social life with little sense of being an isolated community or a cultural backwater. Highlights of the year are the August round of agricultural shows and the Christmas and New Year Ba' games in the streets of Kirkwall. Ample variety is provided by the activities of Young Farmer's Clubs, Rural Institutes, sport, and all kinds of clubs and societies. Amateur drama flourishes, and music-making is popular both in schools and in the community. The St Magnus Festival in Kirkwall and the Pier Arts Centre in Stromness provide high-points in the Arts. A culture which reflects the Orkney identity is to be found in the internationally known poetry and prose of Edwin Muir (1887–1952), Eric Linklater (1899–1974), and George Mackay Brown (1921–1996) and in the music of Sir Peter Maxwell Davis. Sometimes one wonders by what quirk such a small society consistently produces these rare figures of imagination and genius.

In the nineteenth century Scandinavian countries sought their identity in their peasant roots and their Norse past. An offshoot of this movement was represented by Alfred Johnston (1859–1947) who founded the Viking Club (now the Viking Society for Northern Research) and continued to manage its affairs for 50 years. Joseph Storer Clouston (1870–1944) was a historian whose scholarship and whose infectious enthusiasm made his *History of Orkney* (1932) one of the most admired Orkney books. Hugh Marwick (1885–1965) was headmaster of Kirkwall Grammar School, Director of Education, and a magisterial scholar, author of *The Orkney Norn* and *Orkney Farm-names*. Ernest Marwick (1915–77) was a writer whose unassuming manner and lucid writing style concealed an unrivalled knowledge of Orkney's history and folklore. In the general public there is a widespread interest in the past, and a recognition of its importance as an extra dimension of identity; schools succeed in communicating this enthusiasm to their pupils. There is a seemingly unending stream of books about Orkney, many published locally, an excellent library and archive with good local collections, a weekly newspaper, the *Orcadian* (founded 1854), a magazine, the *Orkney View*, and a local radio station which broadcasts every morning and evening, often in the infectious intonations of the Orkney dialect. Yet dialect is not in a healthy state—its vocabulary is continually diluted and its grammar ignored. The days are long gone when schools suppressed dialect as a matter of deliberate policy yet, despite an *Orkney Dictionary* and other material designed for use in schools, it seems likely that schools will be no more successful in preserving dialect than they once were in trying to abolish it.

In the nineteenth century local government in Orkney, as elsewhere in Scotland, was in the hands of the Commissioners of Supply. Since the Commissioners were non-elected, and membership depended on the ownership of land worth £100 scots per annum, the Commissioners were the political expression of a landlord-dominated society. The property qualification, however, was modest and the number of Commissioners was quite large, rising from 35 in 1731 to 112 in the early nineteenth century, before declining to 70 in 1869.[48] Much smaller numbers usually turned up to conduct county business which was relatively uncomplicated, consisting of the gathering of *cess* (national taxation), the levying of *rogue money* to apprehend and prosecute criminals, and the collection of a rate to finance asylums and prisons. A proliferation of Boards and committees independent of the Commissioners of Supply developed such as Parochial Boards (1845) to administer Poor Relief, and School Boards (1872) to manage the schools of each parish. School Boards generally were effective in building the new schools which universal education required, but occasionally were diverted from their main purposes as, for example, when the Rousay School Board became the battleground between General Burroughs and the crofters he had evicted.[49] The creation of County Councils in 1889 reformed this untidy structure and placed it under democratic control, but the first County Council generated little enthusiasm. Interest continues to be sporadic and in a small community where few put themselves forward for election the quality of candidates is often not high. Many seats are uncontested, and public disaffection frequently results in the sitting Councillor being defeated if he or she is opposed. The Authority has a thoroughly justified pride in its ownership and upkeep of St Magnus Cathedral, but is unlikely ever to initiate any project of similar grandeur and imagination—and Councillors would be voted out by a horrified electorate if they suggested any such scheme.

One issue which provoked a vigorous campaign was the fear that Orkney might be amalgamated with Highland Region as a result of the Wheatley Committee's proposals for the reform of local government. Vocal opposition in both Orkney and Shetland, and the harassment of Willie Ross, Secretary of State for Scotland, when he toured the islands, won 'Island Authority' status in 1975.[50] Orcadians were reasonably satisfied with the outcome: the town councils of Kirkwall and Stromness were abolished, and a single-tier Authority carried out most of the functions which on the Scottish mainland were the responsibility of both Regional and District Councils. As long as this two-tier system prevailed, the small Island Authorities had to cope with bureaucratic structures appropriate to the much bigger Regions and Districts on the Scottish mainland, but sometimes they had the advantage that they could take quicker decisions and retain a more personal touch.

Being elected on a non-party basis, Councillors maintain a sturdy independence free from the restrictions of a party-line. Most electors approve of this independence, but the obverse is a certain unpredictability, an over-involvement with trivia and, most seriously, a lack of consistent direction. Individual Councillors tackle immediate problems with enthusiasm, but often lack tried-and-tested policies to allow them to do more than snap at the heels of their officials (which they do with great gusto). One scheme which ended in expensive failure was the Council's plan to develop a short-sea car ferry from Burwick in South Ronaldsay to Gills Bay in Caithness.

When it comes to predicting what lies ahead history can make only a limited contribution. A warning against predicting the future is to be found in the experience of the writer of the *Third Statistical Account* of Flotta who, a few years before the oil was discovered, was unlucky enough to head his final paragraph 'The Future'. Not only the coming of oil but much else in Orkney's economic history suggests that unpredictability is a recurring factor. The rise and sudden collapse of kelp and linen, the wartime activity in Scapa Flow, and the unexpected collapse of the egg industry all suggest that change rather than continuity is likely to be the pattern. In the previous chapter it was predicted that agriculture will probably play a smaller part in the economy, and that it will employ fewer people. This need not produce an empty countryside, since living in the country and working in the towns is becoming an increasingly common pattern.

We may also see changes in the advantages and limitations of Orkney's location. In the first phase of the Industrial Revolution Orkney diversified into kelp, linen, straw-plaiting, fishing, whaling and service with the Hudson's Bay Company, and perhaps this degree of diversification will return. The advent of steam-driven machinery caused industry to locate in large factories on coalfield sites, causing the tide of activity to retreat from Orkney. These sites, however, no longer have the same advantages. Industry is nowadays more likely to be attracted by human resources, by the facilities which a community can offer, and by inducements stemming from the policies of government and the European Union. With some new occupations, especially those using information technology, one location is literally as good as any other, and the drawbacks of remoteness no longer apply. Nevertheless for most industries the high cost of transport remains a major disincentive to locating in Orkney.

There are two ways of looking at Orkney's position. On the one hand Orkney can be envisaged as being at the farthest extremity of a very long line stretching south to the Scottish Parliament in Edinburgh, and beyond to successively remote seats of power in Westminster, Brussels and Strasbourg. But the end-of-the-line is not the only model. In Viking times Orkney lay at the centre of a web of communications reaching out to the Hebrides and Ireland, to Shetland, Faroe, Iceland and beyond, as well as to Norway, Denmark, Scotland and England. Today some of these places are more difficult to reach by public transport than they were in a Viking longship. The twinning of Orkney with Hordaland, the activities of the Orkney-Norway Friendship Society, the re-establishment of better links with Shetland are all small steps in breaking free of the 'end-of-the-line' mentality, and rediscovering the opportunities of a central position in the northern world.

Measurement of Land

Urisland, uresland, eyrisland, ounceland: (1) a small district used for taxation and administrative purposes (2) a district forming a sub-division of a parish.

Pennyland: one-eighteenth of an urisland, being a unit used mainly to define proportionate shares and obligations.

Mark: a unit used for most transactions involving land (but not payment of skat). Originally the mark was the amount of land which could be bought for 1 mark of money (= £⅔). Later the mark was somewhat variable. There were most commonly 3 or 4 marks in a pennyland.

Skatland: one-quarter of an urisland = 4½ pennylands.

Plank: (1) a consolidated block of land (2) an area 40 fathoms square = an approximation to the Scots acre. *To plank:* to consolidate run-rig by creating planks.

Weights and Measures

24 marks = 1 setten
6 settens or lispunds = 1 meil
24 meils = 1 last

Span: an archaic unit approximately equal to 5 lispunds.
Chalder: an old Scottish unit of dry measure containing 15 bolls.

Notes
1. The setten was used to measure grain. The lispund, which was the same weight, was used to measure butter.
2. In 1826 the meil was legally defined as 177 lbs 12 oz., thus the mark was 0.56 kg., the setten 13.44 kg., the meil 80.65 kg., and the last 1,935.5 kg. All weights had been much less in earlier times.
3. Weights were further complicated by the use of two weigh-bars. Weights on the *bere-pundlar* were two-thirds of those on the *malt pundlar* (see H.Marwick, 'Old-time Weights and Measures').

Glossary

Admiralty: a legal jurisdiction over maritime matters including wreck and piracy.

Auld Bow: (1) an inner dyke surrounding the central part of a township (2) the area enclosed by that dyke.

Auld Earldom: (1) the lands which the Earls of Orkney held from the King of Norway (in contrast to their personal or 'conquest' lands) (2) Sometimes applied in a more restricted sense to the skat-paying part of these lands (in contrast to the 'bordland').

Backs: areas of rough grass within the hill-dyke, usually located on the periphery of a township.

Bailie Court: a parish or island court with powers delegated by the Sheriff (or Steward) to deal with agricultural management, petty crime, weights and measures, and the maintenance of a watch against invasion.

Bismar: a weigh-beam.

Bordland: the principal farms of the Earls of Orkney, identifiable by immunity from skat payments.

Bu: a large farm; a single farm (as opposed to a multi-tenanted run-rig township).

Cess: Scottish tax (assessment).

Common grazing: land used in common (but not necessarily owned in common).

Commonty: an area of rough land deemed to be owned in common by the proprietors of the adjacent arable land.

Conquest land: land acquired by its owner other than by inheritance, for example by purchase; more specifically the lands so acquired by Earl William Sinclair (1434-1470).

Cottar: a sub-tenant given a house and a small area of land in return for labour services.

Croft: (1) a small farm held directly from the landowner (2) a small farm defined as a croft by the 1886 Crofters' Act, the main stipulation being that it paid a rent of less than £30 per annum.

Crofters' Commission: the land court established by the 1886 Crofters' Act, its main powers being to set fair rents and to cancel arrears.

Davach: a land unit resembling the urisland found in the north of Scotland (but not in Orkney).

Earldom Estate: see: bordland, auld earldom, conquest, kingsland.

Feu: an agreement which gave perpetual occupancy of a property to the feuar in return for an annual payment (the feu duty).

Forcop: a skat paid at highly variable rates calculated in 'pennies' and paid in 'pennyworths'.

Goding: a principal members of the earl's *hird*.

Goodman: one of 'the best men' or men of highest social standing; a member of the Lawting.

Hawk-hens (halk-hens): a skat payment of hens made to the royal falconer (paid by individual houses at irregular rates).

Hill-dyke: the dyke (= stone or turf wall) which separated the in-bye land from the hill grazing or common.

Hird: the bodyguard or privileged group which formed the entourage of the king or earl.

Impignoration: the act of pledging or pawning; more specifically the transactions of 1468-9 when Orkney and Shetland were pledged by Christian I for the balance of his daughter's dowry.

Kelp: ashes or fused slag produced by the incineration of seaweed and valued for its alkali or iodine content (not properly used for the seaweed itself).

Kenning: a descriptive phrase used as a literary device in Norse poetry instead of the name of a person, animal, object etc.

Kingsland: land 'belonging to the king', often identified in rentals by the term 'pro rege'. Although at one time *kingsland* was assumed to be the Norwegian Crown estates, the term was actually used to refer to land which belonged to the Scottish Crown after 1470, and so included the former earldom.

Kirklands: lands pertaining to individual churches, chapels or prebends (often in contrast to the bishopric estate which pertained to the bishop).

Laird: a landowner of a tenanted estate. *Peedie laird:* ('small landowner', *petty udaller*) owner-occupier of a small property.

Lawman: the chief magistrate whose function also included the presidency of the Lawting.

Lawrightman (1) a member of the Lawting with powers to act under the direction of the Lawman as a magistrate in less important cases (2) a member of a parish Bailie Court (later usage).

Lawting: the head court, particularly its summer sitting.

Leidang: the Norwegian naval levy.

Ley: land left uncultivated either because it is untenanted or as part of a crop rotation.

Mark: the smallest denomination of Orkney weight: see 'Weights and Measures' (2) a unit of currency = £⅔ (3) a unit of land value, originally the land which was worth one mark of money: see 'Measurement of Land'.

Meadow skift, kappaskyft: a system whereby sections of meadow cut for hay changed hands each year.

Odal: see udal.

On ca': ('on call') a system whereby cottars were required to provide labour services often of an ill-defined nature.

Perambulation: the inspection, measurement and re-allocation of run-rig land.

Pennyworths: a scale of payments expressed in money but actually paid in produce. The main rates were: 1 lispund of butter = 4 pennies, 1 meil of bere = 4 pennies, 1 meil of malt = 6 pennies, and 1 meil of flesh = 6 pennies.

Prebend: an ecclesiastical endowment commonly intended for the service of an altar dedicated to a saint. *Prebendary:* the priest who provided the service and received the income from the endowment.

Pundlar: a weigh-beam.

Quoy: a field or small enclosure.

Quoyland: a technical term for land which had been recently reclaimed and was not liable to skat.

Ranselman: a member of the parish or island Bailie Court empowered to 'ransel', to search for stolen property.

Roithmen: Councillors; members of the Lawting.

Rikest men: 'best men or Goodmen'; members of the Lawting.

Run-rig: a system of holding land in scattered and intermingled shares, which were liable to periodic redistribution.

Shead: a block of arable land containing a number of rigs.

Skat: a payment in butter, malt, meat, poultry and sometimes money, made by both owners of property and by tenants of the earldom and bishopric estates.

Skatland: (1) land which was subject to skat (2) the overseas lands belonging to the Norwegian king (3) one-quarter of an ounceland (urisland) = 4½ pennylands.

Skatfaa: the confiscation of property for failure to pay skat.

Skat merts: a skat payment of slaughtered cattle at the rate of one per urisland.

Stent: the part of the butter skat paid in butter (in contrast to the remainder paid in 'pennyworths').

Steward, Steward-depute: the Sheriff.

Sysselman: a Norwegian royal official, originally acting alongside Harald Maddadsson and John I, and later found as governor at times when there was no earl.

Tack: a lease. *Tacksman:* the holder of a lease, particularly the person who paid the King of Scots a fixed sum for the right to collect rent and other revenue from land which had once belonged to the Earl or Bishop of Orkney.

Teind: tithe, a church tax.

Toft: house site and immediate surrounds.

Township: a community of farmers grouped together by common agricultural practices, for example by farming in run-rig or making use of common grazings.

Townsland: run-rig land (in contrast to 'tunmal').

Tunmal: (1) land adjacent to the house site and toft, regarded as being attached to it rather than held in run-rig (2) a recent enclosure similarly attached to a farm and not held in run-rig (3) more generally, a field.

Udal Land: privately owned land originally characterised by being held by unwritten right and being divisible among heirs.

Wattle: a payment of one pennyworth per pennyland, originally deriving from the obligation to provide food and accommodation to the earl, his followers and officials.

Notes to the Text

Chapter One
Pictish Orkney
Notes to pp.1-23

1. H.Marwick, 'Antiquarian Notes on Sanday', 22.
2. G.Marwick, *The Old Roman Plough*, 12.
3. Jakobsen, *The Dialect and Place-names of Shetland*, 66; Waugh, 'Place-name Evidence for Scandinavian Settlement in Shetland'.
4. Historia Norvegiae, *ESSH* 1, 330-1.
5. Foster, *Picts, Gaels and Scots*, 17-18.
6. Foster, *Picts, Gaels and Scots*, 17.
7. Brøgger, *Ancient Emigrants*, 66-7.
8. Smith, *Howe*, 140, 149, 152; Buteaux, *Settlements at Skaill*, 237.
9. Smith, *Howe*, 159.
10. Graham-Campbell and Batey, *Vikings in Scotland*, 18-23.
11. Hawkes, *Pytheas*.
12. Rivet and Smith, *Place-names of Roman Britain*, 434, 469.
13. Nicoaisen, 'Scandinavians and Celts in Caithness', 84-5.
14. Rivet and Smith, *Place-names of Roman Britain*; Nicolaisen, 'Scandinavians and Celts in Caithness'.
15. Wallace, *Description of Orkney*, 87; *OSA* Shapinsay: Johnston, 'The Romans in Orkney and Shetland'.
16. Smith, *Howe*, 287-8; Hedges, *Bu, Gurness and the Brochs of Orkney*, Part 2, 311; *RCAHMS* 2, No.406.
17. Childe, *Skara Brae*.
18. Wainwright, *The Problem of the Picts*, 1-5.
19. Dumville, 'A Note on the Picts in Orkney'.
20. Sommerfelt, 'On the Norse Form of the Name of the Picts'.
21. Nicolaisen, *Scottish Place-names*, 149-172; Nicolaisen, *The Picts and their Place-names*.
22. Rhys, 'The Inscriptions and Language of the Northern Picts'; Jackson, 'The Pictish Language' in Wainwright, *The Problem of the Picts*.
23. Forsyth, 'The Ogham-inscribed Spindle Whorl from Buckquoy'; Forsyth, 'Language in Pictland'; Forsyth, 'The Case against Non-Indo-European Pictish'.
24. De Situ Albanie, *ESSH* 1, cxv-cxix.
25. *Adomnán's Life of Columba*, 166-7.
26. *Adomnán's Life of Columba*, 189.
27. Duncan, *Scotland; the Making of the Kingdom*, 43.
28. Annals of Ulster, *ESSH* 1, 86.
29. Tigernach Annals, *ESSH* 1, 191.
30. Annals of Ulster, *ESSH* 1, 190.
31. Annals of Ulster, *ESSH* 1, 212.
32. Tigernach Annals, *ESSH* 1, 226;
33. *ECMS* 2, Fig.230b.
34. *ECMS* 2, 26. Figs.22 and 23.
35. Brand, *Brief Description*, 21-2; Barry, *History*, 85-6.
36. Geoffrey of Monmouth, *History of the Kings of Britain*, 277; *SAEC*, 12n., 13n.
37. *The Annals of Clonmacnoise*, s.a.717 AD.
38. *RCAMS* 2, 5 and Fig.57.
39. Ritchie, 'The Archaeological Evidence of Daily Life', 22.
40. Thomson, 'The Ladykirk Stone'.
41. Thomson, 'The Ladykirk Stone'.
42. Smith, *Howe*, 149; Buteux, *Settlements at Skaill*, 237.
43. Scott, 'The Celtic Church in Orkney'.
44. H.Marwick, *Orkney Farm-names*, 1.
45. MacQuarrie, *The Saints of Scotland*, 50-73.
46. *Adomnán's Life of Columba*, 166-7.
47. *Adomnán's Life of Columba*, 206-7.
48. Historia Norvegiae, *ESSH* 1, 330-1.
49. RCAHMS 3, No.1734; Scott, 'The Celtic Church in Orkney', 47.
50. Islendingabók, *ESSH* 1, 340; Jóhannesson, *Íslendinga saga*, 3-11.
51. Bell and Dickson, 'Excavations at Warebeth'.
52. Liber de Mensura Orbis Terrarum, *ESSH* 1, 341.
53. Fordun, 41.

54. *OS*, c.29-30.
55. *OS*, c.42, 44, 52.
56. Thomson, *1492 Rental*, xix.
57. Foster, *Picts, Gaels and Scots*, 90.
58. Skene, *Celtic Scotland* 1, 277-8 and 2, 229-232.
59. Kirby, 'Bede and the Pictish Church'; *Curadán, Boniface and the Early Church at Rosemarkie*.
60. Veitch, 'The Columban Church in Northern Britain', 636-9.
61. Henderson, *The Picts*, 124-6.
62. Lamb, 'Papil, Picts and Papar'; Lamb, 'Carolingian Orkney and its Transformation'; Lamb, 'Pictland, Northumbria and the Carolingian Empire'.
63. It might be thought unlikely that the distinction between 'kirk' and 'chapel' would survive language changes from Pictish to Norse to Scots. The distinction is, however, necessary to Lamb's theory since it allows him to discard St Peter 'chapels' on the Brough of Birsay, Holm, Swona and Muckle Skerry which do not fit easily into his proto-parish network.
64. *RCAHMS* , No.810; *ECMS* 2, 20-1.
65. Lamb, 'Pictland, Northumbria and the Carolingian Empire', 44.
66. H.Marwick, 'Antiquarian Notes on Papa Westray', 33-4.
67. *OS*, c.111.
68. Brand, *Brief Description*, 87; *NSA* Westray.
69. Lowe, *St Boniface Church*; Marwick, 'Antiquarian Notes on Papa Westray'.
70. Lamb, 'Papil, Picts, and Papar', 22.
71. *Bede's Ecclesiastical History* 2, c.4; Mac-Quarrie, *The Saints of Scotland*, 2-3, 216-8.
72. *RCAHMS* 3, No.1266.
73. Smith, *Howe*.
74. Ritchie, 'Excavations at Buckquoy'; Ritchie, 'Birsay around AD 800'.
75. Buteux, *Settlements at Skaill*.
76. Small et al., *St.Ninian's Isle and its Treasure*.
77. Graham-Campbell, 'A Lost Pictish Treasure'.
78. Curle, *Pictish and Norse Finds from the Brough of Birsay*.

Chapter Two
***Orkneyinga Saga* and the Early Jarls**
Notes to pp.24-39

1. Taylor, *Orkneyinga Saga*, 33-109.
2. *OS* c.4; *Heimskringa*, Harald Fairhair's saga c.22, St Olaf's saga, c.99.
3. Annals of Ulster, *ESSH*, Vol.1, 255.
4. *ESSH*, Vol.1, 255-7.
5. Andersen, *Samlingen av Norge*, 79-83.
6. *Eyrbyggja saga*, c.1.
7. *Laxdæla saga*, c.2.
8. *Landnámabók*, c.13.
9. *OS*, c.5; *Laxdæla saga*, c.4.
10. Wars of the Irish with the Foreigners, *ESSH* 1, 276.
11. Annals of Ulster, *ESSH* 1, 279.
12. Ó Corráin, 'The Vikings in Scotland and Ireland in the Ninth Century'.
13. *OS*, c.5.
14. *Heimskringla*, Harald Fairhair's saga, c.22.
15. St Olaf's saga, c.99.
16. Shetelig, *Viking Antiquities*, part 1, 25; Harald Fairhair's saga, c.19;
17. *ESSH* 1, 393, 396.
18. A.O.Anderson, *ESSH* 1, 392-3; Shetelig, *Viking Antiquities* 1, 24-5; Sawyer, 'Harald Fairhair and the British Isles'; Smyth, *Scandinavian Kings in the British Isles*, 68-71.
19. *OS*, c.4; *Heimskringla*, Saga of Magnus Barefoot, c.10.
20. *OS*, c.3, 41.
21. *OS*, c.17; *St Olaf's saga*, c.105.
22. *Sverre's saga*, c.125.
23. *OS*, c.5.
24. *Caithness & Sutherland Recs.*, No.9; Crawford, 'The Making of a Frontier', 38-9.
25. *OS*, c.5.
26. *OS*, c.6.
27. *Landnámabók*, c.309.
28. Whaley, *The Poetry of Arnórr jarlaskáld*, 267.
29. Mundal, 'The Orkney Earl and Scald, Torf Einarr' discusses Gro Steinland's doctoral thesis, 'Det hellige bryllup og norren kongeideologi'.
30. *OS*, c.4.
31. *OS*, c.5.

32. *OS*, c.6.
33. Historia Norvegiae, *ESSH* 1, 330-1.
34. *Saxo Grammaticus.*
35. Bibire, 'The Poetry of Earl Rognvaldr's Court', 208-9, 224.
36. Barnes, *The Runic Inscriptions of Maeshowe*, 178-186.
37. Duald Mac-Firbis Fragment III, *ESSH* 1, 292-4.
38. Shetelig, *Viking Antiquities* 1, 25-7.
39. Turville-Petre, 'The Genealogist and History', 7.
40. *OS*, c.1-3; Sørenson, 'The Sea, the Flame and the Wind'.
41. *OS*, c.8.
42. *OS*, c.8.
43. *Heimskringla*, King Harald Fairhair's saga, c.6. Similarly: *Egil's saga*, c.4.
44. *St Olaf's Saga*, c.99. King Olaf makes the same claim in *OS*, c.18.
45. Discussed in Johnston, 'Fiscal Antiquities', and in Crawford, *Scandinavian Scotland*, 119-203.
46. *OS*, c.11. Another instance of a reluctance to serve outside Orkney is found in *OS*, c.14.
47. *OS*, c.76.
48. *OS*, c.7.
49. Rudolf Simek, *Dictionary of Northern Mythology*, 249.
50. Ynglinga Saga, c.6.
51. A further sarcastic Odin-touch is the implied comparison of Thorir the Silent who failed to avenge his father and Viðar the Silent, son of Odin, who like Torf Einar did destroy his father's killer. See: Mundal, 'Torf Einarr', 254-5.
52. Mundal, 'Torf Einarr', 253.
53. Mundal, 'Torf Einarr', 253.
54. The killing of King Ælla by the cutting of blood-eagle has provoked a similar controversy about the reality or otherwise of blood-eagles. See: Roberta Frank, (1) 'Viking Atrocity' (2) 'The Blood Eagle Again' (3) 'Ornithology and the interpretation of skaldic verse'; Einarsson (1) 'De Normannorum Atrociate' (2) 'The Blood-eagle; an Observation on the Ornithological Aspect'.

Chapter Three
Place-names and the Pictish-Norse Transition
Notes to pp.40-55

1. Barnes, *The Norn Language of Orkney and Shetland*, 1-5.
2. *REO*, No.93 (1482-3).
3. *REO*, No.97 (1490).
4. Sandnes, 'Bu of Orphir, Burn of Gueth—a Gaelic Pattern of Orkney Place-names?'.
5. Munch, 'Geographical Elucidations'; Andersen, 'Per Andreas Munch'.
6. Jakobsen, *Etymological Dictionary of the Norn Language in Shetland.*
7. Jakobsen, *The Dialect and Place-names of Shetland*, 63.
8. Jakobsen, 'Shetlandsøerne Stednavne'
9. H.Marwick, 'Celtic Place-names in Orkney'.
10. H.Marwick, 'Celtic Place-names in Orkney'.
11. Wainwright, *The Northern Isles*, 102-5.
12. Foote, 'Pre-Viking Contacts between Orkney and Scandinavia', 180-2.
13. Marwick, *Orkney Farm-names*, 6, 23, 38.
14. Rivet and Smith, *The Place-names of Roman Britain*, 215.
15. Rivet and Smith, *The Place-names of Roman Britain*, 215, 185 note 1.
16. Wainwright, *The Northern Isles*, 162.
17. Summarised in I.Crawford, 'War or Peace'.
18. Brøgger, *Ancient Emigrants*, 66-7.
19. H.Marwick, *Place-names of Rousay*, 18-9.
20. Sawyer, *The Age of the Vikings.*
21. Smith, 'War or Peace Re-visited'.
22. Ritchie, 'Excavation of Pictish and Viking-age Farmsteads at Buckquoy', 192.
23. Gelling, 'The Norse Buildings at Skaill'.
24. Hunter,'The Early Norse Period'.
25. Nicholson and Dockrill, 'Old Scatness Broch', 74-5.
26. Morris, 'Raiders, Traders and Settlers', 85.
27. Graham-Campbell and Batey, *Vikings in Scotland*, 163.

28. Batey and Sheehan, 'Viking Expansion and Cultural Blending in Britain and Ireland', 137.
29. Stevenson, 'Pictish Art', in Wainwright, *The Problem of the Picts*, 128; Stevenson, 'Christian Sculpture in Norse Shetland'. The evidence has recently been re-assessed in Smith, 'War or Peace Re-visited'.
30. Lamb, 'Carolingian Orkney and its Transformation'.
31. Barnes, *The Norn Language of Orkney and Shetland*, 8; Graham-Campbell and Batey, *Vikings in Scotland*, 65
32. Wainwright, *The Northern Isles*, 114.
33. Barnes, *The Norn Language of Orkney and Shetland*, 8.
34. Brothwell et al., 'Biological Characteristics'; Roberts, 'Genetic Affinities'; Harvey et al., 'Relationships of the Orcadians'.
35. Wilson et al., 'Genetic Evidence for Different Male and Female Roles during Cultural Transitions in the British Isles'.
36. Clouston, 'A Fresh View of the Settlement of Orkney'.
37. I.Crawford, 'War or Peace'.
38. Smith, 'War or Peace Re-visited'.
39. Annals of Ulster, *ESSH*, Vol.1, 255.
40. Morris, 'Raiders, Traders and Settlers', 83.
41. Barnes, *The Norn Language of Orkney and Shetland*, 7.
42. Historia Norvegiae, *ESSH* 1, 330-1.
43. War of the Irish with the Foreigners, *ESSH* 1, 276; Annals of Ulster, *ESSH* 1, 279.
44. Sawyer, *The Age of the Vikings*, 148-176.
45. Helle, 'The History of the Early Viking Age in Norway'. 252-3, citing T.Iversen, 'Trelldommen; Norsk Slaveri i Middelalderer', unpublished PhD, Bergen.
46. Thomson, 'Some Settlement Patterns in Medieval Orkney'.
47. I.Crawford, 'War or Peace', 264; Smith, 'War or Peace Re-visited'.
48. *ESSH* 1, 256, 258. 259, 263-5.
49. Marwick also argued that the absence of *bólstaðr*-names might imply that the Norse left the island in peace. However, earlier in this chapter it has been shown that place-name generics cannot normally be used for close dating in the Viking Age.
50. Lamb, 'Carolingian Orkney and its Transformation', 268.
51. Holder-Egger, 'Vita Findani'; Christiansen, 'The People of the North', Löwe, 'Findan von Rheinau'; Thomson, 'St Findan and the Pictish Norse Transition'; Lowe, *St Boniface Church*, 8-9; Lamb, 'Papil, Picts and Papar'.
52. Dickins, 'An Orkney Scholar: Hugh Marwick'.
53. Grønneberg, *Jakobsen and Shetland*, 82.
54. Marwick, 'Antiquarian Notes on Stronsay'.
55. Marwick, 'Orkney Farm-name Studies'.
56. Marwick, *Orkney Farm-names*, 249.
57. Nicolaisen, 'Norse Settlement in the Northern and Western Isles'.
58. Marwick, 'Orkney Farm-name Studies', 26.
59. Marwick, 'Orkney Farm-name Studies', 30-1.
60. Andersen, 'When was Regular Taxation Introduced?'.
61. Thomson, 'Orkney Farm-name Chronology', 48-50.
62. Thomson, 'Orkney Farm-name Chronology', 53-62.

Chapter 4
Earl Sigurd and the Raven Banner
Notes to pp.56-68

1. *OS*, c.8.
2. *Heimskringla*, Saga of Hakon the Good, c.4.
3. Smyth, *Warlords and Holy Men*, 226-7; Crawford, *Scandinavian Scotland*, 61-2.
4. Seeberg, 'Five Kings'.
5. *OS*, c.8; Heimskringla, Saga of Hakon the Good, c.3-5; *Anglo-Saxon Chronicle*, s.a.948 and 954; *ESSH* 1, 455-462; Smyth, *Warlords and Holy*

Men, 206-8; Crawford, *Scandinavian Scotland*, 61-2.

6. *Heimskringla*, Harald Fairhair's saga, c.46.
7. *Heimskringla*, Hakon the Good's saga, c.5.
8. *ESSH* 1, 468-9.
9. *Heimskringla*, Olaf Tryggvisson's saga, c.17.
10. *Heimskringla*, Hakon the Good's saga, c.3.
11. *OS*, c.8.
12. *Laxdæla saga*, c.4; *St Olaf's saga*, c.99.
13. Cowan, 'Caithness in the Sagas', 29-31.
14. Nicolaisen, 'The Scandinavians and Celts in Caithness'; Waugh, 'Caithness; an Onomastic Frontier Zone'.
15. *OS* (Taylor), 356; Clouston, *History*, 24n.
16. *OS*, c.9.
17. Foote, 'Observations on Orkneyinga Saga', 196.
18. *OS*, c.10.
19. *OS*, c.11.
20. *Njal's saga*, c.85.
21. *OS*, c.10.
22. *Fordun*, 174-5.
23. *OS*, c.11; *Njal's saga*, c.85.
24. Annals of Ulster, Annals of Innisfallen, *ESSH* 1, 489-490.
25. Annals of Ulster, *ESSH* 1, 494.
26. *Njal's saga*, c.85.
27. *Njal's saga*, c.88.
28. Annals of Ulster; Tigernach Annals, *ESSH* 1, 494.
29. *Eyrbyggia Saga*, c.29.
30. *Eyrbyggia Saga*, introduction, 11.
31. *Njal's saga*, c.84-5.
32. *ESSH* 1, 485n.
33. Graham-Campbell, *Viking-age Gold and Silver of Scotland*, 34-48, 51-2,131-141; Graham-Campbell, 'Northern Hoards of Viking-age Scotland', 180-1.
34. *OS*, c.12; *Heimskringla*, Olaf Trygvesson's saga, c.52; *St Olaf's saga*, c.99; *Theoderic*, 12-3.
35. *Anglo-Saxon Chronicle*, 129; *Heimskringla*, Olaf Trygvesson's saga, c.32.
36. *OS*, c.12.

37. *Heimskringla*, Olaf Trygvesson's saga, c.31
38. *OS*, c.11; Smyth, *Scandinavian Kings in the British Isles*, 249, 269-270.
39. *Scriptores Rerum Danicarium*, Langabek, 1774; Jesch, 'England and Orkneyinga Saga', 226-7, 232-5.
40. Thorsteinsson, 'The Viking Burial Place at Pierowall'.
41. Kaland, 'Westnessutgravningene på Rousay'.
42. Owen and Dalland, *Scar; a Viking Boat Burial*, 188.
43. H.Marwick, 'Antiquarian Notes on Stronsay', 70.
44. H.Marwick, 'Antiquarian Notes on Sanday'; E.Marwick, *Folklore of Orkney and Shetland*, 42.
45. E.Marwick, 'The Stone of Odin', 31-5.
46. Lamb, 'Carolingian Orkney and its Transformation', 269.
47. *OS*, c.65; *OS*, Taylor 383.
48. *Flateyjarbók* 4, 242-5; Dasent, *Orkneyingers saga*, 369-373; Owen and Dalland, *Scar; a Viking Boat Burial*, 5-11.
49. *OS*, c.12; *Njal's saga*, c.153-6.
50. Magnusson, *Viking Expansion Westwards*, 75.
51. *Njal's saga*, c.153-4.
52. Thorstein Side-Hall's saga, *ESSH* 1, 529-30.
53. *ESSH* 1, 536n.
54. *Njal's saga*, c.155.
55. *Njal's saga*, c.156.
56. Scott, *The Pirate*, Note A.
57. *Njal's saga*, c.156.

Chapter 5
Earl Thorfinn and the Christian Earldom
Notes to pp.69-87

1. *OS*, c.32; *St Olaf's saga*, c.109.
2. *OS*, c.13, 20.
3. Hudson, 'Cnut and the Scottish Kings', 354.
4. *OS*, c.13; *St Olaf's saga*, c.99.
5. *ESSH*, cxvi.
6. *OS*, c.13.
7. *OS*, c.21.

8. *OS*, c.61.
9. *OS*, c.15.
10. *OS*, c.33.
11. *OS*, c.77.
12. *OS*, c.112.
13. *OS*, c.20.
14. *OS*, c.29, 30.
15. Taylor, 'Some Saga Place-names', 42.
16. Clouston, 'Two Features of the Orkney Earldom'; Clouston, *History*, 36.
17. Steinnes, 'The Huseby System in Orkney'.
18. Smith, 'Shetland in Saga-Time'.
19. *OS*, c.26; Whaley, *The Poetry of Arnórr jarlaskáld*, 306-8.
20. *OS*, c.25.
21. *ESSH* 1, cxvi.
22. Fordun, 270.
23. *SAEC*, 316
24. *OS*, c.15; Taylor, 'Some Saga Place-names', 45.
25. *OS*, c.15.
26. *OS*, c.15.
27. *OS*, c.16; *Icelandic Annals* s.a.1020.
28. *OS*, c.17.
29. *Icelandic Annals* s.a.1021.
30. *OS*, c.17; *St Olaf's saga*, c.106-7.
31. *OS*, c.15; *St Olaf's saga*, c.103.
32. *OS*, c.19.
33. *OS*, c.20.
34. *ESSH* 1, 577n.
35. Whaley, *The Poetry of Arnórr jarlaskáld*, 230-242.
36. In *OS* we find Hlodver 'Hundi' Sigurdsson, Hakon Karl and Holdbodi Hundisson.
37. Skene, *Celtic Scotland* 1, 400-1; Clouston, *History*, 40; Donaldson, 'The Contemporary Scene', 2.
38. Cowan, 'The Historical MacBeth'; Crawford, *Earl & Mormaer*, 5-6; Duncan, *Scotland; the Making of the Kingdom*, 100; Hudson, *Kings of Celtic Scotland*, 140-1.
39. *ESSH* 1, 509.
40. *OS*, c.12; *ESSH* 1, 509.
41. Taylor, 'King Karl Hundason'; Taylor, *Orkneyinga saga*, 361.
42. *ESSH* 1, 551.
43. *ESSH* 1, 571.
44. Discussed in Woolf, 'The Moray Question'.
45. *OS*, c.5.
46. *OS*, c.10.
47. *Njal's saga*, c.85.
48. *ESSH* 2, ii, 176-7.
49. *OS*, c.20.
50. *OS*, c.19.
51. *ESSH* 1, 572.
52. OS c.20
53. *St Olaf's saga*, c.109.
54. *ESSH* 1, 571.
55. Whaley, *The Poetry of Arnórr jarlaskald*, 241.
56. Discussed in Woolf, 'The Moray Question'.
57. *ESSH* 1, 551.
58. Hudson, 'Cnut and the Scottish Kings', 354-5.
59. Barrow, 'MacBeth and Other Mormaers of Moray', 114-5.
60. *ESSH* 1, 569.
61. *ESSH* 1, 571.
62. *OS*, c.33; Donaldson, 'The Contemporary Scene', 3.
63. *OS*. c.32.
64. Whaley, *The Poetry of Arnórr jarlaskáld*, 262-3; Crawford, *Scandinavian Scotland*, 75.
65. *OS*, c.20.
66. *OS*, c.20. Further possible links between Thorfinn and Macbeth with Fife are discussed in Simon Taylor, 'The Scandinanvians in Fife'.
67. *Anglo-Saxon Chronicle* s.a.1031. (D and E text).
68. *St Olaf saga*, c.140; Hudson, 'Cnut and the Scottish Kings', 350.
69. Hudson, 'Cnut and the Scottish Kings', 359.
70. *OS*, c.21.
71. *OS*, c.21.
72. *OS*, c.22; Whaley, *The Poetry of Arnórr jarlaskald*, 243-5; Crawford, *Scandinavian Scotland*, 233.
73. *OS*, c.23.
74. *OS*, c.24.
75. *St Olaf saga*, c.116.
76. *OS*, c.25; *Morkinskinna*, c.4, contains a similar but not identical account of the Battle of Rauðabjorg.
77. Taylor, 'Some Saga Place-names', 43; Clouston, *History*, 47-9.
78. H.Marwick, 'Antiquarian Notes on Stronsay', 65.

79. *OS*, c.29.
80. *OS*, c.93, 94.
81. *ESSH* 2, 1; Jesch, 'England and Orkneyinga Saga', 225.
82. *OS*, c.31.
83. *Orkney & Shetland Recs.*, No.1.
84. Crawford, 'Birsay and the Early Earls and Bishops'; Crawford, 'Bishops of Orkney in the Eleventh and Twelfth Centuries'.
85. Cruden, 'Earl Thorfinn the Mighty and the Brough of Birsay'; Cruden, 'Excavations at Birsay'.
86. Lamb, 'The Cathedral and the Monastery', 42.
87. Lamb, 'The Cathedral of Christchurch'; Lamb, 'The Cathedral and the Monastery'.
88. Morris, *The Birsay Bay Project* 2, 11-31.
89. Rendall, 'Birsay's Forgotten Palace'.
90. Lamb, 'The Cathedral and the Monastery', 43-4.
91. *OS*, c.31.
92. *St Olaf's saga*, c.56.
93. *OS*, c.32.

Chapter 6
The Martyrdom of St Magnus
Notes to pp.88-100

1. *OS*, c.34; *Heimskringla, King Harald's saga*, c.83
2. *Heimskringla, King Harald's saga*, c.87.
3. *Shorter Magnus saga*, 22
4. *OS*, c.35. Note that the saga at no point describes an equal division of the earldom between Thorfinn and Brusi.
5. *OS*, c.36; Thomson, 'St Magnus'.
6. Power, 'Magnus Barelegs' Expeditions to the West'.
7. *OS*, c.38; *Heimskringla, Magnus Barelegs' saga*, c.12.
8. Ágrip, c.50.
9. Maund, *Gruffudd ap Cynan*.
10. Moore, 'Gruffudd ap Cynan', 20
11. *OS*, c.39.
12. Mooney, *St Magnus*; Brown, *Magnus*; Brown, 'The Magnus Miracles were Manifest'.
13. *Heimskringla, Saga of Magnus Barelegs*, c.25.
14. Foote, 'Observations on Orkneyinga Saga', 204-5.
15. *OS*, c.40.
16. *OS*, c.40.
17. Maund, *Gruffudd ap Cynan*, 19, 74-5, 152.
18. Dickins, 'Orkney Raid on Wales', 47; Jesch, 'Norse Historical Traditions and the Historia'.
19. *Heimskringla, Magnus Barelegs' Saga*, c.9-10; Jesch, 'Norse Historical Traditions and the Historia'.
20. *Longer Magnus Saga*, 251.
21. *OS*, c.43.
22. *Longer Magnus Saga*, 252.
23. *Longer Magnus Saga*, 251, 258.
24. *OS*, c.46.
25. *OS*, c.45.
26. Dickins, 'St Magnus and his Countess'.
27. *OS*, c.45.
28. Stancliffe and Cambridge, *Oswald*, 233; Thomson, 'St Magnus'.
29. *Longer Magnus Saga*, 257-8.
30. Brut y Tywyssion, *ESSH* 2, 144.
31. See attempts at dating the martyrdom in *OS*, c.51.
32. *OS*, c.66,76,77.
33. Crawford, 'Birsay and the Early Earls and Bishops of Orkney'; Crawford, 'Bishops of Orkney'.
34. A later date for Bishop William's appointment is sometimes suggested on the grounds that an episcopate of 66 years is impossibly long.
35. Crawford, 'Bishops of Orkney', 11.
36. *SAEC*, 164.
37. *SAEC*, 165.
38. *SAEC*, 164.
39. *Longer Magnus Saga*, 263.
40. *Longer Magnus Saga*, 264-5.
41. *OS*, c.49; *Shorter Magnus Saga*, c.12.
42. *OS*, c.74-5.
43. Reid, 'Remains of St Magnus'.
44. *OS*, c.56.
45. H.Marwick, *Orcadian*, 24 Jan., 14 Feb. and 9 May 1957; OA D31/37/1.
46. *OS*, c.57; For the shrine being located *over* the altar, see: Mooney, 'Further Notes on Saints' Relics and Burials', 35.

47. *OS*, c.57
48. *St Olaf Saga*, c.97
49. Jexlev, 'The Cult of Saints in Early Medieval Scandinavia'.
50. Leslie, *History of Scotland*.
51. *Boece*, 277.
52. *Hakonar Saga*, 271
53. Blindheim, St Magnus in Scandinavian Art'; Crawford, *St Magnus Cathedral*, plates 3, 7, 8 and 9.
54. *OS*, c.52.
55. *Longer Magnus Saga*, 239-240, 247-8. and 268-270. Master Robert has sometimes been identified as an Oxford prior, Robert of Cricklade (see: Guðmundsson, *Orkneyinga saga*, xlvi-xlvii).
56. The word 'Amen', for example, appears when the author ceases to quote the sermon and begins to use the miracle list.
57. Matthew 3, v.9; Luke 3, v.8.
58. Theoderic, c.19, introduction xix-xx.
59. 'The four main virtues' are the cardinal or natural virtues of prudence, temperance, fortitude and justice, as opposed to the 'theological virtues'— faith, hope and charity.
60. *Longer Magnus Saga*, 248.
61. Barrow, 'The Kings of Scotland and Durham'.

Chapter Seven
St Rognvald and the Twelfth Century Renaissance
Notes to pp.101-112

1. Crawford, *St Magnus Cathedral and Orkney's Twelfth Century Renaissance*.
2. *OS*, c.52.
3. Taylor, *Orkneyinga Saga*, 388n.
4. *OS*, c.55.
5. *OS*, c.41-2.
6. *OS*, c.61. Sigurd was the former boy-king in Orkney, son of Magnus Barelegs.
7. *OS*, c.62.
8. *OS*, c.63.
9. *OS*, c.53, 63.
10. *OS*, c.68.
11. *OS* c.56, 57.
12. *OS* c.57
13. *OS* c.57.
14. Diploma, 416.
15. *OS* c.68; Crawford, 'St Magnus and St Rognvald', 32 n.6
16. Clouston, *History*, 157-168.
17. Peterkin, *Rentals* (1500), 76.
18. Thomson, 'Some Settlement Patterns in Medieval Orkney', 342-5.
19. *OS*, c.67, 97.
20. *OS*, c.66.
21. Clouston, 'The Battle of Tankerness'; Marwick, 'Leidang in the West'; Marwick, 'Naval Defence in Norse Scotland'; Williams, 'Land Assessment and Military Organisation in the Northern Settlements in Scotland'.
22. Dated from Icelandic Annals, *ESSH* 2, 190.
23. Crawford, 'The Cult of St Magnus in Shetland'; Thomson, 'St Magnus'.
24. Clouston, 'The Battle of Tankerness'.
25. Pálsson and Edwards, *Orkneyinga Saga*, c.75.
26. Cambridge, 'The Romanesque Cathedral at Kirkwall'.
27. *OS*, c.76; A more literal interpretation is found in Johnson, 'Fiscal Antiquities', 138, and in Clouston, *History*, 90.
28. *OS*, c.86-89.
29. Bibire, 'The Poetry of Earl Rognvald's Court'.
30. *OS*, c.66-108.
31. *OS*, c.108.
32. *OS*, c.108.
33. *OS*, c.82.
34. *OS*, c.64.
35. *OS*, c.77.
36. *OS*, c.78.

Chapter Eight
Harald Maddadsson
Notes to pp.113-127

1. Crawford. 'The Earldom of Caithness'; Topping, 'Harald Maddadsson'.
2. *Sverre's saga*, 156.
3. Magnus Erlendsson, Harald Hakonsson, Paul Hakonsson, Erlend Haraldsson, Rognvald Kolsson and Harald the Younger.

4. *OS*, c.92, 93.
5. *OS*, c.77. By 1138, the apparent date of the mission, Bishop John of Glasgow had resigned from his see and had become a monk: see Duncan, *Scotland; The Making of the Kingdom*, 261. Latterly Bishop John seems to have been out of favour, so it is possible his mission to Orkney was earlier than appears from *Orkneyinga saga*.
6. *OS*, c.77. This chapter first states that Harald was fostered by Rognvald, then it states that he was fostered by Thorbjorn Clerk. It appears that Rognvald adopted him as heir, but that the actual management of the young earl was committed to Thorbjorn.
7. *SAEC*, 189n.
8. *OS*, c.77
9. *OS*, c.85.
10. *Heimskringla*, Saga of the Sons of Harald, c.13.
11. *Morkinskinna*, c.97.
12. *OS*, c.91; *Heimskringla*, Saga of the Sons of Harald, c.1; *Morkinskinna*, c.97; Taylor, A.B., 'Eystein Haraldsson in the West'.
13. Johnsen, 'The Payments from the Hebrides and the Isle of Man to the Crown of Norway'.
14. *OS*, c.92.
15. *OS*, c.92.
16. The king is named as 'Malcolm' in *OS*, c.92, but he was more probably David I.
17. *OS*, c.92.
18. *OS*, c.92.
19. *OS*, c.92-5.
20. *OS*, c.93.
21. *OS*, c.94.
22. Dated from *Icelandic Annals*, s.a.1158.
23. *OS*, c.103; Taylor, 'The Death of Earl Rognvaldr'.
24. Anderson, 'Wimund, Bishop and Pretender'.
25. *OS*, c.33.
26. *RRS* 1, introduction, 12-3.
27. If Ingibjorg was a daughter of Thorfinn (rather than his widow), and if Thorfinn's mother was a daughter of Malcolm II (rather than of Malcolm, Mormaer of Moray), Malcolm III and Ingibjorg would be second cousins.
28. *OS*, c.105, 109.
29. Duncan, *Scotland; The Making of the Kingdom*, 166.
30. *ESSH* 2, 233n.
31. *ESSH* 2, 249n.
32. *ESSH* 2, 266.
33. Fordun 2, 252.
34. *ESSH* 2, 347-8.
35. Fordun 2, 270.
36. Ingigerd's marriage to Erik *stagbrellr* was in 1154 (*OS*, c.94) and Harald was the eldest son of their six children (*OS*, c.104), so it is likely that he was born c.1155 or soon after.
37. Fordun 2, 263; *ESSH* 2, 301; *RSS*, introduction, 11-14.
38. *SAEC*, 278.
39. Fordun 2, 264.
40. *ESSH* 2, 271.
41. Poole, *Domesday Book to Magna Carta*, 307.
42. *ESSH* 2, 272-3.
43. *OS*, c.105-108
44. *Sverre's saga*, c.119.
45. *SAEC*, 316-8.
46. *Sverre's saga*, c.118-120.
47. *Sverre's saga*, c.120.
48. *Icelandic Annals*, s.a.1168.
49. *Sverre's saga*, c.125; Imsen, 'Earldom and Kingdom'.
50. Imsen, 'Earldom and Kingdom', 3.
51. Thomson, *1492 Rental*, xix.
52. Cruden, 'The Founding and Building of the Twelfth-Century Cathedral of St Magnus'; Cambridge, 'The Romanesque Cathedral at Kirkwall'; Thurlby, 'Aspects of the Architectural History of Kirkwall Cathedral'.
53. *OS*, c.99.
54. Clouston, *History*, 195-6.
55. *OS*, c.84, 109.
56. *OS*, c.84.
57. *APS* 1, No.106; Topping, 'Harald Maddadsson', 109-112.
58. *DN* 2, No.2; *Orkney & Shetland Records* 1, part 1, No.13.
59. 'The Rental of the Bischop of Orknayis landis within Cathnes'; Saint-Clair, 'The Bishopric of Orkney; References to Lands in Caithness'.

60. *RSS* 1, No.179 refers to what appears to the same community as 'monks of Dunfermline'.
61. Barrow, *The Charters of King David I*, 127; *Orkney & Shetland Records* 1, part 1, No.11.
62. *ESSH* 1, cxviii.
63. Crawford, 'The Earldom of Caithness', 28.
64. Crawford, 'Peter's Pence'.
65. Lawrie, *Annals of the Reigns of Malcolm and William*, 340; *Orkney & Shetland Records* 1, part 1, 22-4.
66. Fordun 2, 271.
67. Fordun 2, 270.
68. *SAEC*, 316.
69. *SAEC*, 316-8.
70. *ESSH* 2, 347-8.
71. *SAEC*, 316-8.
72. Fordun 2, 270.
73. *SAEC*, 317; Fordun 2, 270.
74. *SAEC*, 317.
75. *Icelandic Annals*, s.a.1098; *SAEC*, 316-8; *OS*, c.109.
76. Rognvald was not first buried at St Mary's (Burwick?) as stated by Torfaeus who carelessly takes *Flatyjarbók's* dating of Rognvald's death 'five days after the Feast of the Assumption of the Blessed Virgin' and turns it into an interment at a church of the Blessed Virgin (see: Torfaeus, 142).
77. *OS*, c.104.
78. *OS*, c.46.
79. *OS*, c.109.
80. *OS*, c.109.
81. Fordun, 272, states that Harald secured peace on this occasion for the payment of £2000 of silver. Fordun telescopes events: it seems likely that this payment is the same as mentioned by Roger of Howden who places the payment after the wounding of Bishop John (see below).
82. *SAEC*, 316-8. Because Harald had been so long married to Hvarföð, it has been suggested that this requirement was actually made at an earlier date.
83. Fordun 2, 270; *OS*, c.112.
84. *OS*, c.110.
85. Bain 1, 234; Crawford, 'Peter's Pence', 20n.

86. *OS*, c.111; Fordun 2, 271-2.
87. Anderson, *Orkneyinga Saga*, xliii; *Orkney & Shetland Records* 1, part 1, 24-6; Crawford, 'Norse Earls and Scottish Bishops', 135.
88. Taylor, *Orkneyinga Saga*, 410.
89. *OS*, c.112
90. *Inga saga*, 235.
91. *OS*, c.112.

Chapter 9
Earl John and His Successors
Notes to pp.128-137

1. *Inga saga*, 235.
2. *Inga saga*, 235-6.
3. *Norges Gamle Love* 2, 403.
4. *Inga saga*, 236.
5. David's death is recorded in *Icelandic Annals*, s.a.1214, *ESSH* 2, 397.
6. *Hakonar saga*, c.20.
7. *Hakonar saga*, c.22.
8. *Hakonar saga*, c.45.
9. *Hakonar saga*, c.77.
10. *Hakonar saga*, c.101.
11. *Hakonar saga*, c.162.
12. *Hakonar saga*, c.166.
13. Fordun, 274.
14. *OS*, c.105, 112.
15. Fordun, 278; Barrow, 'MacBeth and other Mormaers of Moray', 121-2.
16. Fordun, 274. From the wording of the passage in Fordun it is equally possible that the hostage was the daughter of David, John's brother and co-earl. David, however, is seldom visible in the record, so it is usually assumed that she was a daughter of John.
17. Crawford, 'The Earldom of Caithness and the Kingdom of Scotland', 28-30.
18. Chronicle of Melrose, *ESSH* 2, 449.
19. Duncan, *Scotland: the Making of the Kingdom*, 528.
20. *Flateyjarbók* 3, 139; Dasent, *Orkneyingers saga*, 232-3. Note that Dasent's translation of this passage is somewhat misleading. For spans of butter: see Thomson, *1492 Rental*, xi-xii.

21. Annals of Dunstable, *SAEC*, 336-7.
22. *Caithness & Sutherland Recs.*, No.10; Annals of Dunstable, *ESSH* 2, 337.
23. Fordun, 284-5.
24. *Icelandic Annals*, s.a.1222, *ESSH* 2, 451-2.
25. Crawford, 'Norse Earls and Scottish Bishops', 136.
26. *Caithness & Sutherland Recs.*, Nos.5, 6, 7.
27. *Caithness & Sutherland Recs.*, No.9.
28. *Caithness & Sutherland Recs.*, No.10.
29. Dasent, *Orkneyingers' saga*, 232-3.
30. Annals of Dunstable, *ESSH* 2, 337.
31. Fordun, 285.
32. *Icelandic Annals*, s.a.1226.
33. Clouston, *History*, 218-9.
34. *Orkney and Shetland Recs.*, No.18.
35. *Hakonar saga*, c.168.
36. Dated from *Icelandic Annals*, s.a.1031.
37. *Hakonar saga*, c.170-1.
38. *Hakonar saga*, c.171; *RCAHMS* 2, No.619.
39. *Hakonar saga*, c.172; *ESSH* 2, 484.
40. *Hakonar saga*, c.173.
41. *Diploma*, 406, 416.
42. Crawford, 'The Earldom of Caithness', 34.
43. *OS*, c.105, 109.
44. *Hakonar saga*, c.173.
45. Crawford, 'The Earldom of Caithness', 34.
46. Crawford, 'The Earldom of Caithness', 34.
47. *Diploma*, 406, 416.
48. Crawford, 'The Earldom of Caithness', 34.
49. *Icelandic Annals*, s.a.1239.
50. Translated from Crawford, 'The Earldom of Caithness', 36. The document is dated 1373.
51. Crawford, 'The Earldom of Caithness'.
52. *Hakonar saga*, c.225.
53. One reason for thinking that Gilbert might have been a minor is that he was not present with the Orkneymen in Norway when Hakon *unge* was given the title of king (1240).
54. *Orkney & Shetland Recs.*, No.20.
55. *Icelandic Annals*, s.a.1256.

Chapter 10
King Hakon's Expedition and the Loss of the Hebrides
Notes to pp.138-147

1. Andersen, 'King Hakon the Old before the Bar of History'; Helle, 'Norwegian Consolidation and Expansion'.
2. Young, *History of the Isle of Man*, 75-140.
3. *Inga saga*, 234-6; *ESSH* 2, 387.
4. *Inga saga*, 234-6.
5. *Hakonar saga*, 150-4; McDonald, *Kingdom of the Isles*, 88-9.
6. *Hakonar saga*, 248-9.
7. *Hakonar saga*, 265-7.
8. *Hakonar saga*, 270; Crawford, *Scandinavian Scotland*, 75.
9. *Hakonar saga*, 271; McDonald, *The Kingdom of the Isles*, 100-2.
10. *Hakonar saga*, 327.
11. *Hakonar saga*, 339-40.
12. John Langlifsson may have been a son of Langlif, daughter of Earl Harald Maddadsson.
13. *Hakonar saga*, 345.
14. *Hakonar saga*, 322-3.
15. *Hakonar saga*, 346.
16. *Hakonar saga*, 342.
17. *Hakonar saga*, 363.
18. *Chronicle of the Kings of Man and the Isles*, f.49v.
19. *ESSH* 2, 607.
20. *Hakonar saga*, 363. The term 'urisland' is lost in Dasent's translation.
21. Simpson, *The Castle of Bergen and the Bishop's Palace in Kirkwall*, 65-77.
22. *Saga of Magnus Hakonsson*, 375.
23. *Fordun*, 296.
24. *Saga of Magnus Hakonsson*, 377.
25. *APS* 1, 420; *ESSH* 2, 655-6.
26. *ESSH* 2, 656.
27. *Hakonar saga*, 345.
28. Crawford, 'The Earldom of Caithness', 37-9.
29. *ER* 1, 13; Crawford, 'The Earldom of Caithness, 38.
30. Pálsson, 'Hakonar saga; Portrait of a King', 50.
31. *Norges Gamle Love* 3, 403; Crawford, 'Earls of Orkney and Caithness', 163.
32. *Icelandic Annals*, s.a.1273 and 1276.

33. *APS* 1, 423.
34. Crawford, *Earls of Orkney and Caithness*, 129.
35. *ESSH* 2, 694; *SHR* 69, 1990.
36. Anderson, 'Notes regarding the Death of Princess Margaret'; Prestwich, 'Edward I and the Maid of Norway'.
37. Hossack, *Kirkwall in the Orkneys*, 50.
38. Mss letter, George Chalmers to David Riddoch 16 May 1801, OA D/10.
39. Anderson, 'Notes regarding the Death of Princess Margaret'.
40. *OS* (Anderson), introduction, lii-liv; Helle, 'Norwegian Foreign Policy', 155-6.
41. Crawford, *Earls of Orkney and Caithness*, 122.

Chapter 11
Angus and Strathearn
Notes pp.148-159

1. Crawford, 'Weland of Stiklaw'; Crawford, 'North Sea Kingdoms'.
2. Barron, 'Robert the Bruce in Orkney, Caithness and Sutherland'.
3. Barrow, *Robert Bruce*, 237-40.
4. *Boece*, 277; Thomson, 'The Ladykirk Stone'.
5. *REO*, No.1.
6. *RMS* 1, App.1, No.19.
7. *REO*, No.1.
8. *Saint-Clairs*, 85.
9. *RMS* 1, App.2, No.716.
10. *DN* 2, Nos.168 and 170; *REO*, Nos.4, 5; H.Marwick, 'Two Orkney Letters'.
11. The early forms of these names are discussed in H.Marwick, *Orkney Farm-names*.
12. The Orkney mark of land is not the same as the Scottish 'merk of Old Extent'. The Orkney marks are discussed in Thomson, *1492 Rental*, xx-xxi.
13. Translated from *Diploma*, 407. The Scots translation of the *Diploma* (but not the earlier Latin original) goes on to state that the Norwegian king had ordered that all charters and written evidence should be delivered to Malise so that he could prove his right to the earldom (*Diploma*, 402).
14. *RMS* 1, App.2, No.716.
15. *RSS* David II, No.77; Boardman, *The Early Stewart Kings*, 30.
16. Nicholson, *Scotland; the Later Middle Ages*, 154-6.
17. Crawford, *The Earls of Orkney*, 171.
18. *RMS* 1, App.1, No.150.
19. Boardman, *The Early Stewart Kings*, 30.
20. It is usually assumed that Guttorm Sperra was a descendant of Ivar Spera who was recorded as a member of the Shetland Lawting in 1309 (*Shetland Documents* 1, No.3). The family's landed interests also appear in a 1386 dispute (*Shetland Documents* 1, No.13). The family is discussed in Crawford, 'The Pledging of the Islands' (Shetland).
21. *The Diploma*, 408 and 417, makes it clear that Erngisl possessed only a part of the earldom lands.
22. *Saint-Clairs*, 92.
23. *Saint-Clairs*, 92.
24. Anderson, *Orkneyinga Saga*, introduction, lix.
25. Anderson, *Orkneyinga Saga*, introduction, lix.
26. *DN* 2, 337; *Saint-Clairs*, 94.
27. *RSS*, David II, No.203.
28. Anderson, *OS*, lxxvii.
29. *Shetland Documents* 1, No.5.
30. *Shetland Documents* 1, No.7.
31. *Shetland Documents* 1, No.6.
32. *Shetland Documents* 1, No.5.
33. REO, No.8; *Shetland Documents* 1, No.12; *DN* 1, No.404.
34. Seaver, *The Frozen Echo*, 149.
35. Crawford, *The Earls of Orkney and Caithness*, 229-231.
36. *Shetland Documents* 1, No.19.
37. *REO*, No.8, note.
38. *DN* 1, No.258.
39. *Shetland Documents* 1, No.14.
40. *RMS* 1, No.614; Boardman, *The Early Stewarts*, 99n.
41. *RMS* 1, No.615.
42. *RMS* 1, No.600.
43. *RMS* 1, No.601.
44. *REO*, No.9 and 10; Imsen, 'Earldom and Kingdom', 9.
45. *REO*, No.10.

Chapter 12
The Sinclair Earldom
Notes to pp.160-171

1. *Saint-Clairs*, 96-102.
2. *REO*, No.2.
3. Anderson, *Orkneyinga Saga*, introduction, lxi.
4. *RMS* 1, Nos.369, 370.
5. A testimonial dating from 1422 regarding the ancestry of James Cragy of Huip implies that Henry's claim to the earldom was by virtue of his marriage to Isabella ('Elizabeth') rather than as her son (*REO*, No.16). Since the testimonial was attested by the Lawman and numerous witnesses it needs to be taken seriously. The possibility of an error of transcription is discussed in *ER* 8, introduction, lxxvi. Any doubt is removed by a charter in which Henry described David Sinclair as his brother, and Isabella as David's mother, and therefore his own (*RMS* 1, No.284).
6. *DN* 2, p.353; *REO*, No.11.
7. *DN* 2, 337; *Saint-Clairs*, 94.
8. *REO*, 94.
9. *Icelandic Annals*, s.a.1382.
10. Burns, *Papal Letters of Clement VII*, lvii, 100.
11. Burns, *Papal Letters of Clement VII*, lvii, 160.
12. Sir Walter Haliburton, Sir Patrick Hepburn, Sir Alexander Haliburton, Sir John Edmondstone, George Abernethy and Sir William Ramsay
13. Printed in *Saint-Clairs*, 510-1.
14. Crawford, 'The Pledging of the Islands' (Shetland), 38-40.
15. *Saint-Clairs*, 511.
16. *DN* 18, No.34.
17. *Icelandic Annals*, s.a.1389.
18. *REO*, No.20. While it is usually assumed that the castle was built by Earl Henry I, it is possible that it was constructed by his son, Henry II, although less likely because of Henry II's tenuous contacts with Orkney.
19. *Saint-Clairs*, 276.
20. Hay, *Genealogie of the Sainteclaires*.
21. Quoted in *Saint-Clairs*, 101.
22. Major, *The Voyages of the Venetian Brothers Nicolo and Antonio Zeno*; Pohl, *Prince Henry Sinclair*.
23. Fitzhugh and Ward, *Vikings; the North Atlantic Saga*, 309; Seaver, *The Frozen Echo*, 121-2, 131.
24. Kirsten A. Seaver, 'Unanswered Questions', in William W.Fitzhugh and Elisabeth I. Ward (eds), *Vikings: the North Atlantic Saga*, Washington, USA, 2000, 274, 277.
25. Seaver, *The Frozen Echo*, 149.
26. B.Smith, 'Henry Sinclair's Fictitious Trip to America'. Lucas's translation of the Zeno account appears as an appendix to this paper.
27. *Icelandic Annals*, s.a.1349.
28. *DN* 18, No.34.
29. *Shetland Documents* 1, No.14.
30. *RMS* 1, No.824; *Shetland Documents* 1, No.15; *REO*, No.12.
31. Anderson, *OS*, introduction lxvii; *RMS* 1, App.2, 1732.
32. Peterkin, *Rentals* (1500), 59, 76.
33. *ER* 5, 54; *Saint-Clairs*, 98.
34. *Diploma*, 408, 418.
35. When the *Diploma* describes Henry's death as 'there' (Latin, 'inibi'), the word appears to refer to Orkney. Brian Smith, however, has pointed out that 'there' might refer to 'his country' and so Henry might have died in Scotland, possibly in a border skirmish against the English.
36. Holinshed, *The Scottish Chronicle*, 16; Saint-Clair, 102.

Chapter 13
Orkney at the End of the Middle Ages
Notes to pp.172-188

1. The evidence for the date of Henry II's death is discussed in *Saint-Claires*, 109.
2. Since the date of the death of Henry I is uncertain, it is possible that he rather than Henry II was the Earl of Orkney captured at Homildon Hill.
3. Brown, *James I*, 14-9.

4. Holinshed, *The Scottish Chronicle*, 50; *Saint-Clairs*, 103-111; Crawford, *The Earls of Orkney and Caithness*, 245-6.
5. *Shetland Documents* 1, No.20.
6. *RMS* 1, App.1, No.150.
7. *Diploma*, 408, 418.
8. H.Marwick, 'Sir David Menzies'.
9. Brown, *James I*, 179.
10. For this relationship see: *REO*, No.30.
11. Barbara Crawford has suggested that Thomas Sinclair may have had charge of the Crown estates in the islands.
12. *REO*, No.18.
13. *Saint-Claires*, 109.
14. NAS, Adv.Ms.35, 2, 4(i).
15. Imsen, 'Earldom and Kingdom', 17; Crawford, 'The Orkney Arms'.
16. *REO*, No.18.
17. *REO*, No.18.
18. *REO*, No.14.
19. *REO*, No.15.
20. *REO*, No.18.
21. *REO*, No.16. The difficulties presented by the descent set out in Craigie's testimonial are discussed in Chapter 12, note 5.
22. *REO*, No.18.
23. *REO*, No.17.
24. Clouston, *History*, 244; H.Marwick, 'Sir David Menzies', 14.
25. *REO*, No.18.
26. H.Marwick, 'Sir David Menzies', 14.
27. *REO*, No.19.
28. *REO*, No.19.
29. Imsen, *Norsk Bondekommunalisme* 1, 173.
30. *RRS, David II*, No.233.
31. Crawford, *The Earls of Orkney and Caithness*, 271-2.
32. *REO*, No.209.
33. *Diploma*; Crawford in *The Earls of Orkney and Caithness*, 45-56, shows that, although the extant Latin version is dated 1443, internal evidence demonstrates that it was composed prior to William's installation in 1434.
34. *REO*, No.20; *NGL*, No.74.
35. *NGL* 2, 403; Imsen, 'King Magnus and his Liegemen's Hirdskrå'; Imsen, 'Earldom and Kingdom', 3.
36. 'Earldom and Kingdom', 4-5.
37. *NGL* 2, ser.III, 1, No.79.
38. Imsen, 'Earldom and Kingdom'.
39. Imsen, 'Earldom and Kingdom'.
40. Crawford, *The Earls of Orkney and Caithness*, 195, suggests that there were probably no sysselmen when earls ruled the islands. Imsen, 'Earldom and Kingdom', suggests that sysselmen may have continued to be appointed to act alongside earls.
41. The Avignon bishops, Robert Sinclair, Alexander Vaus and William Stephenson, and the Roman bishops, John (Rector of Fetlar), Henry (Bishop of Gardar) and John Pak (Benedictine of Colchester) are discussed in Troels Dahlerup, 'Orkney Bishops and Suffragans'.
42. Seaver, *The Frozen Echo*, 145.
43. *REO*, No.16.
44. Imsen, Public Life, 59.
45. *ER* 8, 364,
46. *OS*, c.110; Dasent, *OS*, 232-3; Taylor, *OS*, 93-4; *Sturlunga Saga*, 338-9.
47. Clouston, 'The Lawrikmen of Orkney'; Clouston, 'The Goodmen and Hirdmen of Orkney'.
48. Numerous 'Lawrightmen' are found at a later date when the title was routinely applied to members of the Parish Bailie courts, see: p.321.
49. *REO*, No.174.
50. Imsen, 'Earldom and Kingdom', 11.
51. Imsen, (1) *Norske Bondekommunalisme* (2) 'Public Life in Shetland and Orkney' (3) 'Earldom and Kingdom'.
52. *REO*, No.19.
53. *Seyðabrævið*.
54. *REO*, No.14.
55. Fellows-Jensen, 'Tingwall, the Significance of the Name'.
56. REO No.30.
57. For example, *REO*, No.30.
58. For example, *REO*, No.34 and 35.
59. Owen, 'Tuquoy'; Lamb, 'The Hall of Haflidi'.
60. Barrett, 'Fish Trade in Norse Orkney'; Lowe, *St Boniface Church*, 152-5.

Chapter 14
The Marriage Treaty and the Pawning of the Islands
Notes to pp.189-205

1. The main works dealing with the Impignoration are: Mooney, *Charters*, 96-118; Crawford, 'Pledging of Orkney and Shetland'; Crawford, 'The Pawning of Orkney and Shetland'; Hørby, 'Christian I and the Pawning of Orkney'; Crawford, 'The Pledging of the Islands' (Shetland); Donaldson, 'Sovereignty and Law in Orkney and Shetland'.
2. *APS* 1, 423.
3. Donaldson, 'Sovereignty and Law', 16.
4. Brøgger, *Ancient Emigrants*, 184; Anderson, *Robert Stewart*, 17.
5. Crawford, 'The Pawning of Orkney and Shetland', 40.
6. *DN* 2, No.691; Marwick, *The Orkney Norn*, xxii.
7. *Sverre's saga*, c.104.
8. Gade, *The Hanseatic Control of Norwegian Commerce*.
9. Friedland, 'Hanseatic Merchants and their Trade with Shetland', 88.
10. *Icelandic Annals*, 275.
11. Thomson, 'Fifteenth Century Depression'.
12. Danielsen et al., *Norway, a History*, 90-2.
13. Johnston, 'Orkney and Shetland Folk', 93.
14. Marwick, *The Orkney Norn*, xxvi-xxix; Barnes, *The Norn Language*, 21-8.
15. Brown, *James I*, 158.
16. Brown, *James I*, 162-3.
17. Dunlop, *Bishop Kennedy*, 103.
18. Nicholson, *Scotland; the Later Middle Ages*, 396.
19. Hay, *Genealogie of the Sainteclairs of Rosslyn*.
20. Dunlop, *Bishop Kennedy*, 382.
21. Dunlop, *Bishop Kennedy*, 405.
22. *Saint-Clairs*, 121.
23. *ER* 6, 209; Nicholson, *Scotland; the Later Middle Ages*, 360, 373.
24. *DN* 8, No.276.
25. Crawford, 'The Pawning of Orkney and Shetland', 36.
26. Crawford, 'William Sinclair', 235-6.
27. Seaver, *The Frozen Echo*, 195.
28. Hørby, 'Christian I and the Pawning of Orkney', 54-7; Crawford, 'The Pawning of Orkney and Shetland', 39.
29. Dunlop, *Bishop Kennedy*, 204.
30. *DN* 7, No.423.
31. Clouston dated the reply to Christian I's letter to 1460, believing it was dated according to the Norwegian calendar (*REO*, 51n.). Dunlop considered the raid by the Islesmen followed the death of James II and so dated the letter to 1461 (*Bishop Kennedy*, 213n). However, the letter dated 29 February appears to refer to James II as still alive, so Clouston's date is to be preferred.
32. *REO*, No.22. On grounds of handwriting it has been suggested that Earl William might have dictated the reply to a scribe whom he is known to have used.
33. MacDonald, *History of the MacDonalds*, 36; Clouston, *History*, 253-5.
34. *REO*, No.23.
35. MacDonald, *History*, 37. Earl William had some limited experience of warfare in the north of England.
36. Munro, *Acts of the Lords of the Isles*, 307-8.
37. MacDonald, *History of the MacDonalds*, 37.
38. *REO*, No.22.
39. *REO*, No.23.
40. Dunlop, *Bishop Kennedy*, 204n.
41. Crawford, 'The Pawning of Orkney and Shetland', 42.
42. Peterkin, *Rentals* (1500), 74.
43. Crawford, 'The Pawning of Orkney and Shetland', 42.
44. Mooney, *Charters*, 111.
45. *DN* 5, 610f.
46. Mooney, *Charters*, 111.
47. *RSS* 1, No.1031.
48. Mooney, *Charters*, 110.
49. *APS* 2, 85.
50. Crawford, 'The Pawning of Orkney and Shetland', 44.
51. Crawford, 'William Sinclair', 245.

52. Mooney, *Charters*, 110.
53. The treaty and a translation is printed in Mooney, *Charters*, 96-109.
54. Crawford, 'The Pledging of the Islands' (Shetland).
55. Clouston, *History*, 258.
56. Discussed in Mooney, *Charters*, 112-8, and Donaldson, 'Sovereignty and Law', 21.
57. Hørby, 'Christian I and the Pawning of Orkney', 58.
58. Mooney, *Cathedral and Royal Burgh*, 14, 187, 190, 204.
59. Thomson, *1492 Rental*, xix.
60. Mooney's views found acceptance at the 1950 Viking Congress in Shetland.
61. Mooney, *Charters*, 107.
62. Ballantyne and Smith, *Shetland Documents*, No.26.
63. Donaldson, 'Sovereignty and Law in Orkney and Shetland', 17-20; Crawford, 'Pledging of Orkney and Shetland', 167-8.
64. Nevis Institute, *The Shetland Report*, 179-185.
65. Donaldson, 'Sovereignty and Law', 19.
66. Nicholson, *Scotland; the Later Middle Ages*, 399.
67. *RMS* 2, No.998.
68. *RMS* 2, No.999.
69. *RMS* 2, No.999.
70. *RMS* 2, No.1000.
71. *RMS* 2, No.1001.
72. *RMS* 2, Nos.996 and 997.
73. *RMS* 2, No.1001.
74. Crawford, 'William Sinclair', 252.
75. *ER* 8, 224-5.
76. *APS* 2, 102; Ballanyne and Smith, *Shetland Documents*, No.27.

Chapter 15
Taxing and Renting Land in Norse Orkney
Notes to pp.206-219

1. Thomson, *1492 Rental*; Peterkin, *Rentals* (1500).
2. Thomson, *1492 Rental*, ix.
3. Thomson, 'Ouncelands and Pennylands', 36.
4. Thomson, *1492 Rental*, xi-xii, 58.
5. *Orkneyinga Saga*, (Anderson), 200.
6. Andersen, 'When was Annual Taxation introduced in the Norse Islands of Britain?'.
7. H.Marwick, *Orkney Farm-names*, 210-1.
8. Rental of the Bishop of Orknayis Landis within Cathnes; *RMS* 4, No.1669.
9. *REO*, No.187.
10. Imsen, *Norsk Bondekommunalisme*, Vol.1, 207.
11. Clouston, 'The Orkney Bailies and their Wattel'; Thomson, *1492 Rental*, xv-xvi.
12. *OS*, c.92.
13. *OS*, c.65, 74.
14. *Hakonar Saga*, c.328.
15. H.Marwick, *Orkney Farm-names*, 211.
16. Ane Abbreviatioun of the Rental', SRO RH 9/15/169.
17. Balfour, *Oppressions*, 6.
18. Thomson, *1492 Rental*, xvi.
19. Wallace, *Description of Orkney*, 21.
20. Thomson, *1492 Rental*, xvi.
21. Since the Orkney-Shetland marks of land are based on an estimate of purchase price, they are quite different from Scottish 'Marks of Old Extent' which are based on an estimate of annual renting value.
22. Thomson, *1492 Rental*, xix-xxi.
23. Thomas, 'Ancient Valuation', 269.
24. Thomas, 'What is a Pennyland?', 258.
25. Thomas, 'What is a Pennyland?', 258; 'Ancient Valuation', 200-205.
26. H.Marwick, *Orkney Farm-names*, 211.
27. Bangor-Jones, 'Ouncelands and Pennylands', 15.
28. H.Marwick, 'Leidang in the West'; H.Marwick, 'Naval Defence'.
29. There is a full discussion of Marwick's leidang theories in Williams, 'Land Assessment and Military Organisation'.
30. Bannerman, *Studies in the History of Dalriada*.
31. Easson, 'Ouncelands and Pennylands'; Megaw, 'Note on Pennyland and Davoch'; Bannerman, *Studies in the History of Dalriada*.
32. Crawford, 'Peter's Pence'; Crawford,

'Norse Earls and Scottish Bishops';
DN 7, No.2; Innes, *Registrum Monasterii Passelet*, 125.

33. Crawford, 'Peters Pence', 18.
34. Nightingale, 'The Evolution of Weight-Standards'; Spufford, *Money and its Uses*, 223.
35. B.Smith, *Toons and Tenants*, xvi-xvii.
36. Ballantyne and Smith, *Shetland Documents* 1, No.59.
37. Andersen, 'When was Regular Annual Taxation Introduced?'.
38. *OS*, c.20.
39. *OS*, c.29.
40. *OS*, c.76.
41. *RMS*, ii, No.3136; Duncan and Brown, 'Argyll and the Isles'.
42. Ballantyne & Smith, *Shetland Documents*, Vol.1, No.2.

Chapter 16
Under Scottish Rule, 1468–1513
Notes to pp.220-232

1. Nicolson, *Scotland; the Later Middle Ages*, 461-2.
2. Manson, 'Shetland in the Sixteenth Century', 202.
3. Anderson, *Earl Robert*, 17.
4. *RSS* 1, No.755; Ballantyne and Smith, *Shetland Documents 1195-1579*, No.35; Smith, 'In the Tracks of Bishop Andrew'.
5. *ER* 8, 224-5.
6. *ER* 8, xlviii.
7. Smith, 'In the Tracks of Bishop Andrew'.
8. *RMS* 8, No.1376.
9. *ER* 8, lix.
10. Thomson, *1492 Rental*, vii-xxii.
11. *ER* 8, 483, 613.
12. *Pundlar Process*.
13. *REO*, No.126.
14. *ER* 8, 363.
15. *ER* 16, 140, 178.
16. *ER* 8, xlviii; Smith, 'Shetland, Scandinavia, Scotland', 27-8.
17. *ER* 8, 275 and passim; Thomson, *1492 Rental*, p.xvi.
18. Peterkin, *Rentals*; Thomson, *1492 Rental*.
19. Thomson, 'The Landscape of Medieval Birsay'.
20. Thomson, 'Some Settlement Patterns in Medieval Orkney'.
21. *OS*, c.67, 97.
22. *OS*, c.94, 102.
23. Thomson, 'The Landscape of Medieval Birsay', 66-7.
24. Steinnes, 'The Huseby System'; Thomson, 'Some Settlement Patterns'.
25. Thomson, *1492 Rental*, 68.
26. Thomson, 'Some Settlement Patterns'.
27. Peterkin, *Rentals*, (1500), 11.
28. Crawford, 'William Sinclair', 240-3.
29. Thomson, *1492 Rental*, xix-xx.
30. Thomson, 'Fifteenth Century Depression'.
31. Sverre's Saga, 156-7.
32. J.Storer Clouston, *The Orkney Parishes*, parish introductions.
33. Thomson, *1492 Rental*, xix.
34. Saint-Clair, *Saint-Clairs*, 298-9.
35. Crawford, 'William Sinclair', 245-6.
36. *RMS* 2, No.1804.
37. *APS* 2, 213.
38. *RMS* 2, Nos.1842, 1843, 1844.
39. Mooney, *Charters*, 1-33.
40. *RMS* 2, No.1974; full text in Peterkin, *Rentals*, 14-16.
41. Brian Smith, 'In the Tracks of Bishop Andrew'.
42. Thomson, *1492 Rental*, xiii-xiv, 86.
43. Thomson, 'Fifteenth Century Depression'.
44. Thomson, *1492 Rental*, 60, 61.
45. Thomson, *1492 Rental*, xxi.
46. Peterkin, *Rentals* (1500), 59, 76; *ER*, v, 54.
47. Peterkin, *Rentals* (1500), 78.
48. Balfour, *Odal Rights*, 47-9; Clouston, *History*, 259.
49. *RSS* 1, No.1031.
50. *Orkney & Shetland Recs.*, 56; Crawford, 'Sir David Sinclair'.
51. *RMS* 2, No.2583.
52. *RMS* 2, No.2620.
53. *RSS* 1, Nos.755 and 1031.
54. Thomson, *1492 Rental*, p.xviii.
55. *RMS* 8, No.1894. and *RMS* 9, No.2030.
56. *Saint-Clairs*, 301.
57. *Saint-Clairs*, 300-1.

58. Calder, *History*, 93-4.
59. *ER* 14, 32.

Chapter 17
The Summerdale Years
Notes to pp.233-246

1. *Shetland Documents*, No.51; a copy is printed in *REO*, No.25.
2. *REO*, No.38.
3. *REO*, Nos.40 and 41.
4. *Shetland Documents* 1, No.44.
5. *ER* 14, 32, 416; *ER* 15, 61.
6. *ER* 15, lxviii, 151-2.
7. *RMS* 3, No.260.
8. *RMS* 3, No.457.
9. NAS CS6/19/67
10. *ER* 15, 16 and 17 passim.
11. *ER* 15, 455.
12. James Sinclair's widow was later pursued for the theft of Margaret Sinclair's rents (see: *Shetland Documents*, No.57).
13. Crawford, 'William Sinclair', 252-3.
14. Crawford, 'William Sinclair', 252-3.
15. Crawford, 'William Sinclair', 252.
16. Crawford, 'Sir David Sinclair of Sumburgh'.
17. Peterkin, *Notes*, Appendix, No.1; *Shetland Documents*, No.34.
18. *Shetland Documents* 1, No.36.
19. *Shetland Documents* 1, No.37.
20. *Shetland Documents* 1, No.45.
21. Clouston, *History*, 285, 287.
22. Anderson, *Robert Stewart*, 23.
23. Clouston, *History*, 286.
24. *Shetland Documents*, No.51; *REO*, No.25.
25. *Saint-Claires*, 190.
26. *Shetland Documents*, No.51; *REO*, No.25.
27. Anderson, *Earl Robert*, 22-3.
28. Leslie, *The History of Scotland*.
29. Peterkin, *Notes*, 90.
30. Summerdale is discussed in Clouston, 'The Battle of Summerdale', Clouston, *History*, 279-292, Clouston, 'Sir James Sinclair of Brecks', and Anderson, *Robert Stewart*, 22-4.
31. *Shetland* Documents 1, No.51; *REO*, No.25.

32. A later tradition tells how the earl was killed escaping from the battlefield; see: Calder, *History of Caithness*, 96-7; *Saint-Claires*, 488-9.
33. Holinshed, *History of Scotland*, states that 500 were killed.
34. Calder, *History of Caithness*, 96-7; *Saint-Claires*, 488-9.
35. Hossack, *Kirkwall in the Orkneys*, 20.
36. *Shetland Documents* 1, No.51; *REO*, No.25.
37. *RMS* 3, No.988.
38. Clouston, *History*, 291.
39. Christensen, 'The Earl of Rothes in Denmark'.
40. Donaldson, 'Problems of Sovereignty and Law', 39-40.
41. Goudie, *Celtic and Scandinavian Antiquities*, 129-31.
42. H.Marwick, *Merchant Lairds* 2, 45-6.
43. Donaldson, 'Sovereignty and Law', 37.
44. *REO*, No.110.
45. *RRS* 2, No.1697; *RMS* 3. No.1479.
46. *REO*, Nos.45 and 46; Clouston, 'Sir James Sinclair'.
47. *RMS* 3, No.1479; *REO*, No.114.
48. Barry, *History*, 246.
49. Mooney, *Charters*, 1-28.
50. Stewart, 'The Final Folios of Adam Abell's *Roit or Quheill of Tyme*', 233-4.
51. Barry, *History*, 246.
52. *RSS* 2, No.2999.
53. *RSS* 2, No.2088.
54. *Shetland Documents*, No.57.
55. *RSS* 2, No.2999.
56. *Shetland Documents*, No.64.
57. *RSS*, 2, No.3151; *Shetland Documents*, No.65; Low, *Tour*, 208-210.
58. Adams and Fortune, *Alexander Lindsay*, 13.
59. Donaldson *James V-James VII*, 58.
60. Adams and Fortune, *Alexander Lindsay*.
61. Hossack, *Kirkwall in the Orkneys*, 64.
62. Balfour, *Odal Rights*, 52.
63. *RMS* 3, No.2233.
64. *REO*, No.27.
65. *REO*, No.27.
66. *ER* 21, 325-7.
67. Craven, *History of the Church in Orkney, to 1558*, 144, quoting Mackenzie mss.

68. *RMS* 3, No.3275.
69. *Shetland Documents*, No.86.
70. *Saint-Clairs*, 134-5.
71. *REO*, No.49.
72. *Shetland Documents*, No.64, note.
73. Anderson, *Robert Stewart*, 32.
74. NAS CS6/6/119.
75. Strype, *Ecclesiastical Memorials* 3, 86-7; Clowes, *The Royal Navy* 2, 473; Buchanan, *The History of the Kirk of Scotland* 16, 396; *OLM* 1, 303. Pitscottie (*The Historie and Chronicles of Scotland* 2, 118) dates the attack to 1556. English sources put the dead at 500 (*CSP* Spanish, 320).

Chapter 18
The Reformation
Notes to pp.247-261

1. Cuthbert, *A Flame in the Shadow*.
2. Donaldson, 'Adam Bothwell' in *Reformed by Bishops*.
3. Fawcett, 'Kirkwall Cathedral', 109.
4. Hossack, *Kirkwall in the Orkneys*, 33.
5. Simpson, *The Castle of Bergen and the Bishop's Palace in Kirkwall*, 65-7.
6. Printed in Cant and Firth, *Light in the North*, 121-2.
7. Clouston, 'The Old Prebends of Orkney'; Mackenzie Mss.
8. *RMS* 6, No.154; Peterkin, *Rentals* (1595), 81.
9. Craven, *History of the Church in Orkney, 1558-1662*, 157.
10. Clouston, 'The Old Prebends of Orkney', 33-4.
11. Peterkin, *Rentals*, (1500), 91; (1627), 89; *RMS* 6, No.1038.
12. Lamb, *Archaeological Sites of Sanday and North Ronaldsay*, No.176.
13. *RMS* 4, No.1758.
14. *RMS* 9, No.1075; *RMS* 9, No.1344; Peterkin, *Rentals* (1595), 111-2.
15. Peterkin, *Rentals* (1595), 56.
16. Peterkin, *Rentals* (1627), 94.
17. *RMS* 11, No.46.
18. Peterkin, *Rentals* (1500), 91.
19. Thomson, 'Settlement Patterns at Tuquoy'; Thomson, 'The Landscape of Burness'.

20. Anderson, *Robert Stewart*, 13.
21. Cuthbert, *A Flame in the Shadows*, 116.
22. Peterkin, *Rentals*, (Appendix), 18-25; *REO*, No.236; *RMS* 3, No.3102.
23. The Archdeacon of Shetland is not mentioned; at that time the Provost, Malcolm Halcro, retained the position (see: Cant, 'The Constitution of St Magnus Cathedral', 111.
24. Hossack, *Kirkwall in the Orkneys*, 65.
25. *REO*, No.236.
26. *RMS*, No.2232.
27. Peterkin, *Rentals* (Documents), 21.
28. Peterkin, *Rentals* (1500), 91.
29. Cant, 'The Constitution of St Magnus Cathedral', 107.
30. *DN* 1, No.42; Cant, 'Norwegian Influences', 129.
31. Printed in Cant and Firth, *Light in the North*, 122-3; Andersen, 'The Orkney Church of the Twelfth and Thirteenth Centuries', 61.
32. Donaldson, *Reformed by Bishops*, 24-5.
33. Donaldson, *Reformed by Bishops*, 25.
34. *RMS* 3, No.2882.
35. Haren, *Papal Letters*, 15.
36. *REO*, No.131.
37. Anderson, *Robert Stewart*, 32-3.
38. Cuthbert, *A Flame in the Shadows*, 141-4.
39. The books in Bothwell's library are discussed in D.Shaw, 'Adam Bothwell'.
40. Napier, *Memoirs of John Napier of Merchison*, 234-5.
41. Donaldson, 'Adam Bothwell', 21-3.
42. *RSS* 5, No.589.
43. Simpson, 'Noltland Castle', 143.
44. Simpson, 'Noltland Castle', 144.
45. Sanderson, *Scottish Rural Society*, 174-5.
46. *RMS* 3, No.1479; *REO*, No.114.
47. *REO*, No.115.
48. *RMS* 3, No.3101.
49. *REO*, No.164.
50. Sanderson, *Scottish Rural Society*, 80.
51. Donaldson, 'Adam Bothwell', 25.
52. Donaldson, 'Adam Bothwell', 20.
53. Since 'Ka' is a surname which was frequently found in Kirkwall, it is not entirely certain that James Skea is the same person as James Ka.
54. *RSS* 4, No.916.
55. Anderson, *Robert Stewart*, 37.

56. *RMS* 4, No.1668.
57. Clouston, *History*, 279-280.
58. *Orkney & Shetland Recs.*, No.68.
59. Donaldson, 'Adam Bothwell', 27.
60. Napier, *Memoirs of John Napier of Merchison*, 68.
61. Donaldson, 'Adam Bothwell', 27.
62. Donaldson, 'Adam Bothwell', 27.
63. Crawford, 'An Unrecognised Statue of Earl Rognvald'.
64. Anderson, *Robert Stewart*, 35.
65. Craven, *The Church in Orkney, 1558-1662*, 17.
66. Donaldson, 'Adam Bothwell', 31.
67. Anderson, *Robert Stewart*, 39.
68. *Orkney & Shetland Recs.*, No.65.
69. Leith, 'The Bellendens and the Palace of Stenness'.
70. *RMS* 4, No.1710.
71. *RMS* 4, No.2472.
72. *RMS* 4, No.1759.
73. *RMS* 4, No.1758.
74. *RMS* 4, No.1758.
75. *REO*, No.236.
76. H.Marwick, *Place-names of Rousay*, 29.
77. Angus, *Protocol Book of Mr Gilbert Grote*, No.229.
78. Clouston, *History*, 296-8.
79. *REO*, 167.
80. Hossack, *Kirkwall in the Orkneys*, 226.
81. Donaldson, 'Adam Bothwell', 34-5.
82. Donaldson, 'Adam Bothwell', 32.
83. Craven, *History of the Church in Orkney, 1558-1662*, 32.
84. Craven, *History of the Church in Orkney, 1558-1662*, 21.

Chapter 19
Earl Robert Stewart
Notes to pp.262-276

1. Anderson, *Robert Stewart*, 52.
2. Edward Sinclair of Eday was the only Sinclair to obtain a major feu, but his branch of the family had been absent from Orkney for several generations.
3. Anderson, *Robert Stewart*, 1-7.
4. Knox, *A History of the Reformation* 1, 260.
5. Keith, *History of the Church of Scotland*, 271-2.
6. *RSS* 5, part 1, No.2078.
7. Anderson, *Robert Stewart*, 46.
8. *APS* 2, 102; *Shetland Documents* 1, No.27.
9. *RMS* 3, No.988.
10. Peterkin, *Notes on Orkney and Zetland*, 106-8.
11. Anderson, *Robert Stewart*, 57.
12. *APS* 3, 254.
13. *RSS* 5, part 1, No.2078.
14. Anderson, *Robert Stewart*, 47.
15. *REO*, No.164.
16. *REO*, No.52.
17. *REO*, Nos.53, 54.
18. *RSS* 5, part 2, No.2529; *REO*, No.55.
19. *RSS* 5, part 2, Nos.3530, 3535.
20. Anderson, *Robert Stewart*, 56.
21. *REO*, No.56.
22. Anderson, *Robert Stewart*, 57.
23. Anderson, *Robert Stewart*, 57-8.
24. Anderson, *Robert Stewart*, 62.
25. Donaldson, 'Adam Bothwell', 43.
26. Angus, *Protocol Book of Mr Gilbert Grote*, No.318.
27. Mooney, *Charters*, 80; MacKenzie, *Grievances*, 36.
28. Angus, *Protocol Book of Mr Gilbert Grote*, No.319.
29. *RPC* 2, 340.
30. Craven, *History of the Church in Orkney (1558-1662)*, 21.
31. Hossack, *Kirkwall in the Orkneys*, 226.
32. Angus, *Protocol Book of Mr Gilbert Grote*, Nos.182, 184.
33. Hossack, *Kirkwall in the Orkneys*, 323.
34. Clouston, *The Orkney Parishes*, 226.
35. *REO*, No.162.
36. Craven, *History of the Church in Orkney (1558-1662)*, 20-1.
37. *Shetland Documents* 1, No.216; Balfour, *Oppressions*, 3-11.
38. Anderson, *Robert Stewart*, 87.
39. RSS 5, part 1, No.2078.
40. *REO*, No.27.
41. *APS* 2, 244.
42. *RMS* 2, No.1844. Bishop William Tulloch and Bishop Andrew, the first Scottish tacksmen, were not explicitly created Justice.
43. *APS* 3, 41; Donaldson, 'Sovereignty and Law', 26-7.
44. Crawford, 'William Sinclair', 253.

45. *REO*, No.239; *RPC* 2, 488-9, 517-8; Anderson, *Robert Stewart*, 95, 147; Donaldson, 'Sovereignty and Law', 31; Clouston, *History*, 303.
46. OA D23/5.
47. *Shetland Documents* 1, No.216.
48. *Shetland Documents* 1, No.216.
49. Anderson, *Robert Stewart*, 93.
50. *Shetland Documents* 1, No.216.
51. *Shetland Documents* 1, No.230.
52. *Shetland Documents* 1, No.233.
53. *RPC* 2, 669.
54. Anderson, *Robert Stewart*, 105.
55. *RSS* 8, No.91.
56. *RMS* 5, No.263; *APS* 3, 254-5.
57. *RMS* 5, No.836.
58. Clouston, *History*, 303.
59. *REO*, No.71.
60. *REO*, No.73.
61. *REO*, 164-5n.
62. *REO*, No.193.
63. *REO*, No.193.
64. Imsen, *Norsk Bondekommunalisme* 1, 207.
65. *RSS* 5, part 1, No.3530.
66. *Shetland Documents* 1, No.216.
67. *REO*, No.187.
68. *Orkney & Shetland Recs.*, No.72.
69. *RPC* 4, 216.
70. *RMS* 5, No.263; *RSS* 8, 2617.
71. Anderson, *Robert Stewart*, 113.
72. *RMS* 5, No.1354.
73. *REO*, No.193.
74. Goudie, *The Celtic and Scandinavian Antiquities of Shetland*, 213-229.
75. Anderson, *Robert Stewart*, 114.
76. *Shetland Times*, 25 October 1985.
77. Anderson, 'The Armada and the Northern Isles; Manson, 'The Fair Isle Spanish Armada Shipwreck'.

Chapter 20
Earl Patrick Stewart
Notes to pp.277-286

1. Anderson, *Black Patie; the Life and Times of Patrick Stewart, Earl of Orkney, Lord of Shetland*.
2. The folklore aspects of Patrick are discussed in Anderson, *Black Patie*, 1-13.
3. Clouston, *History*, 307.
4. Notably Balfour, *Oppressions*, and Balfour, *Odal Rights and Feudal Wrongs*.
5. Anderson, 'The Stewart Earls of Orkney', 45.
6. Anderson, 'Earl Patrick and his Enemies', 45.
7. The 'caschielaws', an obscure form of torture, are discussed in Anderson, *Black Patie*, Appendix 4.
8. Pitcairn, *Criminal Trials* 1, part 1, 373-7.
9. Larner, *Enemies of God*, 69.
10. Chambers, *Domestic Annals of Scotland* 1, 235.
11. Pitcairn, *Criminal Trials* 1, part 1, 373-7.
12. Pitcairn, *Criminal Trials* 1, part 1, 373-7.
13. Pitcairn, *Criminal Trials* 1, part 1, 373-7; Craven, *History of the Church in Orkney (1558-1662)*, 69.
14. Brand, *A Brief Description*, 176; Hibbert, *Shetland Islands*, 115.
15. Pitcairn, *Criminal Trials* 1, part 1, 373-7.
16. Pringle, 'The Houses of the Stewart Earls', 18-24.
17. Simpson, 'Noltland Castle', 153.
18. Pringle, 'The Houses of the Stewart Earls', 26.
19. Pringle, 'The Houses of the Stewart Earls', 26-33.
20. B.Smith, 'Earl Robert and Earl Patrick in Shetland', 12.
21. Pitcairn, *Criminal Trials* 3, 84; Goudie, *The Diary of the Reverend John Mill*, 178-9.
22. Anderson, *Black Patie*, 6.
23. Pringle, 'The Houses of the Stewart Earls', .
24. *RCAHMS* 1, 52.
25. Bannatyne Club, *The History of James the Sext*, 386-7.
26. Simpson, *The Bishop's Palace*, 74-6.
27. Clouston, *History*, 312-3; Bannatyne Club, *The History of James the Sext*, 386-7.
28. *RPC* 8, 254-5.
29. Hossack, *Kirkwall in the Orkneys*, 42-3.

30. The intended reading is: 'Robert Stewart, son of James V, King of Scots, erected this building'. However, by using the Latin 'rex' (nominative agreeing with 'Robert') instead of 'regis' (genitive agreeing with 'James') the inscription reads: 'Robert Stewart, King of Scots, son of James V...'.
31. Anderson, *Black Patie*, 23-4.
32. *RPC* 5, 436-7, 744; Anderson, *Black Patie*, 54-5.
33. Clouston, *History*, 311.
34. James, 'Description', 51.
35. *REO*, l.
36. Craven, *History of the Church in Orkney (1558-1662)*, 76.
37. Craven, *History of the Church in Orkney (1558-1662)*, 99.
38. *RPC* 5, 436-7, 535-7, 551, 724, 729; Anderson, *Black Patie*, 56-7.
39. *Shetland Documents* 1, No.233.
40. Peter Anderson notes that the claim that Patrick had a force of 600 implies that he had mobilised an improbably high proportion of the Shetland male population.
41. Anderson, *Black Patie*, 53.
42. Anderson, *Black Patie*, 71.
43. *RPC* 8, 254-5.
44. Peterkin, *Rentals* (1595).
45. *Shetland Times*, 8 November 1985. B.Smith, 'Earl Robert and Earl Patrick in Shetland', 12.
46. Peterkin, *Notes*, 85-92.
47. *Shetland Documents* 1, No.216.
48. O'Dell, *Historical Geography of the Shetland Islands*, 128, 192.
49. H.Marwick, 'Antiquarian Notes on Stronsay', 61.
50. Wallace, *Description of Orkney*, 31; James, 'Description', 51.
51. *Orkney & Shetland Recs.*, 215-9; H.Marwick, 'Antiquarian Notes on Stronsay', 61.
52. Wallace, *Description of Orkney*, 31; Martin, *A Description of the Western Isles*, 356-7. D.Cooke, *Notes and Extracts from the Ancient Records of the Burgh of Pittenweem*, 53.
53. Goudie, *The Diary of the Reverend John Mill*, 192.
54. *RMS* 2, No.1376; *RMS* 2, 1845.

55. *RMS* 6, No.1022; Thomson, *1492 Rental*, xvii.
56. Peterkin, *Notes*, 85-92.
57. *RPC* 5, 153, 195-6.
58. Anderson, *Black Patie*, 22.
59. *RPC* 5, 284-5; Anderson, *Black Patie*, 22-3.
60. Peterkin, *Notes*, 58.

Chapter 21
The End of the Earldom
Notes to pp.287-300

1. *RMS* 6, No.1022; Anderson, *Black Patie*, 35.
2. *RMS* 6, No.1038.
3. *RMS* 6, No.1022.
4. Craven, *History of the Church in Orkney, 1558-1662*, 88; Clouston, *History*, 314.
5. *RPC* 5, 624; Anderson, *Black Patie*, 79-80.
6. *RPC* 5, 167.
7. Anderson, *Robert Stewart*, 140.
8. *RPC* 5, 167.
9. Anderson, *Black Patie*, 79.
10. Anderson, *Black Patie*, 80.
11. Anderson, *Black Patie*, 80.
12. *APS* 4, 320; Anderson, *Black Patie*, 80.
13. *HMC Hatfield* 9, 33.
14. Anderson, *Black Patie*, 42.
15. *RPC* 5, 523; Anderson, *Black Patie*,
16. *RPC* 7, 737-8.
17. *RPC* 7, 737-8.
18. *RPC* 7, 737-8.
19. Anderson, *Black Patie*, 60.
20. Anderson, *Black Patie*, 43-5.
21. *Saint-Claires*, 196-200.
22. Peterkin, *Notes*, 55.
23. Anderson, *Black Patie*, 82.
24. Anderson, *Black Patie*, 78.
25. Peterkin, *Rentals* (Appendix), 88-92.
26. Peterkin, *Rentals* (Appendix), 88.
27. Peterkin, *Notes*, 59-60.
28. *Saint-Clairs*, 196-200; Anderson, *Black Patie*, 62.
29. *Saint-Clairs*, 196-200; Anderson, *Black Patie*, 87.
30. Pitcairn, *Criminal Trials*, 3, 81-7.
31. Donaldson, *Shetland Life under Earl Patrick*, 1-15, 106-129

32. *RPC* 9, 611-2.
33. Peterkin, *Notes*, 62-7.
34. *RPC* 9, 59-60.
35. James, *Description*, 51.
36. Mitchell, *History of the Scottish Expedition to Norway*, 133-4.
37. Mitchell, *History of the Scottish Expedition to Norway*, 48-55.
38. Peterkin, *Notes*, 70.
39. Barclay, *The Court Book of Orkney and Shetland*.
40. Barclay, *The Court Book of Orkney and Shetland*, 19-24.
41. Peterkin, *Notes*, 70.
42. Peterkin, *Notes*, 70.
43. Pitcairn, *Criminal Trials* 3, 304.
44. Peterkin, *Notes*, 76.
45. Pitcairn, *Criminal Trials* 3, 311.
46. Pitcairn, *Criminal Trials* 3, 304.
47. Pitcairn, *Criminal Trials* 3, 301.
48. Pitcairn, *Criminal Trials* 3, 296.
49. Pitcairn, *Criminal Trials* 3, 293, 296.
50. Pitcairn, *Criminal Trials* 3, 293.
51. Anderson, *Black Patie*, 100.
52. Pitcairn, *Criminal Trials* 3, 296-8.
53. Akrigg, *Jacobean Pageant*, 83-4.
54. Anderson, *Black Patie*, 114-5.
55. Pitcairn, *Criminal Trials* 3, 286.
56. Pitcairn, *Criminal Trials* 3, 302.
57. Pitcairn, *Criminal Trials* 3, 302.
58. *RMS* 7, No.1119.
59. Pitcairn, *Criminal Trials* 3, 301.
60. Clouston, *History*, 329.
61. H.Marwick, *Orkney*, 99-103.

Chapter 22
Tacksmen, Lairds and Udallers, 1615–1707
Notes to pp.301-314

1. *RPC* 12, 263, 267; *RPC* (2nd ser.) 3, 425, 462, 469.
2. *RPC* (2nd ser.) 3, 172.
3. *RPC* 12, 263, 267.
4. *Pundlar Process*, 7.
5. *RPC* 12, 267.
6. *RPC* 13, 818-9.
7. Anderson, *Black Patie*, 144.
8. *RMS* 7, Nos.1516, 1517 and 1519.
9. *RMS* 8, No.1894; Marwick, *Orkney Farm-names*, 48.
10. NAS CS15/242.
11. NAS RD1/500/f.6; Lamb, *Archaeological Sites of Eday and Stronsay*, No.77.
12. Purves, *Revenues of the Scottish Crown*, 122-4; *RPC* 12, 713.
13. *RPC* 12, 231n.; *RPC* (2nd ser.) 1, xcvi.
14. Hossack, *Kirkwall in the Orkneys*, 247.
15. NAS E4/4/317.
16. *RPC* 12, 263.
17. Purves, *Revenues of the Scottish Crown*, 122-4.
18. *RPC* 13, 384.
19. *RPC* 12, 231.
20. *RMS* 8, No.690; *RPC* 13, 601-2.
21. *RPC* 7, 86.
22. *RPC* (2nd ser.) 5, 309-310.
23. Sir Walter Scott, *Heart of Midlothian*, Note J.; Hossack, *Kirkwall in the Orkneys*, 229-230; Smout, *History of the Scottish People*, 169.
24. Purves, *Revenues of the Scottish Crown*, 122-4; *RMS* 8, Nos.1966 and 2167; *RPC* (2nd ser.) 5, 309-310.
25. Peterkin, *Rentals* (documents), 23-32; *RMS* 7, Nos.1312, 1333, 1334, 1389.
26. Craven, *History of the Church in Orkney, 1558-1662*, 188-194.
27. Peterkin, *Rentals* (documents), 29.
28. Sutherland Graeme, *Pateas Amicis*, 7-8; Hossack, *Kirkwall in the Orkneys*, 250-1; Peterkin, *Rentals* (documents), 26.
29. Hossack, *Kirkwall in the Orkneys*, 78-9; Watt, 'The Ruins of Breckness'.
30. Donaldson, *Scotland; James V to James VIII*, 350.
31. *The Complete Peerage* 9, 295.
32. OA D31/38/3.
33. Peterkin, *Notes*, App.104-6.
34. Wishart, *The Memoirs of Montrose*; Peterkin, *Notes*, 104-6; Marwick, 'A Glimpse of the Great Marquis'; Mooney, *Charters*, 88-90; Mooney, 'The Wreck of the Crown', 1-8; Tudor, *The Orkneys and Shetland*, 583-4.
35. Peterkin, *Notes*, 106-7; Mooney, *Charters*, 88-9.
36. Peterkin, *Notes*, 106-7.
37. Dow, *Cromwellian Scotland*, 19.
38. Miller, *Orkney*, 94.

39. Emerson, *Poetical Description.*
40. Craven, *History of the Church in Orkney, 1558-1662,* 217.
41. Terry, *The Cromwellian Union,* 125.
42. Mackintosh, *Curious Incidents,* 25, 59-66; Hossack, *Kirkwall in the Orkneys,* 339-340.
43. *RMS* 11, No.234; Gifford, *Historical Description of the Zetland Islands,* 38.
44. Hossack, *Kirkwall in the Orkneys,* 244.
45. Aston University, *The Wreck of the Kennermerland;* Henderson, 'Shipwreck in Shetland', 197-202.
46. 'Maunsmas', feast of St Magnus, 13 December.
47. Aston University, *The Wreck of the Kennermerland.*
48. Wallace, *Description of Orkney,* 33-4.
49. Brand, *Brief Description,* 76-7.
50. Marwick, *The Folklore of Orkney and Shetland,* 25.
51. Lamb, *Climate, History and the Modern World,* 209-210.
52. Hazell, 'Icebergs Warning' in *The Orcadian Book of the Twentieth Century,* 85.
53. Discussed at Orkney Science Festival, 1998.
54. Barry, *History* 475-6.
55. *RPC* (2nd ser.) 3, 353, 386.
56. Wallace, *Description of Orkney,* 37.
57. Shaw, *The Northern and Western Isles,* 166.
58. *RPC* (2nd ser.) 5, 284.
59. *RPC* (2nd ser.) 5, 284.
60. *RPC* (2nd ser.) 5, 659.
61. *OSA* Cross & Burness.
62. Brand, *Brief Description,* 40.
63. Mackintosh, *Curious Incidents,* 92-4.
64. OA Orkney Parish Records, Stromness, 27 July 1697.
65. *OSA,* Birsay & Harray.
66. Steuart, *Diary of Thomas Brown,* 60-4.
67. 'Hamesucken', an attack on a person's home; 'bangstrie', violence.
68. *RPC* 16, 473-4.
69. *RPC* 15, 246, 624-5.
70. *RPC* 15, 337-8.
71. *RPC* 15, 329.
72. Hossack, *Kirkwall in the Orkneys,* 89.
73. Petition of Sir Alexander Brand, OA GD.150/2021.

74. Clouston, 'The Orkney Townships', 35.
75. Peterkin, *Rentals* (Appendix), 106-8.
76. Earldom Compt Book, 1721, OA D38/2015/4.
77. *OSA,* Birsay & Harray, 8.
78. Gow, *James Moodie,* 7.
79. Hossack, *Kirkwall in the Orkneys,* 89.
80. Mackintosh, *Curious Incidents,* 86-7, 129.
81. Brand, *Brief Description.* 40-1.
82. Ross, *Orkney and the Earls of Morton,* 12.
83. Ross, *Orkney and the Earls of Morton,* 9-15.
84. Barry, *History,* 265.
85. Smith, *Shetland Life and Trade,* 23-4.
86. Gailey and Fenton, 'The Reverend John Brand'.
87. Brand, *Brief Description,* 40-1.
88. Ross, *Orkney and the Earls of Morton,* 14.
89. Peterkin, *Rentals* (Appendix), 105-6.
90. Thomson, *1492 Rental,* xix-xx, 102.
91. *Pundlar Process,* 34.
92. Larson, *Earliest Norwegian Laws,* Drever, 'Udal Law'; Ryder, 'Udal Law', Custine, 'Udal Law'.
93. Uthel Buik, OA GD1/236/2.
94. *REO,* No.75.
95. Clouston, 'The Orkney Townships', 22-3.
96. Peterkin, *Rentals* (Appendix), 47.
97. Jones, 'Perceptions of Udal Law'.
98. Shaw, *The Northern and Western Isles,* 39.
99. *RMS* 3, No.3103.
100. *Pundlar Process,* 116.
101. *RMS* 11, No.637.
102. Gifford, *Historical Description of the Zetland Islands,* 62.
103. Peace, *Almanac,* 1925, 139-142.
104. Frances Shaw, *The Northern and Western Isles,* 28.

Chapter 23
Old-style Farming
Notes to pp.315-332

1. Clouston, 'The Orkney Townships'; 'The Orkney Pennylands'; 'An Orkney Perambulation'; 'The Run-rig System in Orkney'.

2. Mackenzie, *Orcades.*
3. Thomson, *1492 Rental.*
4. Craven, *Church Life in South Ronaldsay and Burray*, 110.
5. Enumerator's Notebook, 1821.
6. Marwick, *Orkney Farm-names*, 171.
7. Thomson, *1492 Rental*, 38.
8. *RMS* 10, No.607.
9. Clouston, *Orkney Parishes*, 201.
10. *REO*, No.149.
11. Peterkin, *Rentals* (1500), 47.
12. For a discussion of udal rights to the foreshore see: Scottish Law Commission, *Discussion Paper on Law of the Foreshore and Seabed*, 41-5.
13. Thomson, 'John Coventrie Sitting in Justice'; OA D2/47/6.
14. Begg, 'The Bailie Courts of Orkney'.
15. Craven, *Church Life in South Ronaldsay*, 112.
16. Barclay, *Court Book, 1614-5.*
17. Donaldson, *Shetland under Earl Patrick*, 106-129.
18. *Bailie Court Book of St Andrews & Deerness*, 18.
19. Groundwater, *Memories of an Orkney Family*, 39-42.
20. Barry, *History*, 323-4.
21. Wenham, 'Famine and Victuals on the Graemeshall Estate'; SSPCK Minutes P233/4.
22. *Napier Commission Evidence*, 1535.
23. *APS* 9, 462.
24. Thomson, 'Common Land', 80.
25. Thomson, 'Common Land'.
26. Thomson, 'The Landscape of Medieval Birsay', 55.
27. OA Additional Papers 19.
28. Fenton, *The Northern Isles*, 43.
29. Barry, *History*, 372n.
30. Clouston, 'Orkney Townships', 28.
31. *REO*, No.75.
32. Clouston, 'Orkney Townships', 19-20.
33. *REO*, No.85; Clouston, 'Orkney Townships', 20, 31-2; Fenton, *Northern Isles*, 42.
34. Göransson, 'Regular Open Field Patterns'; Dodgshon, *The Origin of British Field Systems*, 32-3; Whyte, *Agriculture and Society*, 150.
35. Clouston, 'Orkney Townships', 26-7.
36. Clouston, 'The Orkney Lands'.
37. Clouston, 'Orkney Townships', 19-20.
38. Clouston, *History*, 354.
39. Petition of David Aitken, OA D13/3/1.
40. Fenton, *The Northern Isles*, 349.
41. Fenton, *The Northern Isles*, 349.
42. *OSA*, South Ronaldsay & Burray.
43. *Bailie Court Book of St Andrews & Deerness.*
44. Clouston, 'Orkney Townships', 25-6; Marwick, *Orkney Norn*, 18-9.
45. Thomson, 'Township, House and Tenant-holding', 120-3.
46. Dodgshon, 'Medieval Rural Scotland', 67.
47. *Seyðabræviδ*, Tórshavn, 1971; G.V.C.Young, *From the Vikings to the Reformation; a Chronicle of the Faroe Islands up to 1538*, 1979, pp.140-153.
48. Lamb, *Climate, History and the Modern World*, 162-177.
49. Mackintosh, *The Orkney Crofters*, 244-6.
50. OA D3, Add.31.
51. *REO*, No.41.
52. *APS* 9, 421.
53. *APS* 9, 462.

Chapter 24
The False Dawn of Agricultural Improvement
Notes to pp.333-348

1. Aberdeen, Plan of the Barony, OA D8/W20; Thomson, 'The Landscape of Medieval Birsay'.
2. *OSA*, Evie & Rendall, 192, 193, 194.
3. Napier Commission Evidence, 1488.
4. Fenton, *The Northern Isles*, 43; Clouston, 'The Orkney Townships', 32.
5. Fenton, *The Northern Isles*, 41-3; Sanderson, *Scottish Rural Society*, 15.
6. Bond and Hunter, 'Flax-growing in Orkney'.
7. Barry, *History*, 363; Shirreff, *General View*, 81.
8. *OSA*, Holm, 21.
9. Fereday, 'William Balfour', 37.
10. Hewison, *The Diary of Patrick Fea*, 84; Marwick, 'An Orkney Jacobite Farmer'.

11. *OSA*, Evie & Rendall, 192; Stronsay & Eday, 304.
12. Peace, *Almanac*, 1925.
13. Martin, *Description of the Western Isles*, 355; Mackaile, 'A Short Relation', 6.
14. Scarth and Watt, 'Agriculture of Orkney', 5.
15. H.Smith, *Shetland Life and Trade*, 22.
16. *RPC* (2nd ser.) 5, 30.
17. Gow, *James Moodie*, 5-9.
18. MacKenzie, *Orchades* (charts).
19. Fereday, *Orkney Feuds*, 11-20.
20. Whyte, *Agriculture and Society*, 124-5.
21. Brand, *Brief Description*, 225; Defoe, *Tour*, iv, 253; Haldane, *The Drove Roads of Scotland*, 103.
22. OA D14/1/4.
23. Tait, 'Farming in a Bygone Age'.
24. William Sinclair v Patrick Fea, OA SC.11/5/27.
25. Marwick, 'Two Eighteenth Century Orkney Inventories'.
26. Fenton, *Scottish Country Life*, 38-9.
27. Thomson, 'Common Land'; Hewison, *Diary of Patrick Fea*, 210-1.
28. Low, *Tour*, 40-1.
29. Fereday, *Lairds*, ii, 418-425.
30. Fereday, *Lairds*, ii, 420; Gordon, *Remarks*, 258.
31. Fereday, *Orkney Feuds*, 89-93.
32. Fereday, *Lairds*, ii, 422-3.
33. Thomson, *The Little General*, 8-42.
34. Map of the Island of Shapinsay, 1846.
35. Garson, *Balfour Village*.
36. *OSA*, Shapinsay, 358.
37. Map of the Island of Shapinsay, 1846.
38. Whittington, 'Agriculture and Society in Lowland Scotland', 145.
39. Sutherland, 'Answer to Remarks on Sir John Sinclair's Agricultural Account of Orkney, November 1795', OA D13/6/12.
40. *OSA*, Shapinsay, 365.
41. Sutherland, 'Answer to Remarks'.
42. Fereday, *The Orkney Balfours*, 143-175.
43. North Riding Record Office, *The Zetland (Dundas) Archive*.
44. Thomson, 'Common Land', 80-1.
45. OA, Map E29.
46. Division of Marwick, OA Additional Papers 19.
47. Fereday, *Samuel Laing*, 201-2.
48. Sutherland, 'Answer to Remarks'.
49. Fereday, *Samuel Laing*, 43-4.
50. E.Marwick, *Journey from Serfdom*; Hossack, *Kirkwall in the Orkneys*, 293.
51. E.Marwick, *Journey from Serfdom*.
52. Sutherland, 'Answer to Remarks'.
53. Lockhart, *Memoirs*, 277.
54. A letter from Robert Scarth to John Watson, quoted in the latter's *Tenancy and Ownership*.
55. Quoted in Schrank, *An Orkney Estate*, 28.
56. Schrank, *An Orkney Estate*.
57. Thomson, 'Common Land'; Adams, *Directory of Former Scottish Commonties*.
58. Thomson, 'The Crofting Pioneer Fringe'.
59. *OSA* Orphir, 78.
60. Adams, *Directory of Former Scottish Commonties*.
61. Scottish Office Agriculture, Environment and Fisheries Department, June Census, 1998.

Chapter 25
Merchant-Lairds and the Great Kelp Boom
Notes to pp.349-362

1. *OS*, c.105.
2. Marwick, *Merchant Lairds* 2, 53.
3. Marwick, *Merchant Lairds* 2, 48.
4. Tucker, *Report upon the Settlement of the Revenues in Scotland*.
5. *NSA*, Kirkwall, 7; a typical ship of the kelp-boom period is described in Hustwick, *The Peggy & Isabella*.
6. Ross, *Sail Ships of Orkney*.
7. Shaw, *The Northern and Western Isles of Scotland*, 166-7.
8. *Sverre's Saga*, 129.
9. Kaland, 'Some Economic Aspects of the Orkneys in the Viking Period'.
10. Lenman, *An Economic History of Modern Scotland*, 21; Marwick, *Merchant Lairds*, 60-2.
11. *REO*, no.18.
12. Shaw, *The Northern and Western Isles of Scotland*, 169-170.
13. Hewison, 'Smuggling in Eighteenth

Century Orkney; Fereday, *Samuel Laing*, 24-5.

14. Smith, *Shetland Life and Trade*, 24-5; Mackaile, 'A Short Relation'.
15. Brand, *Brief Description*, 111.
16. Smith, *Shetland Life and Trade*, 32-5; Marwick, *Merchant Lairds* 2, 47-8.
17. Smith, *Shetland Life and Trade*, 82.
18. Smith, 'Stock-stove Houses'; Fenton, *The Northern Isles*, 111; Stoklund, 'Building Traditions in the Northern World'.
19. Peterkin, Rentals (1500), 87, and (1595), 77, 83.
20. Barclay, *Court Book, 1614-1615*, 31-2.
21. Shaw, *The Northern and Western Isles*, 172.
22. Hossack, *Kirkwall in the Orkneys*, 137-9; Hewison, *Who was Who*, 30-1, 86; Anderson, *Robert Stewart*, 179; Fereday, 'The Lairds of Eighteenth Century Orkney'.
23. Thomson, *Kelp-making in Orkney*, 13-7.
24. Thomson, *Kelp-making in Orkney*, 19-25.
25. *NSA*, St Andrews and Deerness.
26. Thomson, *Kelp-making in Orkney*, 26-33.
27. *OSA* (Withrington and Grant), xvii-xviii.
28. Thomson, *Kelp-making in Orkney*, 34-38.
29. Thomson, *Kelp-making in Orkney*, 39-44.
30. Thomson, *Kelp-making in Orkney*, 44-53.
31. Thomson, *Kelp-making in Orkney*, 60-70.
32. Thomson, *Kelp-making in Orkney*, 65-73.
33. *OSA*, Birsay, 155.
34. *OSA*, Birsay, 15-6.
35. Barry, *History of the Orkney Islands*, 383.
36. Hossack, *Kirkwall in the Orkneys*, 109.
37. Hossack, *Kirkwall in the Orkneys*, 352.
38. Thomson, *Kelp-making in Orkney*, 91-7.
39. *NSA*, Cross & Burness, 109; Miller and Luther-Davies, *Eday and Hoy*, 31-2.
40. Fereday, *Autobiography of Samuel Laing*.
41. Thomson, *The Little General*, 27-9
42. *NSA*, Kirkwall, 1-12.
43. Thomson, *Kelp-making in Orkney*, 46, 48.
44. Thomson, *Kelp-making in Orkney*, 98-100.

Chapter 26
Linen, Fishing and the 'Nor Wast'
Notes to pp.363-377

1. Schrank, 'Cross-roads of the North; Proto-industrialisation in the Orkney Islands'.
2. Bond and Hunter, 'Flax-growing in Orkney from the Norse Period to the Eighteenth Century'; Morris, 'Viking Orkney'; Kaland, 'Some Economic Aspects of the Orkneys in the Viking Period'.
3. Shirreff, *General View of the Agriculture of the Orkney Islands*, App.46-55.
4. Durie, *The Scottish Linen Industry*, 11-20.
5. Durie, *The Scottish Linen Industry*, 115-140.
6. Durie, *The Scottish Linen Industry*, 88.
7. McMath, 'Kirkwall in the Orkneys'.
8. Durie, *The Scottish Linen Industry*, 136.
9. Durie, *The Scottish Linen Industry*, 142n.
10. MacMath, 'Kirkwall in the Orkneys' 36-7.
11. Hepburn, *Letter to a Gentleman*, 21.
12. Hepburn, *Letter to a Gentleman*, 21; Mackintosh, *The Orkney Crofters*, 16.
13. McMath, 'Kirkwall in the Orkneys'.
14. Hepburn, *Letter to a Gentleman*, 20.
15. Wenham, 'From Lintseed to Linen'.
16. Shirreff, *General View of the Agriculture of Orkney*, 89.
17. Wenham, 'From Lintseed to Linen', 29.
18. *OSA*, Birsay & Harray, Evie & Rendall, Holm, Kirkwall.
19. Wenham, 'From Lintseed to Linen', 27.
20. *OSA*, Birsay & Harray, Sandwick & Stromness, Evie & Rendall, Westray.

21. Fenton, *The Northern Isles*, 492.
22. E.Marwick, *Journey from Serfdom*; Durie, *The Scottish Linen Industry*, 106.
23. Shirreff, *General View of the Agriculture of the Orkney Islands*, 62-71.
24. Wenham, 'From Lintseed to Linen', 30.
25. *Edinburgh Encyclopaedia* 16, 1830 s.v. Orkney.
26. E.Marwick, *Journey from Serfdom*.
27. Barry, *History*, introduction to 3rd edition.
28. *NSA*, Kirkwall.
29. Neil, *Tour*, 6-7; *NSA*, Sandwick, 62; Barry, *History*, introduction to 3rd edition.
30. Firth, *Reminiscences of an Orkney Parish*, 50.
31. Dennison, 'Manufacture of Straw Articles'; Fenton, *Northern Isles*, 260-272.
32. *NSA*, Sandwick.
33. Firth, *Reminiscences of an Orkney Parish*, 50.
34. Troup & Eunson, *Stromness*, 17.
35. Miller, *Orkney*, 155.
36. *OSA*, South Ronaldsay & Burray.
37. *OSA*, Orphir; *NSA*, Kirkwall, Brand, *Brief Description*, 31.
38. Low, *Tour*, 18-9; *OSA*, Orphir, Birsay & Harray; *NSA*, Westray.
39. Goudie, *Celtic and Scandinavian Antiquities*, 191.
40. MacInnes, 'The Alexander Graham Case', 114.
41. Dunlop, *The British Fisheries Society*, 9-10.
42. Coull, *The Sea Fisheries of Scotland*, 68.
43. Fea, *The Present State of the Orkney Islands*, 87.
44. Brand, *Brief Description*, 32.
45. *OSA*, Walls & Flotta.
46. Fenton, *The Northern Isles*, 542.
47. *OSA*, Walls & Flotta; *NSA*, Holm.
48. *NSA*, North Ronaldsay, Stronsay & Eday.
49. Low, *Brief Description*, 10-1.
50. *OSA*, Walls & Flotta.
51. *OSA*, Delting (Shetland); *OSA*, Sandwick & Stromness.
52. *NSA*, South Ronaldsay & Burray; Fenton, *The Northern Isles*, 597.
53. Coull, 'Fishing in Orkney'.
54. *NSA*, Stronsay & Eday.
55. Goodlad, *Shetland Fishing Saga*, 132.
56. Dunlop, *The British Fisheries Society*, 185.
57. Fereday, *The Autobiography of Samuel Laing*, 140-4, 207-210.
58. Coull, 'Herring Fisheries in Orkney', 48.
59. Hazell, *The Orcadian Book of the Twentieth Century*, 104-5; Gibson, *The Herring Fishing, Stronsay*.
60. Coull, 'Herring Fisheries in Orkney', 45, 47.
61. Traill, *Vindication of Orkney*.
62. Stromness Museum, *Harvest of Silver*.
63. Coull, 'Herring Fisheries in Orkney', 46.
64. *NSA*, County Report, 214.
65. Coull, 'Herring Fisheries in Orkney', 46.
66. Low, *Tour*, 55; *OSA*, St Andrews & Deerness, Kirkwall; *NSA*, St Andrews, 172.
67. Troup and Eunson, *Stromness*, 5-8.
68. *OSA*, Sandwick & Stromness; Newman, *Company of Adventurers* 1. 175-182.
69. MacKay, *The Honourable Company*, 90.
70. Clouston, 'Orkney and the Hudson's Bay Company'.
71. *OSA*, Sandwick & Stromness.
72. Clouston, 'Orkney and the Hudson's Bay Company'; E.Marwick, 'Chief Factor James Sutherland'; E.Marwick, 'William Tomison'; Shearer, *The New Orkney Book*, 68-9; Bunyan, *No Ordinary Journey*.
73. Troup, *The Ice-bound Whalers*, 11-41.
74. Troup and Eunson, *Stromness*, 6.
75. Hossack, *Kirkwall in the Orkneys*, 412-3.
76. Traill, *Vindication of Orkney*, 68-9.
77. *OSA*, Kirkwall.
78. *Bailie Court Book of St Andrews and Deerness*, 27.
79. *OSA*, Sandwick & Stromness.
80. MacInnes, 'The Alexander Graham Case'.
81. *OSA*, Orphir.
82. *OSA*, Kirkwall.
83. *OSA*, South Ronaldsay & Burray.

84. *NSA*, South Ronaldsay & Burray.
85. Thomson, 'Sober and Tractable?'.
86. *OSA*, Birsay & Harray.
87. Barclay, *Population of Orkney.*
88. *OSA, passim.*
89. Fea, *The Present State of the Orkney Islands*, 78.
90. Wenham, 'Margaret Vedder'.
91. Wenham, 'From Lintseed to Linen'; Wenham, 'Farming and Victuals on the Graemeshall Estate'.

Chapter 27
The Nineteenth Century Agricultural Revolution
Notes to pp.378-394

1. Notably Neil, *Tour.*
2. Troup and Eunson, *Stromness*, 6.
3. Troup and Eunson, *Stromness*, 7.
4. Barclay, *Population of Orkney.*
5. Hewison, *Diary of Patrick Fea*, 210.
6. *NSA* Cross & Burness, 94.
7. Gray, 'North-east Agriculture and the Labour Force'.
8. *NSA* Cross & Burness, 97; E.Marwick, *Journey from Serfdom*; Fereday, *Samuel Laing*, 145-6.
9. *NSA* Holm, 221; Sutherland-Graeme, 'From my Family Papers'; Schrank, *An Orkney Estate*, 40-87.
10. Rousay estate, 'Condition of Leases'; Thomson, *The Little General*, 106-9.
11. E.Marwick, 'Looking Around', OA D31/52/3/6.
12. Thomson, *The Little General*, 55-6.
13. *OSA* Stronsay & Eday, 301n.; Marwick, *The Orkney Norn*, 25.
14. *Orcadian*, 10 November 1855.
15. Poor Law Enquiry, xxi, 238.
16. Poor Law Enquiry, xxiii, 437a.
17. OA SC/11/50/11.
18. Thomson, 'Crofting Pioneer Fringe'.
19. The comment is from Olsen, *Farms and Fanes*, 119, discussing *ruð*-names which are applied to similar places of an earlier date in Norway.
20. OA, Grainger & Miller, Plan of the Commonty of Shapinsay, 1831.
21. Thomson, 'Crofting Pioneer Fringe', 34-6.
22. Thomson, 'The Landscape of Medieval Birsay', 64.
23. Mackintosh, *The Orkney Crofters*, 112.
24. Mackintosh, *The Orkney Crofters*, 112.
25. Thomson, *The Little General*, 42-52.
26. Donaldson, *Northwards by Sea*, 13-7, 103-5.
27. OA D5/3/17.
28. Adams, *A Directory of Former Scottish Commonties*, 165-173.
29. 9 & 10 Vic.c.101; Fenton, *Scottish Country Life*, 23; Thomson, *The Little General*, 116.
30. O'Dell, *Land of Britain*, 199-200; Vink, *De Ontwikkeling van de Agrarische Bedrijsstructuur in Orkney*, 37.
31. General Burroughs' dealings with the Scottish Drainage & Improvement Company, OA D19/7/11.
32. Pringle, 'On the Agriculture of Orkney'.
33. Pringle, 'On the Agriculture of Orkney'; Thomson, 'Crofting Pioneer Fringe'.
34. Pringle, 'On the Agriculture of Orkney'.
35. Information from Professor Minoti Chakravarty-Kaul.
36. Thomson, *The Little General*, 42-80.
37. Barry, *History*, 390.
38. Shirreff, *General View*, 33-5.
39. *NSA* County Report, 215.
40. C.Clouston, *Guide to the Orkney Islands*; Barry, *History*, 3rd edition, introduction; Pringle, 'On the Agriculture of Orkney'; *Orkney Herald*, 3 May 1882; *Scotsman*, 11 May 1883.
41. Hewison, 'Holm Farm Diary',
42. Hunter, *The Making of the Crofting Community* 131-145.
43. Napier Commission Evidence, 1492-7; Skea, *Island Images*, xix; Goodfellow, *Sanday Church History*, 180-2, 380-6.
44. Thomson, *The Little General*, 126-8.
45. Napier Commission Evidence, 1434-1593; Thomson, *The Little General*, 123-134.
46. Thomson, *The Little General.*
47. Mackintosh, *The Orkney Crofters*, v-vii.

48. Mackintosh, *The Orkney Crofters*, 280-4.
49. Thomson, *The Little General*, 155-6.
50. SRO AF 39/33/23.
51. Well described in Groundwater, *Memories of an Orkney Family*.
52. E.Marwick, *Journey from Serfdom*.
53. Power, *Medieval People*, 11-33.
54. Mackintosh, *The Orkney Crofters*, 16.
55. Stove field names from Hewison, *Diary of Patrick Fea*, 210-1.

Chapter 28
Orkney Society in the Eighteenth and Nineteenth Centuries
Notes to pp.395-415

1. Anderson, *Robert Stewart*, 150.
2. *Pundlar Process*; Fereday, *Orkney Feuds*, 36-8, 47-52; Fereday, *Orkney Balfours*, 14, 15, 17, 21.
3. Published in Mackenzie's *General Grievances and Oppressions*.
4. *Pundlar Process*, 47; Hossack, *Kirkwall in the Orkneys*, 408-410.
5. Connor, *Weights and Measures*.
6. Fereday, *Orkney Balfours*, 26-7.
7. Fereday, *The Family of Dundas*; North Riding Record Office, *The Zetland Archive*; Royal Bank of Scotland, *36 St Andrews Square*.
8. North Riding Record Office, *The Zetland Archive*, 21.
9. Flett, 'When Orkney had Four Voters'.
10. Thomson, 'The Eighteenth Century Church', 68-70.
11. Flett, 'When Orkney had Four Voters'.
12. Hewison, *Who was Who*, 76.
13. Sutherland-Graeme, *Orkney and the Last Great War*, 68.
14. Fereday, *Lairds* 1, 12.
15. Sutherland-Graeme, 'Parliamentary Representation'.
16. Flett, 'When Orkney had Four Voters'; Fereday, *Autobiography of Samuel Laing*, 222-228; Mackintosh, *Glimpses of Kirkwall*, 288-294.
17. Thomson, *The Little General*, 11-4, 61-83.
18. Fereday, *The Lairds and Eighteenth Century Orkney*, 243-4.
19. Thomson, *Little General*, 29, 110-1.
20. DAFS, Agricultural Returns.
21. Thomson, *Little General*, 135-144.
22. Irvine, W., *Shapinsay*, 104-5; Shapinsay Folk Studies Project, *The Eviction of the Shapinsay Elders*.
23. Garson, *Balfour Village*.
24. Balfour, *Odal Rights and Feudal Wrongs*; Balfour, *Oppressions*.
25. Balfour, *Ancient Orkney Melodies*.
26. Garson, *Balfour Village*.
27. Valuation rolls.
28. Thomson, 'Eighteenth Century Church'; Craven, *Episcopal Church*, 31.
29. Liddell, *Melancholy Case*.
30. Thomson, 'The Eighteenth Century Church', 68-70.
31. Cuthbert, *Life of George Low*.
32. Low, *Tour*; Low, *History of Orkney*.
33. Smith, *Church in Orkney*, 95-6.
34. OA Mss volume of Thomas Baikie's sermons.
35. OA, St Magnus Kirk Session Records, 13 May 1730.
36. *OSA*, Holm.
37. Thomson, 'Sober and Tractable'.
38. Barry, *History*, 343.
39. Newman, *Company of Adventurers* 1, 180-1.
40. *OSA*, Birsay & Harray.
41. H.Marwick, 'Antiquarian Notes on Stronsay'; Thomson, *Kelp-making*, 74-85.
42. *OSA*, Stronsay & Eday.
43. OSA, Firth & Stenness, D.P.Thomson, *Orkney Through the Centuries*.
44. Haldane, *Journal*.
45. Sutherland, 'Crack-brained Mechanics'.
46. Flett, 'Kirkwall Incorporated Trades'.
47. Fereday, *The Orkney Balfours*, 99-103.
48. Fereday, *The Orkney Balfours*, 103.
49. Barry, *History*, 341-2.
50. Flett, *Lodge Kilwinning*, 47-8.
51. Paterson, *Memoir of Robert Paterson*; Webster, *Kirkwall United Presbyterian Congregation*; Goodfellow, *Dr Robert Paterson*.
52. Napier Commission Evidence, 1492-7, 1533-48.
53. *The Orkney Herald*, 13 June 1892.
54. Acts, i, v.11.

55. Skea, *Island Images*, 38.
56. Firth, *Reminiscences of an Orkney Parish*, 33-4.
57. E.Marwick, 'When Stromness had a Newspaper', in Robertson (ed.), *An Orkney Anthology*, 216-7.
58. Mackay, *Islands Postal History*.
59. Somner, 'The Pentland Firth Mail Service'.
60. Mooney, *Charters*, 1-15.
61. Peterkin, *Rentals* (1627), 84; Fereday, 'From Sang School to Burgh School'.
62. Eunson, 'The Influence of the Education Act', 5.
63. Peterkin, *Rentals* (1627), 87.
64. Peterkin, *Rentals* (1627), 33-98.
65. Presbytery Records, 27 June 1698 and 28 September 1709.
66. Presbytery Records, 4 November 1719 and 3 February 1720.
67. *NSA*, Orphir; *NSA*, South Ronaldsay.
68. *NSA*, Sandwick.
69. Eunson, 'The Influence of the Education Act', 9.
70. Eunson, 'The Influence of the Education Act', 5.
71. OA Minute Book.
72. Introduction to Dennison, *Orkney Folklore*, xi-xii.

Chapter 29
Farming in the Twentieth Century
Notes to pp.416-433

1. The account of the break-up of the estates is mainly based on Valuation Rolls, Earldom Estate Rent Books, correspondence in OA D7/9, and DAFS Agricultural Returns.
2. Thomson, *1492 Rental*, 102.
3. Mackintosh, *The Orkney Crofters*, vi.
4. Marshall, *In a Distant Isle*; Thomson, *The Little General*, 179-180.
5. Trustees of J.C.Traill, Trustees of F.W.T.Burroughs, Trustees of W.G.T.Watt, Trustees of the Stewart Endowment, Creditors of Thomas Traill of Holland.
6. Calder, *History of Caithness*, 214-8.
7. Mss letter 20 January 1898, OA D7/9/57.
8. Mss letter 24 February 1887, OA D7/9/56.
9. Napier Commission, 1527.
10. Maxton, 'Landownership in Scotland', 77-184.
11. Moar, 'Weather and Climate in Orkney'.
12. Hazell, 'Farming in Crisis' in *The Orcadian Book of the Twentieth Century*, 110-2.
13. O'Dell, *The Land of Britain*; Scarth and Watt, 'The Agriculture of Orkney'; Corrigal, 'Seventy Years of Orkney Farming'.
14. Corrigal, 'Seventy Years of Orkney Farming', 49.
15. W.T.Wood, 'Farming Experiences in Orkney'.
16. Maxwell, 'Silage'.
17. There were 8128 cattle in 1855, and the number had increased to 25,416 by 1880.
18. Hazell, 'Farmers rocked by Disease Crisis' in *The Orcadian Book of the Twentieth Century*, 232; Muir, 'Forty Years On; the Tragedy of Foot and Mouth'.
19. Anderson, *Earl Robert*, 133.
20. M.Wood, 'Dairy Cattle'.
21. Hamilton, *Orkney and Shetland Farmers in Denmark*.
22. *TSA*, Kirkwall, 78-9.
23. Windwick, 'Fifty Years of Cheese-making'.
24. Fenton, *The Northern Isles*, 149.
25. *Orkney Economic Review*, No.18, 10.
26. Ludgate, 'The Orkney Egg Industry'; Groat et al., 'The Hen v the Cow'; Cormack, 'Egg Industry Memories'; Bichan, 'Poultry and Horses'.
27. Mackintosh, *The Orkney Crofters*, 236-7.
28. Bichan, 'From the Last Days of the Horse to the Mighty Tractor'.
29. Hazell, 'Hurricane Force Twelve' in *The Orcadian Book of the Twentieth Century*, 210-4.
30. Cromarty, 'The Mogul Tractor'.
31. Hazell, 'Farming in Crisis' in *The Orcadian Book of the Twentieth Century*, 111.
32. W.T.Wood, 'Farming Experiences in Orkney'.

33. Calder, 'The Business Side of Farming'.
34. Although the 1998 census records 1,260 holdings, a more realistic figure is obtained from the number of holdings with tillage (649), or from the number of cattle producers who submit subsidy claims (c.600).
35. *Orcadian*, 16 November 1995.
36. *Orcadian*, 16 November 1995.
37. *Orkney Economic Review*, No.18.
38. J.Thomson et al., 'Brain v Brawn in Agriculture'.

Chapter 30
The Twentieth Century: War and Peace
Notes to pp.434-450

1. Fereday, *The Longhope Battery and Towers*.
2. Hewison, *This Great Harbour, Scapa Flow*, 102-110; Cousins, *The Story of Scapa Flow*, 98-113; Hazell, *The Orcadian Book of the Twentieth Century*, 58-62; E.Marwick, 'The Day that Kitchener Died', in Robertson (ed), *An Orkney Anthology*, 419-423.
3. Hewison, *This Great Harbour, Scapa Flow*, 124-6; Cousins, *The Story of Scapa Flow*, 91-7.
4. Hewison, *This Great Harbour, Scapa Flow*, 127; McBride, 'Opal and Narborough, January 1918'.
5. The well-known poem 'Bloody Orkney' exists in many versions.
6. Van der Vat, *The Great Scuttle*, 128.
7. Van der Vat, *The Great Scuttle*, 158-195; Hewison, *This Great Harbour, Scapa Flow*, 141-157.
8. Hewison, *This Great Harbour, Scapa Flow*, 202-222; Bowman, *The Man who Bought a Navy*; George, *Jutland to Junkyard*.
9. Hewison, *This Great Harbour, Scapa Flow*, 256-261; Weaver, *Nightmare at Scapa Flow*.
10. Cormack and Cormack, *Bolsters, Blocks, Barriers*.
11. E.Marwick, 'Chiocchetti and the Italian Chapel', in Robertson (ed.), *An Orkney Anthology*, 453-6.
12. *TSA*, South Ronaldsay, 184-5.
13. Hewison, *This Great Harbour, Scapa Flow*, 323-8.
14. Hamilton-Baillie, *Coastal Defences in Orkney in Two World Wars*.
15. Hazell, *The Orcadian Book of the Twentieth Century*, 222-3.
16. *TSA*, Sandwick, 177.
17. *TSA*, South Ronaldsay, 193.
18. Firth, *Reminiscences of an Orkney Parish*, 122.
19. Miller, *Orkney*, 147.
20. Hazell, *The Orcadian Book of the Twentieth Century*, 107, 286.
21. *TSA*, Sandwick, 176.
22. *TSA*, Sanday, 117.
23. *TSA*, Sanday, 117.
24. Fenton, *The Northern Isles*, 116-130; Omond, *Orkney Eighty Years Ago*, 27-37.
25. *Orkney Herald*, 17 August 1870.
26. E.Marwick, *The Sufficient Place*.
27. Census 1951, County Report, Orkney.
28. Hossack, *Kirkwall in the Orkneys*, 364.
29. Bannerman, 'Rural Housing'.
30. *Orkney Economic Review*, No.18, 26.
31. Barclay, *The Population of Orkney*, 10.
32. E.Marwick, *Journey from Serfdom*.
33. *TSA*, Rousay, 160.
34. Based on 1991 census.
35. Cormack and Cormack, *The Days of Orkney Steam*.
36. Occidental, *The Flotta Story*; Hazell, *The Orcadian Book of the Twentieth Century*, 290-4.
37. *Orkney Economic Review*, No.18, 19-20.
38. Forsythe, 'Urban Incomers and Rural Change'.
39. *TSA*, Eday, 30.
40. *TSA*, Orphir, 138.
41. Forsythe, 'Urban Incomers and Rural Change'.
42. Thomson, *Kelp-making in Orkney*, 82.
43. Donaldson, *Northwards by Sea*.
44. *Orkney Economic Review*, No.18, 18-25.
45. Fresson, *Air Road to the Isles*; Hazell, *The Orcadian Book of the Twentieth Century*, 118-123.
46. Thomson, *The Little General*, 93-6.

47. E.Marwick, *Orcadian*, 5 April 1973.
48. E.Marwick, *Journey from Serfdom*.
49. Thomson, *The Little General*, 190-205.
50. Hazell, *The Orcadian Book of the Twentieth Century*, 251.

Bibliography and Abbreviations

Adams, I.H., *Directory of Former Scottish Commonties*, 1971.

Adams, I.H., and G.Fortune (eds.), *Alexander Lindsay, a Rutter of the Scottish Seas*, National Maritime Museum, 1980.

Adomnán's Life of Columba (A.O.Anderson and Marjorie O.Anderson, eds.), 1991.

Ágrip = H.J.Driscoll (trans.), *Ágrip af Nóregskonungasogum*, 1995.

Akrigg, G.P.V., *Jacobean Pageant; the Court of King James I*, 1962.

Andersen, Per Sveaas, 'King Hakon the Old before the Bar of History', *Orkney Miscellany* 5, 1973.

Andersen, Per Sveaas, 'Per Andreas Munch and the Beginning of Shetland Place-name Research', in Barbara E. Crawford (ed.), *Essays in Shetland History*, 1984.

Andersen, Per Sveaas, 'The Orkney Church of the Twelfth and Thirteenth Centuries', in Barbara E. Crawford (ed.), *St Magnus Cathedral*, 1988.

Andersen, Per Sveaas, 'When was Regular Annual Taxation Introduced in the Norse Islands of Britain?', *Scandinavian Journal of History* 16, No.2, 1991.

Andersen, Per Sveaas, *Samlingen av Norge og Kristingen av Landet*, (revised edition), Oslo, 1995.

Anderson, A.O., 'Wimund, Bishop and Pretender', *SHR* 7, 1909.

Anderson, Joseph, 'Notes...regarding the Death of Princess Margaret, the Maiden of Norway', *PSAS* 10, 1872/4.

Anderson, Peter D., *Robert Stewart; Earl of Orkney, Lord of Shetland*, 1982.

Anderson, Peter D., 'The Armada and the Northern Isles', *Northern Studies* 25, 1988.

Anderson, Peter D., 'The Stewart Earls of Orkney and the History of Orkney and Shetland', *Northern Studies* 29, 1992.

Anderson, Peter D., *Black Patie; the Life and Times of Patrick Stewart, Earl of Orkney, Lord of Shetland*, 1992.

Anderson, Peter D., 'Earl Patrick and his Enemies', *New Orkney Antiquarian Journal* 1, 1999.

Anderson, Theodore M., and Kari Ellen Gade, *Morkinskinna*, 2000.

Angus, W., (ed.), *Protocol Book of Mr Gilbert Grote, 1552-1573*, 1914.

Antonsson, Haki, *St Magnus of Orkney,* 2007.

APS = T.Thomson and C.Innes (eds.), *Acts of the Parliament of Scotland*, 1814-75.

Aston University Sub-aqua Club, *The Wreck of the Kennermerland*, 1974.

Baikie, Thomas, unpublished sermons OA, OCR, 14/94.

Bailey, Patrick, *Orkney*, 1971.

Bailie Court Book of St Andrews and Deerness, SRO RH.11/62/1.

Bain, J., *Calendar of Documents relating to Scotland*, 1881.

Balfour, David, *Oppressions of the Sixteenth Century in the Islands of Orkney and Shetland*, 1859.

Balfour, David, *Odal Rights and Feudal Wrongs*, 1860.

Balfour, David, *Ancient Orkney Melodies*, 1885.

Ballantyne, John H., and Brian Smith, *Shetland Documents, 1195-1579*, 1999 (cited as Volume 1).

Ballantyne, John H., and Brian Smith, *Shetland Documents, 1580-1611*, 1994 (cited as Volume 2).

Bangor-Jones, Malcolm, 'Ouncelands and Pennylands in Sutherland and Caithness', in L.J.MacGregor and B.E.Crawford, *Ouncelands and Pennylands*, 1987.

Bannatyne Club, *History of James the Sext*, 1825.

Bannerman, Dr., 'Rural Housing', *Journ. OADS* 7, 1932.

Bannerman, J., *Studies in the History of Dalriada*, 1974.

Barclay, R.S., *The Court Book of Orkney and Shetland, 1612-1613*, 1962.

Barclay, R.S., *Population of Orkney, 1755-1961*, 1965.

Barclay, R.S., *The Court Book of Orkney and Shetland*, 1614-1615, 1967.

Barclay, R.S., *Orkney Testaments and Inventories*, 1977.

Bargett, Frank, *Two Millennia of Church and Community in Orkney*, 2000.

Barnes, Michael P., *The Runic Inscriptions of Maeshowe*, Uppsala, 1994.

Barnes, Michael P., *The Norn Language of Orkney and Shetland*, 1998.

Barrett, James H., 'Few know an Earl in Fishing Clothes; Fish Middens and the Economy of Viking Age and Late Norse Earldoms of Orkney and Caithness', unpublished Ph.D, Glasgow, 1995.

Barrett, James H., 'Fish Trade in Norse Orkney and Caithness; a Zooarchaeological Approach', *Antiquity* 71, 1997.

Barrett, James H., et al., 'What Was the Viking Age and When Did it Happen?', *Norwegian Archaeological Review* 33, 2000.

Barratt, James H., et al., 'Diet and Ethnicity during the Viking Colonisation of Northern Scotland; Evidence from Fish Bones and Stable Carbon Isotopes, *Antiquity* 75, 2001.

Barron, E.M., 'Robert the Bruce in Orkney, Caithness and Sutherland', *OLM* 2, part 2, 1909.

Barrow, G.W.S., 'Macbeth and Other Mormaers of Moray', in *The Hub of the Highlands* (Inverness Field Club), 1975.

Barrow, G.W.S., 'The Kings of Scotland and Durham', in David Rollason et al. (eds.), *Anglo-Norman Durham*, 1994.

Barrow, G.W.S., The Charters of King David I, 1999.

Barry, George, *History of the Orkney Islands*, (second edition), 1808.

Batey, Colleen E., and John Sheehan, 'Viking Expansion and Cultural Blending in Britain and Ireland', in William W. Fitzhugh and Elisabeth I. Ward (eds.), *Vikings; the North Atlantic Saga*, Smithsonian Institutution, 2000.

Bede's Ecclesiastical History, (J.A.Giles ed.), 1892.

Begg, James, 'The Bailie Courts of Orkney', *POAS* 2, 3 and 4, 1923-6.

Bell, Bernard, and Camilla Dickson, 'Excavations at Warebeth (Stromness Cemetery) Broch, Orkney', *PSAS* 119, 1989.

Ben, Jo, 'Descriptio Insularum Orchadia', in *MacFarlane's Geographical Collections* 3, 1908.

Bibire, Paul, 'The Poetry of Earl Rognvaldr's Court', in Barbara Crawford (ed), *St Magnus Cathedral and Orkney's Twelfth Century Renaissance*, 1988.

Bichan, Mary, 'From the Last Days of the Horse to the Mighty Tractor', *Orcadian*, Supplement 15 November 1975.

Bichan, Mary, 'Poultry and Horses', *Orcadian*, Supplement, 8 August 1985.

Boardman, Stephen, *The Early Stewart Kings*, 1996.

Boece = Batho, E.C., and Husbands, H.W., (eds.), *The Chronicles of Scotland*. (Hector Boece, *Scottorum Historia*, Paris, 1527, trans. John Bellenden, 1531), 2 vols., 1941.

Bond, J.M, and Hunter, J.R, 'Flax-growing in Orkney from the Norse Period to the Eighteenth Century', *PSAS* 117, 1987.

Bowman, G., *The Man who Bought a Navy*, 1964.

Brand, Rev. J., *A Brief Description of Orkney, Zetland, Pightland Firth and Caithness (1700)*, 1883.

Brøgger, A.W., *Ancient Emigrants*, 1929.

Brothwell, Don, Don Tills and Veronica Muir, 'Biological Characteristics' (of Orcadians), in R.J.Berry and H.N.Firth, *The People of Orkney*, 1986.

Brown, George Mackay, *Magnus*, 1977.

Brown, George Mackay, 'The Magnus Miracles were Manifest', *The Orcadian*, 3 November 1994.

Brown, Michael, *James I*, 1994.

Buchanan, George, *The History of the Kirk of Scotland* (trans. James Aikman), 1827.

Bunyan, Ian, et al., *No Ordinary Journey; John Rae, Arctic Explorer, 1813-1893*, 1993.

Burns, Charles (ed.), *Papal Letters to Scotland of Clement VII of Avignon*, 1976.

Buteux, Simon, *Settlements at Skaill, Deerness, Orkney*, 1997.

Caithness & Sutherland Recs. = A.W.Johnston and Amy Johnston (eds.) *Caithness & Sutherland Records*, Viking Society, 1909 onwards.

Calder, A., 'The Business Side of Farming', *Journ. OADS* 1, 1925/6.

Calder, James T., *History of Caithness*, 1861.

Cambridge, Eric, 'The Romanesque Cathedral at Kirkwall', in Barbara Crawford (ed.), *St Magnus Cathedral and Orkney's Twelfth Century Renaissance*, 1988.

Cant, Ronald G., 'Settlement, Society and Church Organisation in the Northern Isles', in A.Fenton & H.Pálsson (eds.), *The Northern and Western Isles in the Viking World*, 1984.

Cant, Ronald G., 'Norwegian Influences in the Design of the Transitional and Gothic Cathedral', in Barbara Crawford (ed.), *St Magnus Cathedral and Orkney's Twelfth Century Renaissance*, 1988.

Cant, Ronald G., 'The Constitution of St Magnus Cathedral', in Barbara E. Crawford (ed.), *Northern Isles Connections*, 1995.

Childe, V. Gordon, *Skara Brae; a Pictish Village in Orkney*, 1931.

Christensen, T.L., 'The Earl of Rothes in Denmark', in Ian B. Cowan and Duncan Shaw (eds.), *The Renaissance and Reformation in Scotland*, 1983.

Christiansen, Reidar Th., 'The People of the North', *Lochlann* 2, 1962.

Chronicle of the Kings of Man and the Isles, (trans.George Broderick), 1996.

Clouston, C., *Guide to the Orkney Islands*, 1861.

Clouston, J. Storer, 'The Battle of Summerdale', *OLM* 2, part 2, 1909.

Clouston, J. Storer, 'The Lawrikmen of Orkney', *SHR* 14, 1917.

Clouston, J. Storer, 'Two Features of the Orkney Earldom', *SHR* 16, 1918.

Clouston, J. Storer, 'The Orkney Townships', *SHR* 16, 1919.

Clouston, J. Storer, 'The Orkney Bailies and their Wattel', *PSAS*, Vol.55, 1920.

Clouston, J. Storer, 'The Orkney Pennylands', *SHR* 20, 1922.

Clouston, J. Storer, 'The Orkney Lands', *POAS* 2, 1923-4.

Clouston, J. Storer, 'The Goodmen and Hirdmen of Orkney, *POAS* 3, 1924-5.

Clouston, J. Storer, 'An Orkney Perambulation', *SHR* 27, 1925.

Clouston, J. Storer, 'The Old Prebends of Orkney', *POAS* 4, 1925/6.

Clouston, J. Storer, 'The Orkney Bus', *POAS* 5, 1926/7.

Clouston, J. Storer, 'The Battle of Tankerness', *POAS* 6, 1927/8.

Clouston, J. Storer, 'The Run-rig System in Orkney', *Journ.OADS* 2, 1927.

Clouston, J. Storer, *The Orkney Parishes*, 1928.

Clouston, J. Storer, 'A Fresh View of the Settlement of Orkney', *POAS* 9, 1930-1.

Clouston, J. Storer, *History of Orkney*, 1932.

Clouston, J. Storer, 'James Sinclair of Brecks', *POAS* 15, 1936/7

Clouston, J. Storer, 'Orkney and the Hudson's Bay Company', *The Beaver*, December 1936, March and September 1937.

Clowes, W.L., *The Royal Navy*, 1897.

Cormack, A. and A., *Days of Orkney Steam*, 1971.

Cormack, A. and A., *Bolsters, Blocks, Barriers; the Story of the Building of the Churchill Barriers in Orkney*, 1992.

Corrigal, Simon, 'Seventy Years of Orkney Farming', *Journal OADS* 8, 1933.

Coull, J.R., *The Sea Fisheries of Scotland*, 1996.

Coull, J.R., 'Herring Fisheries in Orkney', *Northern Scotland* 18, 1998.

Coull, J.R., 'Fishing in Orkney', in Donald Omand (ed.), forthcoming.

Cousins, G., *The Story of Scapa Flow*, 1965.

Cowan, Edward J., 'Caithness in the Sagas' in John Baldwin (ed.), *Caithness; a Cultural Crossroads*, 1982.

Cowan, Edward J., 'The Vikings in Galloway; a Review of the Evidence', in Richard D. Oram and Geoffrey P. Stell, *Galloway, Land and Lordship*, 1991.

Cowan, Edward J., 'The Historical MacBeth', in W.D.H.Sellar, *Moray: Province and People*, 1993.

Cox, Richard A.V., *The Language of the Ogham Inscriptions of Scotland*, 1999.

Craven, J.B., *History of the Church in Orkney*, 3 vols., 1893, 1897, 1902.

Craven, J.B., *Church Life in South Ronaldsay and Burray*, 1911.

Crawford, Barbara E., 'The Earls of Orkney and Caithness and their Relations with Scotland and Norway', unpublished Ph.D, St Andrews, 1971.

Crawford, Barbara E., 'Weland de Stiklaw; a Scottish Royal Servant at the Norwegian Court', *Historisk Tidskrift* 4, 1973.

Crawford, Barbara E., 'Peter's Pence in Scotland', in G.W.S.Barrow (ed.), *The Scottish Tradition*, 1974.

Crawford, Barbara E., 'The Fifteenth Century Genealogy of the Earls of Orkney', *Medieval Scandinavia* 10, 1976.

Crawford, Barbara E., 'The Orkney Arms', *Orcadian*, 13 July 1978.

Crawford, Barbara E., 'Sir David Sinclair of Sumburgh' in John Baldwin (ed.), *Scandinavian Shetland; an On-going Tradition?*, 1978.

Crawford, Barbara, E., 'The Pledging of the Islands (Shetland) in 1469', in D.J.Withrington (ed.), *Shetland and the Outside World 1469-1969*, 1983.

Crawford, Barbara E., 'Birsay and the Early Earls and Bishops of Orkney', *Orkney Heritage* 2, 1983.

Crawford, Barbara, E., 'The Cult of St Magnus in Shetland', in Barbara Crawford (ed.), *Essays in Shetland History*, 1984.

Crawford, Barbara, E., 'The Earldom of Caithness and the Kingdom of Scotland', in K.J.Stringer (ed.), *Essays on the Nobility of Medieval Scotland*, 1985.

Crawford, Barbara, E., 'William Sinclair, Earl of Orkney, and his Family', in K.J.Stringer (ed.), *Essays on the Nobility of Medieval Scotland*, 1985.

Crawford, Barbara E., 'The Making of a Frontier; the Firthlands from the Ninth to Twelfth Centuries', in John Baldwin (ed.) *Firthlands of Ross and Sutherland*, 1986.

Crawford, Barbara E., *Scandinavian Scotland*, 1987.

Crawford, Barbara E., 'North Sea Kingdoms, North Sea Bureaucrat: a Royal Official Who Transcended National Boundaries' (Weland de Stiklaw), *SHR* 69, 1990.

Crawford, Barbara E., 'Norse Earls and Scottish Bishops in Caithness', in Colleen E.Batey et al., (eds.), *The Viking Age in Caithness, Orkney and the North Atlantic*, 1993.

Crawford, Barbara E., (ed.), 'An Unrecognised Statue of Earl Rognvald', in *Northern Isles Connections*, 1995.

Crawford, Barbara E., *Earl and Mormaer; Norse Pictish Relationships in Northern Scotland*, 1995.

Crawford, Barbara E., 'Bishops of Orkney in the Eleventh and Twelfth Centuries: Bibliography and Biographical List', *Innes Review* 47, no.1, 1996.

Crawford, Barbara E, 1998, 'St Magnus and St Rognvald—the Two Orkney Saints', *Scottish Church History Society Records* 28, 1998.

Crawford, Barbara E., (ed.), *The Papar in the North Atlantic*, 2002.

Crawford, Barbara E., 'The Bishopric of Orkney' in Steinar Imsen's *Ecclesia Nidrosiensis*, Trondheim, 2003.

Crawford, Iain A., 'War or Peace; Viking Colonisation in the Northern and Western Islands of Scotland', in H.Bekker-Nielsen et al., *Proceedings of the Eighth Viking Congress*, 1981.

Cromarty, James, 'The Mogul Tractor', *Orkney Vintage Club Newsletter*, No.3, 1986.

Cruden, Stewart, 'Earl Thorfinn the Mighty and the Brough of Birsay', in K.Eldjárn (ed.), *The Third Viking Congress*, Reykjavik, 1958.

Cruden, Stewart, 'Excavations at Birsay, Orkney', in A.Small (ed.), *The Fourth Viking Congress*, 1965.

Cruden, Stewart, 'The Founding and Building of the Twelfth-Century Cathedral of St Magnus', in Barbara Crawford (ed.), *St Magnus Cathedral and Orkney's Twelfth Century Renaissance*, 1988.

Curle, C.L., *Pictish and Norse Finds from the Brough of Birsay, 1934-74*, 1982.

Custine, D.J., 'Udal Law', *Northern Studies* 32, 1997.

Cuthbert, Olaf, *The Life and Letters of an Orkney Naturalist; Reverend George Low, 1747-95*, 1995.

Cuthbert, Olaf, *A Flame in the Shadows; Robert Reid, Bishop of Orkney 1541-1558*, 1998.

DAFS = Department of Agriculture and Fisheries for Scotland, Agricultural Returns, 1866 onwards.

Dahlerup, Troels, 'Orkney Bishops as Suffragans in the Scandinavian-Baltic Area', in Grant G. Simpson (ed.), *Scotland and Scandinavia*, 1990.

Danielsen, Rolf, et al., *Norway; a History from the Vikings to our own Times*, 1995.

Defoe, D., *Tour through Great Britain in 1724*, 1762.

Dennison, Walter Traill, 'Manufacture of Straw Articles in Orkney', in M.M.Charleston, *Orcadian Papers*, 1905.

Dennison, Walter Traill, 'Remarks on the Agricultural Classes in the North Isles of Orkney', *POAS* 11, 1932.

Dennison, Walter Traill, *Orkney Folklore and Traditions*, 1961.

Dickins, Bruce, 'Orkney Raid on Wales', *POAS* 8, 1928/30.

Dickins, Bruce, 'St Magnus and his Countess', *POAS* 13, 1934/5.

Dickins, B., 'An Orkney Scholar; Hugh Marwick, 1881-1965', *Saga Book* 17, Part 1, 1966.

Diploma = 'Diploma or Deduction concerning the Genealogies of the Ancient Counts of Orkney', printed and translated in Barry, *History*, 1808.

Dip.Norv. = *Diplomatarium Norvegicum*, 1849-1919, Christiania.

Dodgshon, R.A., *The Origin of British Field Systems*, 1980.

Dodgshon, R.A., *Land and Society in Early Scotland*, 1981.

Dodgshon, R.A., 'Medieval Rural Scotland', in G.Whittington and I.D.Whyte (eds.), *An Historical Geography of Scotland*, 1983.

Donaldson, Gordon, *Scotland; James V – James VII*, (Edinburgh History 3), 1965.

Donaldson, Gordon, *Northwards by Sea*, 1966.

Donaldson, Gordon, 'Sovereignty and Law in Orkney and Shetland', *Miscellany II*, Stair Society, 1984.

Donaldson, Gordon, *Reformed by Bishops*, 1987.

Donaldson, Gordon, 'The Contemporary Scene', in Barbara E. Crawford, (ed.), *St Magnus Cathedral and Orkney's Twelfth Century Renaissance*, 1988.

Donaldson, Gordon, 'The Archdeaconry of Shetland', in Barbara E. Crawford (ed.), *Northern Isles Connections*, 1995.

Dow, F.D., *Cromwellian Scotland, 1651-1660*, 1979.

Dumville, D.N., 'A Note on the Picts in Orkney', *Scottish Gaelic Studies* 12, 1976.

Duncan, A.A.M., *Scotland; the Making of the Kingdom*, (Edinburgh History 1), 1975.

Duncan, A.A.M, and A.L.Brown, 'Argyll and the Isles in the Early Middle Ages', *PSAS* 90, 1956/7.

Dunlop, Annie I., *The Life and Times of Bishop Kennedy*, 1950.

Dunlop, Jean, *The British Fisheries Society*, 1978.

Durie, Alistair J., *The Scottish Linen Industry in the Eighteenth Century*, 1979.

Easson, A.R., 'Ouncelands and Pennylands in the West Highlands of Scotland', in L.J.MacGregor and B.E.Crawford (eds.), *Ouncelands and Pennylands*, 1987.

ECMS = Allen, J.Romilly, and Joseph Anderson, *The Early Christian Monuments of Scotland*, 2 vols., 1903 (reprinted 1993).

Einarsson, Bjarni, 'De Normannorum Atrocitate, or the Execution of Royalty by the Aquiline Method', *Saga Book* 23, (Viking Society), 1986

Einarsson, Bjarni, 'The Blood-eagle; an Observation on the Ornithological Aspect', *Saga Book* 23, 1990.

Ekrem, Inger, and Lars Boye Mortensen, *Historia Norvegie*, Copenhagen, 2002.

Eldjárn, Kristján, 'Graves and Grave Goods; Survey and Evaluation', in A.Fenton and H.Pálsson, (eds.), *The Northern and Western Isles in the Viking World*, 1984.

Emerson, J., (attributed), *Poetical Description of Orkney, 1652*, reprinted 1971.

ER = J.G.MacKay and G.P.MacNeill, *Exchequer Rolls of Scotland*, 1897 onwards.

ESSH = A.O.Anderson, *Early Sources of Scottish History*, 2 vols., 1922.

Eunson, D., 'The Influence of the Education (Scotland) Act, 1872, on Education in Orkney', unpublished M.Ed.dissertation, Stirling, 1979.

Eyrbyggia saga = Hermann Pálsson and Paul Edwards (trans.), *Eyrbyggia saga*, 1973.

Faroe Islanders Saga = George Johnston (trans.), *The Faroe Islanders Saga*, 1975.

Fawcett, 'Kirkwall Cathedral; an Architectural Analysis', in Barbara Crawford (ed.), *St Magnus Cathedral and Orkney's Twelfth Century Renaissance*, 1988.

Fea, J., *The Present State of the Orkney Islands, 1775*, 1884.

Fellows-Jensen, Gillian, 'Viking Settlement in the Northern and Western Isles; the Place-name Evidence as seen from Denmark and Danelaw', in A.Fenton & H.Pálsson (eds.), *The Northern and Western Isles in the Viking World*, 1984.

Fellows-Jensen, Gillian, 'Tingwall: the Significance of the Name', in Doreen Waugh (ed.), *Shetland's Northern Links; Language and History*, 1996.

Fenton, A., *Scottish Country Life*, 1976.

Fenton, A., *The Northern Isles; Orkney and Shetland*, 1978.

Fereday, R.P., *The Longhope Battery and Towers*, 1971.

Fereday, R.P., 'From Sang School to Burgh School', in Orkney Islands Council Education Committee, *Kirkwall Grammar School; from Sang School to Comprehensive*, 1976.

Fereday, R.P., *Orkney Feuds and the '45*, 1980.

Fereday, R.P., 'William Balfour after the '45', *Orkney Heritage* 1, 1981.

Fereday, R.P., 'The Lairds of Eighteenth Century Orkney', unpublished Ph.D, Aberdeen, 1983.

Fereday, R.P., 'The Lairds of the Eighteenth Century Orkney', in R.J.Berry and H.N.Firth, *The People of Orkney*, 1986.

Fereday, R.P., *The Orkney Balfours, 1747-99*, 1990.

Fereday, R.P., *A Brief Introduction to the Family of Dundas of Fingask and Kerse*, Word-processed booklet, Orkney Library, 1998.

Fereday, R.P., (ed.), *The Autobiography of Samuel Laing of Papdale, 1780-1868*, 2000.

Finlay, Alison, *Fagrskinna*, 2004.

Firth. John, *Reminiscences of an Orkney Parish*, 1922.

Flatyjarbók = Siguður Nordal, (ed.), *Flatyjarbók*, Akraness, 4 vols., 1944.

Flett, Emile, 'When Orkney had Four Voters', *Orcadian*, 3 April 1997.

Flett, James, 'Kirkwall Incorporated Trades', *POAS* 7, 1928/9.

Flett, James, *Lodge Kilwinning; the Story from 1736*, 1976.

Foote, Peter, 'Observations on Orkneyinga Saga', in Barbara E. Crawford, (ed.), *St Magnus Cathedral*, 1988.

Fordun = W.F.Skene (ed.), *John of Fordun's Chronicle of the Scottish Nation*, 1872 (reprinted 1993).

Forsyth, Katherine, 'The Ogham-inscribed Spindle-whorl from Buckquoy: Evidence for the Irish Language in pre-Viking Orkney', *PSAS* 125, 1995.

Forsyth, Katherine, 'Language in Pictland', in Eric H. Nicoll (ed.), *A Pictish Panorama*, 1995.

Forsyth, Katherine, *Language in Pictland; the Case against Non-Indo-European Pictish*, De Keltische Draak, Utrecht, 1997.

Forsythe, Diana, 'Urban Incomer and Rural Change', *Sociologica Ruralis* 20, No.4, 1980.

Foster, Sally M., *Picts, Gaels and Scots*, 1996.

Frank, Roberta, 'Viking Atrocity and Skaldic Verse; the Rite of the Blood Eagle', *English Historical Review* 99, 1984.

Frank, Roberta, 'The Blood Eagle Again', *Saga Book* 22, 1988.

Frank, Roberta, 'Ornithology and the Interpretation of Skaldic Verse', *Saga Book* 23, 1990.

Fresson, E.E., *Air Road to the Isles*, 1967.

Friedland, K., 'Hanseatic Merchants and their Trade with Shetland', in Donald J. Withrington (ed.), *Shetland and the Outside World, 1469-1969*, 1983.

Gade, J.A., *The Hanseatic Control of Norwegian Commerce*, Leiden, 1951.

Gailey, A., and A.Fenton (eds.), 'The Reverend John Brand and the Bo'ness of the 1690s', Ulster Folk Museum, 1970.

Gammeltoft, Peder, 'Sowing the Wind? Reaping a Crop of Bólstaðr', *Northern Studies* 32, 1998.

Garson, Sheila, *Balfour Village; the Development of an Estate Village and its Relationship to Agricultural Improvement*, unpublished dissertation, Aberdeen University Continuing Education, 1999.

Gelling, P.S., 'The Norse Buildings at Skaill, Deerness, and their Immediate Predecessor', in A.Fenton, and H.Pálsson, (eds.), *The Northern and Western Isles in the Viking World*, 1984.

George, S.C., *From Juland to Junkyard*, 1973.

Genzmer, Felix, 'Sage und Wirklichkeit in der Geschichte von der ersten Orkadenjarlen', *Historische Zeitschrift* 168, 1943.

Gibson, W.M., *The Herring Fishing, Stronsay*, 1984.

Gifford, Thomas, *Historical Description of the Zetland Islands, 1733*, 1879.

Gammeltoft, Peder, and Bent Jørgensen (eds.), *Names through the Looking Glass*, Copenhagen, 2006.

Gammeltoft, Peder, et al. (eds.), *Cultural Contacts in the North Atlantic Region*, 2005.

Gammeltoft, Peder, *The Place-name Element bólstaðr in the North Atlantic Area*, 2001 (Copenhagen).Goodfellow, Alexander, *Sanday Church History*, 1912.

Goodfellow, Alexander, *Dr Robert Paterson of Orkney*, 1920.

Goodlad, C.A., *Shetland Fishing Saga*, 1971.

Göransson, S., 'Regular Open Field Patterns in England and Scandinavian Solskifte', *Geografiska Annaler* 44 (b), 1961.

Gordon, Principal, *Remarks Made in a Journey to the Orkney Islands*, *Archaeologica Scotica* 1.

Gorrie, Daniel, *Summers and Winters in the Orkneys*, n.d.

Goudie, Gilbert, (ed.), *The Diary of the Reverend John Mill*, 1889.

Goudie, Gilbert, *The Celtic and Scandinavian Antiquities of Shetland*, 1904.

Gow, Sylvia, *James Moodie, Younger of Melsetter*, 1976.

Graham-Campbell, James, 'A Lost Pictish Treasure (and Two Viking Age Gold Arm-rings) from the Broch of Burgar, Orkney', *PSAS* 115, 1985.

Graham-Campbell, James, 'Northern Hoards of Viking-age Scotland', in Colleen E. Batey et al., (eds.), *The Viking Age in Caithness, Orkney and the North Atlantic*, 1993.

Graham-Campbell, James, *The Viking-age Gold and Silver of Scotland*, 1995.

Gray, Malcolm, 'North-east Agriculture and the Labour Force', in A.A.MacLaren (ed.), *Social Class in Scotland*, 1976.

Groat, William, et al., 'The Hen v the Cow' (debate), *Journ. OADS* 8, 1933.

Grönneberg, Roy, *Jakobsen and Shetland*, 1981.

Groundwater, Henrietta, *Memories of an Orkney Family*, 1967.

Gunn, John, (ed.), *The Orkney Book*, 1900.

Guðmundsson, Finnbogi, 'On the Writing of the Orkneyinga Saga', in Colleen Batey et.al. (eds.), *The Viking Age in Caithness, Orkney and the North Atlantic*, 1993.

Häfstrom, G., 'Atlantic and Baltic Earldoms', in P.Foote and D.Strömback (eds.), *Proceedings of the Sixth Viking Congress*, Uppsala, 1971.

Hakonar saga = G.W.Dasent, *The Saga of Hacon*, 1894 (reprinted 1997).

Haldane, A.R.B., *The Drove Roads of Scotland*, 1973.

Haldane, J., *Journal of a Tour through the Northern Counties of Scotland and the Orkney Islands*, 1798.

Hamilton, Sir R.W., *Orkney and Shetland Farmers in Denmark*, 1925.

Hamilton-Baillie, J.R.E., Coastal Defences in Orkney in Two World Wars, 1979.

Harvey, Robin, Diana Suter and Don Tills, 'Relationships of Orcadians; the View from Faroe', in R.J.Berry and H.N.Firth (eds.), *The People of Orkney*, 1986.

Hawkes, C.F.C., *Pytheas; Europe and the Greek Explorers*, 1977.

Hay, R.A., *Genealogie of the Sainteclaires of Rosslyn*, 1835.

Hazell, Howard, *The Orcadian Book of the Twentieth Century*, 2000.

Heimskringa = Samuel Laing, *Heimskringa*, 1844 (frequently reprinted).

Hedges, John W., *Bu, Gurness and the Brochs of Orkney*, 2 parts, 1987.

Helle, Knut, 'Norwegian Consolidation and Expansion during the Reign of King Hakon Hakonsson', *Orkney Miscellany* 5, 1973.

Helle, Knut, *Norge blir en Stat*, Bergen, 1974.

Helle, Knut, 'Norwegian Foreign Policy and the Maid of Norway', *SHR* 69, 1990.

Helle, Knut, 'The History of the Early Viking Age in Norway', in Howard B. Clarke, Máire Ni Mhaonaigh and Raghnall Ó Floinn (eds.), *Ireland and Scandinavia in the Early Viking Age*, 1998.

Helle, Knut, (ed.), *Cambridge History of Scandinavia* 1, n.d.

Henderson, George, *The Norse Influence on Celtic Scotland*, 1910.

Henderson, Isobel, *The Picts*, 1967.

Hepburn, Thomas (attributed), *A Letter to a Gentleman from his Friend in Orkney, 1757*, 1885.

Hewison, W.S., 'Holm Farm Diary', *Orkney Miscellany* 2, 1954.

Hewison, W.S., 'Smuggling in Eighteenth Century Orkney', *Orkney Miscellany*

3, 1956.

Hewison, W.S., *This Great Harbour; Scapa Flow*, 1985.

Hewison, W.S., *The Diary of Patrick Fea of Stove, Orkney, 1766-1796*, 1997.

Hewison, W.S., *Who was Who in Orkney*, 1998.

Hibbert, Samuel, *A Description of the Shetland Islands (1822)*, 1891.

Historia Norvegiae = Kunin, Devra, (trans.), *A History of Norway and the Passion of the Blessed Óláfr*, 2001.

Hørby, K., 'Christian I and the Pawning of Orkney', *SHR* 48, 1969.

Holinshed, R., *The Scottish Chronicle*, 1805.

Hossack, B.H., *Kirkwall in the Orkneys*, 1900.

Holder-Egger, O., 'Vita Findani', *Monumenta Germanicae Historica Scriptorum* 15, 1.

Hudson, Benjamin T., 'Cnut and the Scottish Kings', *English Historical Review* 107, 1992.

Hudson, Benjamin T., *Kings of Celtic Scotland*, Westport, Conn., 1994.

Hunter, James, *The Making of the Crofting Community*, 1976.

Hunter, John R., *Rescue Excavations on the Brough of Birsay*, n.d.

Hunter, John R., 'The Early Norse Period' in K.J.Edwards and I.B.M.Ralston (eds.), *Scotland; Environment and Archaeology, 8000 BC–AD 1000*, 1997.

Hustwick, Ian, *The Peggy & Isabella; the Story of an Eighteenth Century Orkney Sloop*, 1996.

Icelandic Annals = G.Storm, *Islandske Annaler indtil 1578*, Christiania, 1888.

Imsen, Steinar, *Norsk Bondekommunalisme*, 2 vols., Trondheim, 1990 and 1994.

Imsen, Steinar, 'Public Life in Orkney and Shetland, c.1300-1550', *New Orkney Antiquarian Journal*, 1999.

Imsen, Steinar, 'Tingwall and Local Community Power in Shetland during the Reign of Håkon Magnusson, Duke and King' (Conference paper in Shetland, 1999).

Imsen, Steinar, 'King Magnus and his Liegemen's Hirdskrå; a Portrait of the Norwegian Nobility in the 1270s', in Anne E. Duggan, *Nobles and Nobility in Medieval Europe*, 2000.

Imsen, Steinar, 'Earldom and Kingdom; Orkney and the Realm of Norway, 1195-1379', *Historisk Tidskrift* 79, No.2, 2000 (Norway).

Inga Saga = G.W.Dasent, *The Orkneyingers' Saga*, 1894, 234-6.

Innes, Cosmo, (ed.), *Registrum Monasterii Passelet*, 1832.

Irvine, James M., *The Breckness Estate; its Growth and Decline between 1625 and 1922*, unpublished dissertation, Aberdeen University Continuing Education, 1997.

Irvine, James M., *Blaeu's Orkney and Shetland*, 2006.

Irvine, James M., *The Orkney Poll Taxes of the 1690s*, 2003.Irvine, W., *The Isle of Shapinsay*, 1977.

Jackson, K.H., 'The Pictish Language', in F.T.Wainwright (ed.), *The Problem of the Picts*, 1955.

Jakobsen, Jakob, *The Dialect and Place-names of Shetland*, 1897.

Jakobsen, Jakob, 'Shetlandsøerne Stednavne', *Aarbøger for Oldkyndighed og Historie*, Copenhagen, 1901.

Jakobsen, Jakob, 'Nordiske Minder, isser sproglige på Orknøene, *Svenska*

Landsmålen, 1911.

Jakobsen, Jakob, 'Om Orknøenes Historie og Sprog; et Brudstykke', *Danske Studier*, 1919 (translated as 'Orkney's History and Language; a Fragment', *The Orcadian*, 26 May 1921).

Jakobsen, Jakob, *An Etymological Dictionary of the Norn Language in Shetland*, 2 vols., 1928/1932.

Jakobsen, Jakob, *The Place-names of Shetland*, 1936.

James, Richard, 'Description of Shetland, Orkney and the Highlands of Scotland', *Orkney Miscellany* 1, 1953.

Jesch, Judith, 'England and Orkneyinga Saga', in Colleen E. Batey et al., (eds.), *The Viking Age in Caithness, Orkney and the North Atlantic*, 1993.

Jesch, Judith, 'Norse Historical Traditions and *Historia Gruffud vab Kenan*; Magnús berfoettr and Haraldr håfagri', in K.L.Maund (ed.), *Gruffudd ap Cynan*, 1996.

Jexlev, Thelma, 'The Cult of Saints in Early Medieval Scandinavia', in Barbara E. Crawford, *St Magnus Cathedral*, 1988.

Jóhannesson, Jón, *Íslendinga saga; a History of the Old Icelandic Commonwealth*, Manitoba, 1974.

Johnsen, A.O., 'The Payments from the Hebrides and the Isle of Man to the Crown of Norway', *SHR* 48, 1969.

Johnston, A.W., 'The Romans in Orkney and Shetland', *OLM* 1, part 7, 1908.

Johnston, A.W., 'Fiscal Antiquities of Orkney and Shetland', *OLM* 9, parts 1, 3 and 4, 1921/1933.

Johnston, A.W., 'Orkney and Shetland Folk', *OLM* 7, 1914.

Jones, Michael R.H., 'Perceptions of Udal Law in Orkney and Shetland', in Doreen Waugh and Brian Smith (eds.), *Shetland's Northern Links*, 1996.

Kaland, S., 'The Settlement of Westness, Rousay', in Colleen Batey et al. (eds.), *The Viking Age in Caithness, Orkney and the North Atlantic*, 1993.

Kaland, S., 'Some Economic Aspects of the Orkneys in the Viking Period', *Norw. Arch. Rev.* 15, 1982.

Kelley, David H., 'The Claimed Irish Origin of Clan Munro', *The American Genealogist* 45, No.2, 1969.

Kirby, D.P., 'Bede and the Pictish Church', *Innes Review* 24, 1973.

KLNM = Kulturhistorisk Lexicon for Nordisk Middelalder, 22 vols., Copenhagen and elsewhere.

Landnámabók = Hermann Pálsson and Paul Edwards (trans.), *The Book of Settlements, Landnámabók*, Manitoba, 1972.

Lamb, H.H., *Climate, History and the Modern World*, 1982.

Lamb, R.G., 'The Cathedral of Christchurch and the Monastery of Birsay', *PSAS* 105, 1974.

Lamb, R.G., *The Archaeological Sites of Sanday and North Ronaldsay*, 1980.

Lamb, R.G, 'The Hall of Haflidi', *Orcadian*, 23 July 1981.

Lamb, R.G, *The Archaeological Sites and Monuments of Eday and Stronsay*, 1984.

Lamb, R.G., 'Carolingian Orkney and its Transformation', in Colleen E. Batey et al., (eds.), *The Viking Age in Caithness, Orkney and the North Atlantic*, 1993.

Lamb, Raymond G., 'Papil, Picts and Papar', in Barbara E. Crawford (ed.), *Northern Isles Connections*, 1995.

Lamb, Raymond G., 'Pictland, Northumbria and the Carolingian Empire', in Barbara E. Crawford (ed.), *Conversion and Christianity in the North Sea World*, St Andrews, 1998.

Larner, Christina, *Enemies of God; the Witch-hunt in Scotland*, 1981.

Larson, L.M., *The Earliest Norwegian Laws*, New York, 1935.

Lawrie, A.C., *Annals of the Reigns of Malcolm and William, Kings of Scotland*, 1910.

Laxdæla saga = Magnus Magnusson and Hermann Pálsson (trans.), *Laxdæla saga*, 1969.

Leith, P., 'The Bellendens and the Palace of Stenness', *POAS* 14, 1936/7.

Legenda = *Legenda de Sancto Magno* (1) Islendzk Fornrit xxxiv, 1965, 303-8 (2) Dasent, *Orkneyingers' Saga*, 302-4.

Leslie, John, *The History of Scotland*, 1888/95.

Liddell, Francis, *The Melancholy Case of Mr Francis Liddell*, 1808.

Low, Rev. George, *A Tour through the Islands of Orkney and Schetland (1774)*, 1978.

Low, Rev. George, (Olaf D. Cuthbert, ed.), *Low's History of Orkney*, 2001.

Lowe, Christopher, *St Boniface Church, Orkney*, 1998.

Löwe, H., 'Findan von Rheinau; Eine Irische Perigrinatio im 9 Jarhundert', *Studi Medievali*, 3rd ser. 26, 1, Spoleto, 1985.

Ludgate, Rachel, 'The Orkney Egg Industry, 1800s-1970s', *Orkney View*, Nos. 71-4, 1997.

McBride, Keith, 'Opal and Narborough, January 1918', *Mariners' Mirror* 85, No.2, 1999.

MacDonald, Aidan, *Curadán, Boniface and the Early Church at Rosemarkie*, 1994.

MacDonald, Hugh, (attributed), 'History of the MacDonalds', in J.R.N.MacPhail (ed.), *Highland Papers* 1, 1914.

McDonald, R. Andrew, *The Kingdom of the Isles*, 1997.

MacFarlane's Geographical Collections = A.Mitchell (ed.), *MacFarlane's Geographical Collections*, 3 vols., 1906 onwards.

MacInnes, Ian, 'The Alexander Graham Case', *Orkney Heritage* 1, 1981.

MacKaile, M., 'A Short Relation of the Most Considerable Things in the Orkney Islands', in *MacFarlane's Geographical Collections* 3, 1908.

MacKay, D., *The Honourable Company*, Toronto, 1937.

Mackay, J.A., *Islands Postal Series No.7, Orkney and Stroma*, 1979.

Mackenzie, James, *The General Grievances and Oppressions of the Islands of Orkney and Shetland*, 1836.

Mackenzie Manuscript (by James Mackenzie), OA D8/5.

Mackenzie, Murdoch, *Orcades*, 1750.

Mackintosh, W.R., *Glimpse of Kirkwall and its People in Olden Times*, 1887.

Mackintosh, W.R., *The Orkney Crofters; their Evidence and Statements*, 1889.

Mackintosh, W.R., *Curious Incidents from the Ancient Records of Kirkwall*, 1892.

MacMath, J.M.N., 'Kirkwall in the Orkneys', *Linen Leaves* 1, 3 (British Linen Bank Staff Magazine), 1949.

MacQuarrie, Alan, *The Saints of Scotland*, 1997.

Magnusson, Magnus, *Viking Expansion Westwards*, 1973.

Major, R.H., *The Voyages of the Venetian Brothers Nicolo and Antonio Zeno*, 1873.

Manson, T.M.Y., 'Historical Problems of Shetland', in W.D.Simpson (ed.), *The*

Viking Congress, 1954.

Manson, T.M.Y., 'The Fair Isle Spanish Armada Shipwreck', in G.W.S.Barrow (ed.), *The Scottish Tradition; Essays in Honour of Ronald Gordon Cant*, 1974.

Manson, T.Y.M., 'Shetland in the Sixteenth Century', in Ian Cowan and Duncan Shaw (eds.), *The Renaissance and Reformation in Scotland*, 1983.

Marshall, George, *In a Distant Isle; the Orkney Background of Edwin Muir*, 1987.

Martin, Martin, *Description of the Western Isles of Scotland*, reprinted 1970.

Marwick, E.W., *Journey from Serfdom*, unpublished, OA D31/24/3.

Marwick, E.W., *The Folklore of Orkney and Shetland*, 1975.

Marwick, E.W., 'William Tomison; Pioneer of the Fur Trade', *Alberta Historical Review* 10, No.4, 1962.

Marwick, E.W., 'Chief Factor James Sutherland and his Orkney Correspondence', *The Beaver*, 1966.

Marwick, E.W., 'The Stone of Odin', *PSAS* 107, 1975.

Marwick, E.W., *The Sufficient Place*, unpublished, OA.

Marwick, G., *The Old Roman Plough*, 1936.

Marwick, Hugh, 'Celtic Place-names in Orkney', *PSAS* 57, 1923.

Marwick, Hugh, 'Antiquarian Notes on Papa Westray', *POAS* 3, 1924-5.

Marwick, Hugh, 'Antiquarian Notes on Stronsay', *POAS* 5, 1926-7.

Marwick, Hugh, 'Sir David Menzies of Weem', *POAS* 6, 1927-8.

Marwick, Hugh, *The Orkney Norn*, 1929.

Marwick, Hugh, 'A Glimpse of the Great Marquis', *POAS* 8, 1929-30.

Marwick, Hugh, 'An Orkney Jacobite Laird', *Journ.OADS* 12, 1930.

Marwick, Hugh, 'Orkney Farm-name Studies', *POAS* 9, 1930/1.

Marwick, Hugh, 'Two 18th Century Orkney Inventories', *POAS* 12, 1933/4.

Marwick, Hugh, 'Leidang in the West', *POAS* 13, 1934/5.

Marwick, Hugh, 'Old-time Weights and Measures', *POAS* 15, 1937-9.

Marwick, Hugh, *Merchant-Lairds of Long Ago*, 2 vols., 1939.

Marwick, Hugh, *The Place-names of Rousay*, 1947.

Marwick, Hugh, 'Naval Defence in Norse Scotland', *SHR* 28, 1949.

Marwick, Hugh, *Orkney*, 1951.

Marwick, Hugh, *Orkney Farm-names*, 1952.

Marwick, Hugh, 'Two Orkney Letters of AD 1329', *Orkney Miscellany* 4, 1957.

Maxton, J.P., 'Landownership in Scotland in its Relation to the Economic Development of Agriculture in the Period 1871-1921', unpublished B.Litt., Oxford University, 1930 (Queen Elizabeth House).

Maxwell, P., 'Silage', *Journ. OADS* 1, 1925/6.

Miller, Ronald, *Orkney*, 1976.

Miller, Ronald, and Susan Luther Davies, *Eday and Hoy; a Development Survey*, (Univ. of Glasgow), n.d.

Mitchell, T., *History of the Scottish Expedition to Norway in 1612*, 1886.

Moar, W.J., 'Climate and Weather in Orkney', *Journ.OADS* 6, 1931.

Monmouth, Geoffrey of, *The History of the Kings of Britain*, 1982.

Mooney, Harold L., 'The Wreck of the Crown; the Covenanters in Orkney', *Orkney Miscellany* 2, 1954.

Mooney, John, 'Further Notes on Saints' Relics and Burials in St Magnus Cathedral, *POAS* 6, 1927-8.

Mooney, John, *St Magnus, Earl of Orkney*, 1935.

Mooney, John, *Royal Charters and Records of the City of Kirkwall*, 1952.

Morkinskinna = Andersson, Theodore M., and Kari E. Gade (trans.), *Morkinskinna; the Earliest Chronicle of the Norwegian Kings*, Cornell University, 2000.

Morris, Christopher D., *The Birsay Bay Project*, 2 vols., 1989 and 1996.

Morris, Christopher D., and D. James Rackham (eds.), *Norse and Later Settlement and Subsistence in the North Atlantic*, 1992.

Morris, Christopher D., 'Raiders, Traders and Settlers', in H.B.Clarke, Máire Ni Mhaonaigh and Raghnall Ó Floinn (eds.), *Ireland and Scandinavia in the Early Viking Age*, 1998.

Muir, Tom, 'Forty Years On; the Tragedy of Foot and Mouth', *Orkney View*, No.93, 2000.

Munch, P.A., 'Geographical Elucidations of the Scottish and Irish Local Names occurring in the Sagas', *Memoires de la Societé des Antiquaires du Nord*, 1845-1860.

Munch, P.A., *Det Norske Folks Historie*, Christiana, 1852-9.

Mundal, Else, 'The Orkney Earl and Scald Torf-Einarr and his Poetry', in Colleen E. Batey et al. (eds.), *The Viking Age in Caithness, Orkney and the North Atlantic*, 1993.

Munro, Jean, and R.W, *Acts of the Lords of the Isles*, 1986.

Napier Commission = *Evidence taken by HM Commissioners of Inquiry into the Condition of the Crofters and Cottars in the Highlands and Islands of Scotland*, 1884.

Neil, Patrick, *A Tour through Some of the Islands of Orkney and Shetland*, 1806.

Newman, Peter C., *Company of Adventurers*, 1985.

Nevis Institute, *The Shetland Report; a Constitutional Study*, 1978.

NGL = *Norges Gamle Love*, (1) Ser.1 to 1387 = R.Keyser and P.A.Munch, Christiania, 5 vols., 1846 (2) Ser.2 1388-1604, A.Taranger, Christiania, 4 vols., 1903-12.

Nicolaisen, W.F.H., 'Norse Settlement in the Northern and Western Isles; Some Place-name Evidence', *SHR* 48, 1969.

Nicolaisen, W.F.H., *Scottish Place-names*, 1976.

Nicolaisen, W.F.H., 'The Scandinavians and Celts in Caithness', in J.Baldwin (ed.), *Caithness; a Cultural Cross-roads'* 1982.

Nicolaisen, W.F.H. *The Picts and their Place-names*, 1996.

Nicholson, R.A., and S.J.Dockrill, *Old Scatness Broch, Shetland: Retrospect and Prospect*, 1998.

Nicolson, Ranald, *Scotland; the Later Middle Ages (Edinburgh History of Scotland 2)*, 1974.

Nightingale, Pamela, 'The Evolution of Weight-Standards and the Creation of New Monetary and Commercial Links in Northern Europe', *Economic History Review* 38, 1985.

Njal's saga = G.W.Dasent, *The Story of Burnt Njal*, n.d.

North Riding Record Office, *The Zetland (Dundas) Archive*, 1971.

NSA = New Statistical Account = *The Statistical Account of the Orkney Islands*, 1842.

OA = Orkney Archives.

OADS = Orkney Agricultural Discussion Society.

Occidental Oil Company, *The Flotta Story*, 1977.

Ó Corráin, Donnchadh, 'The Vikings in Scotland and Ireland in the Ninth Century', *Peritia* 12, 1998.

O'Dell, A.C., *Historical Geography of the Shetland Islands*, 1939.

O'Dell, A.C., *The Land of Britain; Part 4; Orkney*, (Report of the Land Utilisation Survey of Great Britain), 1939.

OLM = Old Lore Miscellany, Viking Society.

Olsen, Magnus, *Farms and Fanes of Ancient Norway*, 1928.

Omand, Christine (trans.), 'The Life of Saint Findan', in R.J.Berry and H.N.Firth (eds.), *The People of Orkney*, 1986.

Omond, James, *Orkney Eighty Years Ago*, 1911.

Orkney & Shetland Recs. = A.W.Johnston and A.Johnston (eds.), *Orkney & Shetland Records*, Viking Society, 1907 onwards.

Orkney Islands Council, *Orkney Economic Review*, 1998.

OS = Orkneyinga Saga = (1) Islendzk Fornrit xxxiv, 1965 (2) G.W.Dasent, *Icelandic Sagas III, Orkneyingers' Saga*, 1894 (3) A.B.Taylor, (trans.) *Orkneyinga Saga*, 1938 (4) Pálsson, H., and Edwards, P., (trans.), *Orkneyinga Saga*, 1981. References are to Taylor's translation unless cited otherwise.

OSA = Old Statistical Account = (1) Sir John Sinclair, *The Statistical Account of Scotland*, 1791-9 (2) J.Storer Clouston, *The Orkney Parishes*, 1928 (3) D.J.Withrington and I.R.Grant, *The Statistical Account of Scotland*, xix, Orkney and Shetland, 1978. References are to Clouston's edition unless cited otherwise.

Owen, Olwyn A., 'Tuquoy, Westray, Orkney', in Colleen Batey et al. (eds.), *The Viking Age in Caithness, Orkney and the North Atlantic*, 1993.

Owen, Olwyn, and Dalland, Magnar, *Scar; a Viking Boat Burial on Sanday, Orkney*, 1999.

Olwyn Owen (ed.), *The World of Orkneyinga Saga*, 2005.

Omand, Donald, (ed.), *The Orkney Book*, 2003.

Pálsson, Hermann, 'Hakonair Saga; Portrait of a King', *Orkney Miscellany* 5, 1973.

Papar Project, http://www.paparproject.org.uk

Paterson, John, *Memoir of Robert Paterson D.D.*, 1874.

Peace's Orkney Almanac and County Directory, annual.

Peterkin, Alexander, *Rentals of the Ancient Earldom and Bishoprick of Orkney*, 1820.

Peterkin, Alexander, *Notes on Orkney and Shetland*, 1822.

Phelpstead, Carl, 'A Viking Pacifist?' in David Clark and Carl Phelpstead (eds.), *Old Norse made New'*, 2007.

Pitcairn, R., *Criminal Trials in Scotland*, 3 vols., 1833.

POAS = Proceedings of the Orkney Antiquarian Society.

Pohl, Frederick J., *Prince Henry Sinclair; his Voyage to the New World in 1398*, 1974.

Poor Law Enquiry = Parliamentary Papers; Royal Commission on the Poor Laws in Scotland, 1844.

Power, Eileen, *Medieval People*, 1937.

Power, Rosemary, 'Magnus Barelegs' Expeditions to the West', *SHR* 65, 2, 1986.

Prestwich, Michael, 'Edward I and the Maid of Norway', *SHR* 69, 1990.

Pringle, Denys, 'The Houses of the Stewart Earls in Orkney and Shetland', *New Orkney Antiquarian Journal* 1, 1999.

Pringle, R.O., 'On the Agriculture of the Islands of Orkney', *Trans. Highland & Agric. Soc.*, 4th ser. 6, 1874.

PSAS = Proceedings of the Society of Antiquaries of Scotland.

Pundlar Process = Printed legal papers, Orkney Library, 333Y.

Purves, W., *Revenues of the Scottish Crown, 1681*, 1897.

RCAHMS = The Royal Commission on the Ancient Monuments of Scotland, *Inventory of the Ancient Monuments of Orkney and Shetland*, 3 vols., 1946.

Reid, R.W., 'Remains of Saint Magnus and St Rognvald entombed in Saint Magnus Cathedral, Kirkwall, Orkney', *Biometrika* 18, 1 & 2, 1926.

Rendall, Robert, 'Birsay's Forgotten Palace', *Orkney Herald*, 21 April 1959.

Renfrew, C., (ed.), *The Prehistory of Orkney*, 1985.

Rental of the Bishop of Orknayis Landis within Cathnes, Adv.Mss.47/7/19 (iv), National Library of Scotland.

REO = J. Storer Clouston, *Records of the Earldom of Orkney*, 1914.

Rhys, John, 'The Inscriptions and Language of the Northern Picts', *PSAS* 26, 1891/2.

Ritchie, Anna, 'Excavations of the Pictish and Viking-age Farmsteads at Buckquoy', *PSAS* 108, 1976/7.

Ritchie, Anna, 'Birsay around AD 800', *Orkney Heritage* 2, 1983.

Ritchie, Anna, 'The Archaeological Evidence for Daily Life', in Eric H. Nicoll, *A Pictish Panorama*, 1995.

Rivet, A.L.F., and Colin Smith, *The Place-names of Roman Britain*, 1979.

RMS = John Maitland Thomson, *Registrum Magni Sigilli Regum Scotorum; The Register of the Great Seal of Scotland*, 10 vols., reprinted 1984.

RPC = J.H.Burton et al., *Register of the Privy Council of Scotland*, 1877 onwards.

Roberts, Derek F., 'Genetic Affinities' (of Orcadians), in R.J.Berry and H.N.Firth (eds.), *The People of Orkney*, 1986.

Robertson, John D.M. (ed.), *An Orkney Anthology; Selected Works of Ernest Walker Marwick*, 1991.

Ross, Jane, *Orkney and the Earls of Morton*, 1977.

Ross, Sinclair, *Sail Ships of Orkney*, 1954.

Royal Bank of Scotland, *36 St Andrews Square, Edinburgh*, n.d.

RRS = G.W.S.Barrow and others, *Regesta Regum Scotorum*, 8 vols., 1960 onwards.

RSS = *Registrum Secreti Sigilli Regum Scottorum; Register of the Privy Seal of Scotland.*

Ryder, Jane, 'Udal Law', *Northern Studies* 25, 1988.

Rygh, O., *Norske Gaardnavne*, Christiania, 1898.

SAEC = A.O.Anderson, *Scottish Annals from English Chronicles*, 1908.

Saga of Magnus Hakonsson = *G.W.Dasent (trans)*, The Saga of Hacon, *374-387, 1894 (reprinted 1997)*.

Saint-Clair, Roland, 'The Bishopric of Orkney; References to Lands in Caithness', *OLM* 4, part 1.

Saint-Clairs = Roland Saint-Clair, *The Saint-Clairs of the Isles*, Auckland, 1898.

Sanderson, M.H.B, *Scottish Rural Society in the Sixteenth Century*, 1982.

Sandnes, Berit, 'The Bu of Orphir, Burn of Gueth—a Gaelic Pattern of Naming', *Northern Studies* 32, 1997.

Sawyer, Peter, *The Age of the Vikings*, second edition 1971.

Sawyer, Peter, 'Harald Fairhair and the British Isles', in R.Boyer (ed.), *Les Vikings et leur Civilisation*, Paris, 1976.

Saxo Grammaticus = Hilda Ellis Davidson (trans.), *Saxo Grammaticus, the History of the Danes*, 1998.

Scarth, R., and Watt, G., 'Agriculture of Orkney', *Trans. Highland & Agric. Soc.*, 5th series 2, 1939.

Schrank, Gilbert, 'Crossroad of the North: Proto-Industrialisation in the Orkney Islands, 1730-1840', *Journal of European Economic History* 21, No.2, 1992.

Schrank, G., *An Orkney Estate; Improvements at Graemeshall, 1827-1888*, 1995.

Schroder, Virginia, *Bloody Orkney*, 2006.

Scott, A.B., 'The Celtic Church in Orkney', *POAS* 4, 1925/6.

Scott, Sir Walter, *The Pirate*, 1822.

Scottish Law Commission, *Discussion Paper on Law of the Foreshore and Seabed*, Discussion Paper 113, 2001.

Seaver, Kirsten A., *The Frozen Echo; Greenland and the Exploration of North America ca A.D.1000-1500*, Stanford University, 1996.

Senior, W.H., and W.B.Swan, *Survey of Agriculture in Caithness, Orkney and Shetland*, 1972.

Sephton, J., *Saga of King Sverri of Norway*, 1899.

Seyðabrævið (Sheep Letter), Tórshavn, 1971.

Shapinsay Folk Studies Project, *The Eviction of the Shapinsay Elders from their Homes, 1847*, 1985.

Shaw, Duncan, 'Adam Bothwell; a Conserver of the Renaissance in Scotland', in Ian B.Cowan and Duncan Shaw (eds.), *The Renaissance and Reformation in Scotland*, 1983.

Shaw, Frances, *The Northern and Western Isles of Scotland*, 1980.

Shearer, John, et al., *The New Orkney Book*, 1966.

Shetelig, Haakon, *Viking Antiquities in Great Britain and Ireland*, Oslo, 5 parts, 1940.

Shirreff, J., *General View of the Agriculture of the Orkney Islands*, 1814.

SHR = *Scottish Historical Review*.

Sigmundson, S., 'A Critical Review of the Work of Jakob Jakobsen and Hugh Marwick', in A.Fenton & H.Pálsson (eds.), *The Northern and Western Isles in the Viking World*, 1984.

Simpson, W.D., 'Noltland Castle, Westray', in Mooney, *Charters* (only in the Spalding Club edition), 1952.

Simpson, W.D., *The Castle of Bergen and the Bishop's Palace in Kirkwall*, 1961.

Sinclair, Sir John, *General View of the Agriculture of the Northern Counties and Islands of Scotland*, 1785.

Simek, Rudolf, *Dictionary of Northern Mythology*, 1993.

Skea, B.I., *Island Images*, 1982.

Skene, W.F., *Celtic Scotland*, 3 vols., 1876.

Small, Alan, Charles Thomas and David Wilson, *St.Ninian's Isle and its Treasure*, 2 vols., 1973.

Smart, Veronica, 'The Penny in the Pennyland', *Northern Studies* 22, 1985.

Smith, Beverley Ballin, *Howe; Four Millennia of Orkney Prehistory*, 1994.

Smith, Beverley Ballin, et al., *West over Sea*, 2007.

Smith, Brian, 'Stock-stove Houses', *Shetland Folk Book* 7, 1980.

Smith, Brian, 'Shetland in Saga Time; Re-reading the Orkneyinga Saga', *Northern Studies* 25, 1988.

Smith, Brian, 'In the Tracks of Bishop Andrew Pictoris of Orkney and Henry Phankouth, Archdeacon of Shetland', *Innes Review*, xl, 1989.

Smith, Brian, 'Shetland, Scandinavia, Scotland, 1300-1700, in Grant G. Simpson (ed.), *Scotland and Scandinavia*, 1990.

Smith, Brian, 'Earl Robert and Earl Patrick in Shetland', *New Orkney Antiquarian Journal* 1, 1999.

Smith, Brian, *Toons and Tenants*, 2000.

Smith, Brian, 'Henry Sinclair's Fictitious Trip to America', *New Orkney Antiquarian Journal* 2, 2000.

Smith, Brian, 'War or Peace Re-visited', forthcoming, *Northern Studies*.

Smith, Hance, *Shetland Life and Trade*, 1984.

Smith, John, *The Church in Orkney*, 1907.

Smout, T.C., *A History of the Scottish People*, 1969.

Smyth, Alfred P., *Scandinavian Kings in the British Isles*, 1977.

Smyth, Alfred P., *War Lords and Holy Men*, 1984.

Sommerfelt, A., 'On the Norse Form of the Name of the Picts and the Date of the First Norse Raids on Scotland, *Lochlann* 1, 1958.

Somner, G., 'The Pentland Firth Mail Service', *Marine News* 17, n.d.

Sørenson, Preben Meulengracht, 'The Sea, the Flame and the Wind', in Colleen Batey et al. (eds.), *The Viking Age in Caithness, Orkney and the North Atlantic*, 1993.

Spufford, Peter, *Money and its Uses in Medieval Europe*, 1988.

Stancliffe, Claire, and Cambridge, Eric, *Oswald; Northumbrian King to European Saint*, 1995.

Steffánsson, Jón, 'Bishop Bjarne Kolbeinsson, the Skald', *OLM* 1, part 1, 1907-8.

Steinnes, Asgaut, 'The Huseby System in Orkney', *SHR* 44, 1959.

Steuart, A.F., (ed.), *Diary of Thomas Brown*, 1898.

Stevenson, R.B.K., 'Christian Sculpture in Norse Shetland', *Fróðkapparit* (Faroe), 28-9, 1981.

Stewart, Alasdair, 'The Final Folios of Adam Abell's *Roit or Quheill of Tyme*', in Janet Hadley Williams (ed.), *Stewart Style 1513-1542: Essays on the Court of James V*, 1996.

Stewart, John, *Shetland Place-names*, 1987.

Stoklund, B., 'Building Traditions in the Northern World', in A.Fenton & H.Pálsson (eds.), *The Northern and Western Isles in the Viking World*, 1984.

Stromness Museum, *Harvest of Silver*, 1976.

Strype, J., *Ecclesiastical Memorials relating to...Mary*, 1822.

Sutherland, Paul J., 'Turbulent Mechanics and Crack-brained Fellows; Sidelights on the Arrival of the Secession Church in Kirkwall', unpublished dissertation, Aberdeen University Continuing Education, 1996.

Sutherland-Graeme, P., *Orkney and the Last Great War*, 1915.

Sutherland-Graeme, P., *Pateas Amicis*, 1936.

Sutherland-Graeme, P., 'The Parliamentary Representation of Orkney, 1794-1900', *Orkney Miscellany* 1, 1953.

Sverre's saga = J.Sephton (trans.), *Saga of King Sverri of Norway*, 1899.

Tait, W.S., 'Farming in a Bygone Age', *Journ. OADS* 9, 1936.

Taylor, A.B., 'Some Saga Place-names', *POAS* 9, 1930/1.

Taylor, A.B., 'The Death of Earl Rognvaldr', *POAS* 10, 1931/2.

Taylor, A.B., 'Karl Hundasom, King of Scots', *PSAS* 71, 1936.

Taylor, A.B., 'Eystein Haraldsson in the West', in Alam Small, *Fourth Viking Congress*, 1965.

Taylor, Simon, 'The Scandinavians in Fife and Kinross', in Barbara E. Crawford (ed.), *Scandinavian Settlement in Northern Britain*, 1995.

Terry, C.S., *The Cromwellian Union*, 1902.

Theoderic = Theodricus Monachus, (D. and I. McDougal trans.) *Historia de Antiquitate Regum Norwagiensium*, 1998.

Thomas, Charles, 'Sculptured Stones and Crosses from St Ninian's Isle and Papil', in Alan Small et al., *St Ninian's Isle and its Treasure*, Vol.1, 1973.

Thomas, F.W.L., 'What is a Pennyland?', *PSAS* 6, 1883/4.

Thomas, F.W.L., 'Ancient Valuation of Land in the West of Scotland', *PSAS* 8, 1885/6.

Thomson, William P.L., 'Common Land in Orkney', *Orkney Heritage* 1, 1981.

Thomson, William P.L., *The Little General and the Rousay Crofters*, 1981.

Thomson, William P.L., *Kelp-making in Orkney*, 1983.

Thomson, William P.L., 'Fifteenth Century Depression in Orkney; the Evidence of Lord Henry Sinclair's Rentals', in Barbara Crawford, (ed.), *Essays in Shetland History*, 1984.

Thomson, William P.L., 'The Crofting Pioneer Fringe in Nineteenth Century Shapinsay', *Northern Studies* 22, 1985.

Thomson, William P.L., 'St Findan and the Pictish-Norse Transition', in R.J.Berry and H.N.Firth (eds.), *The People of Orkney*, 1986.

Thomson, William P.L., 'Ouncelands and Pennylands in Orkney and Shetland', in L.J.MacGregor and B.E.Crawford (eds.), *Ouncelands and Pennylands*, St Andrews, 1987.

Thomson, William P.L., 'The Eighteenth Century Church in Orkney', in H.W.M. Cant and H.N.Firth (eds.), *Light in the North*, 1989.

Thomson, William P.L., 'Settlement Patterns at Tuquoy, Westray, Orkney', *Northern Studies* 27, 1990.

Thomson, William P.L., 'Sober and Tractable? The Hudson's Bay Men in their Orkney Context', *Scottish Local History* 28, 1993.

Thomson, William P.L., 'Some Settlement Patterns in Medieval Orkney', in Colleen Batey et.al. (eds.), *The Viking Age in Caithness, Orkney and the North*

Atlantic, 1993.

Thomson, William P.L., 'Orkney Farm-names; a Re-assessment of their Chronology', in Barbara E. Crawford (ed.), *Scandinavian Settlement in Northern Britain*, 1995.

Thomson, William P.L., 'The Landscape of Medieval Birsay', in Barbara E. Crawford (ed.), *Northern Isles Connections*, 1995.

Thomson, William P.L., *Lord Henry Sinclair's 1492 Rental of Orkney*, 1996.

Thomson, William P.L., 'Township, House and Tenant Holding; the Structure of Run-rig Agriculture in Shetland', in Val Turner (ed.), *The Shaping of Shetland*, 1998.

Thomson, William P.L., 'The Landscape of Burness in the Viking Age', in Olwyn Owen and Magnar Dalland, *Scar*, 1999.

Thomson, William P.L., 'John Coventrie Sitting in Judgement', *Orkney View*, December 2000.

Thomson, William P.L., 'The Ladykirk Stone', *New Orkney Antiquarian Journal* 2, 2002.

Thomson, William P.L., 'St Magnus; an Exploration of his Sainthood', in Doreen Waugh (ed.), in Doreen Waugh (ed.), *The Faces of Orkney; Stones, Skalds and Saints*, 2003.

Thomson, William P.L., *Orkney: Land and People*, 2008.

Thorsteinsson, Arne, 'The Viking Burial Place at Pierowall, Westray, Orkney', in Bjarni Niclasen (ed.), *The Fifth Viking Congress*, Tórshavn, 1968.

Thurlby, Malcolm, 'Aspects of the Architectural History of Kirkwall Cathedral', *PSAS* 127, 1997.

Topping, P., 'Harald Maddadsson; Earl of Orkney and Caithness', *SHR* 62, 1983.

Traill, W., *Vindication of Orkney*, 1823.

Troup, J., *The Ice-bound Whalers*, 1987.

Troup, J., and F.Eunson, *Stromness; 150 Years a Burgh*, 1967.

TSA = *Third Statistical Account* = Ronald Miller (ed.), *The Third Statistical Account of Scotland*, Vol.xxa, The County of Orkney, *1985*.

Tucker, Thomas, *Report upon the Settlement of the Revenues in Scotland*, 1824.

Tudor, John, *The Orkneys and Shetland*, 1883.

Turville-Petre, Joan, 'The Genealogist and History; Ari to Snorri', *Saga Book* 20, 1978/9.

Van der Vat, D., *The Great Scuttle*, 1982.

Veitch, R, 'The Columban Church in Northern Britain', *PSAS* 127, 1997.

Vink, B., *De Ontwikkeling van de Agrarische Bedrijsstructuur in Orkney, 1840-1930*, unpublished thesis, Catholic University of Nijmegen, 1983.

von See, Klaus, 'Der Skalde Torf-Einar Jarl', *Beiträge zur Geschichte der deutschen Spache und Literatur*, (Tübingen) 82, 1960.

Wainwright, F.T., *The Problem of the Picts*, 1955.

Wainwright, F.T., *The Northern Isles*, 1962.

Wallace, James, *Description of Orkney (1700)*, 1883.

Watson, J., *Tenancy and Ownership*, (Cobden Club Essay), n.d., (c.1891).

Watt, W.G.T., 'The Ruins of Breckness', in M.M.Charleston, *Orcadian Papers*, 1905.

Waugh, Doreen, 'Place-name Evidence for Scandinavian Settlement in Shetland', *Review of Scottish Culture* 7, 1991.

Waugh, Doreen, 'Caithness; an Onomastic Frontier Zone', in Colleen E. Batey et al., (eds.), *The Viking Age in Caithness, Orkney and the North Atlantic*, 1993.

Waugh, Doreen J., (ed.), *Stones, Skalds and Saints,* 2003.

Weaver, H.J., *Nightmare at Scapa Flow*, 1980.

Webster, David, *The History of the Kirkwall United Presbyterian Congregation*, 1910.

Wenham, Sheena, 'From Lintseed to Linen; the Manufacture of Linen on an Orkney Estate, 1770-1818', *The Making of Modern Orkney*, (Continuing Education, Aberdeen University), 1995.

Wenham, Sheena, 'Margaret Vedder, Orkney, 1788; Her Household Goods and Body Clothes', *Review of Scottish Culture* 10, 1996-7.

Wenham, Sheena, 'Famine and Victuals on the Graemeshall Estate', in Doreen Waugh (ed.), *The Faces of Orkney, Stones, Skalds and Saints*, 2001.

Wenham, Sheena, *A More Enterprising Spirit*, 2001.

Whaley, Diana, 'The Kings' Sagas', in Anthony Faulkes and Richard Perkins, *Viking Revaluations*, 1993.

Whaley, Diana, *The Poetry of Arnórr jarlaskáld*, 1998.

Whittington, G., 'Agriculture and Society in Lowland Scotland, 1750-1870', in Whittington, G., and I.D.Whyte (eds.), *An Historical Geography of Scotland*, 1983.

Whyte, I.D., *Agriculture and Society in Seventeenth Century Scotland*, 1979.

Wickham-Jones, Caroline, *Orkney, a Historical Guide*, 1998.

Wishart, G., *The Memoirs of James, Marquis of Montrose*, 1893.

Williams, D.G.E., 'Land Assessment and Military Organisation in the Northern Settlements in Scotland, c.900-1266 AD', Unpublished Ph.D., St Andrews, 1996.

Williams, Gareth, and Paul Bibire, *Sagas, Saints and Settlements*, 2004.

Wilson et al., 'Genetic Evidence for Different Male and Female Roles during Cultural Transitions in the British Isles', *Proc. National Academy of Science* (USA) 98, No.9, 2001.

Windwick, Norman, 'Fifty Years of Cheese-making', *Orkney View*, No.66, 1996.

Wood, Marcus W.T., 'Dairy Cattle', *Orcadian*, Supplement, 8 August 1985.

Wood, W.T., 'Farming Experiences in Orkney', *Journ.OADS* 7, 1928.

Woolf, Alex, 'The Moray Question and the Kingship of Alba in the Tenth and Eleventh Centuries', *SHR* 79, 2000.

Young, G.V.C., *From the Vikings to the Reformation; a Chronicle of the Faroe Islands up to 1538*, 1979

Young, G.V.C., *The History of the Isle of Man under the Norse*, 1981.

Index

Abell, Adam, 242
Aberdeen, 98, 310
Aberdeen, Alexander, surveyor, 333-4, 342
Aberdeen, William, surveyor, 342
Abune-the-Hill, Birsay, 224
Acredale, 335
Act anent lands lying run-rig, 332
Act for the division of commonties, 332, 347
Adalbert, Archbishop of Hamburg-Bremen, 85
Adalbert, Bishop of Orkney, 85
Adam, Bishop of Caithness, 130, 184, 208
Adam, Chaplain of Orkney, 126
Adam of Bremen, 85
Admiralty, 244, 267, 285-6, 452
Adomnán, 8, 9, 14
Aedán mac Gabráin, 9
Afreka, first wife of Harald Maddadsson, 118, 126, 135
Agneta (Annot), dau. of Earl Malise, 152
Agricola, croft, Shapinsay, 4, 340
Agricola, Roman general, 4-5
Agriculture, 315-32, 333-48, 378-94, 416-33
    Agricultural Holdings Act, 419
    Contractors, 422, 429-30
    Depression, 389-90, 416-20
    Holdings (Also see: Cottars, crofts), 311-2, 381
    Improvement, 378-94
    Labour (Also see: farm servants), 422, 429-30
    Machinery, 411, 428-9
    Subsidies, 420-421, 430-1,
Airigh-names, see: Place-names
Aitken, David, surveyor, 326
Alexander de Ard, 153, 157-9, 160, 163-4, 173
Alexander I, King of Scots, 89, 118
Alexander II, King of Scots, 130-1, 135, 136, 140
Alexander III, King of Scots, 140, 144, 145, 146, 149, 189
Alginates, 361
Allhallow court, 186, 245
Anderson, Duncan, 153, 163
Anderson, Peter, historian, 236, 263, 269

Andreas, son of Rafn, 184
Andrew, Bishop of Caithness, 123
Andrew (Pictoris), Bishop of Orkney, 220, 227, 228, 247, 252
Andro and Graith, ship of King's Lynn, 246
Anglesey, 61
Angus earls, 130, 134-7, 148-50, 181, 185, 189
Angus, Earl of Moray, 117
Annand, James, prebendary of St John, 260
Anne of Denmark, wife of James VI, 275
Annual of Norway, 144, 156, 194, 199
Archdeaconry of Shetland, 220
Ari, Icelandic historian, 15
Ark of Noy, 285
Ark, The (croft), 382
Armada, 276
Armour, Rev. Matthew, 390, 410
Arne Lorja, sysselman, 127, 182
Arnfinn Thorfinsson, Earl of Orkney, 29, 57
Arnkell Einarsson, Earl of Orkney, 29, 56-7
Arnór jarlaskald, 72, 76, 80, 81, 84
Arnot, Sir John, 288, 290, 293, 294, 301
Artabláir, 10
Asleif, mother of Sweyn Asleifsson, 109
Audfin, Bishop of Bergen, 154
Auld bow (dyke), 328, 452
Auld earldom land, 106, 225, 452
Ausdale, Caithness, 127
Auskerry, 241
Avelshay, Rousay, 198
Ayre Mills, Kirkwall, 427

Ba', The, 447
Backaskaill, Papa Westray, 51
Baikie estate, 215, 341
Baikie, James of Tankerness (17th cent.), 309, 314
Baikie, James of Tankerness (19th cent.), 384
Baikie, Thomas, boat-builder, 349
Baikie, Rev. Thomas, 405
Bailies and Bailie courts, 211, 312, 321-3, 325, 327, 347, 452
Balaclava, 382

Balfour castle, 340, 402, 422
Balfour estate, 420
Balfour Mains, 340, 422, 431
Balfour Village (Also see: Shoreside), 403
Balfour, Alison, witch, 278-9, 301
Balfour, David, 229, 256, 384, 386, 401, 403, 416, 419, 431
Balfour, Gilbert, 254-5, 257, 258-9, 264, 265, 266, 278, 281
Balfour, James, of Pittendreich, 254, 263
Balfour, John, Sheriff-depute, 264
Balfour, John, 338, 399-400
Balfour, John (1780-1799), 400
Balfour, Michael, 278, 281-2
Balfour, Thomas, 339, 340, 374, 383, 386, 400, 431,
Balfour, William, 336, 400
Balfour, Captain William, 382, 400
Ballarat, 382
Banff, 158, 170
Bannockburn, Battle of, 98, 148
Barley (Also see: Bere), 221, 423, 424, 429
Barony, Birsay, 224
Barry, Rev. George, 241, 339-340, 373, 404, 406, 408
Bayern, The, 435
Beaton, James, of Clouk, 312
Bellenden, George, Sheriff-depute, 264
Bellenden, Sir John, of Auchnoull, 252-9, 262, 263, 265
Bellenden, Katherine, 253, 254
Bellenden, Lewis, Justice-clerk, 254, 274
Bellenden, Patrick, 254, 259, 264, 266, 267, 275, 278, 281, 289
Bendigo, 382
Benkoren, unidentified monastery, 122
Bere, beremeal (Also see: Barley), 221, 245, 266, 308, 344, 393, 424
Bergen, 121, 141, 154, 190, 240-1
Bergfinn, Skatisson, 97
Berryhill, Burray, 382
Binnas Kirk, Papa Westray, 20
Birsay, 3, 97, 104, 207, 221-4, 248, 252, 257, 271, 272, 333, 334,
Birsay warriors sculptured stone, 11
Birsay, Brough of, 44, 86, 334
Birsay, Earl's palace, 272, 278, 279=80, 296, 307, 334
Birsay, Lower palace, 334
Bishop's Palace, Kirkwall, 143, 236, 246, 248, 250, 278

Bishopric estate, 104-5, 224-5, 228-30, 252-3, 256, 272, 274, 287-92, 298, 301, 304-5, 310, 318-9, 329, 341
Bishopric estate, lands in Caithness, 123, 253
Bismar (weigh-beam), 270, 396, 452
Bister-names, see: Place-names
Bjarni, Bishop of Orkney, 122, 123, 125, 128, 132, 137, 252, 412
Björn Thorleifsson, Governor of Iceland, 195
Black Death, 156, 169, 187, 190, 210, 211, 228
Black, Henry, Capt. of Kirkwall Castle, 290
Black, Thomas, Chamberlain, 283
Blair, Patrick, Sheriff, 307
Blaeu, Johan, map-maker, 40
Blathmac, martyrdom of, 49
Blood eagle, 34, 36, 37-8
Blow High, Rousay, 382
Board of Trustees (for linen), 363, 365
Boardhouse, Birsay, 334
Boats and boatbuilding, 349-51
Bodo, Villein, 393
Body, Rev. Gilbert, 282
Boece, Hector, 282
Boer-names, see: Place-names
Boniface, St, (Curitan), 17, 19, 20
Boniface, St, of Crediton, 17
Bonot, M., Sheriff, 246, 253
Bordland, 48, 106, 170, 184, 223-5, 230, 231, 236, 242, 452
Borthwick, James, master-gunner, 248
Bothwell, Adam, Bishop of Orkney, 247-61, 264, 265, 287, 290
Bothwell, Earl of, and Duke of Orkney, 260, 264
Bothwell, Francis, half brother of George III, Earl of Caithness, 289
Bothwell, Francis, nephew of Adam Bothwell, 258
Braal (Brathwell), Caithness, 130, 158
Braebister, Deerness, 210, 274
Braehead, Rousay, 382
Brand's years (famine), 352
Brand, Rev. John, 331, 351, 368
Brand, Alexander, tacksman, 310
Breckness, 266, 305
Bressay stone, 45-6
Bressigarth, Sanday, 249
Brian Boru, Irish king, 67
Bridei mac Bile, Pictish king, 9-10

Bridei mac Máelchú, Pictish king, 8-9, 14
Brims, Walls, 337
Bristol, 355. 357
British Airways, 447
British Linen Bank, 364
Brittonic languages and place-names, 6-7, 10, 41-2, 50
Brodie, William, 406
Brøgger, A.W, historian, 43, 47
Brough, Bu of, Sanday, 223, 230
Brough, Rousay, 259
Brough, South Ronaldsay, 149
Brown, Alexander, 149, 160
Brown, George MacKay, poet, 91, 447
Brown, Isobel, 268
Brown, James and Robert, pirates, 286
Brown, Margaret, cottar, 402
Brown, Thomas, skipper, 177, 178
Bruce, Isabella, wife of King Eric Magnusson, 147, 148
Bruce, James, earldom chamberlain, 343
Bruce, Laurence of Cultalindie, 270, 278, 281, 283, 291
Bruntland, 382
Brusi Sigurdsson, Earl of Orkney, 29, 69, 72, 75, 79
BSE (Mad cow disease), 431
Bu of Burray, 51, 223, 337, 341, 343,
Bu of... names, see: Place-names
Buchanan, Sir John, of Scotscraig, 303
Buckquoy, Birsay, 7, 19, 22, 44-5
Burgar's Bay, Kirkwall, 441, 442
Bummacks, 381
Burness, Sanday, 248
Burrafirth, Shetland, 285
Burray, 252, 253. 260, 298, 308, 337, 370, 404, 419
Burray hoard, 62
Burray Village, 370, 436
Burroughs, General F.W.T., 339, 388, 390, 391, 400, 401, 416, 418, 448
Burwick, South Ronaldsay, 223, 449
Butter, 130, 208, 221, 228, 242, 245, 283, 310, 393, 422, 425
Butter skat, 156, 211

Cabbages, 306, 383
Caereni, 4
Caithness, 3, 8, 58, 60, 72, 91, 123, 126-7, 130-1, 135-6, 150, 158, 194
Cairston, 223
Calder, Marcus, factor, 386

Calderwood, Rev. David, 410
Calfsound, Eday, 302-3
Calixtus II, Pope, 95
Canisby, Caithness, 123
Cantick Head, 336
Cara, Park of, 336-7
Carbisdale, Battle of, 305-6
Carness, 297
Carness, Laurence, Lawman, 267
Carrick, Earldom of, 302-3
Carts, 337, 338
Castleton, Caithness, 419
Cattle, 3, 130, 208, 221, 336-7, 343, 383, 421, 423-4, 432
Cecilia, dau. of K. Hakon IV, 140
Charles I, King of Great Britain, 280, 301, 305
Charles II, King of Great Britain, 304, 307
Charles VI, King of France, 195
Cheese, 425
Childe, Gordon, archaeologist, 6
Christchurch, Birsay, 85-6, 95, 97, 104, 271
Christian I, King of Norway-Denmark, 183, 189, 194-5, 198, 199, 229
Christian III, King of Norway-Denmark, 240
Christian, Sir, of Tain, 156
Christopher, King of Norway-Denmark, 196
Church discipline, 405-6, 410
Churchill Barriers, 436-8
Claudius, Roman emperor, 4, 6
Claymore Creamery, 425
Claymore Oil Field, 444
Clearances, 339-341, 383, 388, 390, 392
Cleat, Sanday, 391
Cleat, South Ronaldsay, 149
Clement VII, Pope, 163
Clere, Sir John, English admiral, 246
Clickhimin, Broch of, Shetland, 12
Climate, climate changes, 169, 328, 377
Clontarf, Battle of, 60, 67-8
Clouk, Stromness, 312
Clouston, J. Storer, 47, 70-2, 106, 122, 162, 206, 226, 236, 240, 257, 281, 300, 315, 448
Clouston, Rev. William, 375, 404
Clow, John, schoolmaster, 412
Coal, 355
Cod, 187, 368-9, 378
Coins, coinage, 217, 270, 351

Coll, 60
Cologne pennies, 217
Colonsay, 60
Columba, St, 8, 9, 98
Colville, Henry, parson of Orphir, 278-9
Combine harvesters, 429
Commissioners of Supply, 448
Common land, commonty, 210, 273, 274, 311, 317-319, 322, 323, 336, 337-9, 347, 381, 383, 384, 387, 392, 452
Compensation for improvements, 384, 419
Complaint anent...Robert Stewart, 266, 272, 274
Complaint of the People of Orkney, 178
Comyn, Walter, Earl of Menteith, 135
Conquest land, 170, 203-4, 225-6, 228, 233, 235, 240, 268, 452
Convention of Royal Burghs, 368
Cooperhouse, Birsay, 310
Copenhagen, 175, 176, 350
Corgill, James, James and John, 312, 325
Cormac ua Liatháin, 8, 14
Cornavii, 4
Corpus Christi eagle, 17
Corrigal Farm Museum, 324
Corse, Bu of, 296, 425
Corsmay, Yanis, Bremen merchant, 267
Costa, 51, 224
Cottars, 345, 353, 379-81, 402, 452
Country Acts, 321, 352
County Council, 448
Court Book of 1612-3, 294
Court of Perambulation and Ogang, 273, 274
Court of Session, 249, 253, 260, 265, 347
Cox & Danks, salvage company, 435
Crab Ha', 383
Craigie, Hugh, MP, 352
Craigie, James, 176
Craigie, James, of Braes, 427
Craigie, Magnus, merchant, 352
Craigie, William, merchant, 352
Craigie, William, of Gairsay, 309, 352
Craigie, William, Steward, 352
Crantit, St Ola, 343
Crawford, Barbara, 136
Crofters' Act of 1886, 382, 391, 392, 419, 421
Crofters' Commission, 383, 391, 417, 427, 452
Crofts, crofters, 381, 417, 419, 443
Cromwellian occupation, 306, 350

Crop rotations, 422
Cross Kirk, Sanday, 252
Cross Kirk, Westray, 187
Cross School, Sanday, 414
Cubbie Roo's Castle, Wyre, 133
Curitan, 17, 19
Currey, rebel, 306
Cyderhall, 28

Dairying, 425
Dál Riata, 6, 9, 59, 61, 78, 214
Dales, The, 59, 78
Damsay, 117
Daniel, William, artist, 401
Danzig, 285, 286
Davach (unit of land), 214, 452
David Haraldson, Earl of Orkney, 128, 180
David I, King of Scots, 89, 104, 109, 113, 114, 116, 118, 123
David II, King of Scots, 152, 153, 179
Davis Straits, 373
Davis, Sir Peter Maxwell, composer, 447
Death duties, 420
Deer, 3, 12, 117
Deer Forest Commission, 391
Deer Sound, 371
Deerness, 22, 75, 210, 230, 274, 289, 303, 310, 353
Dennison, Walter Traill, 414, 440
Desmene, 224
Dialect, see: Language
Dick, Alexander, Cathedral provost, 259, 304
Dick, Sir William, of Braid, 259, 303-4
Dicuil, 16
Digro, Rousay, 392
Diploma or Genealogy of the Earls, 105, 134, 150, 170, 173, 179, 183
Dirmait, King of Ui-Meith, 119
Dishington, John, Sheriff-depute, 283
Disruption, 410
Distilling, 424
Dogfish, 367
Donaldson, Gordon, Professor, 202, 269
Dons (families of Spanish descent), 276
Dornoch, Dornoch Firth, 28, 123, 131, 290
Douglas, Alexander, of Spynie, 307, 314
Douglas, Egidia, wife of Earl Henry II, 172, 192
Douglas, Elizabeth, first wife of Earl William, 192, 194, 235

Douglas, Gavin, poet, 232
Douglas, James, 4th Earl of Morton, 266, 271
Douglas, James, 10th Earl of Morton, 306
Douglas, James, 11th Earl of Morton, 336, 341
Douglas, James, 14th Earl of Morton, 395-7
Douglas, Robert, of Blackerstoune, 303
Douglas, William, of Nithsdale, 172
Douglas, William, 7th Earl of Morton, 304, 305, 306
Douglas, William, 9th Earl of Morton, 306-7, 311, 318, 319
Drainage, Drainage loans, 324, 333-4, 336, 343, 383, 388, 416, 431
Drever, David, of Huip, 369
Droving trade, 337
Drummond, Sir John, 170
Dufnjal, cousin of Magnus and Hakon, 92
Dumbarton, 293, 295, 355
Duncan I, King of Scots, 76, 80
Duncansby, 4, 78, 106, 109
Dundas, Sir Laurence, 338, 341-2, 397-9
Dundas, Thomas, MP, 399
Dundee, 266, 275, 357
Dungalsnipa, Battle of, 60, 78
Dunkirk, The, 283, 284, 290, 294
Dunnet, Dunnet Head, Caithness, 4, 123
Dunnottar, 9, 27
Dunskeath castle, 119
Durcadale, Birsay, 382
Dykes, Fossil, 383, 387
Dykes, Hill, 317, 322, 323, 333, 387, 452
Dykes, Inner, 328
Dykes, Picky, 1
Dysart, 193, 203, 245

Earl Sigurd (ship), 444
Earl Thorfinn (ship), 444
Earl's Palace, Kirkwall, 280, 290, 278
Earldom estate, 106, 176, 206, 295, 301, 319, 329, 341-3, 352, 417, 420, 452
East India Company, 339, 388, 399
Eday, 258, 289-90, 302-3, 336, 360, 379, 382, 445
Edgar, King of Scots, 89, 118
Education, 400, 404, 409, 412, 414, 444
Edward I, King of England, 146
Edward IV, King of England, 197
Edward the Confessor, King of England, 92

Edwin, King of Northumbria, 11
Egg Marketing Board, 427
Egglespethir, Pictish church, 19
Eggs, 388, 393, 421, 437
Egilsay, 93-7, 252,
Einar (Torf Einar), Earl of Orkney, 30-9, 56, 57, 116, 279
Einar Klining, 58
Einar Harðkjotr, 58
Einar Sigurdsson, Earl of Orkney, 29, 69, 70, 74
Eithne, wife of Earl Hlodver, 29, 59
Ekkjalsbakki (Dornoch Firth), 28, 78
Elections, 399, 400, 408, 448
Electricity, 424, 439, 442
Elizabeth, The, 286
Ellen, The, 373
Ellibister, 207, 208
Elphinstone, Col. Robert, tacksman, 309-10
Elphinstone, Euphemia, 262
Elphinstone, Gavin, 266, 269
Elsness, Sanday, 391
Elwick, Shapinsay, 141, 248
Emigration, 360, 376, 411, 442-3
Emilia, sister of Count Maurice, 280
Enclosing, 336, 338, 339-41, 343
Enlargement of crofts, 391
Enstabillie, Sandwick, 170
Environmental issues, 431-2
Eric the Pomeranian, King of Norway, 165, 169, 175, 179, 196
Erik Blood-axe, King of Norway, 29, 48, 56, 59, 60, 62
Erik, King of Norway, 146, 147, 189
Erlend Haraldsson, Earl of Orkney, 89, 101, 109, 116-7, 118
Erlend I Einarsson, Earl of Orkney, 56-7
Erlend II Thorfinnsson, Earl of Orkney, 88, 89
Erling Vidkunnsson, Norwegian regent, 150
Ermingarde, Queen of Narbonne, 108
Erngisl Suneson, Earl of Orkney, 152-3, 157, 182
Erskine, John, Merchant, 364
Estates, Break up of, 416-22
Etherdouer castle, 119
Evangelicalism, 407-11, 440
Evie, 224, 252, 253, 254, 259, 298, 334, 336
Exports, 344, 339

Eyjarskeggjar ('Island Beards'), 120-1
Eyrbyggia saga, 25, 61
Eyrislands: see: Urislands
Eystein, King of Norway, 95, 113, 115,
Eysteinsdalr (Ausdale), Caithness, 127
Eyvind úrashorn, 70

Fa' Doon, 382
Fair Isle, 108, 276
Falcons, falconers: see: Hawks
Famine, 179, 307-9, 335, 358, 368
Fararkaup (Icelandic tax), 210
Farm buildings, 343, 425, 438
Farm servants, 380-1, 407, 422, 429
Farm size, 430
Faroe, 16, 41, 169, 185, 300, 328, 351,
    415
Fea, James, author, 376
Fea, James, of Clestrain, 339
Fea, James, of Whitehall, 352
Fea, Patrick, 336, 364, 379
Feelie Ha', 382
Female labour, 364, 366
Fences, wire, 347
Fencibles, The Orkney & Shetland, 374
Fenton, Alexander, 191
Fetlar, Shetland, 42, 163
Feuing land, 238, 241-2, 255-9, 263, 303,
    304-5, 314, 452
Findan, St, 50, 64
Findláech, Ruler of Moray, 77, 78, 80
Finlayson, John, Sheriff-depute, 295-7,
    302
Finn-men, 1, 308
Firth, 309, 318
Firth, John, 328
Fishing, 3, 168, 171, 187, 190, 246, 275,
    283, 284-5, 292, 317, 341, 367, 368-
    71, 407, 417
Flatjarbók, 66, 130, 131
Flax, 335, 343, 363-4
Flett, Barbara of Gruthay, 331
Flett, Robert, of Netherbrough, 326
Flodden, Battle of, 248
Florevåg, Battle of, 27, 121, 124, 139,
    180, 219, 226
Flotta, 42, 252, 253, 298, 444
Flying Kestrel, 435
Foinaven Oil Field, 444
Folklore, 65, 191, 414-5, 448
Foot-and-Mouth, 422
Forcop (a skat), 208, 210, 211, 452

Fordun, John of, historian, 16, 60, 118, 124,
    130
Fortesque, Archer, of Swanbister, 13, 384,
    386
Foulsie, Gilbert, Prebendary of St John,
    260
Fox, Charles James, MP, 408
Frakok of Dale, 102, 104, 112
Fraser, Simon, 150
Fraser, Margaret, 150
Frederick II, King of Norway-Denmark,
    267
Free Church, 410
Freskin de Moravia, 136
Fresson, Captain E.E., 447
Freya Geo, Stronsay, 64

Gairlies, Lord, 326
Gairsay, 107, 207, 208, 268, 278, 352,
    404
Gaius, King of Orkney, 11
Galilee, Sanday, 382
Galloway, Earl of, 337-9, 341, 396, 398
Gardameles, Sanday, 351
Garden's seed catalogues, 422
Garth-names, see: Place-names.
Gilbert I, Earl of Orkney, 134, 136
Gilbert II, Earl of Orkney, 134, 136, 137
Gilbert, Bishop of Caithness, 131
Gilbert, Bishop of Hamar, 141
Gilli, Earl in Coll or Colonsay, 29, 60, 61,
    67
Gills Bay, Caithness, 449
Girnel, Kirkwall, 294, 297
Glass-making, 355
Glims Holm, 436
Glymsdrapa, 26
Godbold, King of Orkney, 11
Godfrey, King of Man, 61
Godings, 106-7, 133-4, 137, 184, 211,
    215, 452
Goding ship, Loss of, 133, 185
Goedelic languages and place-names, 6
Gold, Andrew, chamberlain, 343, 419
Goodmen, 156, 173-4, 184, 187, 452
Gordon, Helen, 234, 241
Gordon, James, merchant, 364
Graeme, Alexander Sutherland, admiral,
    345-6, 365, 399
Graeme, Jean, 'Lady Graemeshall', 365
Graeme, Patrick, sheriff, 365, 377
Graemeshall estate, 305, 345-7, 365, 404

Graham, Alexander, Stromness merchant, 374
Graham, George, Bishop of Orkney, 252, 301, 304-5,
Graham, James, Marquis of Montrose, 305
Graham, John, of Breckness, 305
Graham, Patrick, Bishop of St Andrews, 220
Graham, Patrick, of Graemeshall, 305
Grain, 179, 190, 209, 221, 228, 282, 294, 343, 344, 350, 377, 389, 424
Grammar School, Birsay, 412
Grammar School, Kirkwall, 50, 143, 250, 251, 361, 412, 414
Granderie, Commissions of, 322
Grandison, Viscount, 306-7
Grass, 326, 338, 341, 343, 422, 423, 424
Graven, Archibald, fiddler, 280
Greenland, 168, 191, 351, 371
Gregory IX, Pope, 137
Greloð, wife of Earl Thorfinn Skull-splitter, 29, 57
Grieve, John, of Myrtle Lane, Sanday, 383, 384
Grim Ormson, 154
Grimbister, Firth, 318
Grimbister, Ann, Alexander and Magnus, 318
Grimond, Jo, MP, 440
Grimsetter, 437
Groat, Henry, in Herston, 321
Gruffydd ap Cynan, King of Gwynedd, 90, 91, 93
Grukalty, Shapinsay, 5
Gunn, John, author, 414
Gunnas, King of Orkney, 11
Gunnhild, daughter of Earl Harald Maddadsson, 135
Gunnhild, mother of Earl (St) Rognvald, 89, 102
Gunnhild, wife of Erik Blood-axe, 57
Gunni of Westray, 105
Gunni Olafsson, 116
Gurness, Broch of, 2, 6-7
Guthorm, Earl of Orkney, 28, 30
Gwynn, David, pirate, 285

Hacksness, Sanday, 223
Hafrsfjord, Battle of, 24, 27
Hakon Hakonsson IV, King of Norway, 138-145, 211
Hakon Jonsson, sysselman, 154-7, 162, 164, 165, 168, 174

Hakon the Good, King of Norway, 29, 56, 57
Hakon *ungi*, King of Norway, 137
Hakon V, King of Norway, 169
Hakon VI, King of Norway, 155
Hakon Paulsson, Earl of Orkney, 88-97, 102
Hakon, Earl in Norway, 61
Hakonar saga, 129, 134, 136, 142, 144
Halcro, Sir Hugh, prebendary, 259
Halcro, Magnus, precentor, 256, 258, 259, 260, 267, 268, 272-3
Halcro, Magnus (senior), Cathedral provost, 259
Halcro, Sir Nicolas, precentor, 259
Halcro, Patrick, 298
Halcro, South Ronaldsay, 148, 256, 259, 314
Haldane, Robert and James, evangelists, 407
Halfdan, Longlegs, 29, 33, 36-8, 57
Hallad, Earl of Orkney, 29-30, 31
Halves and Thirds, 71, 206
Hamburg-Bremen, Archbishopric, 94
Hamilton, Sir Robert, MP, 425
Hampshire, HMS, 434
Hanef *ungi*, sysselman, 132-4
Hans, King of Norway-Denmark, 235
Hanseatic merchants, 190, 270, 285, 310, 351, 368
Harald Fairhair, King of Norway, 24, 29, 47, 52, 56, 214
Harald Gilli, King of Norway, 103
Harald Hakonsson, Earl of Orkney, 101
Harald Hardrada, King of Norway, 84, 88
Harald II, King of Man and the Isles, 140
Harald Maddadsson, Earl of Orkney, 113-127
    Adopted as co-earl, 108, 114
    Rules in Rognvald's absence, 108
    Payment to King Eystein, 115-6
    War of the Three Earls, 116-7
    Exercises right of hospitality, 211
    Shetland detached from earldom, 219
    Post-Florevåg settlement, 27-8, 121-2, 128, 180
    Relations with Caithness bishops, 123
    His marriages, 118, 126, 135
    Relations with Norway, 113, 115-6, 120-2
    Relations with Scotland, 113-4, 124-7
    Kills Harald the Younger, 124-5

Attacks Bishop John, 20, 123
Pays fine for Caithness, 127
Kills Arne Lorja, 182
Gifts to church, 122
Estimate of his career, 127
Harald the Younger, Earl of Orkney, 73, 89, 118, 120, 122, 124-5
Harald, son of Earl John, 129, 132
Hareck, 68
Harray, 314, 382, 390
Hatston, 437, 442
Hartsyde, Margaret, 303
Háttalykill, 32
Hávamál, 36
Havard Harvest-happy, Earl of Orkney, 29, 58
Hawks, hawk-hens, 154, 208, 212, 222, 234, 452
Hay, 130, 323, 327, 422, 423
Hay, John, of Balbithan, 395
Hay, Father R.A, genealogist, 166, 193
Hay, George, 4th Earl of Kinnoul, 304, 305
Heather House, 382
Hebrides, 126, 138-145
Heimskringla, 33, 56, 360
Helena, dau. of Earl Harald Maddadsson, 135
Helga of Dale, 102
Hell, Birsay, 382
Helliehow, Sanday, 65
Helsingborg, 173
Henbister, Holm, 19
Henderson, William, Dingwall herald, 270
Henry I, King of England, 92, 95
Henry II, King of England, 119
Henry III, Emperor, 85
Henry VIII, King of England, 241
Henry, Bishop of Gardar and Orkney, 168
Henry, Bishop of Orkney, 85, 141, 144
Henry, son of Harald Maddadsson, 129
Herboga, dau. of Harald Maddadsson, 135
Herding, 323, 327, 392
Herdis Thorvaldsdatter, 165
Hermits, 14, 16
Herring, 320, 369-71
Herston, 316-9, 320, 321, 323, 326, 328, 370
Hervé, Bishop of Bangor, 91
Herwood, Magnus, 220
Hewison, W.S, author, 434
Hides, 242, 245

Highland Airways, 226-7
Hill dykes, 317, 322, 323, 333, 387. 452
Hill Livestock Compensatory Allowance, 431
Hird (bodyguard), 132, 133, 180, 184, 185, 453
Hirdmanstein (hird court), 184, 186, 245, 257
Hirdskrå, 121, 128, 180, 184
Historia Norvegiae, 1-2, 14, 31-2, 48
Hlaupandanes, 70, 74, 86
Hlifolf, steward in Caithness, 126
Hlodver (Hundi), son of Sigurd the Stout, 29, 63, 76-7
Hlodver, Earl of Orkney, 29, 59
Hoip Weill, The, 286
Holland, Eday, 290
Holland, Papa Westray, 391
Holm, 298, 335, 365, 381, 406
Holmganga (trial by combat), 269
Holyrood, Abbey of, 261, 262, 265, 287
Homildon Hill, Battle of, 172
Honorius, Pope, 131
Honyman, Andrew, Bishop of Orkney, 301
Honyman, William, Lord Armadale, 341, 347, 399
Horroldsgarth, Shapinsay, 249
Horses, 3, 13, 22, 322, 355, 383, 423, 427-8
Horwood, Colonel George, 420
Hoskull, Herra, 150
Housebay, Stronsay, 71
Houseby, Birsay, 71
Housgarth, Sanday, 249
Housing, 440-2
Houton, 143
How be-north, Sanday, 248
How, Shapinsay, 248
Howe, Broch of, 3, 22
Hoxa, 149
Hoy, 40, 223, 224, 289, 298, 444
Hrolf, son of Rognvald of Møre, 29, 30, 38
Hrollaug, son of Rognvald of Møre, 30, 38
Hudson's Bay Company, 348, 366, 371-2, 375-6, 378, 406, 412
Hugh, Earl of Chester, 90
Hugh, Earl of Shrewsbury, 90
Hugh, Sir, of Rendall, 198
Huip, Stronsay, 369
Huna, Caithness, 411
Hunting, 12-3, 117, 154, 224

Husabae, Rousay, 71
Huseby system (military farms), 71-2, 206
Hutton, Thomas, chamberlain, 343
Hvalfloð, second wife of Harald
    Maddadsson, 118, 126, 135

Iceland, 15-6, 43, 53, 184, 191, 195, 350,
    371
Immigration, 444
Impignoration of Orkney and Shetland,
    189-205, 240-1, 267-8, 453
Imports, 350
Improvement, agricultural, 333-48
Incorporated Trades of Kirkwall, 408
Infield, 3, 323, 347
Inflation, 209, 270, 375
Inga saga, 128
Ingarth, wife of St Magnus, 92
Ingi, King of Norway, 115
Ingibjorg, dau. of King Eric Magnusson,
    147
Ingibjorg, widow or dau. of Earl Thorfinn,
    81, 89, 117
Ingibjorg, wife of Sigurd of Westness, 106
Ingirid, dau. of Earl Rognvald Kolsson, 89,
    118
Inglis, Thomas, factor, 221
Inkerman, 382
Innocent III, Pope, 123, 126
Installation of Earls, 180
Installation of Pictish kings, 11-3
Inskyft, 331
Iona, 25, 49, 60
Irving, Edward, 272
Irving, Gilbert, 272
Irving, James, of Sebay, 255-6
Irving, John, Edinburgh lawyer, 346
Irving, Magnus, 272
Irving, William, 272
Isabella of Strathearn, 152-3, 160, 170,
    173
Isbister, 207
Isbister, Joseph, Factor at Albany Fort, 372
Island Authorities, 449
Isle of Man, 24, 63
Islendingabók, 15
Italian Chapel, 436

Jakobsen, Jakob, 41, 50
James I, King of Scots, 172, 179, 192
James II, King of Scots, 192, 194, 195,
    196

James III, King of Scots, 183, 189, 196, 199,
    203-5, 225, 235
James IV, King of Scots, 220, 252
James V, King of Scots, 240-6, 249, 252,
    262
James VI, King of Scots, 260, 274, 280,
    286, 287, 290, 301, 303
James, Richard, antiquary, 282
Jarteinabók (Miracle Book), 99
Jehovah's Witnesses, 440
Joanna, Angus heiress, 136
Jofrey, Bishop of Orkney, 137
John Haraldsson, Earl of Orkney, 128-132
    Makes peace with Norway, 128
    Involved in MacWilliam rebellions, 129-
        130
    Treaty with William the Lion, 130
    His unnamed hostage daughter, 130,
        135
    Part in murder of Bishop Adam, 130-1
    Makes peace with Alexander II, 131
    Visits Norway, 129
    Aids expedition to Hebrides, 129
    His murder, 132, 182, 180
John II, Earl of Orkney, 146, 147
John Langlifsson, 141
John o' Groat Journal, 411
John of Colchester, Bishop of Orkney, 176
John of Dounreay, 156
John, Bishop of 'Atholl', 114
John, Bishop of Caithness, 20, 85, 123,
    126, 130
John, King of England, 126
John, Lord of the Isles, 152
John, Rector of Fetlar, Bishop of Orkney,
    163, 168, 182
Johnston, A.W., 191, 447-8
Johnston, Nicol, of Langskaill, Birsay, 310
Jómvikingadrápa, 122
Justice, Justiciary, 227, 233, 241, 244,
    245, 267-8, 293
Jutland, Battle of, 434

Ka, James, protestant, 257
Kalf Skurfa, 30
Kali, Saebjornsson, 102
Kari Solmundsson, 61
Karny Kirk, Sanday, 248
Katherine, Countess, widow of Magnus V,
    149-50, 213, 219
Kelp, 352-362
    Introduction of, 352

Cutting and drying seaweed, 331, 353-4, 420
Kelp kilns, 354, 355, 356
Appearance, quality, 355, 453
Implements, 355
Trade, 353, 355-6, 357, 389
Production and prices, 341, 353, 356-8, 360
Labour demands, 345, 362, 375, 407
Industrial uses, 355-6, 360, 362
Demographic and social consequences, 343, 358-62, 369, 377
Riots, 407
End of kelp-making, 360, 362, 369
Kennedy, James, Bishop of St Andrews, 194
Kennermerland, The, 307, 311
Ketil Flatnose, 25, 29, 32, 57
Kingsland, 122, 162. 201, 226-7, 453
Kinloss, Abbey of, 249
Kintyre, 127, 218
Kirbister-names, see: Place-names
Kirbister, Birsay, 313
Kirkwall, 16, 105, 161, 167, 202, 227, 242, 244, 250, 266, 294, 306, 359-61, 374
Kirkwall Castle, 166, 175, 179, 237, 238, 263, 264, 296, 297-8
Kitchner, Lord, 434
Klondyke, Burray, 382
Knarston, Rousay, 330
Knightson, Thomas, pirate, 352
Knox, John, 254, 262
Kolbein Hruga (Cubbie Roo), 115, 122, 132, 412
König, The, 436
Kormak, Archdeacon of Sodor and Man, 154
Krákumal, 32
Kronprintz Wilhelm, The, 436
Krossuden, The, 141
Kugi of Rapness, 106, 107, 184
Kvikobba, South Ronaldsay, 149

Ladykirk stone, 11-2, 13
Laing, James, sugar planter, 369
Laing, Malcolm, of Papdale, 33, 369
Laing, Samuel, of Papdale, 33, 345, 360, 369, 380, 400, 411
Lamb Holm, 310, 436
Lamb, Raymond, archaeologist, 46, 66, 86, 19-21

Land-names, see: Place-names
Landnámabók, 25, 30, 52, 53
Landownership, 224-6, 416-22
Langlif, dau. of Harald Maddadsson, 135
Langskaill, Birsay, 87, 310, 334
Langskaill, Gairsay, 107, 352
Langskaill, Marwick, 45
Langta, Sanday, 248
Language, 6-7, 10, 50, 191, 414-5, 444-5, 448
Largs, Battle of, 142
Larycht oath, 321
Law and legal system, 185-6, 245, 256, 267-70, 299-300, 312, 321
Law, James, Bishop of Orkney, 282, 287-8, 290-4, 298-9, 301, 304
Lawbook, 174, 185, 273, 277, 299
Lauder, William, chamberlain, 265
Lawman, 130, 155-8, 163, 173-4, 176, 183-4, 198, 244-5, 267, 268, 299, 453
Lawman in Shetland, 239
Lawrie, David, royal messenger, 238
Lawrightmen, 158, 270, 321, 453
Lawting, 155-8, 163, 174-5, 176, 184, 186, 245, 299-300, 453
Laxdæla saga, 25
Laxfirth, Shetland, 283
Legenda de Sancto Magno, 99
Leidang (naval levy), 106, 214, 453
Leith, 222, 234, 245, 350, 357
Lerwick, Shetland, 141, 260
Letters of law or rectitude, 186
Levisgarth, Sanday, 248
Lewis, 116
Ley land, 210, 213, 228, 229, 310, 453
Liddell, Rev. Francis, 375
Lifolf, cook, 96
Ligonier, Frances, wife of Thomas Balfour, 338
Lindsay, Alexander, 244
Lindsay, Thomas, linen merchant, 364, 339
Lindsay, William, linen merchant, 364, 339
Linen, 363-6
Introduction of, 349, 363-4
Growing flax, 363-4, 365
Role of Board of Trustees, 363-4, 365
Role of British Linen Bank, 364
Spinning and weaving, 365-6, 393
Merchants, 364
Export, 365
Water-power, 365

On Graemeshall estate, 365
End of linen-making, 366
Social consequences, 369, 377
Lingro, Broch of, 5
Linklater, Eric, novelist, 447
Linklater, James, Sandwick, 393
Linksness, Tankerness, 242
Literacy, 413
Lizzie Burroughs, The, 413, 447
Ljot Thorfinsson, Earl of Orkney, 29, 58, 59, 78
Lobsters, 368
Loganair, 447
Lombard, 126
Longer Magnus saga, 93, 98
Longhope, 434
Lopness, Sanday, 223, 230, 248, 309, 391
Lords of Norway, 222
Louttit, Alexander, 325
Low, Rev. George, 338, 358, 368, 404, 407
Lübeck, 190, 241
Lucknow, 382
Lulach, King of Scots, 78, 79
Lyking, Sandwick, 223
Lyning, Ingilbert, 154
Lyquoy, 149

MacBeth, King of Scots, 76, 77, 78, 81, 89
MacCallum, Rev. Archibald, 410
MacDonald, John, Lord of the Isles, 196-7
MacDougal, Ewen Duncansson, King in Lorn, 139, 140, 141
MacKay, John D., schoolmaster, 439
Mackenzie, James, 395
Mackenzie, Murdoch, chart-maker, 110, 212, 315,
Mackenzie, Murdo, Bishop of Orkney, 301
MacRuarhi, Dougal, King in Garmoran, 139, 141, 144
MacWilliam family, 117-8, 137
MacWilliam, Donald, 119
MacWilliam, Donald Bán, 129
MacWilliam, Guthred, 129
Maddad, Earl of Atholl, 89, 104, 114
Máel Brigte, 77, 78
Maelbrigte Tusk, 28, 78
Maelmuire, bro. of Malcolm III, 89, 114
Maeshowe, 32, 117
Mager, John, Bailie of Kirkwall, 196
Magnus (St Magnus), Earl of Orkney, 88-100

Supposed racial origins, 191
Relations with Hakon, 93
At Menai Straits, 90-1
George MacKay Brown's *Magnus*, 91
Relations with Scotland, 91-2
Chastity in marriage, 92
Visits Henry I, 92
Martyrdom, 95-7
Elevation to sainthood, 97, 104
Miracles, 97, 104-5, 107
Visionary appearances, 140, 148
Relics, 96, 97
Shrine, 258
Sainthood, 90-1, 92, 97-9, 104-8, 238
Sources for his life, 91, 99, 125
His place in *Orkneyinga saga*, 58
Magnus Barelegs, King of Norway, 16, 27, 90-2, 94, 138-40
Magnus Erlingsson, King of Norway, 113, 118, 120, 121
Magnus II, Earl of Orkney, 134-6, 181
Magnus III, Earl of Orkney, 137, 141-5, 180
Magnus IV, Earl of Orkney, 145-6, 181
Magnus V, Earl of Orkney, 148-9
Magnus the Lawmender, King of Norway, 145, 186, 312
Magnus, King of Man and the Isles, 142, 144
Magnus stones, 97
Mail services, 411
Maitland, John, of Thirlestane, 274
Malcolm II, King of Scots, 60, 63, 69, 76, 77, 80, 81
Malcolm III (Canmore), King of Scots, 81, 89, 100, 113, 117
Malcolm IV, King of Scots, 89, 113
Malcolm, Earl of Angus, 134-6
Malcolm, Ruler of Moray, 77, 79
Malise, Earl of Orkney, 150-3, 157, 160, 162
Malt, malt skat, 16, 208, 210, 211, 213, 221, 242, 308, 351
Man, Kingdom of Man and the Isles, 60, 116, 124, 139, 142, 186, 300
Manor farms, 223-4
Manson, William, under-foud, 285
Manure, 3, 323, 324, 353
Mar, Earldom of, 192, 195
Margaret (St Margaret), wife of Malcolm III, 118
Margaret (The Maid of Norway), Queen of Scots, 146-8

Margaret, Countess of Atholl, 89, 108, 114, 116
Margaret, dau. of Alexander III, 146, 189
Margaret, Queen of Norway, 172
Margaret, the false Margaret, 147
Margaret, wife of James III, 199
Marie Blith, The, 266
Marjory, second wife of Earl Malise, 152
Marks of land, 150, 213, 451
Marks of weight and value, 217, 218, 396, 451
Markgraf, The, 436
Marstrand, Norway, 160, 169
Martello towers, 434
Marts, 221, 222, 242
Marwick, Birsay, 224, 257, 324, 342, 435
Marwick, Ernest, 191, 392, 414, 441, 448
Marwick, Hugh, 41-5, 50, 52, 84, 106, 191, 214-5, 300, 317, 439, 448
Mary of Guelders, queen, 192, 203
Mary of Guise, queen-regent, 256
Mary, Queen of Scots, 254, 258, 260, 263
Mary, Queen of England, 246
Masonic lodge, 408-9
Matilda, Angus heiress, 136
Maxwell, Robert, Bishop of Orkney, 236, 244, 247-8
McHeth, Malcolm, 118
Meadow land, meadow shift, 317, 327, 453
Meal, 221, 242, 351
Meason, James, 322
Meat, 221, 245
Melsetter, 364
Menai Straits, Battle of, 90-1, 102
Menzies, David, of Weem, 173-9, 185, 192
Merchant-lairds, 333, 341, 399, 349-362
Midbea, Westray, 249, 252
Milk, Milk Marketing Board, 425
Moddan, Earl in Caithness, 75, 77, 79
Moddan family, 102. 114
Moncrieff, David, 277
Money of account, 217, 270
Monteith, Robert, of Egilsay, 288, 290, 291, 302
Moodie, Benjamin, of Melsetter, 364
Moodie, Captain James, RN, 336, 337
Moodie, Francis, of Breckness, 305
Moodie, William, 258, 266, 267, 270
Mooney, Rev. Harald, 439
Mooney, John, 91, 201

Moray, Earl of, 240, 244, 263
Moray, Maurice, 152
Mortcloth, 408
Mossbank, Burray, 382
Mowat, John, schoolmaster, 323
Mowat, Patrick, 149
Muir, Edwin, poet, 417, 447
Munch, Per Andreas, 41
Muness Castle, Unst, 283
Munkerhouse, Papa Westray, 20
Munkerhouse, Stromness, 16
Myrtle Lane, Sanday, 383, 384

Napier Commission, 390, 410, 419, 440-1
Narborough, HMS, 435
Narve, Bishop of Bergen, 146
Neap, Nesting, Shetland, 278
Nechtán mac Derile, King of the Picts, 17, 19
Nechtansmere, Battle of, 9
Neill, Patrick, author, 362
New Statistical Account, 379, 389, 439
Newark, Deerness, 230
Newark, Sanday, 391
Newburgh, Aberdeenshire, 170, 227, 234
Nicol Oliverson, 268
Nidaros (Trondheim), Archbishopric of, 139, 154-5, 169, 189, 220
Nithsdale, 192, 194
Niva Mc Oirck, Prince of Orkney, 11
Njal's saga, 59, 61, 67, 78-9
Noltland castle, Westray, 255, 266, 279, 403
Norn language, 191, 448
North Hill Common, Shapinsay, 386, 387
Northlink, 446
North of Scotland College of Agriculture, 422
North of Scotland Shipping Company, 446
North Ronaldsay, 13, 36, 157, 241, 255, 360, 361
Northern Burghs elections, 400, 408
Northumberland Fishing Society, 368
Northumbria, kingdom of, 17-20
Nory, John, royal chaplain, 196, 197
Novell, Ralph, Bishop of Orkney, 94-5

Oats, oatmeal, 344, 423, 424
Occidental Oil Company, 444
Odal rights (also see: Udal tenure), 34, 39, 108
Odal Rights and Feudal Wrongs, 229, 256
Odin, 33, 35-6, 63, 64-6

Ofeig, standard-bearer, 96
Ogham inscriptions, 7, 19
Ogmund krakadanz, 144
Oil, 242, 245, 310, 444
Olaf (St Olaf), King of Norway, 27-8, 74-5, 82, 87, 97-9, 140, 186
Olaf Cuaran, King of Dublin, 56
Olaf Hrofsson, 106, 107, 109
Olaf Trygvesson, King of Norway, 63
Oliver rósti, 102, 104, 107, 109, 111
Olsone, Janet, beggar, 310
Omond, Robert, Herston, 321
On ca' (on call) work, 353, 379-80, 390, 393, 453
Opal, HMS, 435
Orc, Orkas, Cape Orkas, Orcades, 4, 42
Orcadia (ship), 444
Orcadian, The (newspaper), 382, 411, 448
Orkney & Shetland American (newspaper), 443
Orkney & Zetland Chronicle (newspaper), 411
Orkney & Zetland Telegraph (newspaper), 411
Orkney Agricultural Discussion Society, 422, 433
Orkney Antiquarian Society, 50
Orkney Book, The, 414
Orkney Dictionary, 448
Orkney Egg Producers, 427
Orkney Herald, The (newspaper), 448
Orkney Heritage Society, 33
Orkney View (magazine), 448
Orkneyinga saga, 24-39, 56, 59, 66, 67, 76, 90, 95, 99, 117,
Ormlie castle, Thurso, 124
Orphir, 110, 111, 224, 238-40, 259, 298, 375, 445
Osmundwall, 40, 63
Ouncelands, see: Urislands.
Out Skerries, Shetland, 283, 307
Owner-occupancy, 390, 401, 416-22

P & O Shipping Company, 446
Pacock, Gilbert, 279
Papa Stronsay, 15, 16, 84, 218, 241
Papa Westray, 15, 16, 20-1, 49, 50, 187, 257
Papa-names, see: Place-names
Papae, clergy, 14-7, 21, 45
Papdale, Kirkwall, 15, 16, 33, 246, 295, 352, 360, 422

Papdale, Battle of, 246
Papey Geo, Wick, 14
Papil, West Burra, Shetland, 21, 45
Paplay, Holm, 15, 16, 225, 226
Paplay, South Ronaldsay, 15, 20, 326
Paplay, Thomas, 278
Parliament Close, Kirkwall, 244
Parochial Boards (Also see: Poor Relief), 448
Paterson, Dr Robert, 409
Paul I Thorfinnsson, Earl of Orkney, 88, 89, 108
Paul II Hakonsson, Earl of Orkney, 101, 105, 109
Pawning of Orkney and Shetland, see: Impignoration,
Peat, 3, 37, 303, 323, 356, 379
Peche, Sir Bernard, 148-9
Pemberton, John, Quaker, 407
Pennylands, 61-2, 150, 206-19, 315-7, 319, 329, 334, 451
Pennyworths, 209, 211, 217, 221, 228, 270, 453
Pentland Firth, 6, 124, 148
Pentland Skerries, 150
Perambulations, 273, 325-7, 342, 453
Perth, Treaty of, 144, 145, 149, 179, 194, 267
Peter's Pence, papal tax, 123, 154-5, 189, 216
Peterkin, Sheriff Alexander, 263, 384, 411
Peterkirks, 19-20, 231
Petrie, David, factor, 346
Phankouth, Henry, 220
Philippa, Queen, 177
Pickaquoy, 1, 51, 248
Picts, 1-23
    Artefacts, 23, 43-4
    Bishops, 21, 50
    Books, 16, 22
    Church, 13-22
    Kingship, 8-9, 11-3, 16-7
    Identified with supernatural, 1-2
    Language, 3, 6-7, 10, 41, 46, 50
    Matrilinear succession, 3
    Relations with Norse, 10, 44-50
    Sculpture, 10, 18, 21, 10-2, 16, 17, 20-3
    Settlements, 22-3
    Ships, 10
    Symbols, 10
Pierowall, Westray, 64

Pigs, 3, 4, 221, 269, 294, 322, 327, 383, 425
Piper Oil Field, 444
Pirate, The, (novel), 345, 403
Pirates and privateers, 264, 267, 270, 272, 275, 286, 310, 352
Pisgah, 382
Place-names, 40-55
    Airigh-names, 41-2
    Akr-names, 53
    Boer-names, 51-4
    Brittonic names, 6-7, 10, 41-2, 50
    Bruntland, 382
    Bu of-names, 51-4
    Bister (bólstaðr) names, 51-4, 110
    Celtic names, 6-7, 10, 41-2, 50
    Chronology, 45, 52-4
    Division-names, 53, 330
    Garth-names, 51-4
    Goedelic, 6
    Heathen names, 64-5
    Island-names, 40, 42
    Kirbister-names, 53
    Land-names, 51-54
    Measurable characteristics, 54
    Papa-names, 15-6, 20, 49
    Picky and Pett (Pict) names, 1
    Pit-names, 6-7
    Quoy (kví) names, 45, 51-4, 273, 327, 453
    Reclamation-names, 382
    Rig names, 324
    Setter-names, 51-4
    Skaill (skáli) names, 45, 51-4
    Staðir-names, 51-4, 317
    Stove-names, 351
    Streams and lochs, 40
Planking, 333-5
Plógsland (unit of land), 218
Plough silver, 210
Ploughs, 306, 336, 342, 429
Plover Ha', 383
Pomona Egg Packers, 427
Pomponius Mela, geographer, 4
Pool, Sanday, 10, 22, 43
Poor relief, 406, 410, 420
Population, 228, 369-70, 375-6, 380, 442-5
Post Office, 411
Potatoes, 335-6, 422, 423
Poultry, 222, 388, 393, 423, 424, 425-7, 437, 438

Prebends, 248-9, 259, 453
Press gang, 373
Pro rege land, 226-7
Ptolemy, geographer, 4
Public Money Drainage Act, 384
Pultneytown, Wick, 370
Pundlar, Pundlar Process, 395, 396, 453
Purgatory, Birsay, 382
Pytheas of Massila, 4

Quandale, Rousay, 170, 384, 388, 390, 392
Quham, Rousay, 170
Quoy-names, see: Place-names
Quoygreen, Herston, 316, 317, 320, 327
Quoygrew, Westray, 187
Quoyland (tax-free land), 273, 327, 453

Radio Orkney, 448
Rae, John, Arctic explorer, 372, 373
Rafn, Lawman in Caithness, 130, 184
Ragnar Loðbrók, 32
Ragnhild, dau. of Erik Blood-axe, 29, 57, 58-9
Ranselmen, 197, 321, 453
Rapness, Westray, 225
Rattar, Caithness, 337
Rattle Up, 382
Raven banners, 66-8
Ravenna Cosmography, 42
Ravenscraig, 203, 227, 234, 245
Ravie Hill, 224, 333-4
Reclamation, 213, 311, 328, 336, 343, 379, 382, 383, 386, 389, 416, 421, 431
Redcastle, 119, 235
Redpath, James, Sheriff-depute, 264
Reformation, 220, 247-61
Reginald III, King of Man, 140
Regulus (Orkney sub-king), 8-9, 14
Reid, Robert, Bishop of Orkney, 246, 247, 260
Rendall, 207, 208, 334
Rendall, Robert, 272
Rennibister, Firth, 309
Rent, 156, 175, 206, 208, 282, 350, 384, 417
Rentals (1492, 1500, 1595), 162, 170, 198, 206, 208, 219, 224, 228, 283, 315
Reuter, Admiral Ludwig von, 435
Richan, Esther, 259

Richan, Captain William, 359
Rigs, Rig-names, 324, 325-6, 333-4, 393
Rikest men, 156, 184, 454
Ring money, 63
Roads, 420
Robert I, the Bruce, King of Scots, 148, 149
Robert II, the Steward, King of Scots, 152, 158, 192
Robert III, King of Scots, 172, 192
Robert's Haven, Caithness, 187
Robert, Master, preacher, 99-100
Roderick, grandson of Somerled, 218
Roger of Howden, historian, 124
Rognvald Kali Kolsson (St Rognvald) Earl of Orkney
    His immediate ancestors, 89, 102-3
    Assumes name of Rognvald, 103
    Vows to build cathedral, 104
    Invades Orkney, 107
    Accepted as earl, 108
    Founds cathedral, 99-100, 108
    Raises tax for cathedral, 35, 218
    Co-earl with Harald Maddadsson, 125
    His crusade, 108, 115
    War of the Three Earls, 116-7
    Protects monks at Dornoch, 123
    His poetry, 32, 101-12
    Relations with Scotland, 109
    Relations with Sweyn Asleifsson, 109
    His assassination, 117
    Buried in cathedral, 125
    His cult, 125
    Sources for his life, 125
Rognvald Brusisson, Earl of Orkney, 16, 29, 73, 82, 103, 106, 218
Rognvald Gudrodsson, King of Man, 126, 184
Rognvald, Earl of Møre, 24, 29, 30, 31, 32, 33, 48, 89
Rognvald, son of Halfdan the Black, 32
Rognvald, son of Somerled, 216
Roithmen, 185, 245, 454
Roll-on Roll-off ships, 444
Roman contacts, 4-6
Ronaldsvoe, South Ronaldsay, 443
Ros-Cuissine, 10
Rosemarkie, 17
Roslin, 160, 193, 227, 249
Ross, 59
Ross, Alexander, 312
Ross, Willie, Secretary of State for Scotland, 449

Rosslyn Chapel, Roslin, 193
Rotations, 343
Rothiesholm, Stronsay, 248
Round Church, Orphir, 111
Rousay, 64, 106, 170, 198, 259, 272-3, 289, 390, 360, 388, 389, 445, 447
Royal Mail, The, (ship), 412
Royal Oak, HMS, 436
Royal Society for the Protection of Birds, 431
Run-rig, 186, 208, 235, 265, 315-32, 334-5, 342, 360, 454

Sabiston, 207
Saint-Clair, Roland, historian, 166-8
Salamander, The, 243
Salt manufacture, 303
Sanday, 10, 22, 66, 157, 209, 212, 230, 241, 255, 289, 335, 391, 444,
Sandwick, 19, 170, 252, 289, 298, 365
Sang school, Kirkwall, 250, 412
Sangster, John, factor, 338
Sawyer, Peter, historian, 43
Saxo Grammaticus, 32
Saxter oath, 322
Scalloway, Scalloway castle, 279, 283
Scapa, 143, 364
Scapa Flow, 224, 317, 368, 435-8
Scar, Sanday, 64, 65, 379
Scarth, Robert, of Binscarth, 33, 345, 379
Schism, the Great, 163, 176, 182, 189
School Boards, 410, 414, 448
Scott, Sir Walter, 68, 345, 403
Scottish Drainage & Improvement Company, 385
Scrabster, Caithness, 126, 412
Seal of the Orkney Community, 174, 176, 177, 183, 184
Seaweed (Also see: Kelp), 3, 336, 352-4, 361
Sebay, St Andrews, 226, 256, 272, 331
Secession church, 402, 407, 408-9
Selby & Co., lobster merchants, 368
Sellibister school, Sanday, 414
Senchus Fer nAlban, 215
Sermons, 405, 410-1
Set-aside schemes, 431
Setter-names, see: Place-names
Sex ratio, 376
Shapinsay, 5, 42, 141, 289, 298, 339-41, 383, 385, 387, 402-3
Sheads, 324, 325, 331, 454

Sheaf bands, 327
Sheep, 3, 186, 221, 242, 294, 322, 328, 329, 381, 383, 388, 423
Sheep letter (Faroe), 186
Sheeprights (sheep drives), 329
Shetilig, Haakon, 26
Shetland, 24, 73, 103, 107, 121, 149, 154, 160, 166, 169, 172-3, 176, 211, 217, 239, 351, 368, 400, 411
Shetland, Archdeacon of, 176
Shetland Journal, 411
Ships and shipping (also see ships by name), 349-50, 360, 372, 444, 446, 447
Shirreff, John, 345, 365
Shore Street, Kirkwall, 441, 442
Shoreside, Shapinsay (Also see: Balfour Village), 339-40, 403
Short-sea crossing, 449
Shorter Magnus saga, 99
Sigurd Haftorsson, 165
Sigurd Hlodversson, the Stout, Earl of Orkney, 35, 59-68
Sigurd Jatgeirsson, 150
Sigurd of Westness, 106, 108, 184, 211
Sigurd the Crusader, King of Norway, 92, 95, 103
Sigurd the Mighty, Earl of Orkney, 24, 25, 28, 29, 30, 31, 78, 305
Sigurd, son of King Magnus Erlingsson, 121
Sigvaldi Skalgsson, 133
Silage, 422, 423, 424, 429
Sinclair expedition, 294
Sinclair, Sir David, of Sumburgh, 221, 230, 235, 241, 269
Sinclair, David, bro. of Earl Henry I, 169-70
Sinclair, Edward, of Eday, 258, 289-90, 303, 235
Sinclair, Edward, of Strom, 234, 235-46, 257, 262
Sinclair, Elizabeth, dau. of Earl Henry I, 170
Sinclair, George II, Earl of Caithness, 235, 258, 259, 266-7, 289
Sinclair, George III, Earl of Caithness, 235, 288-90, 291, 297-8
Sinclair, Sir Henry, Bailie in Caithness, 149
Sinclair, Henry I, Earl of Orkney, 160-71
  His claim to Orkney, 153
  Installation as earl, 160, 176-7
  Ceremonial role, 169

Relations with Alexander de Ard, 159
  Visits Norway, 160, 165, 169
  Builds castle, 175
  Kills Malise Sperra, 165-6
  Secures lands in Orkney, 169-70
  Killed, 170-1, 172
  Viking image, princely life-style, 166-71
  Identified as Zichmni, 168
  Supposed Atlantic crossing, 168-9
Sinclair, Henry II, Earl of Orkney, 172-4, 181, 211
Sinclair, Lord Henry, 220-32
  His tack, 221
  Head of family, 227
  Appointed Justice, 268
  Butter skat enquiry, 209
  His rentals, 206, 208, 235
  Management of conquest lands, 209 225, 226
  Management of tack, 219-32, 235
  Seizes estate of David Sinclair, 236
  Church appointments, 220-1
  Relatives, 225, 235
  Interest in literature, 232
  At court, 232
  Killed at Flodden, 232
Sinclair, Henry, page, 266
Sinclair, Henry, son of Edward of Strom, 235, 262
Sinclair, Sir James, of Breck, 233-243, 255, 269
Sinclair, John, bro. of Earl Henry II, 172-3
Sinclair, John, Earl of Caithness, 234, 235, 238-40, 288
Sinclair, Sir John, author of *Statistical Account*, 345, 408
Sinclair, Magnus, of Braebister, 210, 274
Sinclair, Magnus, of Warsetter, 235
Sinclair, Magnus, son of Sir David Sinclair, 235
Sinclair, Margaret, widow of Lord Henry, 232, 241, 243, 244
Sinclair, Margaret, dau. of Sir James of Brecks, 260
Sinclair, Marjory, dau. of Earl Henry I, 173
Sinclair, Oliver, of Pitcairns, 235, 240, 244-6, 253, 258, 263, 267, 268
Sinclair, Oliver, of Roslin, son of Earl William, 233, 235, 244
Sinclair (Sanctoclaro), Robert, Dean of Moray, 163, 182
Sinclair, Robert, son of Edward of Strom,

235, 257

Sinclair, William, husband of Isabella of Strathearn, 152

Sinclair, Sir William, of Warsetter, 225, 230, 233-4, 235, 303

Sinclair, Thomas, Bailie of the King of Norway, 160

Sinclair, Thomas, cousin of Earl Henry II, 176, 178

Sinclair, Lord William, son of Lord Henry, 233-40, 244, 268

Sinclair, William, Earl of Orkney, 189-205
    Succeeds as a minor, 174
    Relations with guardian, 175-7
    Seizes power, 177-8, 183, 191-2
    Visits Copenhagen, 176, 179
    Scottish interests, 192
    Visits James I, 177
    Marries Elizabeth Douglas, 192
    Installed as earl, 179
    In France, 193
    His household, 193
    Interest in chivalry, 193
    Campaigns against Douglases, 194
    Marries Marjory Sutherland, 194
    Chancellor of Scotland, 194, 195
    Embassy to England, 197
    Contacts with Scandinavia, 177, 196, 198
    Relations with Denmark, 194, 198
    Apparently deposed, 198
    His conquest lands, 203-4, 225-6, 235, 311, 416
    Patron of St Duthac's Stouk, 248
    Gives up earldom, 203
    Receives Ravenscraig, 203
    Effect of impignoration, 202-3
    His heirs, 223

Sinclair, William, 'the Waster', 199, 227, 233

Sinclair, William, of Eday, 289-90

Sinclair, William, Earl of Caithness, 235, 232, 233, 235

Sinclair, William, son of Lord William, 235

Sites of Special Scientific Interest, 431

Siward of Northumbria, 64

Sixtus IV, Pope, 220

Skaill hoard, 62-3

Skaill, Deerness, 22, 43, 70, 74, 86-7

Skaill, Sandwick, 305, 365

Skaill-names, see Place-names

Skara Brae, 6

Skat, 61-2, 108, 116, 201, 206, 208, 218, 222, 228, 234, 275, 294, 395-6, 454

Skat merts, 208, 212-3, 454

Skat silver, 209, 283-4

Skatfaa, 226, 273

Skatland (quarter of urisland), 214, 451, 454

Skatlands (tributary provinces), 185

Skea, Deerness, 249, 310

Skea, James, protestant, 257

Skeabrae, 437

Skennistoft, Shapinsay, 249

Skittenmire, Battles of, 64

Skuli, brother of Earl Ljot, 29, 59, 78

Skuli, Earl in Norway, 129

Skye, 82, 139, 140, 141

Slaves (thralls), 30, 42, 48, 50

Small Landholders' Act, 419

Small-pox, 405

Smith, Brian, historian, 44, 72

Smuggling, 350-1, 359, 360, 364

Smyth, Patrick, of Braco, 305

Snaekoll Gunnisson, 89, 132, 135

Snelsetter, Walls, 266

Society for the Propagation of Christian Knowledge, 412

Society of Free British Fishery, 368

Sodor and Man, Bishopric of, 139, 220

Soid Brevet (Faroese sheep letter), 328

Soil erosion, 228, 229

Solway Moss, Battle of, 245-6

Somerled, 118, 139, 140

Sound, Shapinsay, 249, 339-40

Sourin, Rousay, 252

South Ronaldsay, 179, 213, 259, 289, 316-8, 326, 336-7, 342

Sovereign, The, 384

Span (a measure of butter), 130, 450

Sparke, Hinrich, Lübeck merchant, 190

Spence, James, banker, 360

Spence, Nicol, 382

Sperra, Gutthorm, 152

Sperra, Malise, 163-6, 170, 173, 176, 225, 228

Squaring, 385, 387

St Andrews, Fife, 177, 179, 220, 256

St Andrews, Orkney, 5, 222, 230, 274, 322

St Augustine's prebend, 248, 250

St Boniface church, Papa Westray, 17, 19, 20-1, 49, 187

St Catherine's quoys, 249

St Catherine's stouk (prebend), 248-9, 259

St Columba's prebend, 259
St Duthac's stouk, 248, 259
St Findan, 50, 64
St Laurence dedications, 21, 239, 248
St Magnus (ship), 446
St Magnus Cathedral,
    Building works, 99-100, 122, 247
    Taxation to fund, 35, 108, 218
    Prebends, 248, 259, 453
    Pilgrimages, 248
    Ownership, 449
    Sanctuary, 173-4
    Bishop Reid's reforms, 250-2
    Public functions, 143, 144, 149, 174,
        186, 239, 280
    Military functions, 246, 265
    Survives Reformation, 258
    Sermons, 405
    Discipline, 405-6
St Magnus Church, Birsay, 86
St Magnus Church, Tingwall, 157
St Magnus Festival, 447
St Margaret's Hope, 142, 147, 337, 370
St Mary's Village, 310, 370, 436
St Mary's Church, Burwick, 11-2, 13
St Ninian (ship), 446
St Ninian dedications, 13-4, 49, 248
St Ninian's Isle, Shetland, 14, 21, 23, 49
St Ola (parish), 252, 258
St Ola (ship), 443, 446
St Olaf's Church, Kirkwall, 97, 248
St Olaf's saga, 26, 34-5
St Paul's Masonic Lodge, 408-9
St Peter's Church, South Ronaldsay, 20, 49
St Tredwell, St Tredwell's chapel, 19, 20
Stamford Bridge, Battle of, 88
Standard, Battle of, 115
Statistical Account (OSA), 376, 407, 438-9
Staðir-names, see: Place-names
Steamships, 384, 403
Steiness, Asgaut, historian, 72, 206
Stenness, 58, 254, 342
Stenness, Palace of, 259
Stent butter, 209, 454
Stewart, Alexander (the Wolf of
    Badenoch), 158
Stewart, Sir Archibald, 352
Stewart, Barbara, wife of Sir James Sinclair,
    242-3
Stewart, Bernard, keeper of Birsay palace,
    296, 297
Stewart, Edward, Bishop of Orkney, 247

Stewart, Sir James, of Burray, 336-7, 395
Stewart, James, of Graemsay, 277, 281
Stewart James, of Killeith, Lord Ochiltree,
    295, 297, 302, 303
Stewart, John, Master of Orkney,
    Kinclaven, Earl of Carrick, 277-9, 281,
    302-3
Stewart, John, son of James V, 252
Stewart, Marie, niece of Earl Robert, 274
Stewart, Patrick, Earl of Orkney, 277-300
    Building programme, 279
    Extravagant life-style, 279-80
    Intended marriage to Emilia, 280-1
    Profits from shipwreck, 285-6
    His property seized by pirates, 285-6
    His debts, 288, 291
    Surety required, 281
    Feud with Earl of Caithness, 289-90
    Feud with Laurence Bruce, 283
    Feud with Eday Sinclairs, 289-90
    Invades Westray, 282
    Visits England, 290
    Charges against him, 290, 292, 294
    Imprisoned, 291, 293
    Deprived of earldom and bishopric,
        293, 295
    Offered keepership of palaces, 295
    His execution, 298
    His reputation, 277, 299-300
Stewart, Robert, Earl of Orkney, 262-76
    His parentage, 262
    Feu of Orkney and Shetland, 263-4,
        271
    Seizes cathedral, 265
    Seizes Kirkwall charters, 266
    His dairy farm, 425
    His laws and law courts, 267-70, 273-5,
        294, 321
    Demands banquets, 211
    Relations with udallers, 264, 273-6,
        313
    Treasonable dealings, 266-7
    Warded in Edinburgh Castle, 266, 270
    Charges against him, 268-70, 274
    Created earl, 272
    Deposed, 274
    Repels invasion, 275
    Pro-Spanish politics, 276
    Death, 276
    Estimate of his rule, 276
Stewart, Robert, son of Earl Robert, 268
Stewart, Robert, son of Earl Patrick, 293-

4, 296-8
Stewart, William, of Maynes, 317
Stews, South Ronaldsay, 13, 149
Stikklestad, Battle of, 99
Stock-stove houses, 351
Stonefield, Burray, 382
Stove-names, see: Place-names
Stove, Sanday, 336, 351, 379-80, 391, 393
Stracathro, Battle of, 117, 118
Strathearn, Earldom of, (also see: Malise),
    150-3, 157
Straw-plaiting, 349, 366-7, 379
Stromness, 298, 367, 370, 372, 374, 411
Stromness News, The, 411
Stronsay, 42, 64, 223, 230, 255, 289, 308,
    336, 352, 359, 369-71, 444
Stubble grazing, 322, 381, 386
Sumarlidi Sigurdsson, Earl of Orkney, 69-
    70, 74
Sumburgh, House of, Shetland, 279
Summerdale, Battle of, 98, 238-40, 288
Sunniva's meal, 155
Surveying and surveyors, 326-7, 342
Sutherland, Alexander, of Dunbeath, 194
Sutherland, Captain James, Lord Duffus,
    341-3
Sutherland, Marjory, second wife of Earl
    William, 235
Sverre's saga, 143
Sverre, King of Norway, 27, 113, 120-1,
    128, 145, 190, 350
Swanbister, Orphir, 384, 386
Sweyn Asleifsson, 109-112
    Parents and relatives, 94, 106, 109, 132
    Kills Sweyn Breastrope, 66
    Heroic lifestyle, 101, 109-11, 120
    Military tactics, 109-12, 116-7
    His hall on Gairsay, 120
    Relations with Earl Rognvald, 109
    Relations with Bishop William, 66, 94,
        109
    Relations with King David I, 105-6
    Identified as John the Wode, 119
    Killed, 120
Sweyn Breastrope, 66, 109, 111
Sydserff, Thomas, Bishop of Orkney, 301
Sygtrygg, Norse King in Dublin, 67
Sysselman (royal officer), 122, 127, 128,
    132, 155-7, 158, 162, 182, 245

Tacitus, Roman historian, 5
Tafts, Sanday, 223, 230, 309

Tait, James, Orphir, 412
Tankerness, 242, 404
Tankerness, Battle of, 107, 109, 111, 112,
    215
Tankerness, Hall of, 251
Tarry Ha', 383
Tarvedunum, 4
Tea, 358
Teinds (tithes), 130, 154, 252, 454
Temperance, 409, 439, 440
Thames Company (fishing), 369
Theophilus, Dr Nicholas, 275
Third Statistical Account, 438-9, 445, 449
Thomas of Kyrkness, Bailie of Kirkwall,
    196
Thomas, Captain F.W.L, 214
Thorbjorn Clerk, 115, 117
Thorbjorn Hornklove, poet, 26
Thorfinn Einarsson, 'Skullsplitter', Earl of
    Orkney, 56-8
Thorfinn Sigurdsson, 'the Mighty', Earl of
    Orkney, 69-87
    Parentage, 69
    Appearance, 70
    Extent of his realm, 81, 87
    Residence in Birsay, 71
    Holds earldom of Caithness, 69, 73
    Visits Norway, 74-5
    Defeats Karl Hundisson, 75-81
    In Fife, 75
    Campaigns in Galloway, 82
    Victory at Vatzfjoðr, 82, 83
    Battle of Rauðabjorg, 83-4
    Kills Rognvald Brussion, 84
    Visits Rome, 84-5
    Obtains a bishop, 85
    Builds Christchurch, 85-7
    Reforms laws, 87
Thorfinn, son of Earl Harald Maddadsson,
    118, 124, 126
Thorfinnsdrápa, 76
Thórir Tréskegg, 30
Thorir, Earl of Møre, 30, 38
Thorkell Fosterer, 70, 74, 84
Thorstein the Red, 25, 28
Thralls, 30, 42, 48, 50
Thurrigar, 194
Thursa Skerry, Muckle Flugga (?), 140
Thurso, 124, 132, 403
Timber, 3, 285, 306, 351
Tingwall, Rendall, 186, 207
Tingwall, Shetland, 166

Toab, St Andrews, 13, 274, 322
Toft (house site), 312, 318, 331, 454
Tomison's Academy, 413
Tomison, William, Governor, Hudson's
    Bay Company, 372, 412
Torfness, 37, 75, 79, 81, 82, 83
Torness, 64
Towback quarry, Eday, 290
Townships, 316-331, 454
Townsland, 324, 325, 326, 331, 454
Tractors, 428
Trade, 350-2, 371, 374, 388-9
Traill, George William, 384, 388, 400
Traill, George, MP, of Hobbister, 400
Traill, J.C., of Rattar, 418-9, 420
Traill, Thomas, of Holland, 418
Traill, Thomas, of Westove, 360, 379
Traill, William, of Frotoft, 360
Travelling shops, 426, 427
Tresness, Sanday, 223
Trows, trolls, 1, 66
Tucker, Thomas, 350
Tulloch, Thomas, Bishop of Orkney, 175-
    7, 179, 183, 186, 196, 248
Tulloch, Thomas, of Fluris, 253, 258
Tulloch, William, Bishop of Orkney, 184,
    197, 198-9, 202, 204, 221, 228, 247
Tunmal, 312, 318, 323, 328, 454
Tuquoy, Westray, 187, 249
Turf, utilisation of, 37, 323, 347
Turgéis, Viking leader, 48
Turnips, 322, 337, 338, 341, 344, 422,
    423
Turolf, Bishop of Orkney, 85
Tuskerbister, 239
Twatt, 437
Twatt, Magnus, Orphir, 412

Ubotamal, fines for serious offences, 158
Udal law, udal tenure, 108, 170, 186, 201,
    235-6, 238, 241-2, 255-6, 263, 269,
    311-4, 317, 319, 329, 416, 453
Ulf the Bad, 66
Unicorn, The, 260, 287
Urban refugees, 445
Urislands, 143, 150, 206-19, 451
Urquhart, Thomas, postmaster, 412
Uspak, 140
Uthel Buik, 312

Valkyries, 68
Van Bassan, 'confident' genealogist, 166

Vanguard, The, 434
Vedder, David, poet, 403
Vedder, Margaret, linen worker, 377
Veizla (wattle), 106, 211, 454
Velocity, The, 384
Viking Club (later 'Society'), 447-8
Viking graves, 49

Wadmell (cloth), 270
Wainwright, F.T., 41-2, 43, 47
Wallace, David, crofter, 335
Wallace, Jim, MSP, 440
Wallace, Rev. James, author, 308
Walls, 63, 289, 298, 337, 342, 368
Walls, Sanday, 223, 230, 248, 309
Ward hills, 322
Wardenburg, Zutpheldus, 220
Warebeth, Stromness, 19
Warenne, Sir John de, 152
Warsetter, Sanday, 225, 230, 391
Water supply, 425
Watson, James, chamberlain, 343
Watson, Rev. James, 375
Watt, William, laird, 360
Wattle (a skat), 106, 208, 211, 454
Weights and measures, 222, 253, 270,
    396, 451
Weland de Stiklaw, 148
Wenham, Sheena, historian, 377
West Brough, Sanday, 391
West End Hotel, Kirkwall, 359
West Hill common, Shapinsay, 339, 340,
    383
Westness, Rousay, 64, 106, 388
Westove, Sanday, 379
Westray, 187, 229, 257, 266, 285, 308,
    314, 336, 342, 444
Whales and whaling, 3, 308, 371-3
Whitehall, Stronsay, 369-71
Wick, 125
Widewall, South Ronaldsay, 317
Wild White Clover, 422
William I, 'the Lion', King of Scots, 73,
    113, 124-7, 129-30, 134
William I, 'the Old', Bishop of Orkney,
    Consecration, 94
    Described as 'intruder', 95
    Role in martyrdom of Magnus, 95
    Links with Egilsay, 93
    Discourages Magnus cult, 97, 104
    Visits Norway, 104
    Supports Earl Rognvald, 104-6

Elevates Magnus to sainthood, 104-5
His bishopric endowed, 105
Relations with King David I, 105-6
Relations with Atholl, 105-6
Relations with Sweyn Asleifsson, 66,
    109
William III, Bishop of Orkney, 154
William IV, King of Great Britain, 408
William IV, Bishop of Orkney, 155-7, 159,
    163, 182
William Thorgilsson, Lawman, 174
Wimund, Bishop of Sodor, 117
Witchcraft, 154, 278-9
Wool, 351
Wrak and waith, 285
Wyre, 133, 352, 384

Yell, Shetland, 42, 107, 217
Yellowley, Triptolemus, 345
Yensta, John, sub-tacksman, 222
York, 56
Yorkstoune, Robert, factor, 221
Young Men's Mutual Improvement
    Society, 414-5

Zawadski, Richard, 431
Zeno, Nicolo and Antonio, 168
Zichmni, identified as Earl Henry I, 16